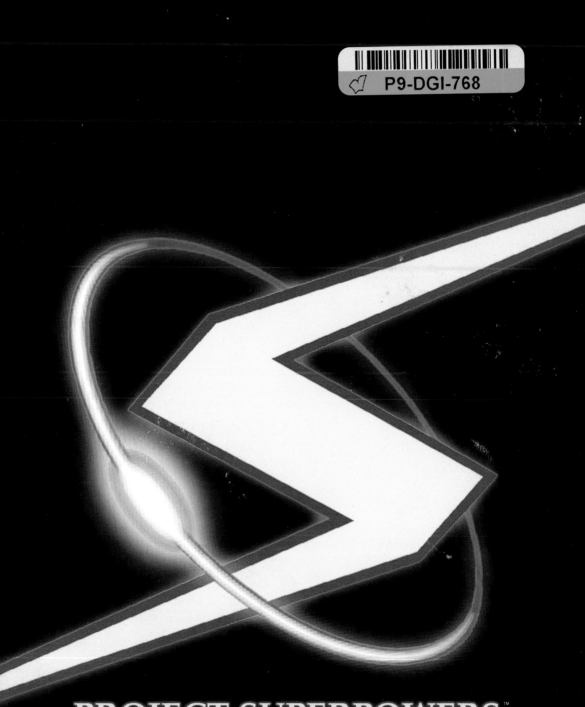

PROJECT SUPERPOWERS™

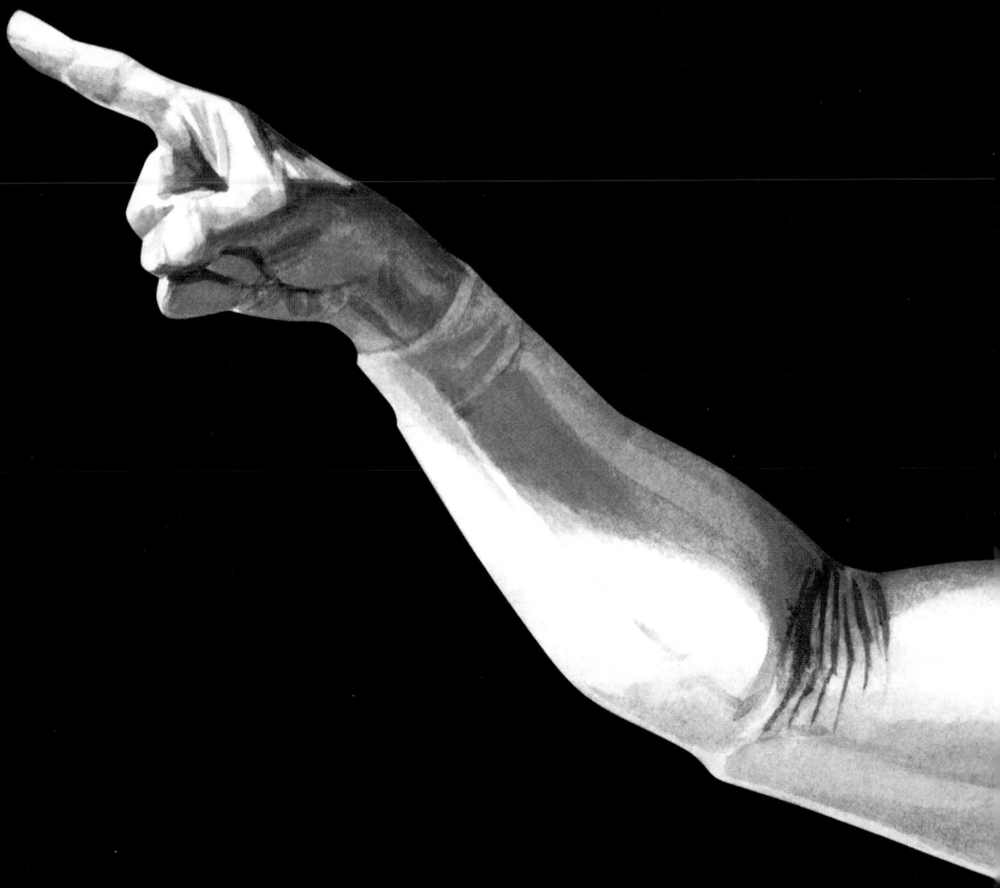

First Printing

Hardcover ISBN-10: 1-933305-91-6
Hardcover ISBN-13: 978-1-93330-591-2

Softcover ISBN-10: 1-60690-014-5
Softcover ISBN-13: 978-1-60690-014-7

10 9 8 7 6 5 4 3 2 1

WWW.DYNAMITEENTERTAINMENT.COM

NICK BARRUCCI   •   PRESIDENT
JUAN COLLADO   •   CHIEF OPERATING OFFICER
JOSEPH RYBANDT   •   ASSOCIATE EDITOR
JOSH JOHNSON   •   CREATIVE DIRECTOR
JASON ULLMEYER   •   GRAPHIC DESIGNER

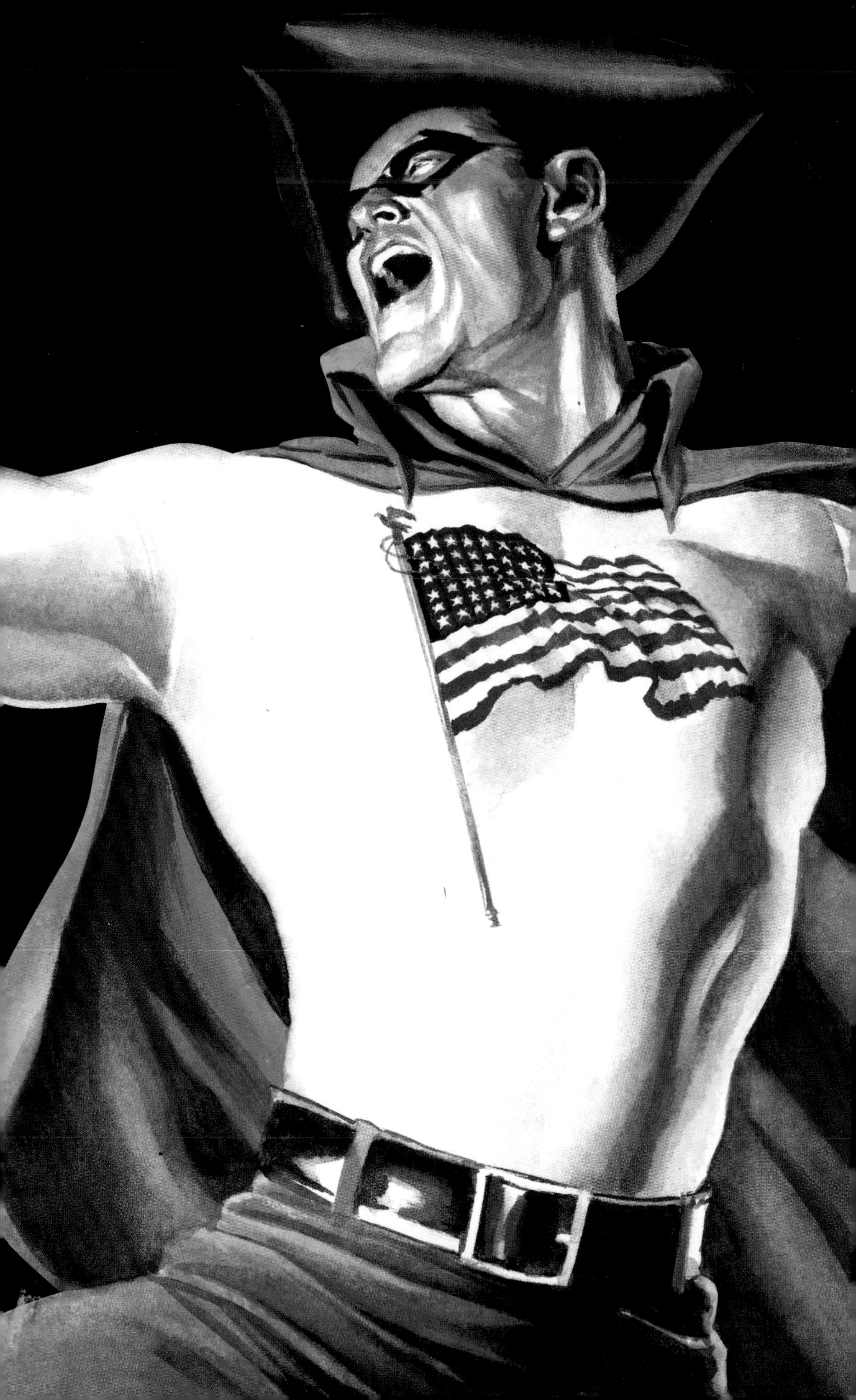

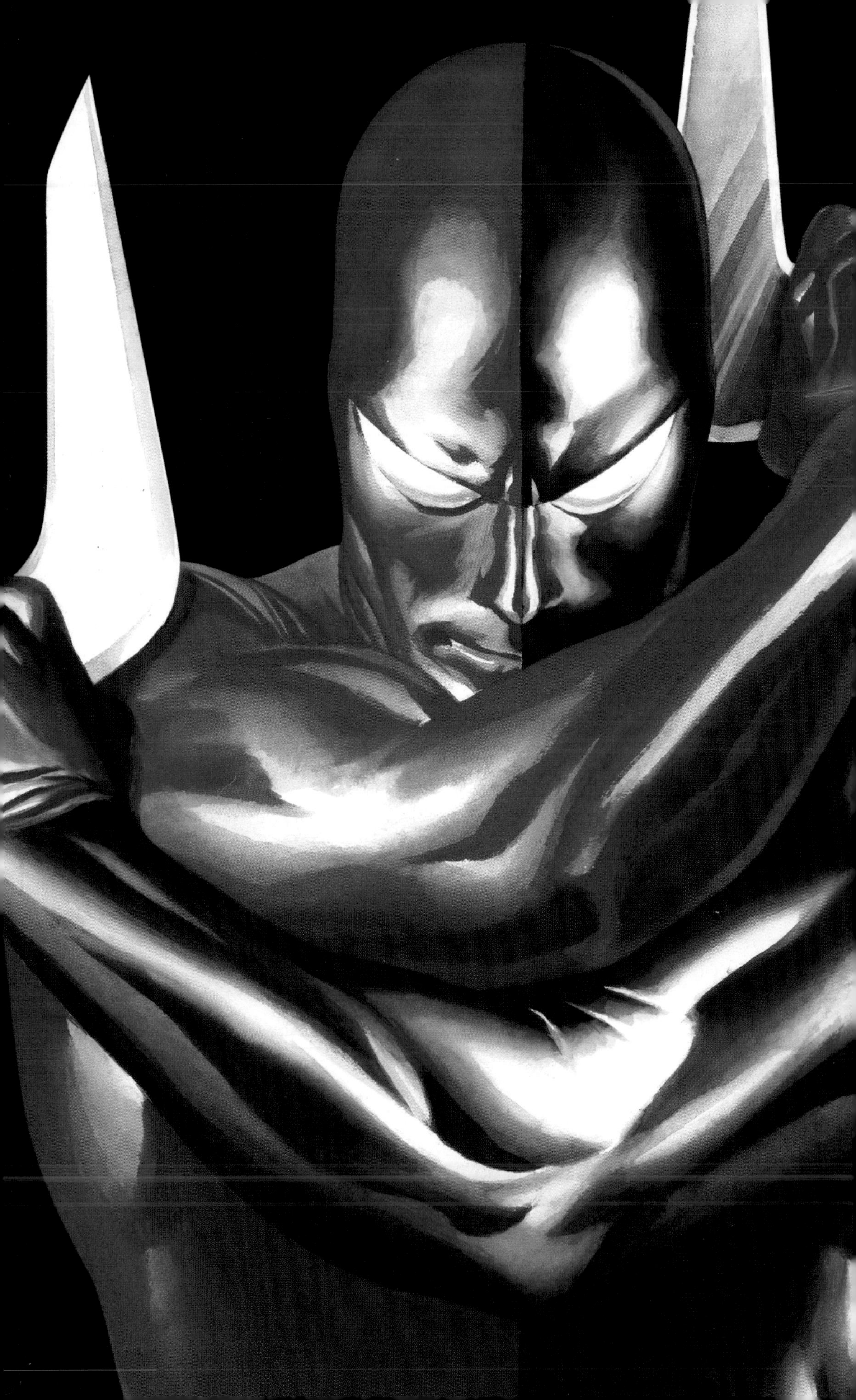

PROJECT SUPERPOWERS™

CHAPTER ONE

STORY
ALEX ROSS
JIM KRUEGER

SCRIPT
JIM KRUEGER

ART
STEPHEN SADOWSKI
(ISSUE 0)
DOUGLAS KLAUBA
(ISSUE 0)
CARLOS PAUL
(ISSUE 1-7)
ALEX ROSS
(PAINTED ART)

COLORS
INLIGHT STUDIO
(ISSUE 0)
DEBORA CARITA
(ISSUE 1-7)

LETTERS
SIMON BOWLAND

COVERS
ALEX ROSS

ART DIRECTION
ALEX ROSS

CONTRIBUTING EDITOR
JOSEPH RYBANDT

COLLECTION DESIGN
JASON ULLMEYER

SPECIAL THANKS TO
T.J. ROSS
JUAN COLLADO
BRIAN HOFACKER

THIS VOLUME COLLECTS ISSUES 0-7
OF PROJECT SUPERPOWERS.

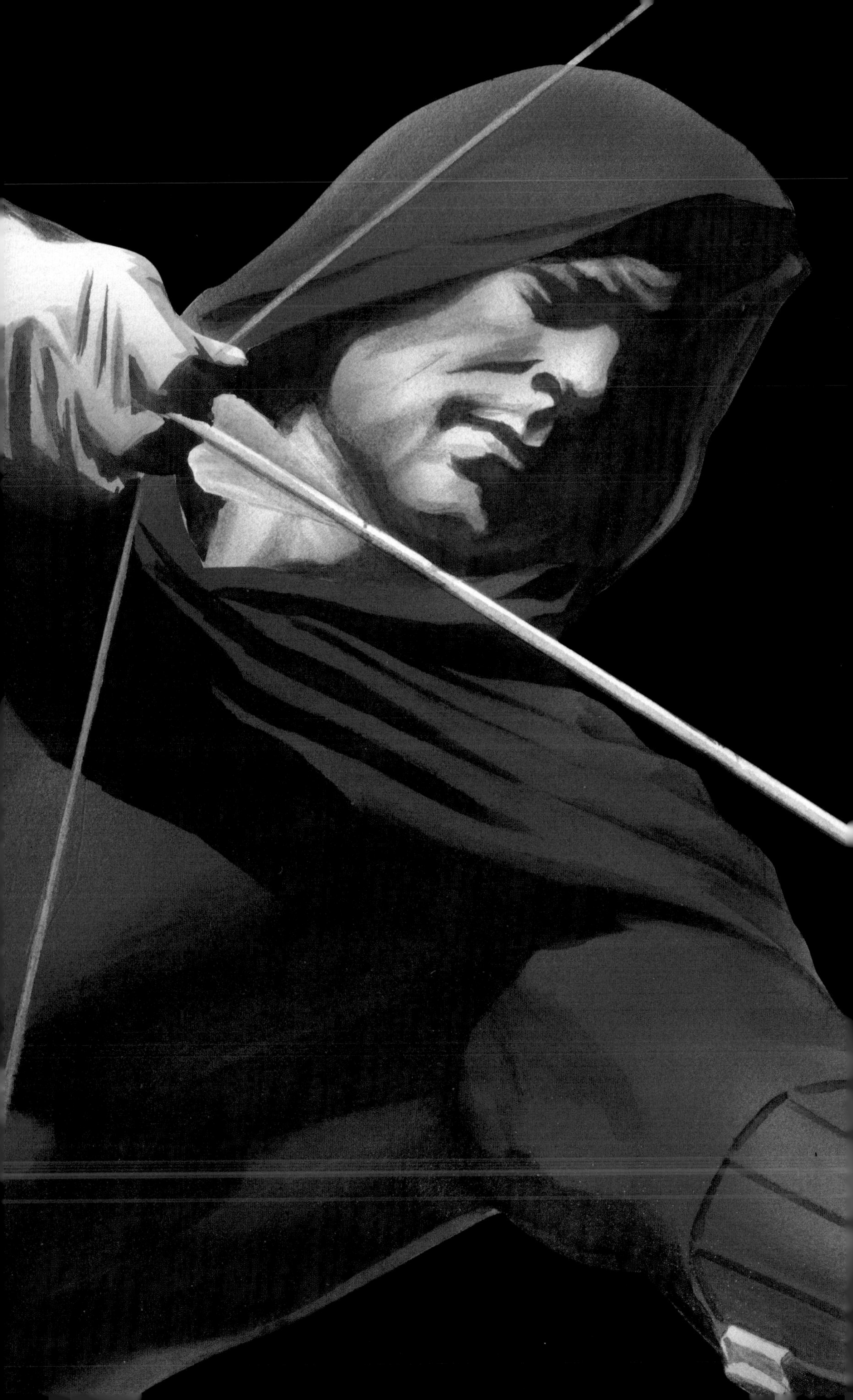

INTRODUCTION

Ideas flow. People talk. One conversation begets another conversation. Sometimes, you feel like Jerry Maguire. You just get in front of the computer and type ideas all night till 4 o'clock in the morning (or later). You write something that makes perfect sense (to you). Then comes the hard part, convincing other people of your vision.

It all began with a scene… something you may have seen played out in movies old and new. There's the mansion on the lake, the old man in front of the fire, glass of booze in hand and his life playing out before his eyes.

And when he sees what he's done as his life and choices play out across his memory, he knows he has to make amends as he's done his friends and allies a great wrong… and he knows he has very little time left to do so…

And from this I thought of more scenes, with more characters and stories… but I was missing something…

All the while I was busy trying to figure this all out, I conveyed my ideas and these scenes to my good friend Alex Ross in one of our regular semi-weekly calls. As we talked, I realized what I was missing (though, to be fair, I think Alex realized it for me) … and Alex (and later writer Jim Krueger who was able to come onboard after wrapping Justice with Alex) was there to help me realize the vision…

And Project Superpowers was born. I'm over-simplifying everything, but you really want to read the collection in your hands, and not me rambling about how it all came together.

But I will say, from all this, it took close to three years until issue #0 saw print and grew into the first chapter of the saga you now hold in your hands; things changed along the way, becoming more solid, but still the story remained rooted as one of betrayal, loss and redemption. The stuff superheroes thrive on, the stuff superpowers are made of.

Without Alex and Jim (and my team at Dynamite: Joe, Juan, Josh, Jason and #1 fan, Brian), it would have remained just a series of scenes, playing out in my head and remaining more dream than reality.

Welcome to Project Superpowers.

Nick Barrucci
President, Dynamite Entertainment

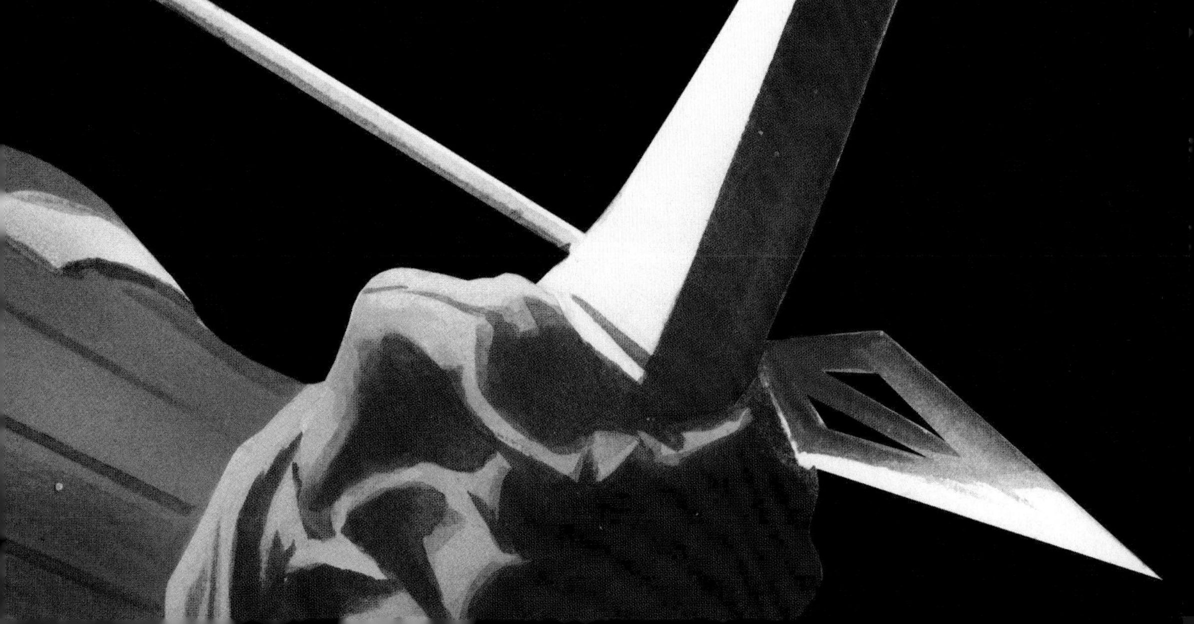

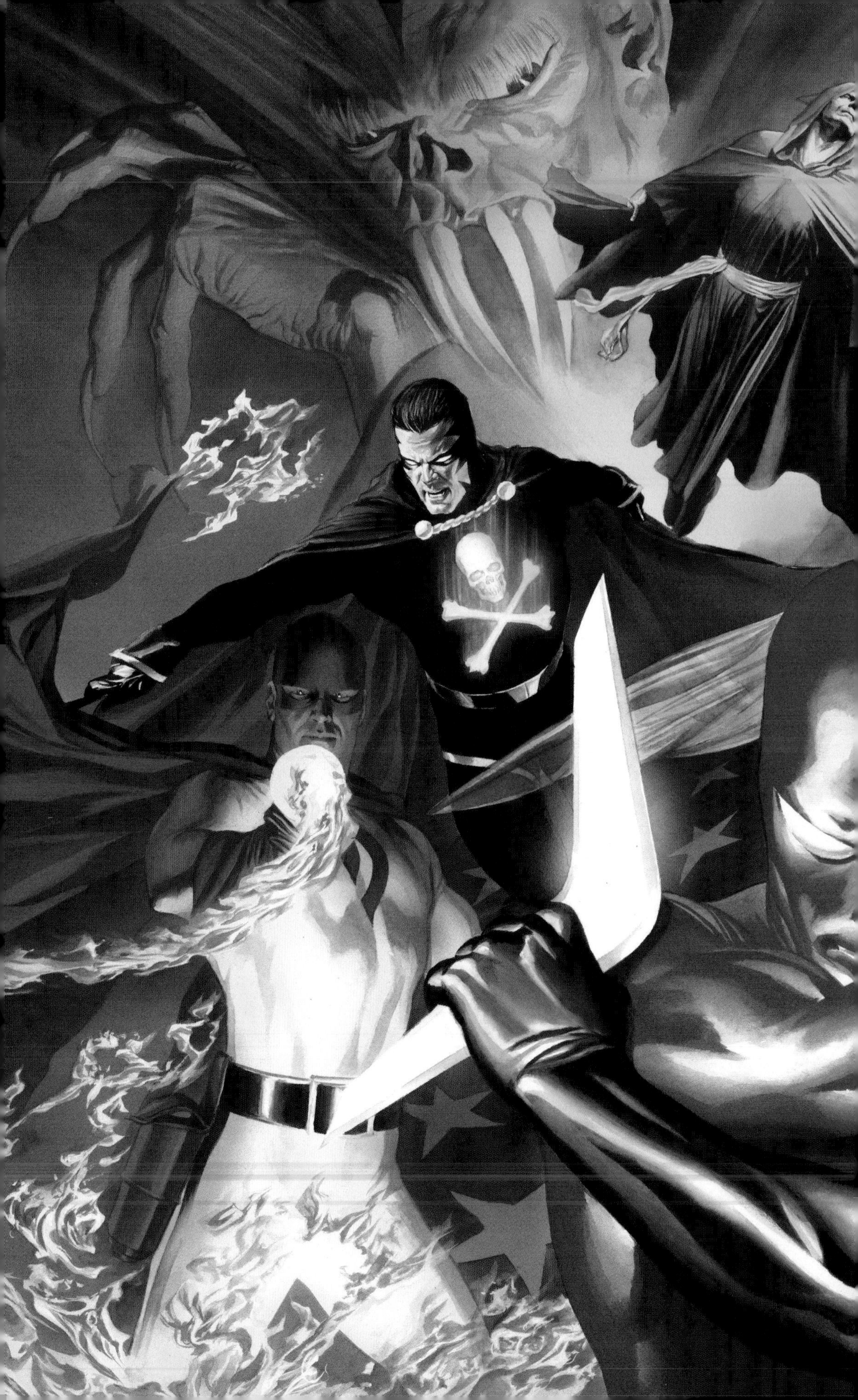

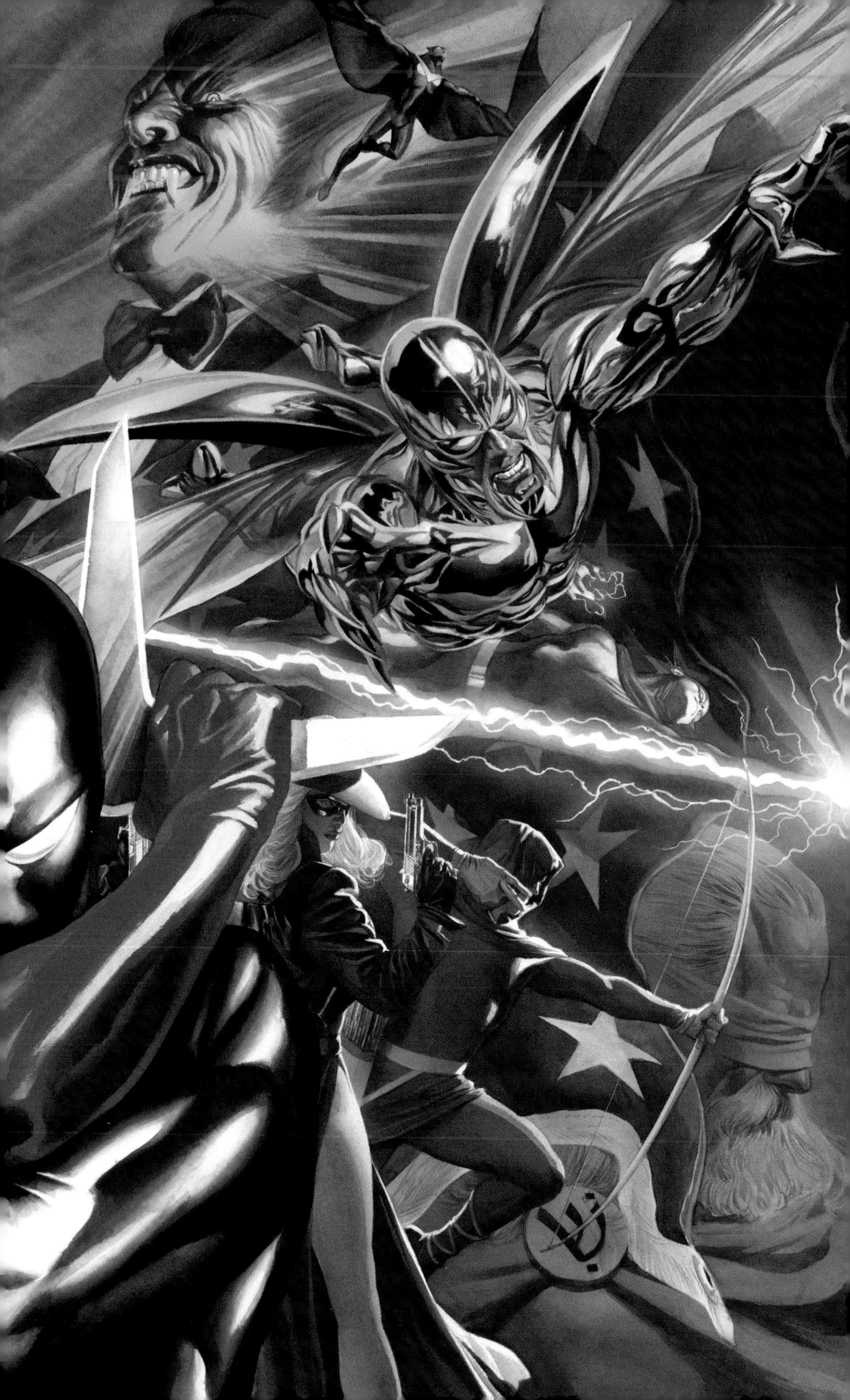

ISSUE

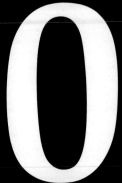

From the dawn of the 20th Century came a new chapter in mankind's history, unleashed during a time of great war and destruction.

It was the beginning of the Age of the Superpowers, yet with the closing of the Second World War, this new spark seemingly flickered and died.

Until now...

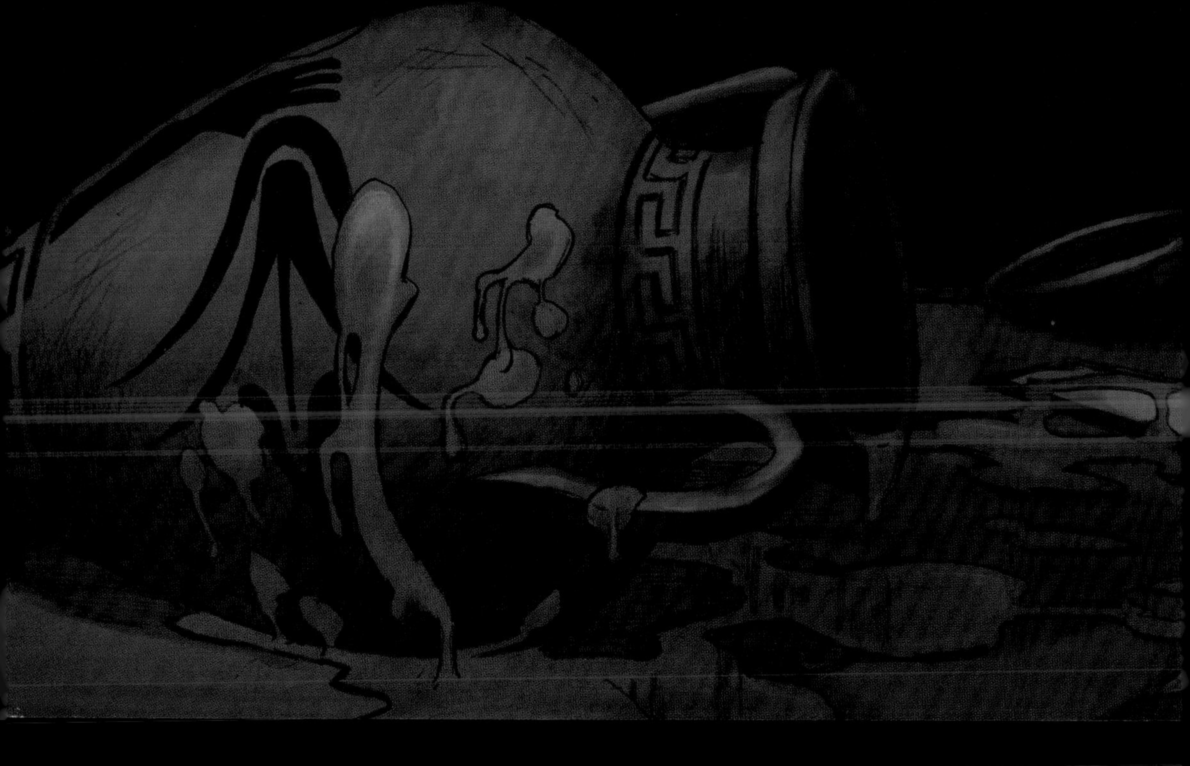

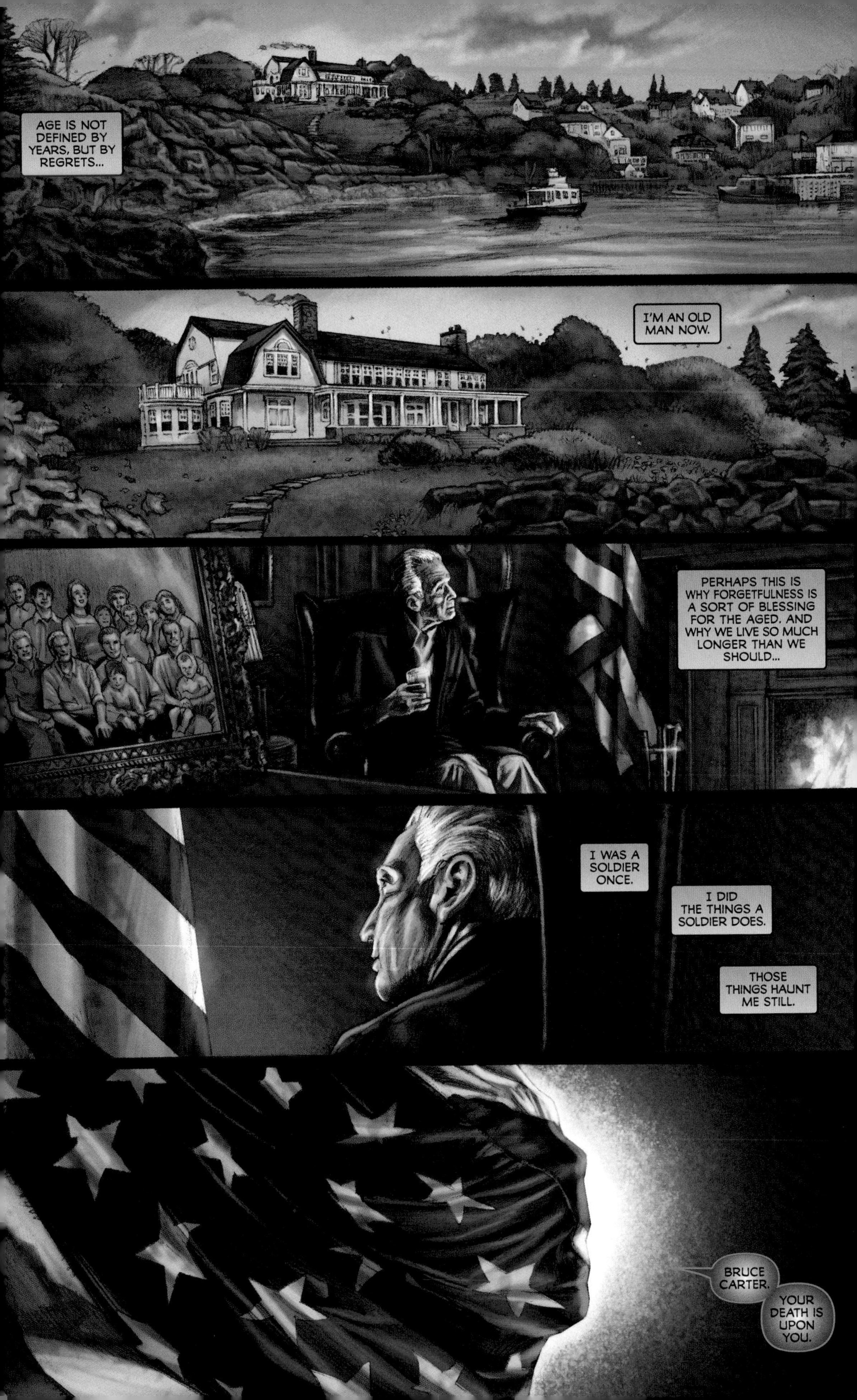
AGE IS NOT DEFINED BY YEARS, BUT BY REGRETS...
I'M AN OLD MAN NOW.
PERHAPS THIS IS WHY FORGETFULNESS IS A SORT OF BLESSING FOR THE AGED. AND WHY WE LIVE SO MUCH LONGER THAN WE SHOULD...
I WAS A SOLDIER ONCE.
I DID THE THINGS A SOLDIER DOES.
THOSE THINGS HAUNT ME STILL.
BRUCE CARTER.
YOUR DEATH IS UPON YOU.

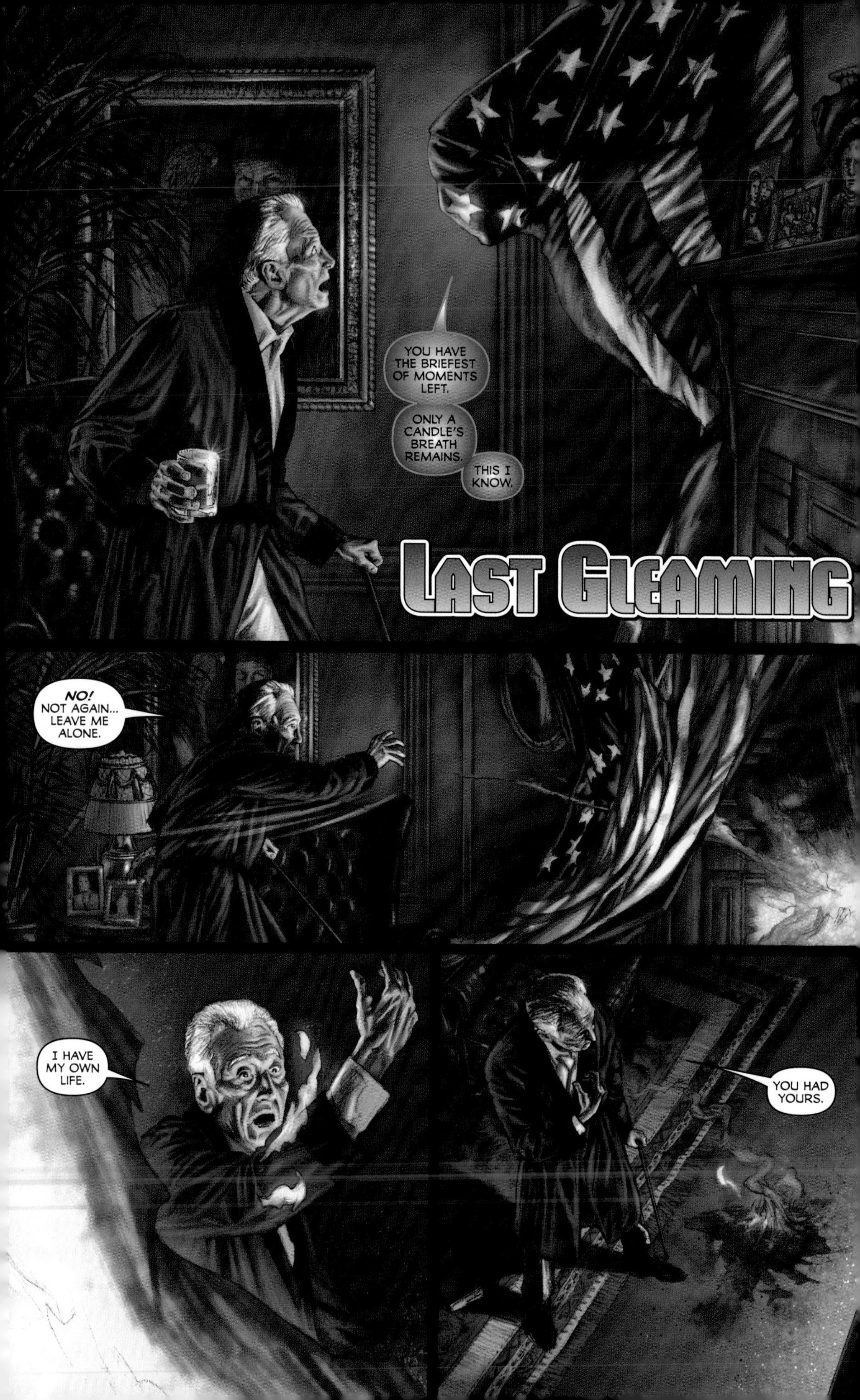
YOU HAVE THE BRIEFEST OF MOMENTS LEFT.
ONLY A CANDLE'S BREATH REMAINS.
THIS I KNOW.
LAST GLEAMING
NO! NOT AGAIN... LEAVE ME ALONE.
I HAVE MY OWN LIFE.
YOU HAD YOURS.

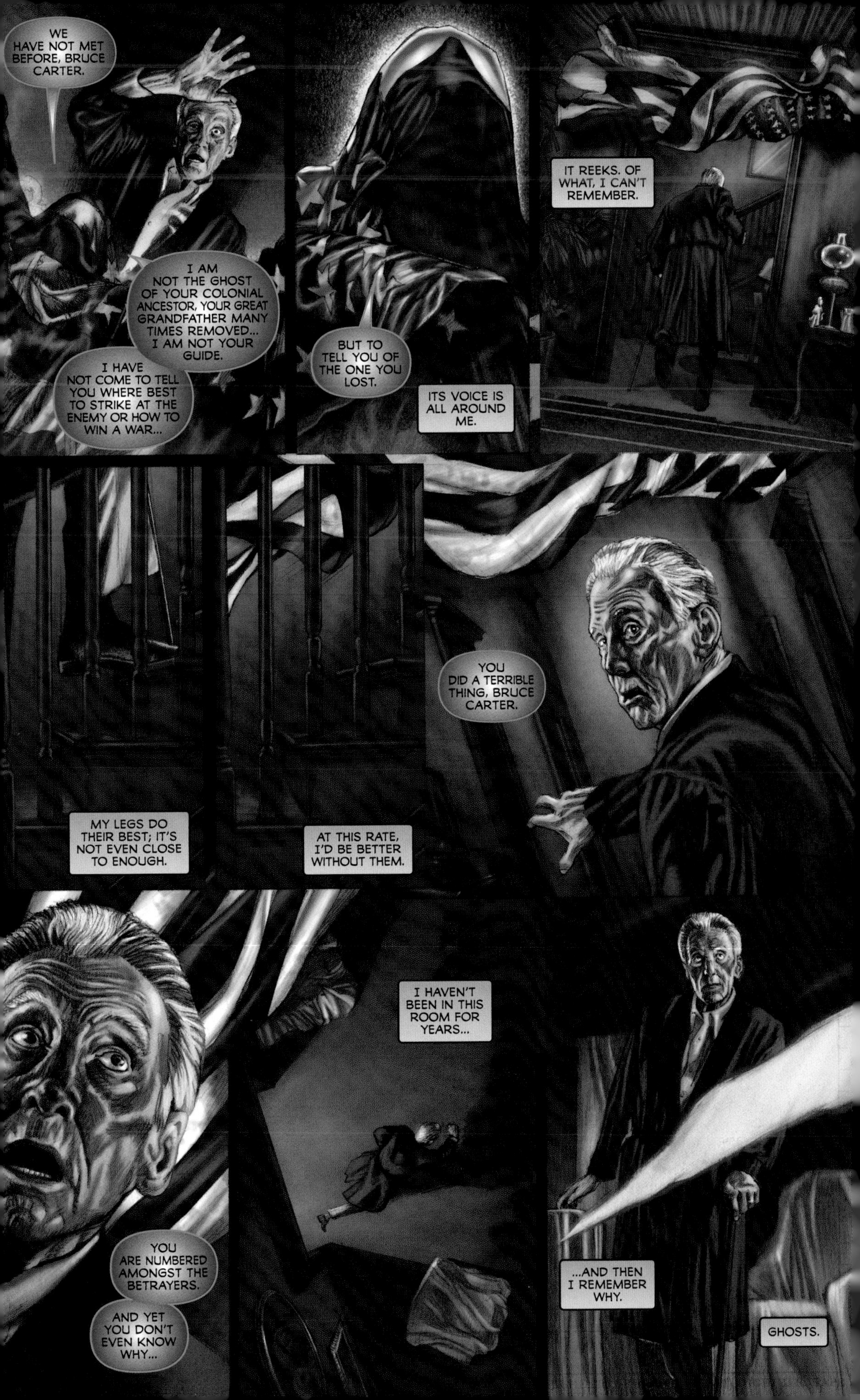
WE HAVE NOT MET BEFORE, BRUCE CARTER.
I AM NOT THE GHOST OF YOUR COLONIAL ANCESTOR, YOUR GREAT GRANDFATHER MANY TIMES REMOVED... I AM NOT YOUR GUIDE.
I HAVE NOT COME TO TELL YOU WHERE BEST TO STRIKE AT THE ENEMY OR HOW TO WIN A WAR...
BUT TO TELL YOU OF THE ONE YOU LOST.
ITS VOICE IS ALL AROUND ME.
IT REEKS. OF WHAT, I CAN'T REMEMBER.
MY LEGS DO THEIR BEST; IT'S NOT EVEN CLOSE TO ENOUGH.
AT THIS RATE, I'D BE BETTER WITHOUT THEM.
YOU DID A TERRIBLE THING, BRUCE CARTER.
YOU ARE NUMBERED AMONGST THE BETRAYERS.
AND YET YOU DON'T EVEN KNOW WHY...
I HAVEN'T BEEN IN THIS ROOM FOR YEARS...
...AND THEN I REMEMBER WHY.
GHOSTS.

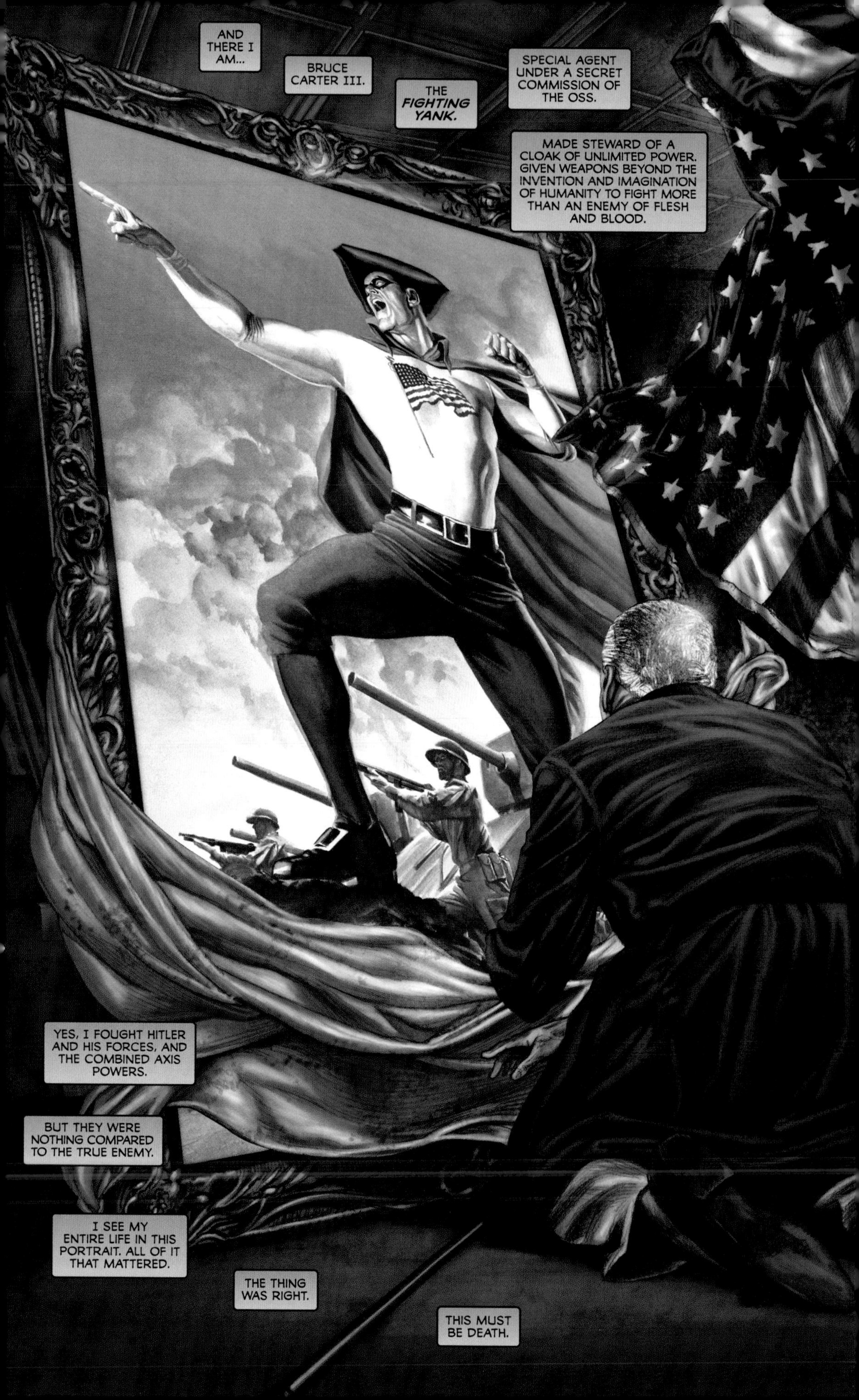
AND THERE I AM...
BRUCE CARTER III.
THE *FIGHTING YANK.*
SPECIAL AGENT UNDER A SECRET COMMISSION OF THE OSS.
MADE STEWARD OF A CLOAK OF UNLIMITED POWER. GIVEN WEAPONS BEYOND THE INVENTION AND IMAGINATION OF HUMANITY TO FIGHT MORE THAN AN ENEMY OF FLESH AND BLOOD.
YES, I FOUGHT HITLER AND HIS FORCES, AND THE COMBINED AXIS POWERS.
BUT THEY WERE NOTHING COMPARED TO THE TRUE ENEMY.
I SEE MY ENTIRE LIFE IN THIS PORTRAIT. ALL OF IT THAT MATTERED.
THE THING WAS RIGHT.
THIS MUST BE DEATH.

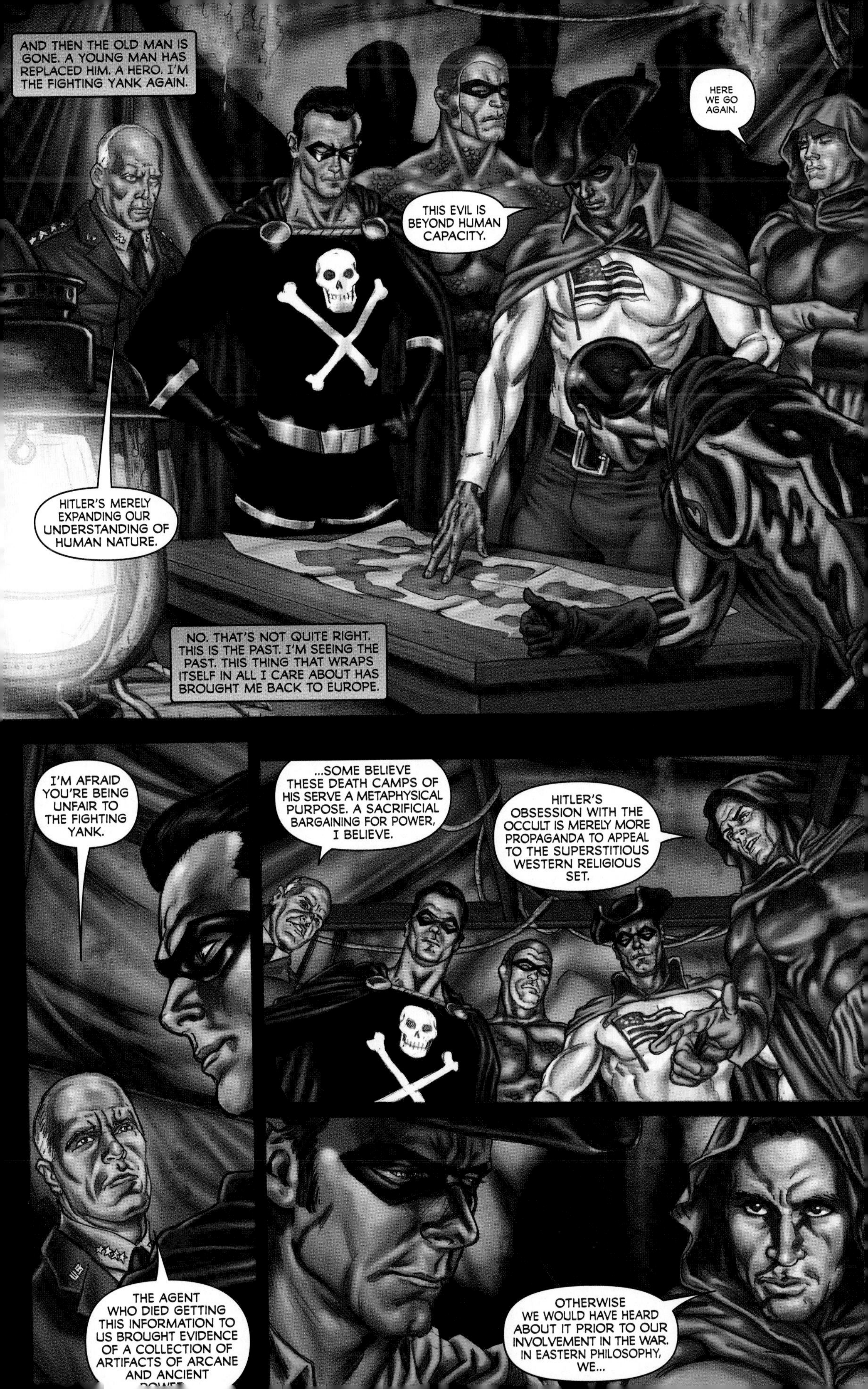
AND THEN THE OLD MAN IS GONE. A YOUNG MAN HAS REPLACED HIM. A HERO. I'M THE FIGHTING YANK AGAIN.
HERE WE GO AGAIN.
THIS EVIL IS BEYOND HUMAN CAPACITY.
HITLER'S MERELY EXPANDING OUR UNDERSTANDING OF HUMAN NATURE.
NO. THAT'S NOT QUITE RIGHT. THIS IS THE PAST. I'M SEEING THE PAST. THIS THING THAT WRAPS ITSELF IN ALL I CARE ABOUT HAS BROUGHT ME BACK TO EUROPE.
I'M AFRAID YOU'RE BEING UNFAIR TO THE FIGHTING YANK.
...SOME BELIEVE THESE DEATH CAMPS OF HIS SERVE A METAPHYSICAL PURPOSE. A SACRIFICIAL BARGAINING FOR POWER, I BELIEVE.
HITLER'S OBSESSION WITH THE OCCULT IS MERELY MORE PROPAGANDA TO APPEAL TO THE SUPERSTITIOUS WESTERN RELIGIOUS SET.
THE AGENT WHO DIED GETTING THIS INFORMATION TO US BROUGHT EVIDENCE OF A COLLECTION OF ARTIFACTS OF ARCANE AND ANCIENT
OTHERWISE WE WOULD HAVE HEARD ABOUT IT PRIOR TO OUR INVOLVEMENT IN THE WAR. IN EASTERN PHILOSOPHY, WE...

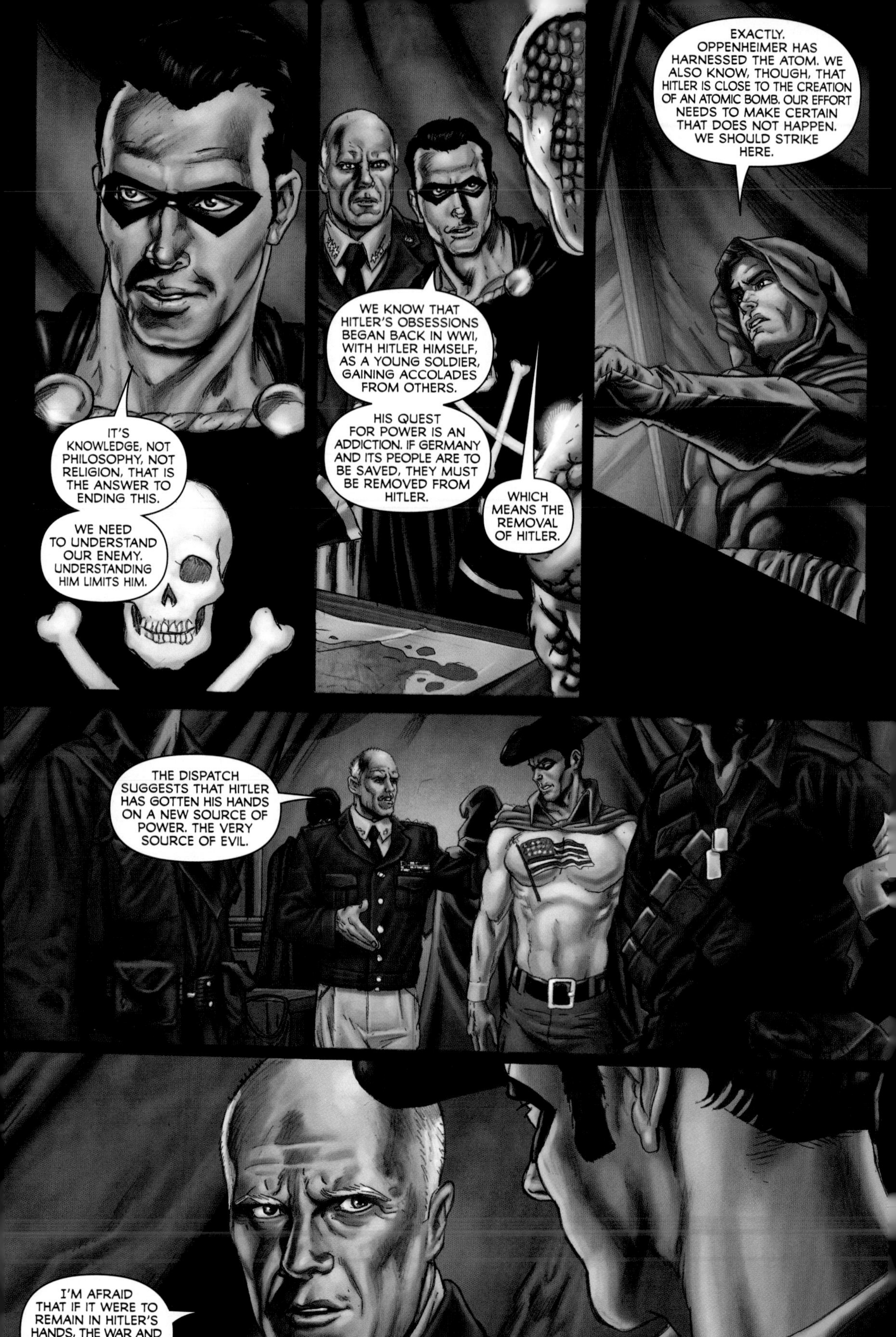
IT'S KNOWLEDGE, NOT PHILOSOPHY, NOT RELIGION, THAT IS THE ANSWER TO ENDING THIS.
WE NEED TO UNDERSTAND OUR ENEMY. UNDERSTANDING HIM LIMITS HIM.
WE KNOW THAT HITLER'S OBSESSIONS BEGAN BACK IN WWI, WITH HITLER HIMSELF, AS A YOUNG SOLDIER, GAINING ACCOLADES FROM OTHERS.
HIS QUEST FOR POWER IS AN ADDICTION. IF GERMANY AND ITS PEOPLE ARE TO BE SAVED, THEY MUST BE REMOVED FROM HITLER.
WHICH MEANS THE REMOVAL OF HITLER.
EXACTLY. OPPENHEIMER HAS HARNESSED THE ATOM. WE ALSO KNOW, THOUGH, THAT HITLER IS CLOSE TO THE CREATION OF AN ATOMIC BOMB. OUR EFFORT NEEDS TO MAKE CERTAIN THAT DOES NOT HAPPEN. WE SHOULD STRIKE HERE.
THE DISPATCH SUGGESTS THAT HITLER HAS GOTTEN HIS HANDS ON A NEW SOURCE OF POWER. THE VERY SOURCE OF EVIL.
I'M AFRAID THAT IF IT WERE TO REMAIN IN HITLER'S HANDS, THE WAR AND THE DEATH CAMPS ARE MERELY THE BEGINNING.

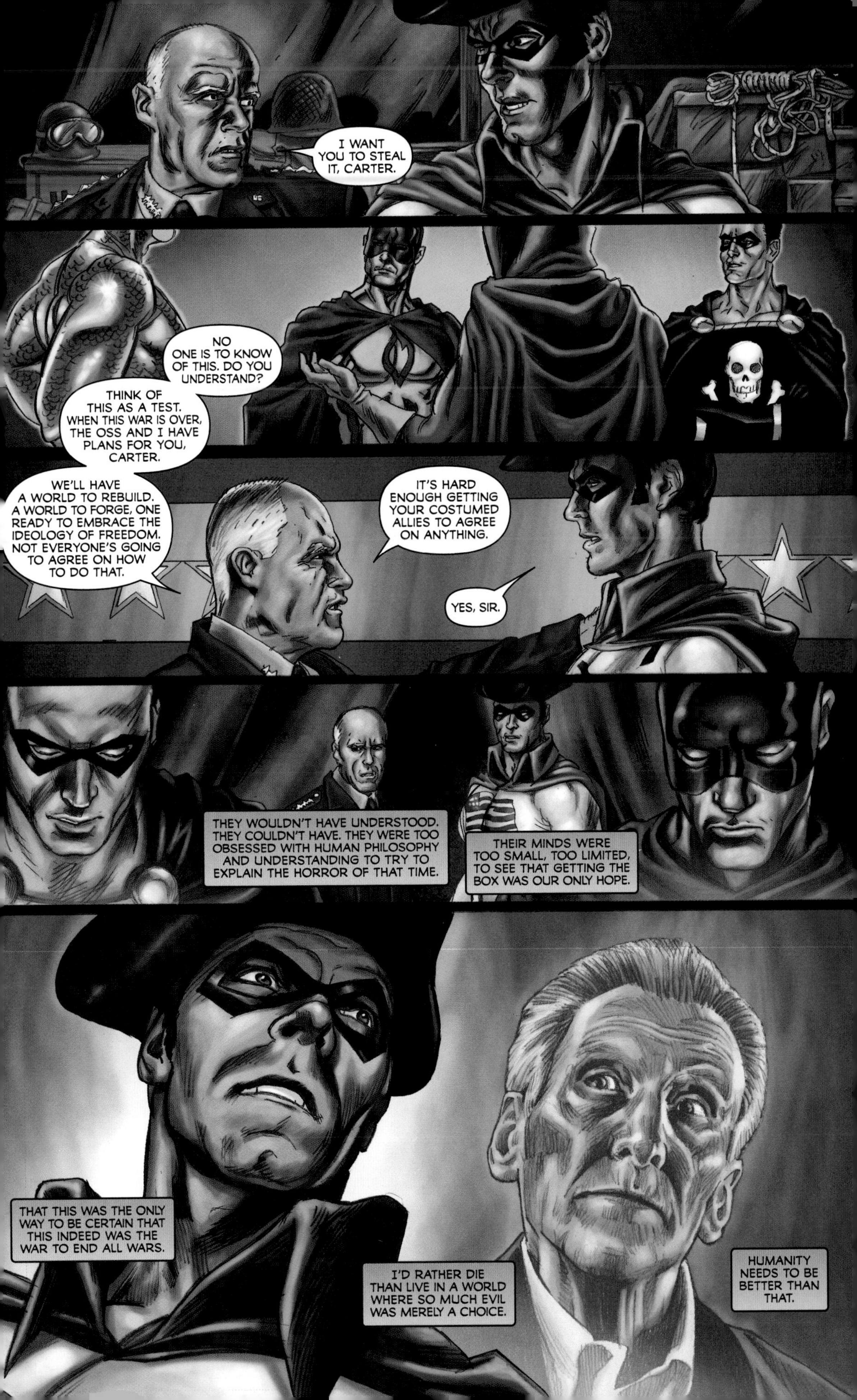
I WANT YOU TO STEAL IT, CARTER.
NO ONE IS TO KNOW OF THIS. DO YOU UNDERSTAND?
THINK OF THIS AS A TEST. WHEN THIS WAR IS OVER, THE OSS AND I HAVE PLANS FOR YOU, CARTER.
WE'LL HAVE A WORLD TO REBUILD. A WORLD TO FORGE, ONE READY TO EMBRACE THE IDEOLOGY OF FREEDOM. NOT EVERYONE'S GOING TO AGREE ON HOW TO DO THAT.
IT'S HARD ENOUGH GETTING YOUR COSTUMED ALLIES TO AGREE ON ANYTHING.
YES, SIR.
THEY WOULDN'T HAVE UNDERSTOOD. THEY COULDN'T HAVE. THEY WERE TOO OBSESSED WITH HUMAN PHILOSOPHY AND UNDERSTANDING TO TRY TO EXPLAIN THE HORROR OF THAT TIME.
THEIR MINDS WERE TOO SMALL, TOO LIMITED, TO SEE THAT GETTING THE BOX WAS OUR ONLY HOPE.
THAT THIS WAS THE ONLY WAY TO BE CERTAIN THAT THIS INDEED WAS THE WAR TO END ALL WARS.
I'D RATHER DIE THAN LIVE IN A WORLD WHERE SO MUCH EVIL WAS MERELY A CHOICE.
HUMANITY NEEDS TO BE BETTER THAN THAT.

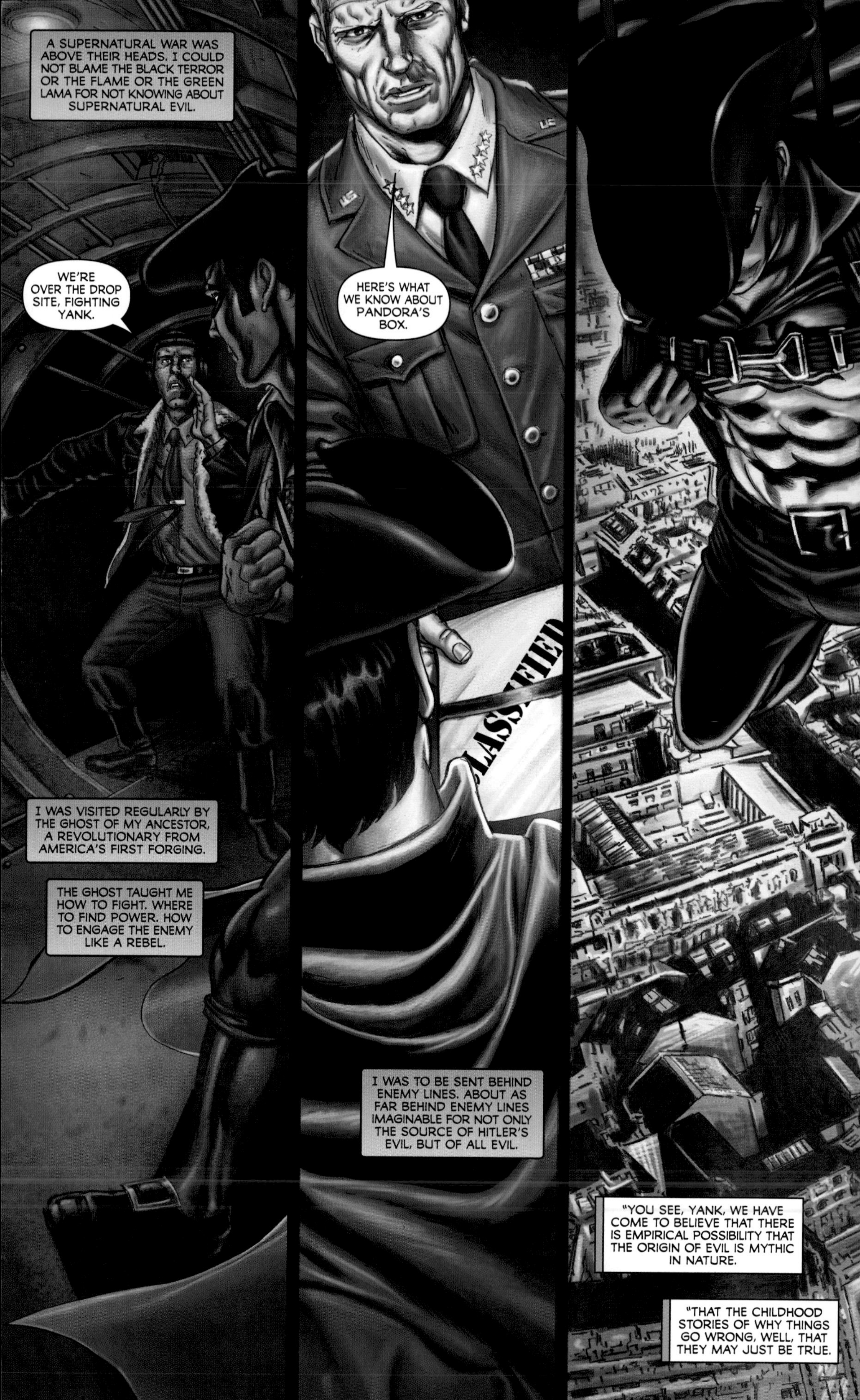
A SUPERNATURAL WAR WAS ABOVE THEIR HEADS. I COULD NOT BLAME THE BLACK TERROR OR THE FLAME OR THE GREEN LAMA FOR NOT KNOWING ABOUT SUPERNATURAL EVIL.
WE'RE OVER THE DROP SITE, FIGHTING YANK.
I WAS VISITED REGULARLY BY THE GHOST OF MY ANCESTOR, A REVOLUTIONARY FROM AMERICA'S FIRST FORGING.
THE GHOST TAUGHT ME HOW TO FIGHT. WHERE TO FIND POWER. HOW TO ENGAGE THE ENEMY LIKE A REBEL.
HERE'S WHAT WE KNOW ABOUT PANDORA'S BOX.
CLASSIFIED
I WAS TO BE SENT BEHIND ENEMY LINES. ABOUT AS FAR BEHIND ENEMY LINES IMAGINABLE FOR NOT ONLY THE SOURCE OF HITLER'S EVIL, BUT OF ALL EVIL.
"YOU SEE, YANK, WE HAVE COME TO BELIEVE THAT THERE IS EMPIRICAL POSSIBILITY THAT THE ORIGIN OF EVIL IS MYTHIC IN NATURE.
"THAT THE CHILDHOOD STORIES OF WHY THINGS GO WRONG, WELL, THAT THEY MAY JUST BE TRUE.

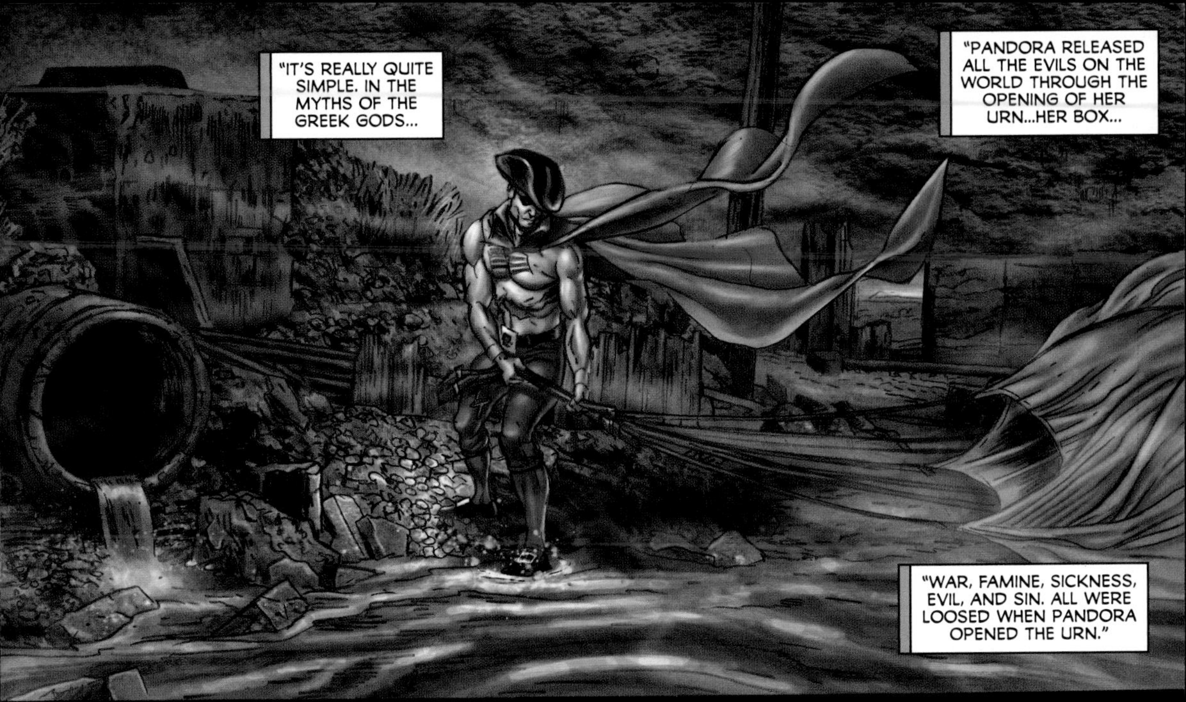
"IT'S REALLY QUITE SIMPLE. IN THE MYTHS OF THE GREEK GODS...
"PANDORA RELEASED ALL THE EVILS ON THE WORLD THROUGH THE OPENING OF HER URN...HER BOX...
"WAR, FAMINE, SICKNESS, EVIL, AND SIN. ALL WERE LOOSED WHEN PANDORA OPENED THE URN."

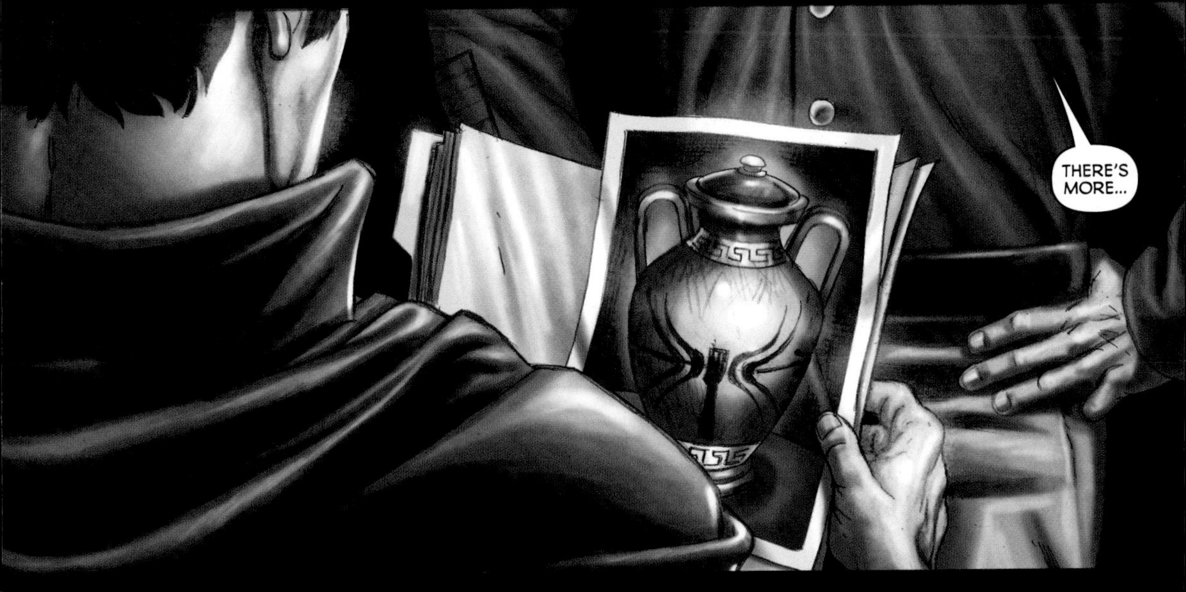
THERE'S MORE...

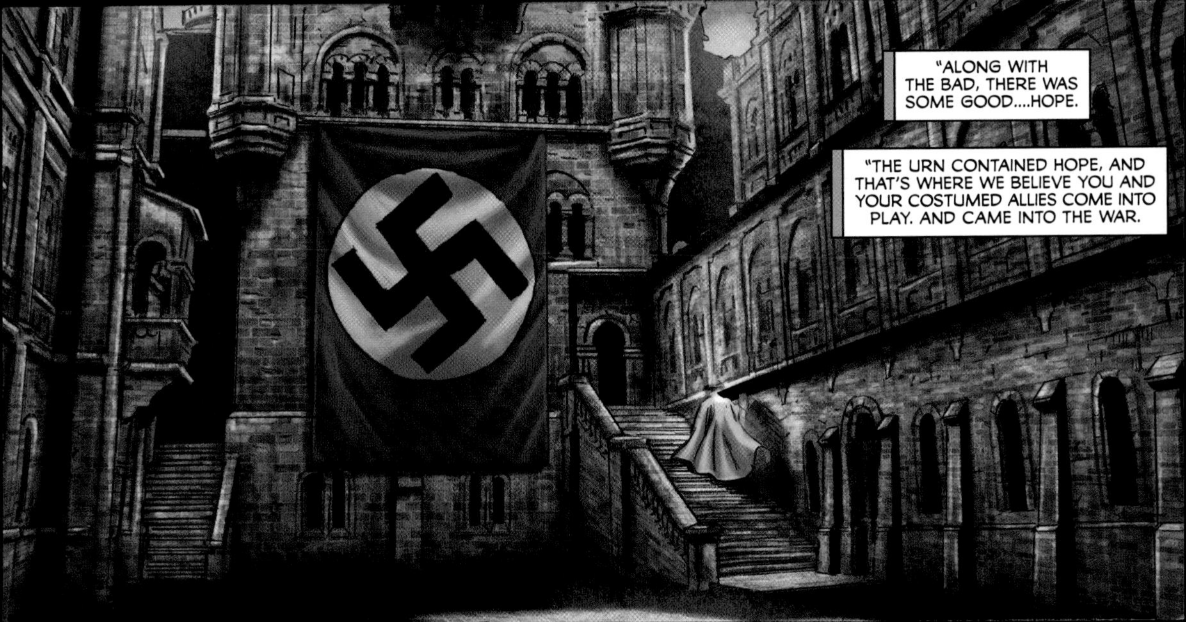
"ALONG WITH THE BAD, THERE WAS SOME GOOD....HOPE.
"THE URN CONTAINED HOPE, AND THAT'S WHERE WE BELIEVE YOU AND YOUR COSTUMED ALLIES COME INTO PLAY. AND CAME INTO THE WAR.

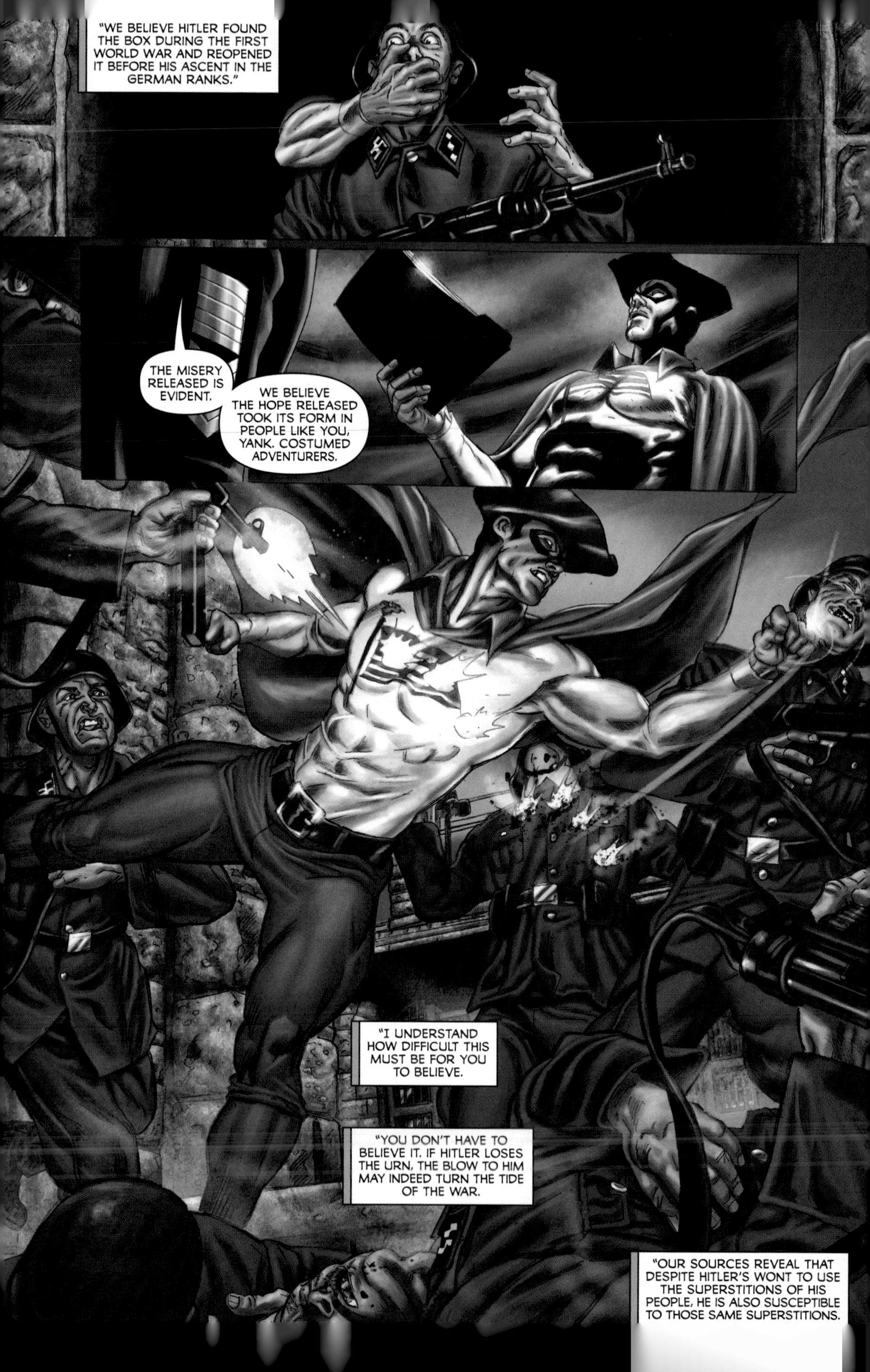
"WE BELIEVE HITLER FOUND THE BOX DURING THE FIRST WORLD WAR AND REOPENED IT BEFORE HIS ASCENT IN THE GERMAN RANKS."
THE MISERY RELEASED IS EVIDENT.
WE BELIEVE THE HOPE RELEASED TOOK ITS FORM IN PEOPLE LIKE YOU, YANK. COSTUMED ADVENTURERS.
"I UNDERSTAND HOW DIFFICULT THIS MUST BE FOR YOU TO BELIEVE.
"YOU DON'T HAVE TO BELIEVE IT. IF HITLER LOSES THE URN, THE BLOW TO HIM MAY INDEED TURN THE TIDE OF THE WAR.
"OUR SOURCES REVEAL THAT DESPITE HITLER'S WONT TO USE THE SUPERSTITIONS OF HIS PEOPLE, HE IS ALSO SUSCEPTIBLE TO THOSE SAME SUPERSTITIONS.

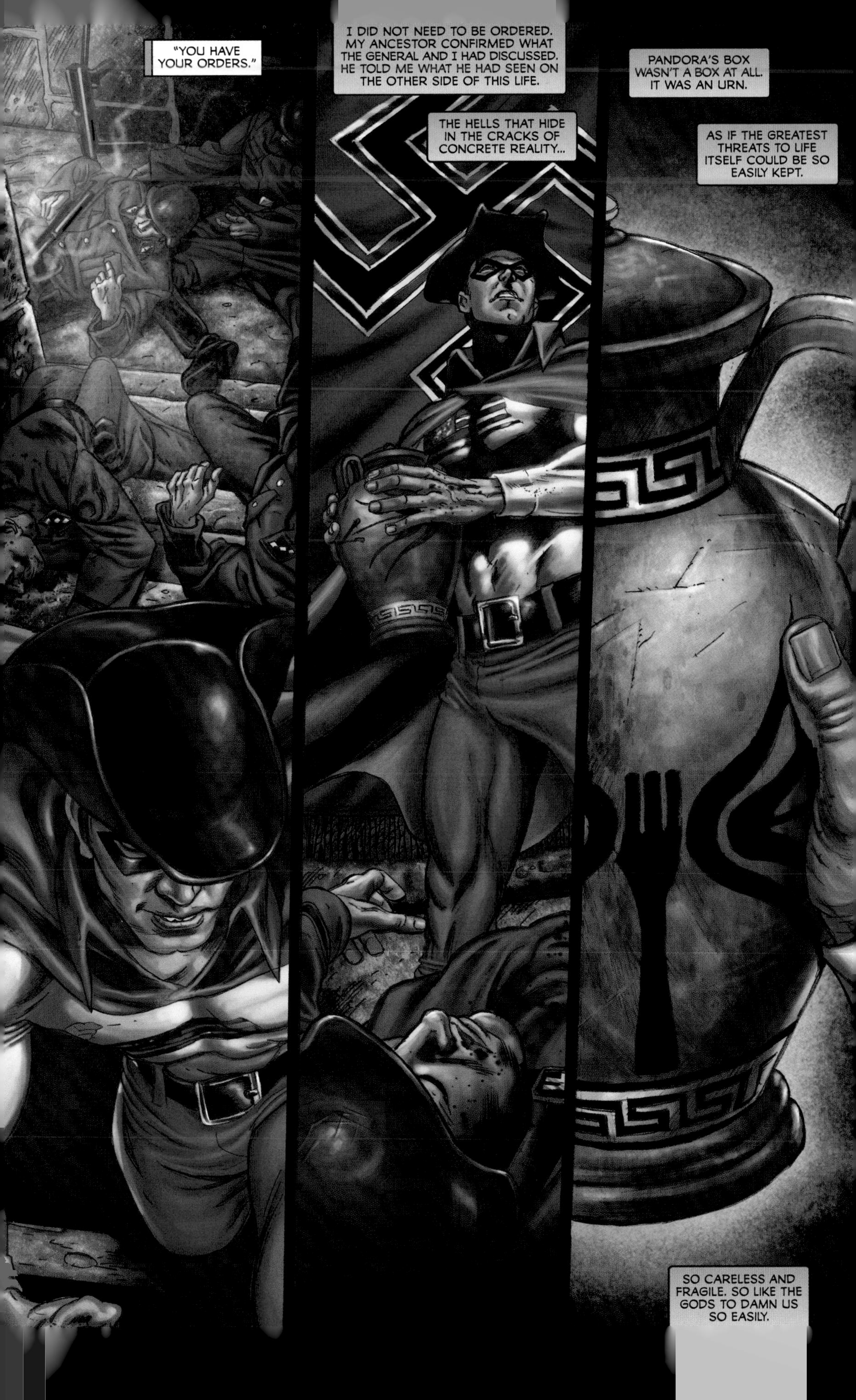
"YOU HAVE YOUR ORDERS."
I DID NOT NEED TO BE ORDERED. MY ANCESTOR CONFIRMED WHAT THE GENERAL AND I HAD DISCUSSED. HE TOLD ME WHAT HE HAD SEEN ON THE OTHER SIDE OF THIS LIFE.
THE HELLS THAT HIDE IN THE CRACKS OF CONCRETE REALITY...
PANDORA'S BOX WASN'T A BOX AT ALL. IT WAS AN URN.
AS IF THE GREATEST THREATS TO LIFE ITSELF COULD BE SO EASILY KEPT.
SO CARELESS AND FRAGILE. SO LIKE THE GODS TO DAMN US SO EASILY.

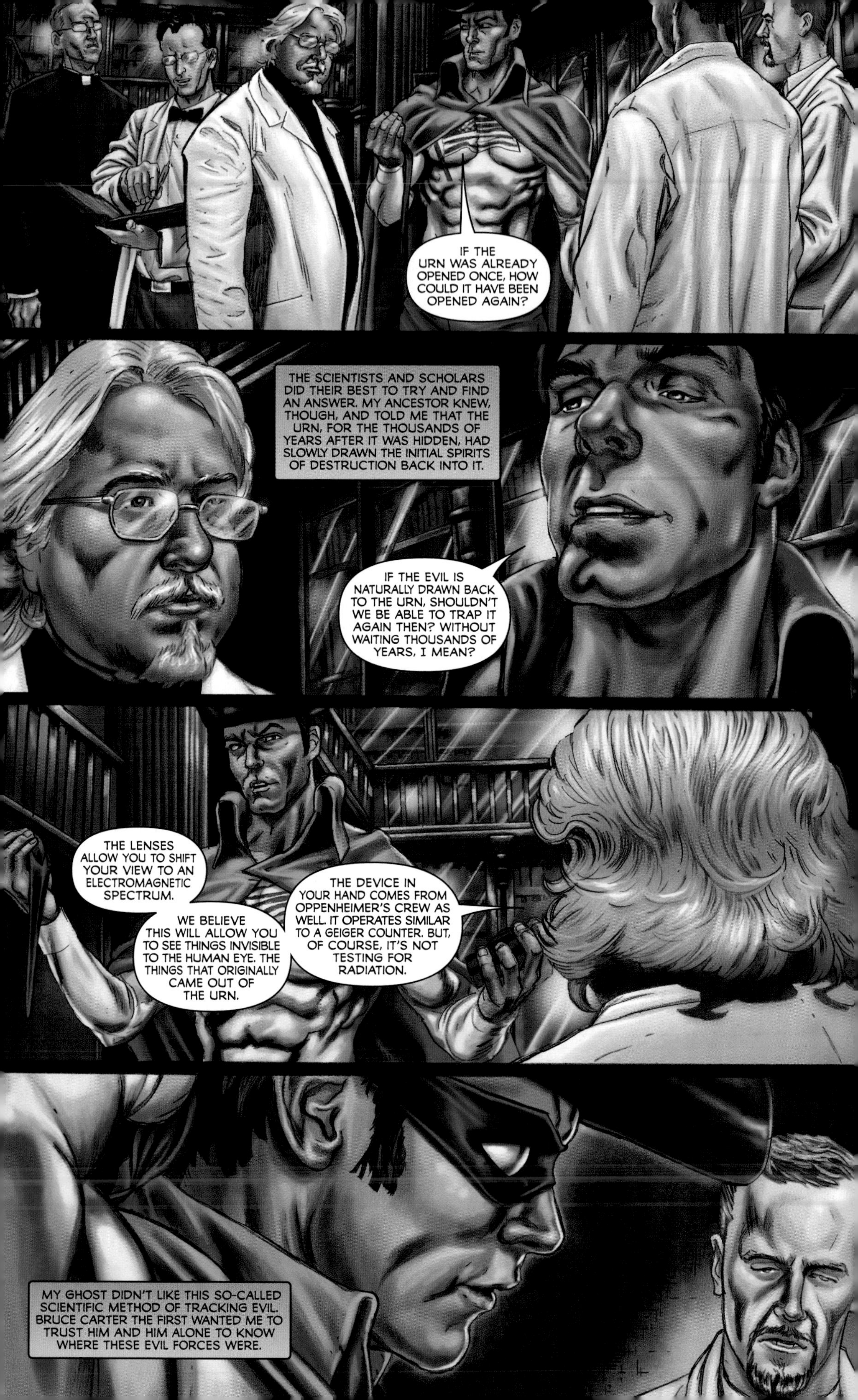
IF THE URN WAS ALREADY OPENED ONCE, HOW COULD IT HAVE BEEN OPENED AGAIN?
THE SCIENTISTS AND SCHOLARS DID THEIR BEST TO TRY AND FIND AN ANSWER. MY ANCESTOR KNEW, THOUGH, AND TOLD ME THAT THE URN, FOR THE THOUSANDS OF YEARS AFTER IT WAS HIDDEN, HAD SLOWLY DRAWN THE INITIAL SPIRITS OF DESTRUCTION BACK INTO IT.
IF THE EVIL IS NATURALLY DRAWN BACK TO THE URN, SHOULDN'T WE BE ABLE TO TRAP IT AGAIN THEN? WITHOUT WAITING THOUSANDS OF YEARS, I MEAN?
THE LENSES ALLOW YOU TO SHIFT YOUR VIEW TO AN ELECTROMAGNETIC SPECTRUM.
WE BELIEVE THIS WILL ALLOW YOU TO SEE THINGS INVISIBLE TO THE HUMAN EYE. THE THINGS THAT ORIGINALLY CAME OUT OF THE URN.
THE DEVICE IN YOUR HAND COMES FROM OPPENHEIMER'S CREW AS WELL. IT OPERATES SIMILAR TO A GEIGER COUNTER. BUT, OF COURSE, IT'S NOT TESTING FOR RADIATION.
MY GHOST DIDN'T LIKE THIS SO-CALLED SCIENTIFIC METHOD OF TRACKING EVIL. BRUCE CARTER THE FIRST WANTED ME TO TRUST HIM AND HIM ALONE TO KNOW WHERE THESE EVIL FORCES WERE.

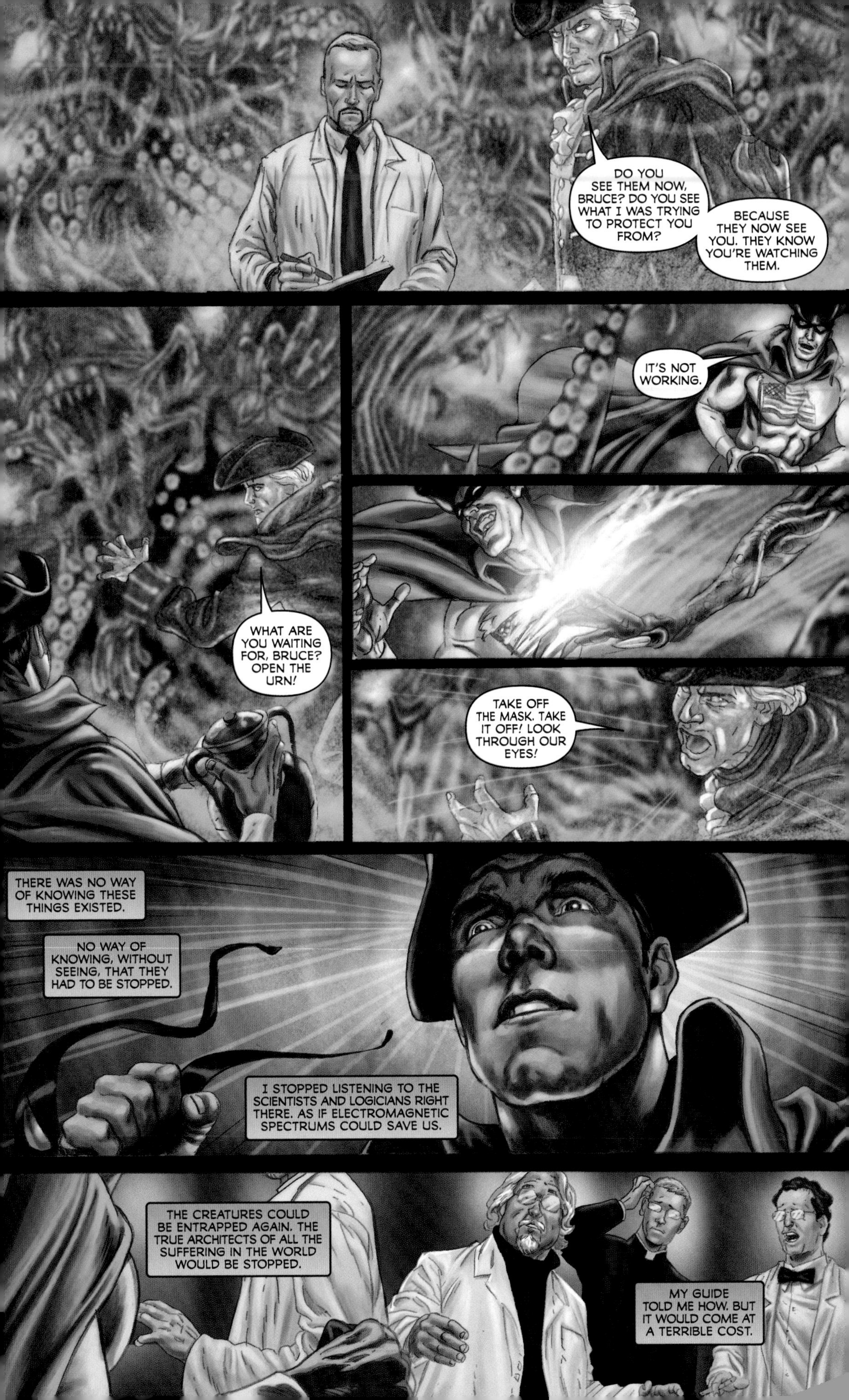
DO YOU SEE THEM NOW, BRUCE? DO YOU SEE WHAT I WAS TRYING TO PROTECT YOU FROM?
BECAUSE THEY NOW SEE YOU. THEY KNOW YOU'RE WATCHING THEM.
WHAT ARE YOU WAITING FOR, BRUCE? OPEN THE URN!
IT'S NOT WORKING.
TAKE OFF THE MASK. TAKE IT OFF! LOOK THROUGH OUR EYES!
THERE WAS NO WAY OF KNOWING THESE THINGS EXISTED.
NO WAY OF KNOWING, WITHOUT SEEING, THAT THEY HAD TO BE STOPPED.
I STOPPED LISTENING TO THE SCIENTISTS AND LOGICIANS RIGHT THERE. AS IF ELECTROMAGNETIC SPECTRUMS COULD SAVE US.
THE CREATURES COULD BE ENTRAPPED AGAIN. THE TRUE ARCHITECTS OF ALL THE SUFFERING IN THE WORLD WOULD BE STOPPED.
MY GUIDE TOLD ME HOW. BUT IT WOULD COME AT A TERRIBLE COST.

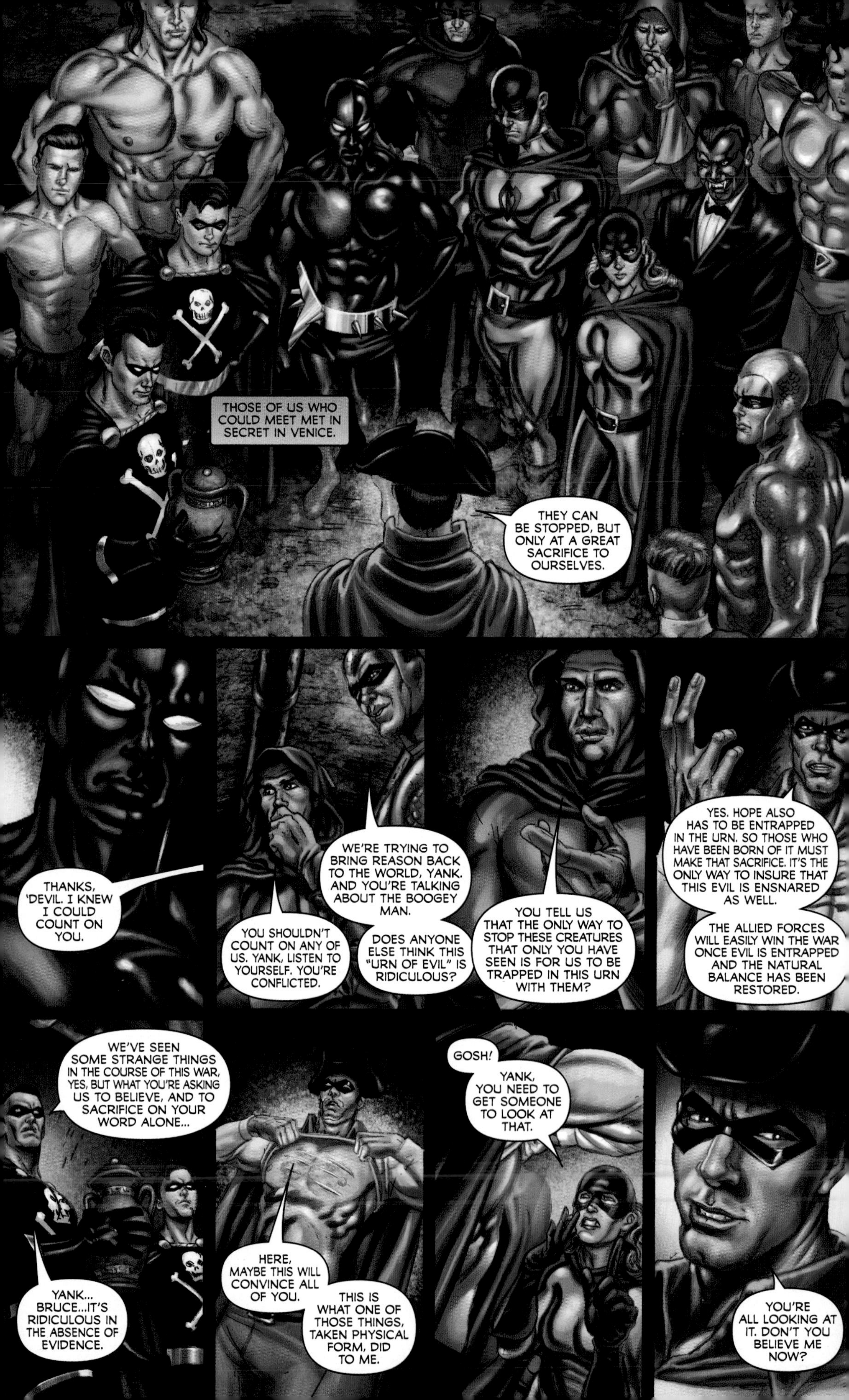
THOSE OF US WHO COULD MEET MET IN SECRET IN VENICE.
THEY CAN BE STOPPED, BUT ONLY AT A GREAT SACRIFICE TO OURSELVES.
THANKS, 'DEVIL. I KNEW I COULD COUNT ON YOU.
YOU SHOULDN'T COUNT ON ANY OF US. YANK, LISTEN TO YOURSELF. YOU'RE CONFLICTED.
WE'RE TRYING TO BRING REASON BACK TO THE WORLD, YANK. AND YOU'RE TALKING ABOUT THE BOOGEY MAN.
DOES ANYONE ELSE THINK THIS "URN OF EVIL" IS RIDICULOUS?
YOU TELL US THAT THE ONLY WAY TO STOP THESE CREATURES THAT ONLY YOU HAVE SEEN IS FOR US TO BE TRAPPED IN THIS URN WITH THEM?
YES. HOPE ALSO HAS TO BE ENTRAPPED IN THE URN. SO THOSE WHO HAVE BEEN BORN OF IT MUST MAKE THAT SACRIFICE. IT'S THE ONLY WAY TO INSURE THAT THIS EVIL IS ENSNARED AS WELL.
THE ALLIED FORCES WILL EASILY WIN THE WAR ONCE EVIL IS ENTRAPPED AND THE NATURAL BALANCE HAS BEEN RESTORED.
WE'VE SEEN SOME STRANGE THINGS IN THE COURSE OF THIS WAR, YES, BUT WHAT YOU'RE ASKING US TO BELIEVE, AND TO SACRIFICE ON YOUR WORD ALONE...
YANK... BRUCE...IT'S RIDICULOUS IN THE ABSENCE OF EVIDENCE.
HERE, MAYBE THIS WILL CONVINCE ALL OF YOU.
THIS IS WHAT ONE OF THOSE THINGS, TAKEN PHYSICAL FORM, DID TO ME.
GOSH!
YANK, YOU NEED TO GET SOMEONE TO LOOK AT THAT.
YOU'RE ALL LOOKING AT IT. DON'T YOU BELIEVE ME NOW?

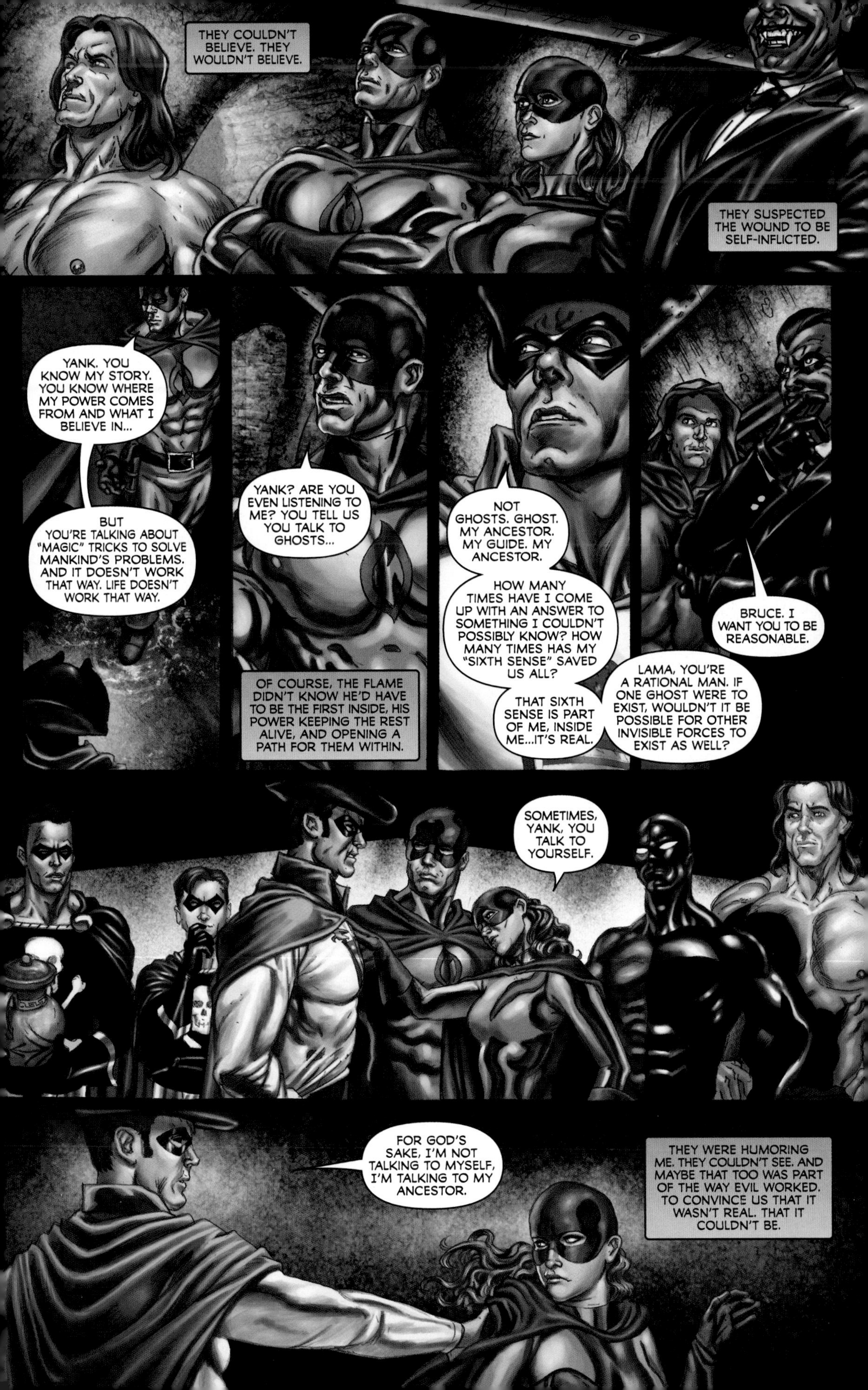
THEY COULDN'T BELIEVE. THEY WOULDN'T BELIEVE.
THEY SUSPECTED THE WOUND TO BE SELF-INFLICTED.
YANK. YOU KNOW MY STORY. YOU KNOW WHERE MY POWER COMES FROM AND WHAT I BELIEVE IN...
BUT YOU'RE TALKING ABOUT "MAGIC" TRICKS TO SOLVE MANKIND'S PROBLEMS. AND IT DOESN'T WORK THAT WAY. LIFE DOESN'T WORK THAT WAY.
YANK? ARE YOU EVEN LISTENING TO ME? YOU TELL US YOU TALK TO GHOSTS...
OF COURSE, THE FLAME DIDN'T KNOW HE'D HAVE TO BE THE FIRST INSIDE, HIS POWER KEEPING THE REST ALIVE, AND OPENING A PATH FOR THEM WITHIN.
NOT GHOSTS. GHOST. MY ANCESTOR. MY GUIDE. MY ANCESTOR.
HOW MANY TIMES HAVE I COME UP WITH AN ANSWER TO SOMETHING I COULDN'T POSSIBLY KNOW? HOW MANY TIMES HAS MY "SIXTH SENSE" SAVED US ALL?
THAT SIXTH SENSE IS PART OF ME, INSIDE ME...IT'S REAL.
BRUCE. I WANT YOU TO BE REASONABLE.
LAMA, YOU'RE A RATIONAL MAN. IF ONE GHOST WERE TO EXIST, WOULDN'T IT BE POSSIBLE FOR OTHER INVISIBLE FORCES TO EXIST AS WELL?
SOMETIMES, YANK, YOU TALK TO YOURSELF.
FOR GOD'S SAKE, I'M NOT TALKING TO MYSELF, I'M TALKING TO MY ANCESTOR.
THEY WERE HUMORING ME. THEY COULDN'T SEE. AND MAYBE THAT TOO WAS PART OF THE WAY EVIL WORKED. TO CONVINCE US THAT IT WASN'T REAL. THAT IT COULDN'T BE.

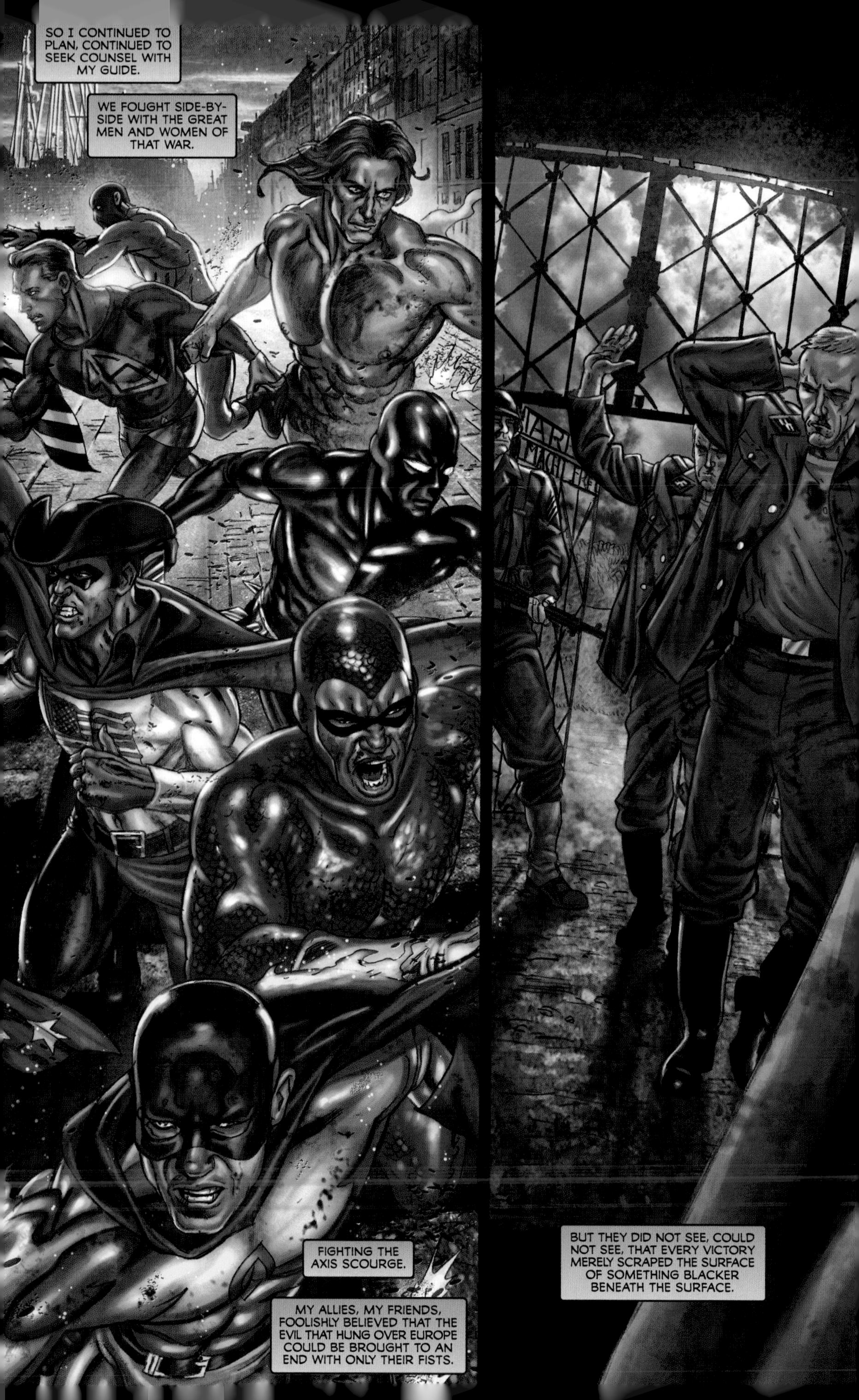
SO I CONTINUED TO PLAN, CONTINUED TO SEEK COUNSEL WITH MY GUIDE.
WE FOUGHT SIDE-BY-SIDE WITH THE GREAT MEN AND WOMEN OF THAT WAR.
FIGHTING THE AXIS SCOURGE.
MY ALLIES, MY FRIENDS, FOOLISHLY BELIEVED THAT THE EVIL THAT HUNG OVER EUROPE COULD BE BROUGHT TO AN END WITH ONLY THEIR FISTS.
BUT THEY DID NOT SEE, COULD NOT SEE, THAT EVERY VICTORY MERELY SCRAPED THE SURFACE OF SOMETHING BLACKER BENEATH THE SURFACE.

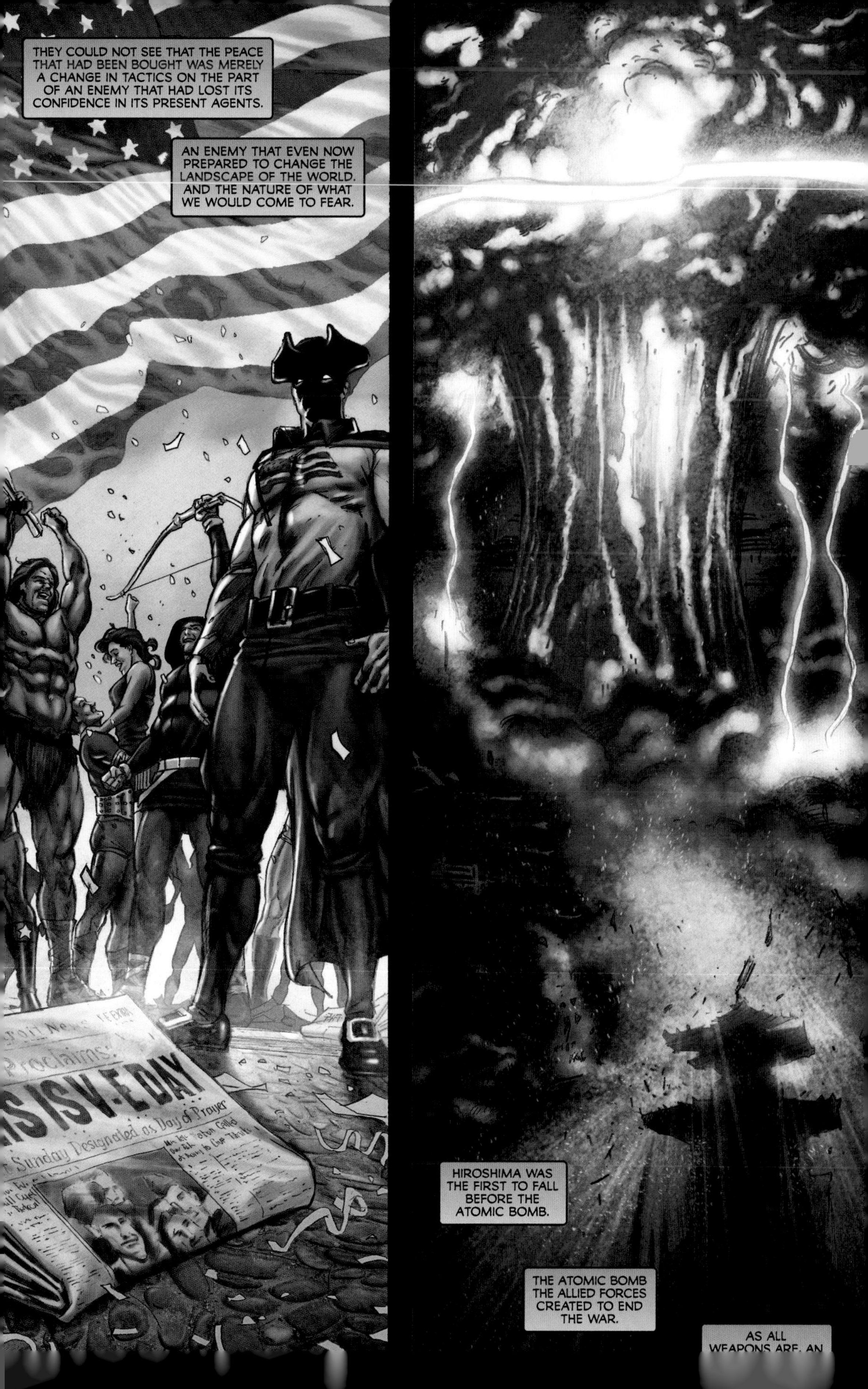
THEY COULD NOT SEE THAT THE PEACE THAT HAD BEEN BOUGHT WAS MERELY A CHANGE IN TACTICS ON THE PART OF AN ENEMY THAT HAD LOST ITS CONFIDENCE IN ITS PRESENT AGENTS.
AN ENEMY THAT EVEN NOW PREPARED TO CHANGE THE LANDSCAPE OF THE WORLD. AND THE NATURE OF WHAT WE WOULD COME TO FEAR.
Proclaims
V-E DAY
Sunday Designated as Day of Prayer
HIROSHIMA WAS THE FIRST TO FALL BEFORE THE ATOMIC BOMB.
THE ATOMIC BOMB THE ALLIED FORCES CREATED TO END THE WAR.
AS ALL WEAPONS ARE, AN

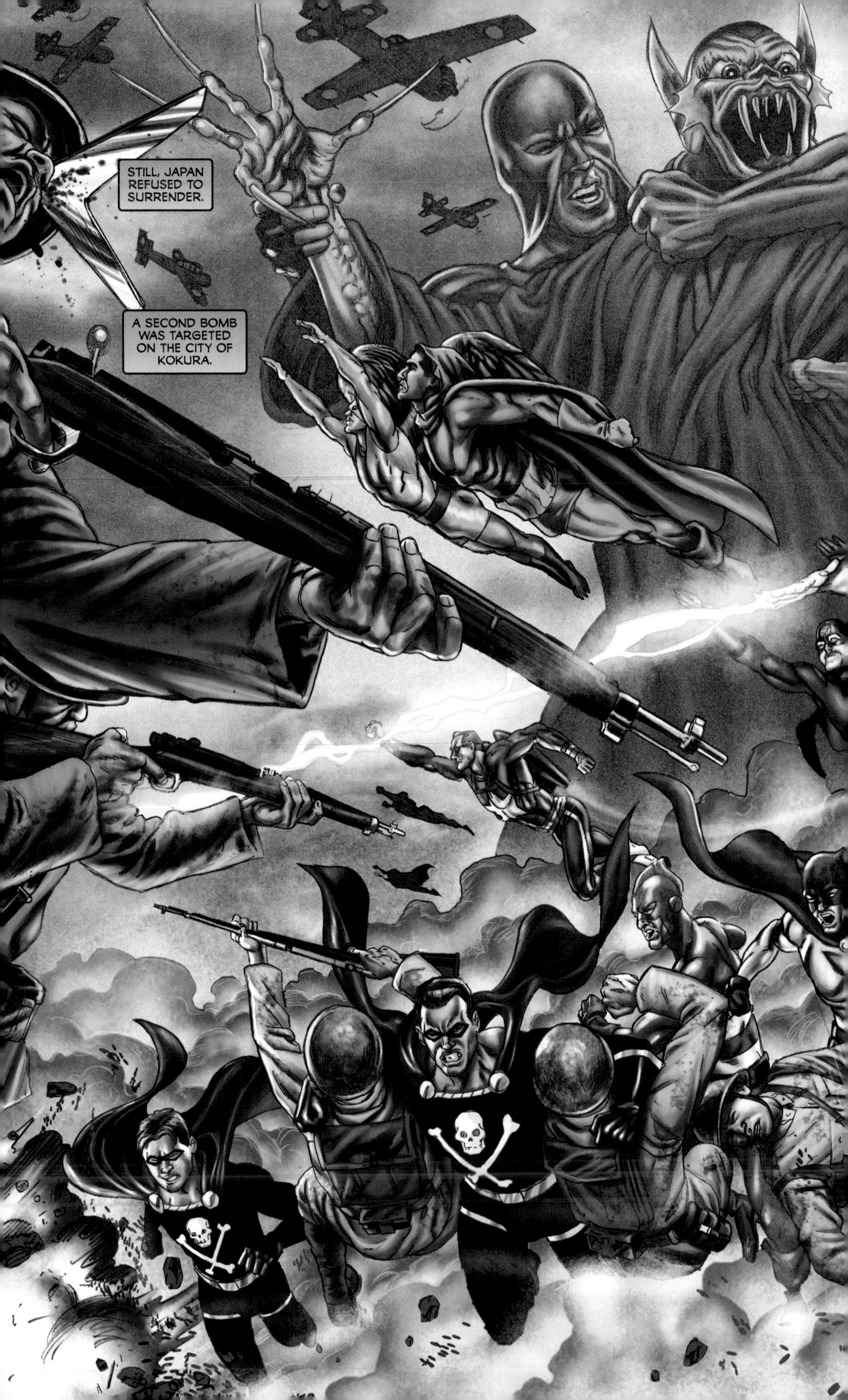
STILL, JAPAN REFUSED TO SURRENDER.
A SECOND BOMB WAS TARGETED ON THE CITY OF KOKURA.

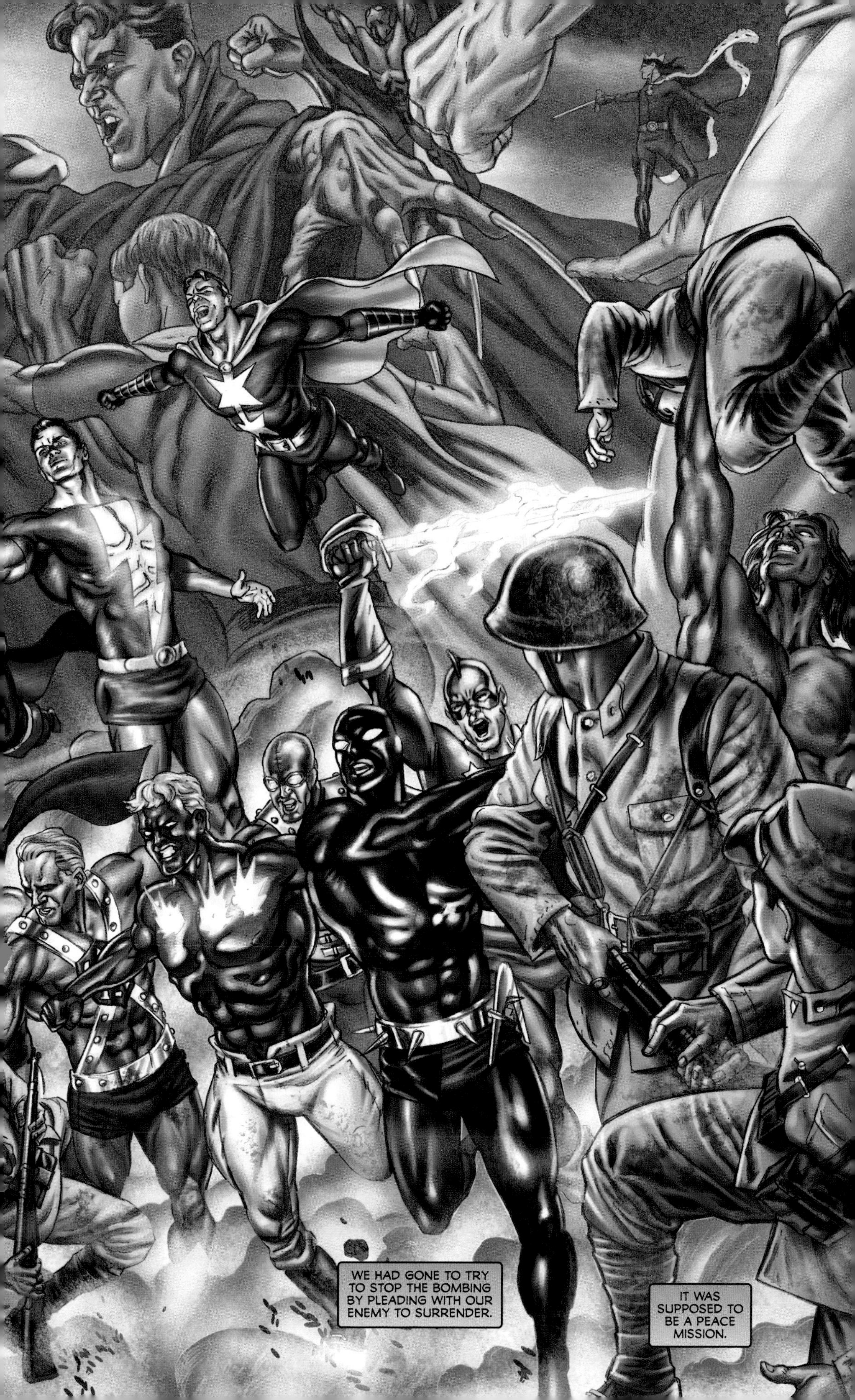
WE HAD GONE TO TRY TO STOP THE BOMBING BY PLEADING WITH OUR ENEMY TO SURRENDER.
IT WAS SUPPOSED TO BE A PEACE MISSION.

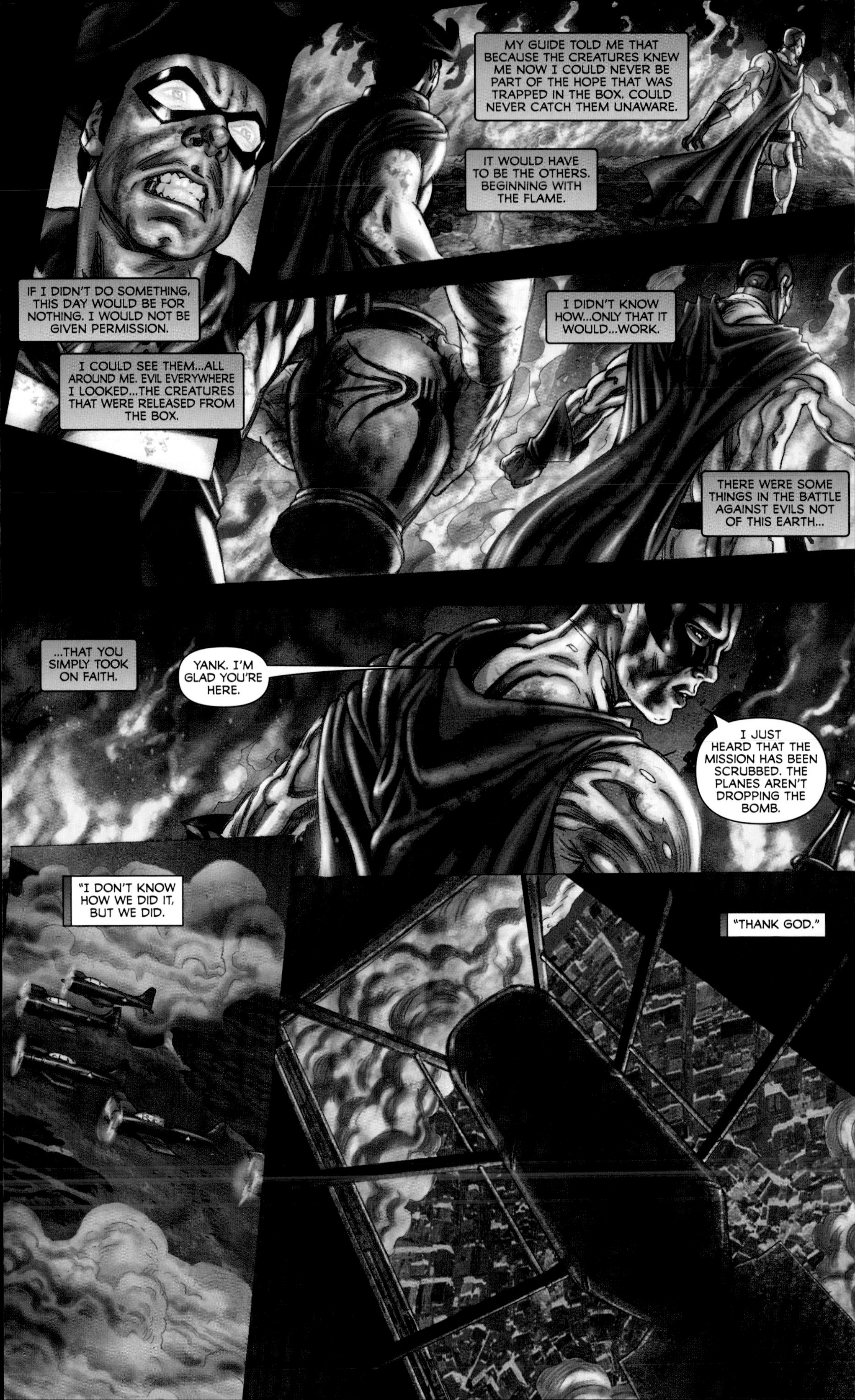
MY GUIDE TOLD ME THAT BECAUSE THE CREATURES KNEW ME NOW I COULD NEVER BE PART OF THE HOPE THAT WAS TRAPPED IN THE BOX. COULD NEVER CATCH THEM UNAWARE.
IT WOULD HAVE TO BE THE OTHERS. BEGINNING WITH THE FLAME.
IF I DIDN'T DO SOMETHING, THIS DAY WOULD BE FOR NOTHING. I WOULD NOT BE GIVEN PERMISSION.
I COULD SEE THEM...ALL AROUND ME. EVIL EVERYWHERE I LOOKED...THE CREATURES THAT WERE RELEASED FROM THE BOX.
I DIDN'T KNOW HOW...ONLY THAT IT WOULD...WORK.
THERE WERE SOME THINGS IN THE BATTLE AGAINST EVILS NOT OF THIS EARTH...
...THAT YOU SIMPLY TOOK ON FAITH.
YANK. I'M GLAD YOU'RE HERE.
I JUST HEARD THAT THE MISSION HAS BEEN SCRUBBED. THE PLANES AREN'T DROPPING THE BOMB.
"I DON'T KNOW HOW WE DID IT, BUT WE DID.
"THANK GOD."

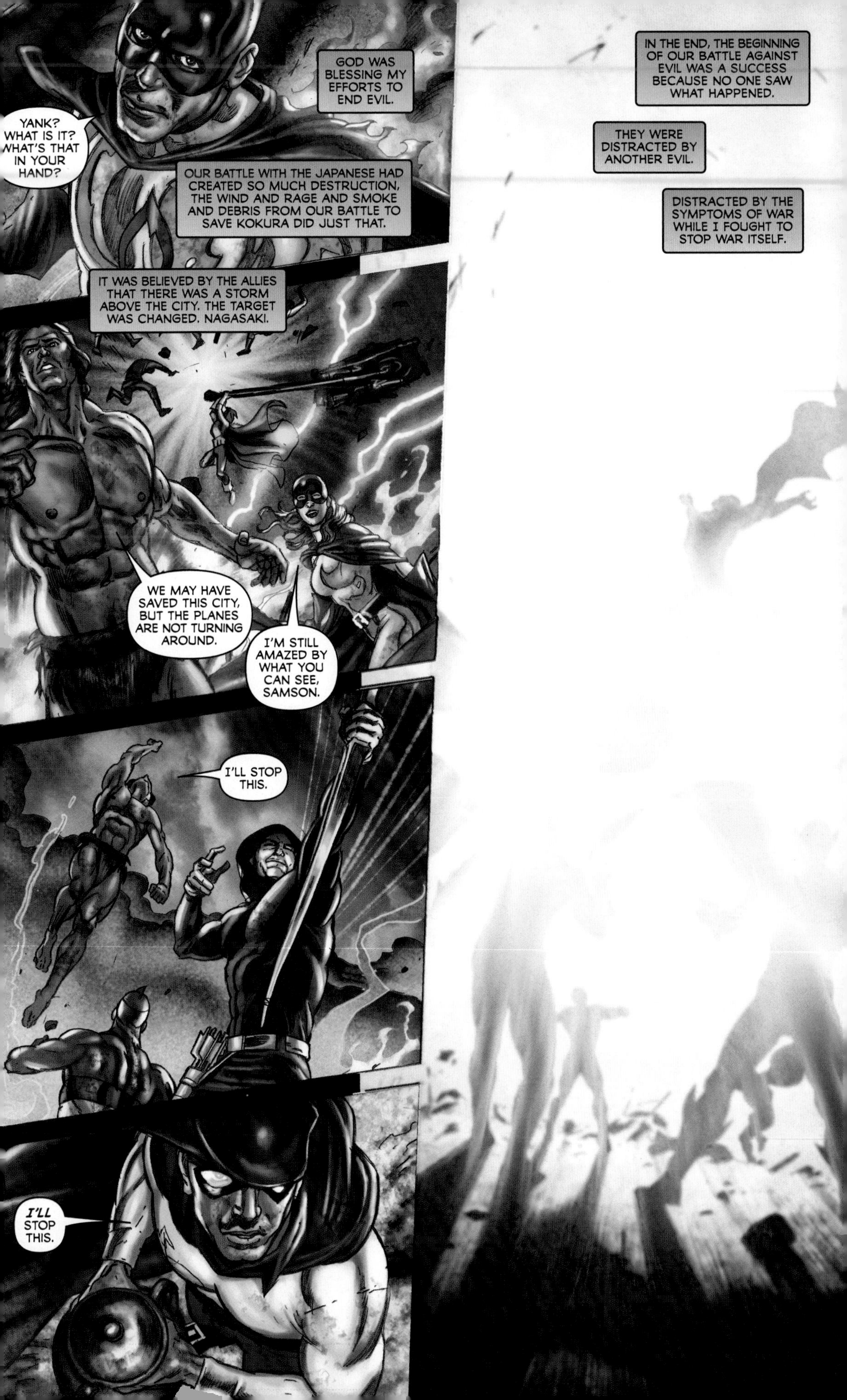
GOD WAS BLESSING MY EFFORTS TO END EVIL.
YANK? WHAT IS IT? WHAT'S THAT IN YOUR HAND?
OUR BATTLE WITH THE JAPANESE HAD CREATED SO MUCH DESTRUCTION, THE WIND AND RAGE AND SMOKE AND DEBRIS FROM OUR BATTLE TO SAVE KOKURA DID JUST THAT.
IT WAS BELIEVED BY THE ALLIES THAT THERE WAS A STORM ABOVE THE CITY. THE TARGET WAS CHANGED. NAGASAKI.
WE MAY HAVE SAVED THIS CITY, BUT THE PLANES ARE NOT TURNING AROUND.
I'M STILL AMAZED BY WHAT YOU CAN SEE, SAMSON.
I'LL STOP THIS.
I'LL STOP THIS.
IN THE END, THE BEGINNING OF OUR BATTLE AGAINST EVIL WAS A SUCCESS BECAUSE NO ONE SAW WHAT HAPPENED.
THEY WERE DISTRACTED BY ANOTHER EVIL.
DISTRACTED BY THE SYMPTOMS OF WAR WHILE I FOUGHT TO STOP WAR ITSELF.

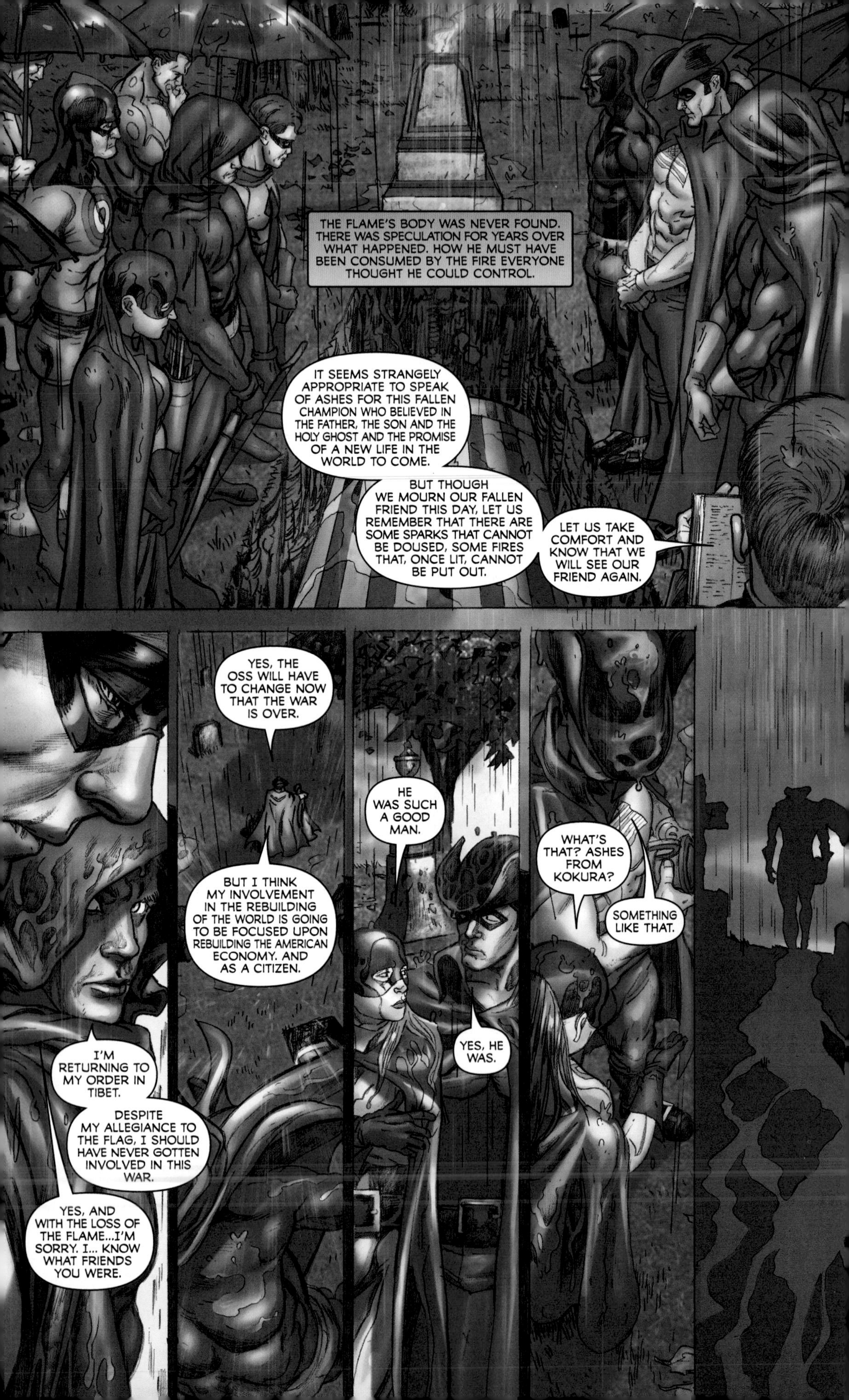
THE FLAME'S BODY WAS NEVER FOUND. THERE WAS SPECULATION FOR YEARS OVER WHAT HAPPENED. HOW HE MUST HAVE BEEN CONSUMED BY THE FIRE EVERYONE THOUGHT HE COULD CONTROL.
IT SEEMS STRANGELY APPROPRIATE TO SPEAK OF ASHES FOR THIS FALLEN CHAMPION WHO BELIEVED IN THE FATHER, THE SON AND THE HOLY GHOST AND THE PROMISE OF A NEW LIFE IN THE WORLD TO COME.
BUT THOUGH WE MOURN OUR FALLEN FRIEND THIS DAY, LET US REMEMBER THAT THERE ARE SOME SPARKS THAT CANNOT BE DOUSED, SOME FIRES THAT, ONCE LIT, CANNOT BE PUT OUT.
LET US TAKE COMFORT AND KNOW THAT WE WILL SEE OUR FRIEND AGAIN.
I'M RETURNING TO MY ORDER IN TIBET.
DESPITE MY ALLEGIANCE TO THE FLAG, I SHOULD HAVE NEVER GOTTEN INVOLVED IN THIS WAR.
YES, AND WITH THE LOSS OF THE FLAME...I'M SORRY. I... KNOW WHAT FRIENDS YOU WERE.
YES, THE OSS WILL HAVE TO CHANGE NOW THAT THE WAR IS OVER.
BUT I THINK MY INVOLVEMENT IN THE REBUILDING OF THE WORLD IS GOING TO BE FOCUSED UPON REBUILDING THE AMERICAN ECONOMY. AND AS A CITIZEN.
HE WAS SUCH A GOOD MAN.
YES, HE WAS.
WHAT'S THAT? ASHES FROM KOKURA?
SOMETHING LIKE THAT.

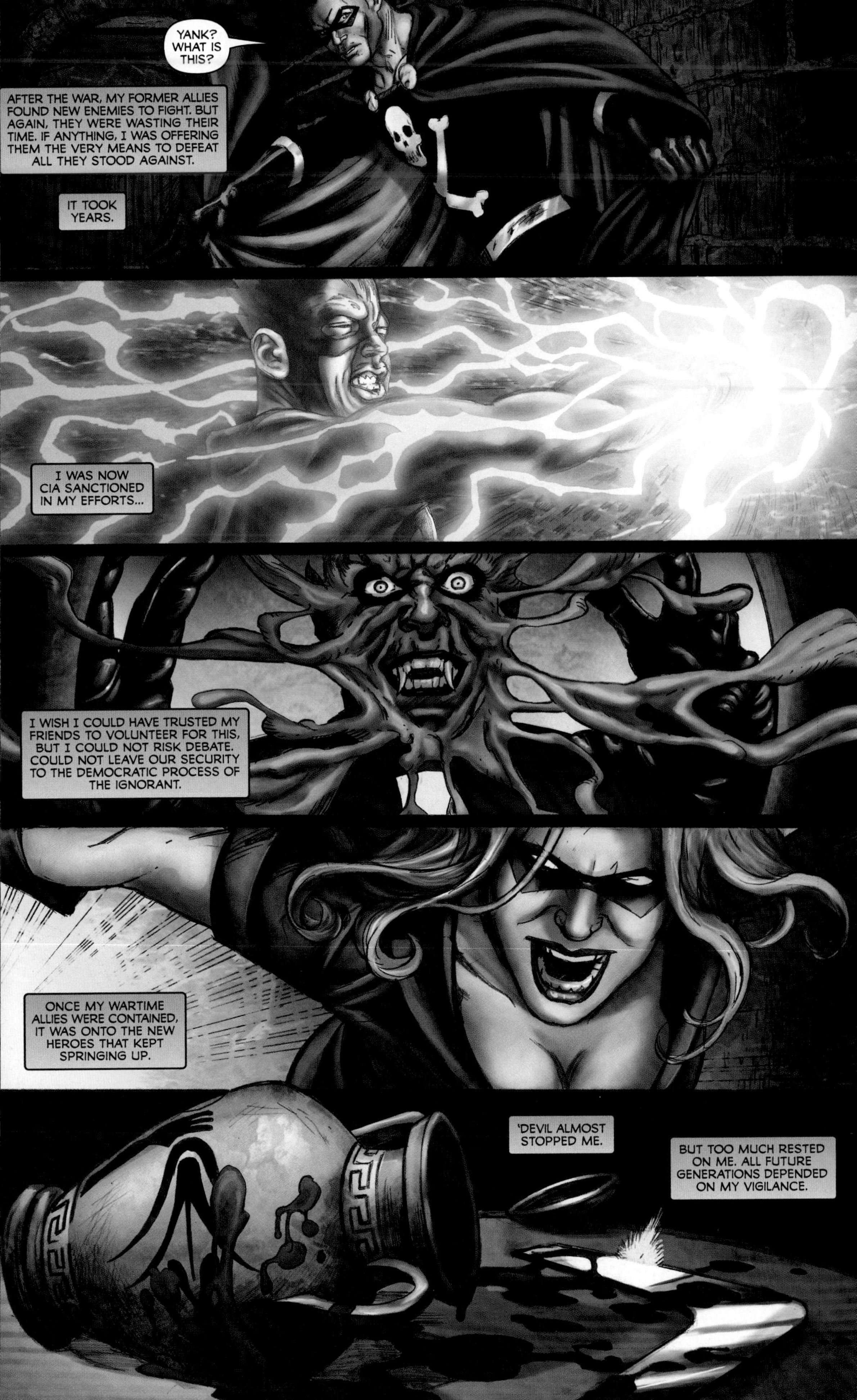
YANK? WHAT IS THIS?
AFTER THE WAR, MY FORMER ALLIES FOUND NEW ENEMIES TO FIGHT. BUT AGAIN, THEY WERE WASTING THEIR TIME. IF ANYTHING, I WAS OFFERING THEM THE VERY MEANS TO DEFEAT ALL THEY STOOD AGAINST.
IT TOOK YEARS.
I WAS NOW CIA SANCTIONED IN MY EFFORTS...
I WISH I COULD HAVE TRUSTED MY FRIENDS TO VOLUNTEER FOR THIS, BUT I COULD NOT RISK DEBATE. COULD NOT LEAVE OUR SECURITY TO THE DEMOCRATIC PROCESS OF THE IGNORANT.
ONCE MY WARTIME ALLIES WERE CONTAINED, IT WAS ONTO THE NEW HEROES THAT KEPT SPRINGING UP.
'DEVIL ALMOST STOPPED ME.
BUT TOO MUCH RESTED ON ME. ALL FUTURE GENERATIONS DEPENDED ON MY VIGILANCE.

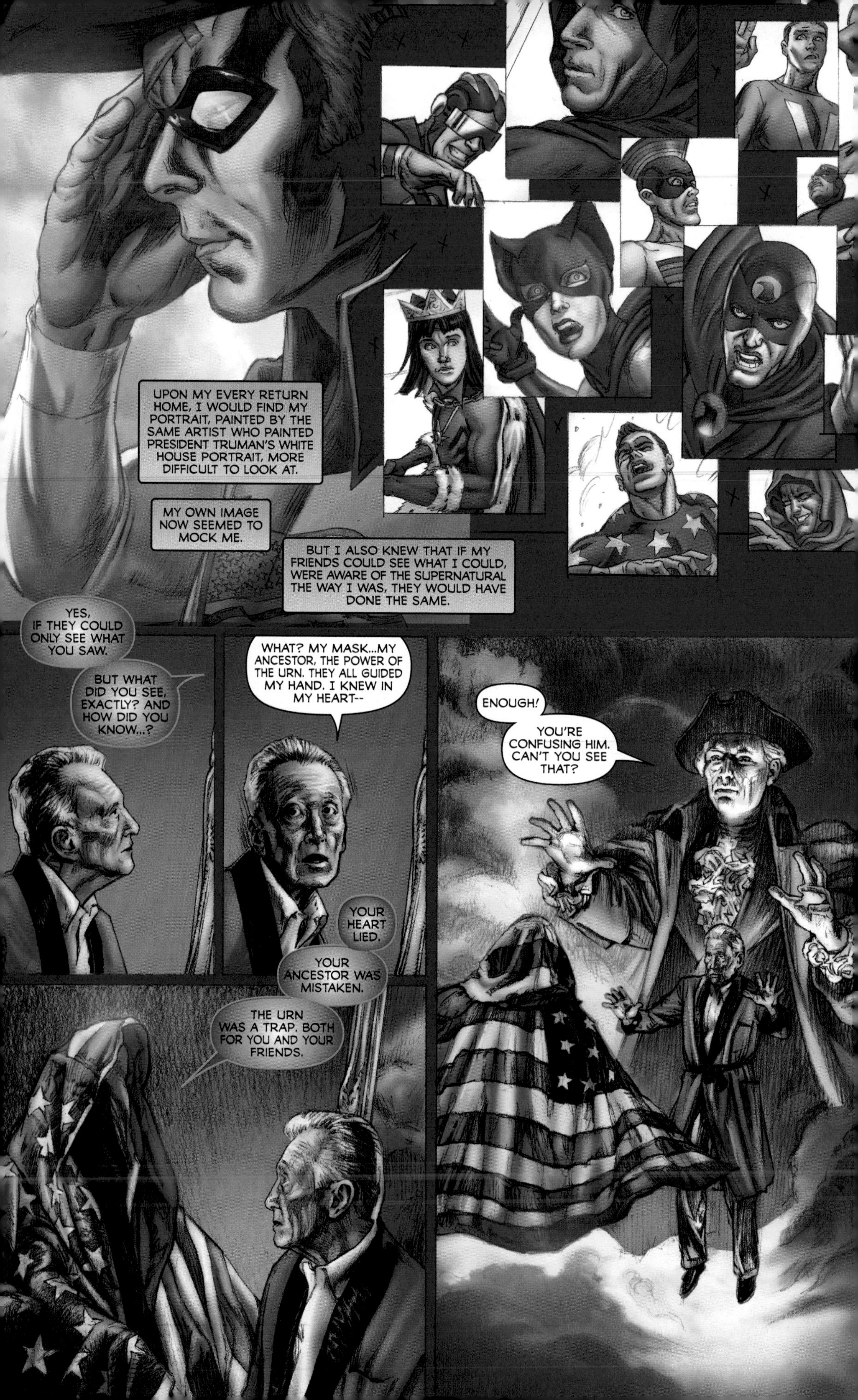
UPON MY EVERY RETURN HOME, I WOULD FIND MY PORTRAIT, PAINTED BY THE SAME ARTIST WHO PAINTED PRESIDENT TRUMAN'S WHITE HOUSE PORTRAIT, MORE DIFFICULT TO LOOK AT.
MY OWN IMAGE NOW SEEMED TO MOCK ME.
BUT I ALSO KNEW THAT IF MY FRIENDS COULD SEE WHAT I COULD, WERE AWARE OF THE SUPERNATURAL THE WAY I WAS, THEY WOULD HAVE DONE THE SAME.
YES, IF THEY COULD ONLY SEE WHAT YOU SAW.
BUT WHAT DID YOU SEE, EXACTLY? AND HOW DID YOU KNOW...?
WHAT? MY MASK...MY ANCESTOR, THE POWER OF THE URN. THEY ALL GUIDED MY HAND. I KNEW IN MY HEART--
YOUR HEART LIED.
YOUR ANCESTOR WAS MISTAKEN.
THE URN WAS A TRAP. BOTH FOR YOU AND YOUR FRIENDS.
ENOUGH!
YOU'RE CONFUSING HIM. CAN'T YOU SEE THAT?

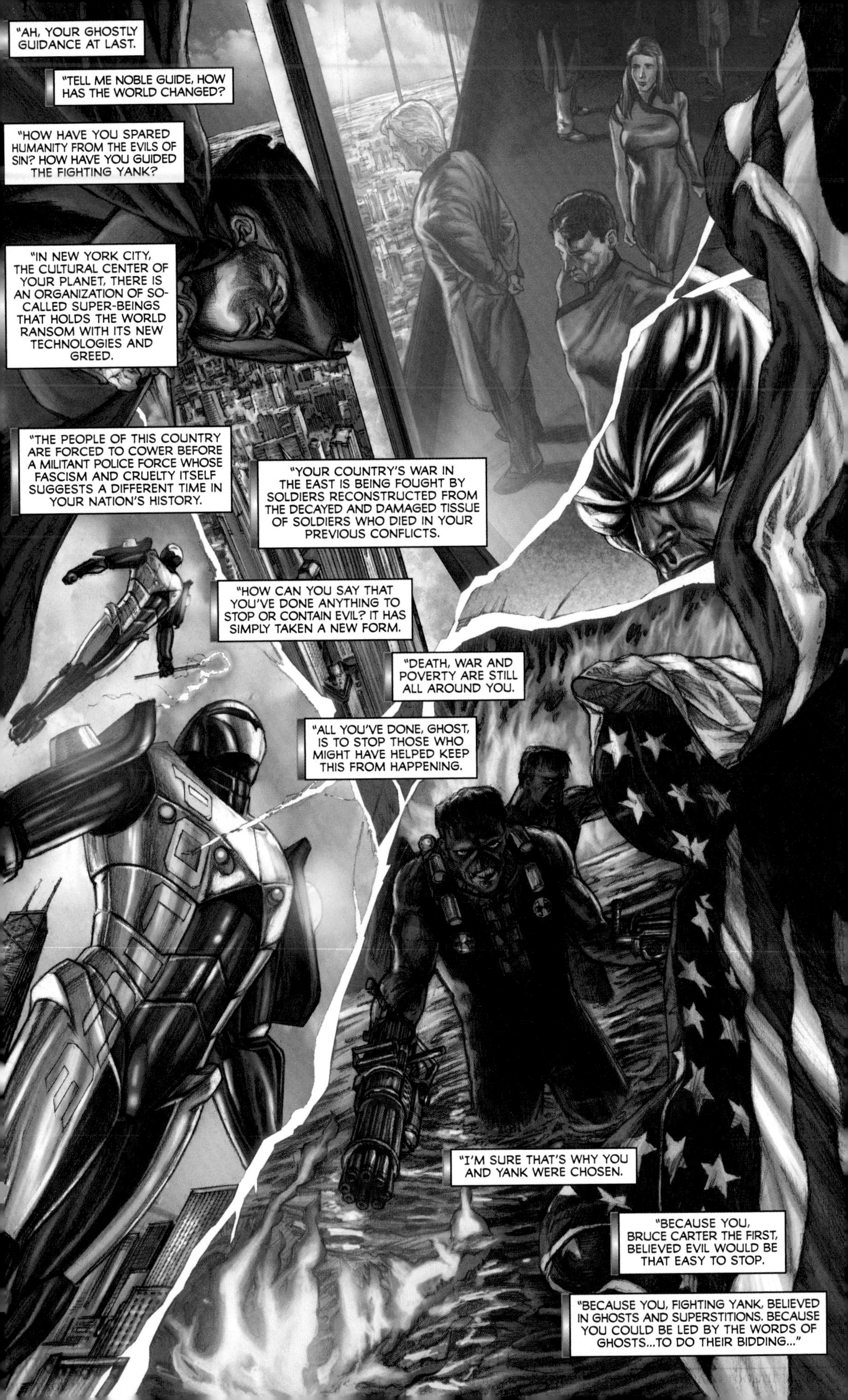
"AH, YOUR GHOSTLY GUIDANCE AT LAST.
"TELL ME NOBLE GUIDE, HOW HAS THE WORLD CHANGED?
"HOW HAVE YOU SPARED HUMANITY FROM THE EVILS OF SIN? HOW HAVE YOU GUIDED THE FIGHTING YANK?
"IN NEW YORK CITY, THE CULTURAL CENTER OF YOUR PLANET, THERE IS AN ORGANIZATION OF SO-CALLED SUPER-BEINGS THAT HOLDS THE WORLD RANSOM WITH ITS NEW TECHNOLOGIES AND GREED.
"THE PEOPLE OF THIS COUNTRY ARE FORCED TO COWER BEFORE A MILITANT POLICE FORCE WHOSE FASCISM AND CRUELTY ITSELF SUGGESTS A DIFFERENT TIME IN YOUR NATION'S HISTORY.
"YOUR COUNTRY'S WAR IN THE EAST IS BEING FOUGHT BY SOLDIERS RECONSTRUCTED FROM THE DECAYED AND DAMAGED TISSUE OF SOLDIERS WHO DIED IN YOUR PREVIOUS CONFLICTS.
"HOW CAN YOU SAY THAT YOU'VE DONE ANYTHING TO STOP OR CONTAIN EVIL? IT HAS SIMPLY TAKEN A NEW FORM.
"DEATH, WAR AND POVERTY ARE STILL ALL AROUND YOU.
"ALL YOU'VE DONE, GHOST, IS TO STOP THOSE WHO MIGHT HAVE HELPED KEEP THIS FROM HAPPENING.
"I'M SURE THAT'S WHY YOU AND YANK WERE CHOSEN.
"BECAUSE YOU, BRUCE CARTER THE FIRST, BELIEVED EVIL WOULD BE THAT EASY TO STOP.
"BECAUSE YOU, FIGHTING YANK, BELIEVED IN GHOSTS AND SUPERSTITIONS. BECAUSE YOU COULD BE LED BY THE WORDS OF GHOSTS...TO DO THEIR BIDDING..."

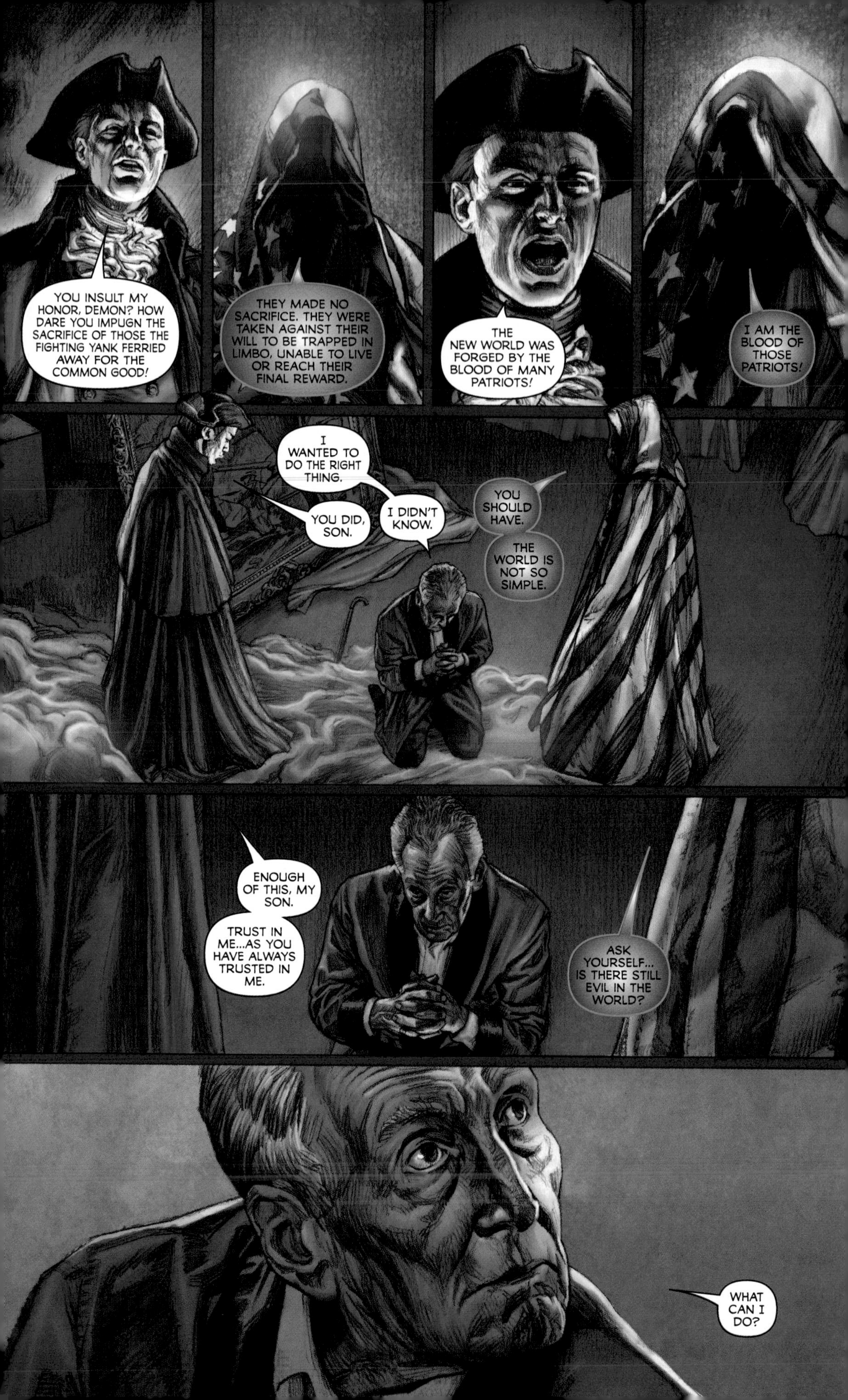
YOU INSULT MY HONOR, DEMON? HOW DARE YOU IMPUGN THE SACRIFICE OF THOSE THE FIGHTING YANK FERRIED AWAY FOR THE COMMON GOOD!
THEY MADE NO SACRIFICE. THEY WERE TAKEN AGAINST THEIR WILL TO BE TRAPPED IN LIMBO, UNABLE TO LIVE OR REACH THEIR FINAL REWARD.
THE NEW WORLD WAS FORGED BY THE BLOOD OF MANY PATRIOTS!
I AM THE BLOOD OF THOSE PATRIOTS!
I WANTED TO DO THE RIGHT THING.
YOU DID, SON.
I DIDN'T KNOW.
YOU SHOULD HAVE.
THE WORLD IS NOT SO SIMPLE.
ENOUGH OF THIS, MY SON.
TRUST IN ME...AS YOU HAVE ALWAYS TRUSTED IN ME.
ASK YOURSELF... IS THERE STILL EVIL IN THE WORLD?
WHAT CAN I DO?

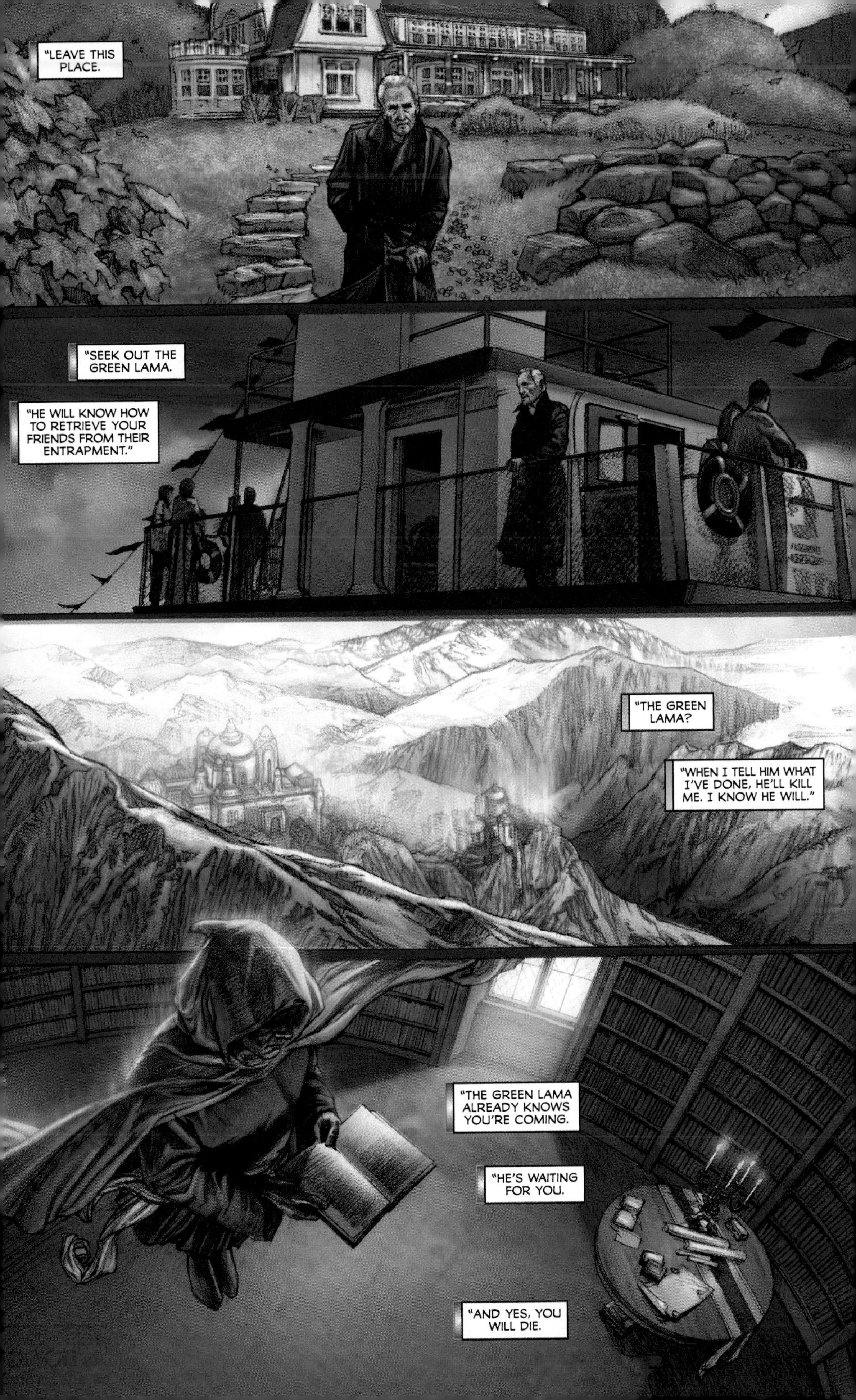
"LEAVE THIS PLACE.
"SEEK OUT THE GREEN LAMA.
"HE WILL KNOW HOW TO RETRIEVE YOUR FRIENDS FROM THEIR ENTRAPMENT."
"THE GREEN LAMA?
"WHEN I TELL HIM WHAT I'VE DONE, HE'LL KILL ME. I KNOW HE WILL."
"THE GREEN LAMA ALREADY KNOWS YOU'RE COMING.
"HE'S WAITING FOR YOU.
"AND YES, YOU WILL DIE.

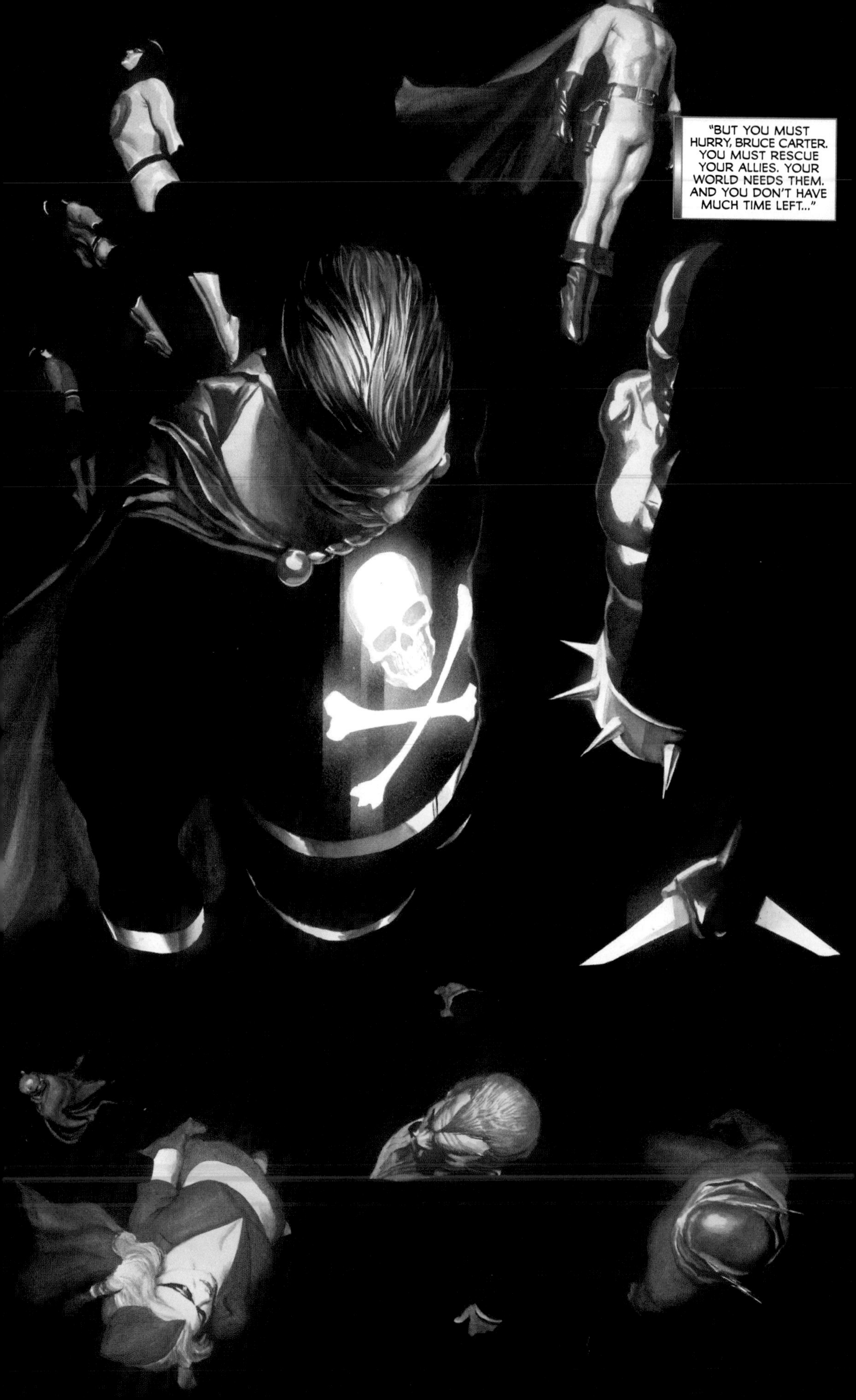
"BUT YOU MUST HURRY, BRUCE CARTER. YOU MUST RESCUE YOUR ALLIES. YOUR WORLD NEEDS THEM. AND YOU DON'T HAVE MUCH TIME LEFT..."

ISSUE

1

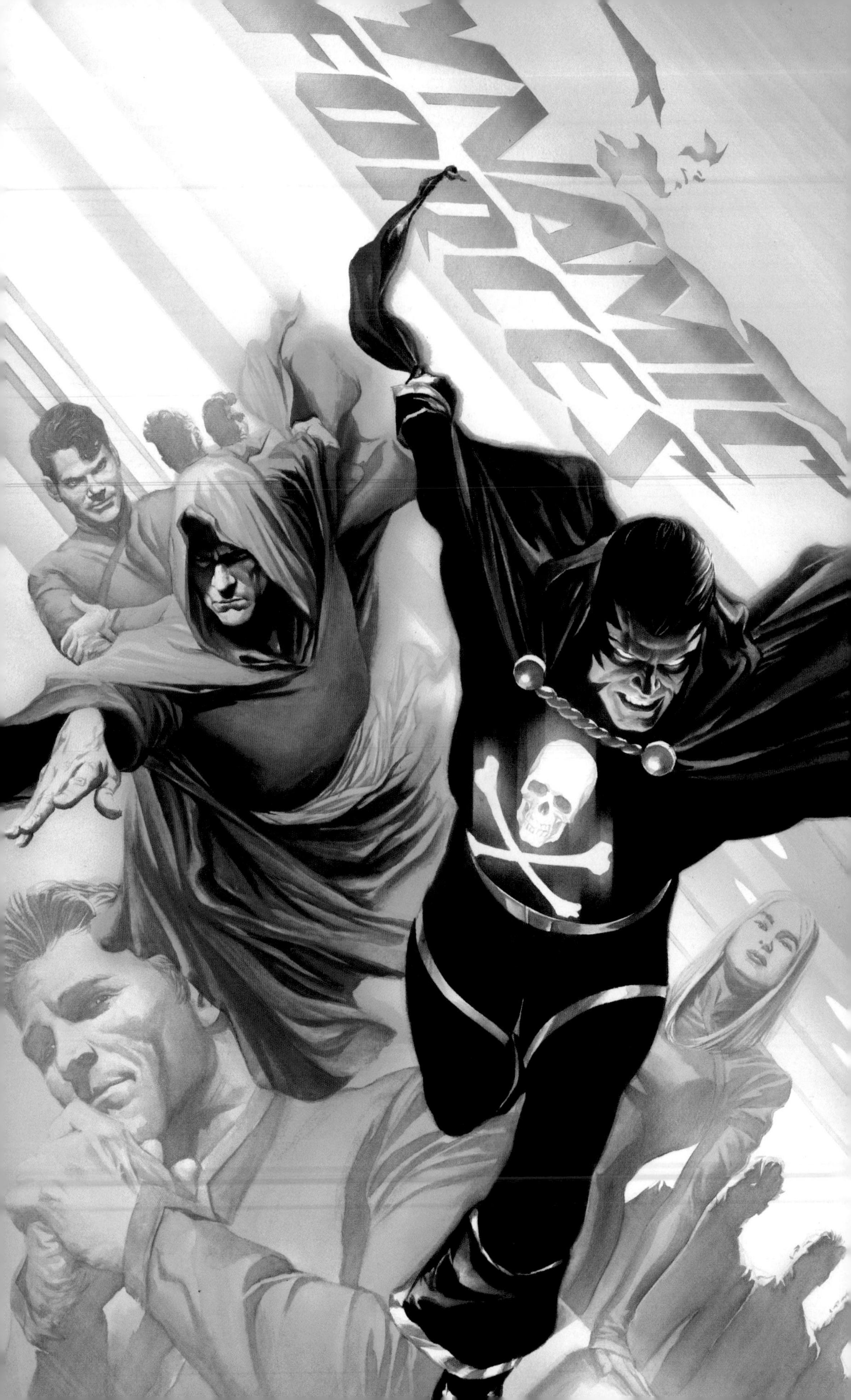

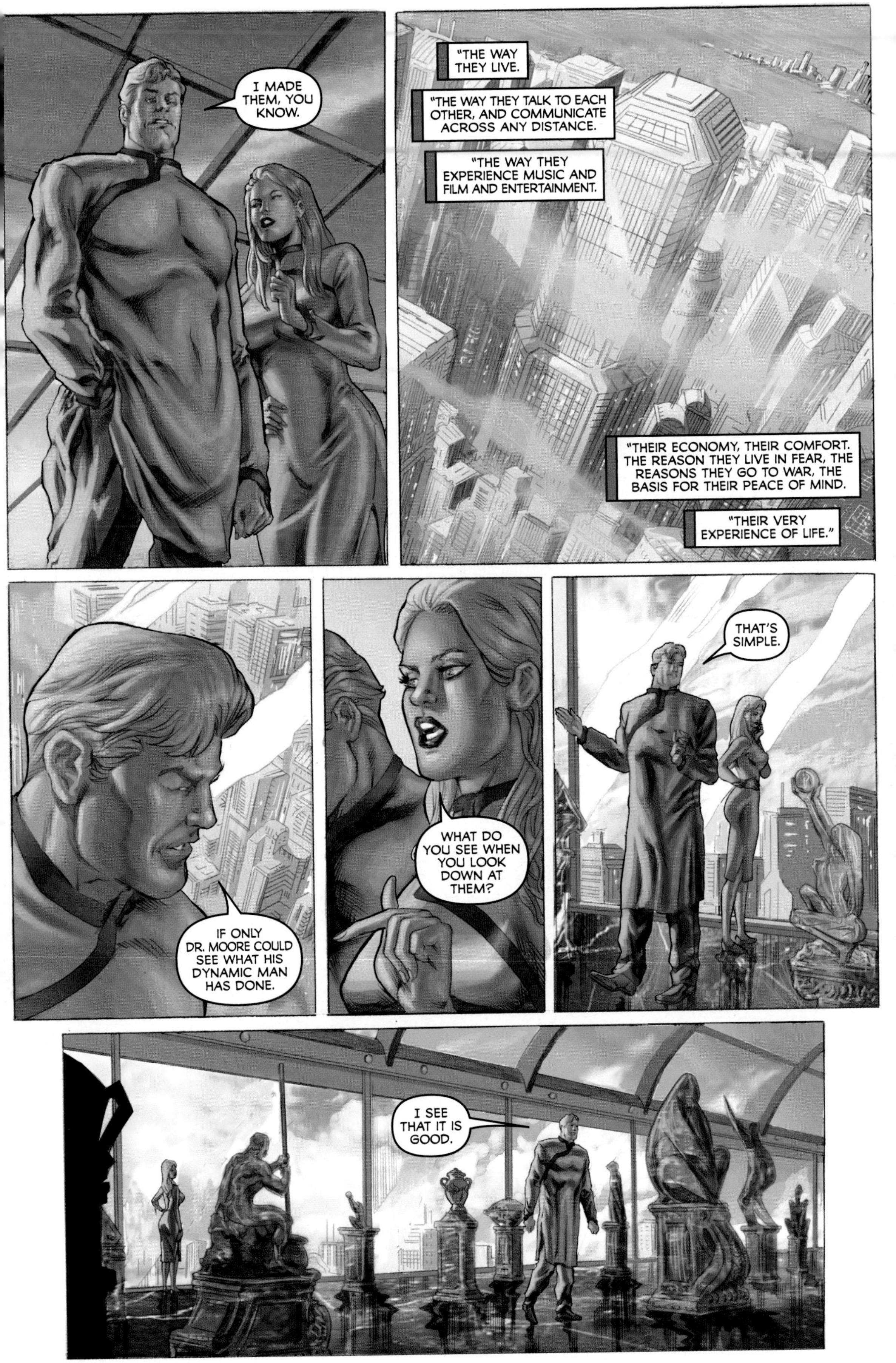
I MADE THEM, YOU KNOW.
"THE WAY THEY LIVE.
"THE WAY THEY TALK TO EACH OTHER, AND COMMUNICATE ACROSS ANY DISTANCE.
"THE WAY THEY EXPERIENCE MUSIC AND FILM AND ENTERTAINMENT.
"THEIR ECONOMY, THEIR COMFORT. THE REASON THEY LIVE IN FEAR, THE REASONS THEY GO TO WAR, THE BASIS FOR THEIR PEACE OF MIND.
"THEIR VERY EXPERIENCE OF LIFE."
IF ONLY DR. MOORE COULD SEE WHAT HIS DYNAMIC MAN HAS DONE.
WHAT DO YOU SEE WHEN YOU LOOK DOWN AT THEM?
THAT'S SIMPLE.
I SEE THAT IT IS GOOD.

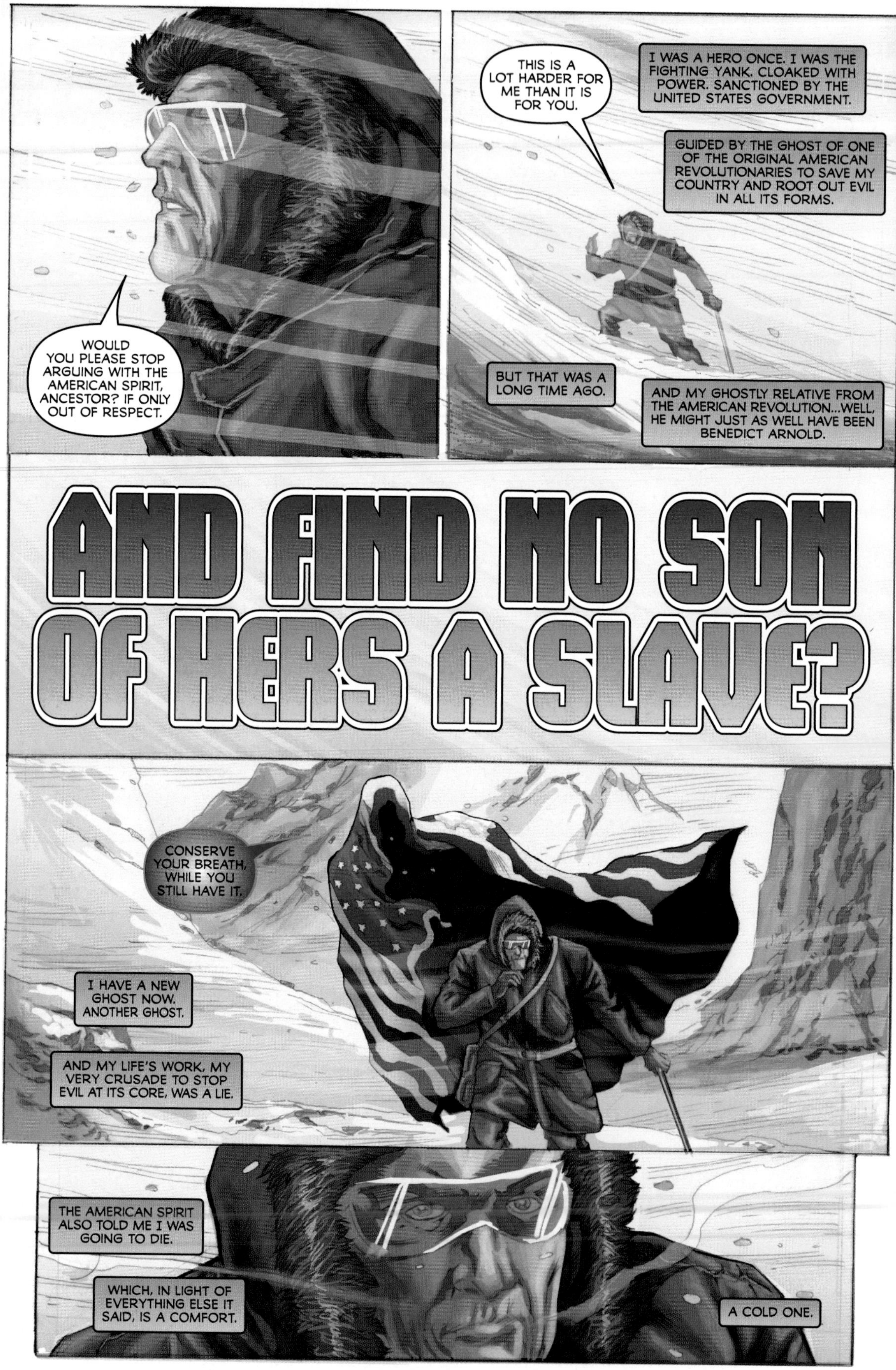
WOULD YOU PLEASE STOP ARGUING WITH THE AMERICAN SPIRIT, ANCESTOR? IF ONLY OUT OF RESPECT.
THIS IS A LOT HARDER FOR ME THAN IT IS FOR YOU.
I WAS A HERO ONCE. I WAS THE FIGHTING YANK. CLOAKED WITH POWER. SANCTIONED BY THE UNITED STATES GOVERNMENT.
GUIDED BY THE GHOST OF ONE OF THE ORIGINAL AMERICAN REVOLUTIONARIES TO SAVE MY COUNTRY AND ROOT OUT EVIL IN ALL ITS FORMS.
BUT THAT WAS A LONG TIME AGO.
AND MY GHOSTLY RELATIVE FROM THE AMERICAN REVOLUTION...WELL, HE MIGHT JUST AS WELL HAVE BEEN BENEDICT ARNOLD.
AND FIND NO SON OF HERS A SLAVE?
CONSERVE YOUR BREATH, WHILE YOU STILL HAVE IT.
I HAVE A NEW GHOST NOW. ANOTHER GHOST.
AND MY LIFE'S WORK, MY VERY CRUSADE TO STOP EVIL AT ITS CORE, WAS A LIE.
THE AMERICAN SPIRIT ALSO TOLD ME I WAS GOING TO DIE.
WHICH, IN LIGHT OF EVERYTHING ELSE IT SAID, IS A COMFORT.
A COLD ONE.

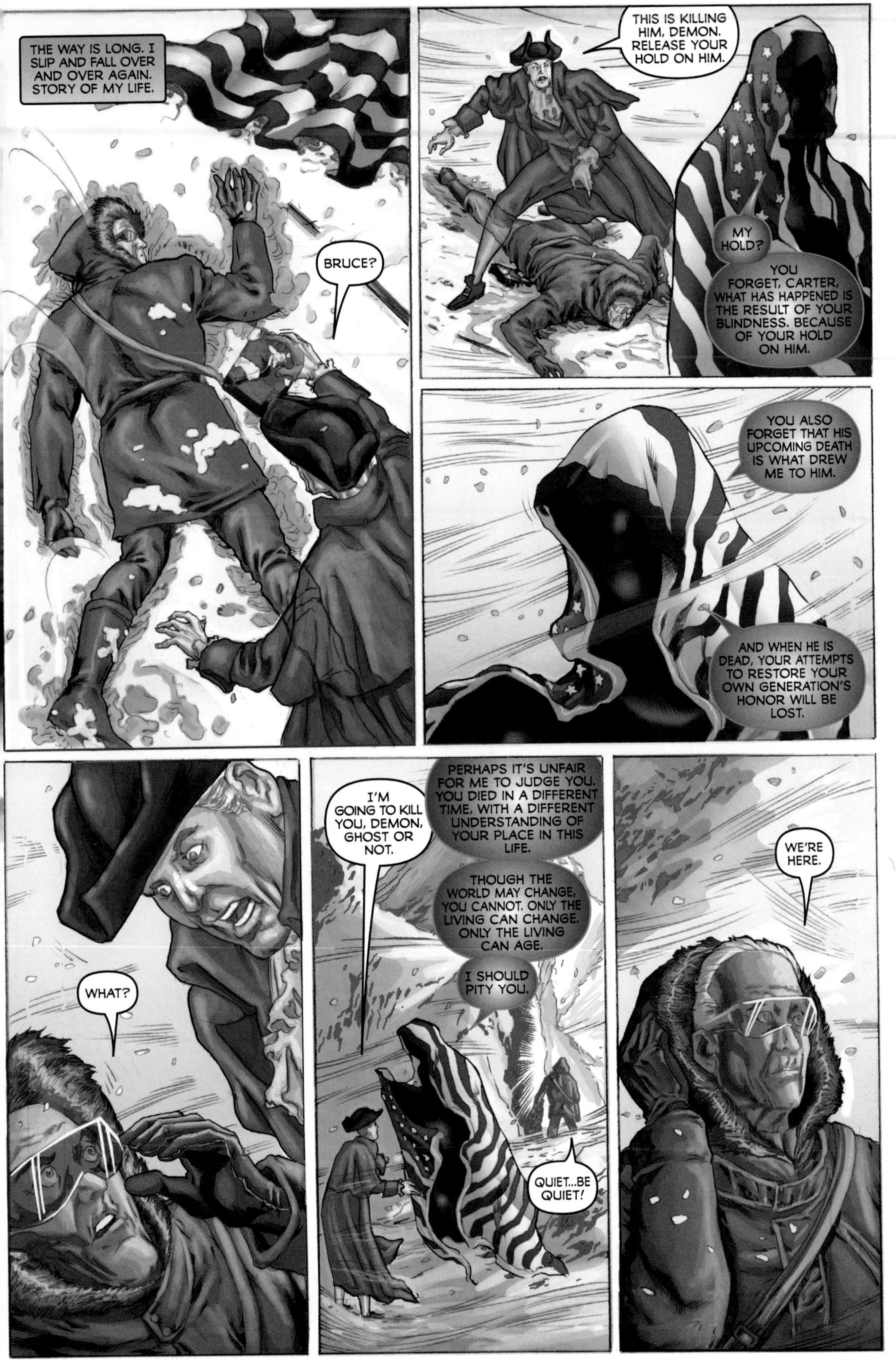
THE WAY IS LONG. I SLIP AND FALL OVER AND OVER AGAIN. STORY OF MY LIFE.
BRUCE?
THIS IS KILLING HIM, DEMON. RELEASE YOUR HOLD ON HIM.
MY HOLD?
YOU FORGET, CARTER, WHAT HAS HAPPENED IS THE RESULT OF YOUR BLINDNESS. BECAUSE OF YOUR HOLD ON HIM.
YOU ALSO FORGET THAT HIS UPCOMING DEATH IS WHAT DREW ME TO HIM.
AND WHEN HE IS DEAD, YOUR ATTEMPTS TO RESTORE YOUR OWN GENERATION'S HONOR WILL BE LOST.
WHAT?
I'M GOING TO KILL YOU, DEMON, GHOST OR NOT.
PERHAPS IT'S UNFAIR FOR ME TO JUDGE YOU. YOU DIED IN A DIFFERENT TIME, WITH A DIFFERENT UNDERSTANDING OF YOUR PLACE IN THIS LIFE.
THOUGH THE WORLD MAY CHANGE, YOU CANNOT. ONLY THE LIVING CAN CHANGE. ONLY THE LIVING CAN AGE.
I SHOULD PITY YOU.
QUIET...BE QUIET!
WE'RE HERE.

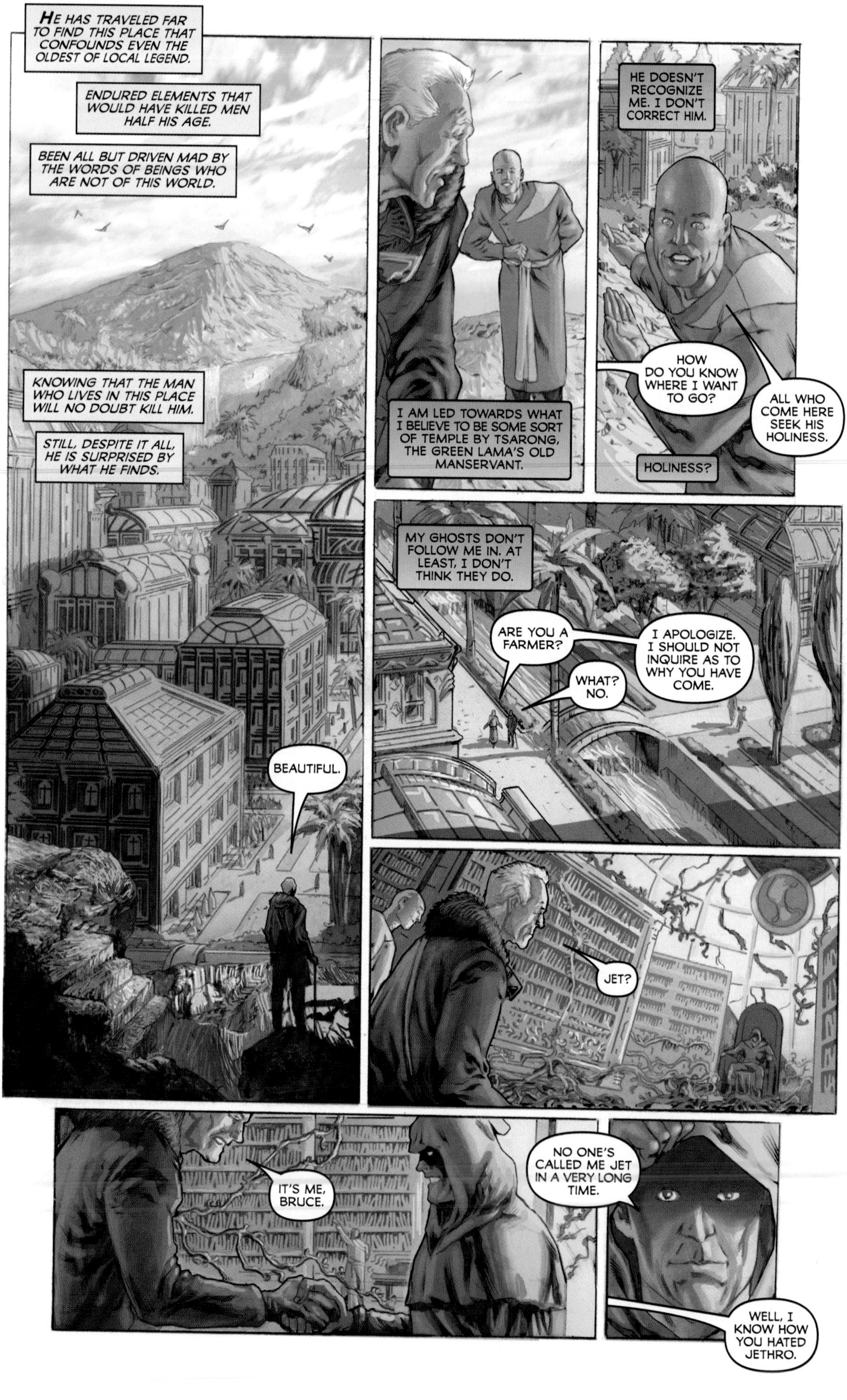
HE HAS TRAVELED FAR TO FIND THIS PLACE THAT CONFOUNDS EVEN THE OLDEST OF LOCAL LEGEND.
ENDURED ELEMENTS THAT WOULD HAVE KILLED MEN HALF HIS AGE.
BEEN ALL BUT DRIVEN MAD BY THE WORDS OF BEINGS WHO ARE NOT OF THIS WORLD.
KNOWING THAT THE MAN WHO LIVES IN THIS PLACE WILL NO DOUBT KILL HIM.
STILL, DESPITE IT ALL, HE IS SURPRISED BY WHAT HE FINDS.
BEAUTIFUL.
I AM LED TOWARDS WHAT I BELIEVE TO BE SOME SORT OF TEMPLE BY TSARONG, THE GREEN LAMA'S OLD MANSERVANT.
HE DOESN'T RECOGNIZE ME. I DON'T CORRECT HIM.
HOW DO YOU KNOW WHERE I WANT TO GO?
ALL WHO COME HERE SEEK HIS HOLINESS.
HOLINESS?
MY GHOSTS DON'T FOLLOW ME IN. AT LEAST, I DON'T THINK THEY DO.
ARE YOU A FARMER?
WHAT? NO.
I APOLOGIZE. I SHOULD NOT INQUIRE AS TO WHY YOU HAVE COME.
JET?
IT'S ME, BRUCE.
NO ONE'S CALLED ME JET IN A VERY LONG TIME.
WELL, I KNOW HOW YOU HATED JETHRO.

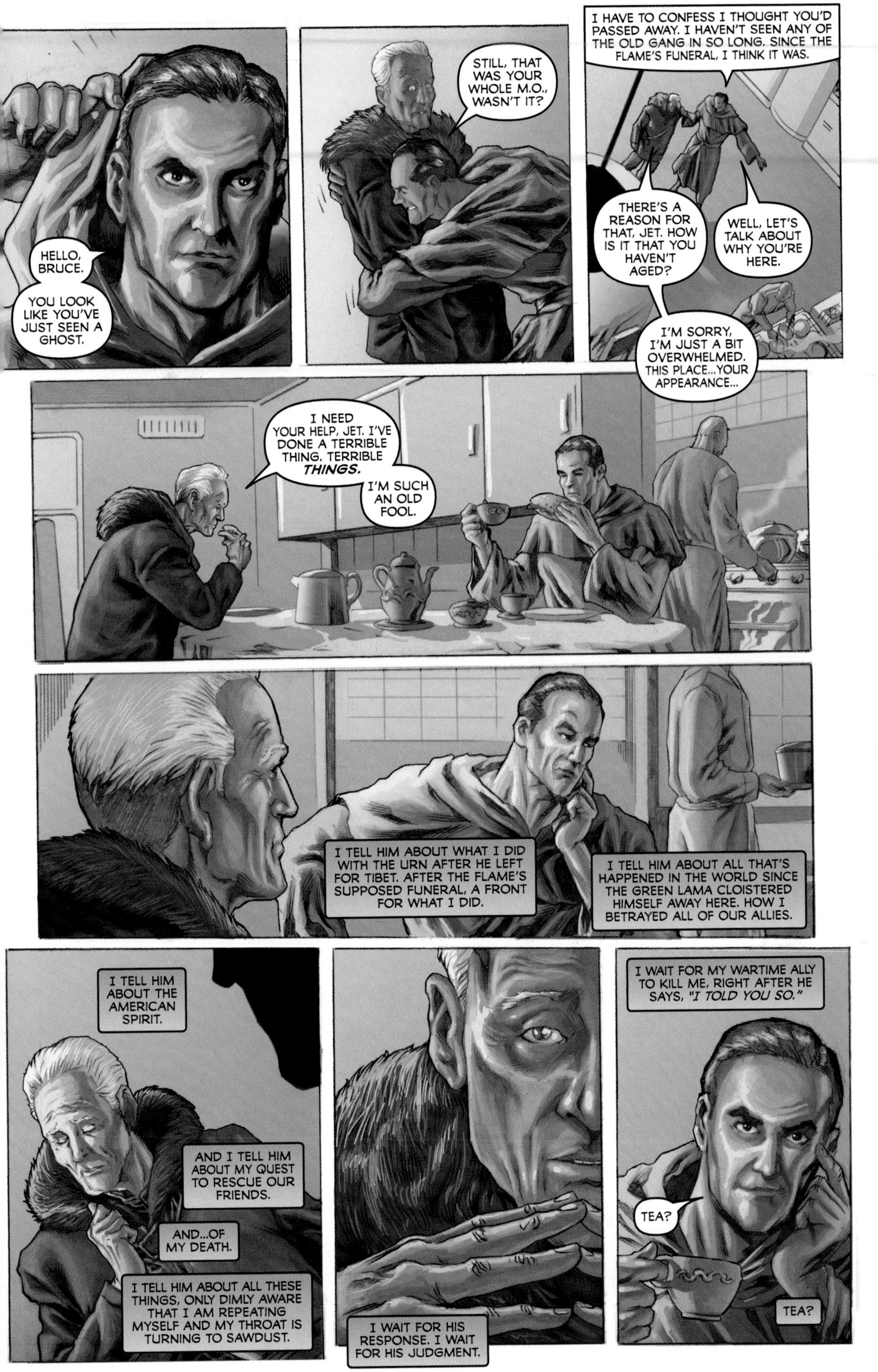
HELLO, BRUCE.
YOU LOOK LIKE YOU'VE JUST SEEN A GHOST.
STILL, THAT WAS YOUR WHOLE M.O., WASN'T IT?
I HAVE TO CONFESS I THOUGHT YOU'D PASSED AWAY. I HAVEN'T SEEN ANY OF THE OLD GANG IN SO LONG. SINCE THE FLAME'S FUNERAL, I THINK IT WAS.
WELL, LET'S TALK ABOUT WHY YOU'RE HERE.
THERE'S A REASON FOR THAT, JET. HOW IS IT THAT YOU HAVEN'T AGED?
I'M SORRY, I'M JUST A BIT OVERWHELMED. THIS PLACE...YOUR APPEARANCE...
I NEED YOUR HELP, JET. I'VE DONE A TERRIBLE THING. TERRIBLE ***THINGS.***
I'M SUCH AN OLD FOOL.
I TELL HIM ABOUT WHAT I DID WITH THE URN AFTER HE LEFT FOR TIBET. AFTER THE FLAME'S SUPPOSED FUNERAL, A FRONT FOR WHAT I DID.
I TELL HIM ABOUT ALL THAT'S HAPPENED IN THE WORLD SINCE THE GREEN LAMA CLOISTERED HIMSELF AWAY HERE. HOW I BETRAYED ALL OF OUR ALLIES.
I TELL HIM ABOUT THE AMERICAN SPIRIT.
AND I TELL HIM ABOUT MY QUEST TO RESCUE OUR FRIENDS.
AND...OF MY DEATH.
I TELL HIM ABOUT ALL THESE THINGS, ONLY DIMLY AWARE THAT I AM REPEATING MYSELF AND MY THROAT IS TURNING TO SAWDUST.
I WAIT FOR HIS RESPONSE. I WAIT FOR HIS JUDGMENT.
I WAIT FOR MY WARTIME ALLY TO KILL ME, RIGHT AFTER HE SAYS, *"I TOLD YOU SO."*
TEA?
TEA?

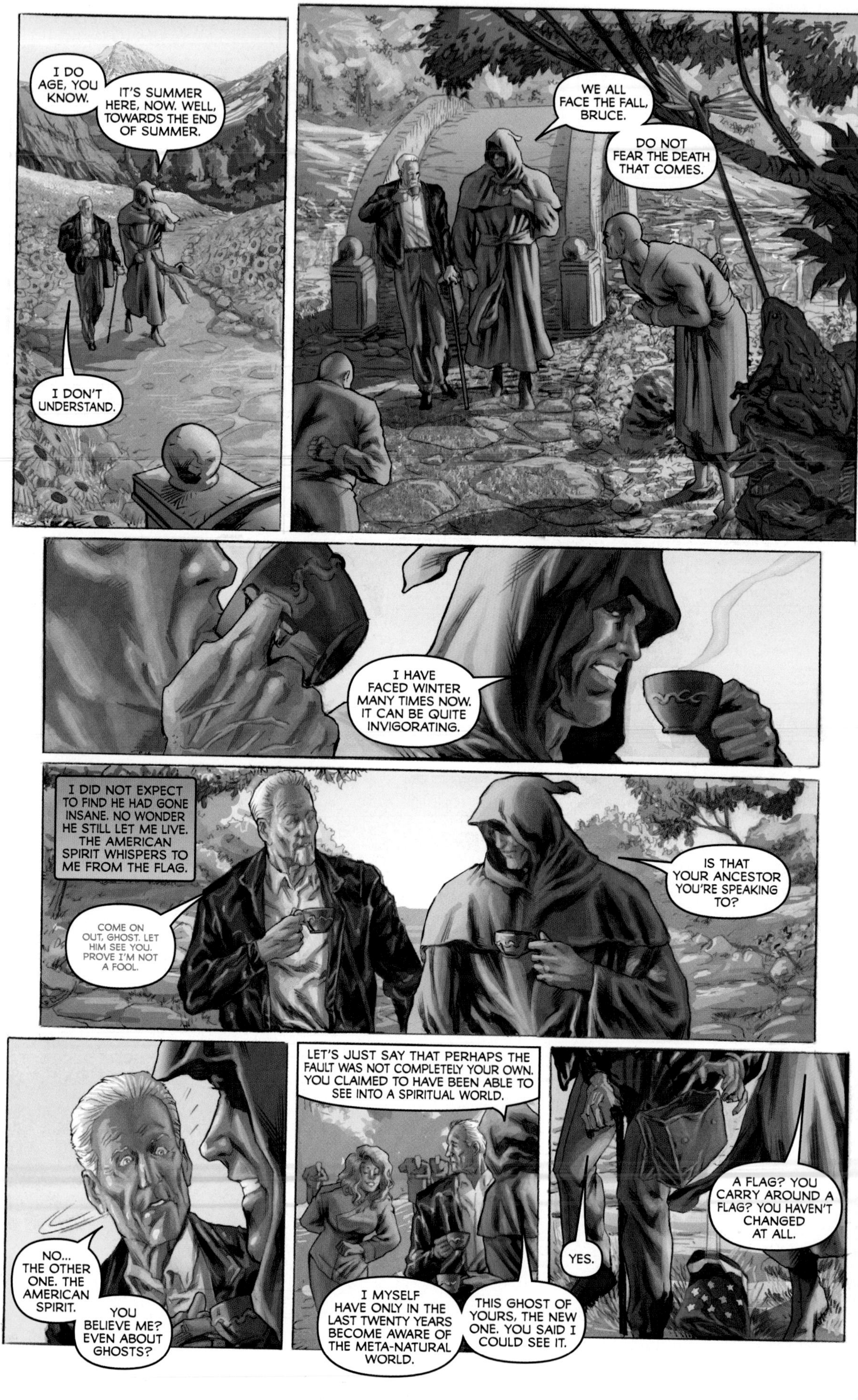
I DO AGE, YOU KNOW.
IT'S SUMMER HERE, NOW. WELL, TOWARDS THE END OF SUMMER.
I DON'T UNDERSTAND.
WE ALL FACE THE FALL, BRUCE.
DO NOT FEAR THE DEATH THAT COMES.
I HAVE FACED WINTER MANY TIMES NOW. IT CAN BE QUITE INVIGORATING.
I DID NOT EXPECT TO FIND HE HAD GONE INSANE. NO WONDER HE STILL LET ME LIVE. THE AMERICAN SPIRIT WHISPERS TO ME FROM THE FLAG.
COME ON OUT, GHOST. LET HIM SEE YOU. PROVE I'M NOT A FOOL.
IS THAT YOUR ANCESTOR YOU'RE SPEAKING TO?
NO... THE OTHER ONE. THE AMERICAN SPIRIT.
YOU BELIEVE ME? EVEN ABOUT GHOSTS?
LET'S JUST SAY THAT PERHAPS THE FAULT WAS NOT COMPLETELY YOUR OWN. YOU CLAIMED TO HAVE BEEN ABLE TO SEE INTO A SPIRITUAL WORLD.
I MYSELF HAVE ONLY IN THE LAST TWENTY YEARS BECOME AWARE OF THE META-NATURAL WORLD.
THIS GHOST OF YOURS, THE NEW ONE. YOU SAID I COULD SEE IT.
YES.
A FLAG? YOU CARRY AROUND A FLAG? YOU HAVEN'T CHANGED AT ALL.

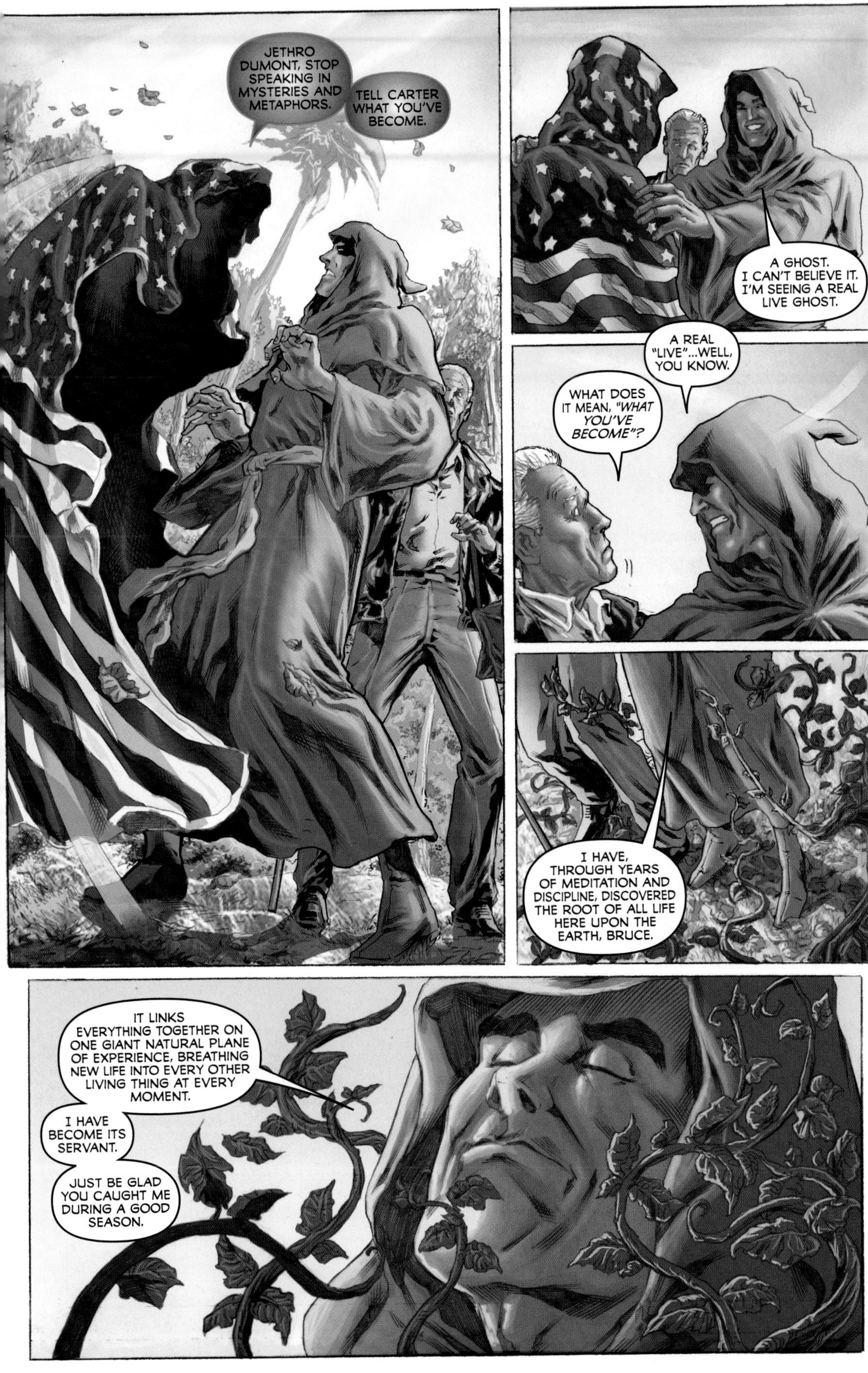
JETHRO DUMONT, STOP SPEAKING IN MYSTERIES AND METAPHORS.
TELL CARTER WHAT YOU'VE BECOME.
A GHOST. I CAN'T BELIEVE IT. I'M SEEING A REAL LIVE GHOST.
A REAL "LIVE"...WELL, YOU KNOW.
WHAT DOES IT MEAN, *"WHAT YOU'VE BECOME"*?
I HAVE, THROUGH YEARS OF MEDITATION AND DISCIPLINE, DISCOVERED THE ROOT OF ALL LIFE HERE UPON THE EARTH, BRUCE.
IT LINKS EVERYTHING TOGETHER ON ONE GIANT NATURAL PLANE OF EXPERIENCE, BREATHING NEW LIFE INTO EVERY OTHER LIVING THING AT EVERY MOMENT.
I HAVE BECOME ITS SERVANT.
JUST BE GLAD YOU CAUGHT ME DURING A GOOD SEASON.

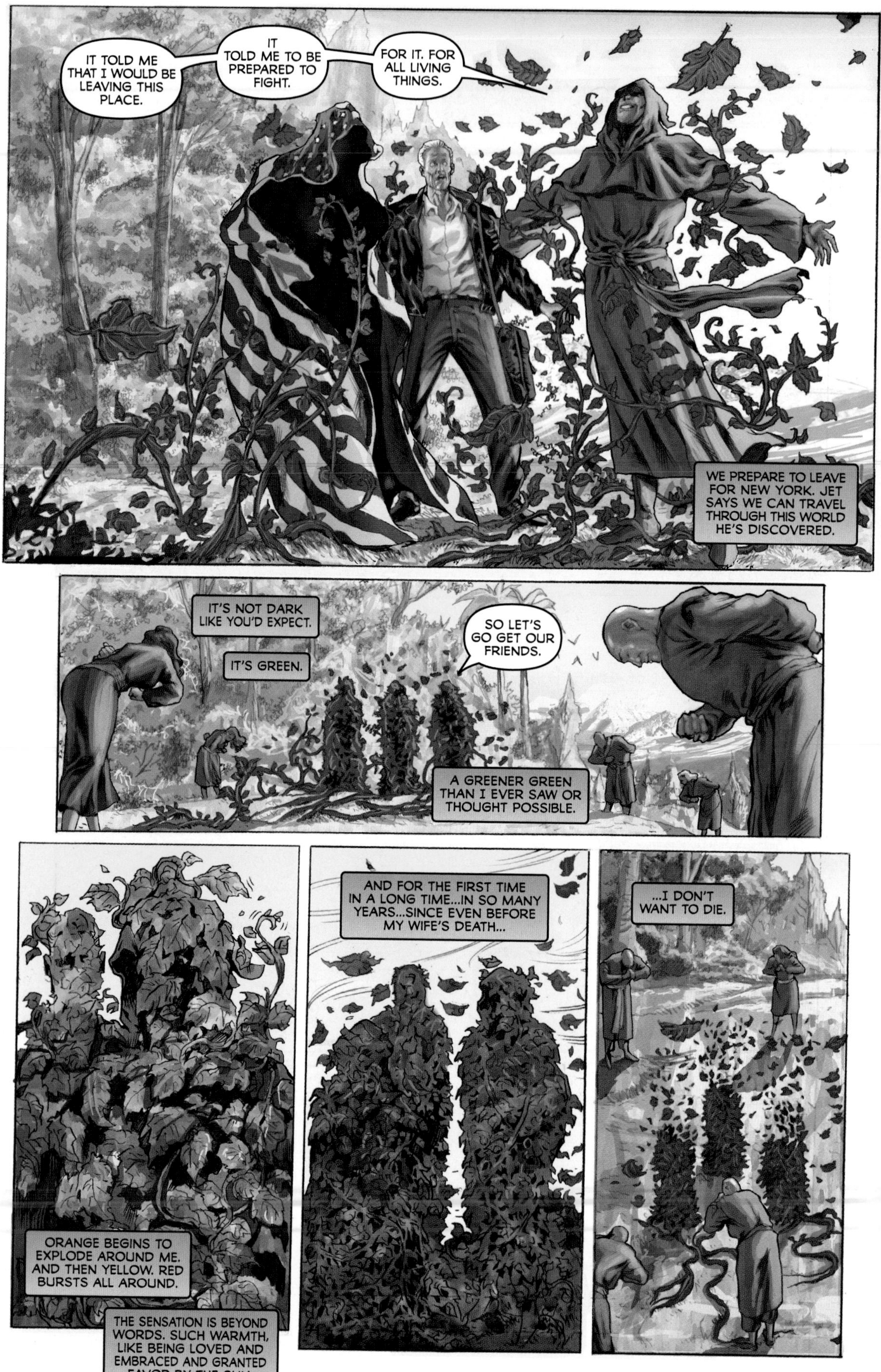
IT TOLD ME THAT I WOULD BE LEAVING THIS PLACE.
IT TOLD ME TO BE PREPARED TO FIGHT.
FOR IT. FOR ALL LIVING THINGS.
WE PREPARE TO LEAVE FOR NEW YORK. JET SAYS WE CAN TRAVEL THROUGH THIS WORLD HE'S DISCOVERED.
IT'S NOT DARK LIKE YOU'D EXPECT.
IT'S GREEN.
SO LET'S GO GET OUR FRIENDS.
A GREENER GREEN THAN I EVER SAW OR THOUGHT POSSIBLE.
ORANGE BEGINS TO EXPLODE AROUND ME. AND THEN YELLOW. RED BURSTS ALL AROUND.
THE SENSATION IS BEYOND WORDS. SUCH WARMTH, LIKE BEING LOVED AND EMBRACED AND GRANTED FAVOR BY THE SUN.
AND FOR THE FIRST TIME IN A LONG TIME...IN SO MANY YEARS...SINCE EVEN BEFORE MY WIFE'S DEATH...
...I DON'T WANT TO DIE.

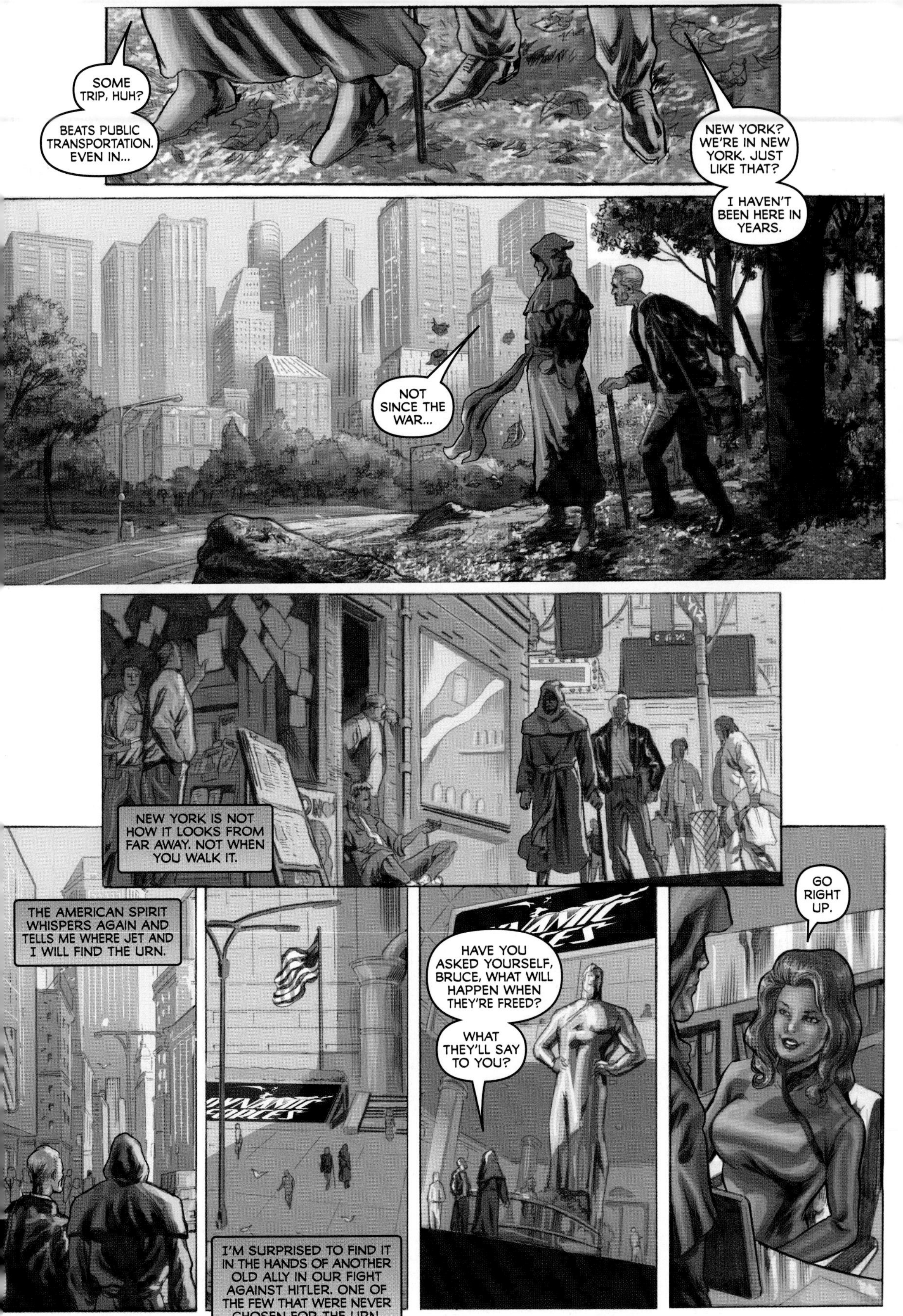
SOME TRIP, HUH?
BEATS PUBLIC TRANSPORTATION. EVEN IN...
NEW YORK? WE'RE IN NEW YORK. JUST LIKE THAT?
I HAVEN'T BEEN HERE IN YEARS.
NOT SINCE THE WAR...
NEW YORK IS NOT HOW IT LOOKS FROM FAR AWAY. NOT WHEN YOU WALK IT.
THE AMERICAN SPIRIT WHISPERS AGAIN AND TELLS ME WHERE JET AND I WILL FIND THE URN.
I'M SURPRISED TO FIND IT IN THE HANDS OF ANOTHER OLD ALLY IN OUR FIGHT AGAINST HITLER. ONE OF THE FEW THAT WERE NEVER CHOSEN FOR THE URN.
HAVE YOU ASKED YOURSELF, BRUCE, WHAT WILL HAPPEN WHEN THEY'RE FREED?
WHAT THEY'LL SAY TO YOU?
GO RIGHT UP.

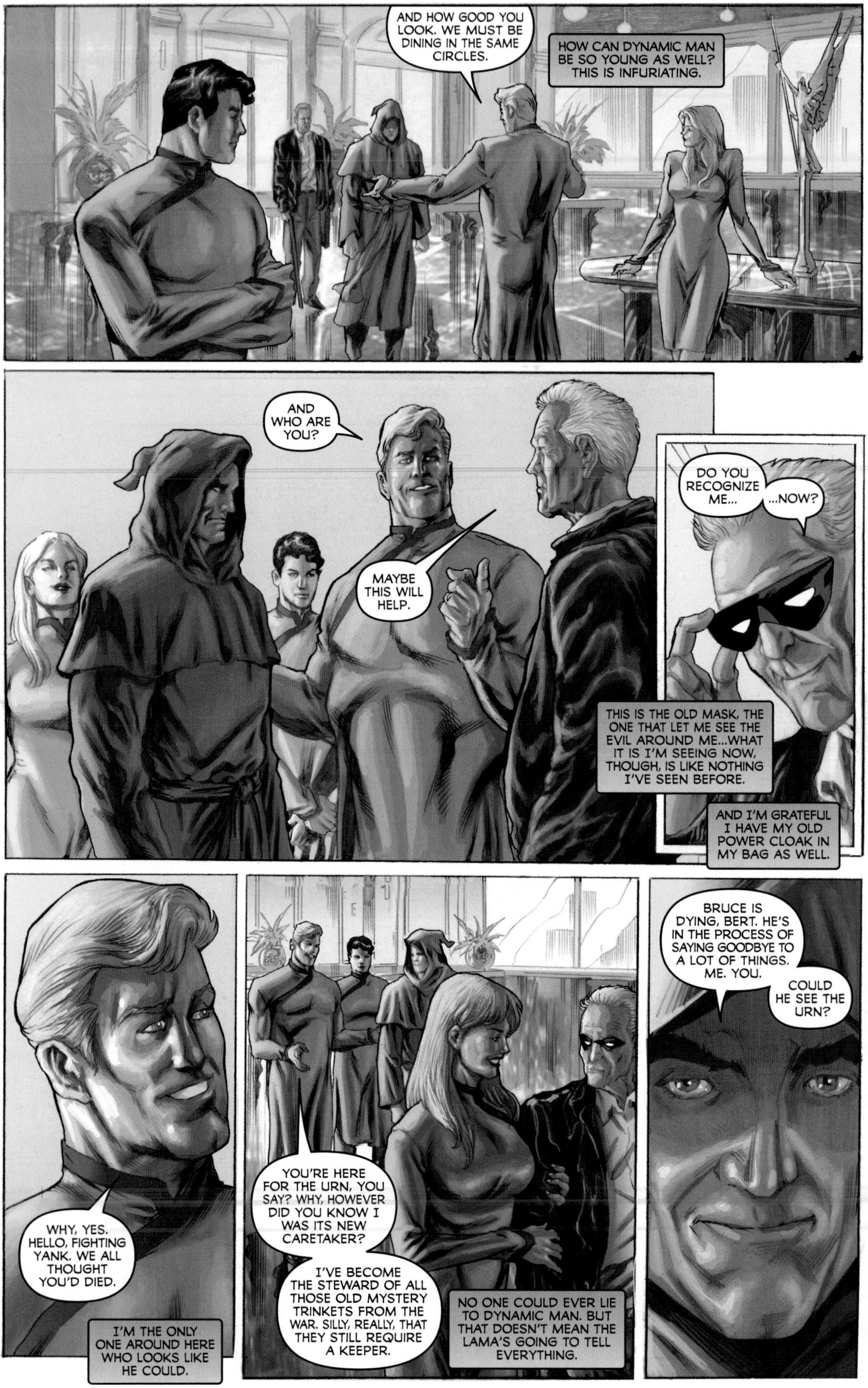
AND HOW GOOD YOU LOOK. WE MUST BE DINING IN THE SAME CIRCLES.
HOW CAN DYNAMIC MAN BE SO YOUNG AS WELL? THIS IS INFURIATING.
AND WHO ARE YOU?
MAYBE THIS WILL HELP.
DO YOU RECOGNIZE ME...
...NOW?
THIS IS THE OLD MASK, THE ONE THAT LET ME SEE THE EVIL AROUND ME...WHAT IT IS I'M SEEING NOW, THOUGH, IS LIKE NOTHING I'VE SEEN BEFORE.
AND I'M GRATEFUL I HAVE MY OLD POWER CLOAK IN MY BAG AS WELL.
WHY, YES. HELLO, FIGHTING YANK. WE ALL THOUGHT YOU'D DIED.
I'M THE ONLY ONE AROUND HERE WHO LOOKS LIKE HE COULD.
YOU'RE HERE FOR THE URN, YOU SAY? WHY, HOWEVER DID YOU KNOW I WAS ITS NEW CARETAKER?
I'VE BECOME THE STEWARD OF ALL THOSE OLD MYSTERY TRINKETS FROM THE WAR. SILLY, REALLY, THAT THEY STILL REQUIRE A KEEPER.
NO ONE COULD EVER LIE TO DYNAMIC MAN. BUT THAT DOESN'T MEAN THE LAMA'S GOING TO TELL EVERYTHING.
BRUCE IS DYING, BERT. HE'S IN THE PROCESS OF SAYING GOODBYE TO A LOT OF THINGS. ME. YOU.
COULD HE SEE THE URN?

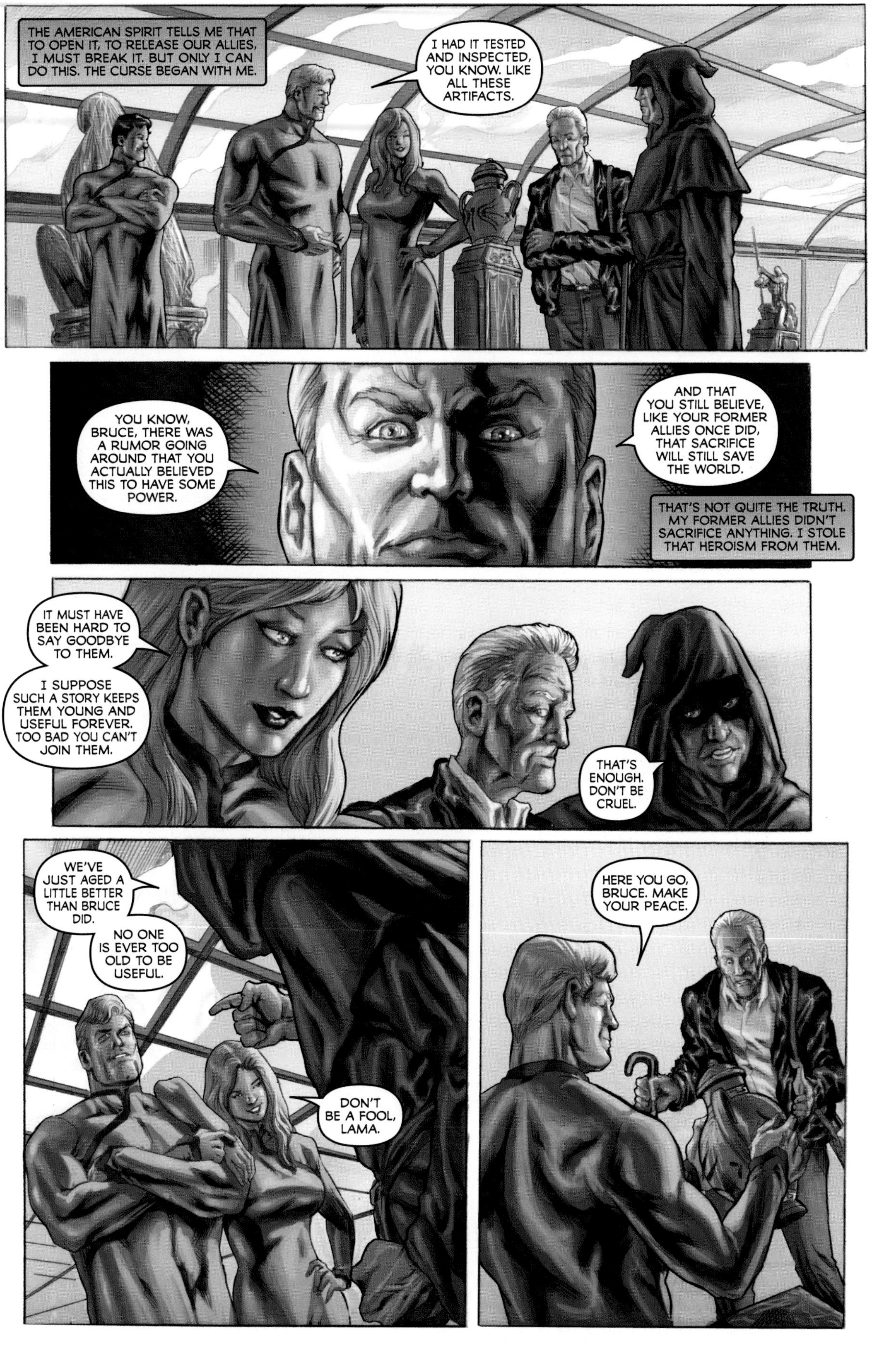
THE AMERICAN SPIRIT TELLS ME THAT TO OPEN IT, TO RELEASE OUR ALLIES, I MUST BREAK IT. BUT ONLY I CAN DO THIS. THE CURSE BEGAN WITH ME.
I HAD IT TESTED AND INSPECTED, YOU KNOW. LIKE ALL THESE ARTIFACTS.
YOU KNOW, BRUCE, THERE WAS A RUMOR GOING AROUND THAT YOU ACTUALLY BELIEVED THIS TO HAVE SOME POWER.
AND THAT YOU STILL BELIEVE, LIKE YOUR FORMER ALLIES ONCE DID, THAT SACRIFICE WILL STILL SAVE THE WORLD.
THAT'S NOT QUITE THE TRUTH. MY FORMER ALLIES DIDN'T SACRIFICE ANYTHING. I STOLE THAT HEROISM FROM THEM.
IT MUST HAVE BEEN HARD TO SAY GOODBYE TO THEM.
I SUPPOSE SUCH A STORY KEEPS THEM YOUNG AND USEFUL FOREVER. TOO BAD YOU CAN'T JOIN THEM.
THAT'S ENOUGH. DON'T BE CRUEL.
WE'VE JUST AGED A LITTLE BETTER THAN BRUCE DID.
NO ONE IS EVER TOO OLD TO BE USEFUL.
DON'T BE A FOOL, LAMA.
HERE YOU GO, BRUCE. MAKE YOUR PEACE.

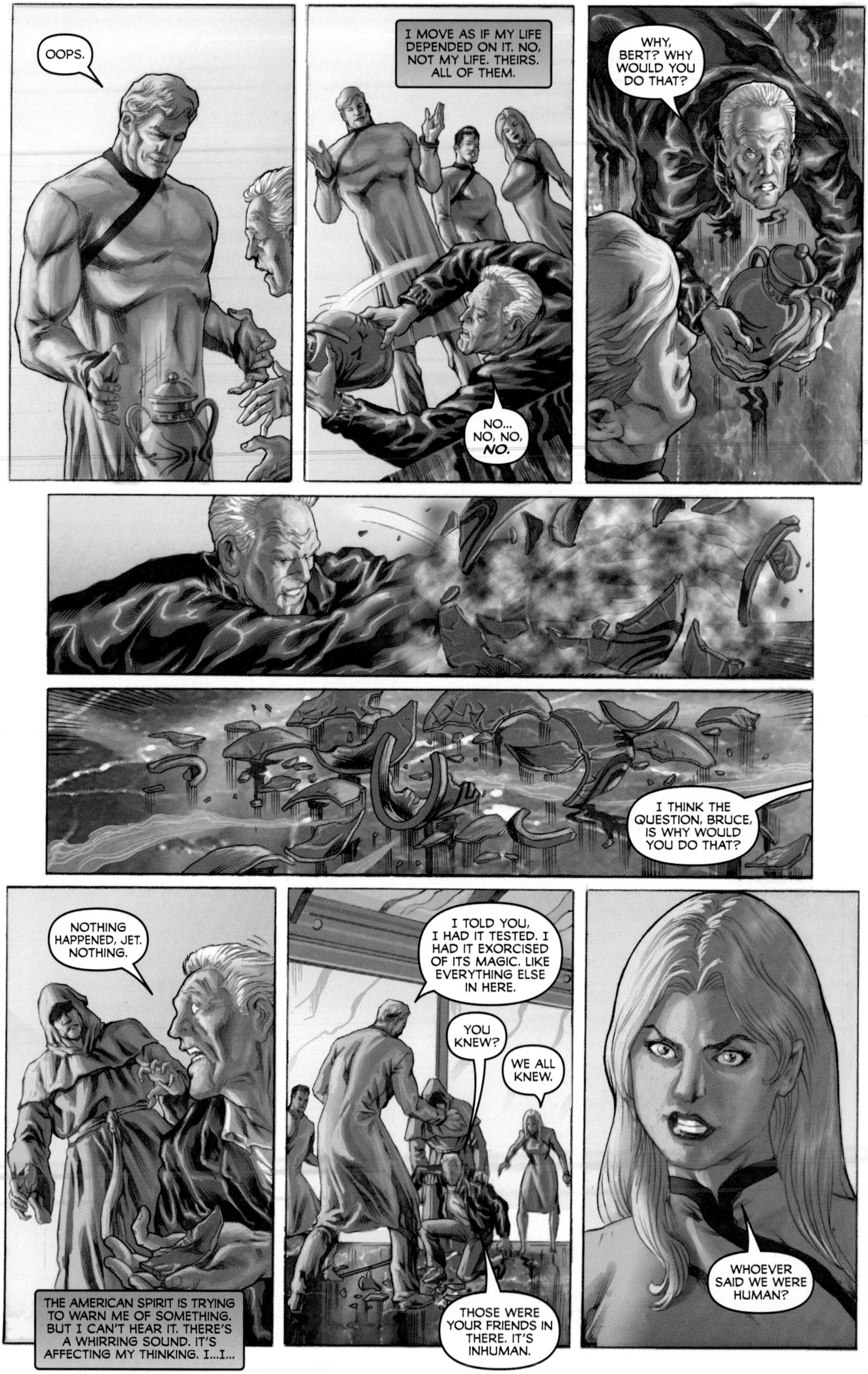
OOPS.
I MOVE AS IF MY LIFE DEPENDED ON IT. NO, NOT MY LIFE. THEIRS. ALL OF THEM.
NO... NO, NO, NO.
WHY, BERT? WHY WOULD YOU DO THAT?
I THINK THE QUESTION, BRUCE, IS WHY WOULD YOU DO THAT?
NOTHING HAPPENED, JET. NOTHING.
THE AMERICAN SPIRIT IS TRYING TO WARN ME OF SOMETHING. BUT I CAN'T HEAR IT. THERE'S A WHIRRING SOUND. IT'S AFFECTING MY THINKING. I...I...
I TOLD YOU, I HAD IT TESTED. I HAD IT EXORCISED OF ITS MAGIC. LIKE EVERYTHING ELSE IN HERE.
YOU KNEW?
WE ALL KNEW.
THOSE WERE YOUR FRIENDS IN THERE. IT'S INHUMAN.
WHOEVER SAID WE WERE HUMAN?

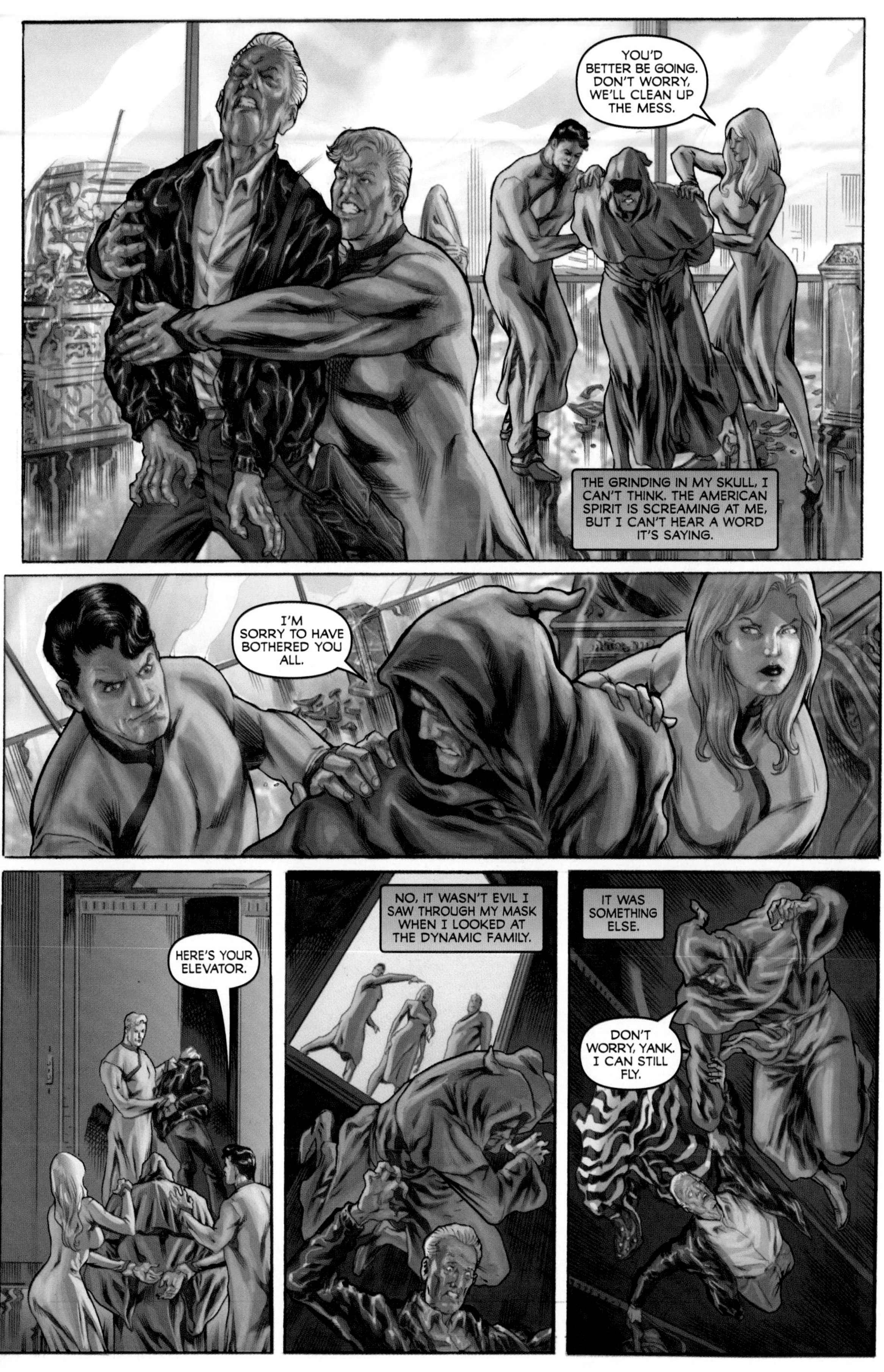
YOU'D BETTER BE GOING. DON'T WORRY, WE'LL CLEAN UP THE MESS.
THE GRINDING IN MY SKULL, I CAN'T THINK. THE AMERICAN SPIRIT IS SCREAMING AT ME, BUT I CAN'T HEAR A WORD IT'S SAYING.
I'M SORRY TO HAVE BOTHERED YOU ALL.
HERE'S YOUR ELEVATOR.
NO, IT WASN'T EVIL I SAW THROUGH MY MASK WHEN I LOOKED AT THE DYNAMIC FAMILY.
IT WAS SOMETHING ELSE.
DON'T WORRY, YANK. I CAN STILL FLY.

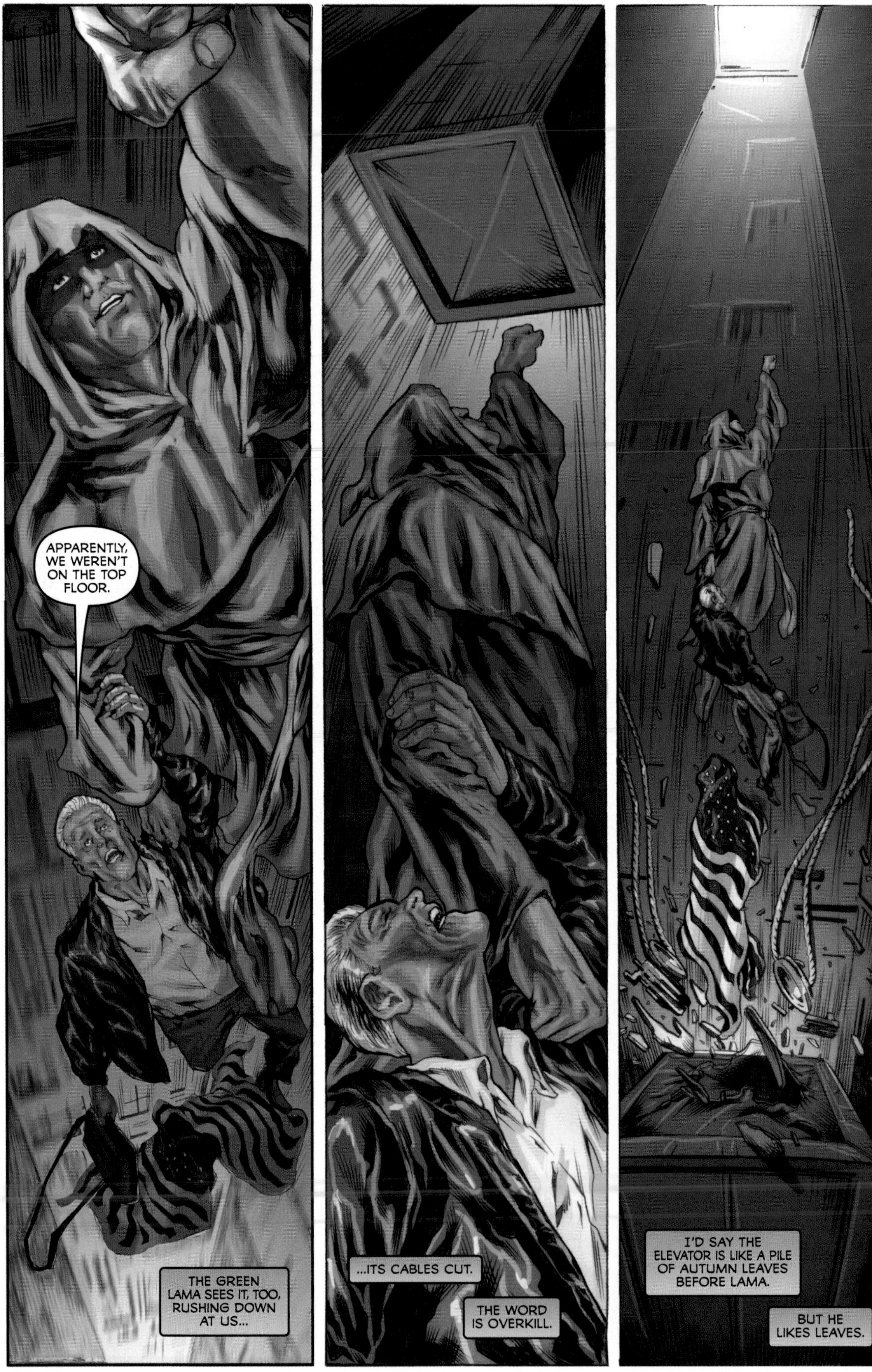
APPARENTLY, WE WEREN'T ON THE TOP FLOOR.
THE GREEN LAMA SEES IT, TOO, RUSHING DOWN AT US...
...ITS CABLES CUT.
THE WORD IS OVERKILL.
I'D SAY THE ELEVATOR IS LIKE A PILE OF AUTUMN LEAVES BEFORE LAMA.
BUT HE LIKES LEAVES.

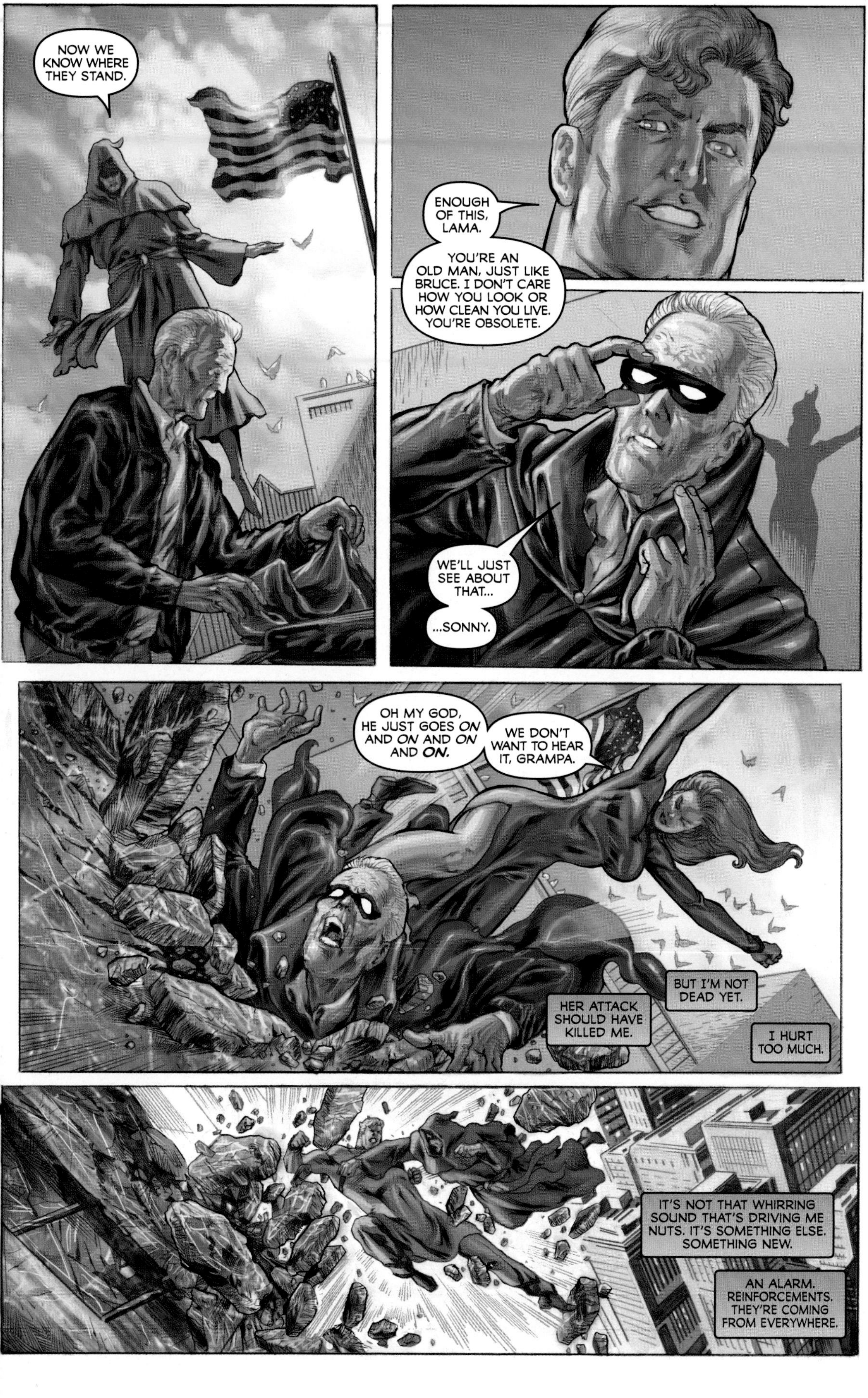
NOW WE KNOW WHERE THEY STAND.
ENOUGH OF THIS, LAMA.
YOU'RE AN OLD MAN, JUST LIKE BRUCE. I DON'T CARE HOW YOU LOOK OR HOW CLEAN YOU LIVE. YOU'RE OBSOLETE.
WE'LL JUST SEE ABOUT THAT...
...SONNY.
OH MY GOD, HE JUST GOES ON AND ON AND ON AND ON.
WE DON'T WANT TO HEAR IT, GRAMPA.
HER ATTACK SHOULD HAVE KILLED ME.
BUT I'M NOT DEAD YET.
I HURT TOO MUCH.
IT'S NOT THAT WHIRRING SOUND THAT'S DRIVING ME NUTS. IT'S SOMETHING ELSE. SOMETHING NEW.
AN ALARM. REINFORCEMENTS. THEY'RE COMING FROM EVERYWHERE.

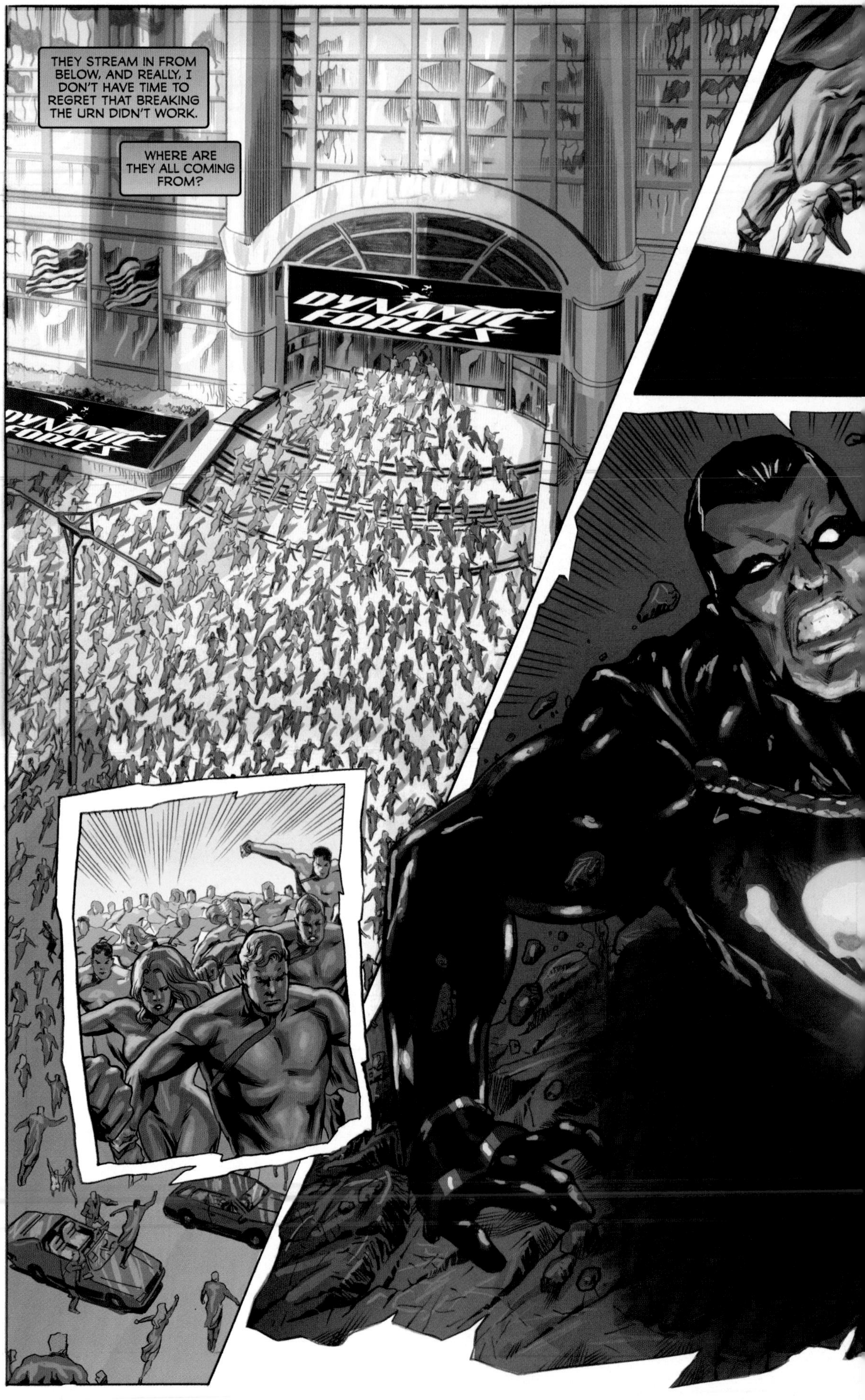
THEY STREAM IN FROM BELOW, AND REALLY, I DON'T HAVE TIME TO REGRET THAT BREAKING THE URN DIDN'T WORK.
WHERE ARE THEY ALL COMING FROM?
DYNAMIC FORCES
DYNAMIC FORCES

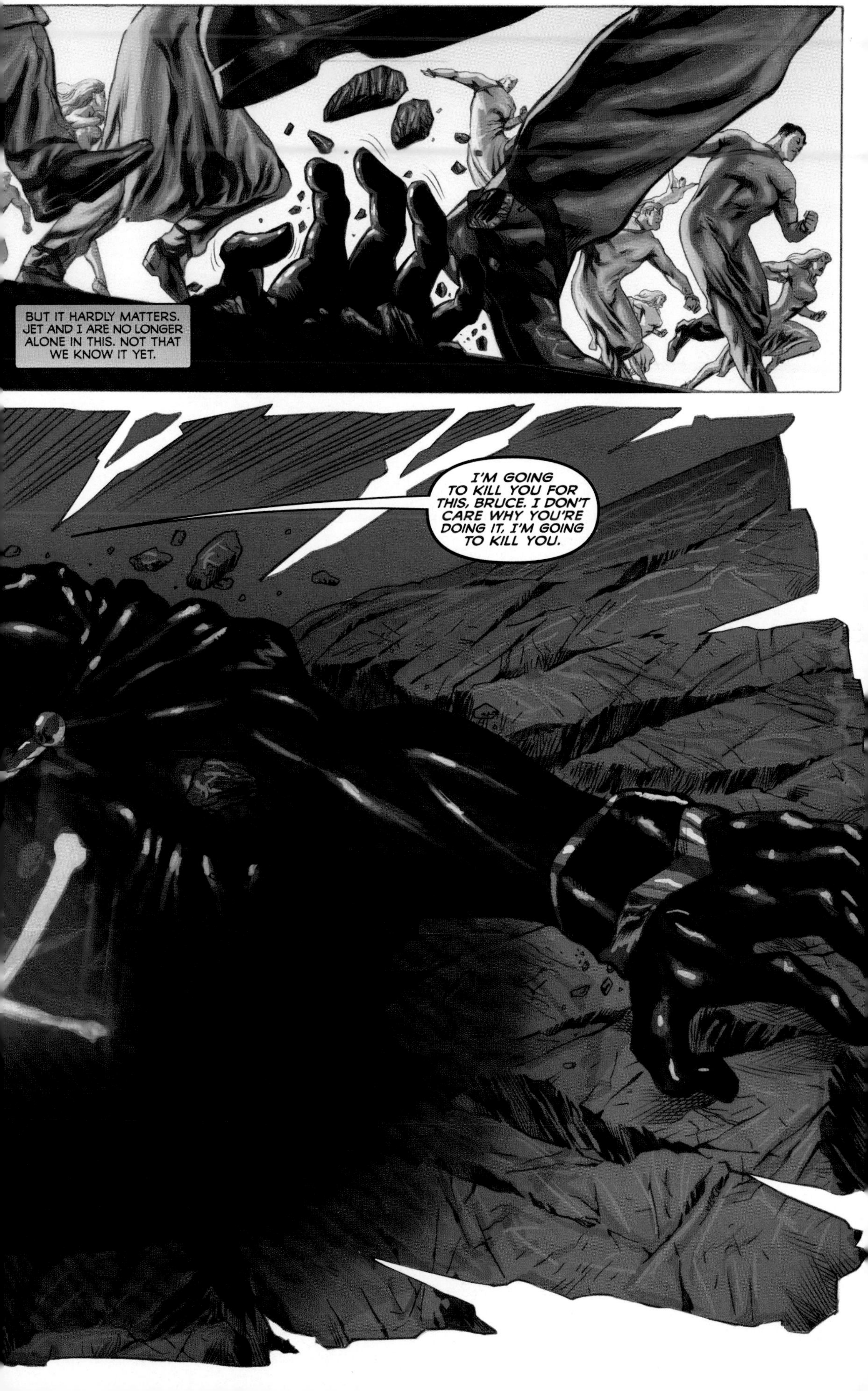
BUT IT HARDLY MATTERS. JET AND I ARE NO LONGER ALONE IN THIS. NOT THAT WE KNOW IT YET.
I'M GOING TO KILL YOU FOR THIS, BRUCE. I DON'T CARE WHY YOU'RE DOING IT, I'M GOING TO KILL YOU.

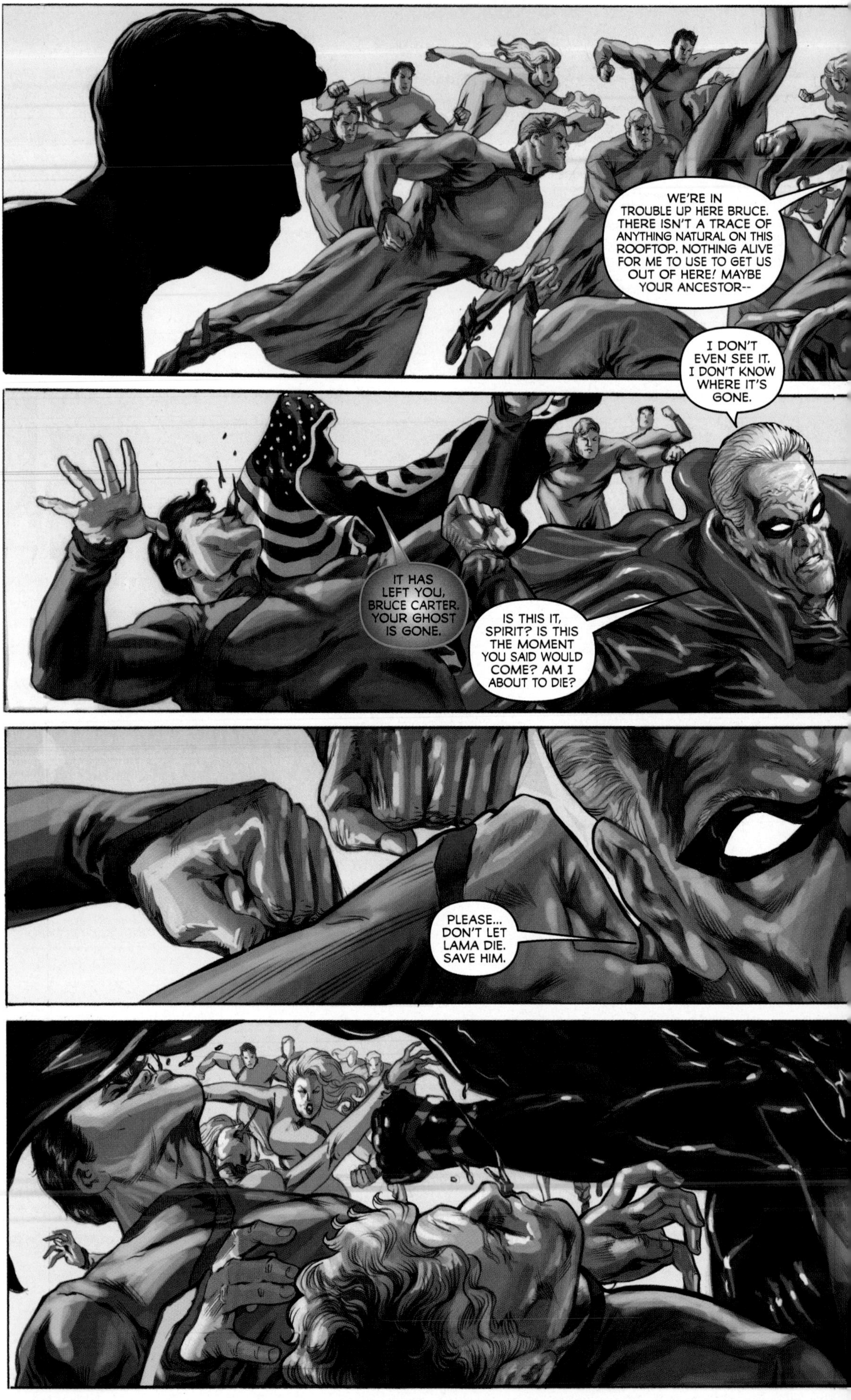
WE'RE IN TROUBLE UP HERE BRUCE. THERE ISN'T A TRACE OF ANYTHING NATURAL ON THIS ROOFTOP. NOTHING ALIVE FOR ME TO USE TO GET US OUT OF HERE! MAYBE YOUR ANCESTOR--
I DON'T EVEN SEE IT. I DON'T KNOW WHERE IT'S GONE.
IT HAS LEFT YOU, BRUCE CARTER. YOUR GHOST IS GONE.
IS THIS IT, SPIRIT? IS THIS THE MOMENT YOU SAID WOULD COME? AM I ABOUT TO DIE?
PLEASE... DON'T LET LAMA DIE. SAVE HIM.

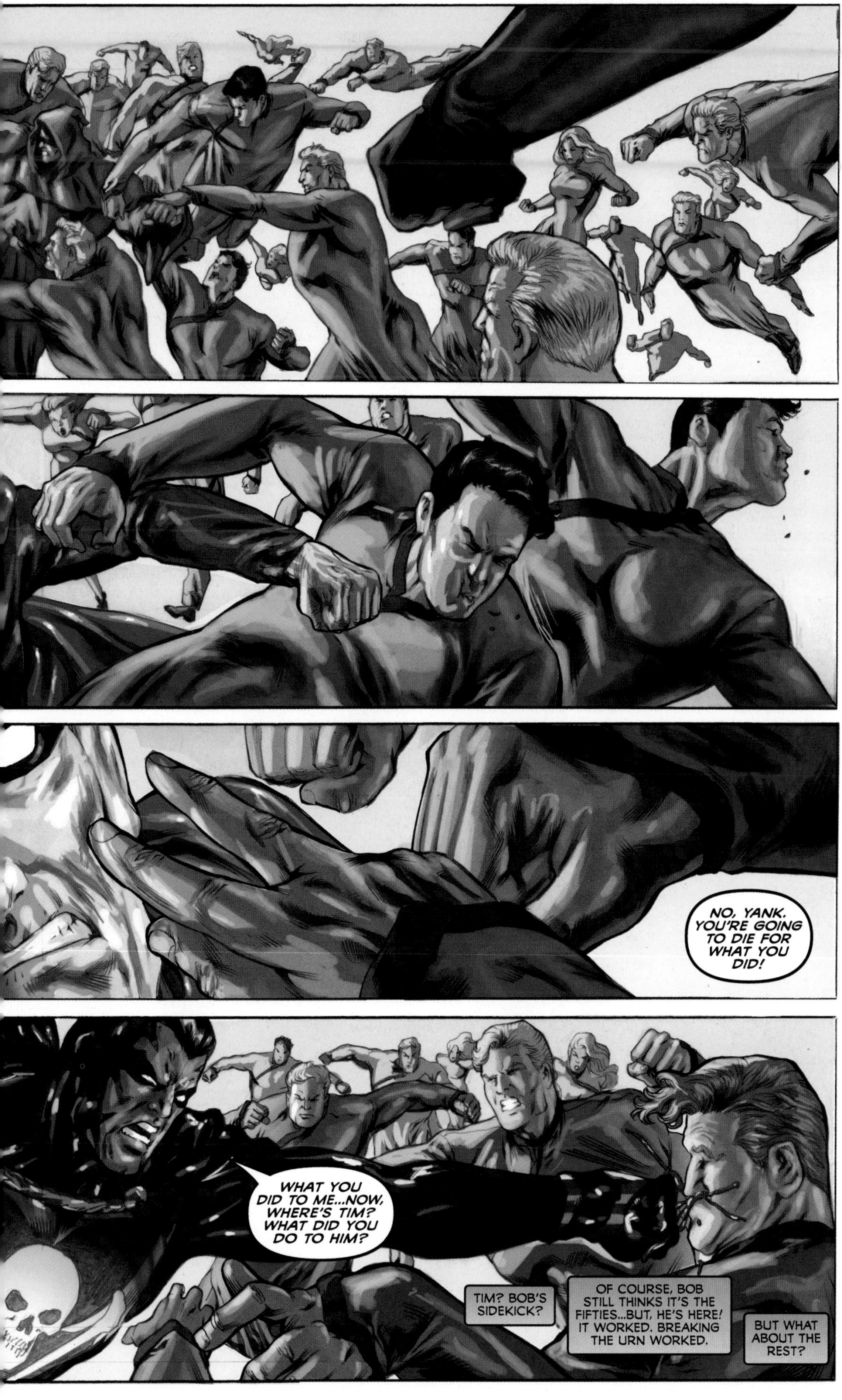
NO, YANK. YOU'RE GOING TO DIE FOR WHAT YOU DID!
WHAT YOU DID TO ME...NOW, WHERE'S TIM? WHAT DID YOU DO TO HIM?
TIM? BOB'S SIDEKICK?
OF COURSE, BOB STILL THINKS IT'S THE FIFTIES...BUT, HE'S HERE! IT WORKED. BREAKING THE URN WORKED.
BUT WHAT ABOUT THE REST?

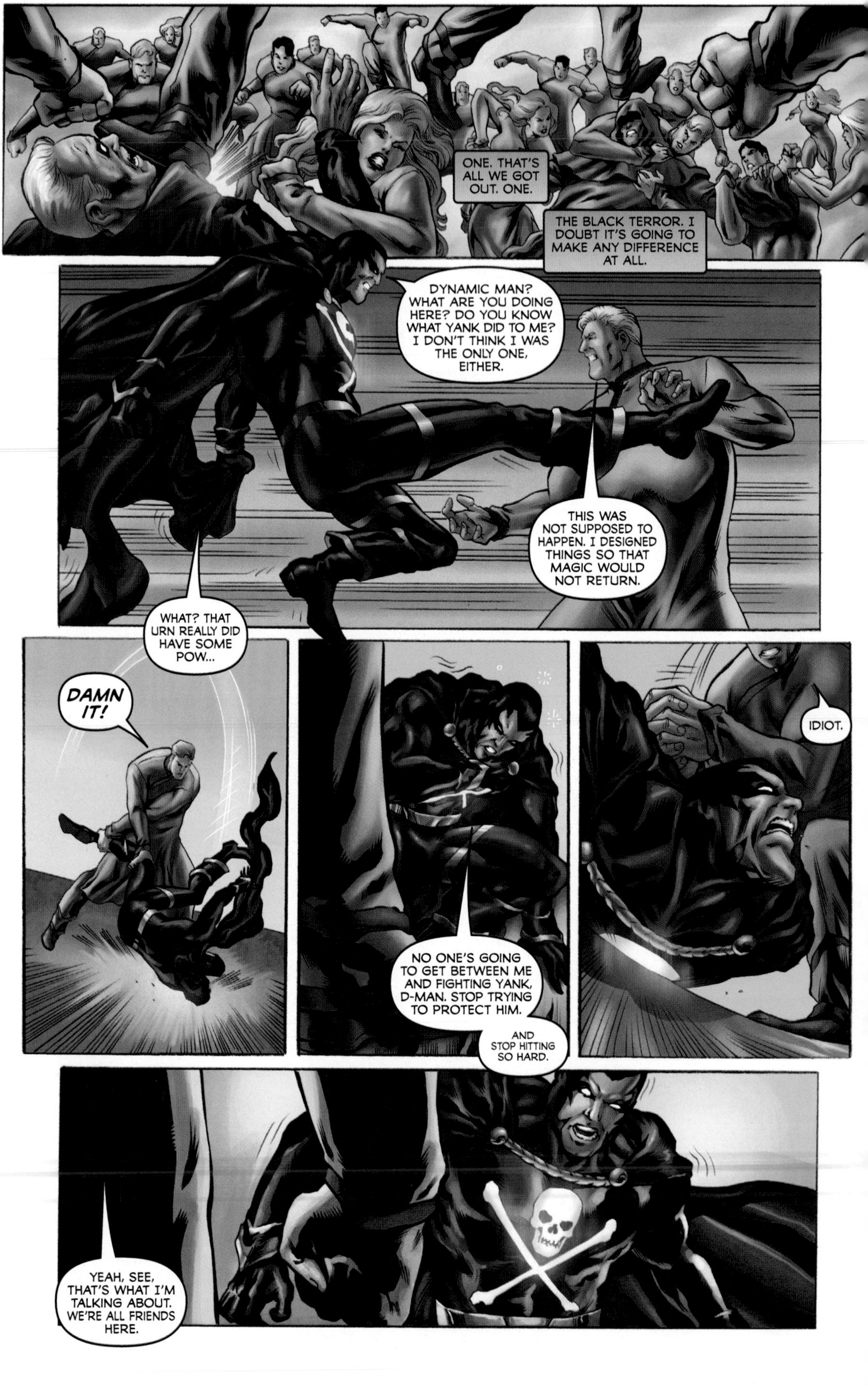
ONE. THAT'S ALL WE GOT OUT. ONE.
THE BLACK TERROR. I DOUBT IT'S GOING TO MAKE ANY DIFFERENCE AT ALL.
DYNAMIC MAN? WHAT ARE YOU DOING HERE? DO YOU KNOW WHAT YANK DID TO ME? I DON'T THINK I WAS THE ONLY ONE, EITHER.
THIS WAS NOT SUPPOSED TO HAPPEN. I DESIGNED THINGS SO THAT MAGIC WOULD NOT RETURN.
WHAT? THAT URN REALLY DID HAVE SOME POW...
DAMN IT!
NO ONE'S GOING TO GET BETWEEN ME AND FIGHTING YANK, D-MAN. STOP TRYING TO PROTECT HIM.
AND STOP HITTING SO HARD.
IDIOT.
YEAH, SEE, THAT'S WHAT I'M TALKING ABOUT. WE'RE ALL FRIENDS HERE.

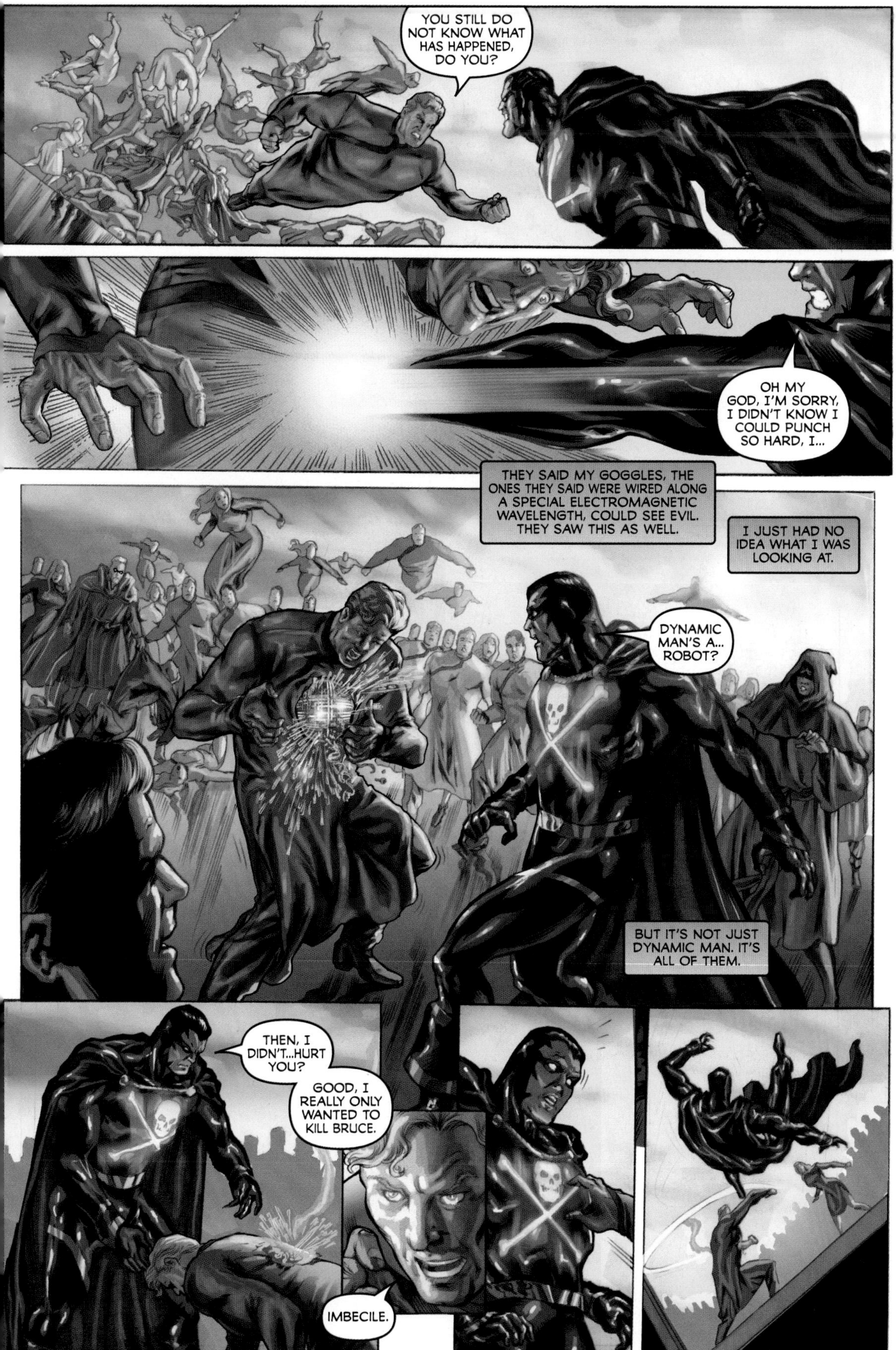
YOU STILL DO NOT KNOW WHAT HAS HAPPENED, DO YOU?
OH MY GOD, I'M SORRY, I DIDN'T KNOW I COULD PUNCH SO HARD, I...
THEY SAID MY GOGGLES, THE ONES THEY SAID WERE WIRED ALONG A SPECIAL ELECTROMAGNETIC WAVELENGTH, COULD SEE EVIL. THEY SAW THIS AS WELL.
I JUST HAD NO IDEA WHAT I WAS LOOKING AT.
DYNAMIC MAN'S A... ROBOT?
BUT IT'S NOT JUST DYNAMIC MAN. IT'S ALL OF THEM.
THEN, I DIDN'T...HURT YOU?
GOOD, I REALLY ONLY WANTED TO KILL BRUCE.
IMBECILE.

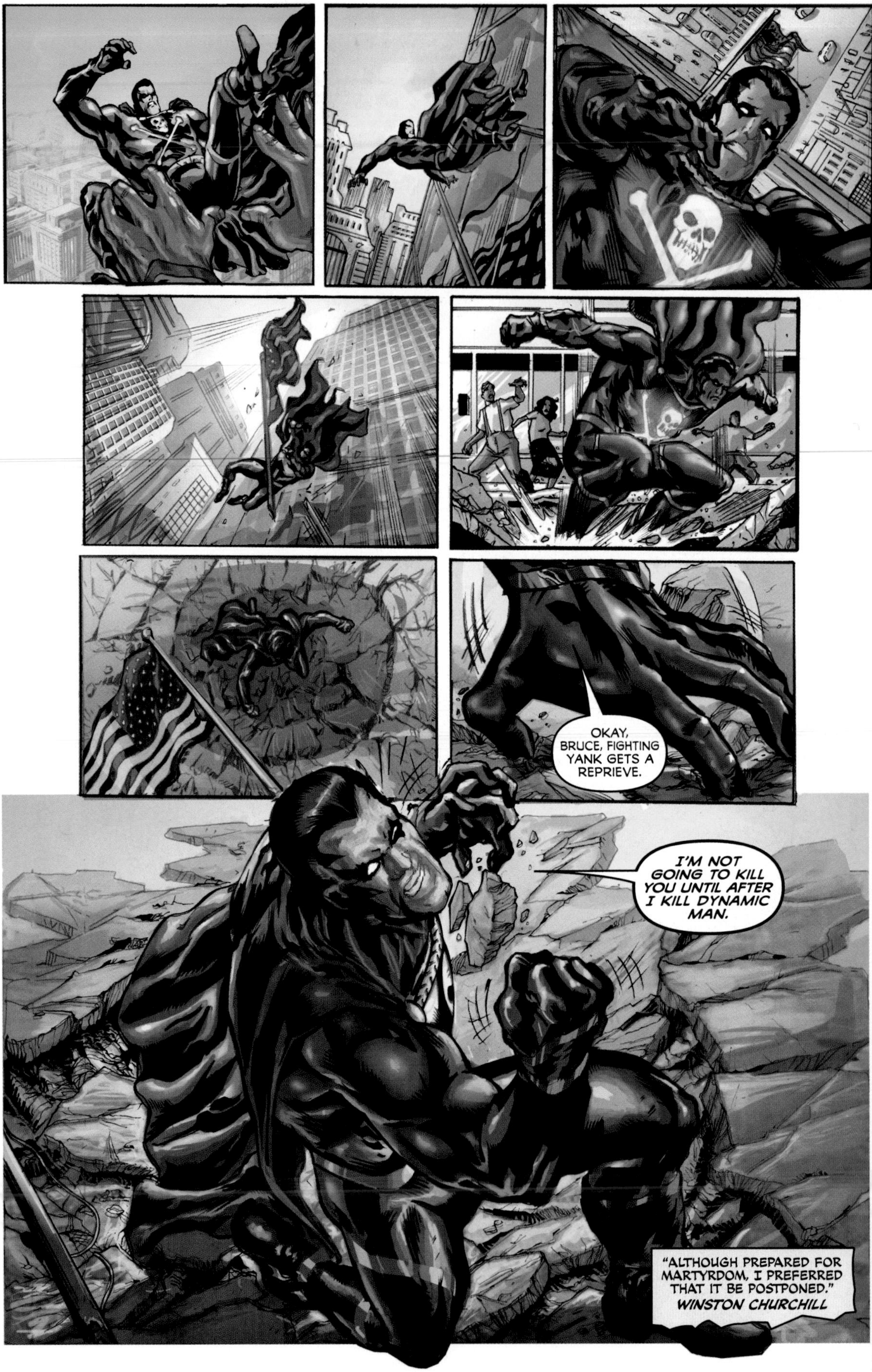
OKAY, BRUCE, FIGHTING YANK GETS A REPRIEVE.
I'M NOT GOING TO KILL YOU UNTIL AFTER I KILL DYNAMIC MAN.
"ALTHOUGH PREPARED FOR MARTYRDOM, I PREFERRED THAT IT BE POSTPONED."
WINSTON CHURCHILL

ISSUE

2

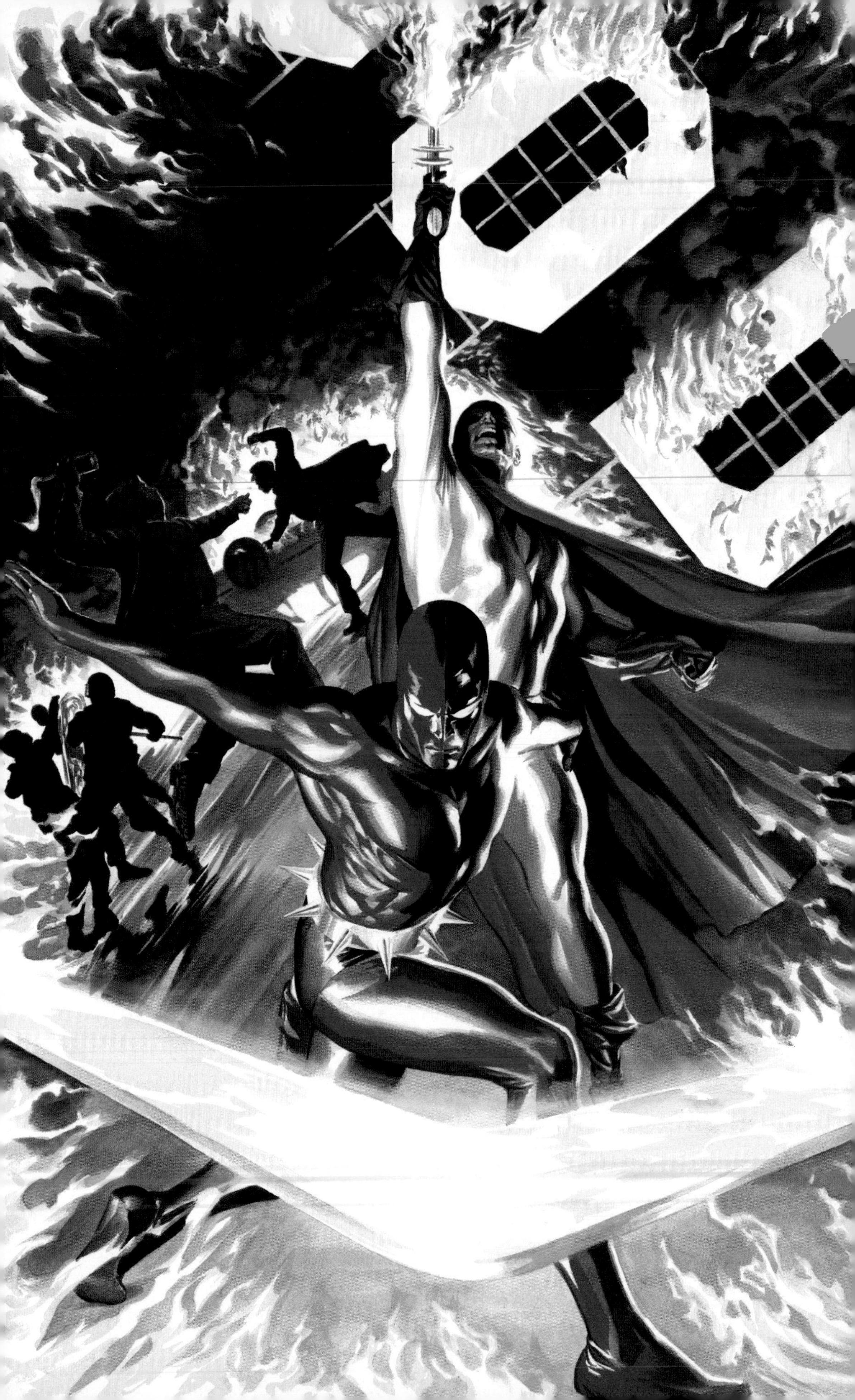

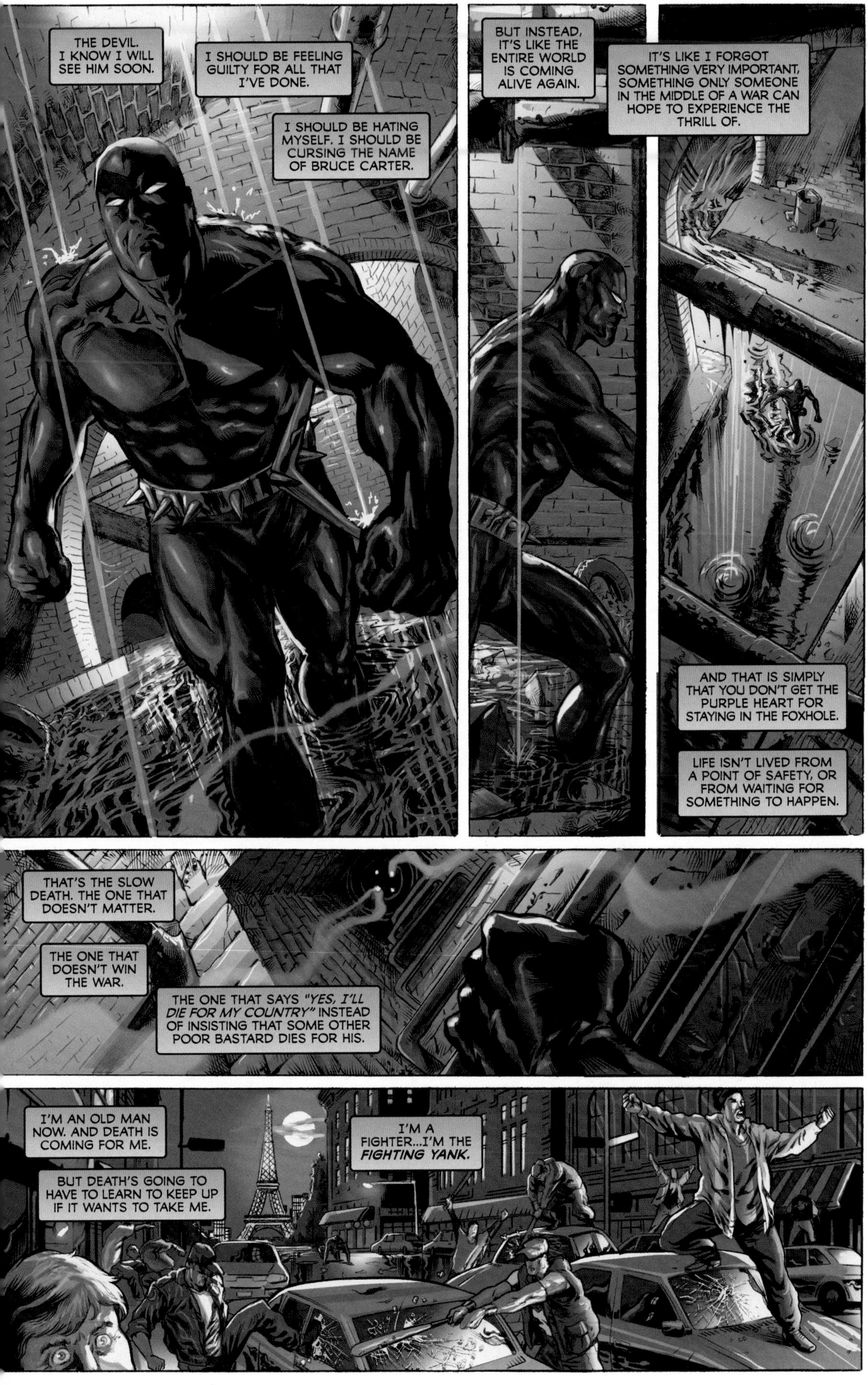
THE DEVIL. I KNOW I WILL SEE HIM SOON.
I SHOULD BE FEELING GUILTY FOR ALL THAT I'VE DONE.
I SHOULD BE HATING MYSELF. I SHOULD BE CURSING THE NAME OF BRUCE CARTER.
BUT INSTEAD, IT'S LIKE THE ENTIRE WORLD IS COMING ALIVE AGAIN.
IT'S LIKE I FORGOT SOMETHING VERY IMPORTANT, SOMETHING ONLY SOMEONE IN THE MIDDLE OF A WAR CAN HOPE TO EXPERIENCE THE THRILL OF.
AND THAT IS SIMPLY THAT YOU DON'T GET THE PURPLE HEART FOR STAYING IN THE FOXHOLE.
LIFE ISN'T LIVED FROM A POINT OF SAFETY, OR FROM WAITING FOR SOMETHING TO HAPPEN.
THAT'S THE SLOW DEATH. THE ONE THAT DOESN'T MATTER.
THE ONE THAT DOESN'T WIN THE WAR.
THE ONE THAT SAYS *"YES, I'LL DIE FOR MY COUNTRY"* INSTEAD OF INSISTING THAT SOME OTHER POOR BASTARD DIES FOR HIS.
I'M AN OLD MAN NOW. AND DEATH IS COMING FOR ME.
BUT DEATH'S GOING TO HAVE TO LEARN TO KEEP UP IF IT WANTS TO TAKE ME.
I'M A FIGHTER...I'M THE ***FIGHTING YANK.***

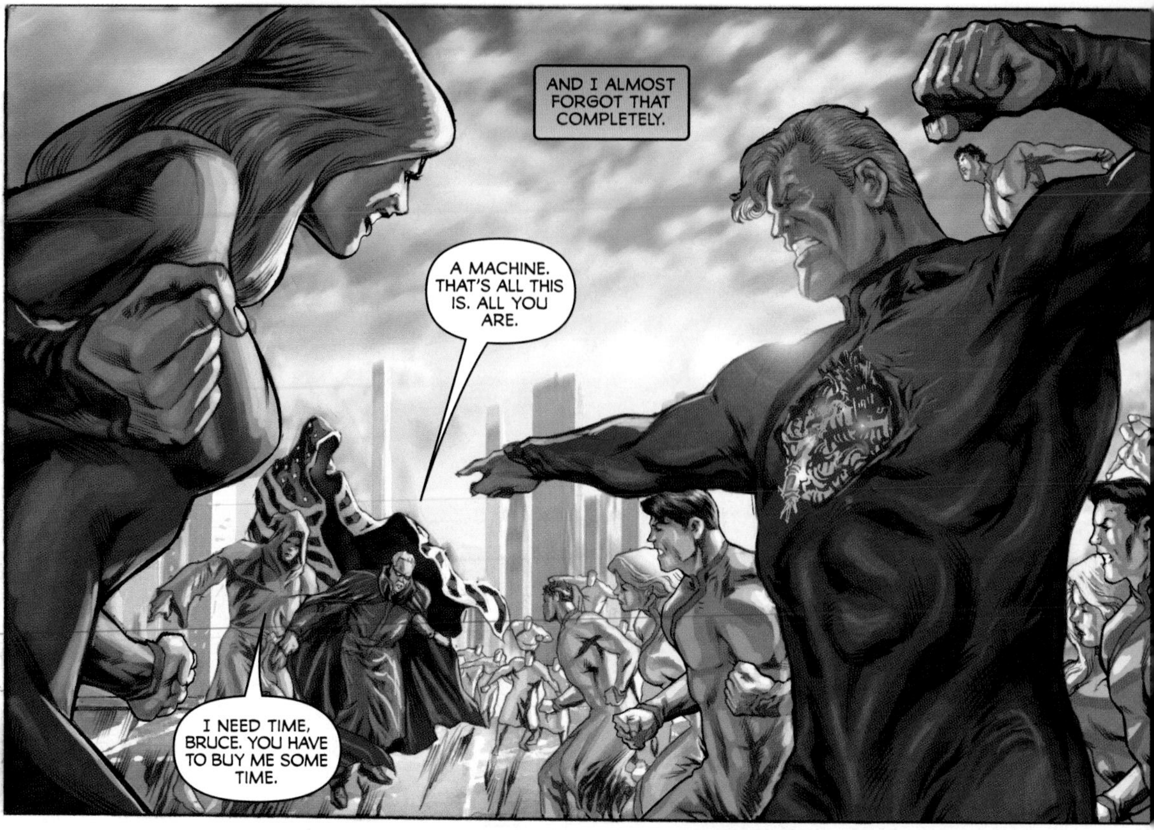
AND I ALMOST FORGOT THAT COMPLETELY.
A MACHINE. THAT'S ALL THIS IS. ALL YOU ARE.
I NEED TIME, BRUCE. YOU HAVE TO BUY ME SOME TIME.

...THE WHITES OF THEIR EYES

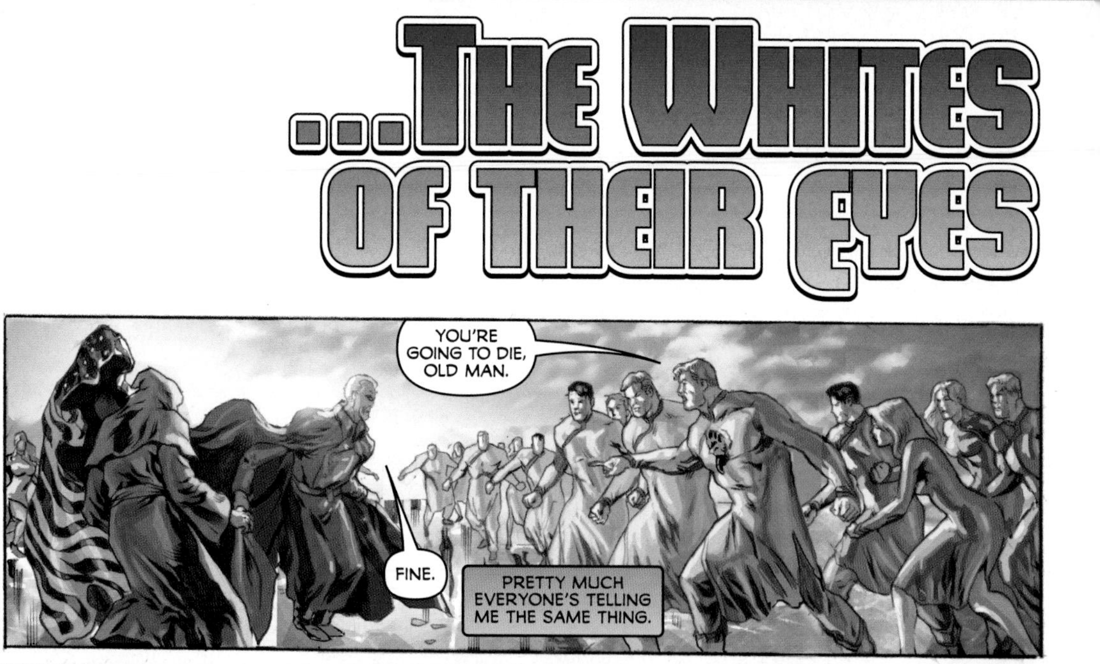
YOU'RE GOING TO DIE, OLD MAN.
FINE.
PRETTY MUCH EVERYONE'S TELLING ME THE SAME THING.

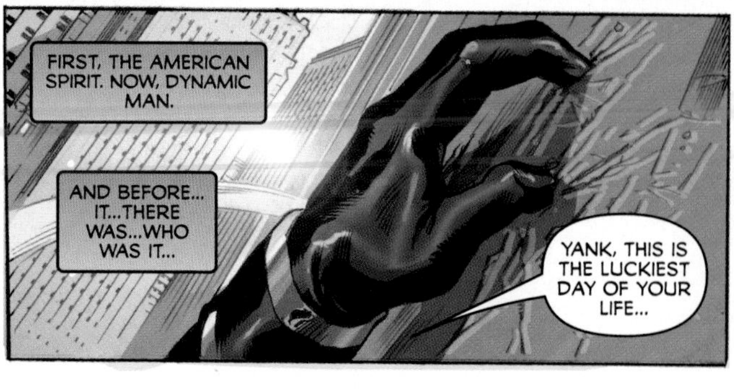
FIRST, THE AMERICAN SPIRIT. NOW, DYNAMIC MAN.
AND BEFORE... IT...THERE WAS...WHO WAS IT...
YANK, THIS IS THE LUCKIEST DAY OF YOUR LIFE...

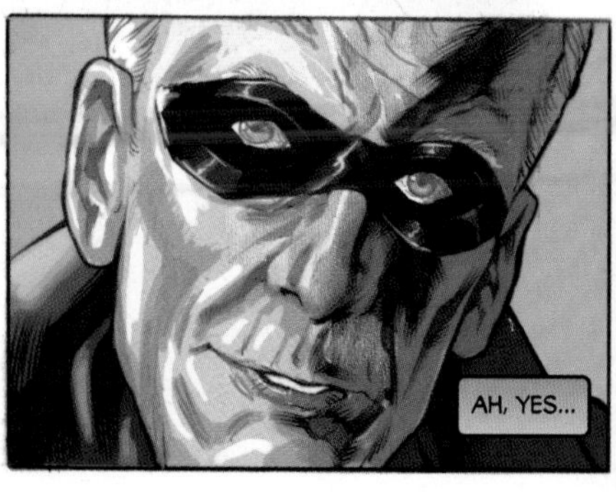
AH, YES...

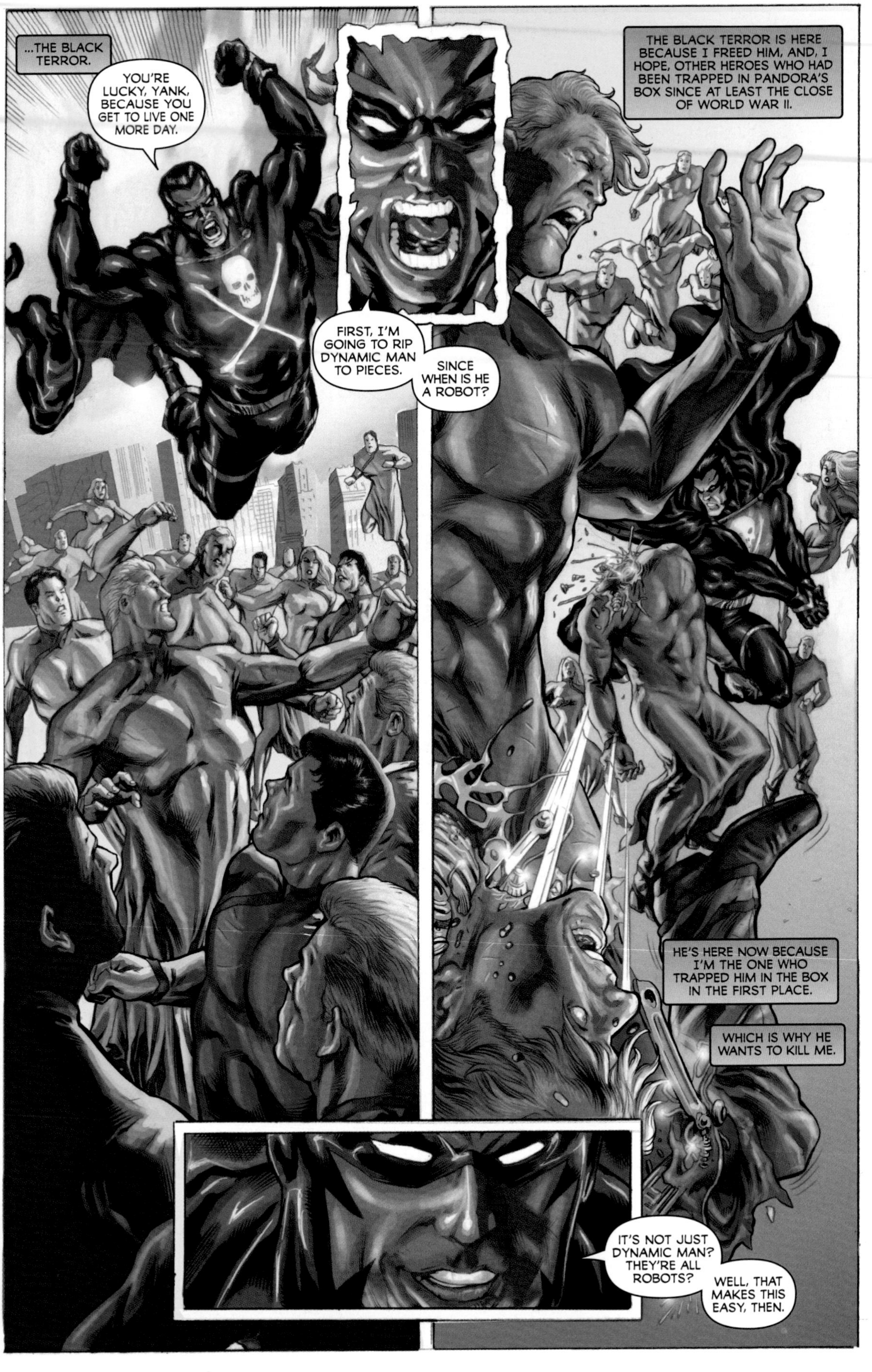
...THE BLACK TERROR.
YOU'RE LUCKY, YANK, BECAUSE YOU GET TO LIVE ONE MORE DAY.
FIRST, I'M GOING TO RIP DYNAMIC MAN TO PIECES.
SINCE WHEN IS HE A ROBOT?
THE BLACK TERROR IS HERE BECAUSE I FREED HIM, AND, I HOPE, OTHER HEROES WHO HAD BEEN TRAPPED IN PANDORA'S BOX SINCE AT LEAST THE CLOSE OF WORLD WAR II.
HE'S HERE NOW BECAUSE I'M THE ONE WHO TRAPPED HIM IN THE BOX IN THE FIRST PLACE.
WHICH IS WHY HE WANTS TO KILL ME.
IT'S NOT JUST DYNAMIC MAN? THEY'RE ALL ROBOTS?
WELL, THAT MAKES THIS EASY, THEN.

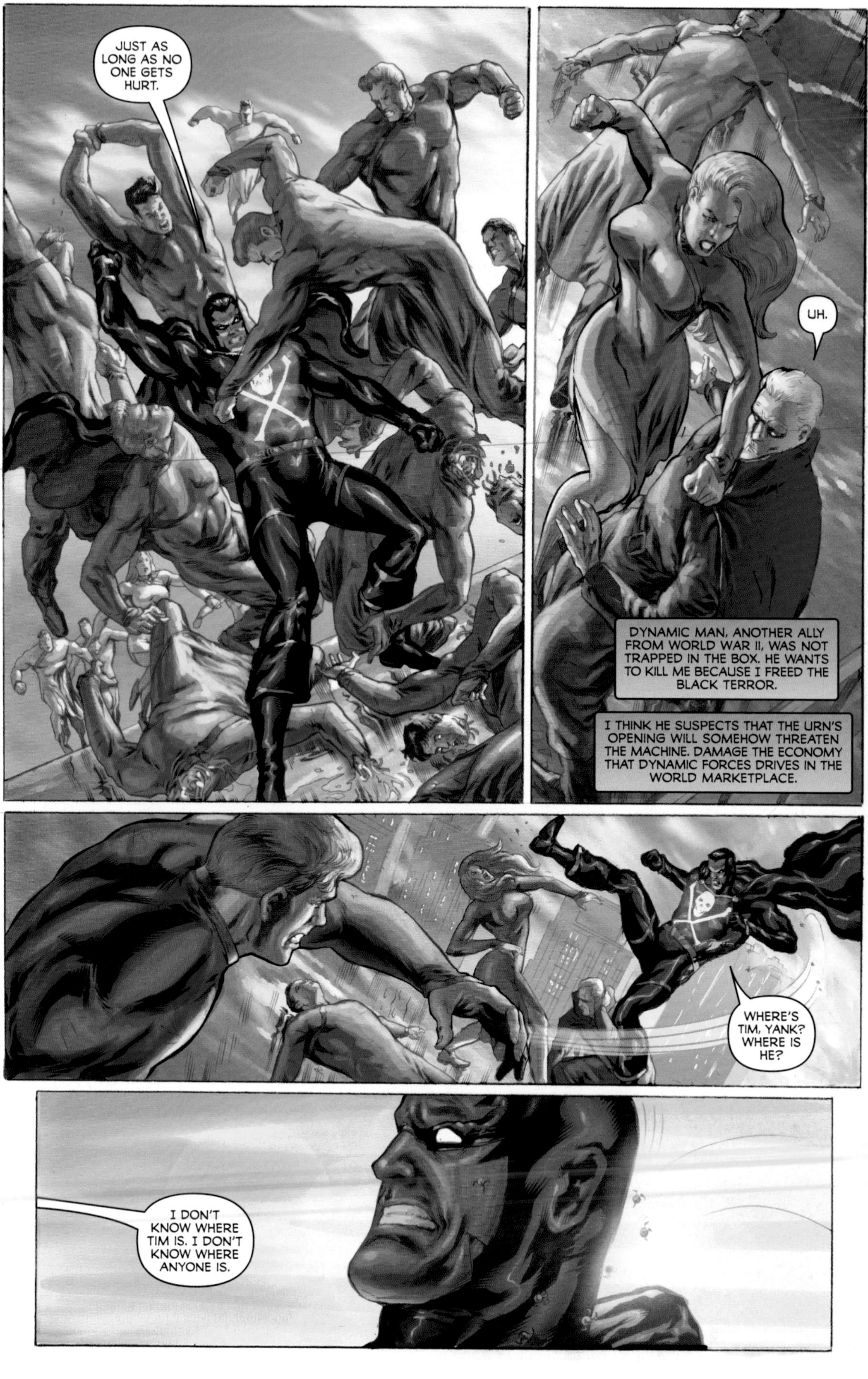
JUST AS LONG AS NO ONE GETS HURT.
UH.
DYNAMIC MAN, ANOTHER ALLY FROM WORLD WAR II, WAS NOT TRAPPED IN THE BOX. HE WANTS TO KILL ME BECAUSE I FREED THE BLACK TERROR.
I THINK HE SUSPECTS THAT THE URN'S OPENING WILL SOMEHOW THREATEN THE MACHINE. DAMAGE THE ECONOMY THAT DYNAMIC FORCES DRIVES IN THE WORLD MARKETPLACE.
WHERE'S TIM, YANK? WHERE IS HE?
I DON'T KNOW WHERE TIM IS. I DON'T KNOW WHERE ANYONE IS.

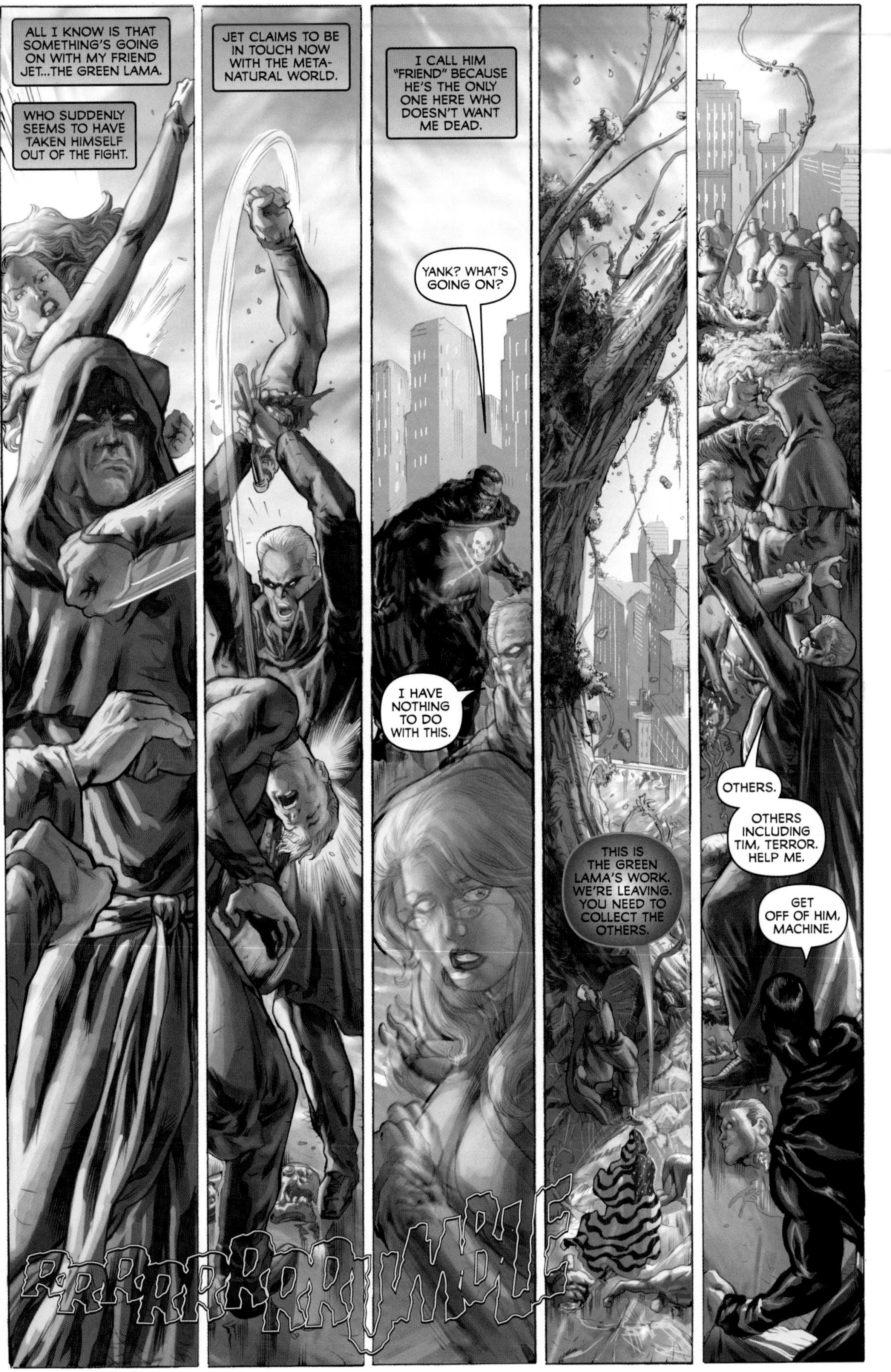
ALL I KNOW IS THAT SOMETHING'S GOING ON WITH MY FRIEND JET...THE GREEN LAMA.
WHO SUDDENLY SEEMS TO HAVE TAKEN HIMSELF OUT OF THE FIGHT.
JET CLAIMS TO BE IN TOUCH NOW WITH THE META-NATURAL WORLD.
I CALL HIM "FRIEND" BECAUSE HE'S THE ONLY ONE HERE WHO DOESN'T WANT ME DEAD.
YANK? WHAT'S GOING ON?
I HAVE NOTHING TO DO WITH THIS.
THIS IS THE GREEN LAMA'S WORK. WE'RE LEAVING. YOU NEED TO COLLECT THE OTHERS.
OTHERS.
OTHERS INCLUDING TIM, TERROR. HELP ME.
GET OFF OF HIM, MACHINE.
RRRRRRRRRUMBLE

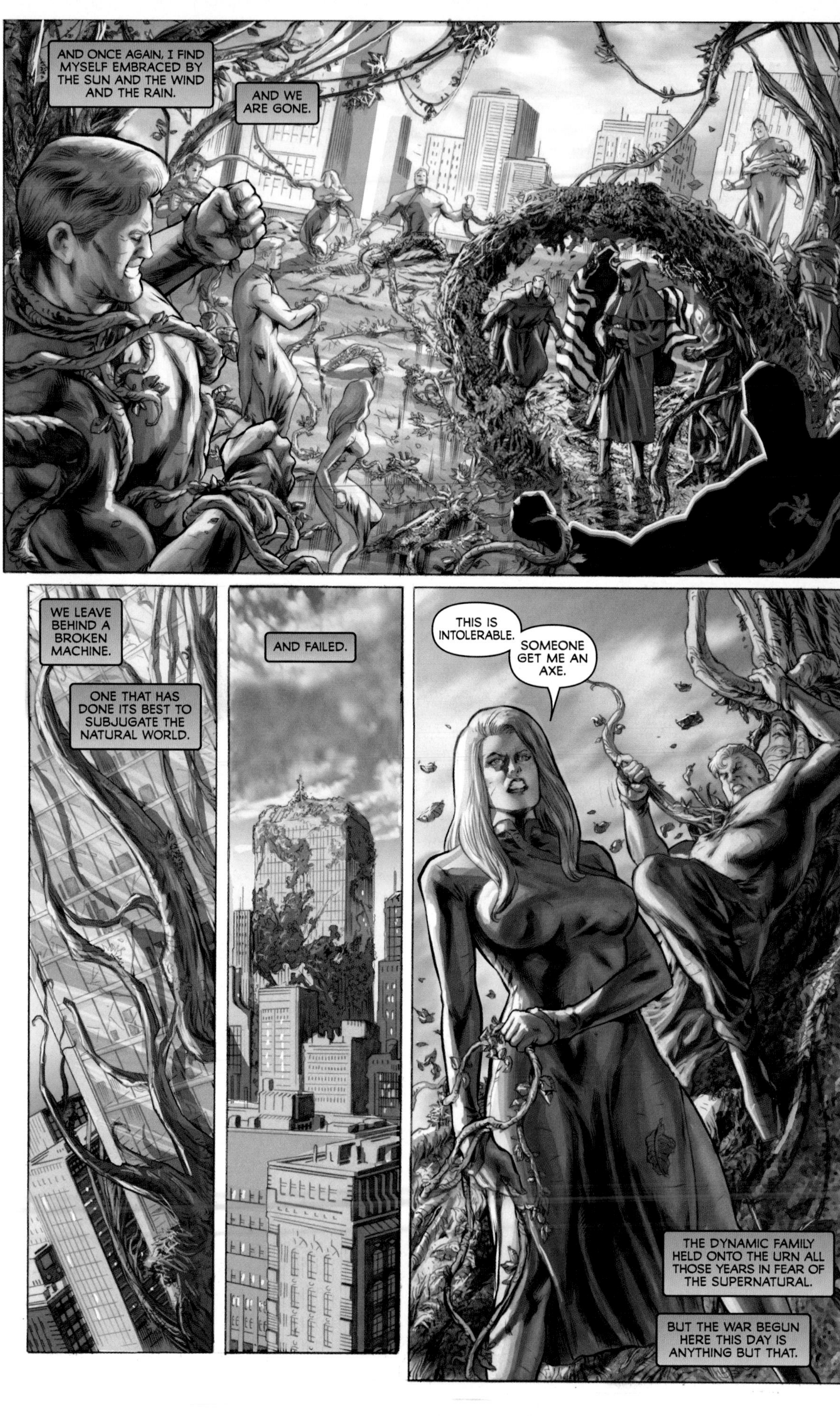
AND ONCE AGAIN, I FIND MYSELF EMBRACED BY THE SUN AND THE WIND AND THE RAIN.
AND WE ARE GONE.
WE LEAVE BEHIND A BROKEN MACHINE.
ONE THAT HAS DONE ITS BEST TO SUBJUGATE THE NATURAL WORLD.
AND FAILED.
THIS IS INTOLERABLE.
SOMEONE GET ME AN AXE.
THE DYNAMIC FAMILY HELD ONTO THE URN ALL THOSE YEARS IN FEAR OF THE SUPERNATURAL.
BUT THE WAR BEGUN HERE THIS DAY IS ANYTHING BUT THAT.

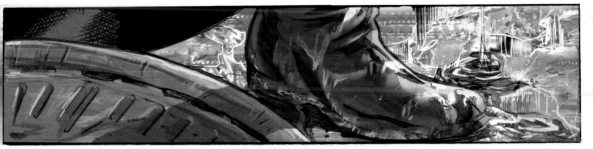

‹LOOK OUT!›*

‹STOP!›

‹PLEASE...›

*TRANSLATED FROM THE FRENCH

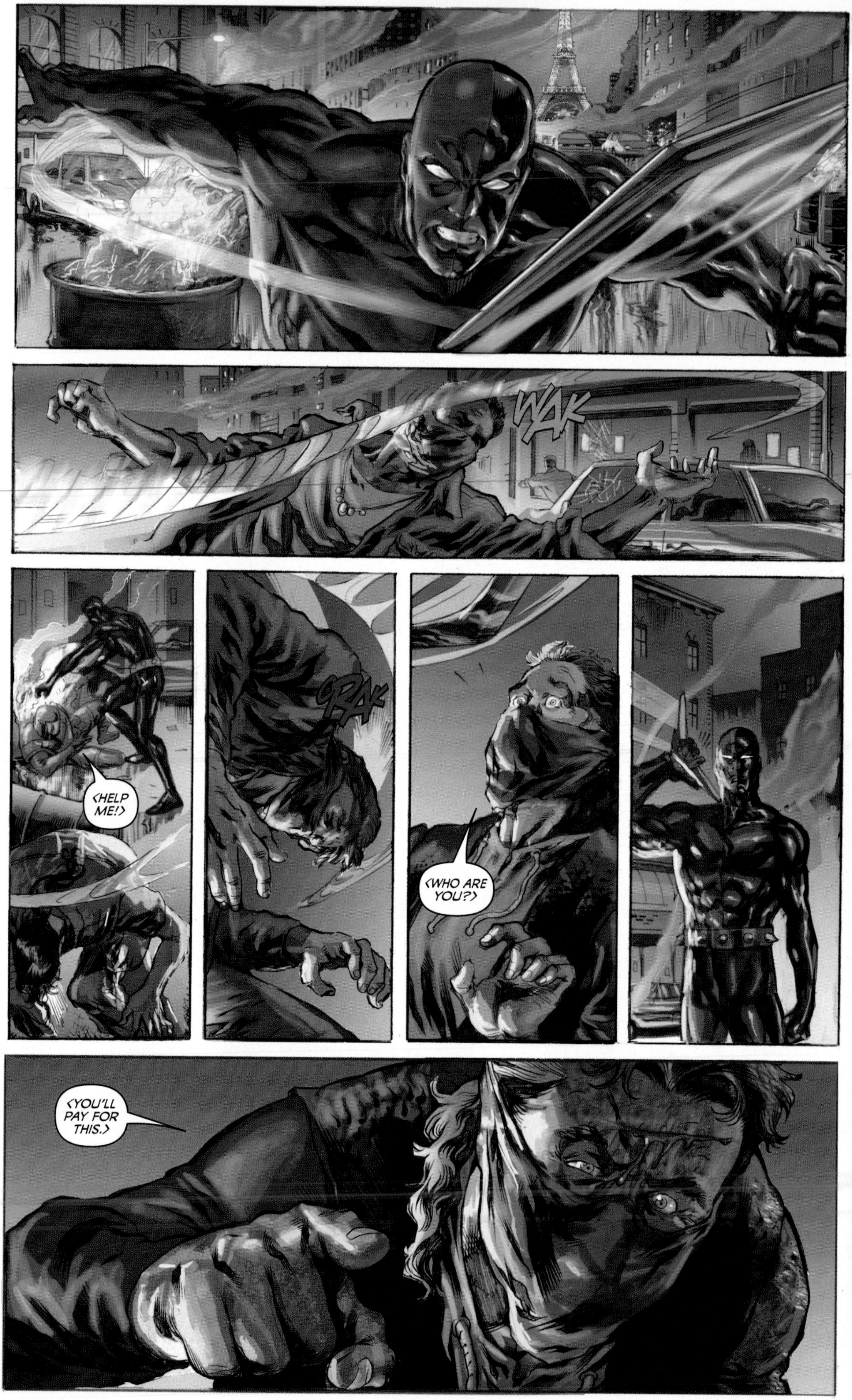
WAK
<HELP ME!>
CRAK
<WHO ARE YOU?>
<YOU'LL PAY FOR THIS.>

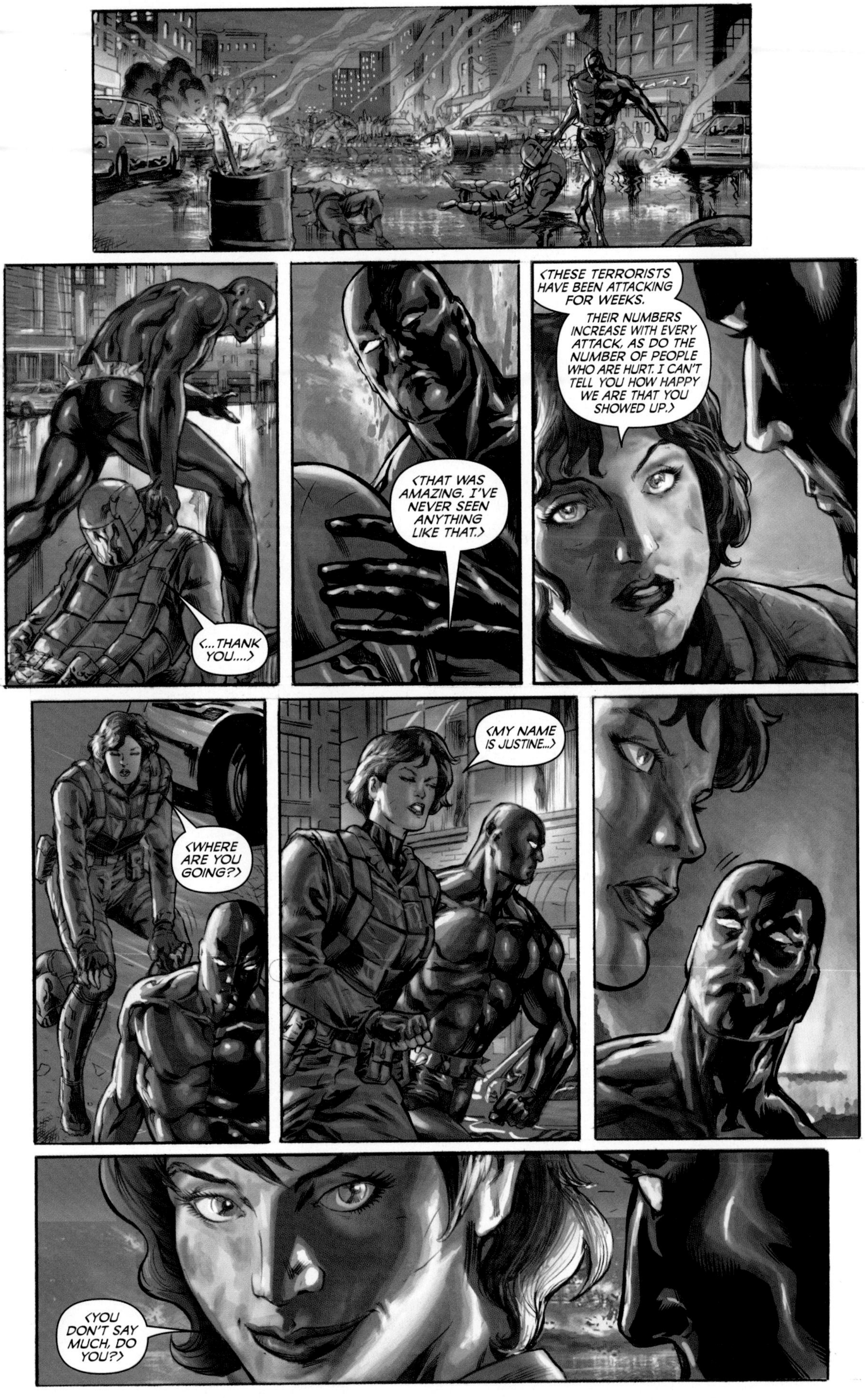

<...THANK YOU....>
<THAT WAS AMAZING. I'VE NEVER SEEN ANYTHING LIKE THAT.>
<THESE TERRORISTS HAVE BEEN ATTACKING FOR WEEKS.
THEIR NUMBERS INCREASE WITH EVERY ATTACK, AS DO THE NUMBER OF PEOPLE WHO ARE HURT. I CAN'T TELL YOU HOW HAPPY WE ARE THAT YOU SHOWED UP.>
<WHERE ARE YOU GOING?>
<MY NAME IS JUSTINE...>
<YOU DON'T SAY MUCH, DO YOU?>

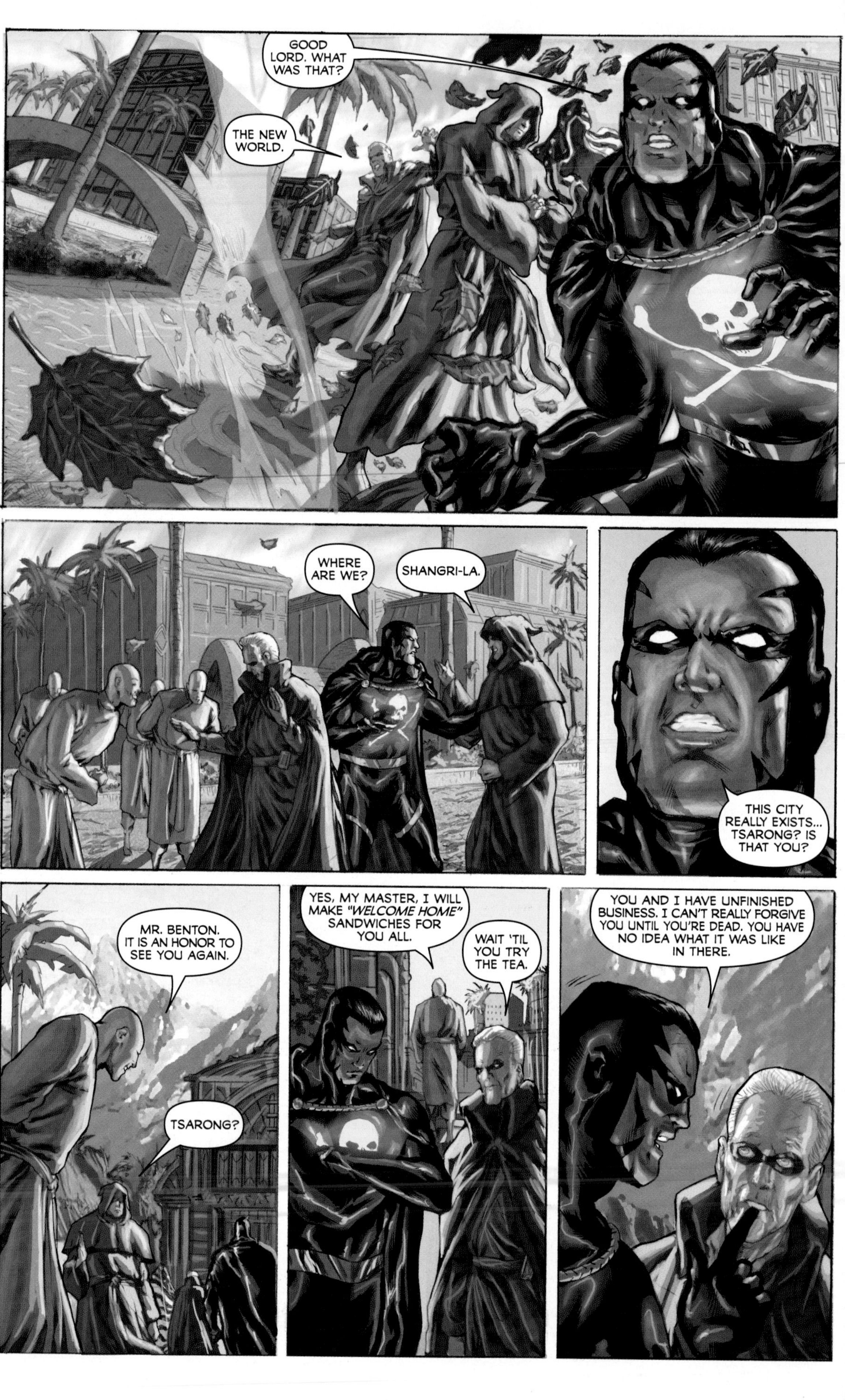

GOOD LORD. WHAT WAS THAT?
THE NEW WORLD.
WHERE ARE WE?
SHANGRI-LA.
THIS CITY REALLY EXISTS... TSARONG? IS THAT YOU?
MR. BENTON. IT IS AN HONOR TO SEE YOU AGAIN.
TSARONG?
YES, MY MASTER, I WILL MAKE "WELCOME HOME" SANDWICHES FOR YOU ALL.
WAIT 'TIL YOU TRY THE TEA.
YOU AND I HAVE UNFINISHED BUSINESS. I CAN'T REALLY FORGIVE YOU UNTIL YOU'RE DEAD. YOU HAVE NO IDEA WHAT IT WAS LIKE IN THERE.

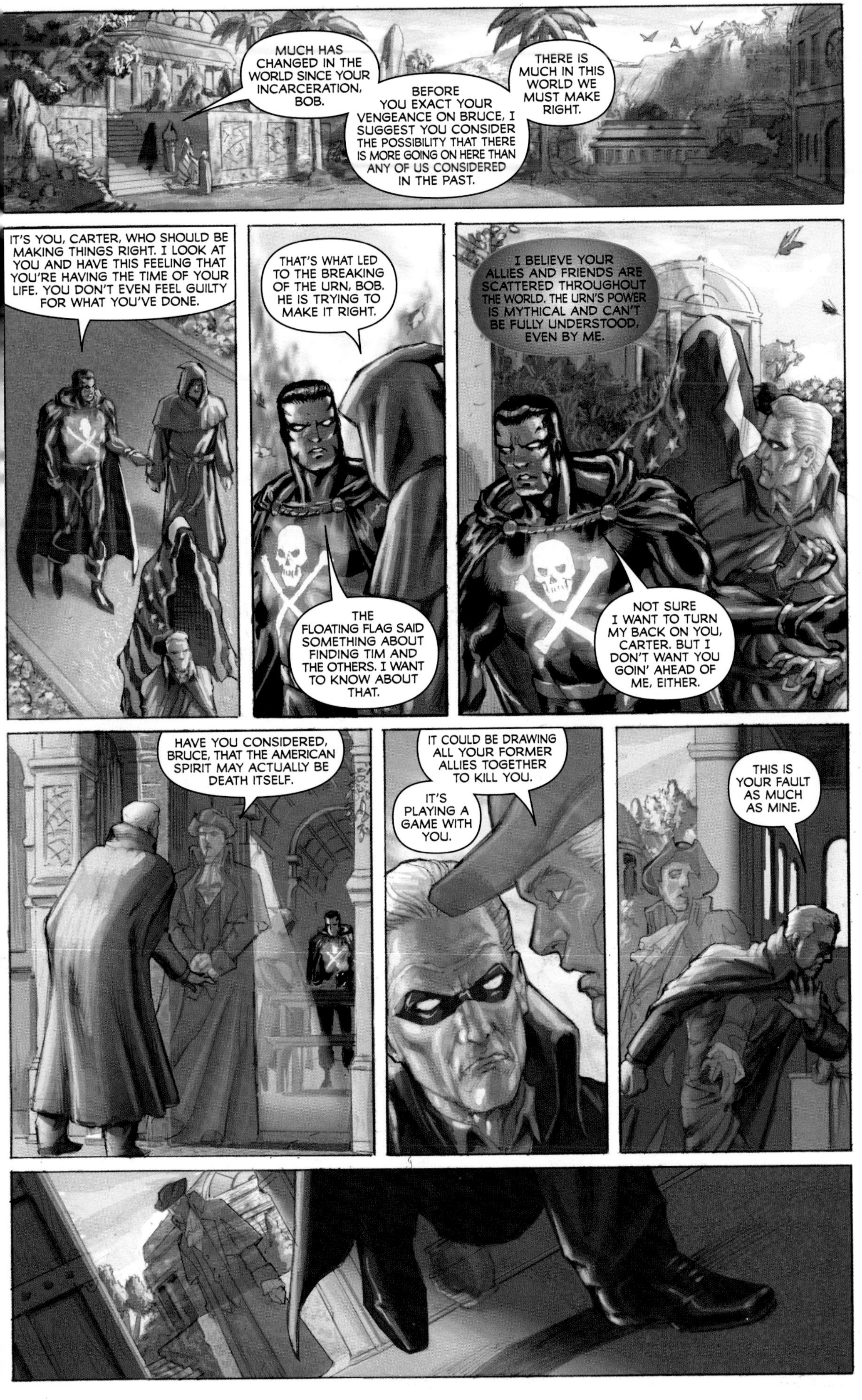
MUCH HAS CHANGED IN THE WORLD SINCE YOUR INCARCERATION, BOB.
BEFORE YOU EXACT YOUR VENGEANCE ON BRUCE, I SUGGEST YOU CONSIDER THE POSSIBILITY THAT THERE IS MORE GOING ON HERE THAN ANY OF US CONSIDERED IN THE PAST.
THERE IS MUCH IN THIS WORLD WE MUST MAKE RIGHT.
IT'S YOU, CARTER, WHO SHOULD BE MAKING THINGS RIGHT. I LOOK AT YOU AND HAVE THIS FEELING THAT YOU'RE HAVING THE TIME OF YOUR LIFE. YOU DON'T EVEN FEEL GUILTY FOR WHAT YOU'VE DONE.
THAT'S WHAT LED TO THE BREAKING OF THE URN, BOB. HE IS TRYING TO MAKE IT RIGHT.
THE FLOATING FLAG SAID SOMETHING ABOUT FINDING TIM AND THE OTHERS. I WANT TO KNOW ABOUT THAT.
I BELIEVE YOUR ALLIES AND FRIENDS ARE SCATTERED THROUGHOUT THE WORLD. THE URN'S POWER IS MYTHICAL AND CAN'T BE FULLY UNDERSTOOD, EVEN BY ME.
NOT SURE I WANT TO TURN MY BACK ON YOU, CARTER. BUT I DON'T WANT YOU GOIN' AHEAD OF ME, EITHER.
HAVE YOU CONSIDERED, BRUCE, THAT THE AMERICAN SPIRIT MAY ACTUALLY BE DEATH ITSELF.
IT COULD BE DRAWING ALL YOUR FORMER ALLIES TOGETHER TO KILL YOU.
IT'S PLAYING A GAME WITH YOU.
THIS IS YOUR FAULT AS MUCH AS MINE.

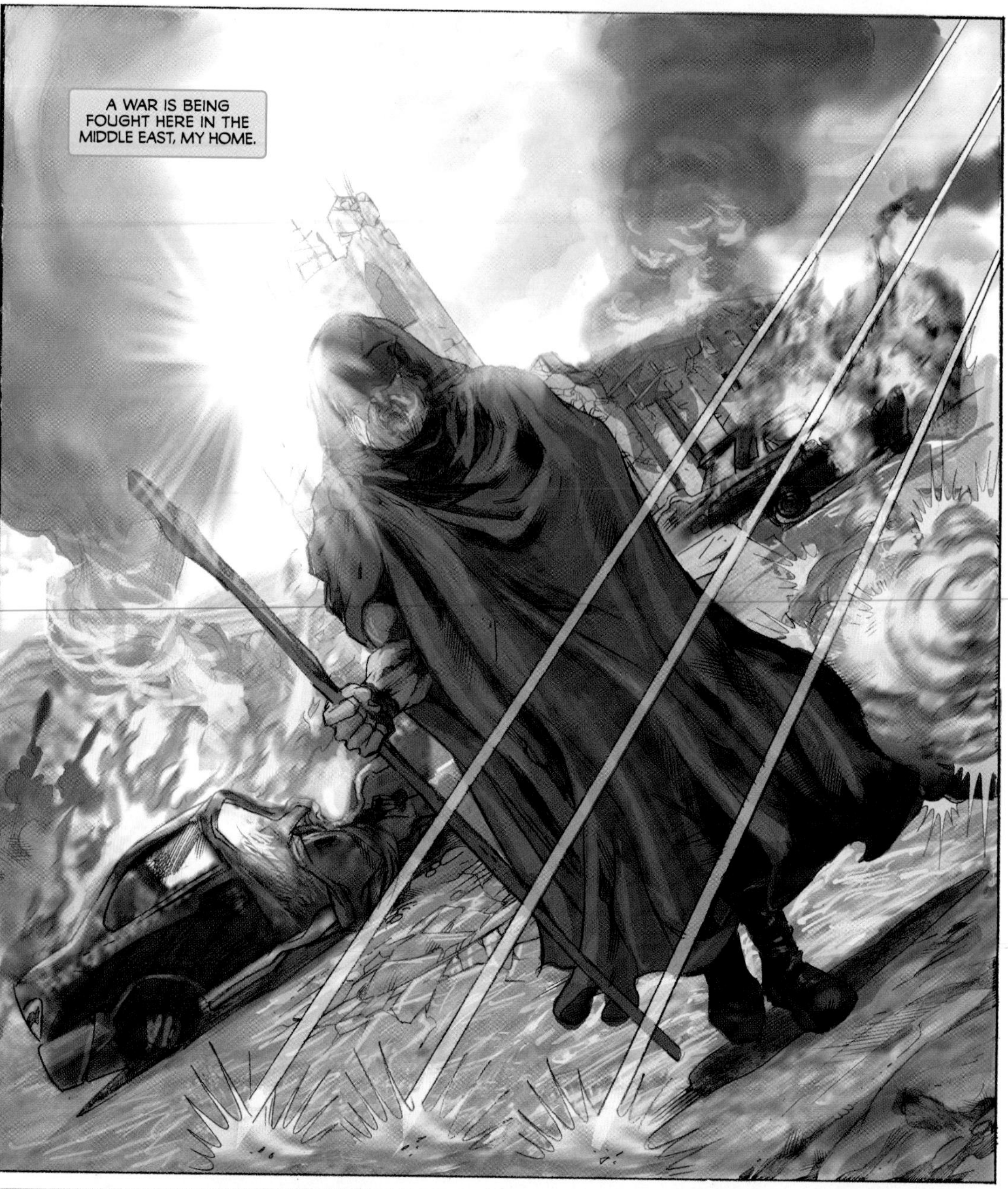
A WAR IS BEING FOUGHT HERE IN THE MIDDLE EAST, MY HOME.

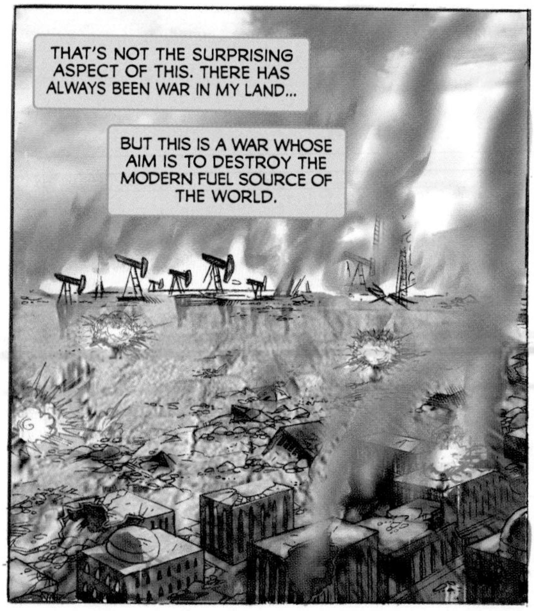
THAT'S NOT THE SURPRISING ASPECT OF THIS. THERE HAS ALWAYS BEEN WAR IN MY LAND...
BUT THIS IS A WAR WHOSE AIM IS TO DESTROY THE MODERN FUEL SOURCE OF THE WORLD.

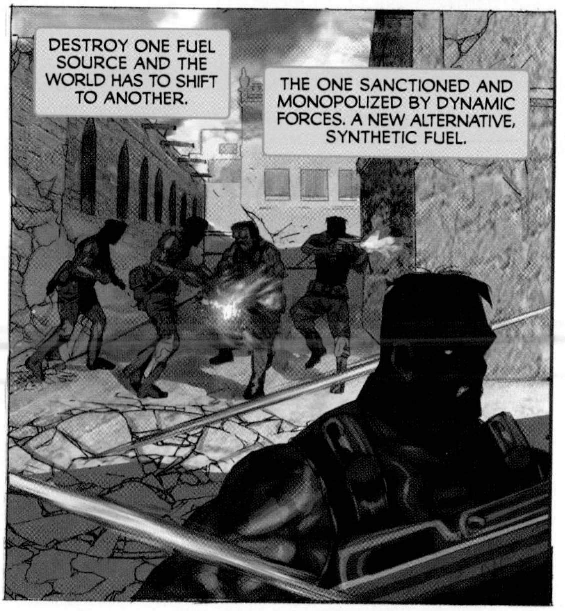
DESTROY ONE FUEL SOURCE AND THE WORLD HAS TO SHIFT TO ANOTHER.
THE ONE SANCTIONED AND MONOPOLIZED BY DYNAMIC FORCES. A NEW ALTERNATIVE, SYNTHETIC FUEL.

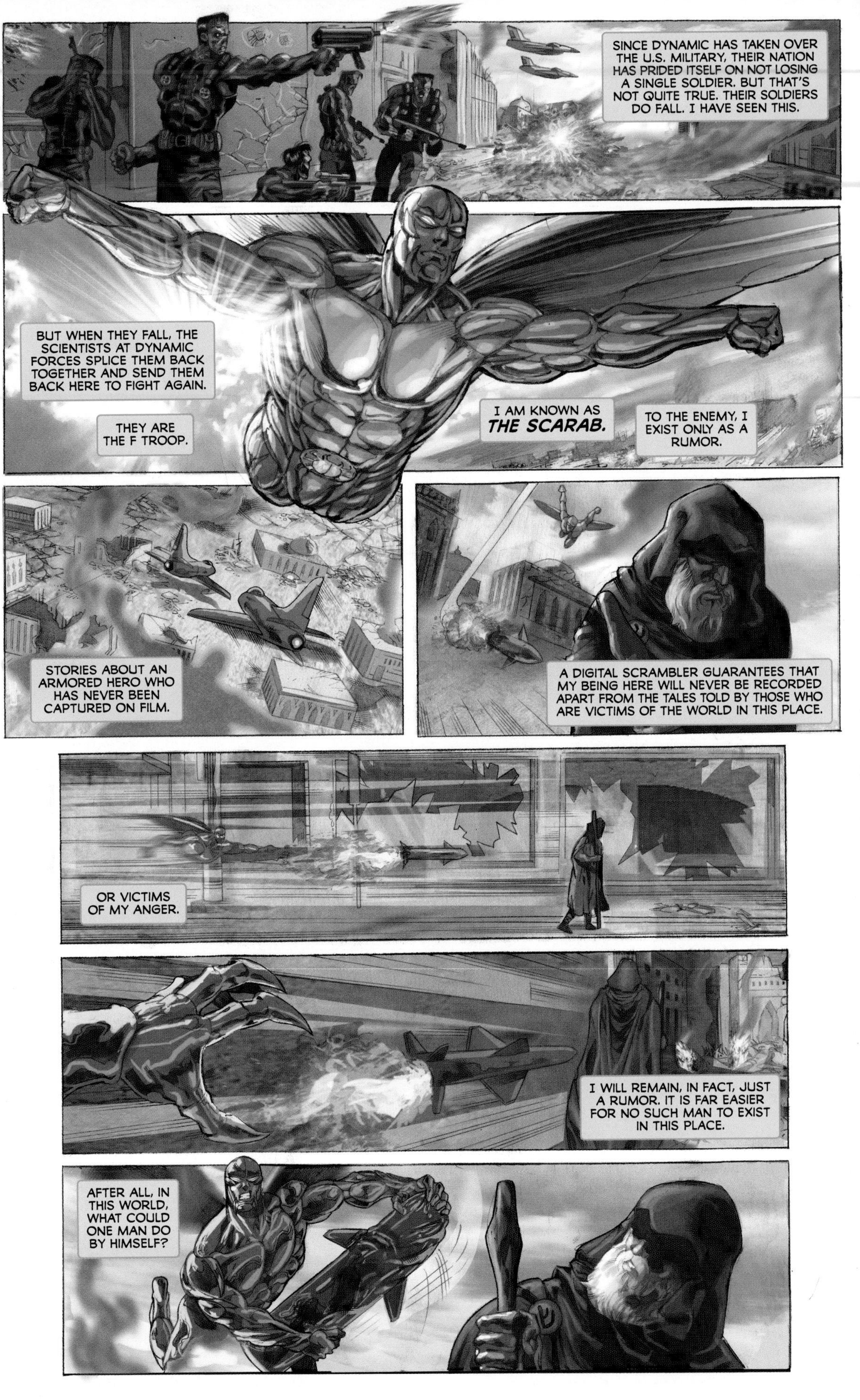
SINCE DYNAMIC HAS TAKEN OVER THE U.S. MILITARY, THEIR NATION HAS PRIDED ITSELF ON NOT LOSING A SINGLE SOLDIER. BUT THAT'S NOT QUITE TRUE. THEIR SOLDIERS DO FALL. I HAVE SEEN THIS.
BUT WHEN THEY FALL, THE SCIENTISTS AT DYNAMIC FORCES SPLICE THEM BACK TOGETHER AND SEND THEM BACK HERE TO FIGHT AGAIN.
THEY ARE THE F TROOP.
I AM KNOWN AS *THE SCARAB.*
TO THE ENEMY, I EXIST ONLY AS A RUMOR.
STORIES ABOUT AN ARMORED HERO WHO HAS NEVER BEEN CAPTURED ON FILM.
A DIGITAL SCRAMBLER GUARANTEES THAT MY BEING HERE WILL NEVER BE RECORDED APART FROM THE TALES TOLD BY THOSE WHO ARE VICTIMS OF THE WORLD IN THIS PLACE.
OR VICTIMS OF MY ANGER.
I WILL REMAIN, IN FACT, JUST A RUMOR. IT IS FAR EASIER FOR NO SUCH MAN TO EXIST IN THIS PLACE.
AFTER ALL, IN THIS WORLD, WHAT COULD ONE MAN DO BY HIMSELF?

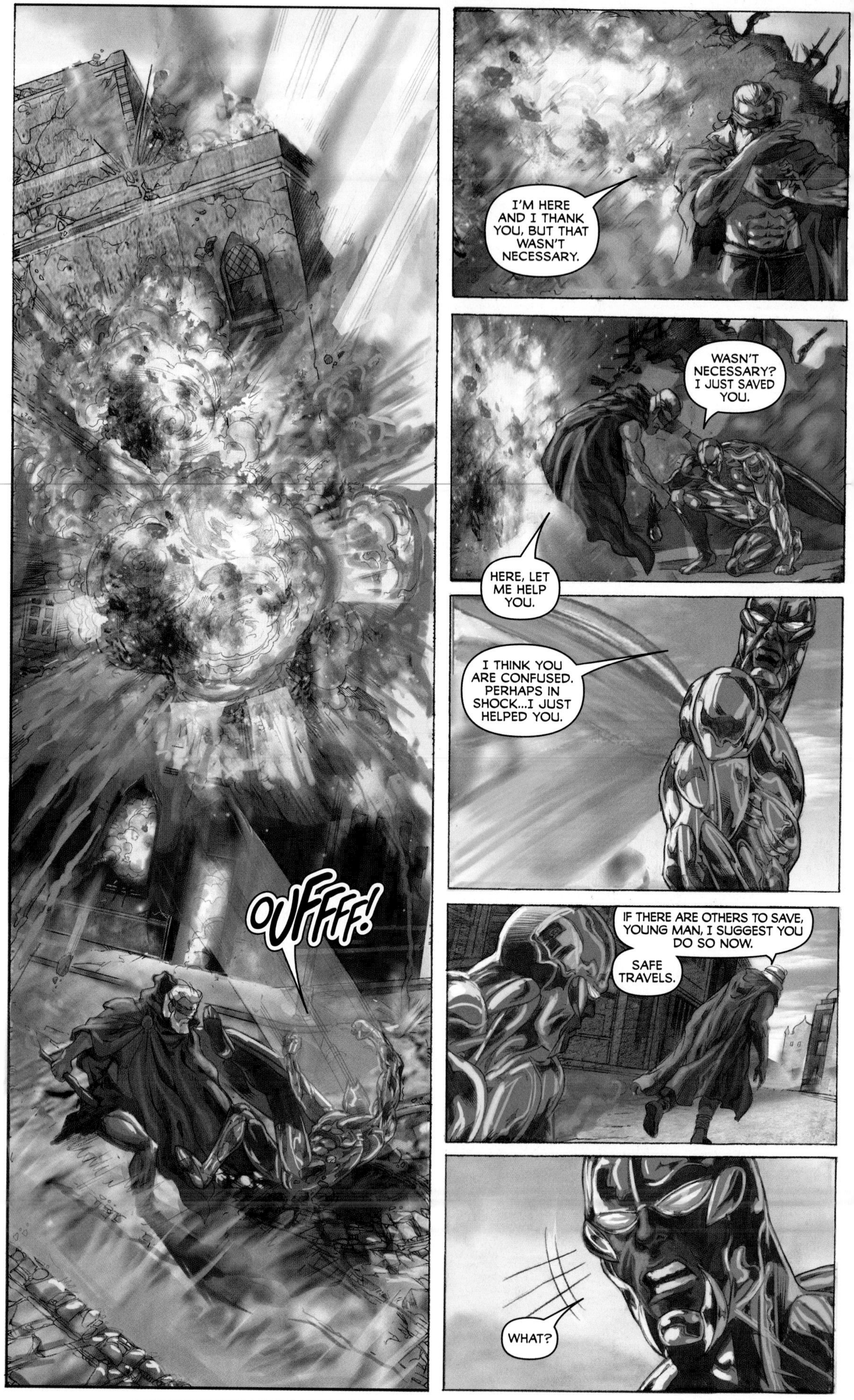
OUFFFF!
I'M HERE AND I THANK YOU, BUT THAT WASN'T NECESSARY.
WASN'T NECESSARY? I JUST SAVED YOU.
HERE, LET ME HELP YOU.
I THINK YOU ARE CONFUSED. PERHAPS IN SHOCK...I JUST HELPED YOU.
IF THERE ARE OTHERS TO SAVE, YOUNG MAN, I SUGGEST YOU DO SO NOW.
SAFE TRAVELS.
WHAT?

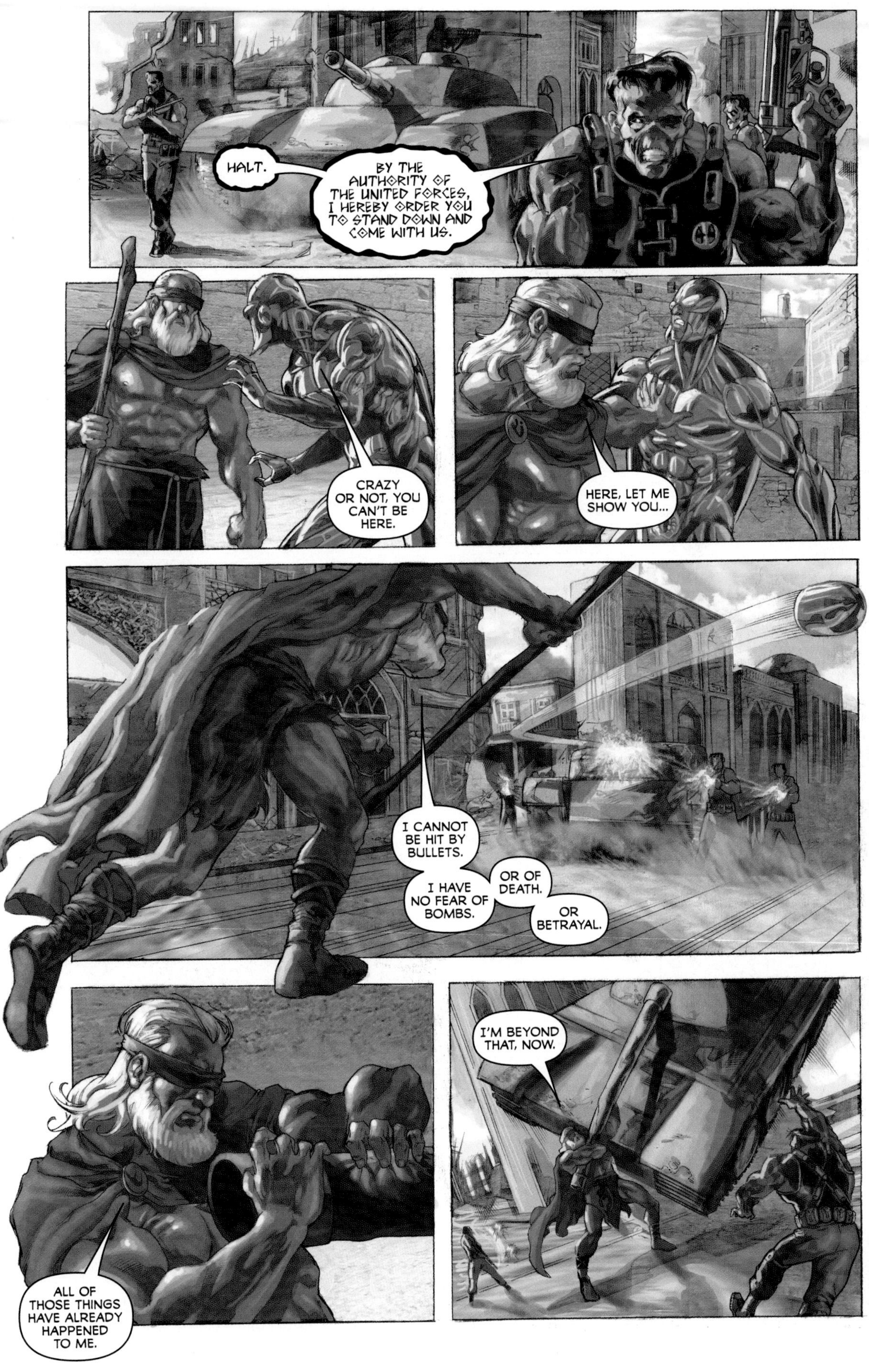
HALT.
BY THE AUTHORITY OF THE UNITED FORCES, I HEREBY ORDER YOU TO STAND DOWN AND COME WITH US.
CRAZY OR NOT, YOU CAN'T BE HERE.
HERE, LET ME SHOW YOU...
I CANNOT BE HIT BY BULLETS.
I HAVE NO FEAR OF BOMBS.
OR OF DEATH.
OR BETRAYAL.
ALL OF THOSE THINGS HAVE ALREADY HAPPENED TO ME.
I'M BEYOND THAT, NOW.

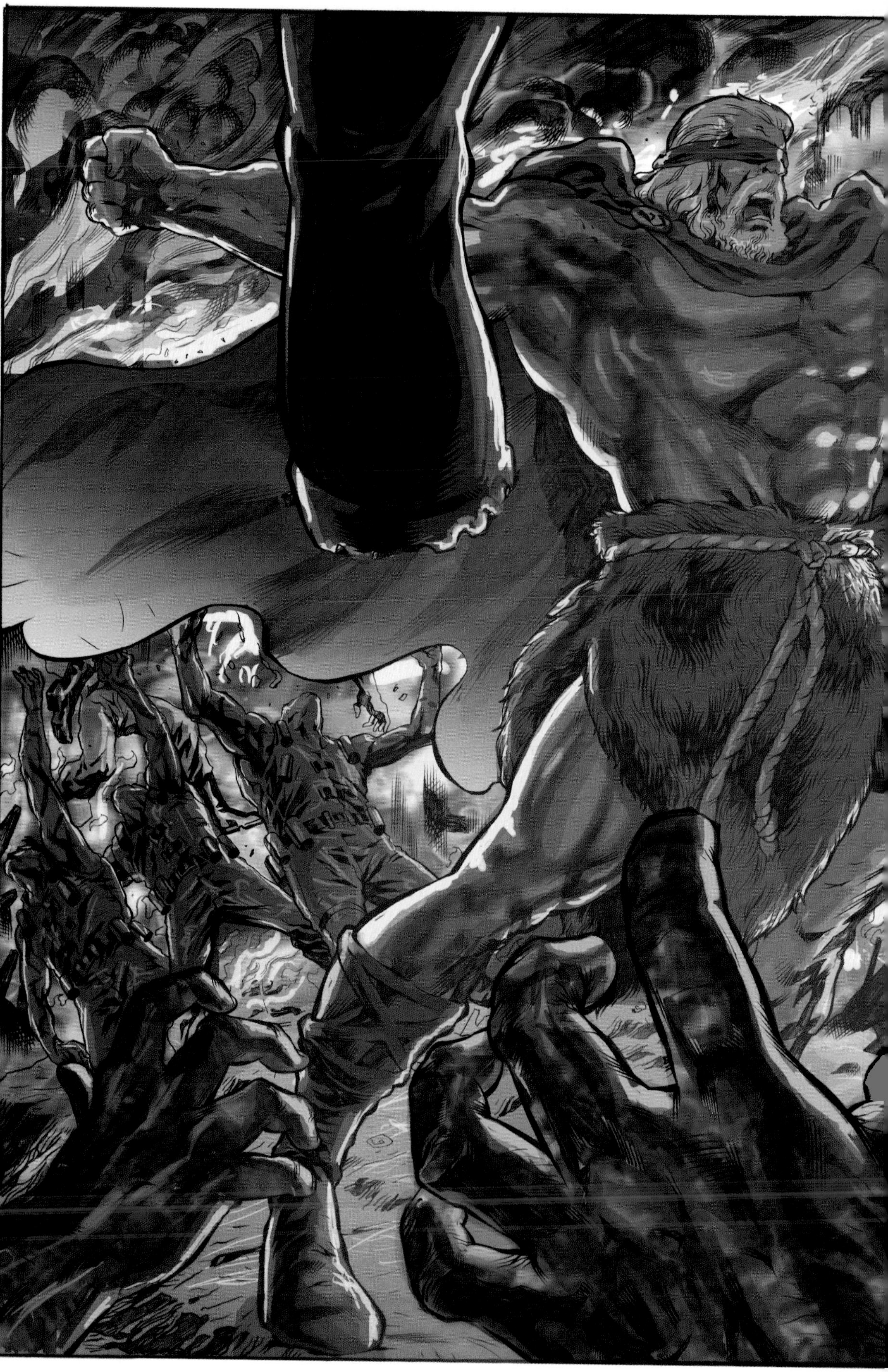

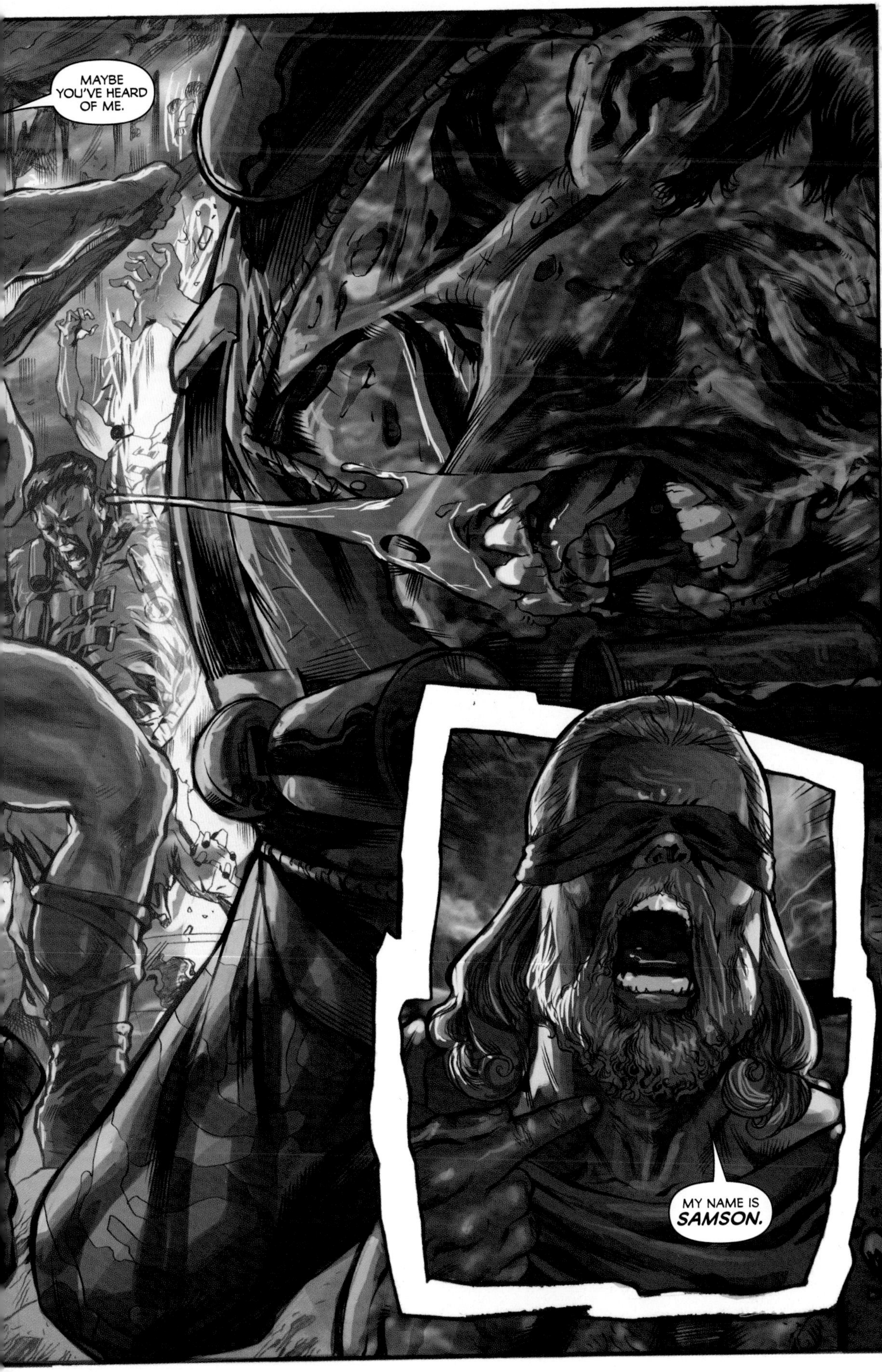
MAYBE YOU'VE HEARD OF ME.
MY NAME IS *SAMSON.*

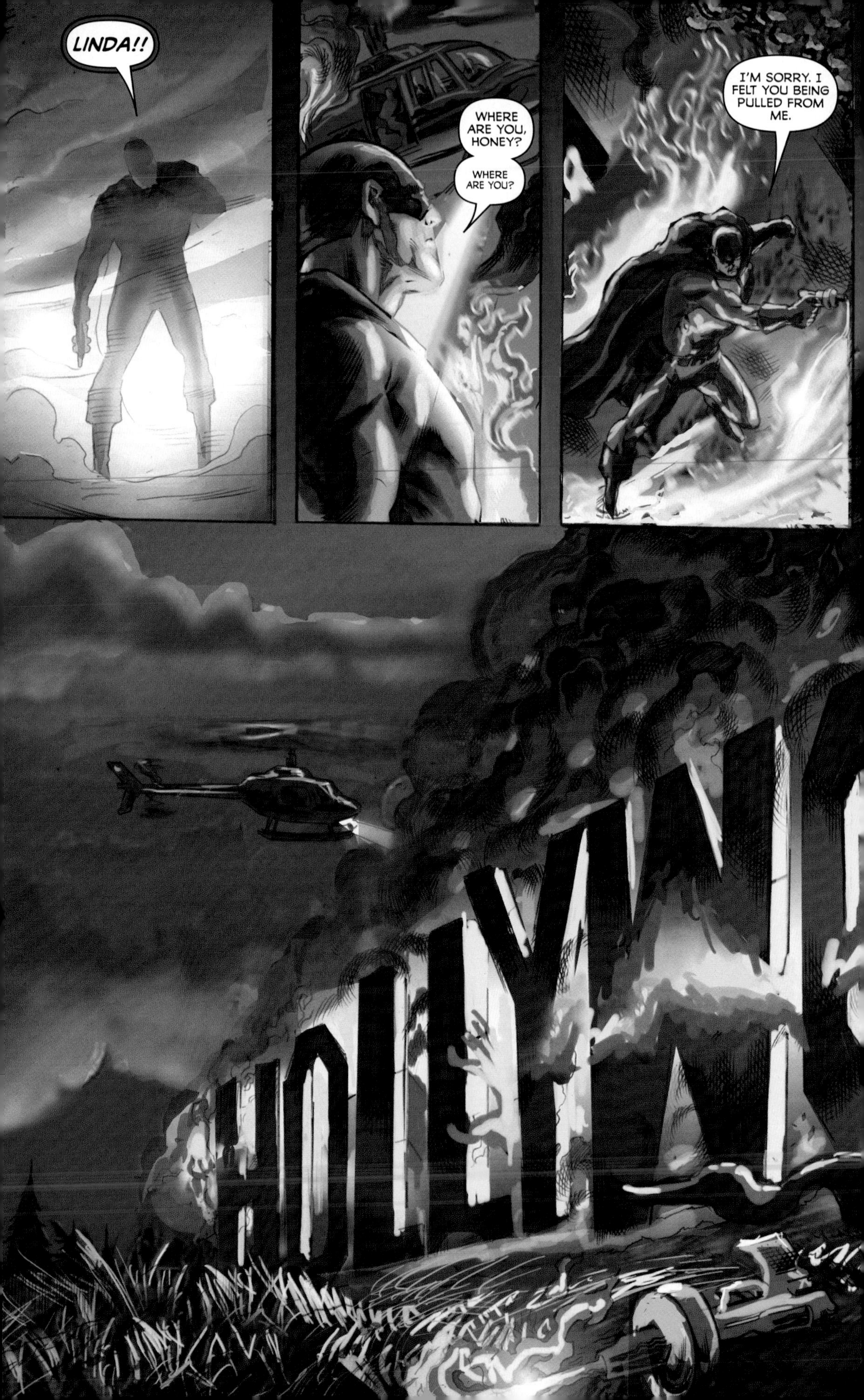
LINDA!!
WHERE ARE YOU, HONEY?
WHERE ARE YOU?
I'M SORRY. I FELT YOU BEING PULLED FROM ME.

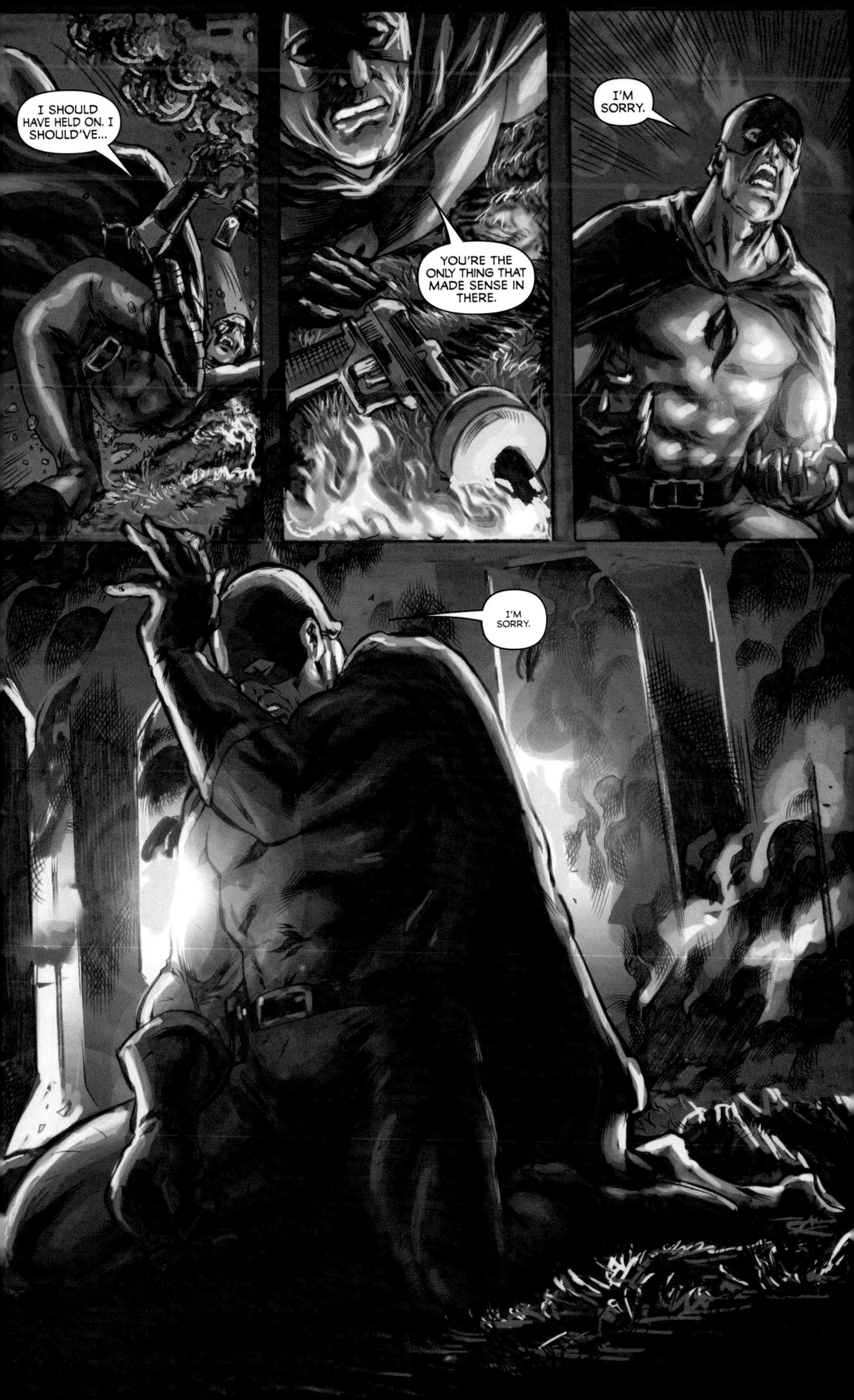
I SHOULD HAVE HELD ON. I SHOULD'VE...
YOU'RE THE ONLY THING THAT MADE SENSE IN THERE.
I'M SORRY.
I'M SORRY.

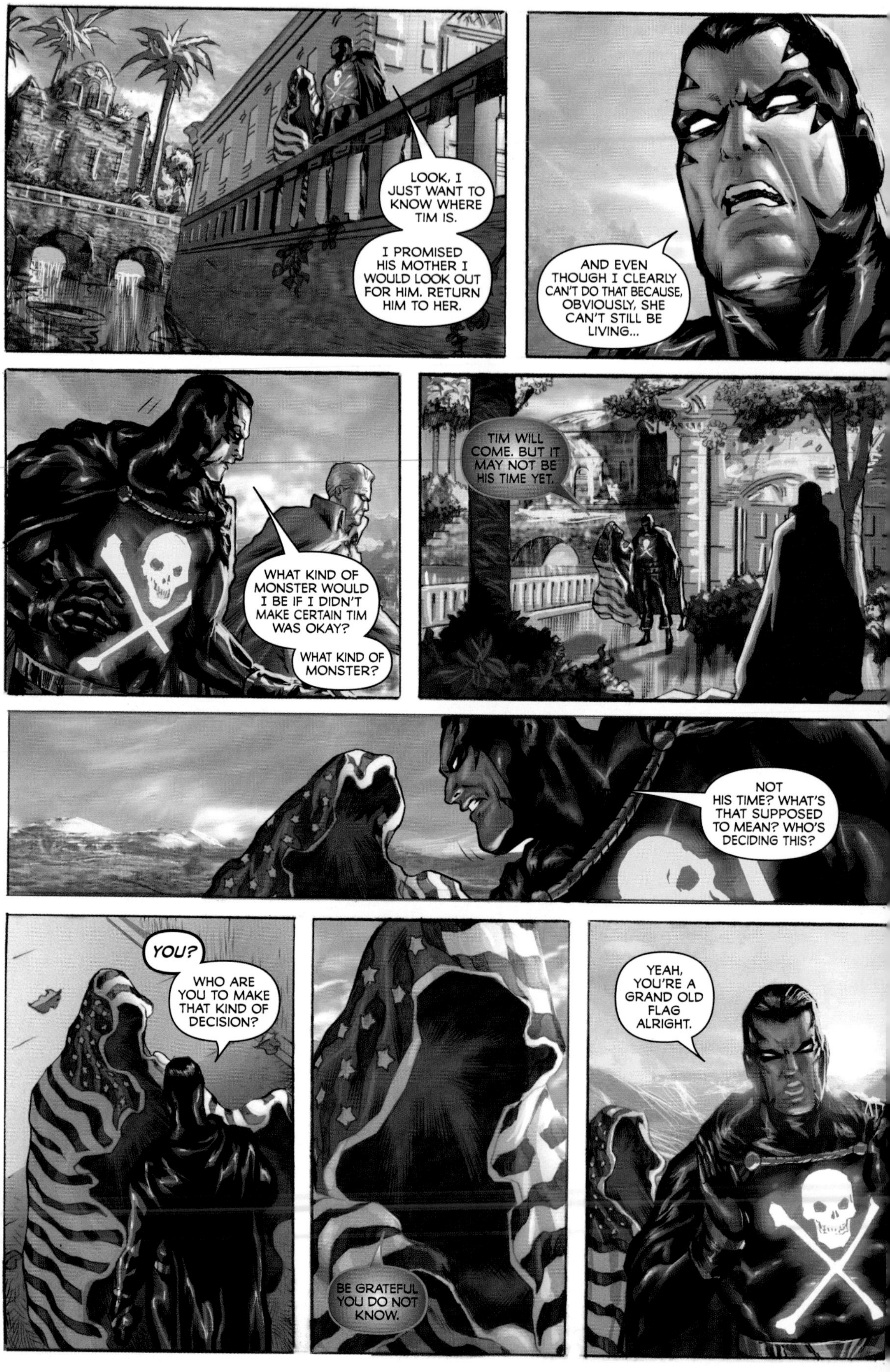
LOOK, I JUST WANT TO KNOW WHERE TIM IS.
I PROMISED HIS MOTHER I WOULD LOOK OUT FOR HIM. RETURN HIM TO HER.
AND EVEN THOUGH I CLEARLY CAN'T DO THAT BECAUSE, OBVIOUSLY, SHE CAN'T STILL BE LIVING...
WHAT KIND OF MONSTER WOULD I BE IF I DIDN'T MAKE CERTAIN TIM WAS OKAY?
WHAT KIND OF MONSTER?
TIM WILL COME. BUT IT MAY NOT BE HIS TIME YET.
NOT HIS TIME? WHAT'S THAT SUPPOSED TO MEAN? WHO'S DECIDING THIS?
YOU?
WHO ARE YOU TO MAKE THAT KIND OF DECISION?
BE GRATEFUL YOU DO NOT KNOW.
YEAH, YOU'RE A GRAND OLD FLAG ALRIGHT.

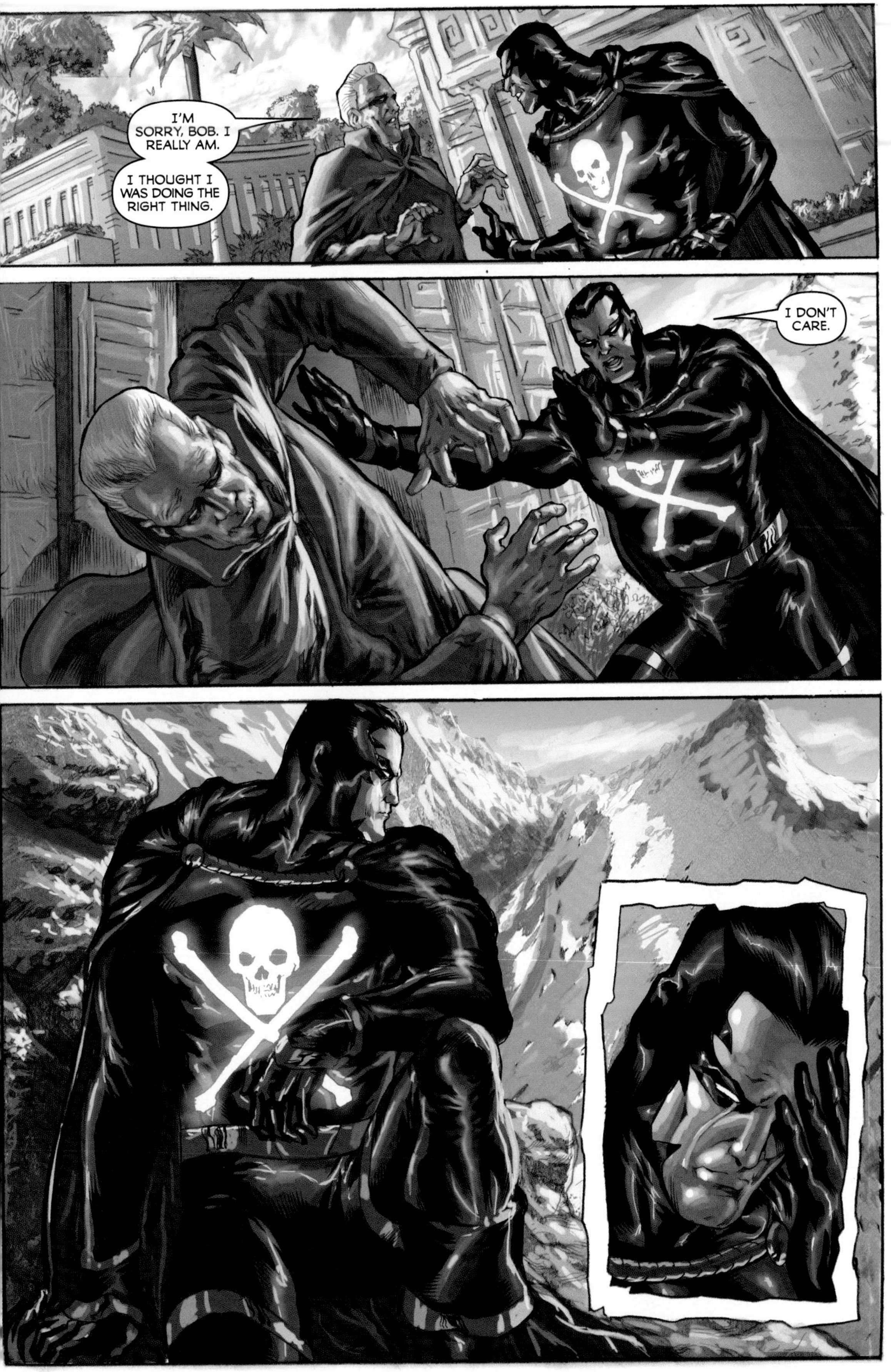
I'M SORRY, BOB. I REALLY AM.
I THOUGHT I WAS DOING THE RIGHT THING.
I DON'T CARE.

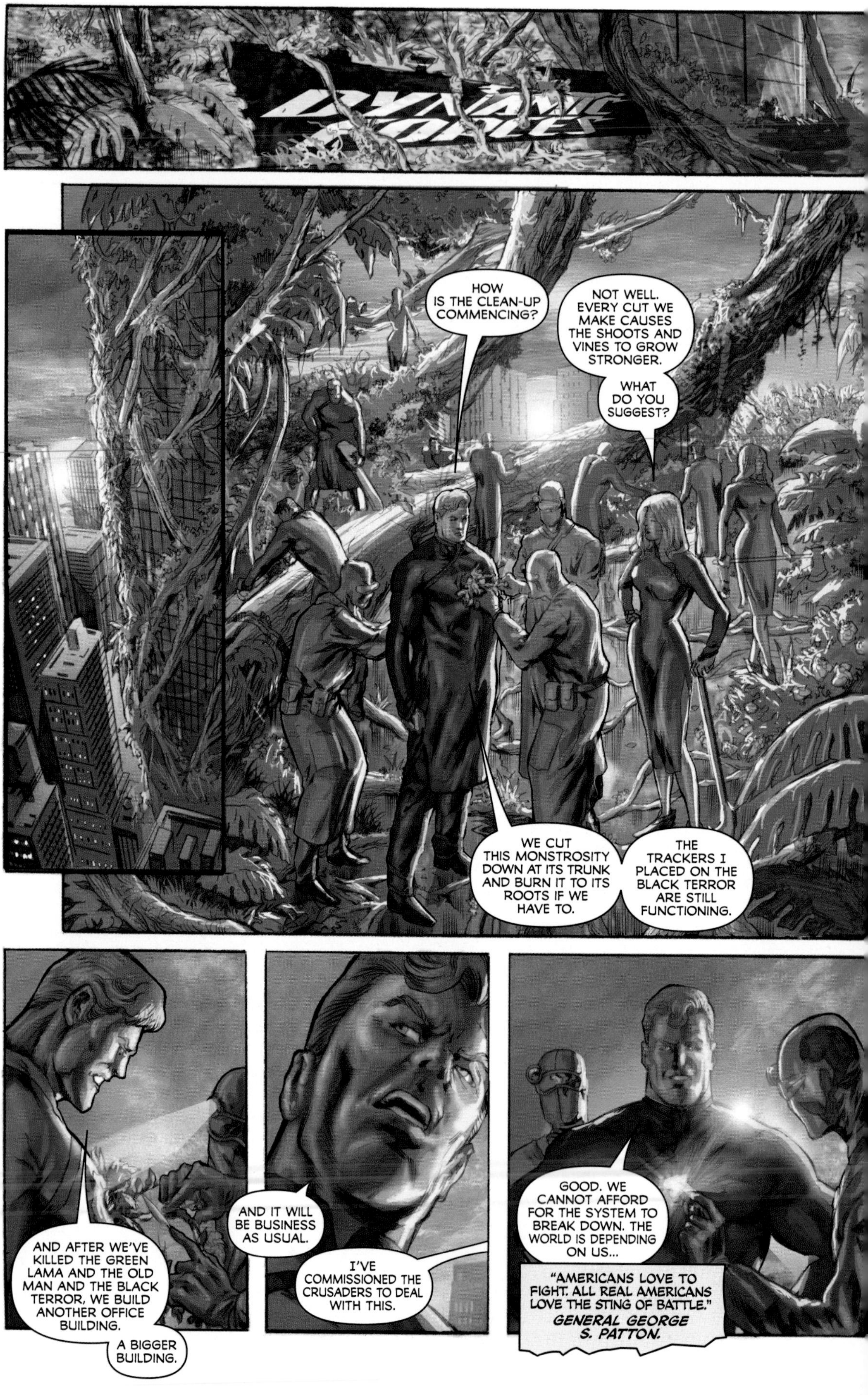
HOW IS THE CLEAN-UP COMMENCING?
NOT WELL. EVERY CUT WE MAKE CAUSES THE SHOOTS AND VINES TO GROW STRONGER.
WHAT DO YOU SUGGEST?
WE CUT THIS MONSTROSITY DOWN AT ITS TRUNK AND BURN IT TO ITS ROOTS IF WE HAVE TO.
THE TRACKERS I PLACED ON THE BLACK TERROR ARE STILL FUNCTIONING.
AND AFTER WE'VE KILLED THE GREEN LAMA AND THE OLD MAN AND THE BLACK TERROR, WE BUILD ANOTHER OFFICE BUILDING.
A BIGGER BUILDING.
AND IT WILL BE BUSINESS AS USUAL.
I'VE COMMISSIONED THE CRUSADERS TO DEAL WITH THIS.
GOOD. WE CANNOT AFFORD FOR THE SYSTEM TO BREAK DOWN. THE WORLD IS DEPENDING ON US...
"AMERICANS LOVE TO FIGHT. ALL REAL AMERICANS LOVE THE STING OF BATTLE."
GENERAL GEORGE S. PATTON.

ISSUE

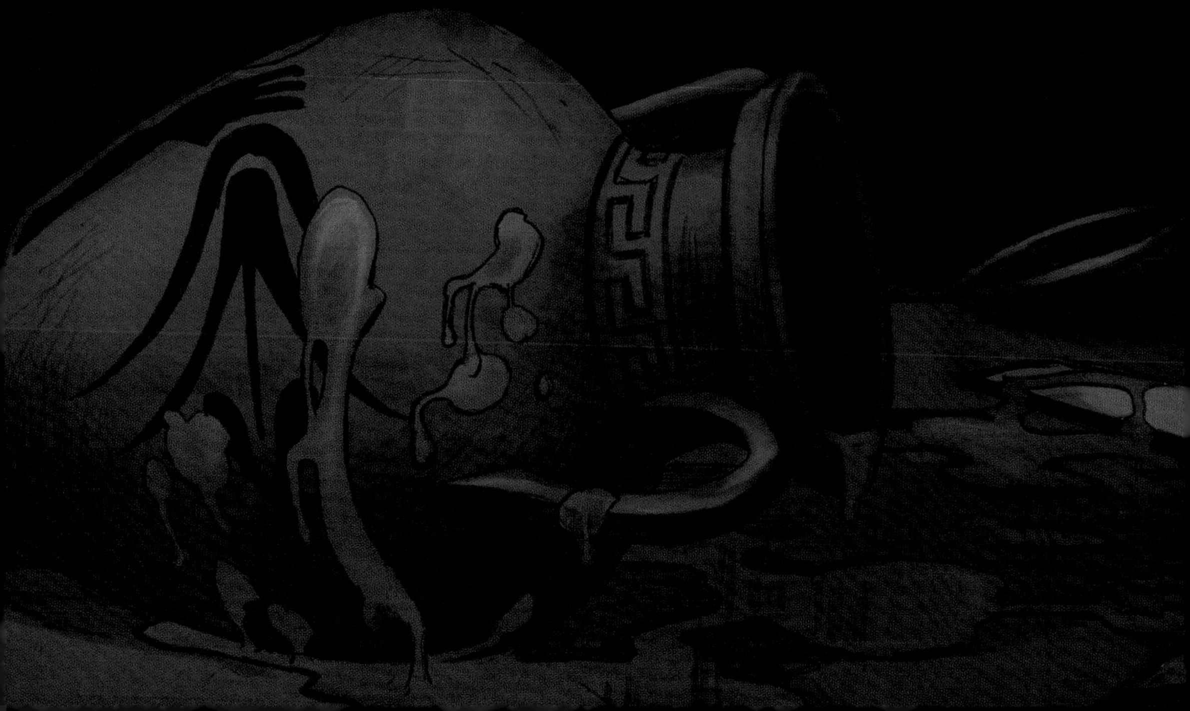

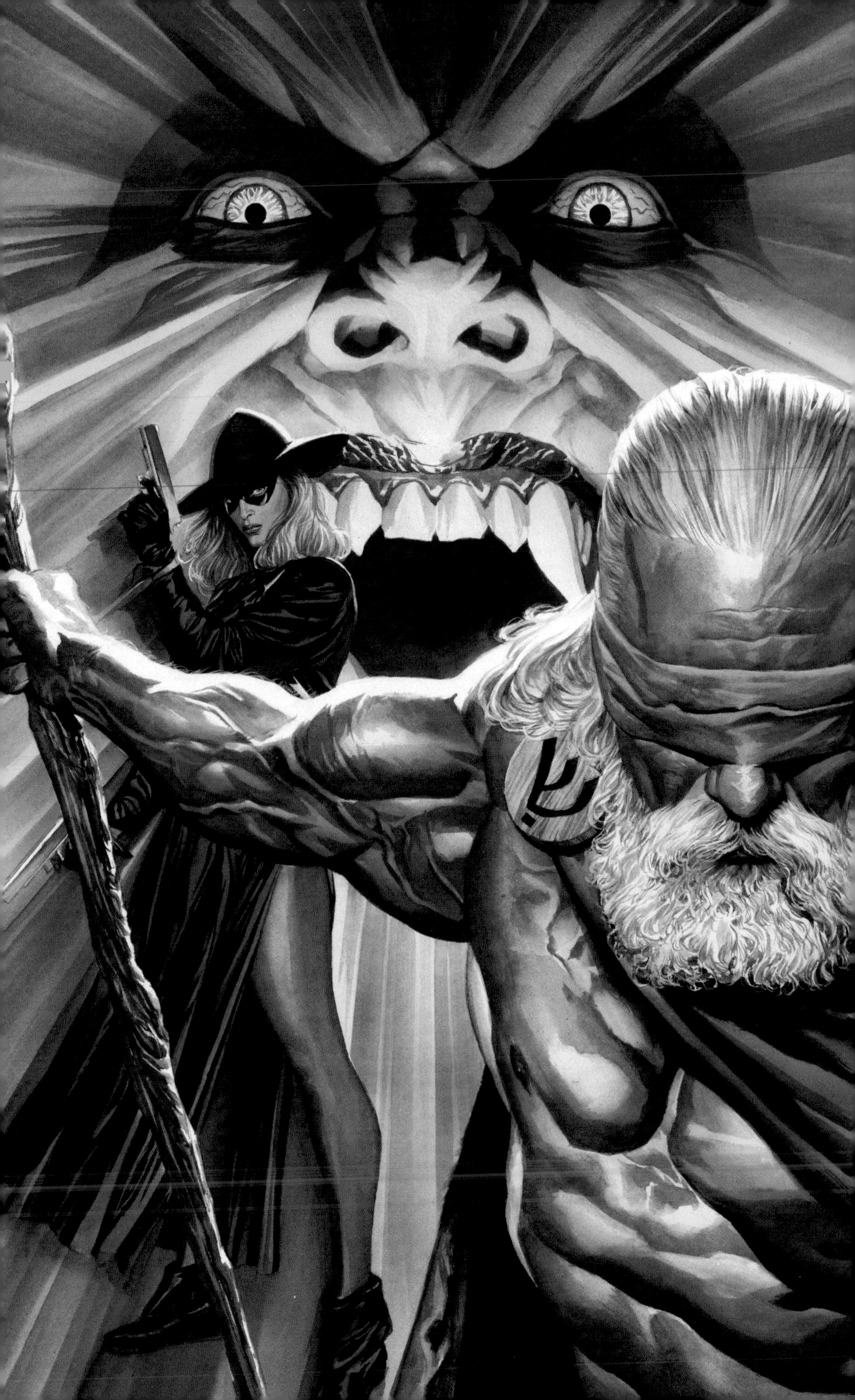

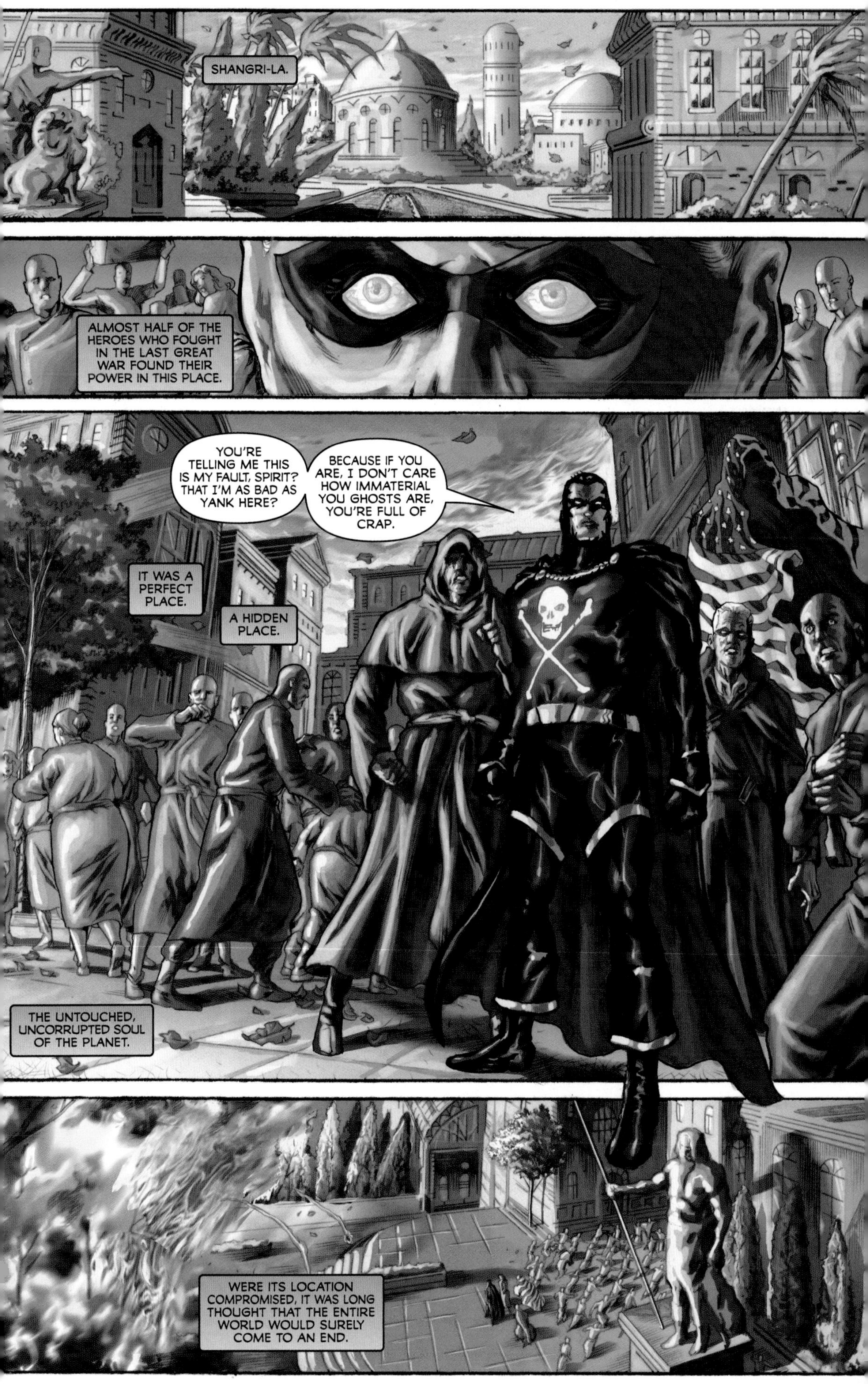
SHANGRI-LA.
ALMOST HALF OF THE HEROES WHO FOUGHT IN THE LAST GREAT WAR FOUND THEIR POWER IN THIS PLACE.
YOU'RE TELLING ME THIS IS MY FAULT, SPIRIT? THAT I'M AS BAD AS YANK HERE?
BECAUSE IF YOU ARE, I DON'T CARE HOW IMMATERIAL YOU GHOSTS ARE, YOU'RE FULL OF CRAP.
IT WAS A PERFECT PLACE.
A HIDDEN PLACE.
THE UNTOUCHED, UNCORRUPTED SOUL OF THE PLANET.
WERE ITS LOCATION COMPROMISED, IT WAS LONG THOUGHT THAT THE ENTIRE WORLD WOULD SURELY COME TO AN END.

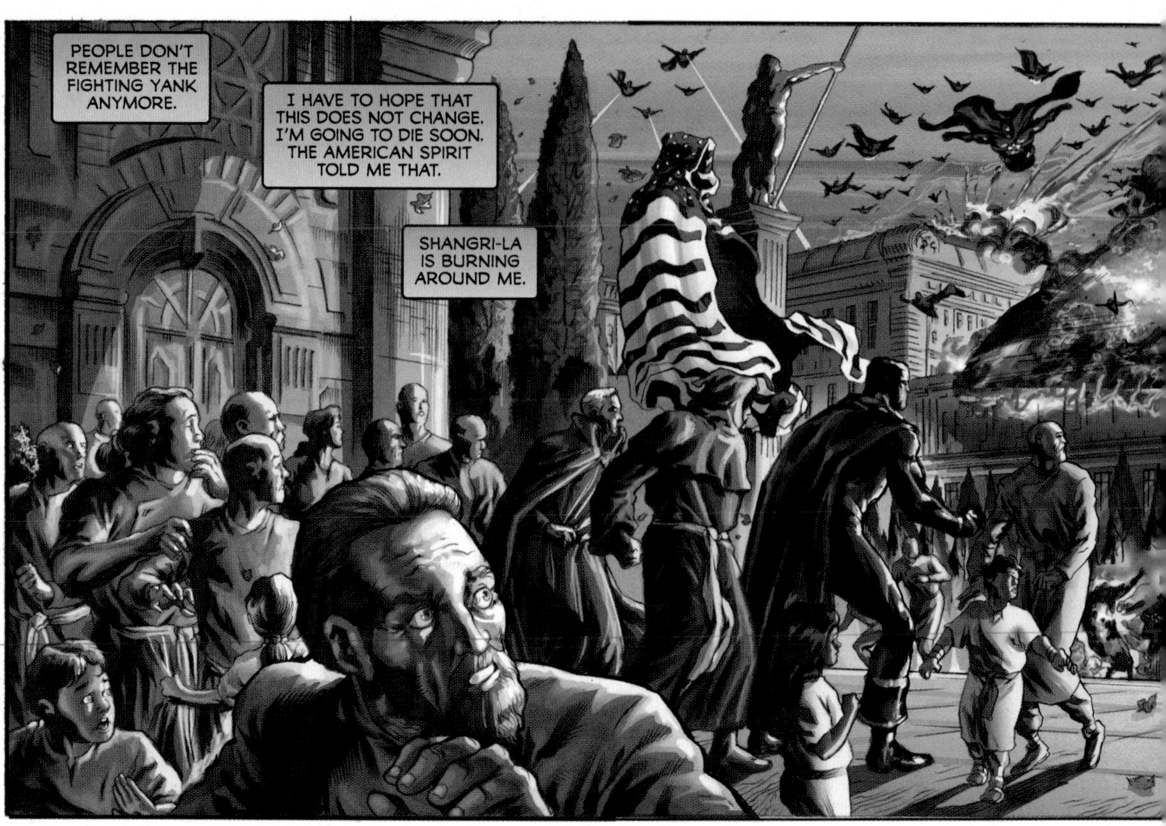
PEOPLE DON'T REMEMBER THE FIGHTING YANK ANYMORE.
I HAVE TO HOPE THAT THIS DOES NOT CHANGE. I'M GOING TO DIE SOON. THE AMERICAN SPIRIT TOLD ME THAT.
SHANGRI-LA IS BURNING AROUND ME.

PROOF THROUGH

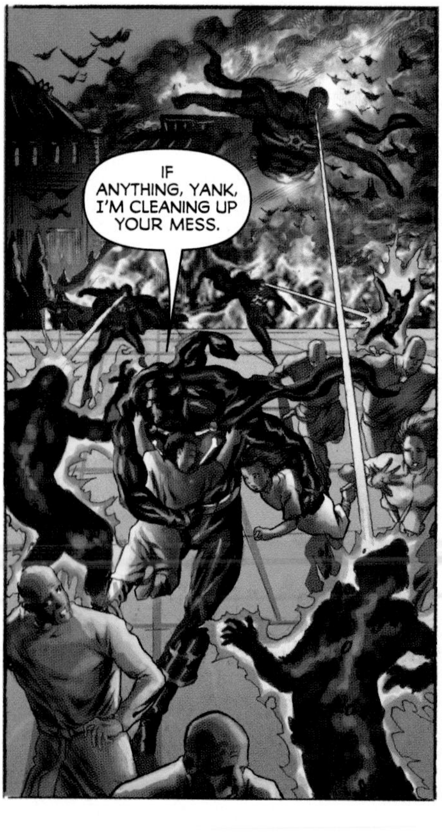
IF ANYTHING, YANK, I'M CLEANING UP YOUR MESS.

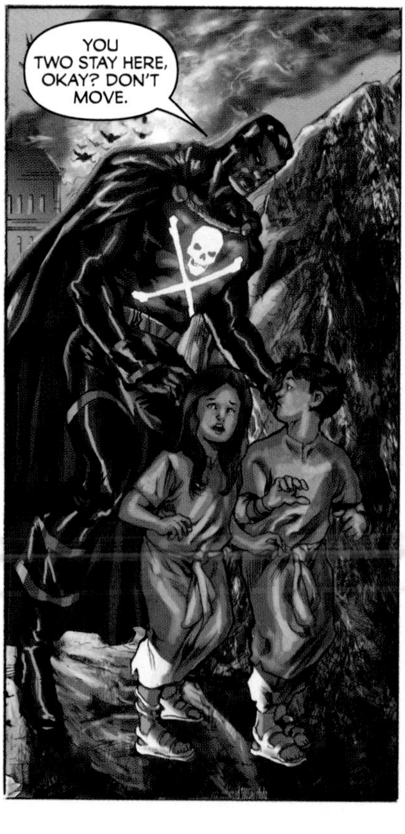
YOU TWO STAY HERE, OKAY? DON'T MOVE.

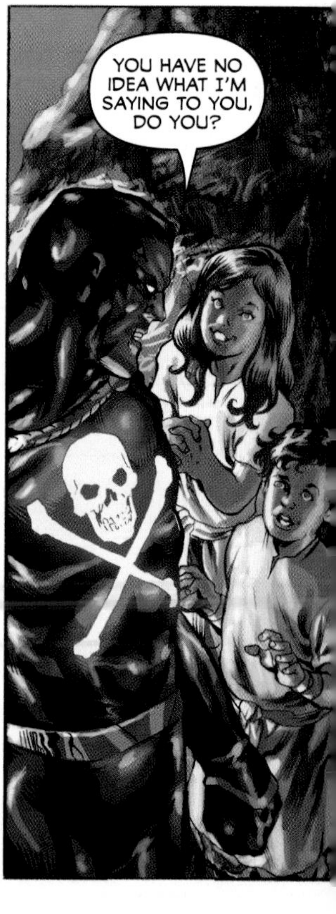
YOU HAVE NO IDEA WHAT I'M SAYING TO YOU, DO YOU?

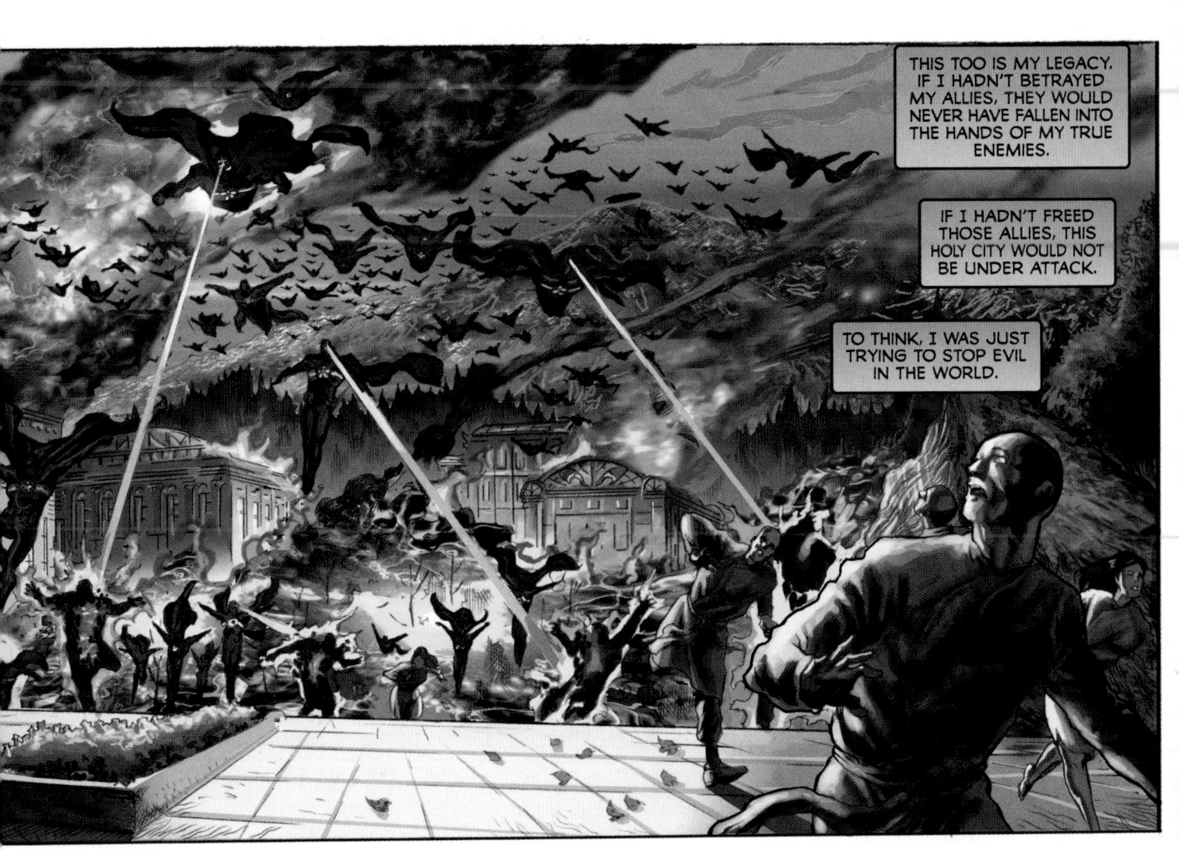
THIS TOO IS MY LEGACY. IF I HADN'T BETRAYED MY ALLIES, THEY WOULD NEVER HAVE FALLEN INTO THE HANDS OF MY TRUE ENEMIES.
IF I HADN'T FREED THOSE ALLIES, THIS HOLY CITY WOULD NOT BE UNDER ATTACK.
TO THINK, I WAS JUST TRYING TO STOP EVIL IN THE WORLD.

THE NIGHT

"IN ITALY, FOR THIRTY YEARS UNDER THE BORGIAS, THEY HAD WARFARE, TERROR, MURDER AND BLOODSHED--THEY PRODUCED MICHELANGELO, LEONARDO DA VINCI AND THE RENAISSANCE. IN SWITZERLAND, THEY HAD BROTHERLY LOVE AND FIVE HUNDRED YEARS OF DEMOCRACY AND PEACE, AND WHAT DID THAT PRODUCE? THE CUCKOO CLOCK!"
HARRY LIME (ORSON WELLES), THE THIRD MAN.

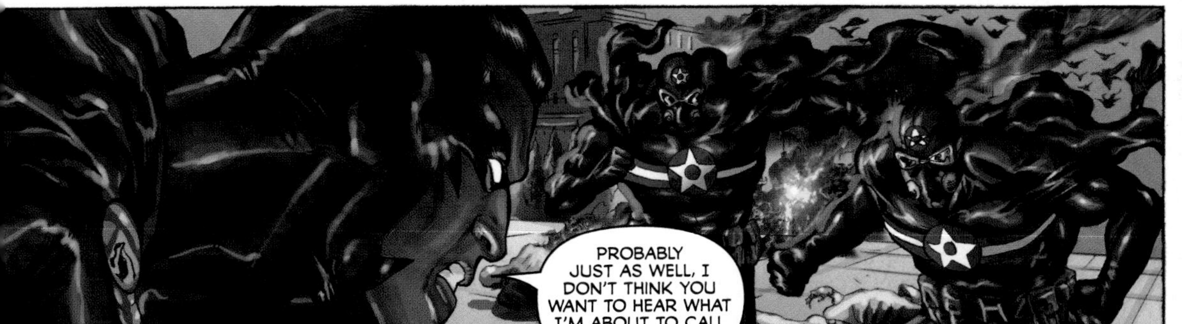
PROBABLY JUST AS WELL, I DON'T THINK YOU WANT TO HEAR WHAT I'M ABOUT TO CALL THESE KILLERS.

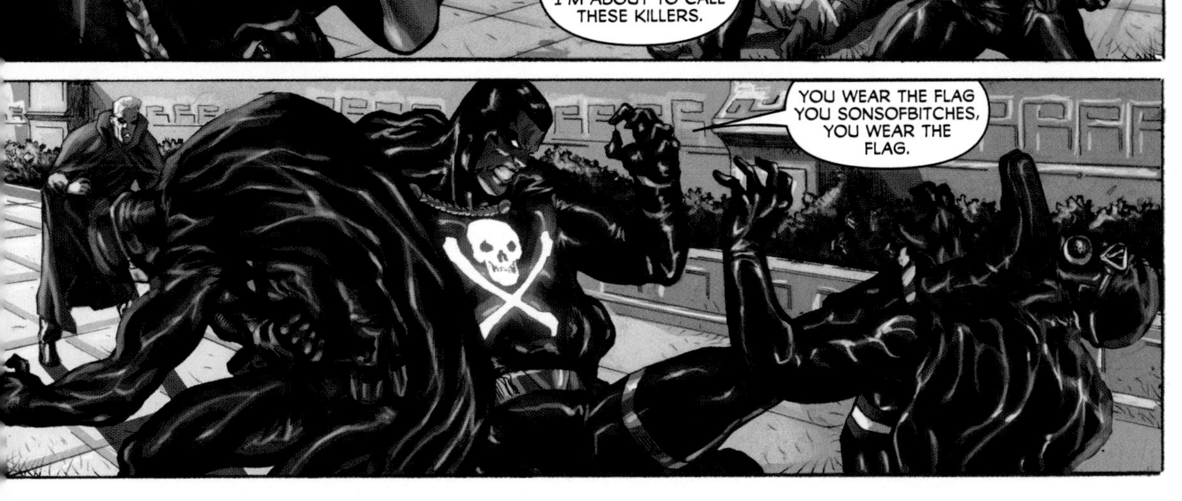
YOU WEAR THE FLAG YOU SONSOFBITCHES, YOU WEAR THE FLAG.

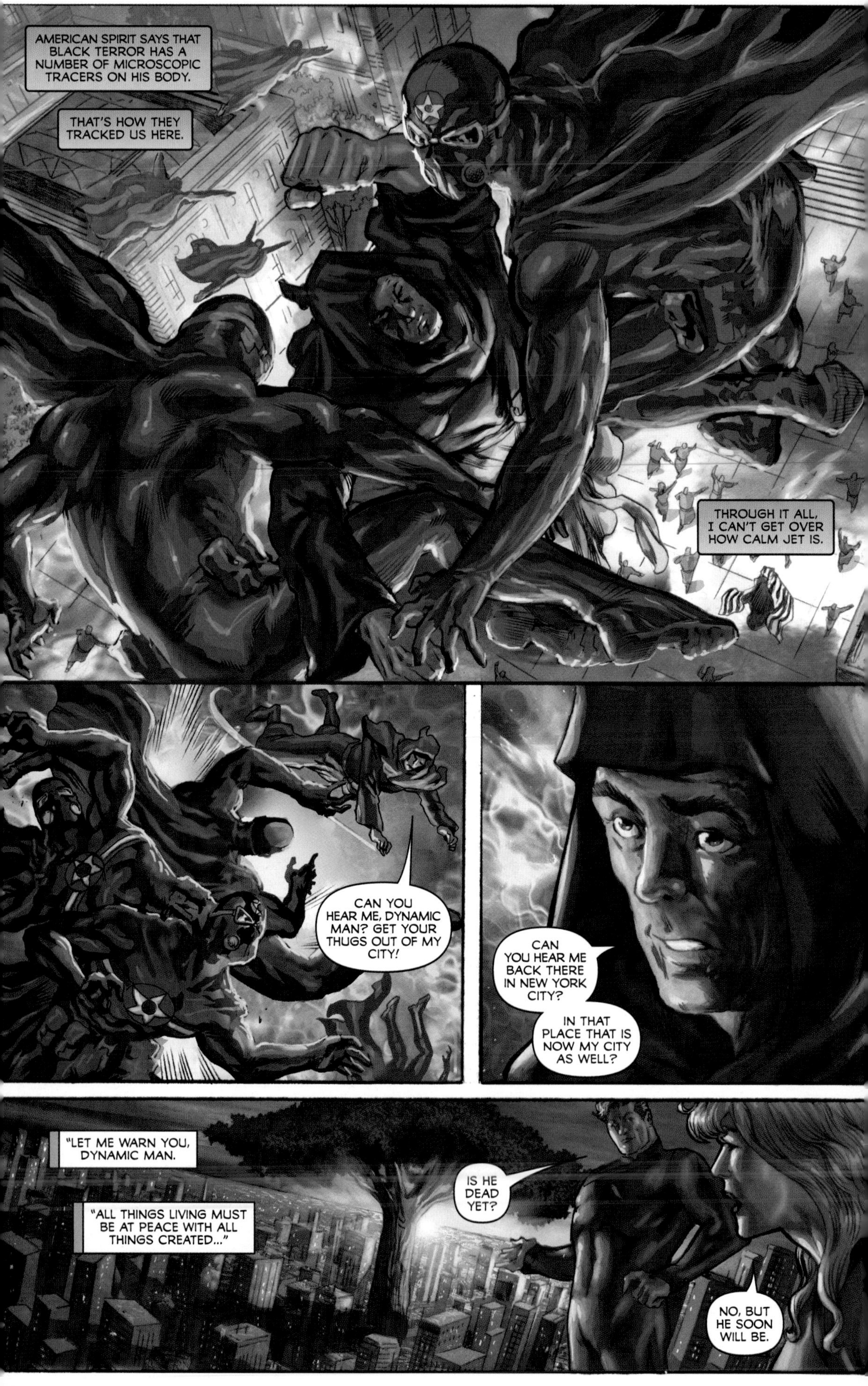
AMERICAN SPIRIT SAYS THAT BLACK TERROR HAS A NUMBER OF MICROSCOPIC TRACERS ON HIS BODY.
THAT'S HOW THEY TRACKED US HERE.
THROUGH IT ALL, I CAN'T GET OVER HOW CALM JET IS.
CAN YOU HEAR ME, DYNAMIC MAN? GET YOUR THUGS OUT OF MY CITY!
CAN YOU HEAR ME BACK THERE IN NEW YORK CITY?
IN THAT PLACE THAT IS NOW MY CITY AS WELL?
"LET ME WARN YOU, DYNAMIC MAN.
"ALL THINGS LIVING MUST BE AT PEACE WITH ALL THINGS CREATED..."
IS HE DEAD YET?
NO, BUT HE SOON WILL BE.

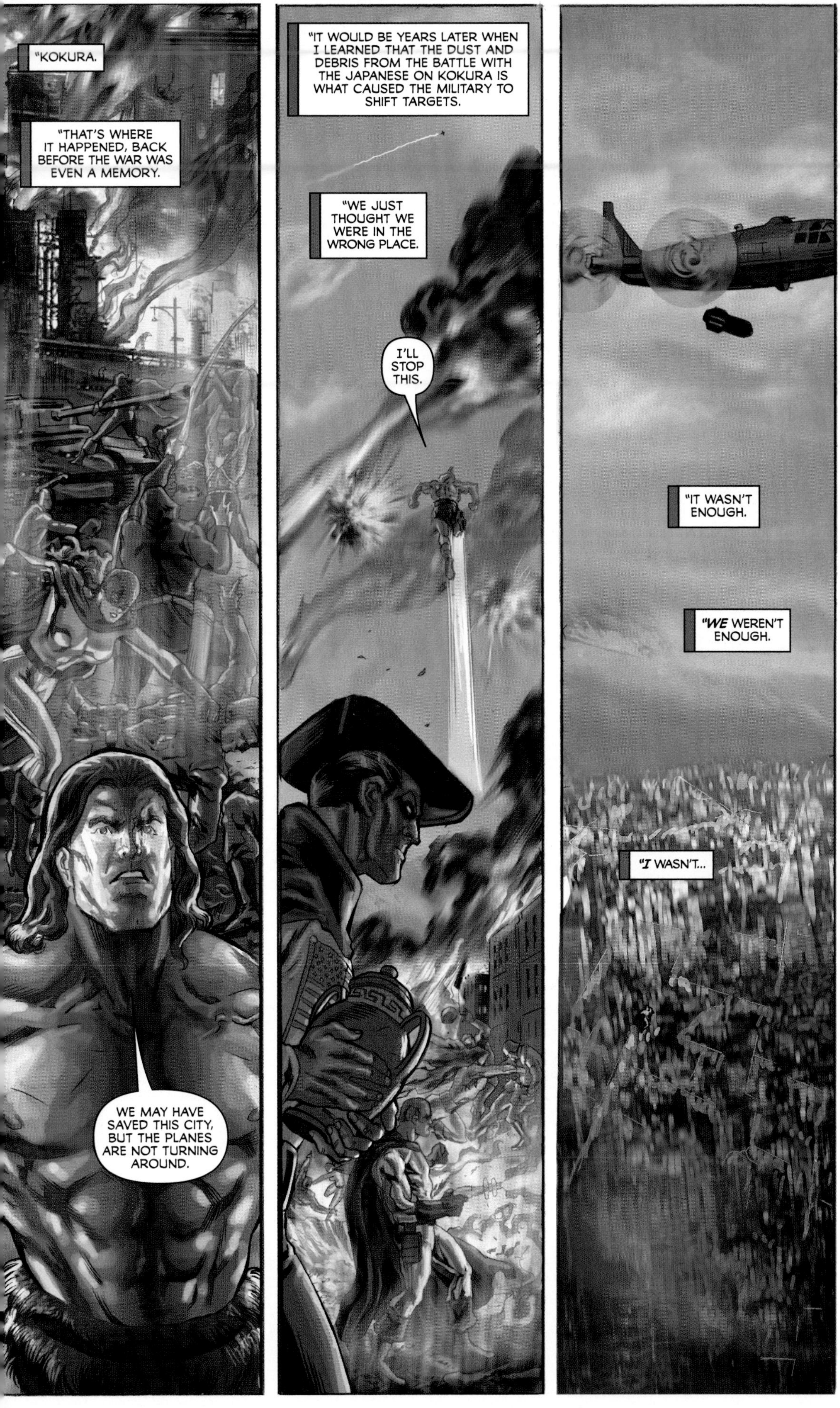
"KOKURA.
"THAT'S WHERE IT HAPPENED, BACK BEFORE THE WAR WAS EVEN A MEMORY.
WE MAY HAVE SAVED THIS CITY, BUT THE PLANES ARE NOT TURNING AROUND.
"IT WOULD BE YEARS LATER WHEN I LEARNED THAT THE DUST AND DEBRIS FROM THE BATTLE WITH THE JAPANESE ON KOKURA IS WHAT CAUSED THE MILITARY TO SHIFT TARGETS.
"WE JUST THOUGHT WE WERE IN THE WRONG PLACE.
I'LL STOP THIS.
"IT WASN'T ENOUGH.
"*WE* WEREN'T ENOUGH.
"*I* WASN'T...

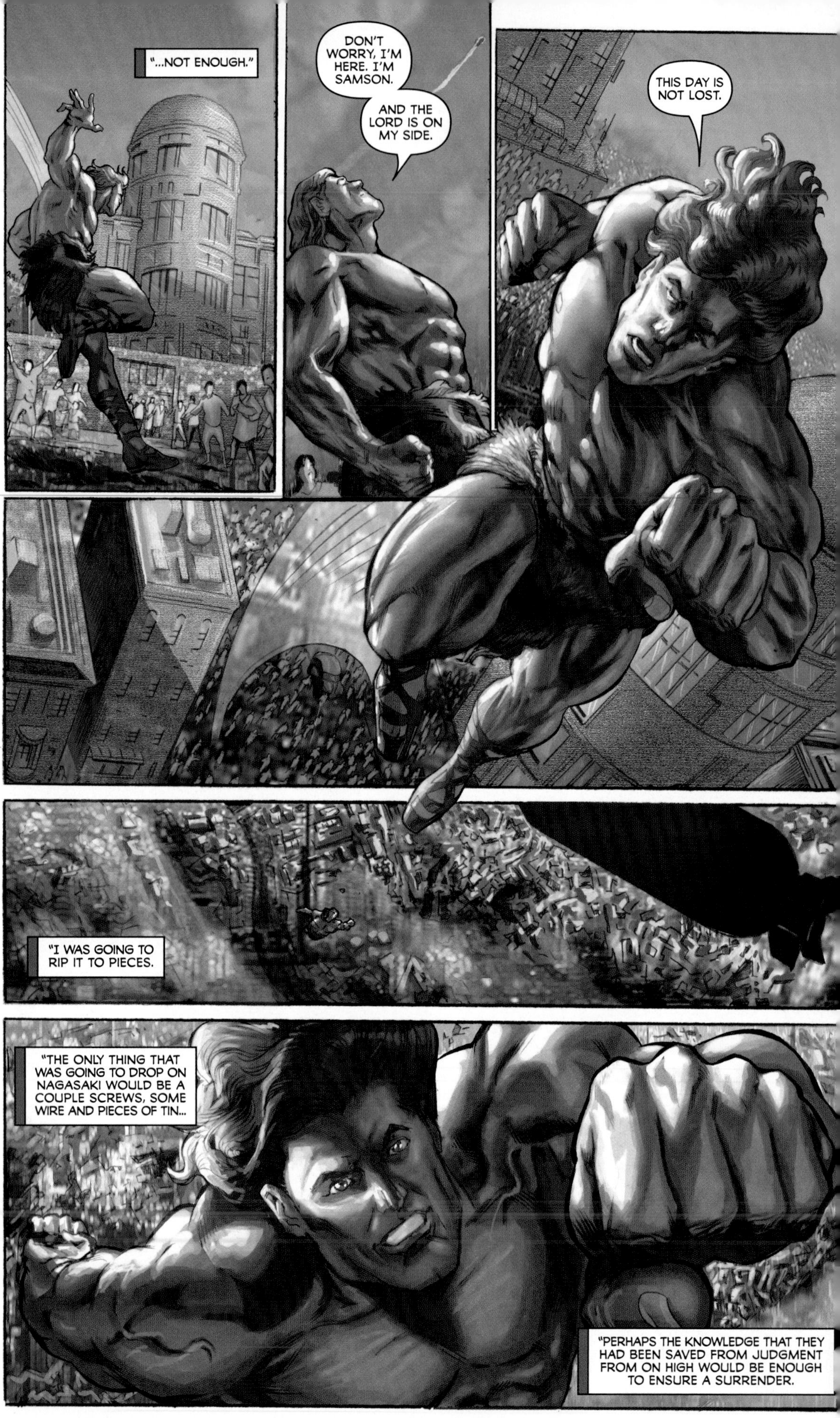
"...NOT ENOUGH."
DON'T WORRY, I'M HERE. I'M SAMSON.
AND THE LORD IS ON MY SIDE.
THIS DAY IS NOT LOST.
"I WAS GOING TO RIP IT TO PIECES.
"THE ONLY THING THAT WAS GOING TO DROP ON NAGASAKI WOULD BE A COUPLE SCREWS, SOME WIRE AND PIECES OF TIN...
"PERHAPS THE KNOWLEDGE THAT THEY HAD BEEN SAVED FROM JUDGMENT FROM ON HIGH WOULD BE ENOUGH TO ENSURE A SURRENDER.

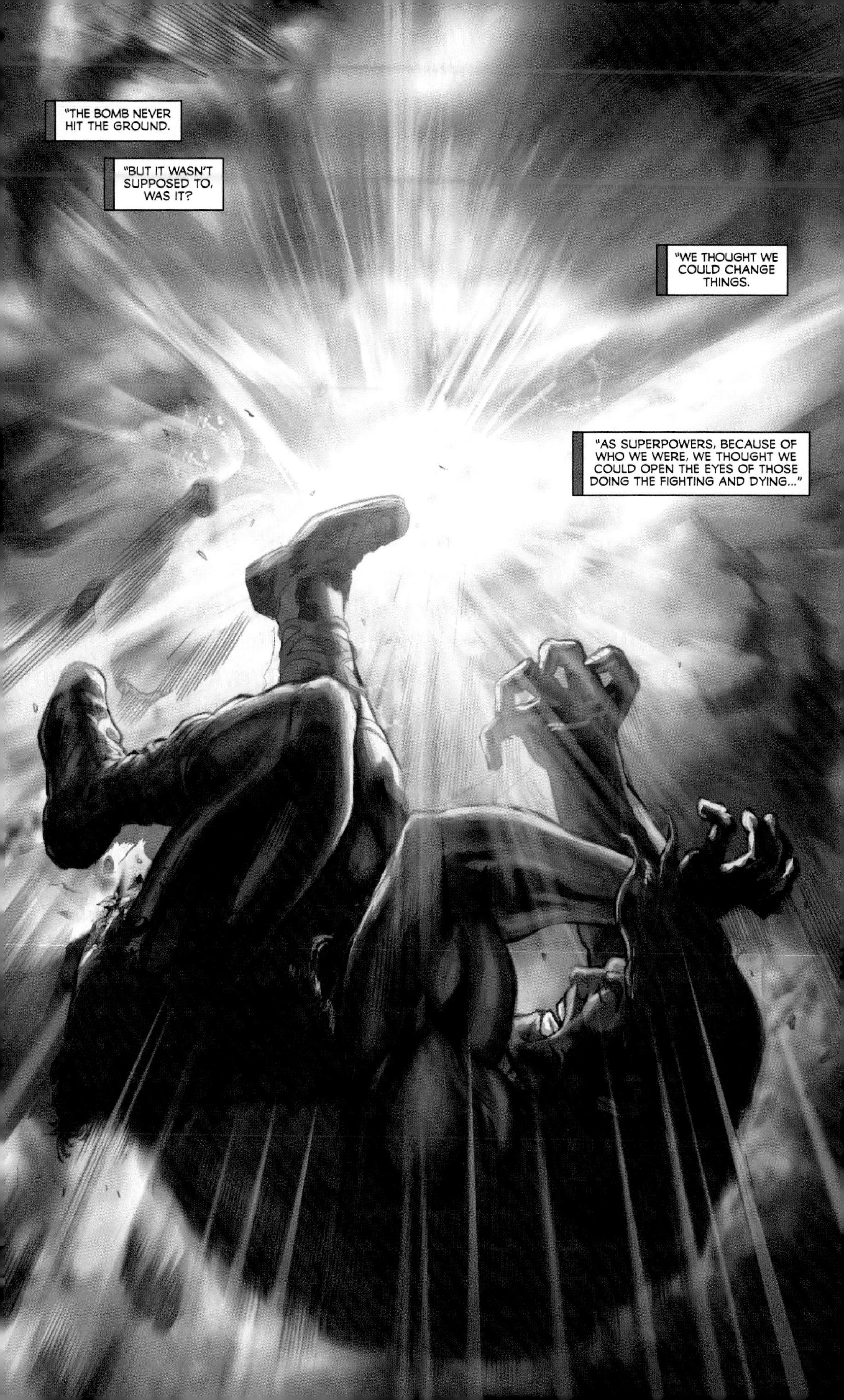
"THE BOMB NEVER HIT THE GROUND.
"BUT IT WASN'T SUPPOSED TO, WAS IT?
"WE THOUGHT WE COULD CHANGE THINGS.
"AS SUPERPOWERS, BECAUSE OF WHO WE WERE, WE THOUGHT WE COULD OPEN THE EYES OF THOSE DOING THE FIGHTING AND DYING..."

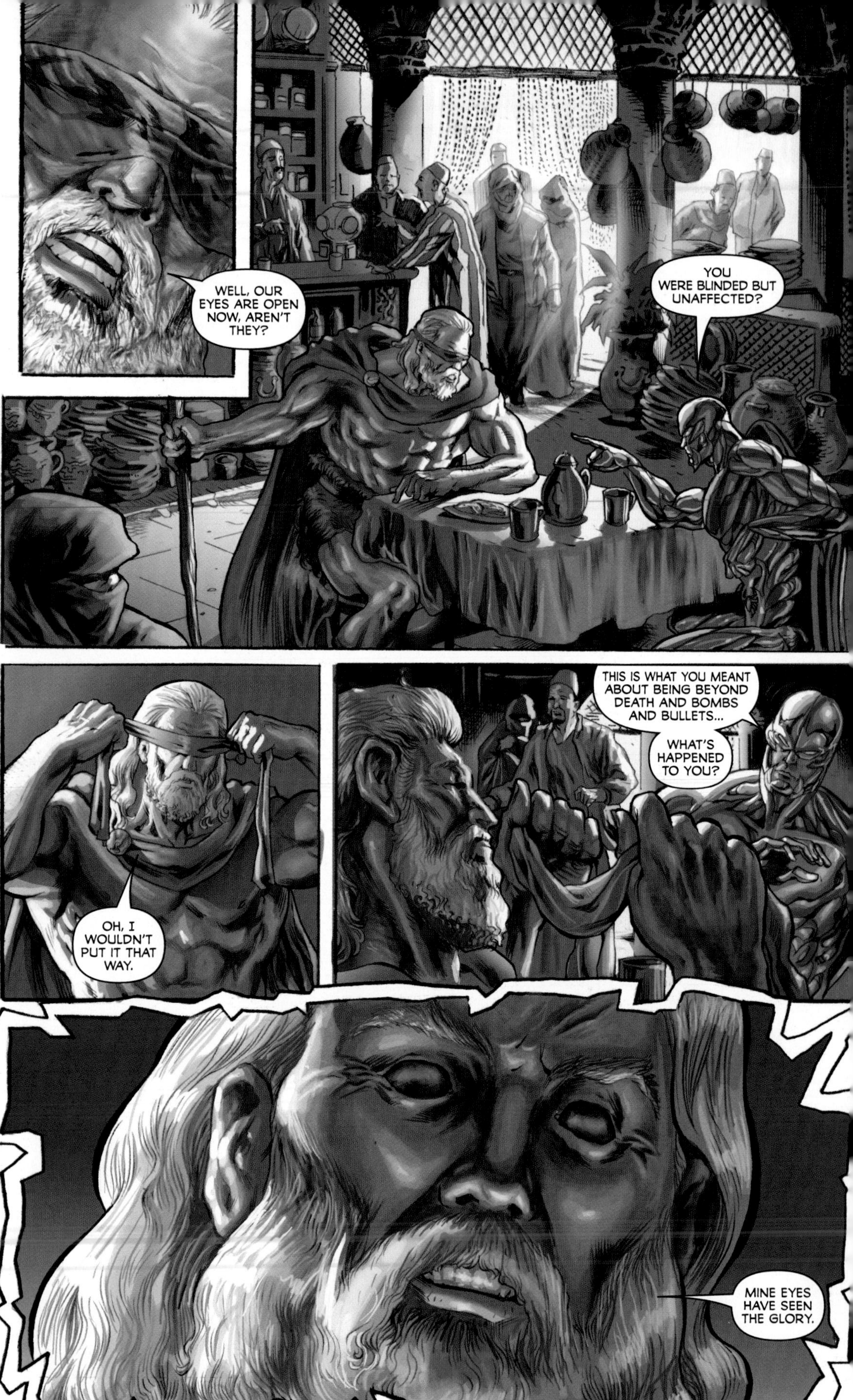
WELL, OUR EYES ARE OPEN NOW, AREN'T THEY?
YOU WERE BLINDED BUT UNAFFECTED?
OH, I WOULDN'T PUT IT THAT WAY.
THIS IS WHAT YOU MEANT ABOUT BEING BEYOND DEATH AND BOMBS AND BULLETS...
WHAT'S HAPPENED TO YOU?
MINE EYES HAVE SEEN THE GLORY.

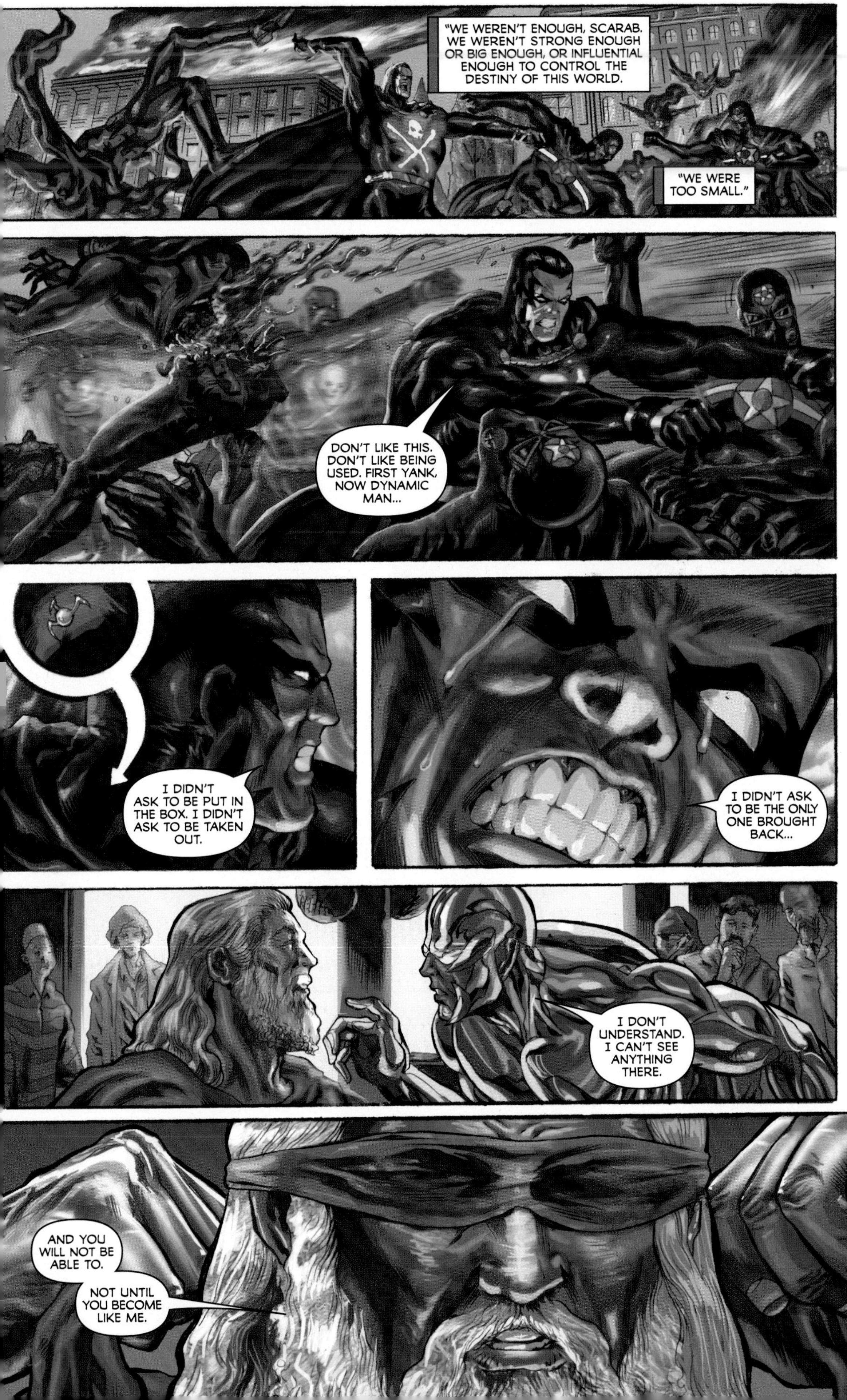
"WE WEREN'T ENOUGH, SCARAB. WE WEREN'T STRONG ENOUGH OR BIG ENOUGH, OR INFLUENTIAL ENOUGH TO CONTROL THE DESTINY OF THIS WORLD.
"WE WERE TOO SMALL."
DON'T LIKE THIS. DON'T LIKE BEING USED. FIRST YANK, NOW DYNAMIC MAN...
I DIDN'T ASK TO BE PUT IN THE BOX. I DIDN'T ASK TO BE TAKEN OUT.
I DIDN'T ASK TO BE THE ONLY ONE BROUGHT BACK...
I DON'T UNDERSTAND. I CAN'T SEE ANYTHING THERE.
AND YOU WILL NOT BE ABLE TO.
NOT UNTIL YOU BECOME LIKE ME.

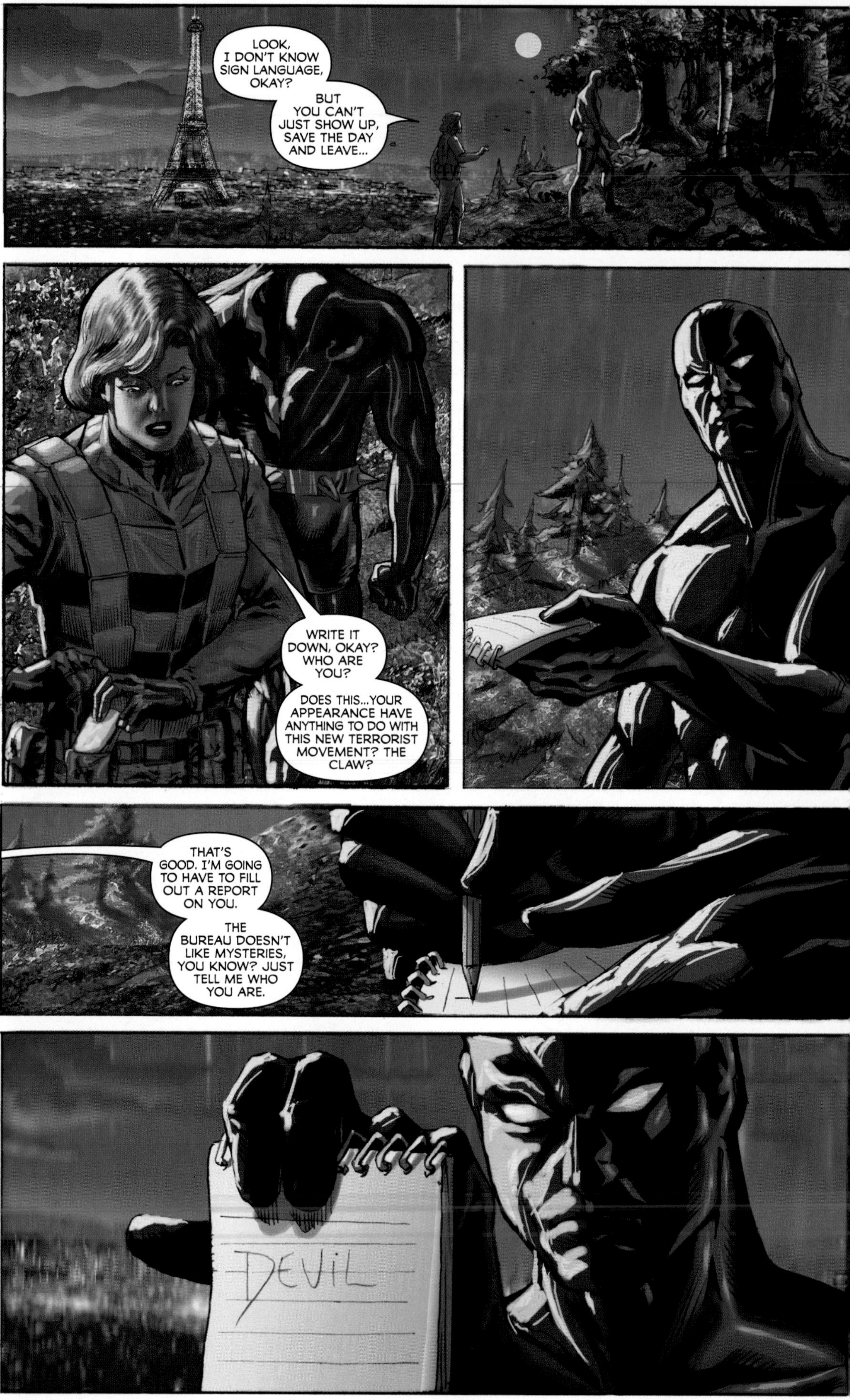
LOOK, I DON'T KNOW SIGN LANGUAGE, OKAY?
BUT YOU CAN'T JUST SHOW UP, SAVE THE DAY AND LEAVE...
WRITE IT DOWN, OKAY? WHO ARE YOU?
DOES THIS...YOUR APPEARANCE HAVE ANYTHING TO DO WITH THIS NEW TERRORIST MOVEMENT? THE CLAW?
THAT'S GOOD. I'M GOING TO HAVE TO FILL OUT A REPORT ON YOU.
THE BUREAU DOESN'T LIKE MYSTERIES, YOU KNOW? JUST TELL ME WHO YOU ARE.
DEVIL

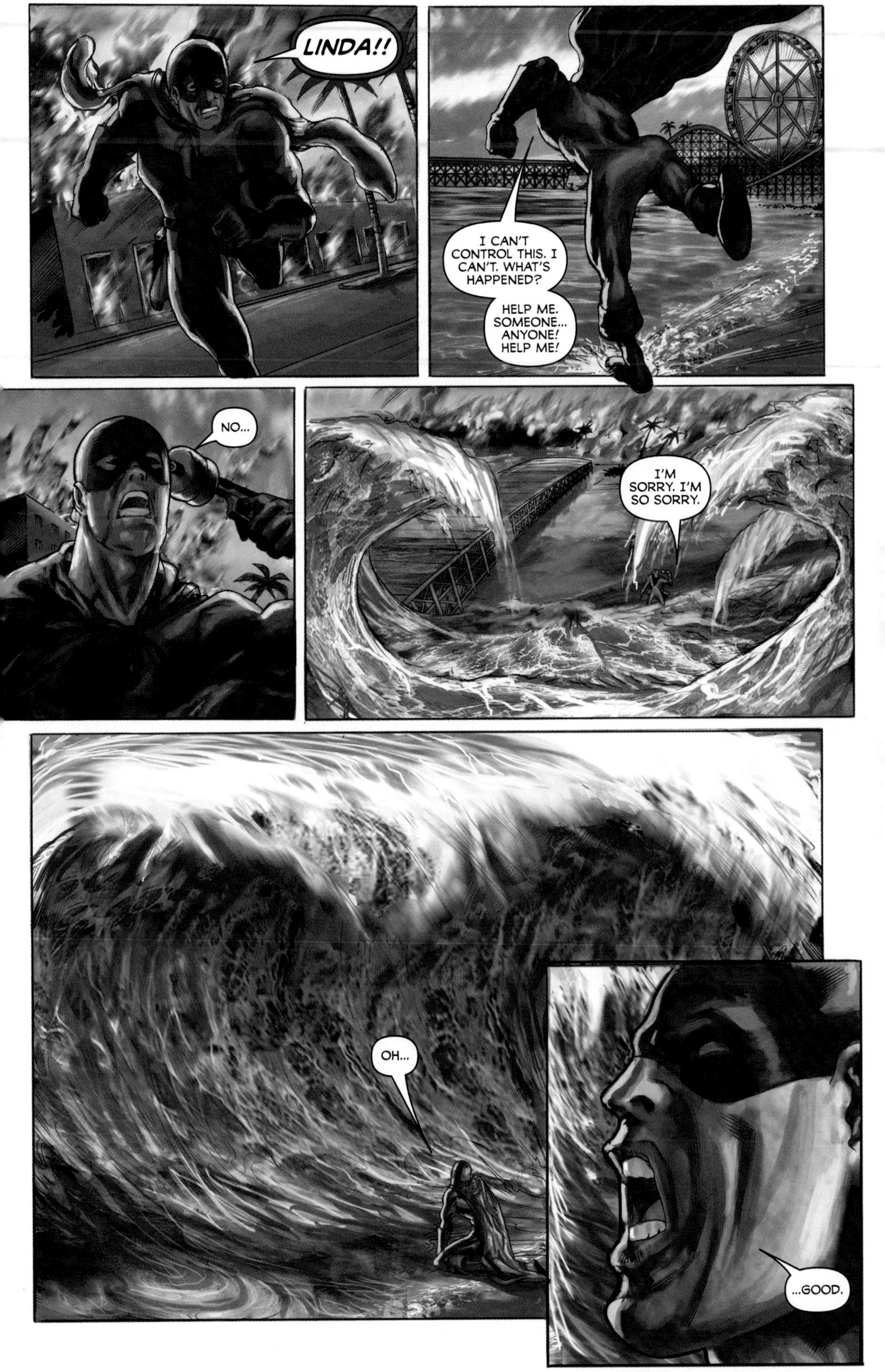
LINDA!!
I CAN'T CONTROL THIS. I CAN'T. WHAT'S HAPPENED?
HELP ME. SOMEONE... ANYONE! HELP ME!
NO...
I'M SORRY. I'M SO SORRY.
OH...
...GOOD.

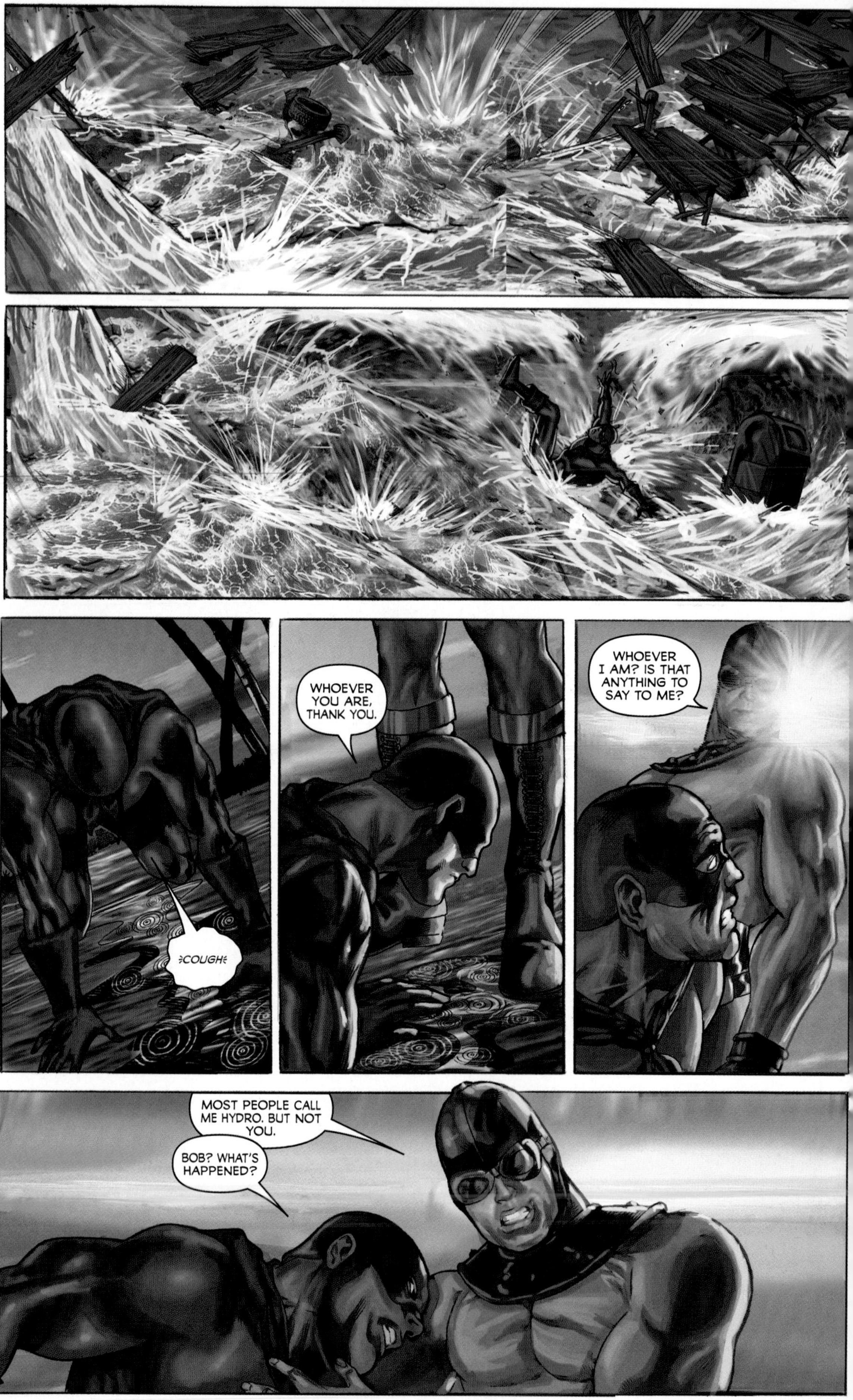

COUGH
WHOEVER YOU ARE, THANK YOU.
WHOEVER I AM? IS THAT ANYTHING TO SAY TO ME?
BOB? WHAT'S HAPPENED?
MOST PEOPLE CALL ME HYDRO. BUT NOT YOU.

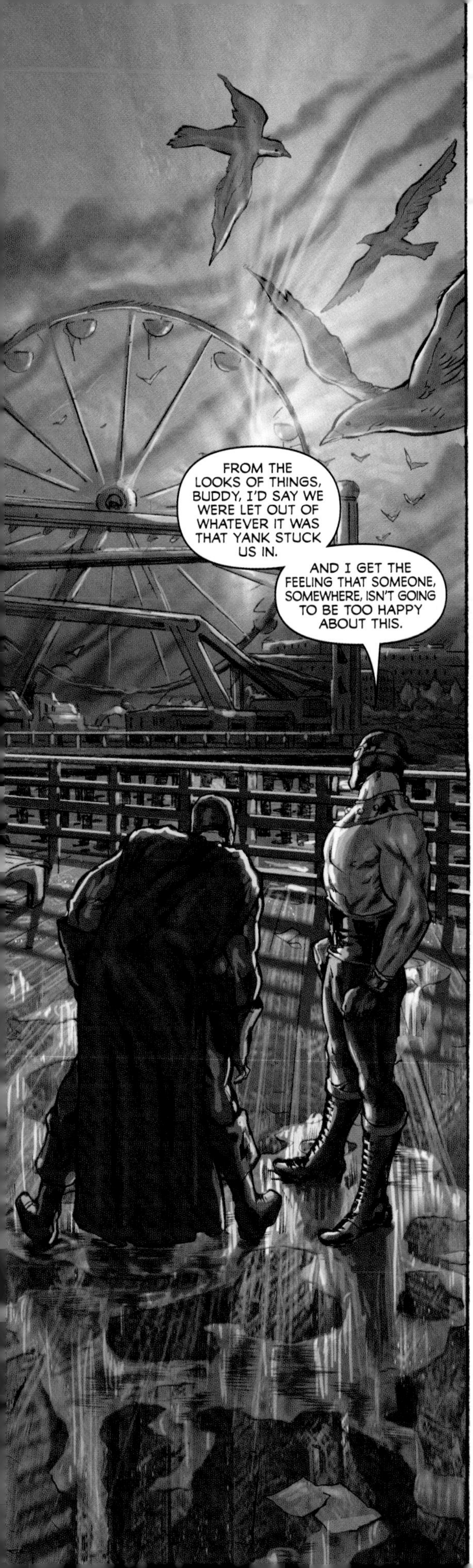
FROM THE LOOKS OF THINGS, BUDDY, I'D SAY WE WERE LET OUT OF WHATEVER IT WAS THAT YANK STUCK US IN.
AND I GET THE FEELING THAT SOMEONE, SOMEWHERE, ISN'T GOING TO BE TOO HAPPY ABOUT THIS.

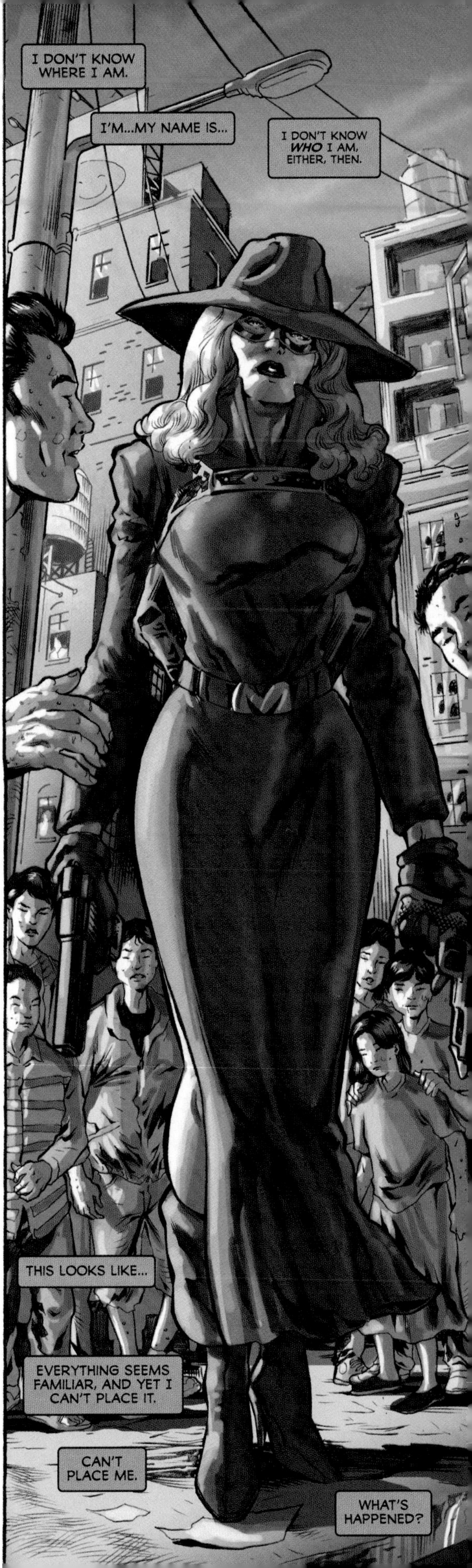
I DON'T KNOW WHERE I AM.
I'M...MY NAME IS...
I DON'T KNOW *WHO* I AM, EITHER, THEN.
THIS LOOKS LIKE...
EVERYTHING SEEMS FAMILIAR, AND YET I CAN'T PLACE IT.
CAN'T PLACE ME.
WHAT'S HAPPENED?

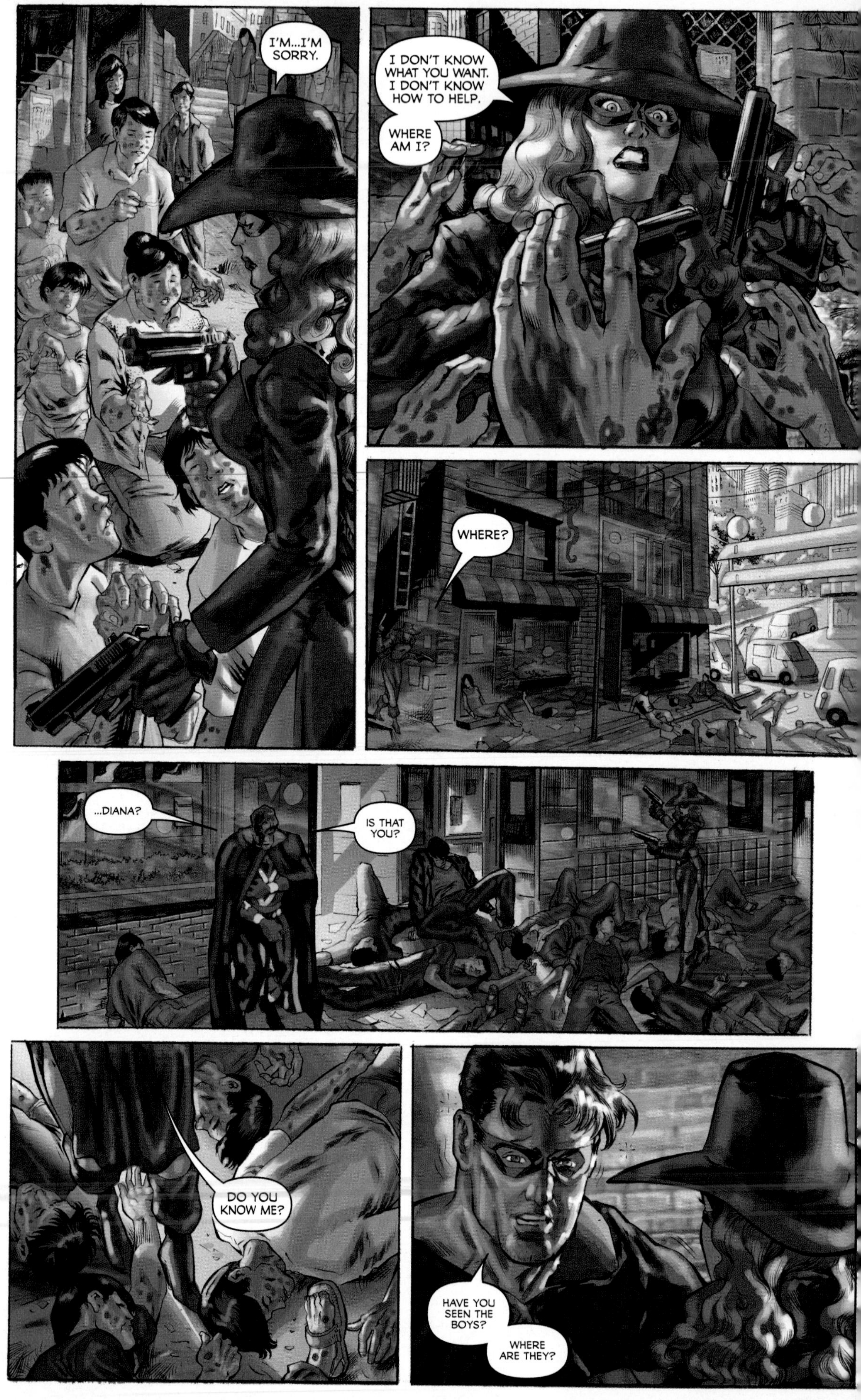
I'M...I'M SORRY.
I DON'T KNOW WHAT YOU WANT. I DON'T KNOW HOW TO HELP.
WHERE AM I?
WHERE?
...DIANA?
IS THAT YOU?
DO YOU KNOW ME?
HAVE YOU SEEN THE BOYS?
WHERE ARE THEY?

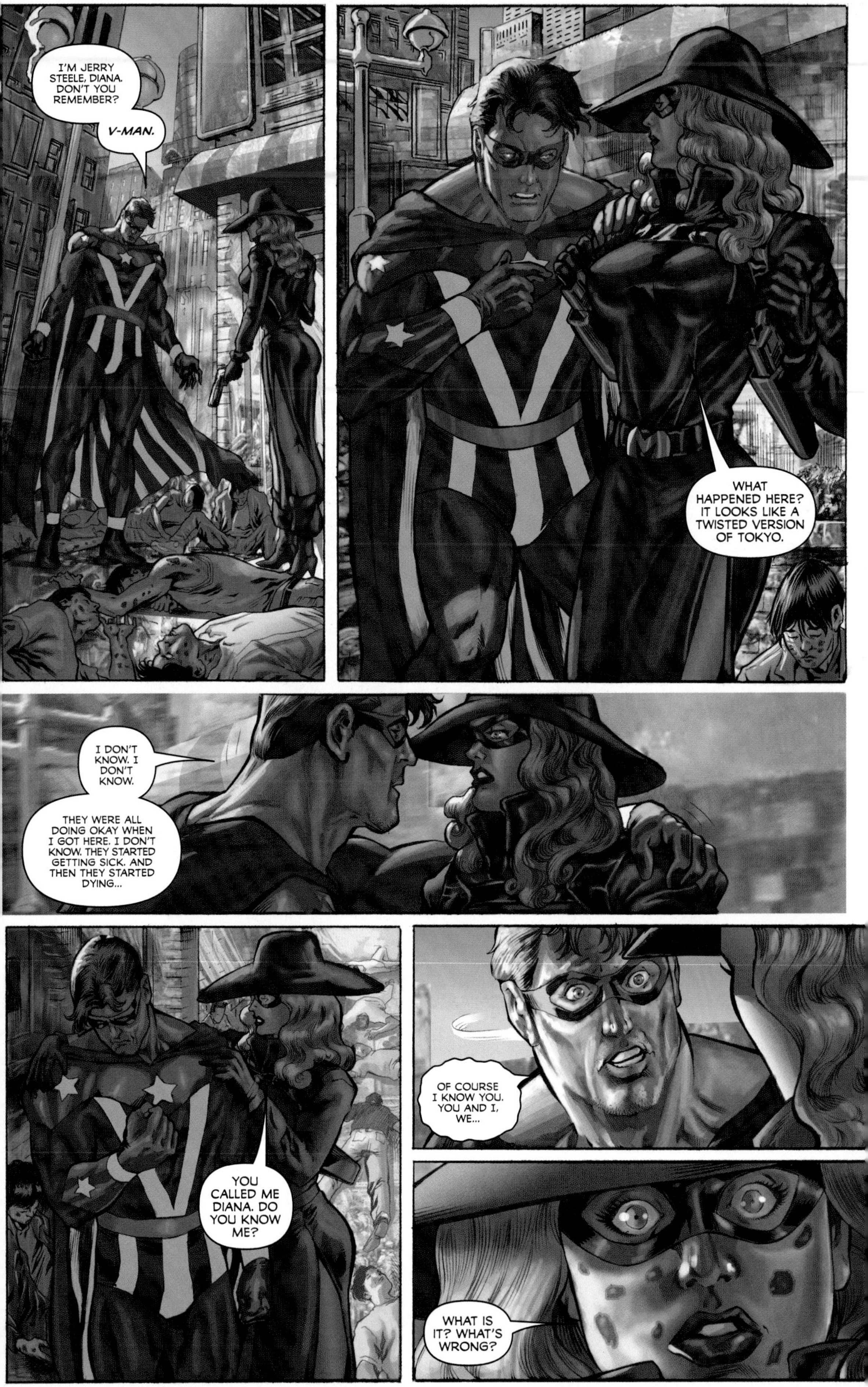
I'M JERRY STEELE, DIANA. DON'T YOU REMEMBER?
V-MAN.
WHAT HAPPENED HERE? IT LOOKS LIKE A TWISTED VERSION OF TOKYO.
I DON'T KNOW. I DON'T KNOW.
THEY WERE ALL DOING OKAY WHEN I GOT HERE. I DON'T KNOW. THEY STARTED GETTING SICK. AND THEN THEY STARTED DYING...
YOU CALLED ME DIANA. DO YOU KNOW ME?
OF COURSE I KNOW YOU. YOU AND I, WE...
WHAT IS IT? WHAT'S WRONG?

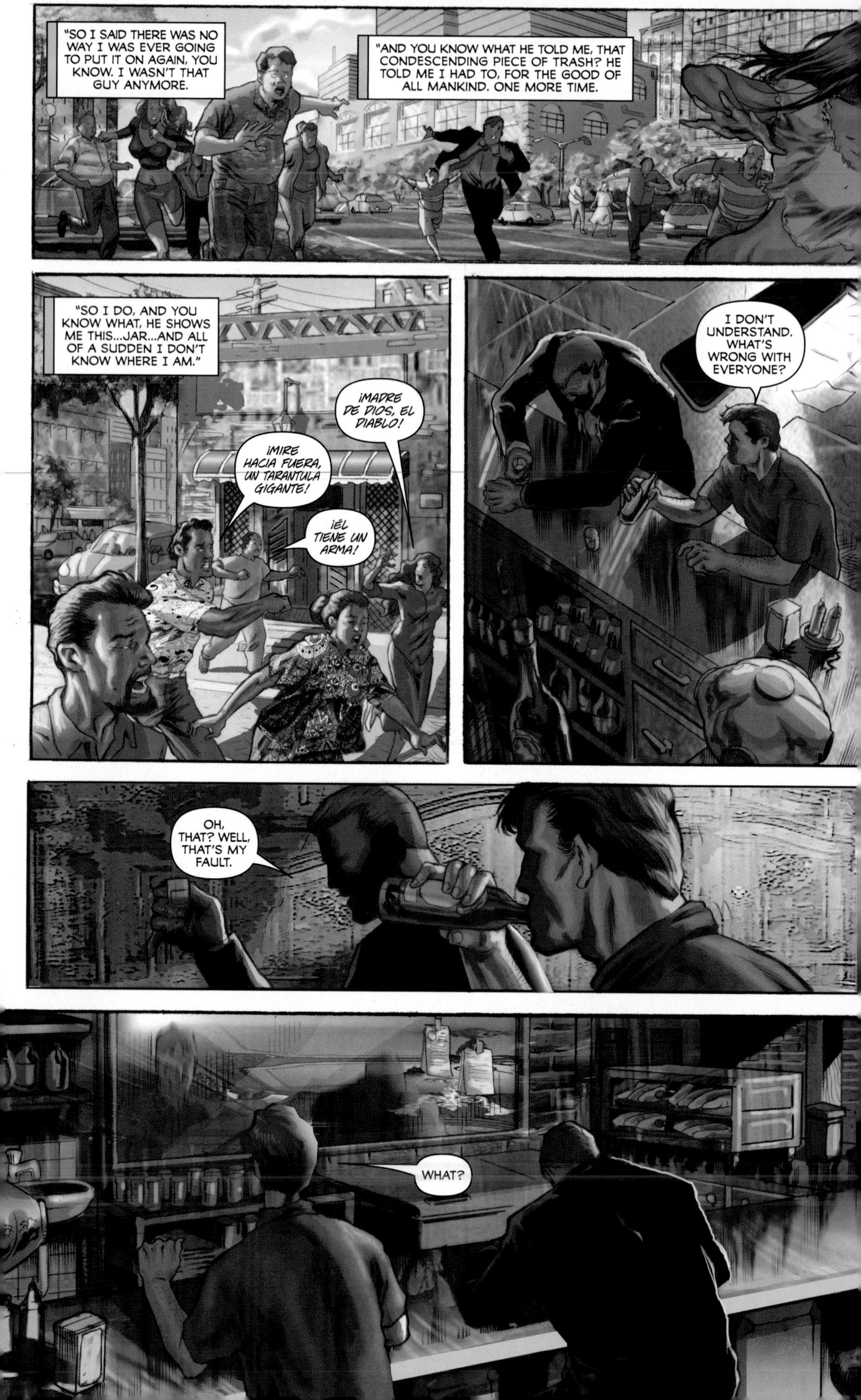
"SO I SAID THERE WAS NO WAY I WAS EVER GOING TO PUT IT ON AGAIN, YOU KNOW. I WASN'T THAT GUY ANYMORE.
"AND YOU KNOW WHAT HE TOLD ME, THAT CONDESCENDING PIECE OF TRASH? HE TOLD ME I HAD TO, FOR THE GOOD OF ALL MANKIND. ONE MORE TIME.
"SO I DO, AND YOU KNOW WHAT, HE SHOWS ME THIS...JAR...AND ALL OF A SUDDEN I DON'T KNOW WHERE I AM."
¡MADRE DE DIOS, EL DIABLO!
¡MIRE HACIA FUERA, UN TARANTULA GIGANTE!
¡ÉL TIENE UN ARMA!
I DON'T UNDERSTAND. WHAT'S WRONG WITH EVERYONE?
OH, THAT? WELL, THAT'S MY FAULT.
WHAT?

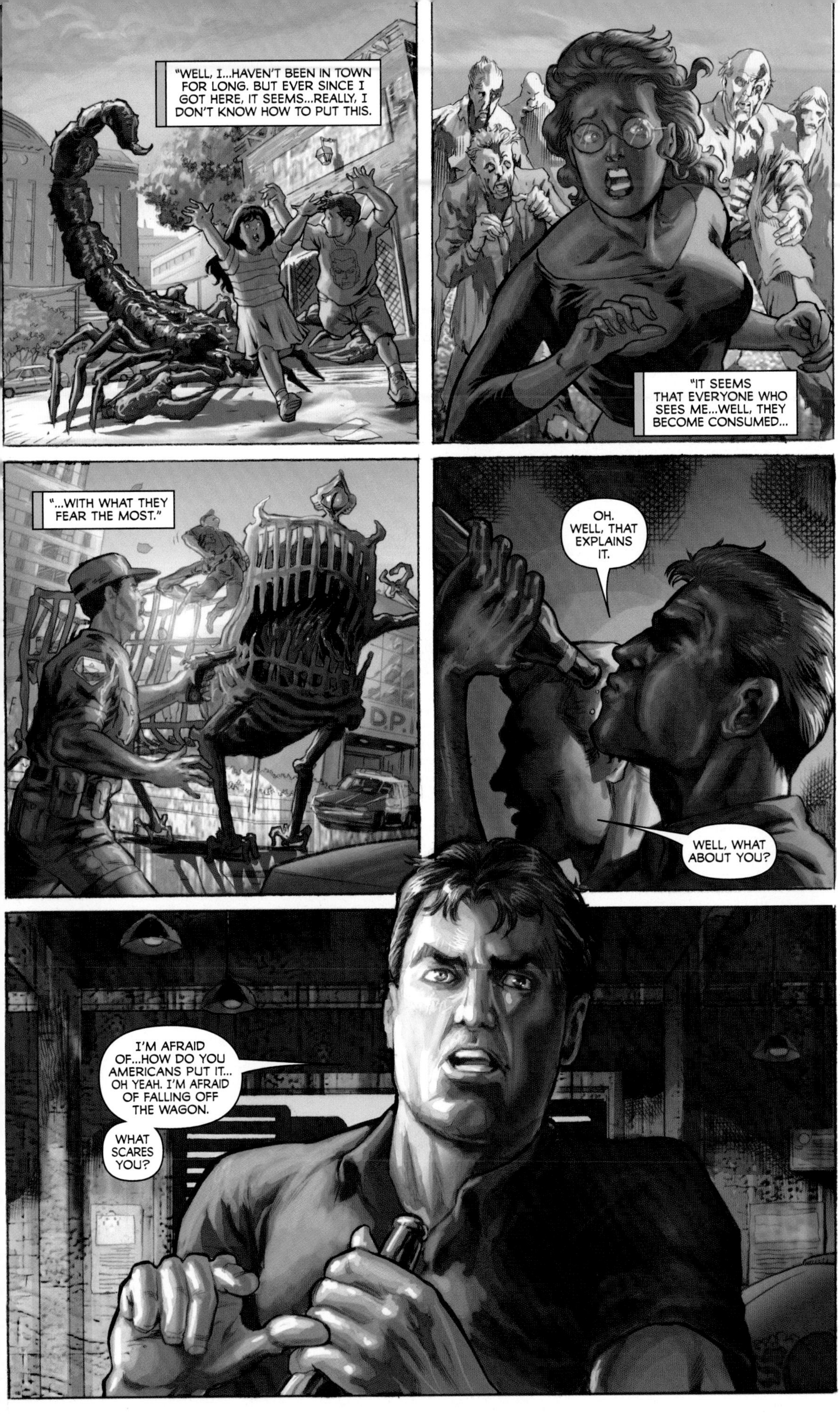
"WELL, I...HAVEN'T BEEN IN TOWN FOR LONG. BUT EVER SINCE I GOT HERE, IT SEEMS...REALLY, I DON'T KNOW HOW TO PUT THIS.
"IT SEEMS THAT EVERYONE WHO SEES ME...WELL, THEY BECOME CONSUMED...
"...WITH WHAT THEY FEAR THE MOST."
OH. WELL, THAT EXPLAINS IT.
WELL, WHAT ABOUT YOU?
I'M AFRAID OF...HOW DO YOU AMERICANS PUT IT... OH YEAH. I'M AFRAID OF FALLING OFF THE WAGON.
WHAT SCARES YOU?

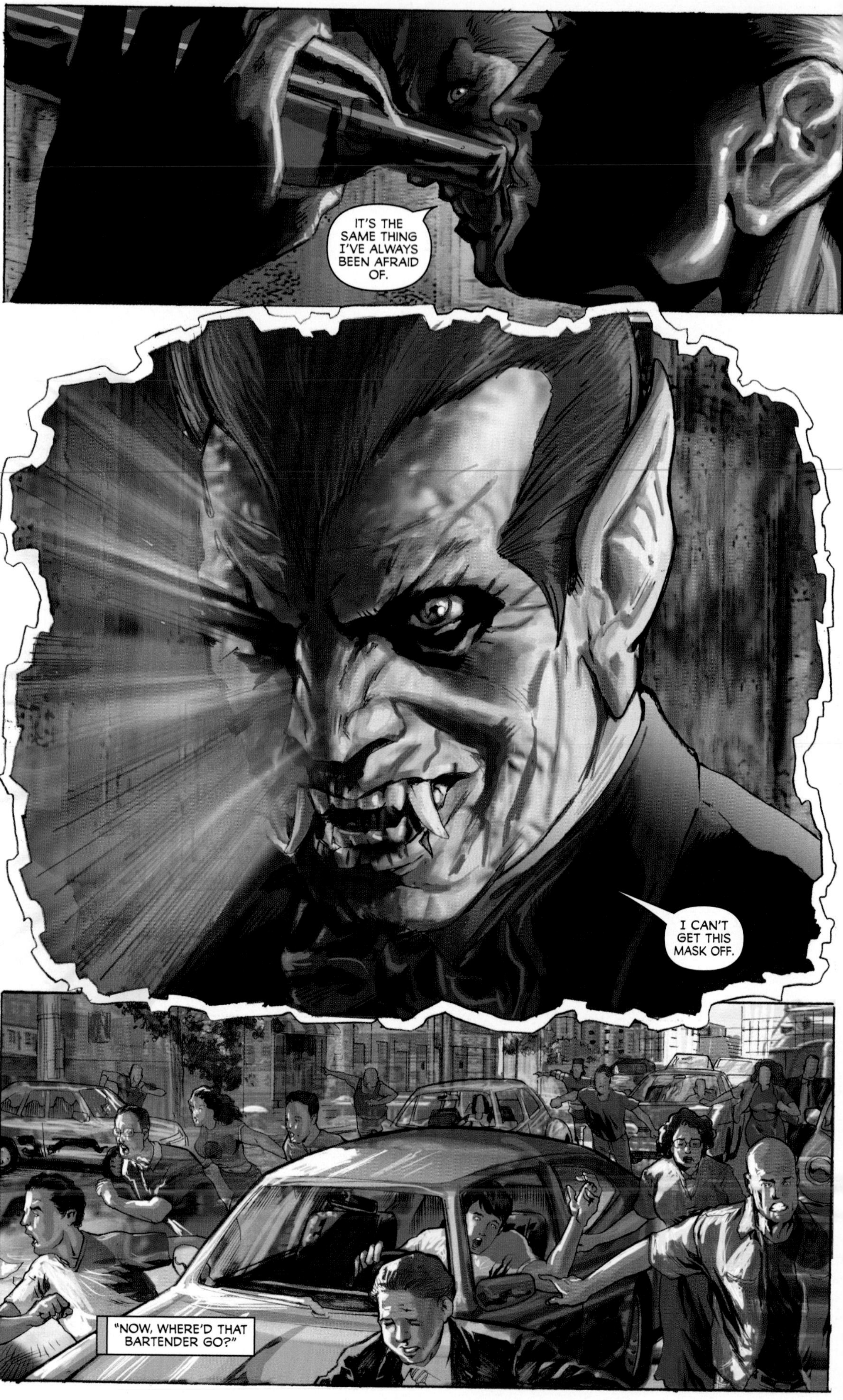
IT'S THE SAME THING I'VE ALWAYS BEEN AFRAID OF.
I CAN'T GET THIS MASK OFF.
"NOW, WHERE'D THAT BARTENDER GO?"

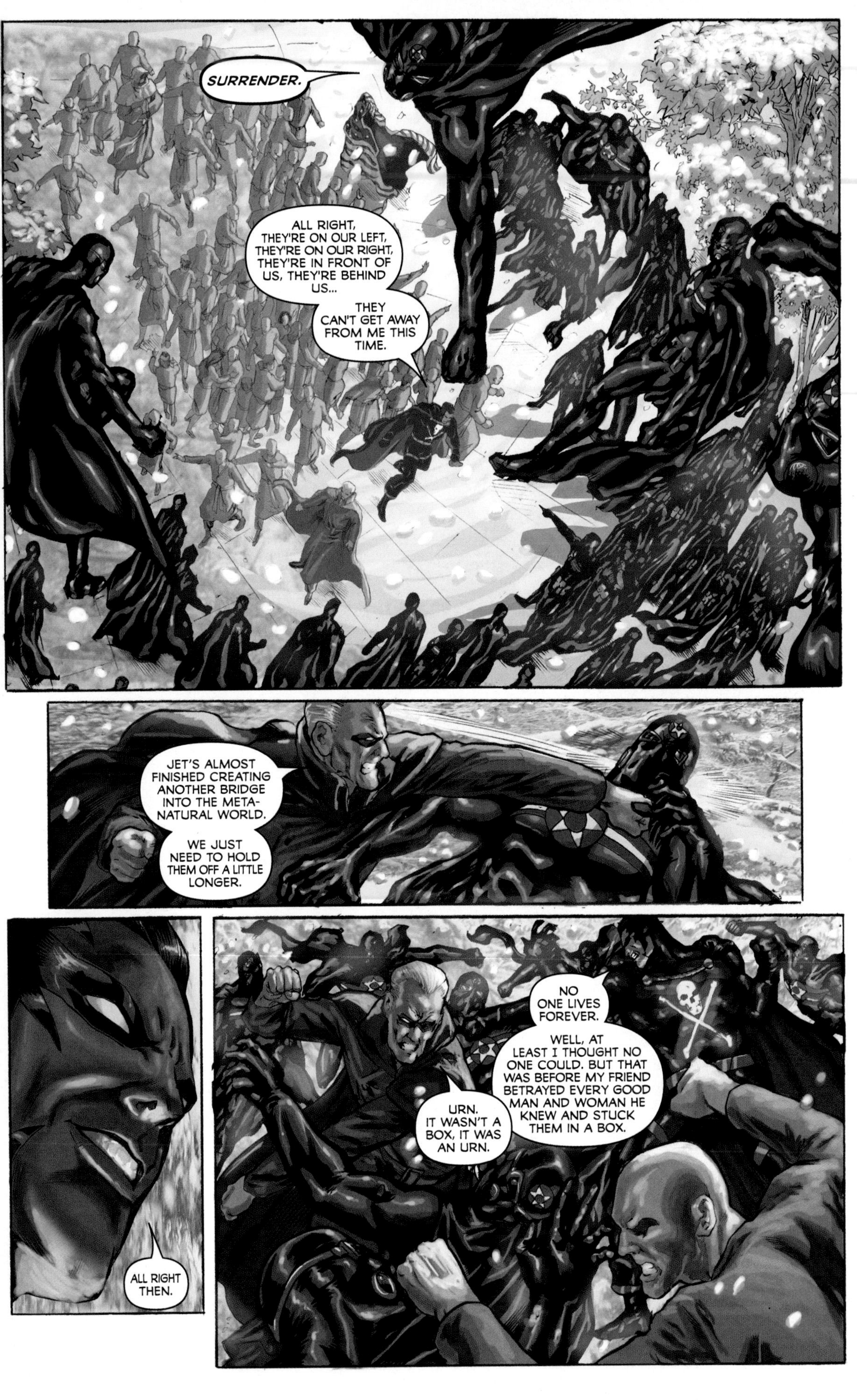
SURRENDER.
ALL RIGHT, THEY'RE ON OUR LEFT, THEY'RE ON OUR RIGHT, THEY'RE IN FRONT OF US, THEY'RE BEHIND US...
THEY CAN'T GET AWAY FROM ME THIS TIME.
JET'S ALMOST FINISHED CREATING ANOTHER BRIDGE INTO THE META-NATURAL WORLD.
WE JUST NEED TO HOLD THEM OFF A LITTLE LONGER.
ALL RIGHT THEN.
NO ONE LIVES FOREVER.
WELL, AT LEAST I THOUGHT NO ONE COULD. BUT THAT WAS BEFORE MY FRIEND BETRAYED EVERY GOOD MAN AND WOMAN HE KNEW AND STUCK THEM IN A BOX.
URN. IT WASN'T A BOX, IT WAS AN URN.

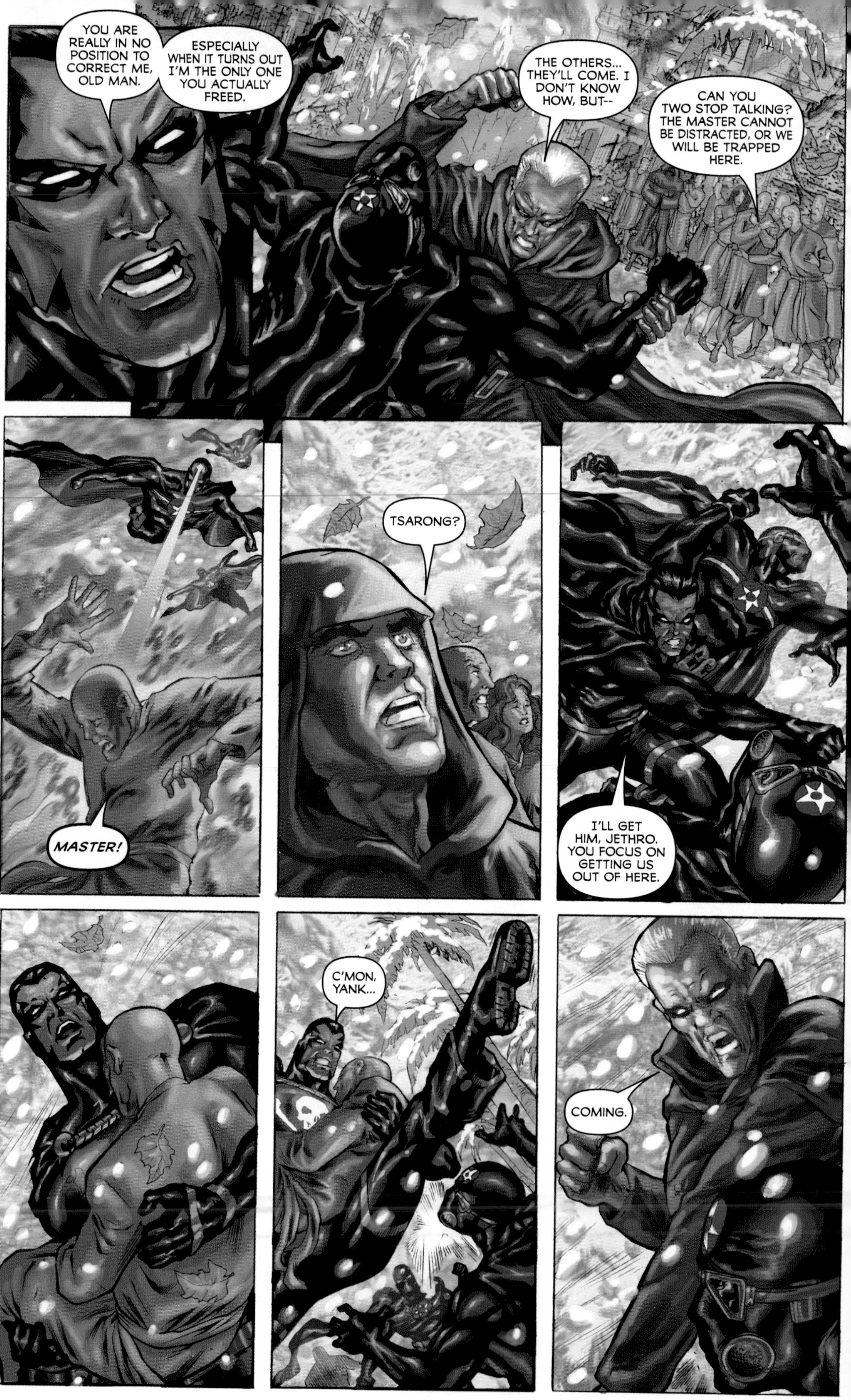
YOU ARE REALLY IN NO POSITION TO CORRECT ME, OLD MAN.
ESPECIALLY WHEN IT TURNS OUT I'M THE ONLY ONE YOU ACTUALLY FREED.
THE OTHERS... THEY'LL COME. I DON'T KNOW HOW, BUT--
CAN YOU TWO STOP TALKING? THE MASTER CANNOT BE DISTRACTED, OR WE WILL BE TRAPPED HERE.
MASTER!
TSARONG?
I'LL GET HIM, JETHRO. YOU FOCUS ON GETTING US OUT OF HERE.
C'MON, YANK...
COMING.

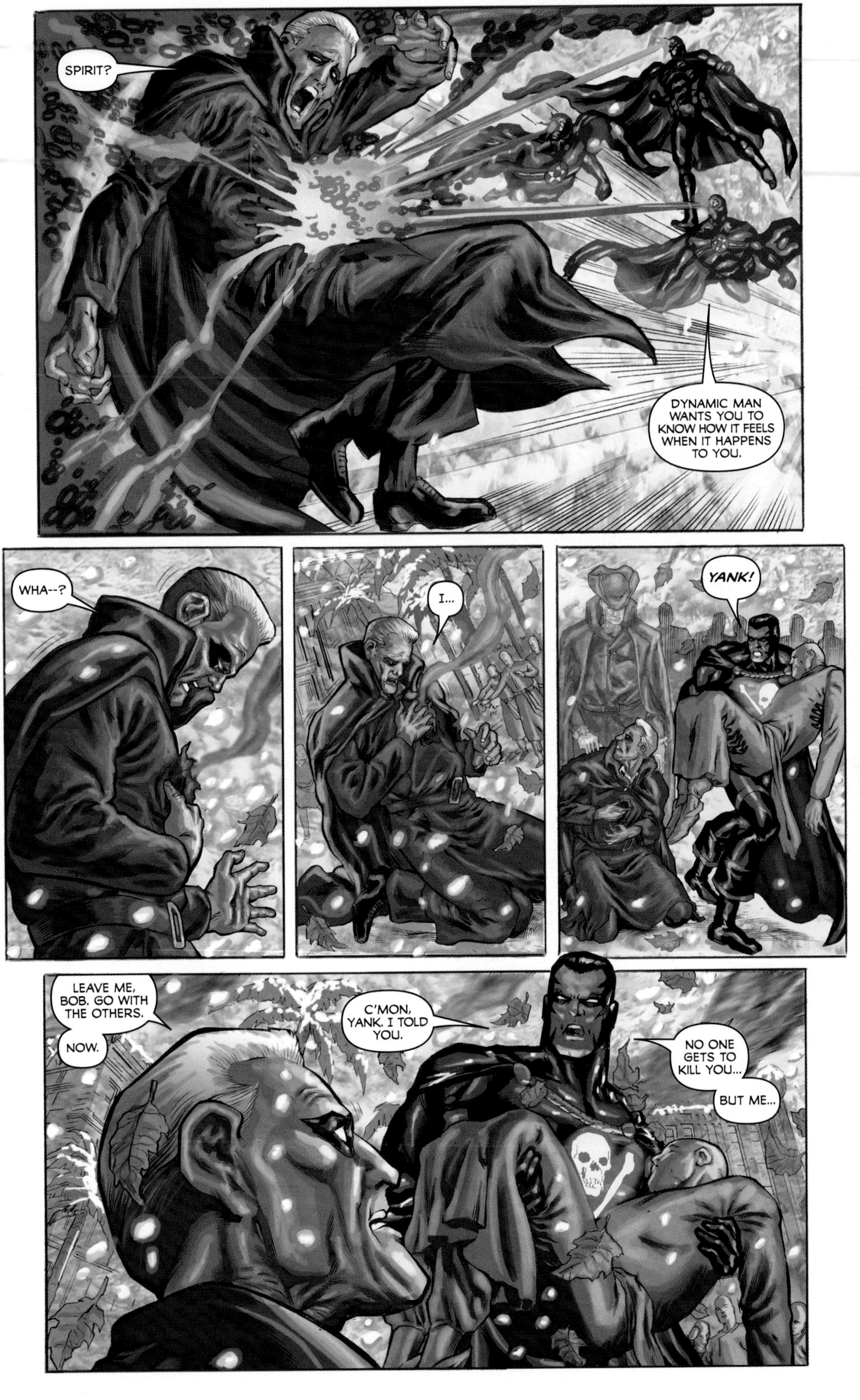
SPIRIT?
DYNAMIC MAN WANTS YOU TO KNOW HOW IT FEELS WHEN IT HAPPENS TO YOU.
WHA--?
I...
YANK!
LEAVE ME, BOB. GO WITH THE OTHERS.
NOW.
C'MON, YANK. I TOLD YOU.
NO ONE GETS TO KILL YOU...
BUT ME...

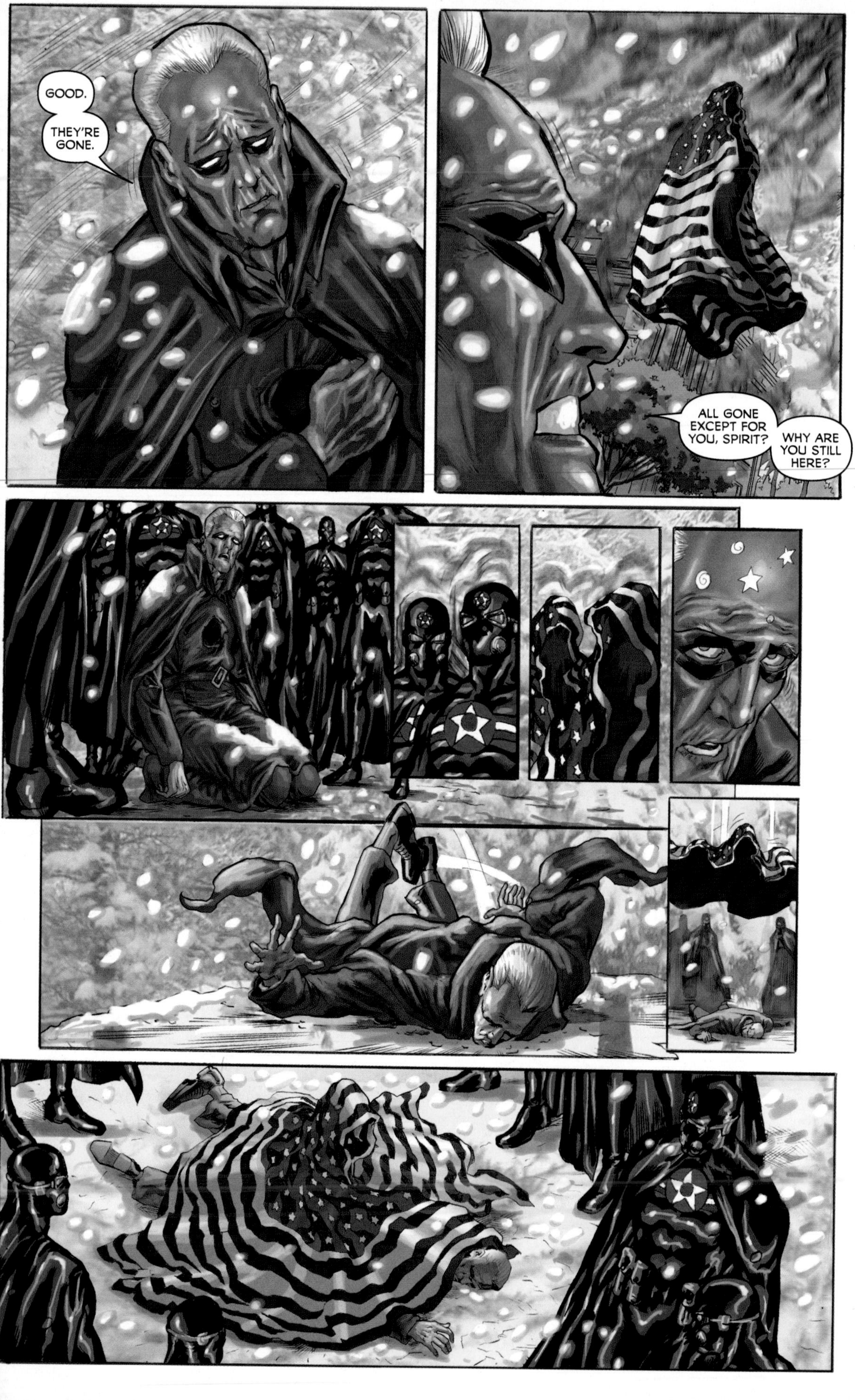
GOOD.
THEY'RE GONE.
ALL GONE EXCEPT FOR YOU, SPIRIT?
WHY ARE YOU STILL HERE?

ISSUE

4

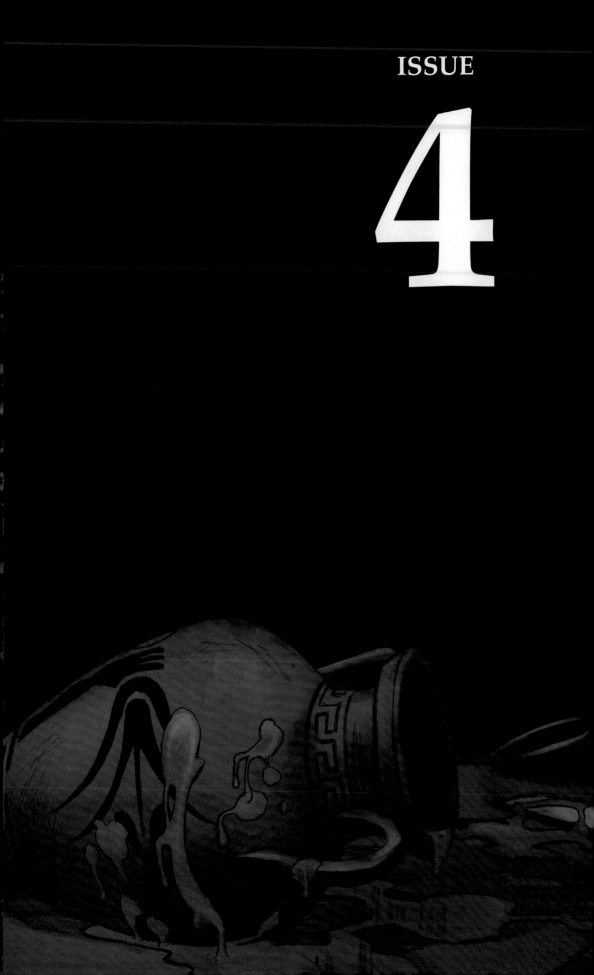

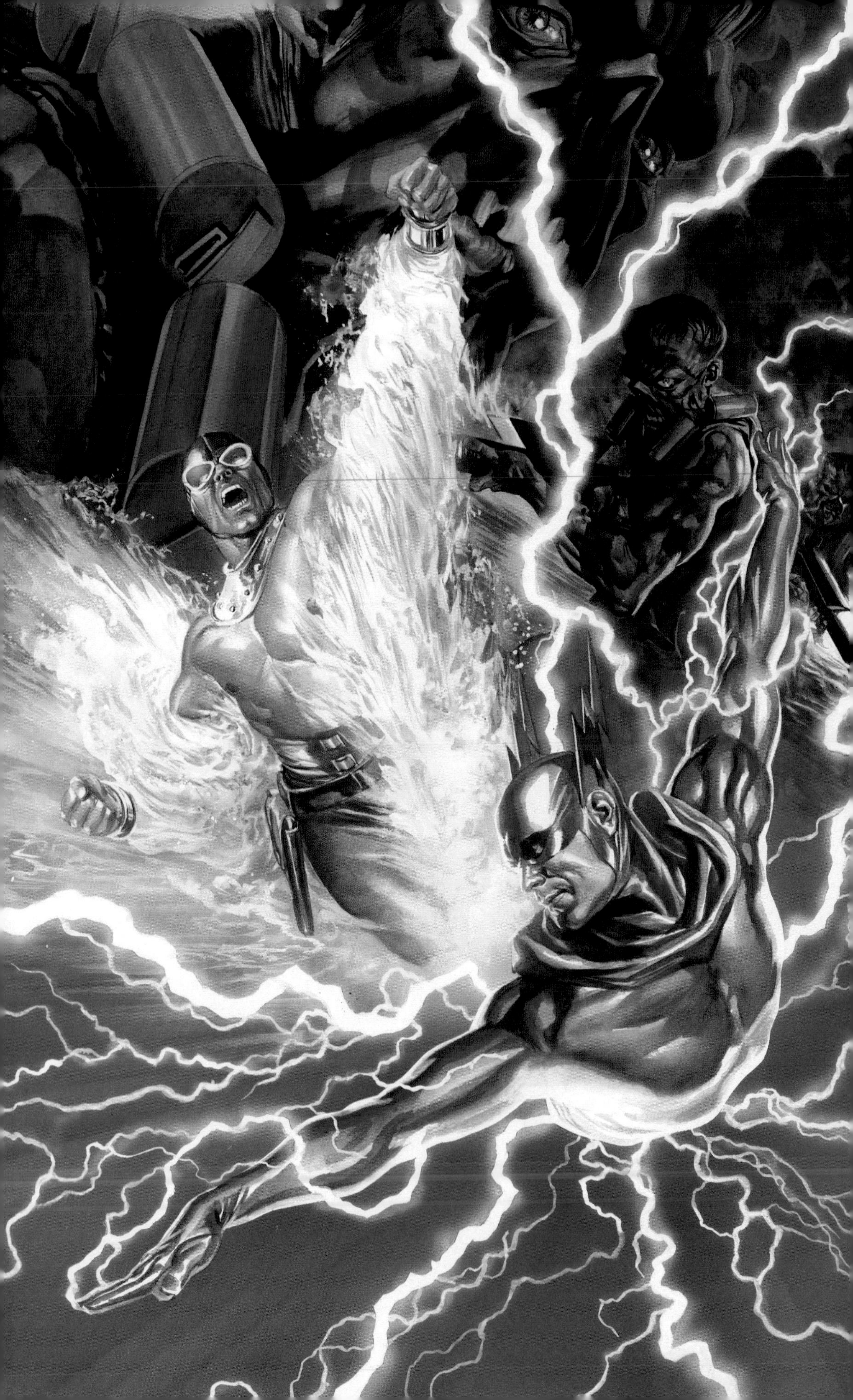

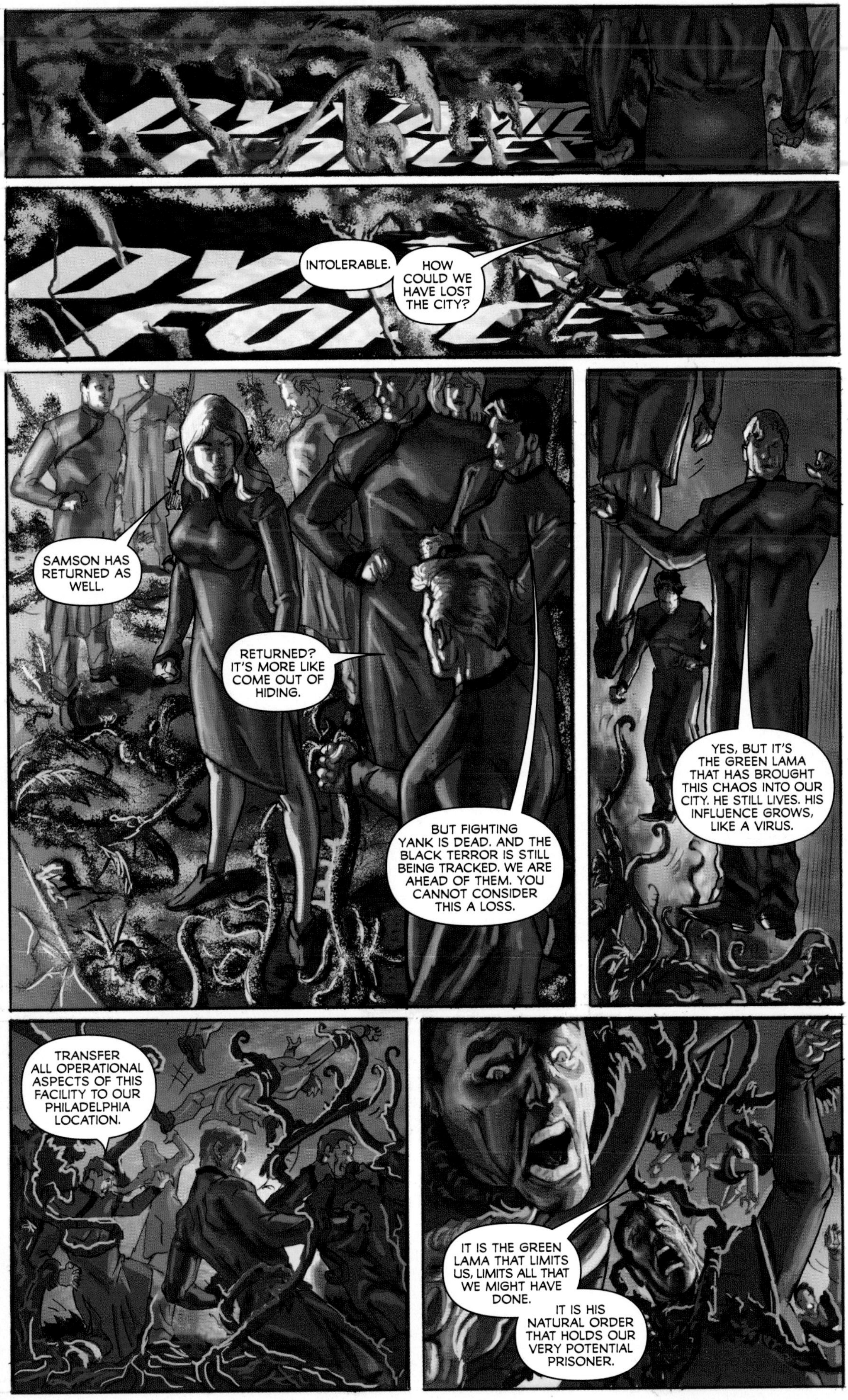
INTOLERABLE.
HOW COULD WE HAVE LOST THE CITY?
SAMSON HAS RETURNED AS WELL.
RETURNED? IT'S MORE LIKE COME OUT OF HIDING.
BUT FIGHTING YANK IS DEAD. AND THE BLACK TERROR IS STILL BEING TRACKED. WE ARE AHEAD OF THEM. YOU CANNOT CONSIDER THIS A LOSS.
YES, BUT IT'S THE GREEN LAMA THAT HAS BROUGHT THIS CHAOS INTO OUR CITY. HE STILL LIVES. HIS INFLUENCE GROWS, LIKE A VIRUS.
TRANSFER ALL OPERATIONAL ASPECTS OF THIS FACILITY TO OUR PHILADELPHIA LOCATION.
IT IS THE GREEN LAMA THAT LIMITS US, LIMITS ALL THAT WE MIGHT HAVE DONE.
IT IS HIS NATURAL ORDER THAT HOLDS OUR VERY POTENTIAL PRISONER.

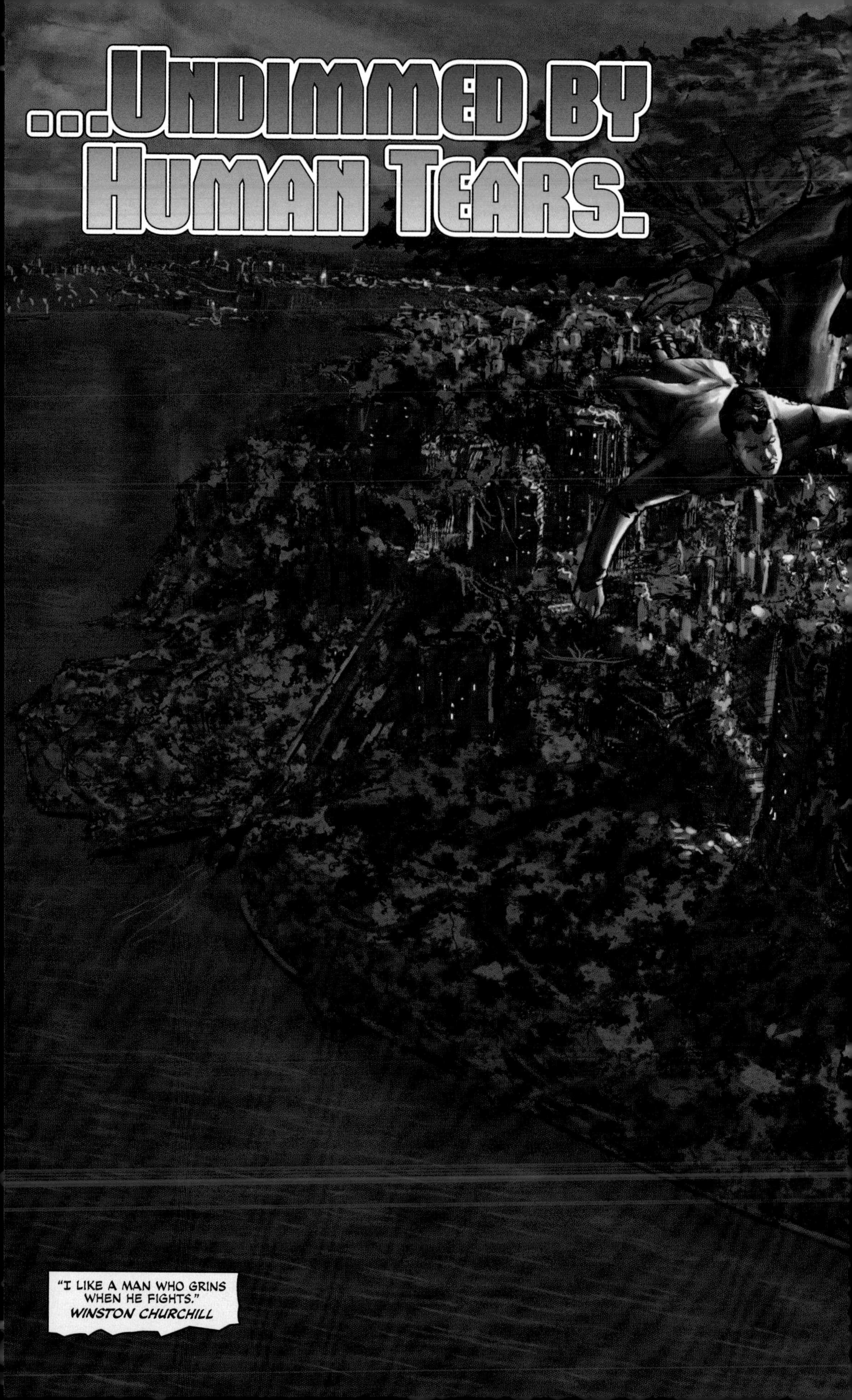
...UNDIMMED BY HUMAN TEARS.
"I LIKE A MAN WHO GRINS WHEN HE FIGHTS."
WINSTON CHURCHILL

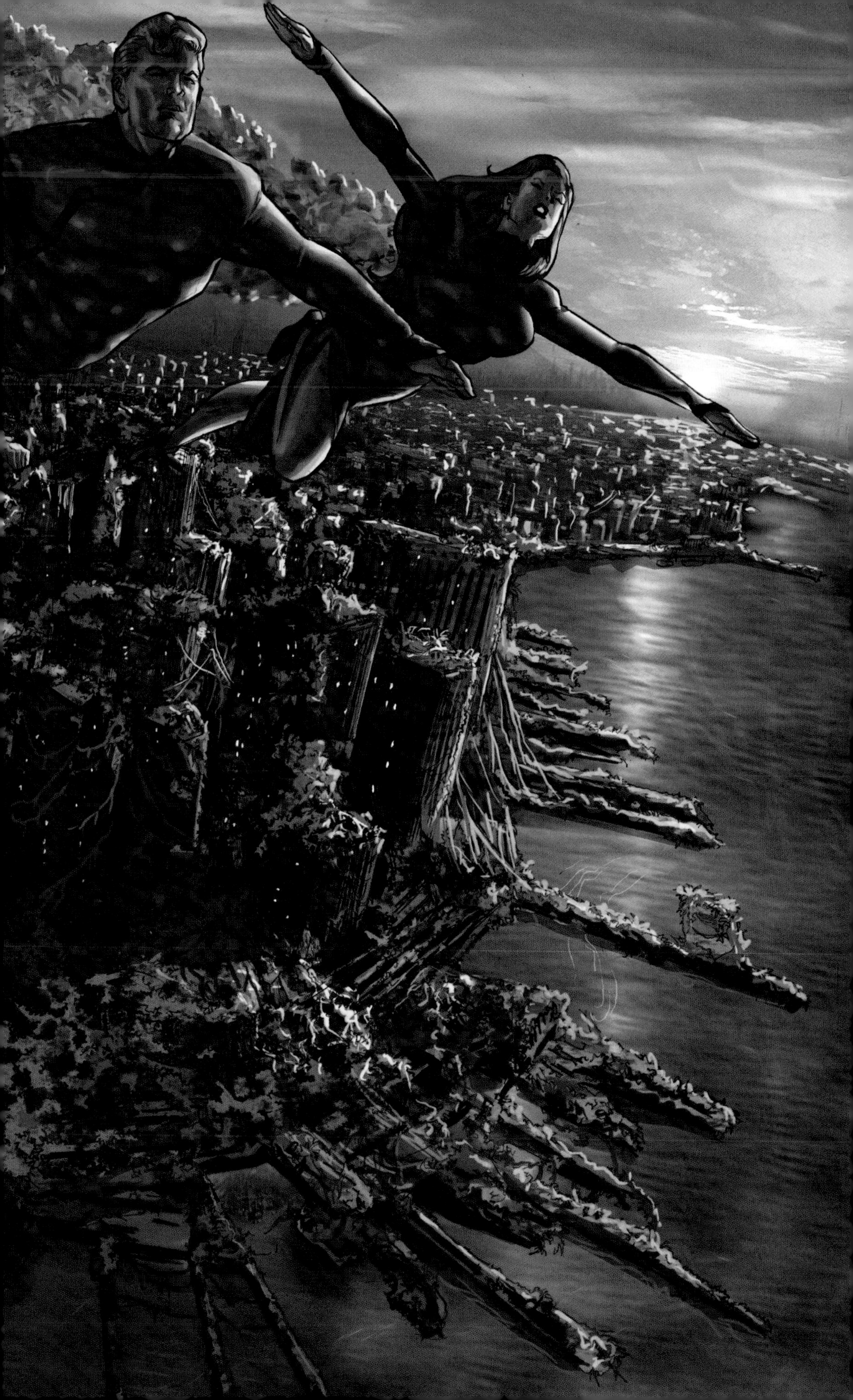

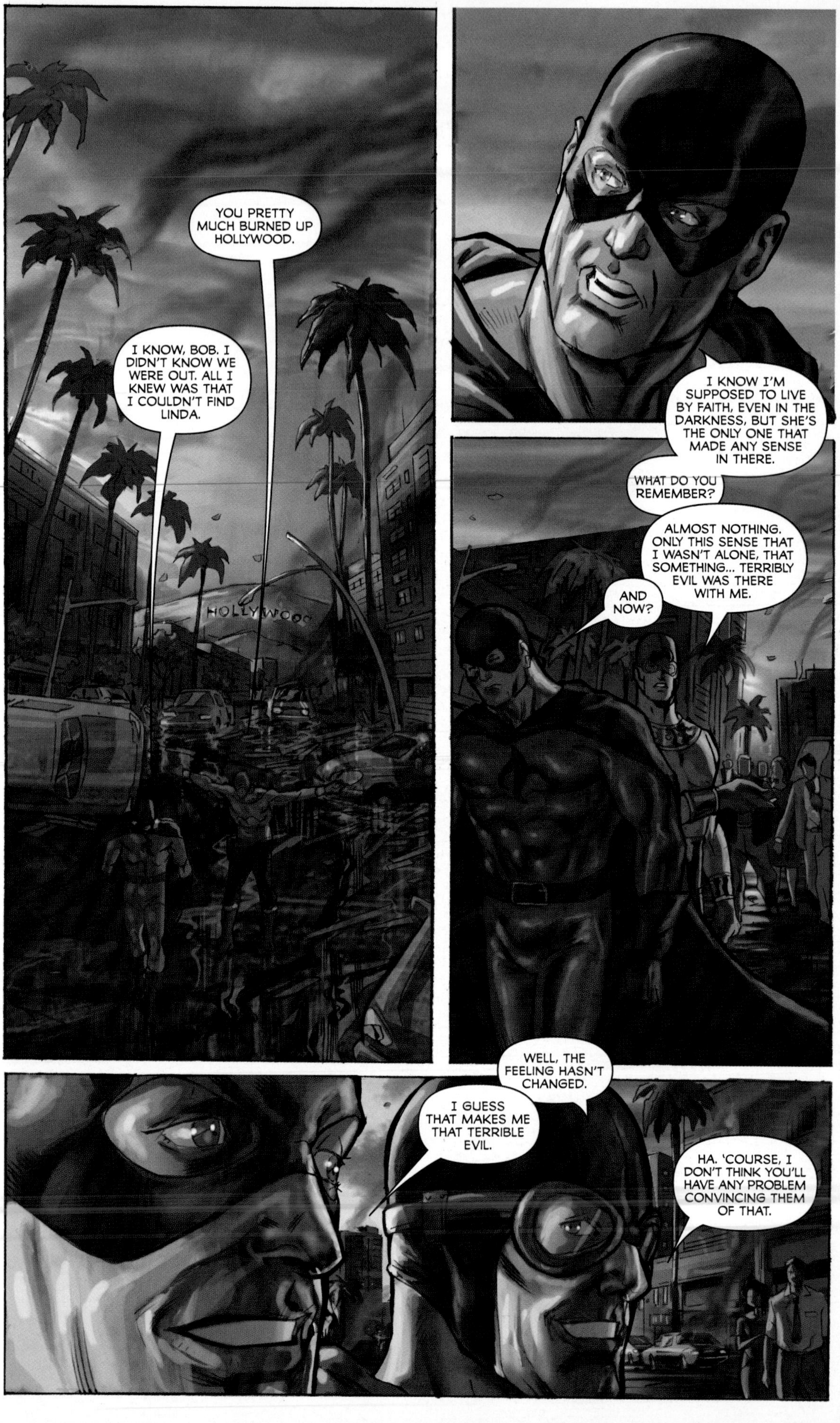
YOU PRETTY MUCH BURNED UP HOLLYWOOD.
I KNOW, BOB. I DIDN'T KNOW WE WERE OUT. ALL I KNEW WAS THAT I COULDN'T FIND LINDA.
HOLLYWOO
I KNOW I'M SUPPOSED TO LIVE BY FAITH, EVEN IN THE DARKNESS, BUT SHE'S THE ONLY ONE THAT MADE ANY SENSE IN THERE.
WHAT DO YOU REMEMBER?
ALMOST NOTHING. ONLY THIS SENSE THAT I WASN'T ALONE, THAT SOMETHING... TERRIBLY EVIL WAS THERE WITH ME.
AND NOW?
WELL, THE FEELING HASN'T CHANGED.
I GUESS THAT MAKES ME THAT TERRIBLE EVIL.
HA. 'COURSE, I DON'T THINK YOU'LL HAVE ANY PROBLEM CONVINCING THEM OF THAT.

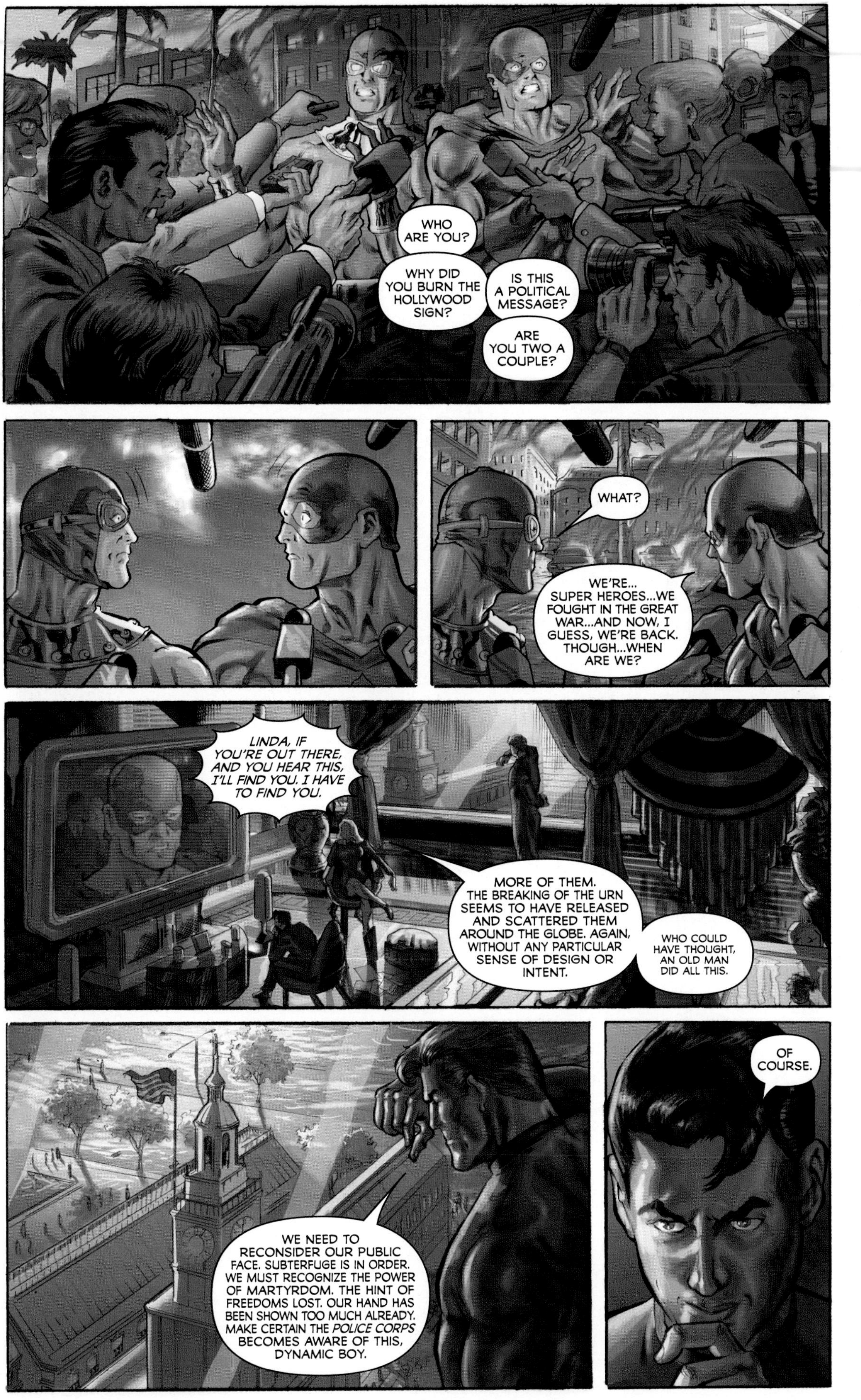
WHO ARE YOU?
WHY DID YOU BURN THE HOLLYWOOD SIGN?
IS THIS A POLITICAL MESSAGE?
ARE YOU TWO A COUPLE?
WHAT?
WE'RE... SUPER HEROES...WE FOUGHT IN THE GREAT WAR...AND NOW, I GUESS, WE'RE BACK. THOUGH...WHEN ARE WE?
LINDA, IF YOU'RE OUT THERE, AND YOU HEAR THIS, I'LL FIND YOU. I HAVE TO FIND YOU.
MORE OF THEM. THE BREAKING OF THE URN SEEMS TO HAVE RELEASED AND SCATTERED THEM AROUND THE GLOBE. AGAIN, WITHOUT ANY PARTICULAR SENSE OF DESIGN OR INTENT.
WHO COULD HAVE THOUGHT, AN OLD MAN DID ALL THIS.
WE NEED TO RECONSIDER OUR PUBLIC FACE. SUBTERFUGE IS IN ORDER. WE MUST RECOGNIZE THE POWER OF MARTYRDOM. THE HINT OF FREEDOMS LOST. OUR HAND HAS BEEN SHOWN TOO MUCH ALREADY. MAKE CERTAIN THE *POLICE CORPS* BECOMES AWARE OF THIS, DYNAMIC BOY.
OF COURSE.

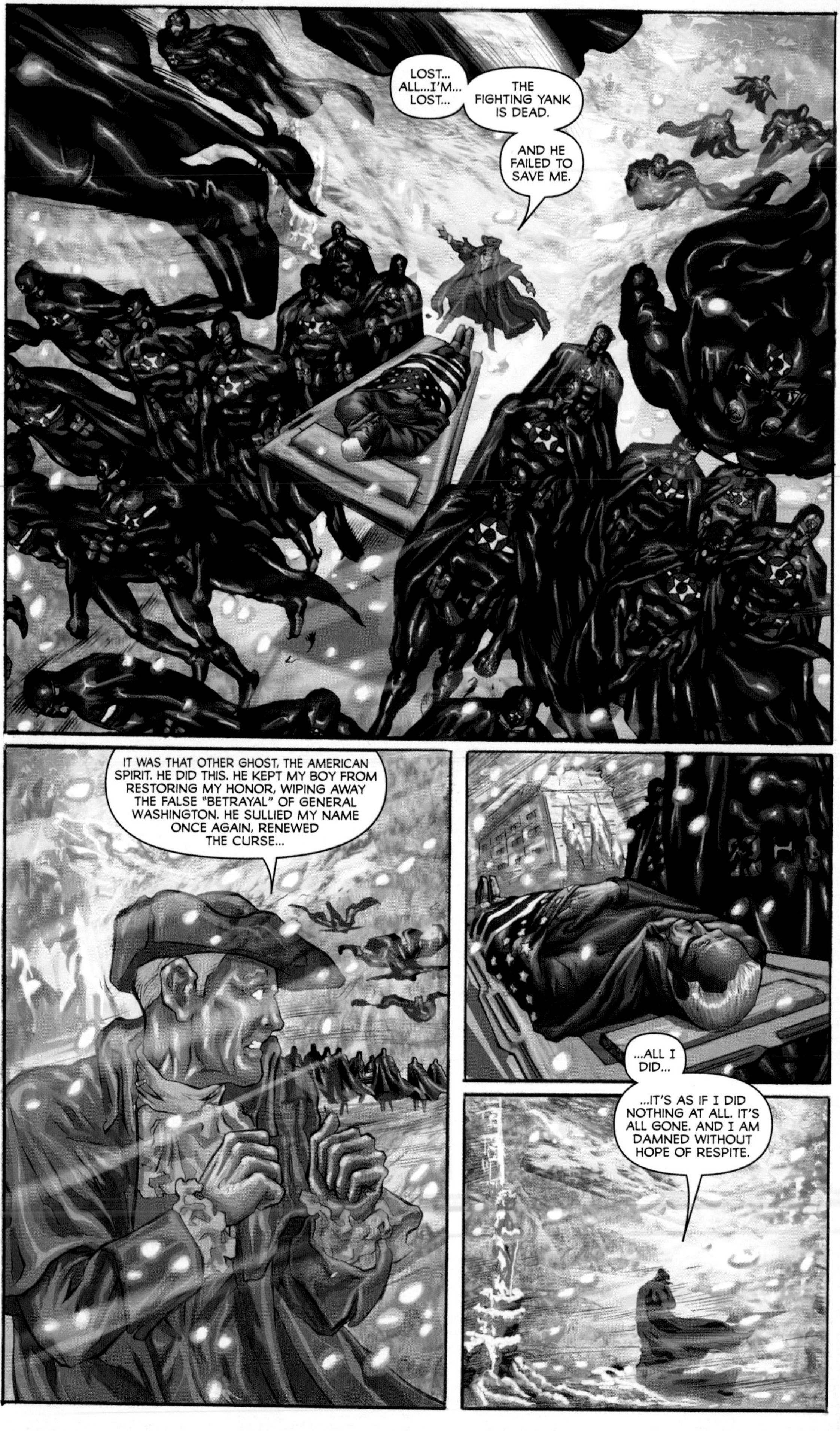
LOST... ALL...I'M... LOST...
THE FIGHTING YANK IS DEAD.
AND HE FAILED TO SAVE ME.
IT WAS THAT OTHER GHOST, THE AMERICAN SPIRIT. HE DID THIS. HE KEPT MY BOY FROM RESTORING MY HONOR, WIPING AWAY THE FALSE "BETRAYAL" OF GENERAL WASHINGTON. HE SULLIED MY NAME ONCE AGAIN, RENEWED THE CURSE...
...ALL I DID...
...IT'S AS IF I DID NOTHING AT ALL. IT'S ALL GONE. AND I AM DAMNED WITHOUT HOPE OF RESPITE.

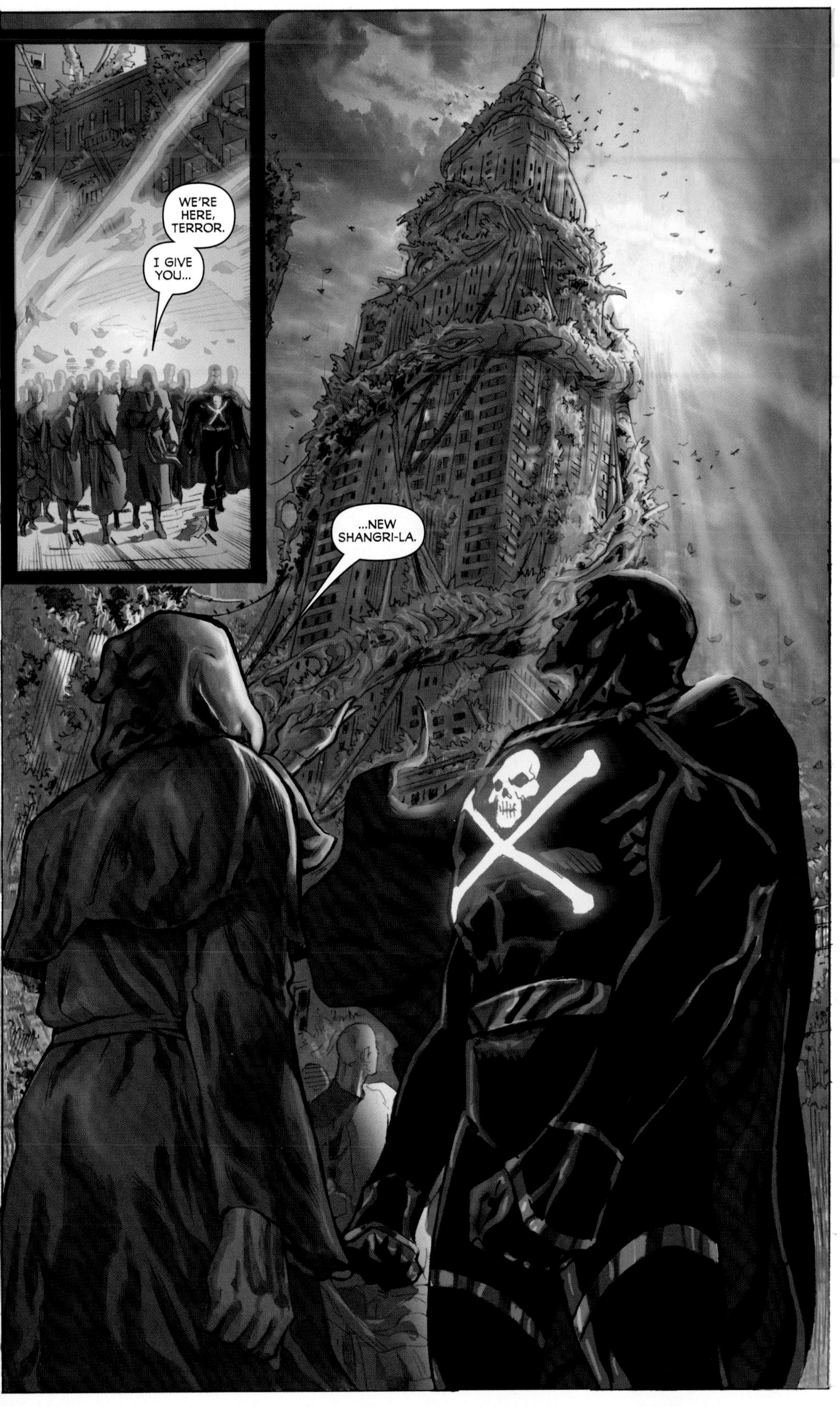
WE'RE HERE, TERROR.
I GIVE YOU...
...NEW SHANGRI-LA.

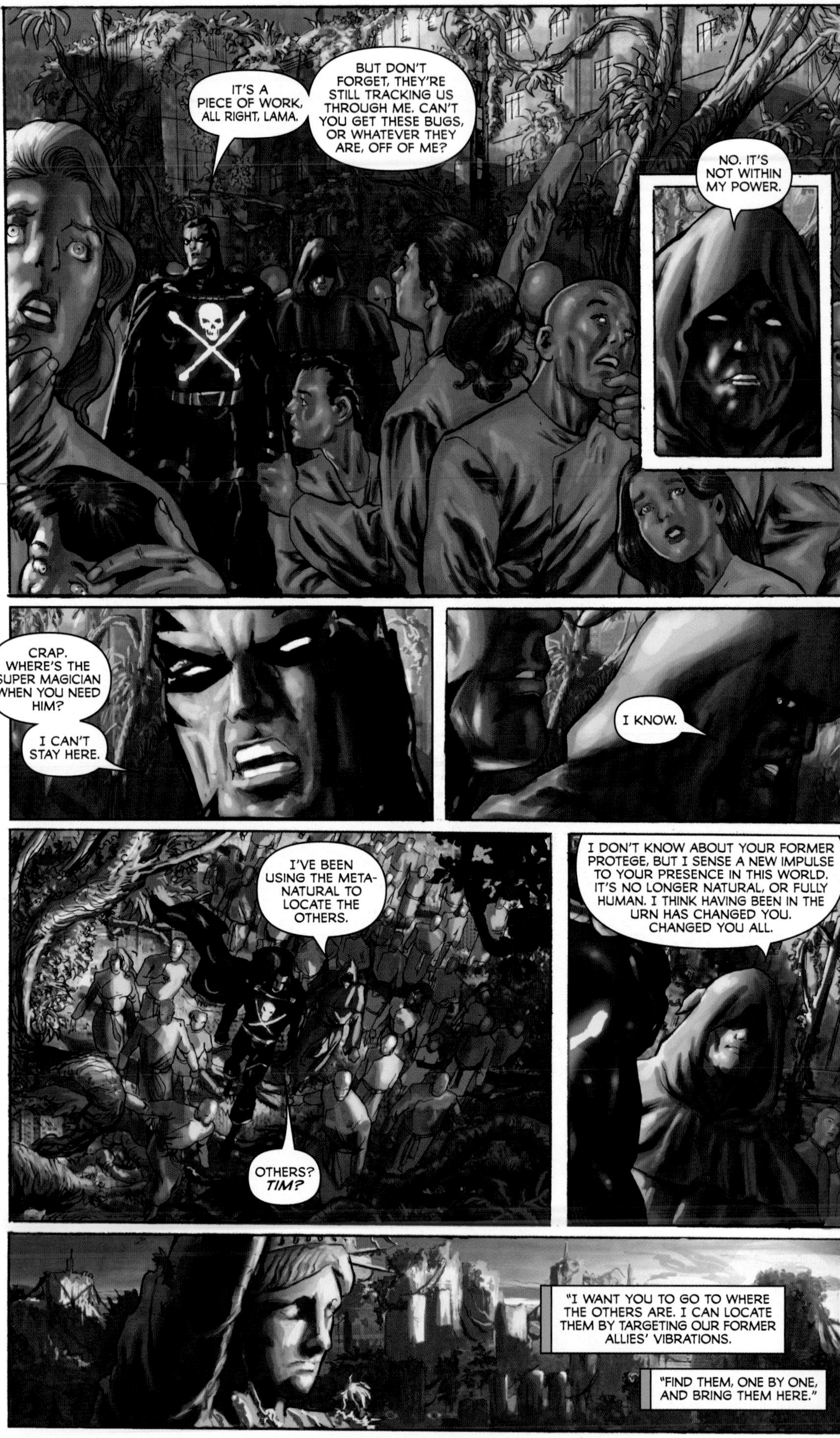
IT'S A PIECE OF WORK, ALL RIGHT, LAMA.
BUT DON'T FORGET, THEY'RE STILL TRACKING US THROUGH ME. CAN'T YOU GET THESE BUGS, OR WHATEVER THEY ARE, OFF OF ME?
NO. IT'S NOT WITHIN MY POWER.
CRAP. WHERE'S THE SUPER MAGICIAN WHEN YOU NEED HIM?
I CAN'T STAY HERE.
I KNOW.
I'VE BEEN USING THE META-NATURAL TO LOCATE THE OTHERS.
OTHERS? *TIM?*
I DON'T KNOW ABOUT YOUR FORMER PROTEGE, BUT I SENSE A NEW IMPULSE TO YOUR PRESENCE IN THIS WORLD. IT'S NO LONGER NATURAL, OR FULLY HUMAN. I THINK HAVING BEEN IN THE URN HAS CHANGED YOU. CHANGED YOU ALL.
"I WANT YOU TO GO TO WHERE THE OTHERS ARE. I CAN LOCATE THEM BY TARGETING OUR FORMER ALLIES' VIBRATIONS.
"FIND THEM, ONE BY ONE, AND BRING THEM HERE."

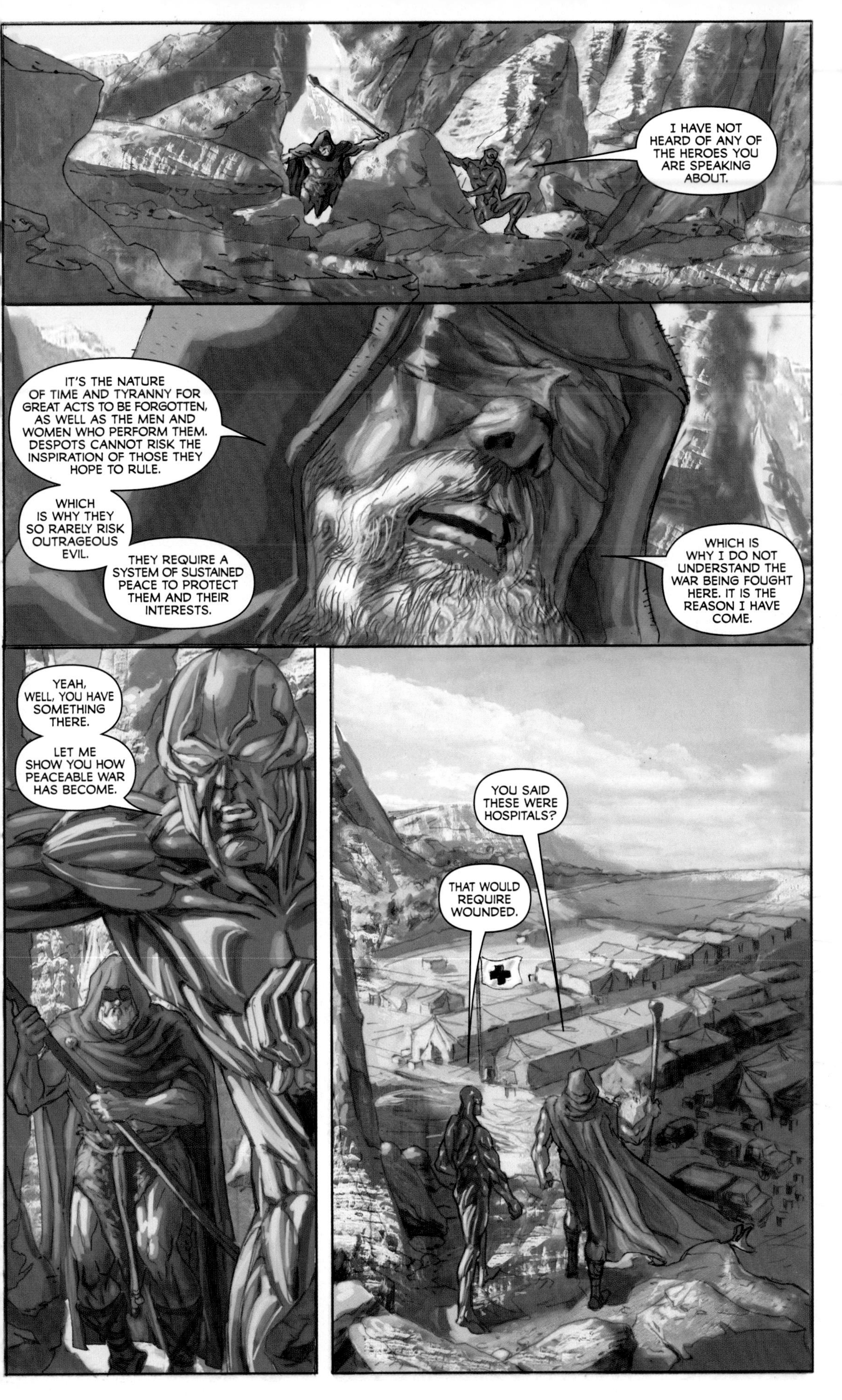
I HAVE NOT HEARD OF ANY OF THE HEROES YOU ARE SPEAKING ABOUT.
IT'S THE NATURE OF TIME AND TYRANNY FOR GREAT ACTS TO BE FORGOTTEN, AS WELL AS THE MEN AND WOMEN WHO PERFORM THEM. DESPOTS CANNOT RISK THE INSPIRATION OF THOSE THEY HOPE TO RULE.
WHICH IS WHY THEY SO RARELY RISK OUTRAGEOUS EVIL.
THEY REQUIRE A SYSTEM OF SUSTAINED PEACE TO PROTECT THEM AND THEIR INTERESTS.
WHICH IS WHY I DO NOT UNDERSTAND THE WAR BEING FOUGHT HERE. IT IS THE REASON I HAVE COME.
YEAH, WELL, YOU HAVE SOMETHING THERE.
LET ME SHOW YOU HOW PEACEABLE WAR HAS BECOME.
YOU SAID THESE WERE HOSPITALS?
THAT WOULD REQUIRE WOUNDED.

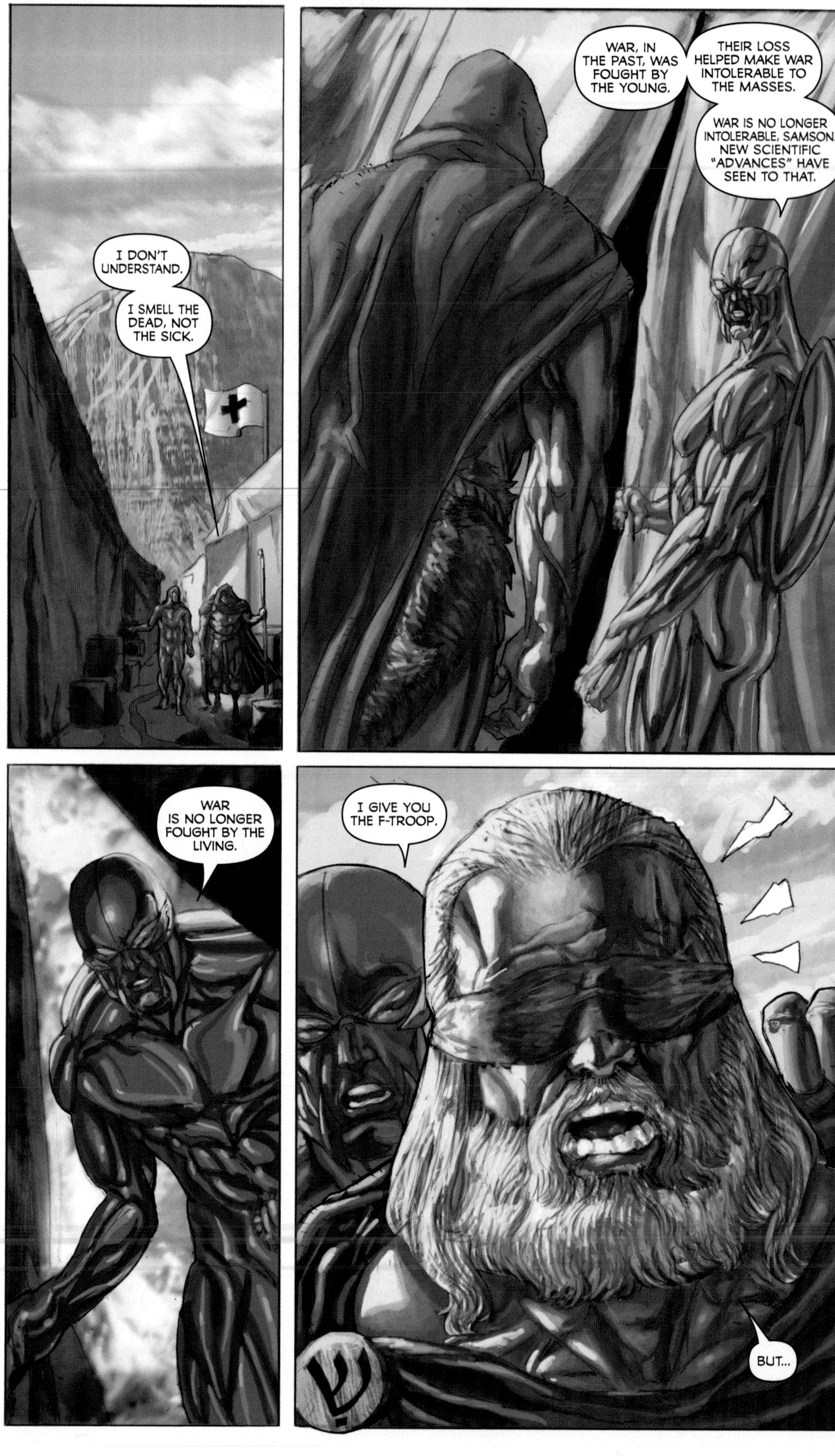
I DON'T UNDERSTAND.
I SMELL THE DEAD, NOT THE SICK.
WAR, IN THE PAST, WAS FOUGHT BY THE YOUNG.
THEIR LOSS HELPED MAKE WAR INTOLERABLE TO THE MASSES.
WAR IS NO LONGER INTOLERABLE, SAMSON. NEW SCIENTIFIC "ADVANCES" HAVE SEEN TO THAT.
WAR IS NO LONGER FOUGHT BY THE LIVING.
I GIVE YOU THE F-TROOP.
BUT...

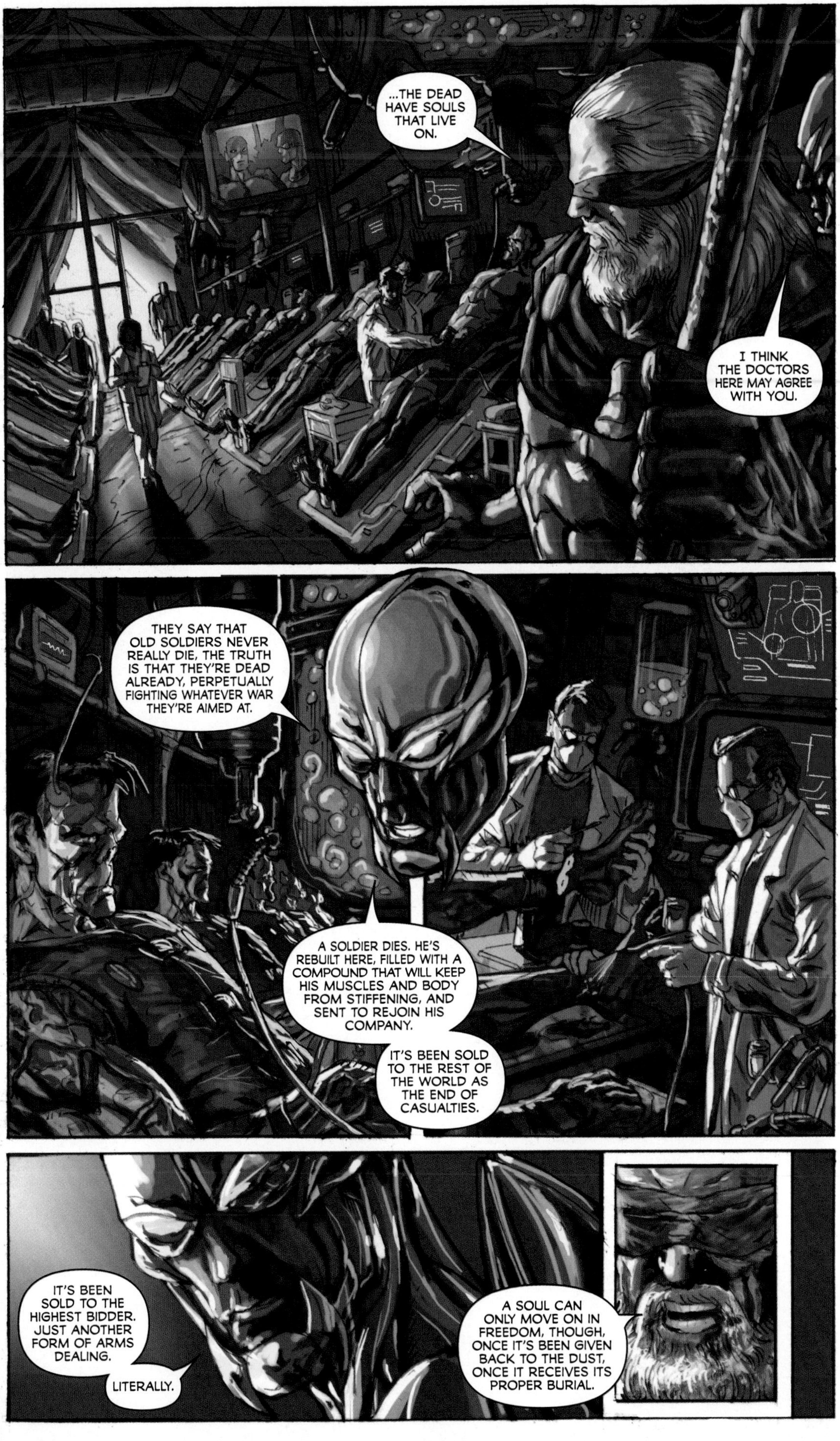
...THE DEAD HAVE SOULS THAT LIVE ON.
I THINK THE DOCTORS HERE MAY AGREE WITH YOU.
THEY SAY THAT OLD SOLDIERS NEVER REALLY DIE, THE TRUTH IS THAT THEY'RE DEAD ALREADY, PERPETUALLY FIGHTING WHATEVER WAR THEY'RE AIMED AT.
A SOLDIER DIES. HE'S REBUILT HERE, FILLED WITH A COMPOUND THAT WILL KEEP HIS MUSCLES AND BODY FROM STIFFENING, AND SENT TO REJOIN HIS COMPANY.
IT'S BEEN SOLD TO THE REST OF THE WORLD AS THE END OF CASUALTIES.
IT'S BEEN SOLD TO THE HIGHEST BIDDER. JUST ANOTHER FORM OF ARMS DEALING.
LITERALLY.
A SOUL CAN ONLY MOVE ON IN FREEDOM, THOUGH, ONCE IT'S BEEN GIVEN BACK TO THE DUST, ONCE IT RECEIVES ITS PROPER BURIAL.

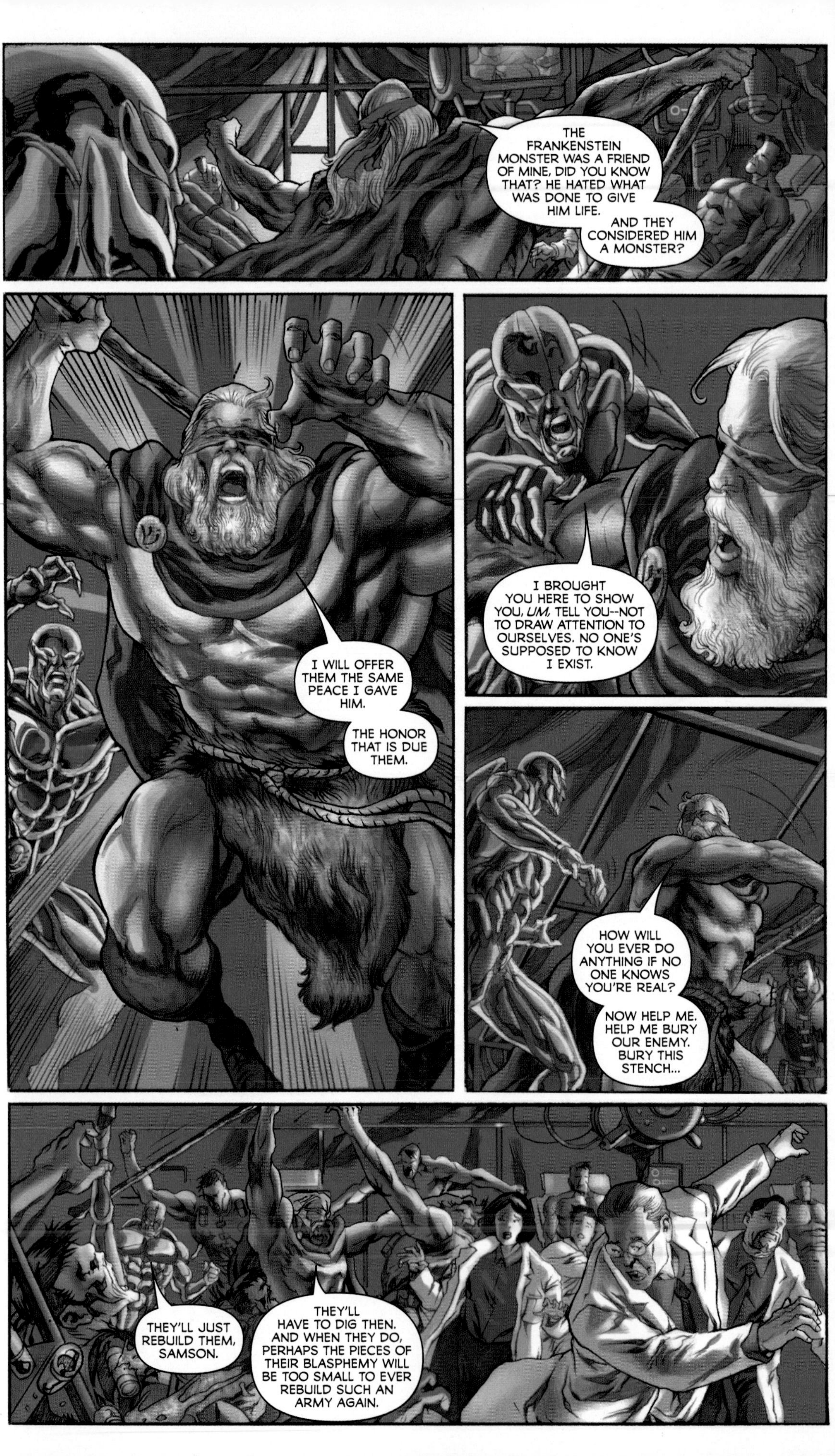
THE FRANKENSTEIN MONSTER WAS A FRIEND OF MINE, DID YOU KNOW THAT? HE HATED WHAT WAS DONE TO GIVE HIM LIFE.
AND THEY CONSIDERED HIM A MONSTER?
I WILL OFFER THEM THE SAME PEACE I GAVE HIM.
THE HONOR THAT IS DUE THEM.
I BROUGHT YOU HERE TO SHOW YOU, *UM,* TELL YOU--NOT TO DRAW ATTENTION TO OURSELVES. NO ONE'S SUPPOSED TO KNOW I EXIST.
HOW WILL YOU EVER DO ANYTHING IF NO ONE KNOWS YOU'RE REAL?
NOW HELP ME. HELP ME BURY OUR ENEMY. BURY THIS STENCH...
THEY'LL JUST REBUILD THEM, SAMSON.
THEY'LL HAVE TO DIG THEN. AND WHEN THEY DO, PERHAPS THE PIECES OF THEIR BLASPHEMY WILL BE TOO SMALL TO EVER REBUILD SUCH AN ARMY AGAIN.

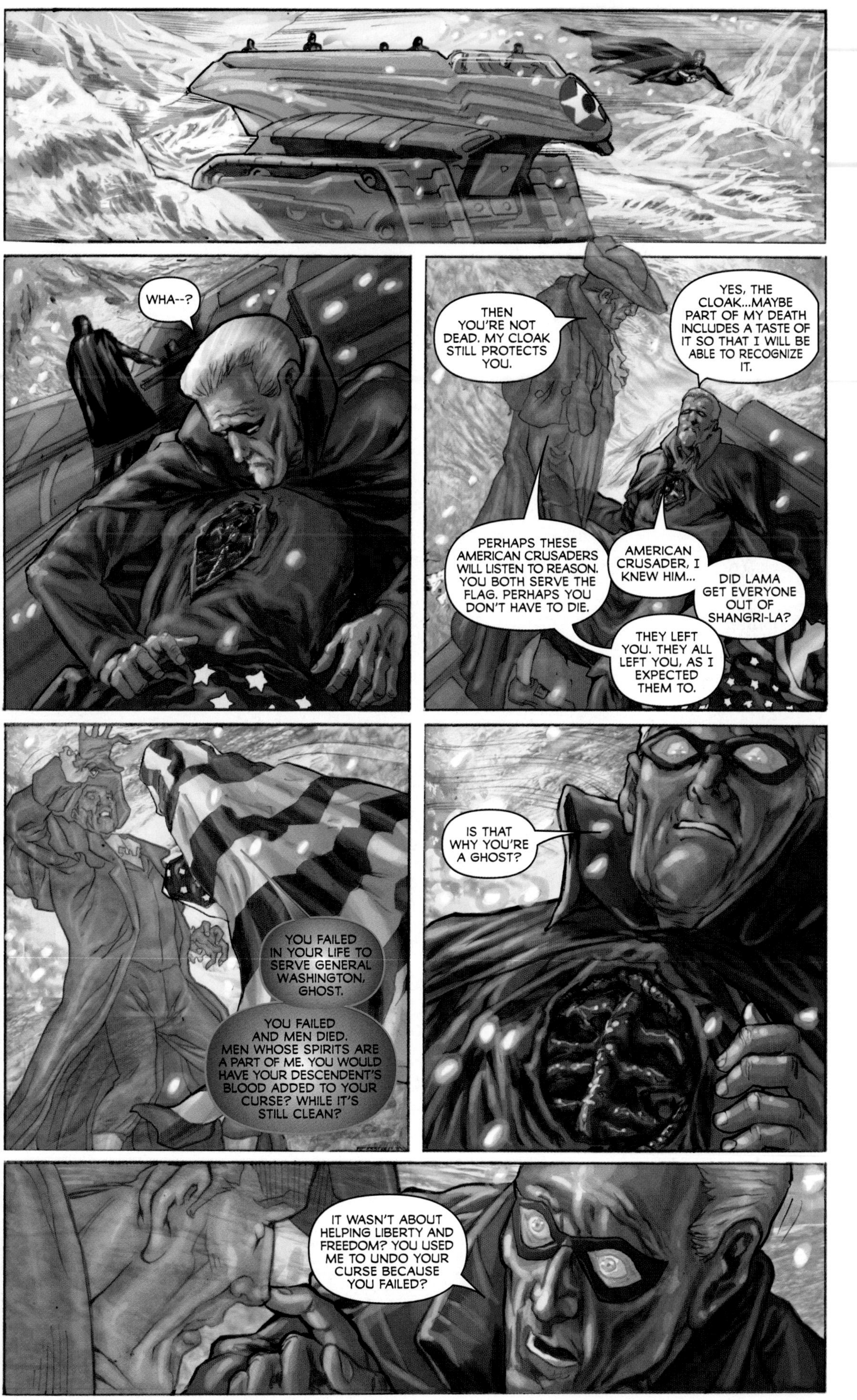
WHA--?
THEN YOU'RE NOT DEAD. MY CLOAK STILL PROTECTS YOU.
YES, THE CLOAK...MAYBE PART OF MY DEATH INCLUDES A TASTE OF IT SO THAT I WILL BE ABLE TO RECOGNIZE IT.
PERHAPS THESE AMERICAN CRUSADERS WILL LISTEN TO REASON. YOU BOTH SERVE THE FLAG. PERHAPS YOU DON'T HAVE TO DIE.
AMERICAN CRUSADER, I KNEW HIM...
DID LAMA GET EVERYONE OUT OF SHANGRI-LA?
THEY LEFT YOU. THEY ALL LEFT YOU, AS I EXPECTED THEM TO.
YOU FAILED IN YOUR LIFE TO SERVE GENERAL WASHINGTON, GHOST.
YOU FAILED AND MEN DIED. MEN WHOSE SPIRITS ARE A PART OF ME. YOU WOULD HAVE YOUR DESCENDENT'S BLOOD ADDED TO YOUR CURSE? WHILE IT'S STILL CLEAN?
IS THAT WHY YOU'RE A GHOST?
IT WASN'T ABOUT HELPING LIBERTY AND FREEDOM? YOU USED ME TO UNDO YOUR CURSE BECAUSE YOU FAILED?

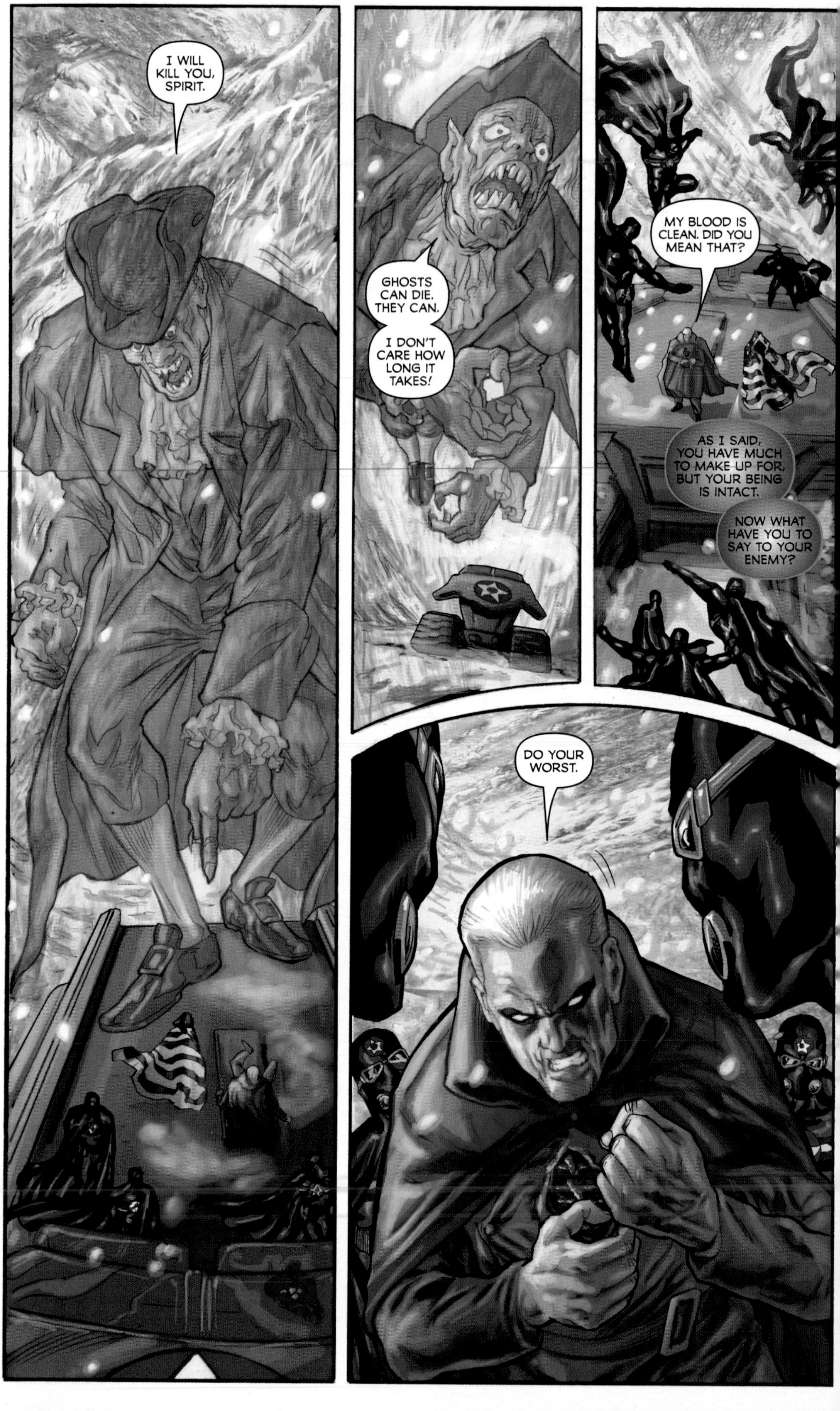
I WILL KILL YOU, SPIRIT.
GHOSTS CAN DIE. THEY CAN.
I DON'T CARE HOW LONG IT TAKES!
MY BLOOD IS CLEAN. DID YOU MEAN THAT?
AS I SAID, YOU HAVE MUCH TO MAKE UP FOR, BUT YOUR BEING IS INTACT.
NOW WHAT HAVE YOU TO SAY TO YOUR ENEMY?
DO YOUR WORST.

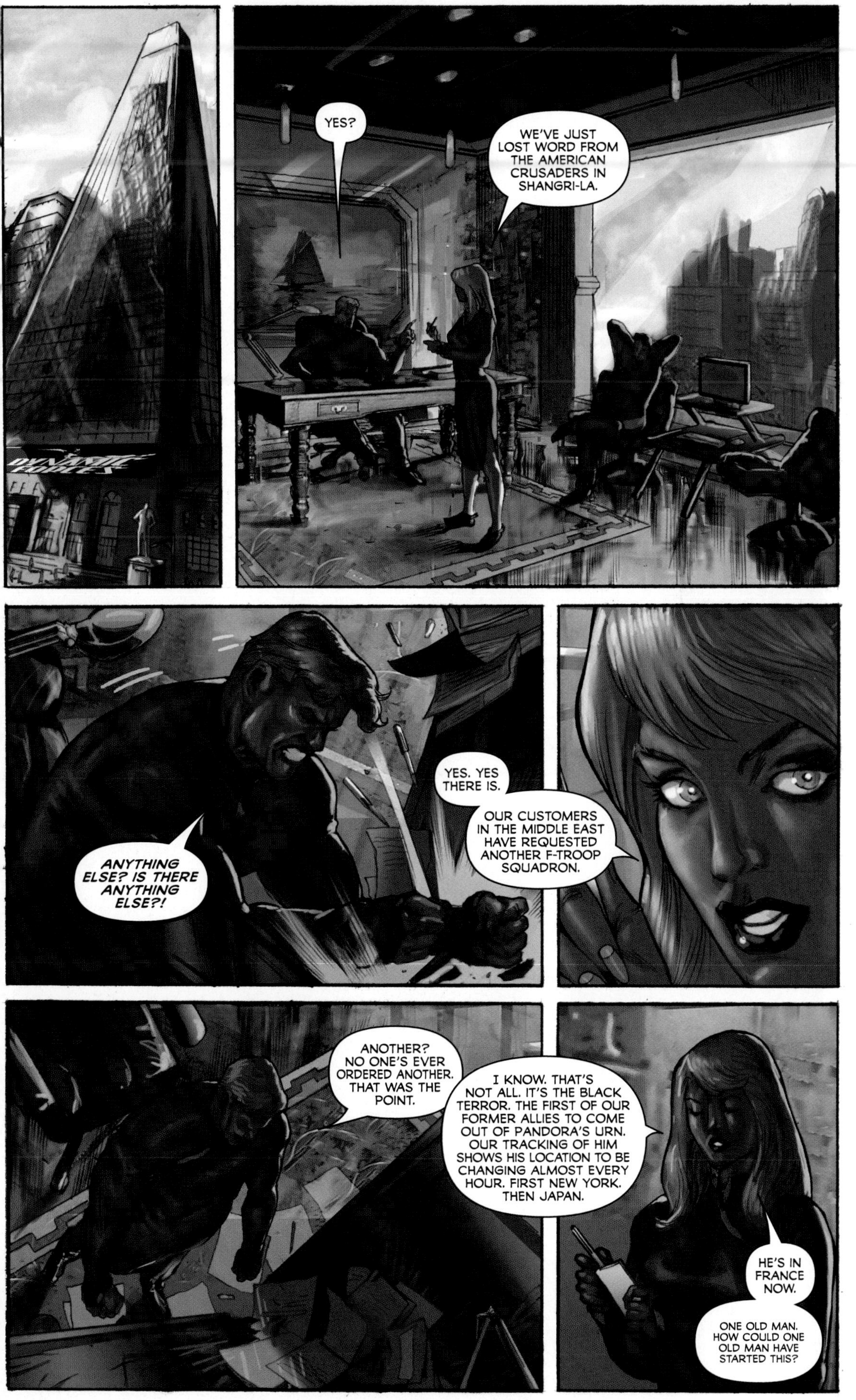
DYNAMIC FORCES
YES?
WE'VE JUST LOST WORD FROM THE AMERICAN CRUSADERS IN SHANGRI-LA.
ANYTHING ELSE? IS THERE ANYTHING ELSE?!
YES. YES THERE IS.
OUR CUSTOMERS IN THE MIDDLE EAST HAVE REQUESTED ANOTHER F-TROOP SQUADRON.
ANOTHER? NO ONE'S EVER ORDERED ANOTHER. THAT WAS THE POINT.
I KNOW. THAT'S NOT ALL. IT'S THE BLACK TERROR. THE FIRST OF OUR FORMER ALLIES TO COME OUT OF PANDORA'S URN. OUR TRACKING OF HIM SHOWS HIS LOCATION TO BE CHANGING ALMOST EVERY HOUR. FIRST NEW YORK. THEN JAPAN.
HE'S IN FRANCE NOW.
ONE OLD MAN. HOW COULD ONE OLD MAN HAVE STARTED THIS?

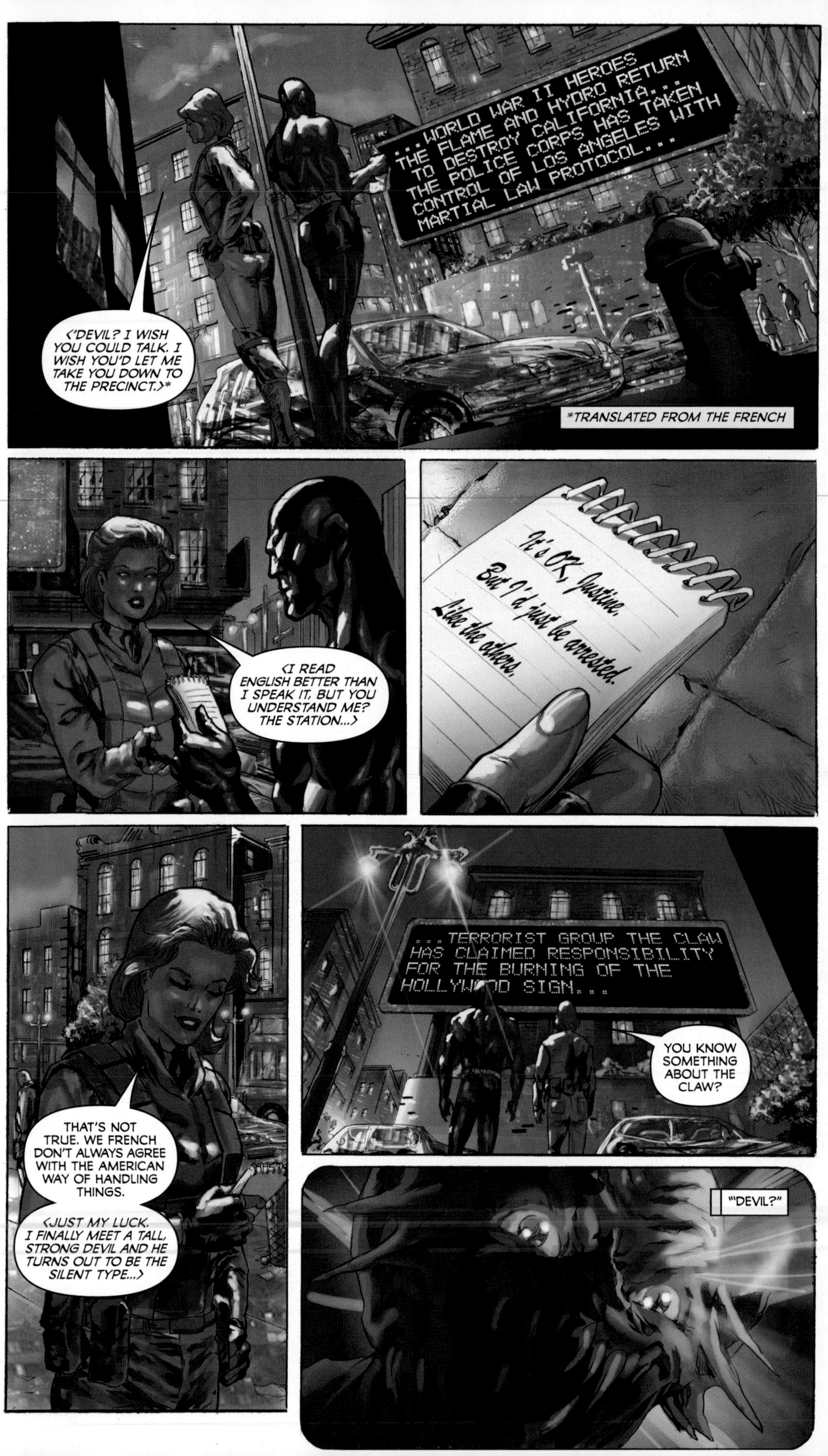
...WORLD WAR II HEROES THE FLAME AND HYDRO RETURN TO DESTROY CALIFORNIA... THE POLICE CORPS HAS TAKEN CONTROL OF LOS ANGELES WITH MARTIAL LAW PROTOCOL...
<'DEVIL? I WISH YOU COULD TALK. I WISH YOU'D LET ME TAKE YOU DOWN TO THE PRECINCT.>*
*TRANSLATED FROM THE FRENCH
<I READ ENGLISH BETTER THAN I SPEAK IT, BUT YOU UNDERSTAND ME? THE STATION...>
It's OK, Justine. But I'd just be arrested. Like the others.
THAT'S NOT TRUE. WE FRENCH DON'T ALWAYS AGREE WITH THE AMERICAN WAY OF HANDLING THINGS.
<JUST MY LUCK. I FINALLY MEET A TALL, STRONG DEVIL AND HE TURNS OUT TO BE THE SILENT TYPE...>
...TERRORIST GROUP THE CLAW HAS CLAIMED RESPONSIBILITY FOR THE BURNING OF THE HOLLYWOOD SIGN...
YOU KNOW SOMETHING ABOUT THE CLAW?
"DEVIL?"

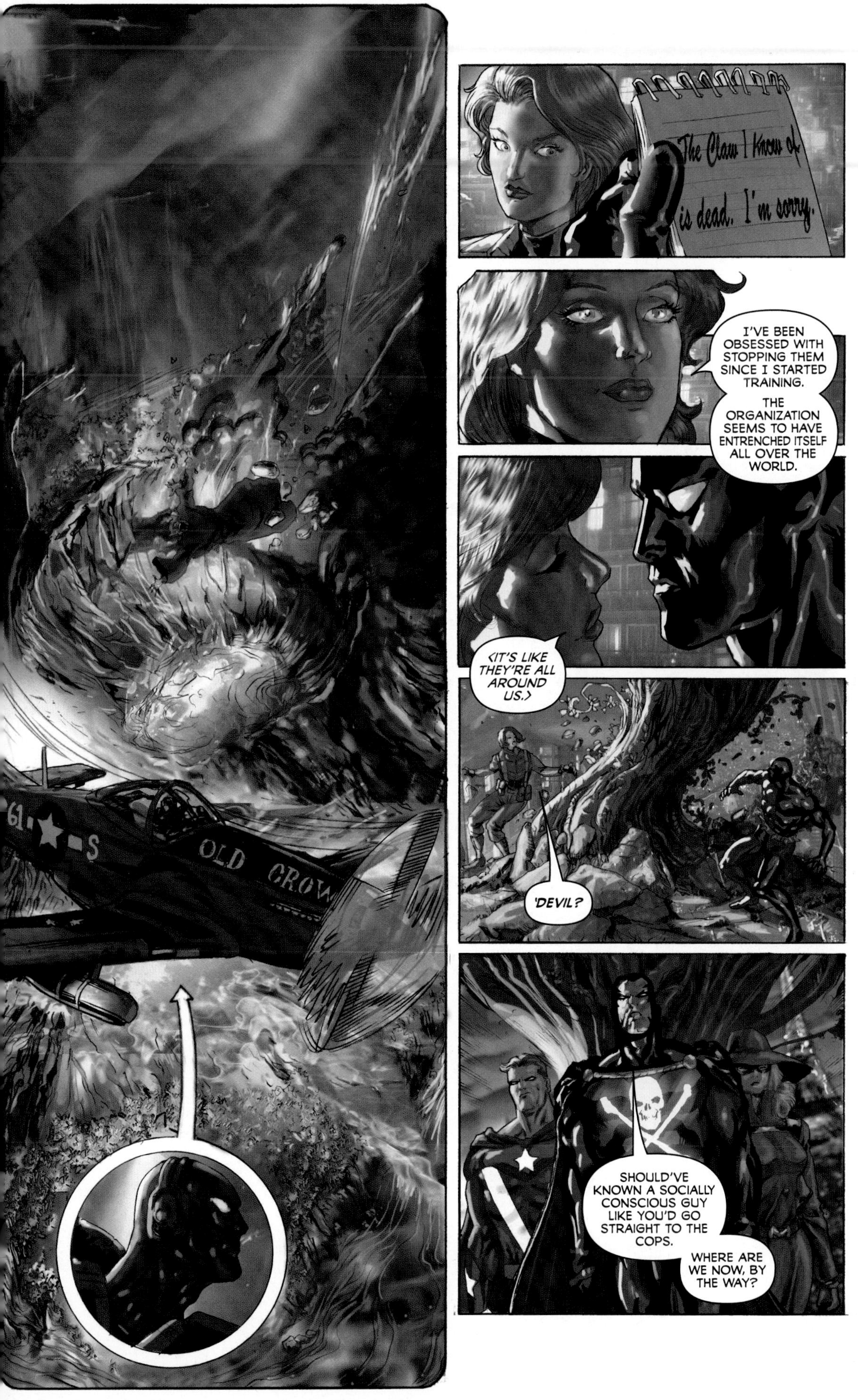
61 S
OLD CROW
The Claw I know of is dead. I'm sorry.
I'VE BEEN OBSESSED WITH STOPPING THEM SINCE I STARTED TRAINING.
THE ORGANIZATION SEEMS TO HAVE ENTRENCHED ITSELF ALL OVER THE WORLD.
<IT'S LIKE THEY'RE ALL AROUND US.>
'DEVIL?
SHOULD'VE KNOWN A SOCIALLY CONSCIOUS GUY LIKE YOU'D GO STRAIGHT TO THE COPS.
WHERE ARE WE NOW, BY THE WAY?

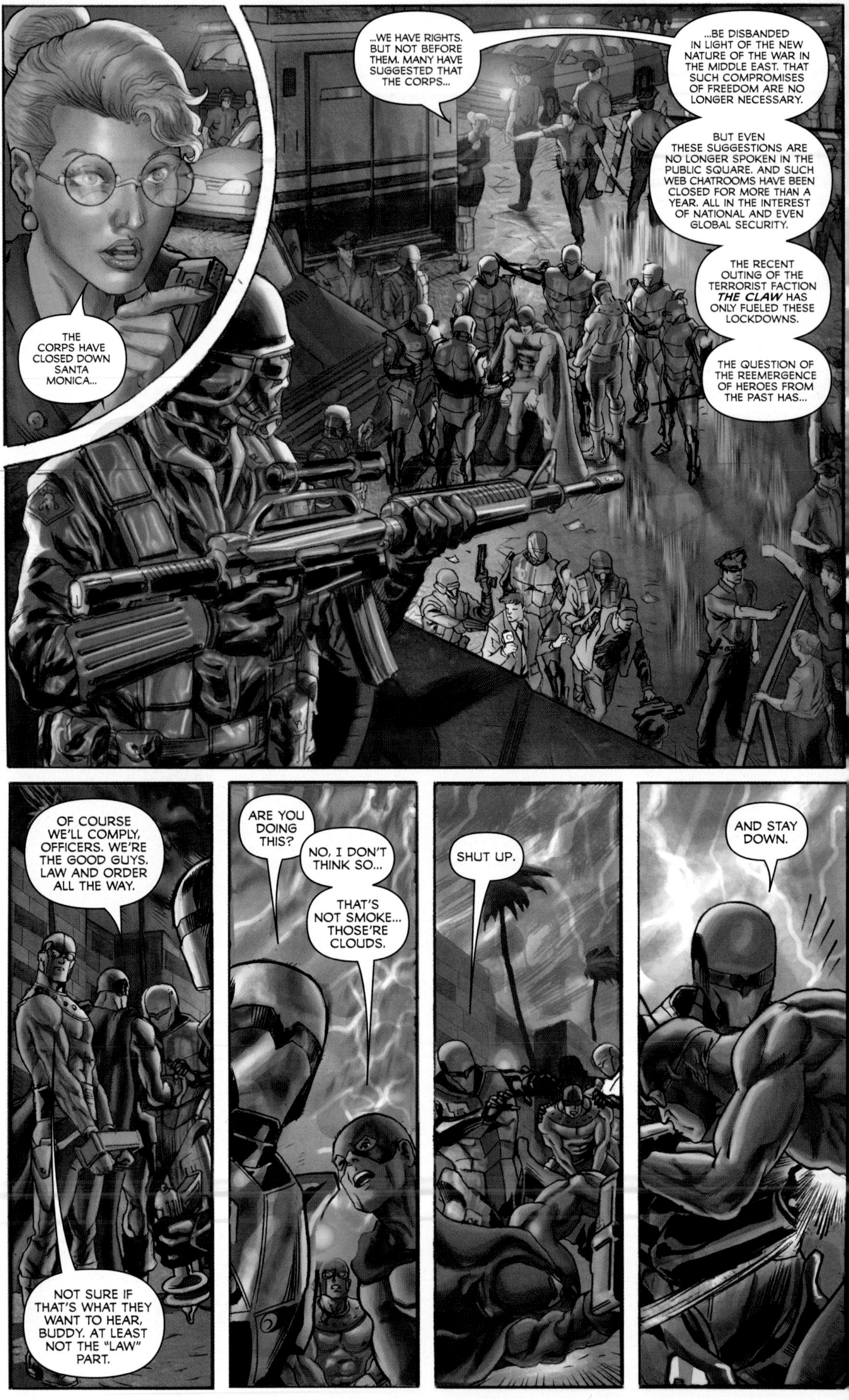
THE CORPS HAVE CLOSED DOWN SANTA MONICA...
...WE HAVE RIGHTS. BUT NOT BEFORE THEM. MANY HAVE SUGGESTED THAT THE CORPS...
...BE DISBANDED IN LIGHT OF THE NEW NATURE OF THE WAR IN THE MIDDLE EAST. THAT SUCH COMPROMISES OF FREEDOM ARE NO LONGER NECESSARY.
BUT EVEN THESE SUGGESTIONS ARE NO LONGER SPOKEN IN THE PUBLIC SQUARE. AND SUCH WEB CHATROOMS HAVE BEEN CLOSED FOR MORE THAN A YEAR. ALL IN THE INTEREST OF NATIONAL AND EVEN GLOBAL SECURITY.
THE RECENT OUTING OF THE TERRORIST FACTION *THE CLAW* HAS ONLY FUELED THESE LOCKDOWNS.
THE QUESTION OF THE REEMERGENCE OF HEROES FROM THE PAST HAS...
OF COURSE WE'LL COMPLY, OFFICERS. WE'RE THE GOOD GUYS. LAW AND ORDER ALL THE WAY.
NOT SURE IF THAT'S WHAT THEY WANT TO HEAR, BUDDY. AT LEAST NOT THE "LAW" PART.
ARE YOU DOING THIS?
NO, I DON'T THINK SO...
THAT'S NOT SMOKE... THOSE'RE CLOUDS.
SHUT UP.
AND STAY DOWN.

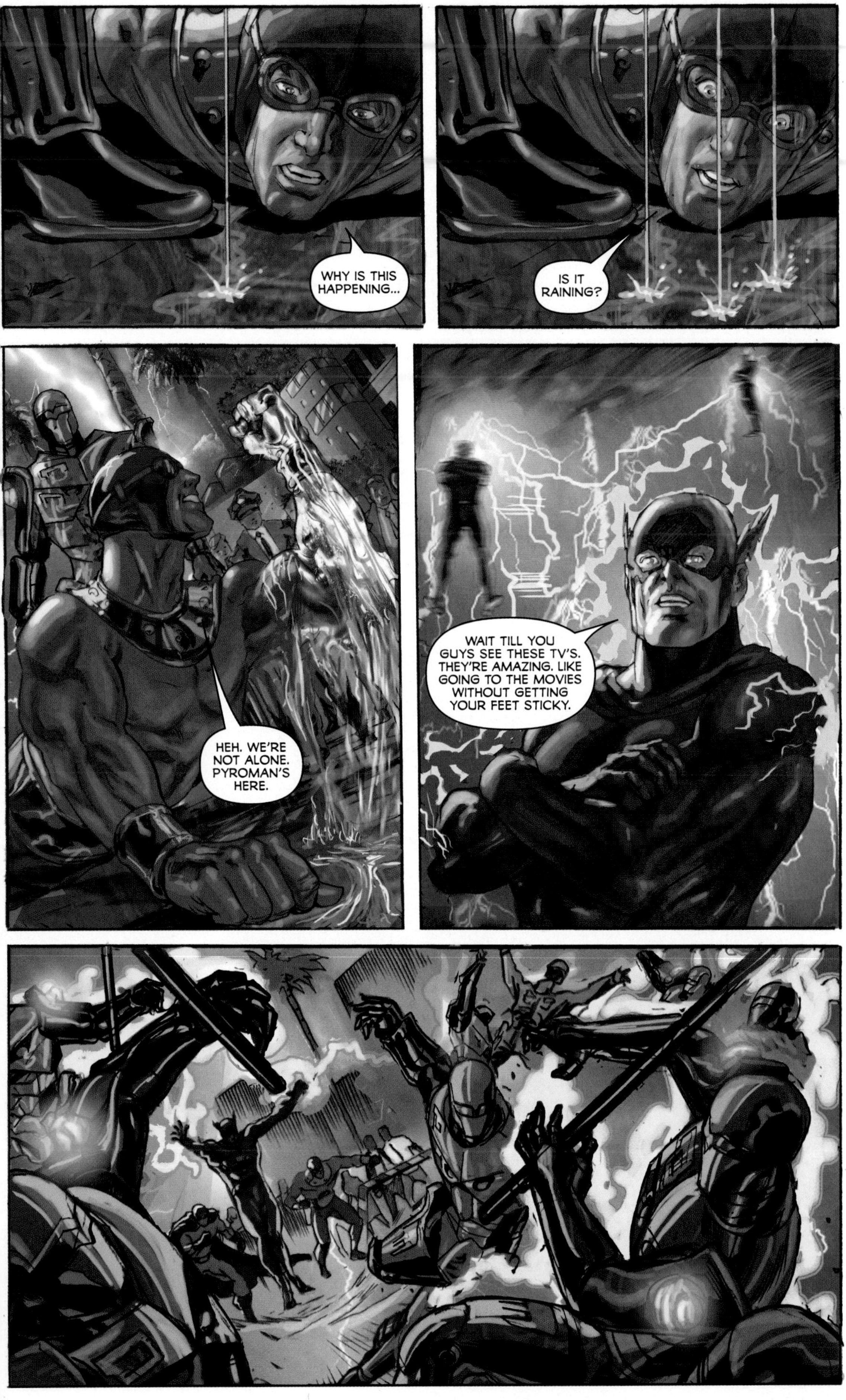
WHY IS THIS HAPPENING...
IS IT RAINING?
HEH. WE'RE NOT ALONE. PYROMAN'S HERE.
WAIT TILL YOU GUYS SEE THESE TV'S. THEY'RE AMAZING. LIKE GOING TO THE MOVIES WITHOUT GETTING YOUR FEET STICKY.

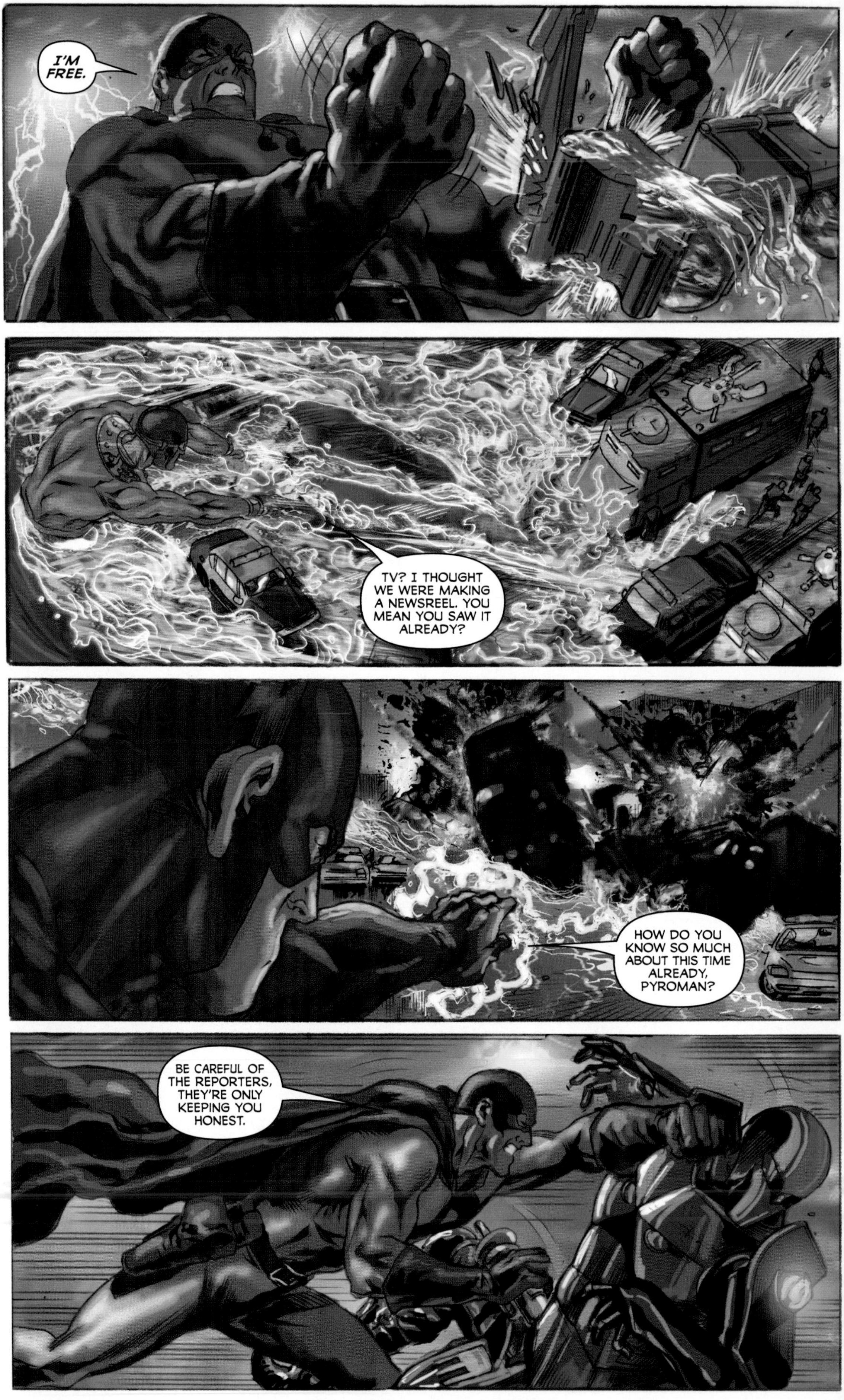
I'M FREE.
TV? I THOUGHT WE WERE MAKING A NEWSREEL. YOU MEAN YOU SAW IT ALREADY?
HOW DO YOU KNOW SO MUCH ABOUT THIS TIME ALREADY, PYROMAN?
BE CAREFUL OF THE REPORTERS, THEY'RE ONLY KEEPING YOU HONEST.

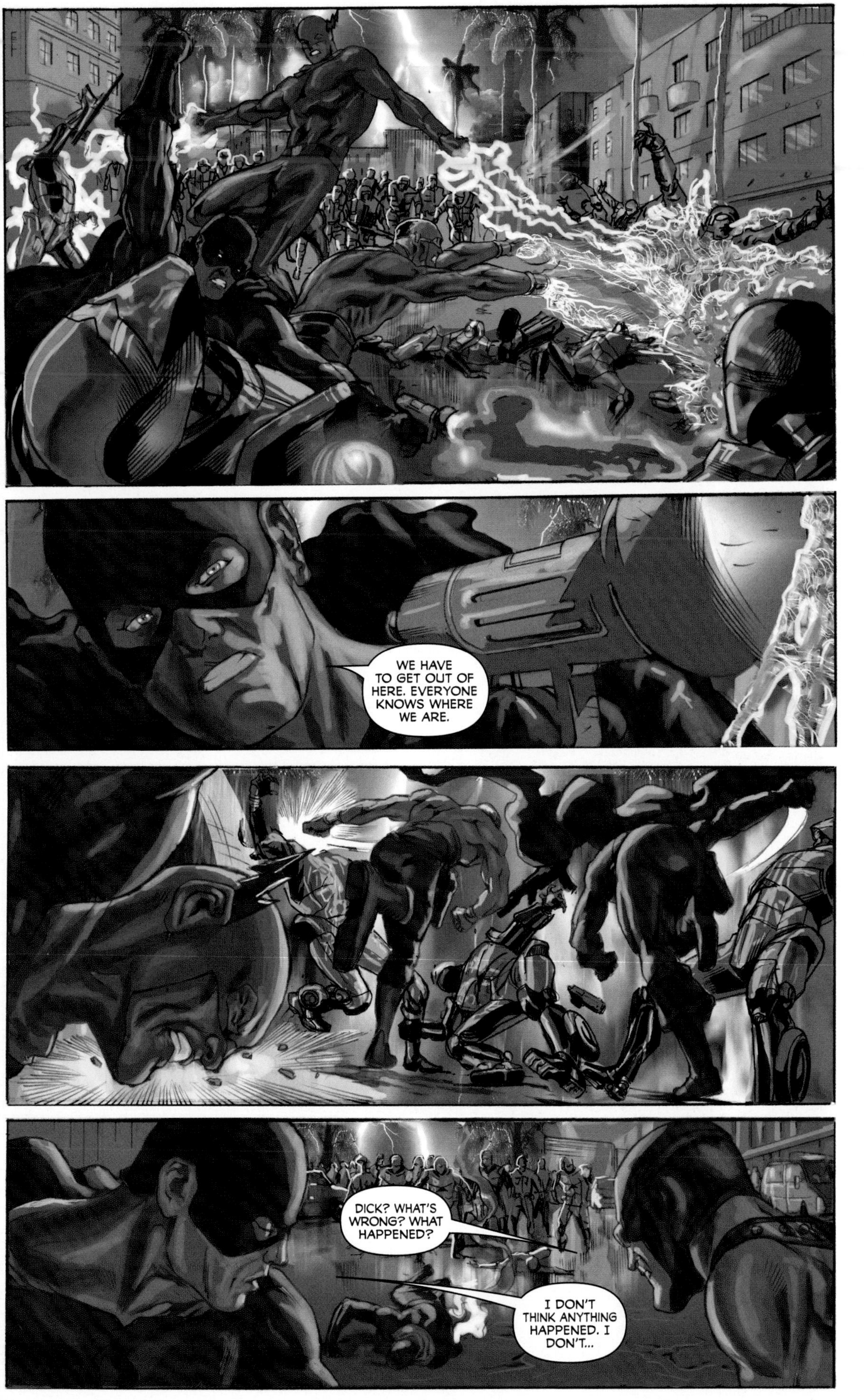
WE HAVE TO GET OUT OF HERE. EVERYONE KNOWS WHERE WE ARE.
DICK? WHAT'S WRONG? WHAT HAPPENED?
I DON'T THINK ANYTHING HAPPENED. I DON'T...

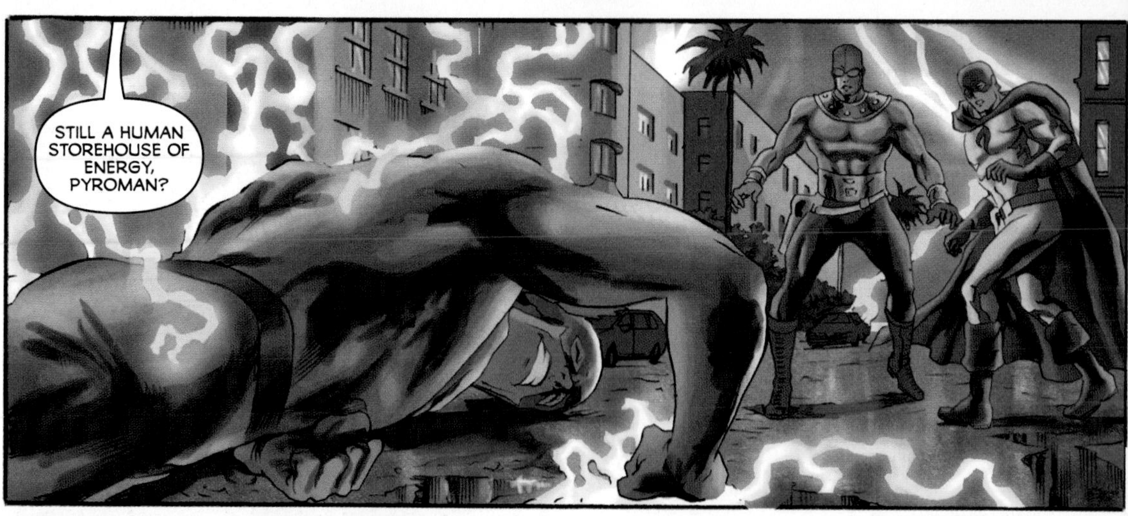
STILL A HUMAN STOREHOUSE OF ENERGY, PYROMAN?

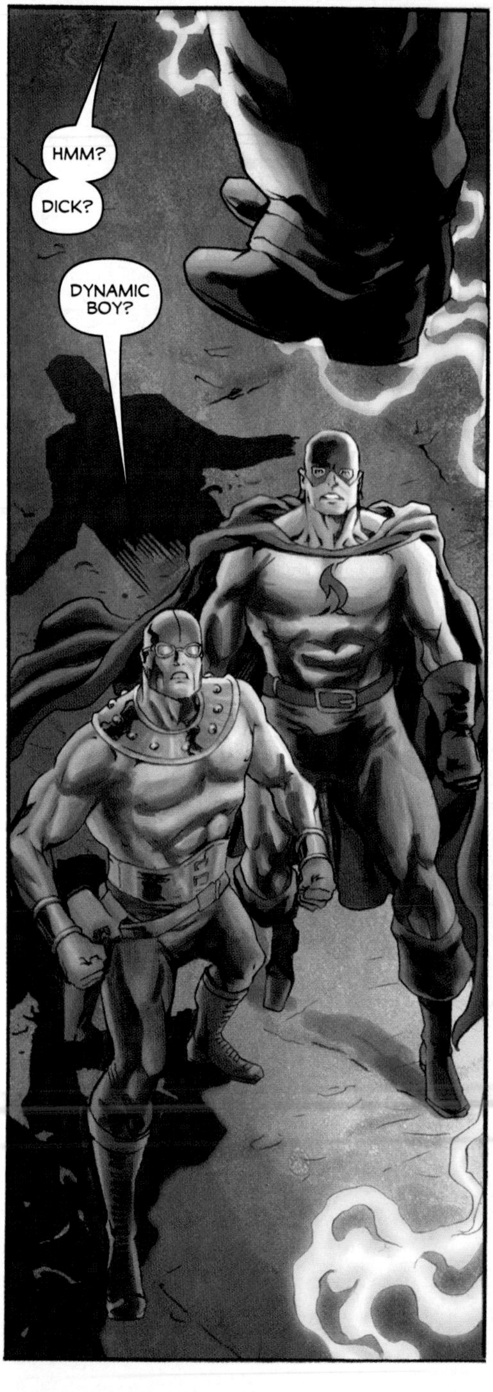
HMM?
DICK?
DYNAMIC BOY?

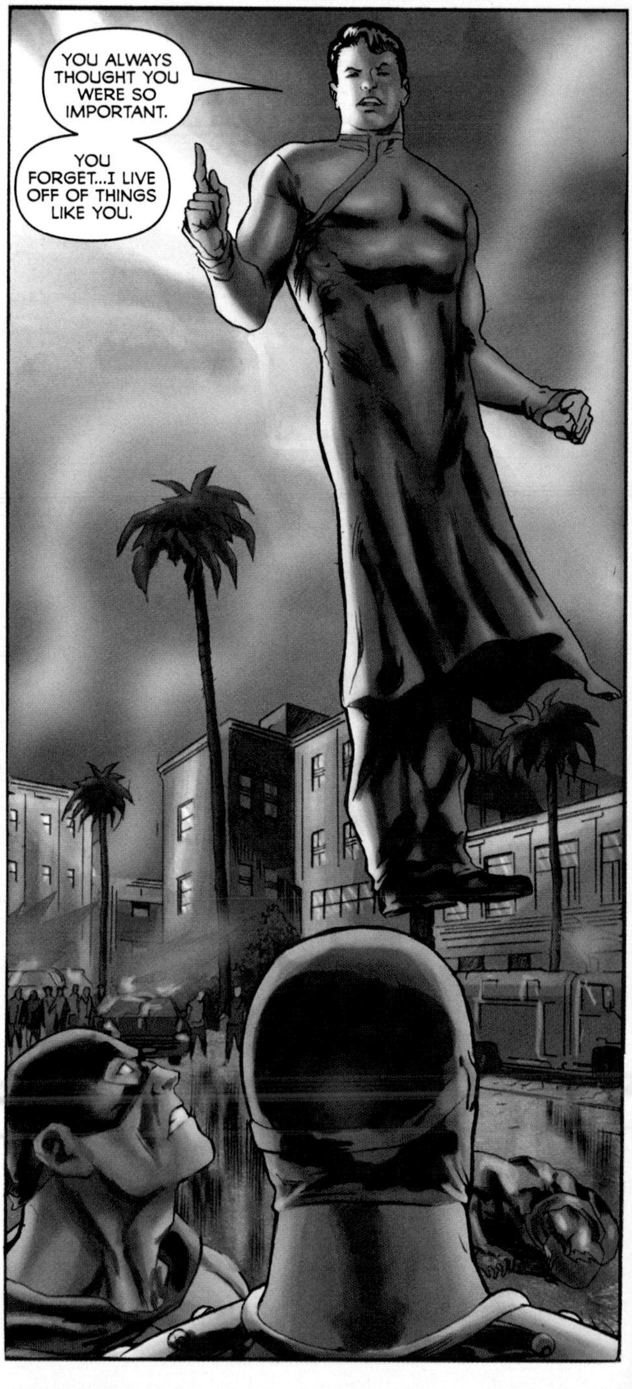
YOU ALWAYS THOUGHT YOU WERE SO IMPORTANT.
YOU FORGET...I LIVE OFF OF THINGS LIKE YOU.

ISSUE

5

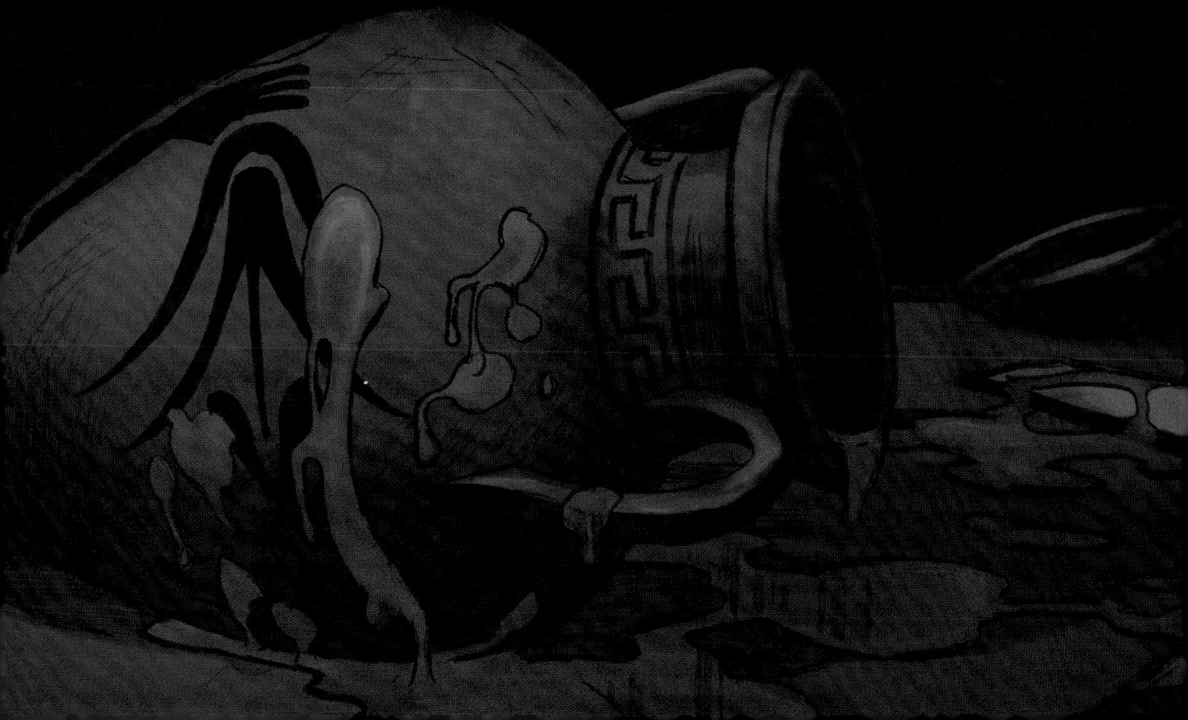

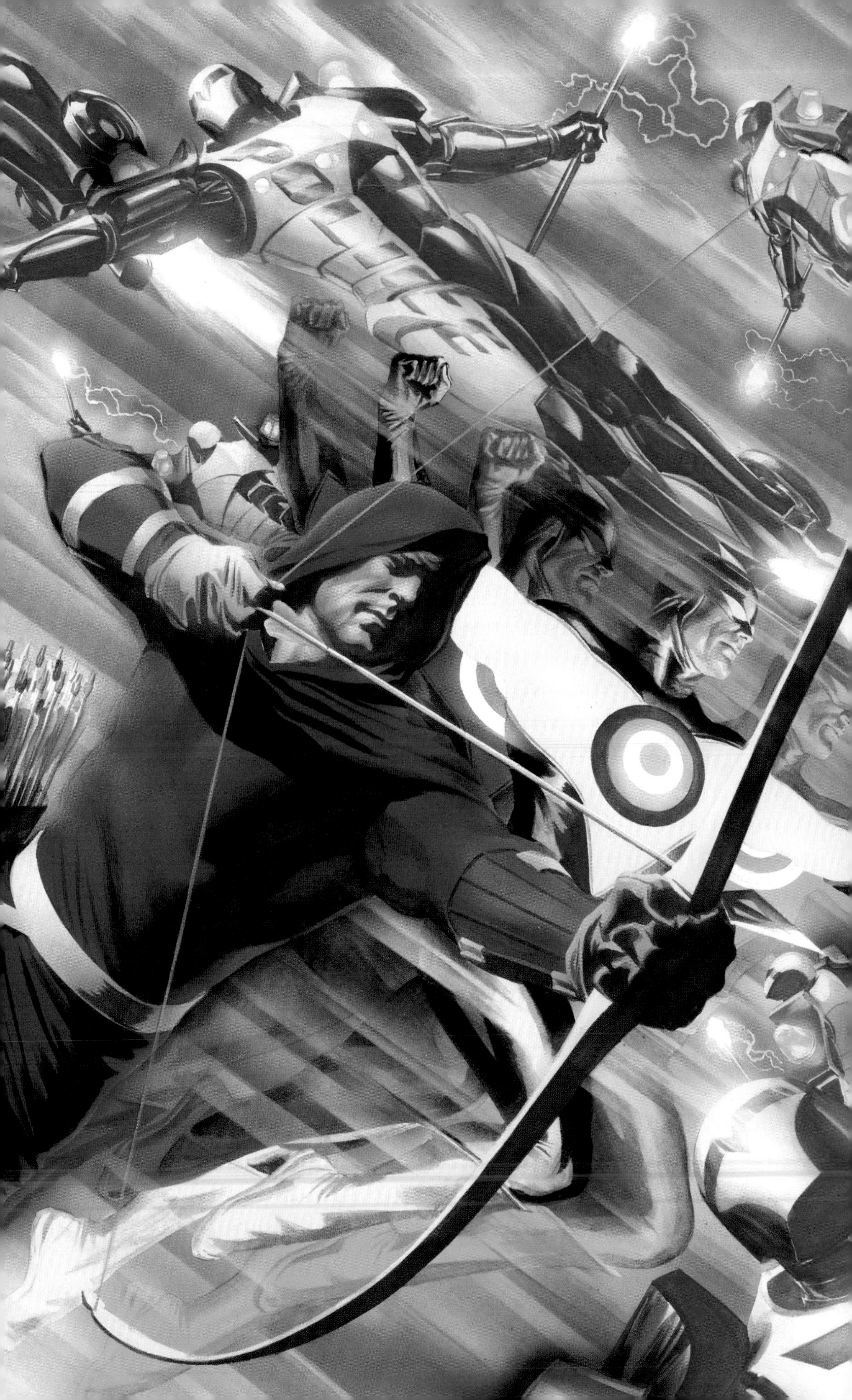

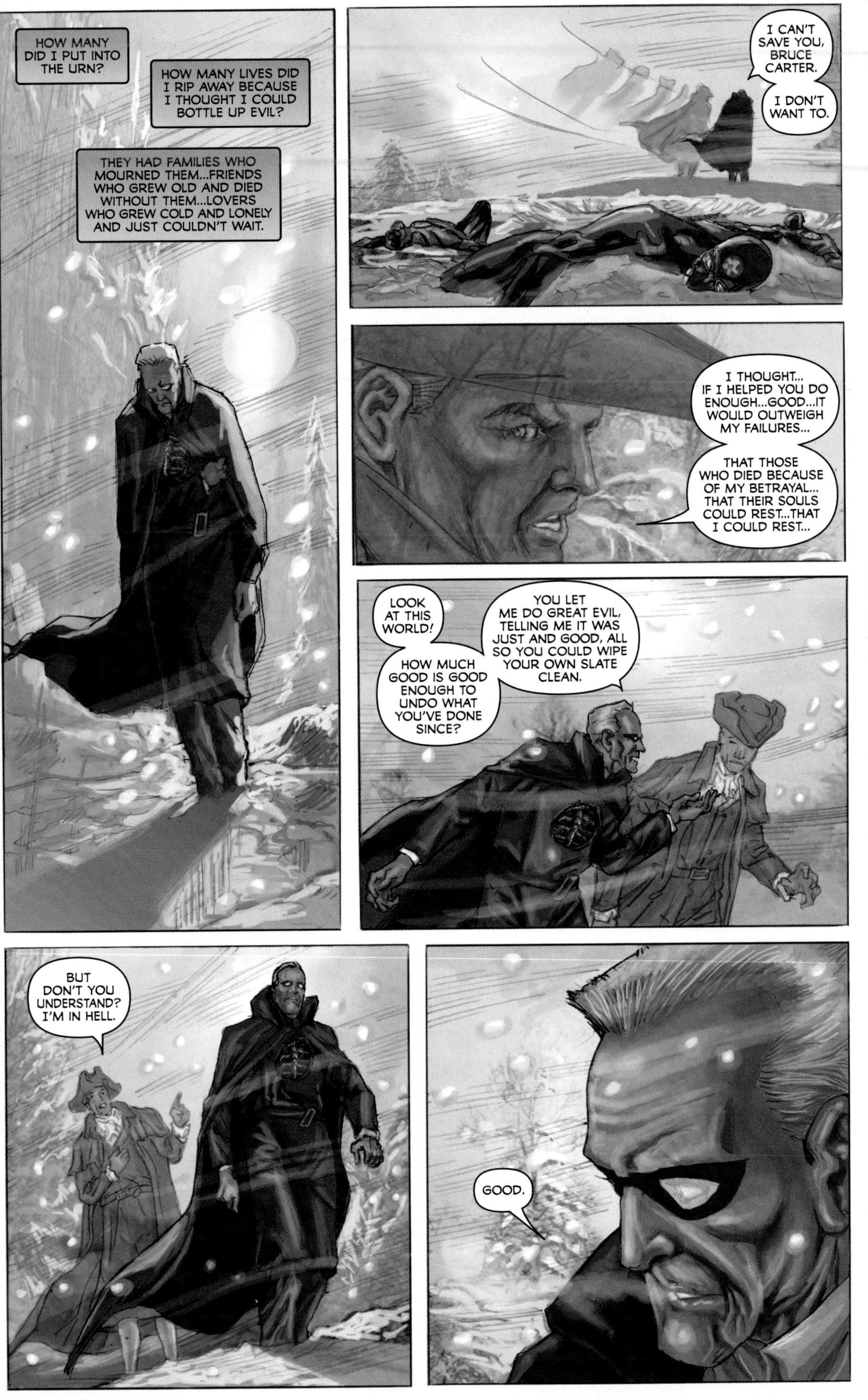
HOW MANY DID I PUT INTO THE URN?
HOW MANY LIVES DID I RIP AWAY BECAUSE I THOUGHT I COULD BOTTLE UP EVIL?
THEY HAD FAMILIES WHO MOURNED THEM...FRIENDS WHO GREW OLD AND DIED WITHOUT THEM...LOVERS WHO GREW COLD AND LONELY AND JUST COULDN'T WAIT.
I CAN'T SAVE YOU, BRUCE CARTER.
I DON'T WANT TO.
I THOUGHT... IF I HELPED YOU DO ENOUGH...GOOD...IT WOULD OUTWEIGH MY FAILURES...
THAT THOSE WHO DIED BECAUSE OF MY BETRAYAL... THAT THEIR SOULS COULD REST...THAT I COULD REST...
YOU LET ME DO GREAT EVIL, TELLING ME IT WAS JUST AND GOOD, ALL SO YOU COULD WIPE YOUR OWN SLATE CLEAN.
LOOK AT THIS WORLD!
HOW MUCH GOOD IS GOOD ENOUGH TO UNDO WHAT YOU'VE DONE SINCE?
BUT DON'T YOU UNDERSTAND? I'M IN HELL.
GOOD.

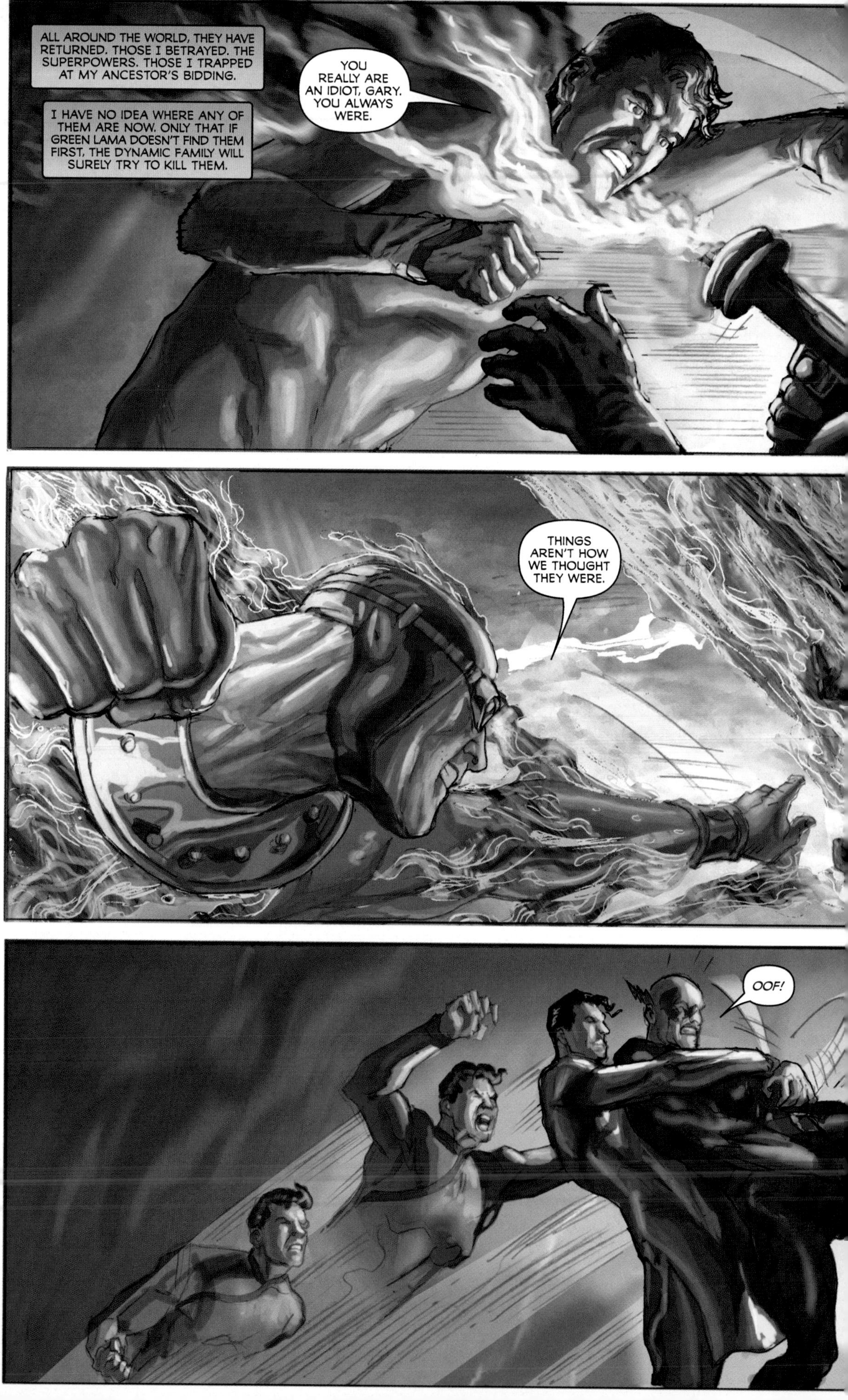
ALL AROUND THE WORLD, THEY HAVE RETURNED. THOSE I BETRAYED. THE SUPERPOWERS. THOSE I TRAPPED AT MY ANCESTOR'S BIDDING.
YOU REALLY ARE AN IDIOT, GARY. YOU ALWAYS WERE.
I HAVE NO IDEA WHERE ANY OF THEM ARE NOW. ONLY THAT IF GREEN LAMA DOESN'T FIND THEM FIRST, THE DYNAMIC FAMILY WILL SURELY TRY TO KILL THEM.
THINGS AREN'T HOW WE THOUGHT THEY WERE.
OOF!

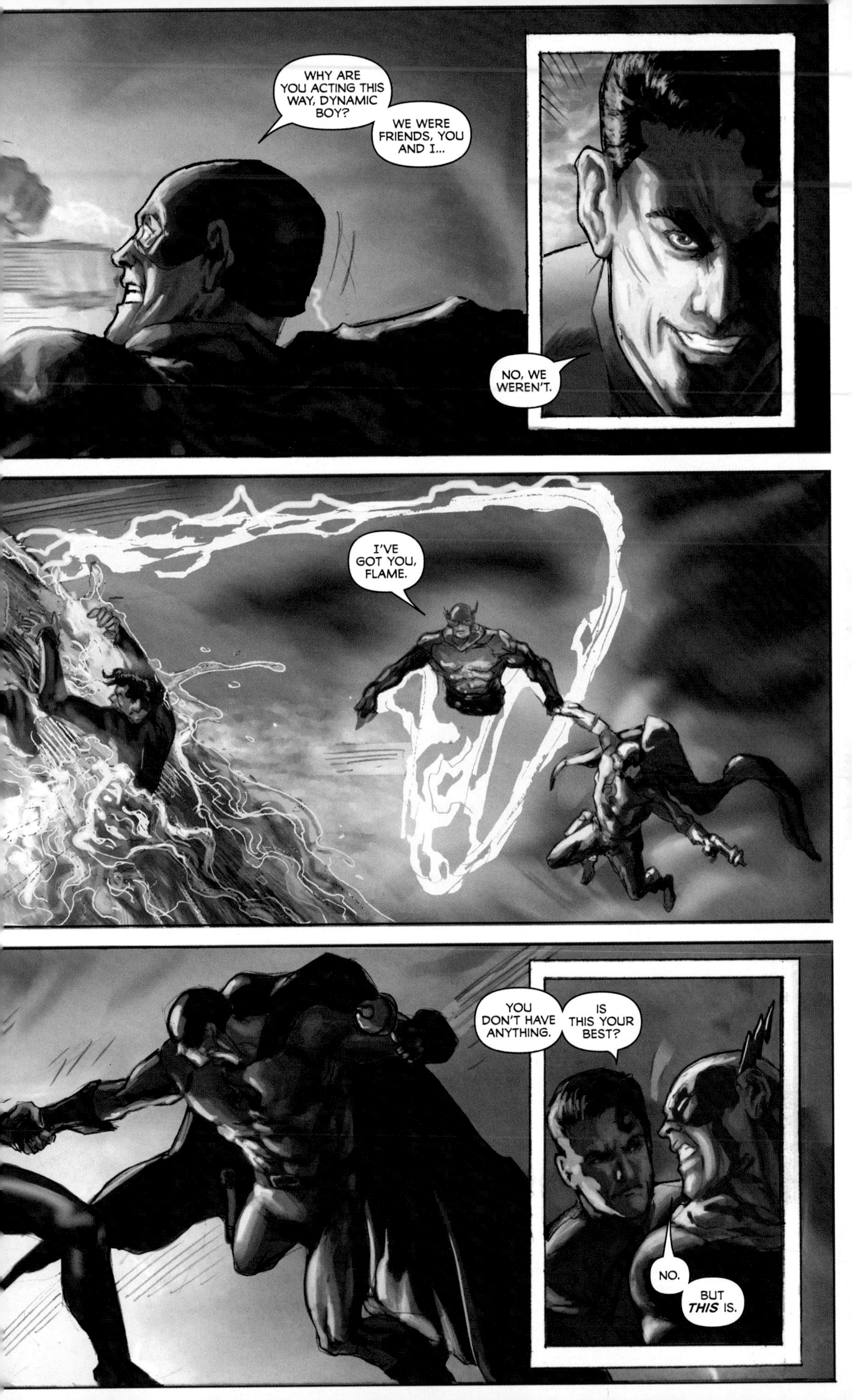
WHY ARE YOU ACTING THIS WAY, DYNAMIC BOY?
WE WERE FRIENDS, YOU AND I...
NO, WE WEREN'T.
I'VE GOT YOU, FLAME.
YOU DON'T HAVE ANYTHING.
IS THIS YOUR BEST?
NO.
BUT *THIS* IS.

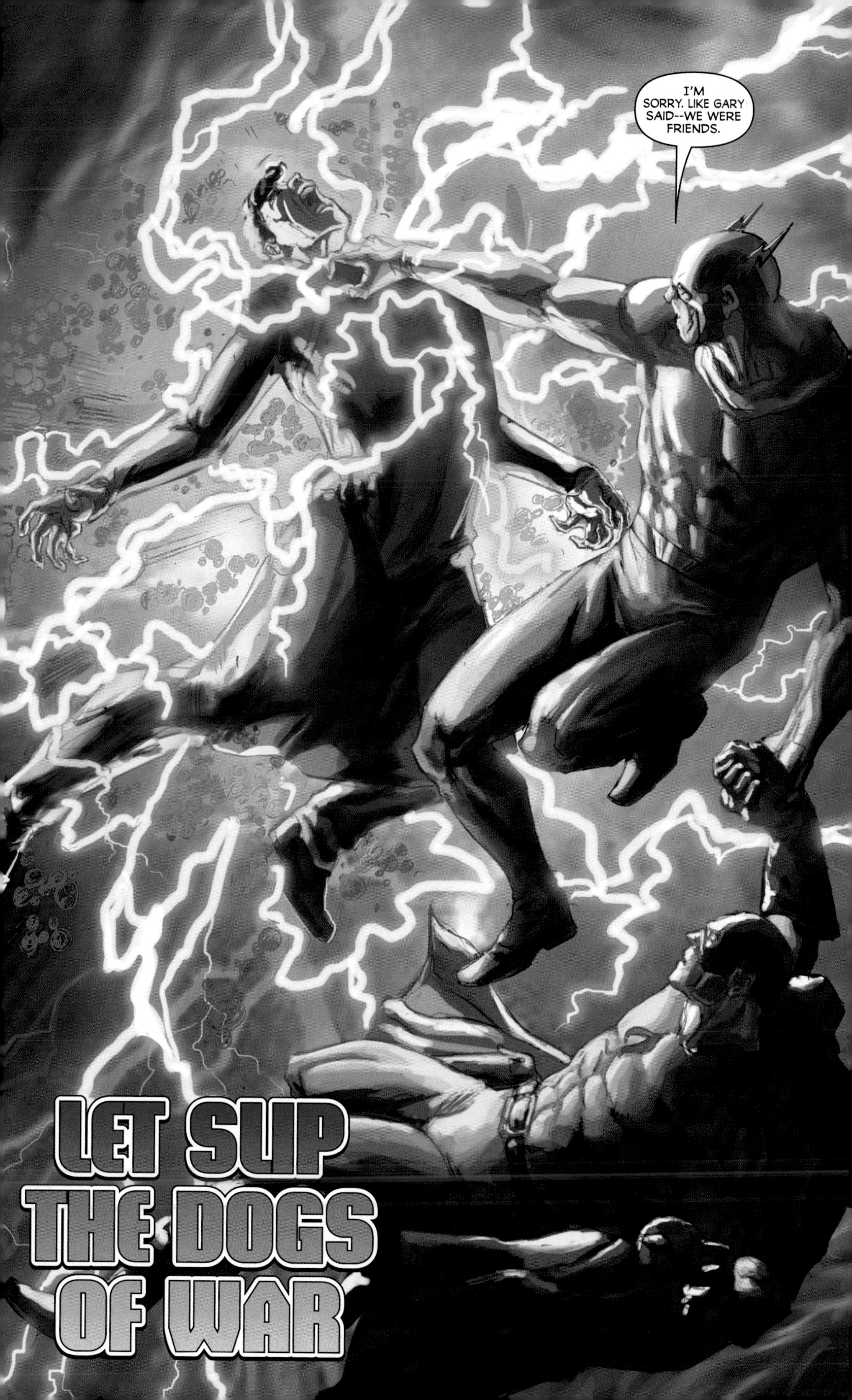
I'M SORRY. LIKE GARY SAID--WE WERE FRIENDS.
LET SLIP THE DOGS OF WAR

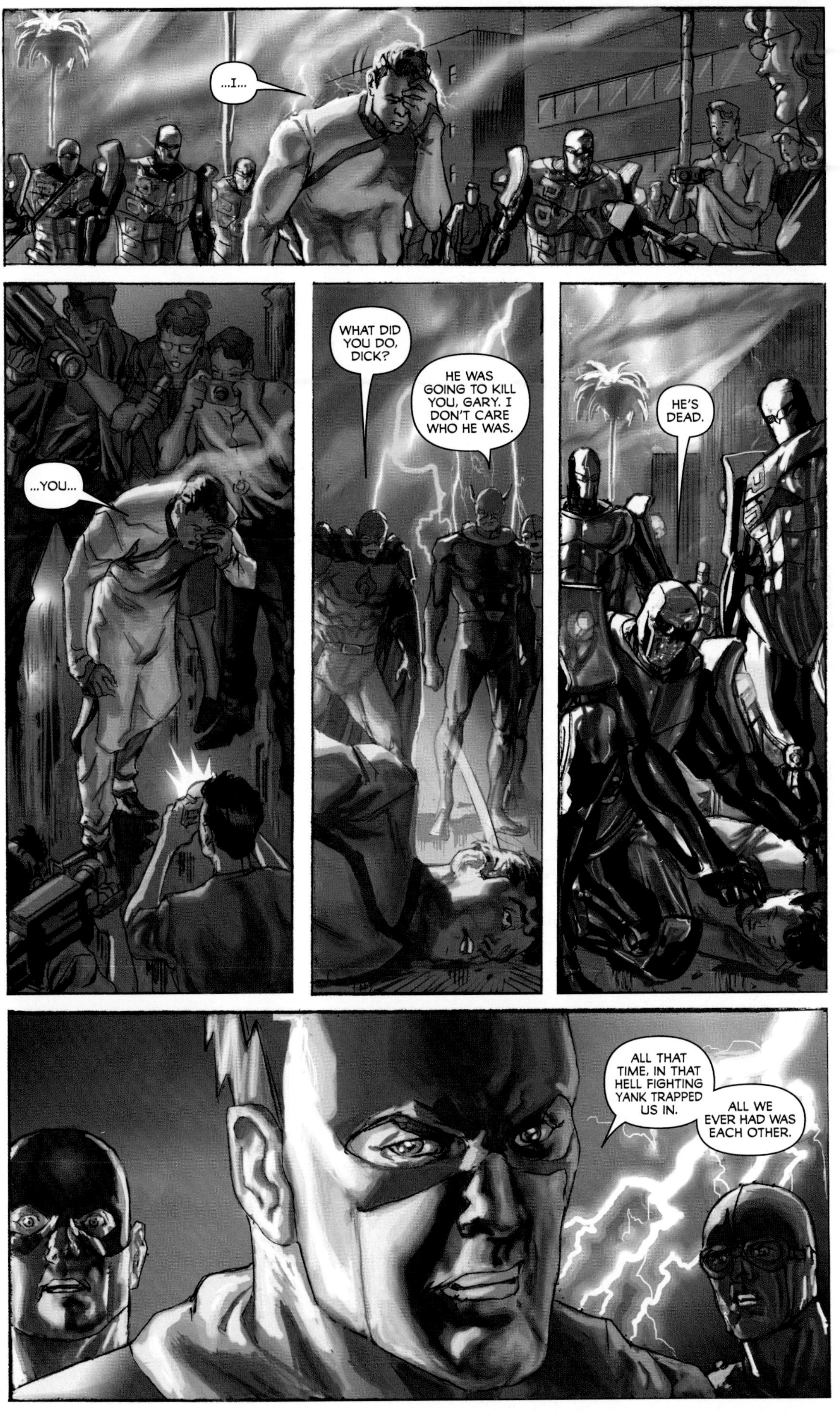
...I...
...YOU...
WHAT DID YOU DO, DICK?
HE WAS GOING TO KILL YOU, GARY. I DON'T CARE WHO HE WAS.
HE'S DEAD.
ALL THAT TIME, IN THAT HELL FIGHTING YANK TRAPPED US IN.
ALL WE EVER HAD WAS EACH OTHER.

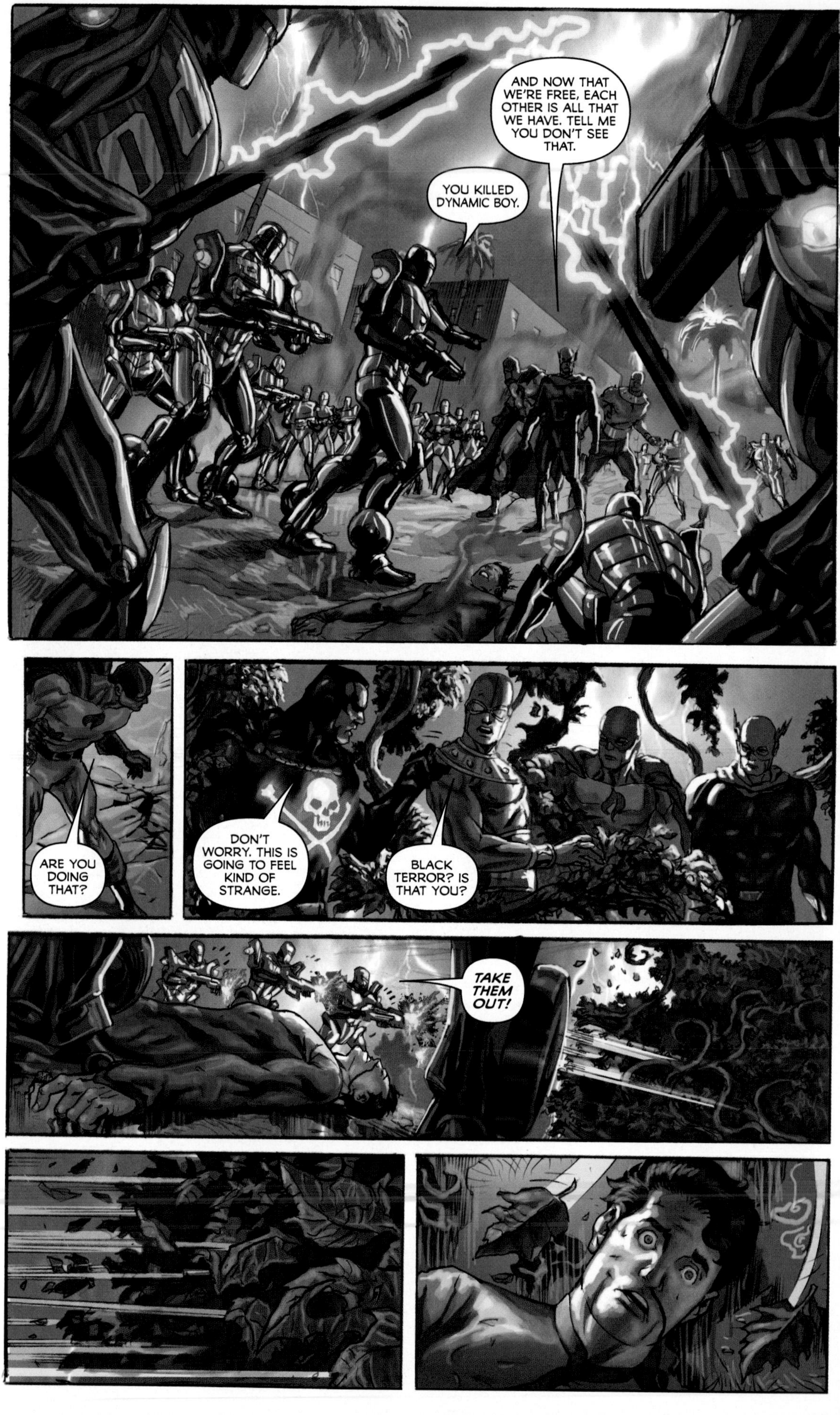

AND NOW THAT WE'RE FREE, EACH OTHER IS ALL THAT WE HAVE. TELL ME YOU DON'T SEE THAT.
YOU KILLED DYNAMIC BOY.
ARE YOU DOING THAT?
DON'T WORRY. THIS IS GOING TO FEEL KIND OF STRANGE.
BLACK TERROR? IS THAT YOU?
TAKE THEM OUT!

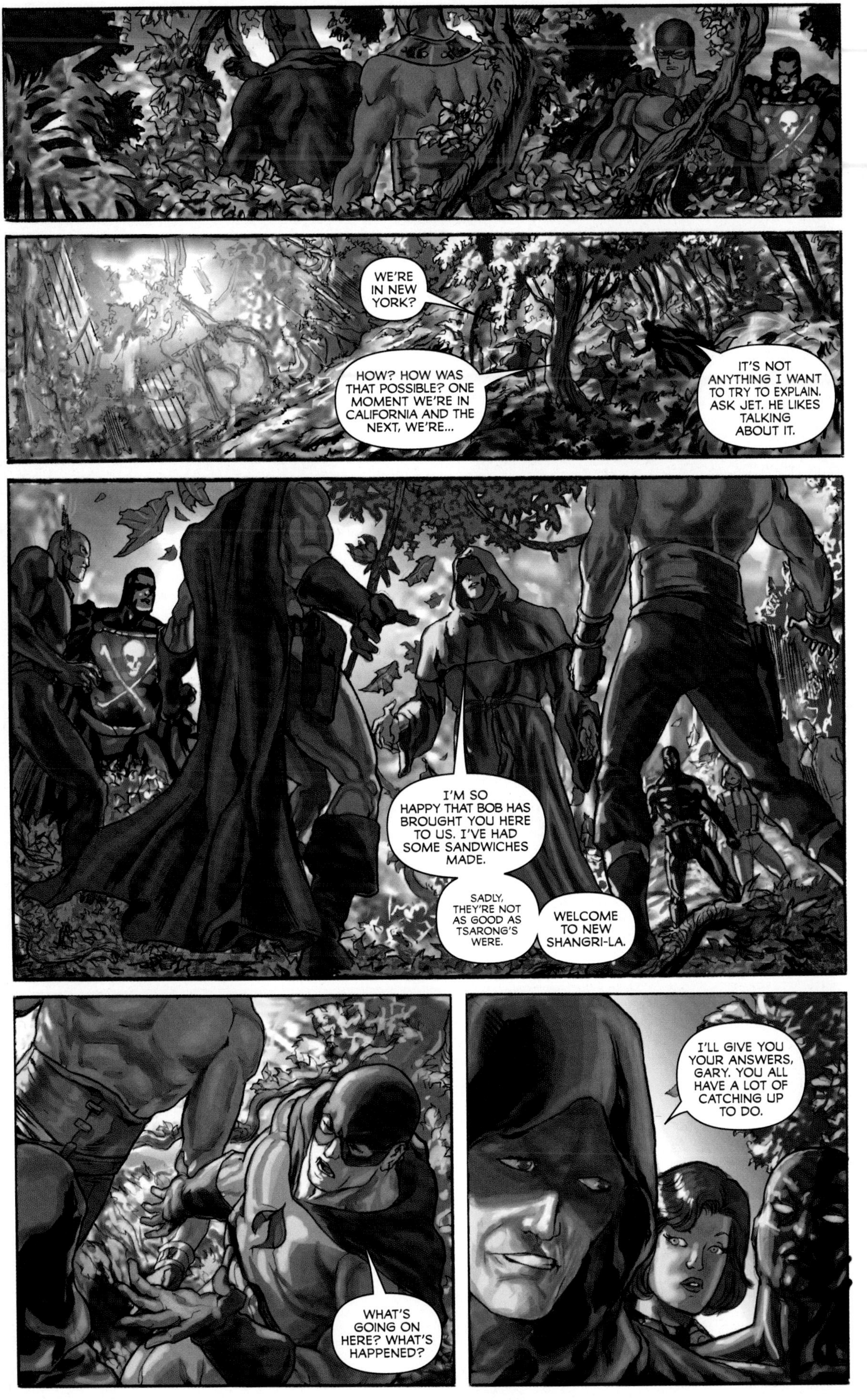
WE'RE IN NEW YORK?
HOW? HOW WAS THAT POSSIBLE? ONE MOMENT WE'RE IN CALIFORNIA AND THE NEXT, WE'RE...
IT'S NOT ANYTHING I WANT TO TRY TO EXPLAIN. ASK JET. HE LIKES TALKING ABOUT IT.
I'M SO HAPPY THAT BOB HAS BROUGHT YOU HERE TO US. I'VE HAD SOME SANDWICHES MADE.
SADLY, THEY'RE NOT AS GOOD AS TSARONG'S WERE.
WELCOME TO NEW SHANGRI-LA.
WHAT'S GOING ON HERE? WHAT'S HAPPENED?
I'LL GIVE YOU YOUR ANSWERS, GARY. YOU ALL HAVE A LOT OF CATCHING UP TO DO.

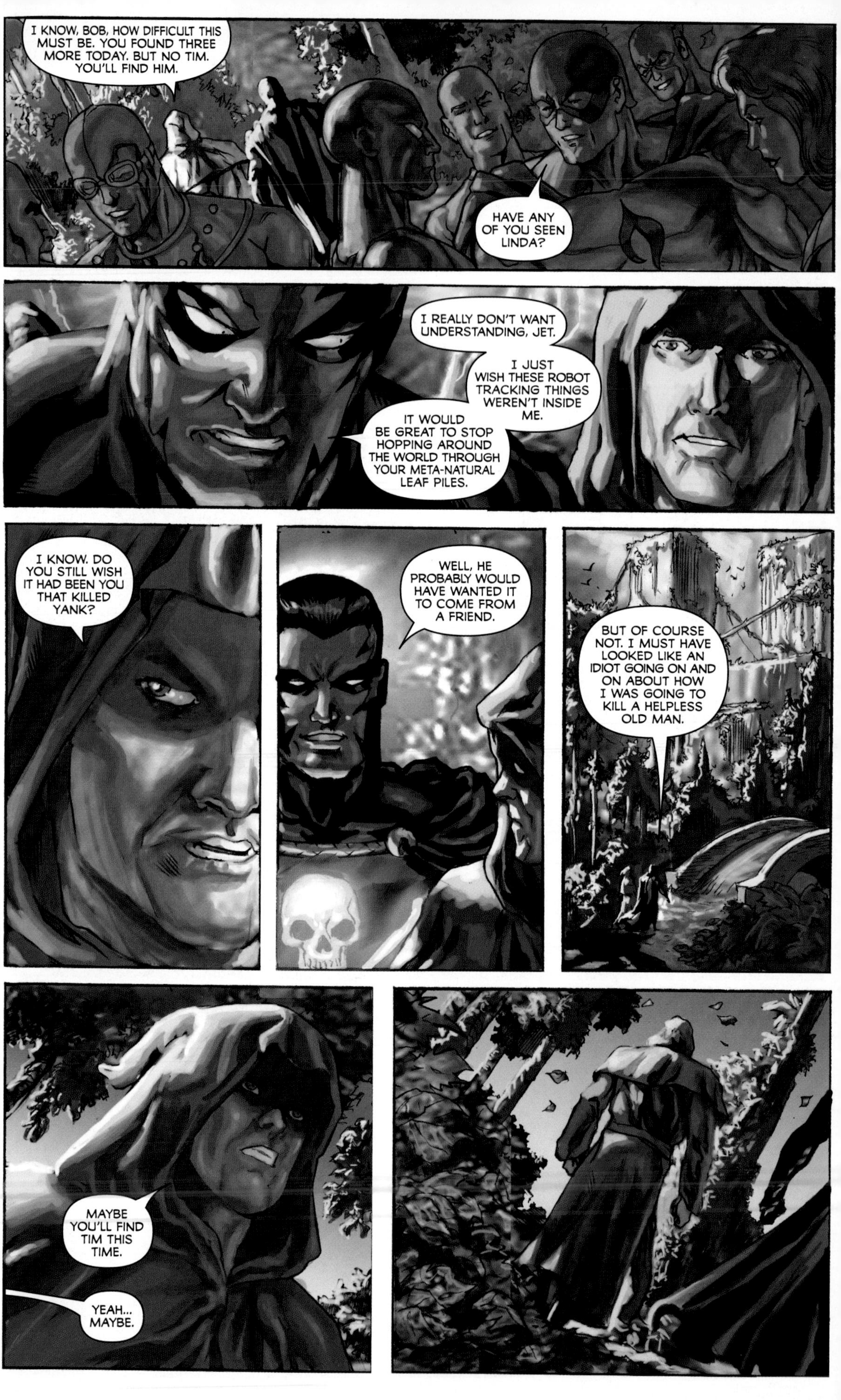
I KNOW, BOB, HOW DIFFICULT THIS MUST BE. YOU FOUND THREE MORE TODAY. BUT NO TIM. YOU'LL FIND HIM.
HAVE ANY OF YOU SEEN LINDA?
I REALLY DON'T WANT UNDERSTANDING, JET.
I JUST WISH THESE ROBOT TRACKING THINGS WEREN'T INSIDE ME.
IT WOULD BE GREAT TO STOP HOPPING AROUND THE WORLD THROUGH YOUR META-NATURAL LEAF PILES.
I KNOW. DO YOU STILL WISH IT HAD BEEN YOU THAT KILLED YANK?
WELL, HE PROBABLY WOULD HAVE WANTED IT TO COME FROM A FRIEND.
BUT OF COURSE NOT. I MUST HAVE LOOKED LIKE AN IDIOT GOING ON AND ON ABOUT HOW I WAS GOING TO KILL A HELPLESS OLD MAN.
MAYBE YOU'LL FIND TIM THIS TIME.
YEAH... MAYBE.

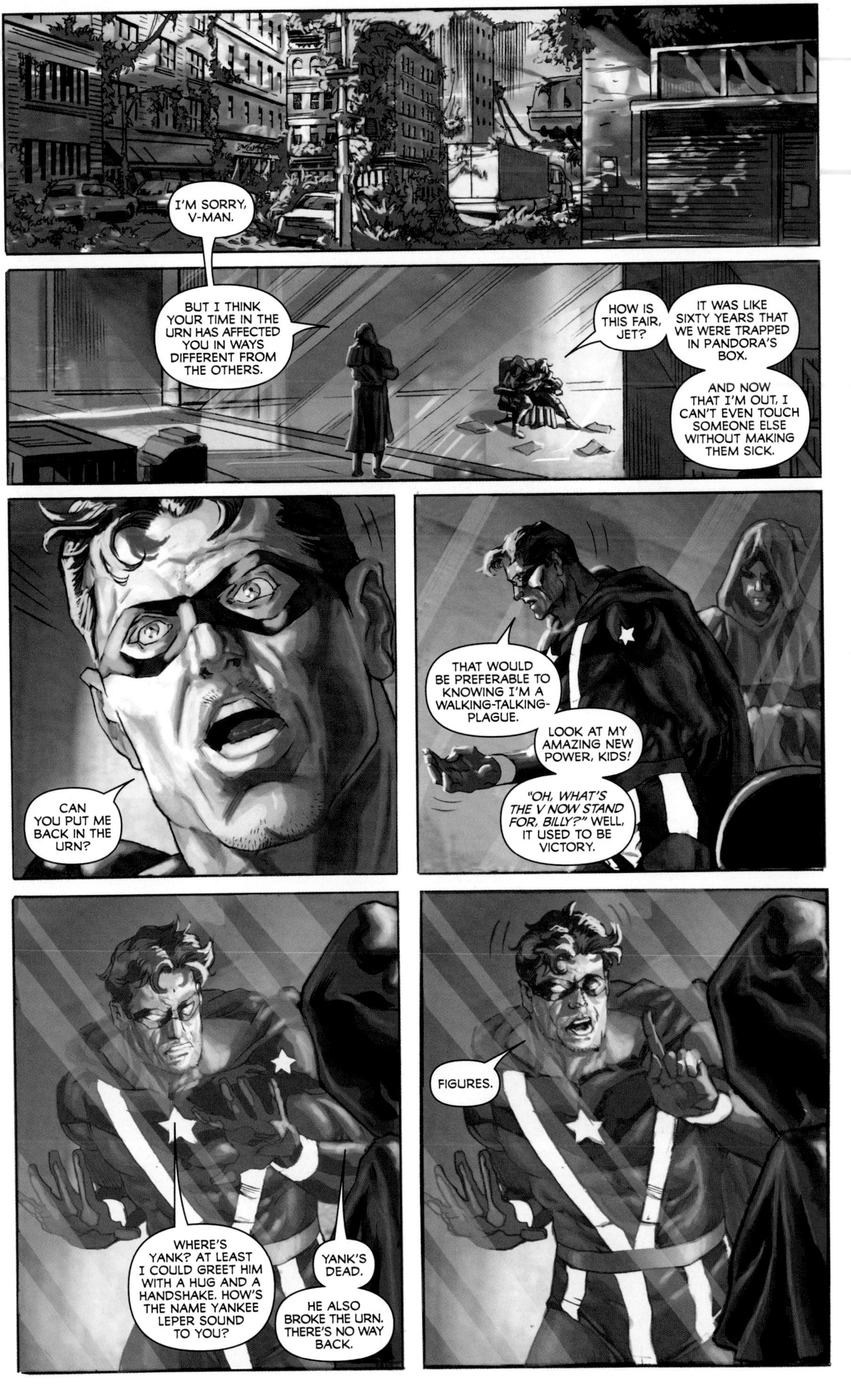
I'M SORRY, V-MAN.
BUT I THINK YOUR TIME IN THE URN HAS AFFECTED YOU IN WAYS DIFFERENT FROM THE OTHERS.
HOW IS THIS FAIR, JET?
IT WAS LIKE SIXTY YEARS THAT WE WERE TRAPPED IN PANDORA'S BOX.
AND NOW THAT I'M OUT, I CAN'T EVEN TOUCH SOMEONE ELSE WITHOUT MAKING THEM SICK.
CAN YOU PUT ME BACK IN THE URN?
THAT WOULD BE PREFERABLE TO KNOWING I'M A WALKING-TALKING-PLAGUE.
LOOK AT MY AMAZING NEW POWER, KIDS!
"OH, WHAT'S THE V NOW STAND FOR, BILLY?" WELL, IT USED TO BE VICTORY.
WHERE'S YANK? AT LEAST I COULD GREET HIM WITH A HUG AND A HANDSHAKE. HOW'S THE NAME YANKEE LEPER SOUND TO YOU?
YANK'S DEAD.
HE ALSO BROKE THE URN. THERE'S NO WAY BACK.
FIGURES.

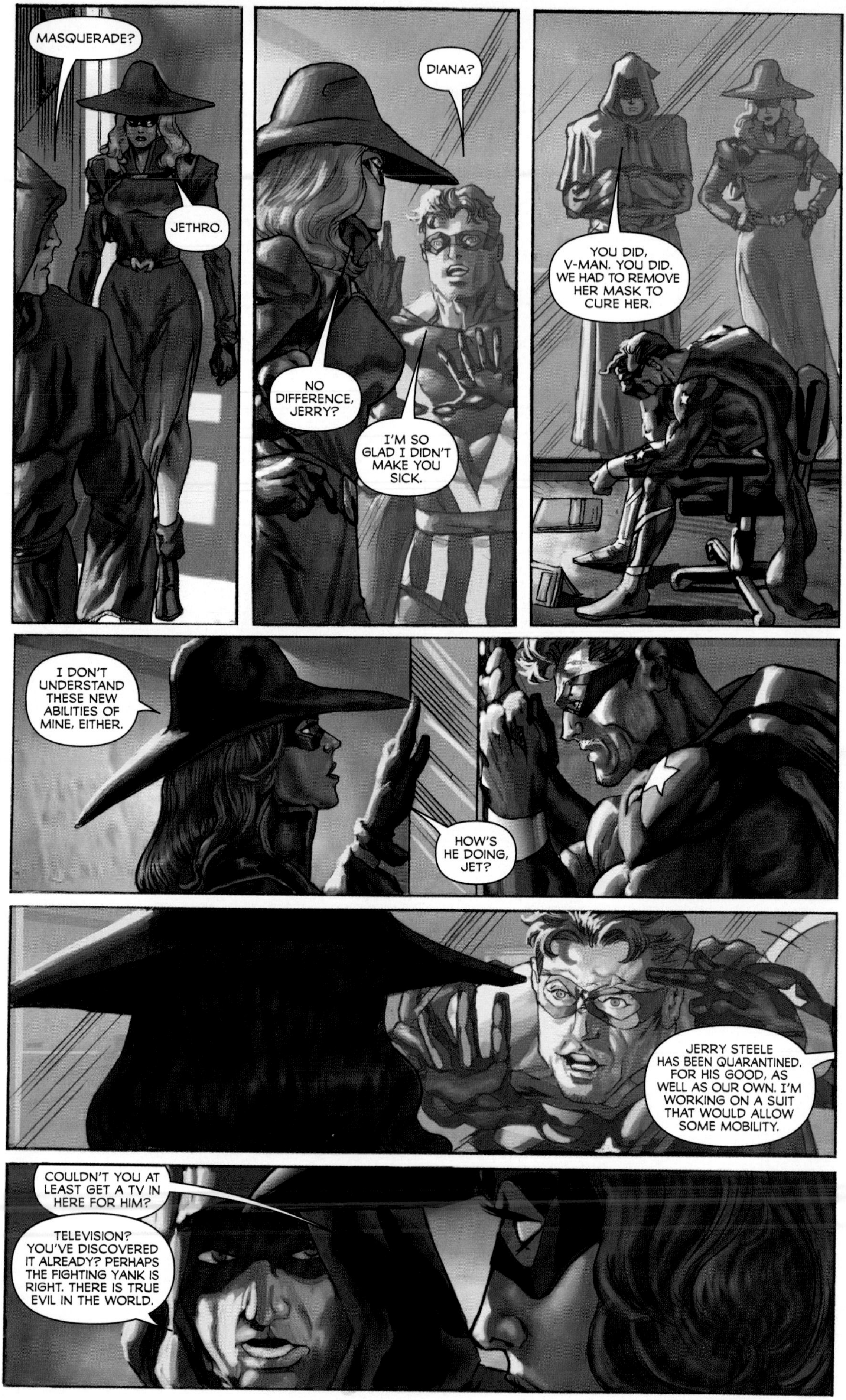
MASQUERADE?
JETHRO.
DIANA?
NO DIFFERENCE, JERRY?
I'M SO GLAD I DIDN'T MAKE YOU SICK.
YOU DID, V-MAN. YOU DID. WE HAD TO REMOVE HER MASK TO CURE HER.
I DON'T UNDERSTAND THESE NEW ABILITIES OF MINE, EITHER.
HOW'S HE DOING, JET?
JERRY STEELE HAS BEEN QUARANTINED. FOR HIS GOOD, AS WELL AS OUR OWN. I'M WORKING ON A SUIT THAT WOULD ALLOW SOME MOBILITY.
COULDN'T YOU AT LEAST GET A TV IN HERE FOR HIM?
TELEVISION? YOU'VE DISCOVERED IT ALREADY? PERHAPS THE FIGHTING YANK IS RIGHT. THERE IS TRUE EVIL IN THE WORLD.

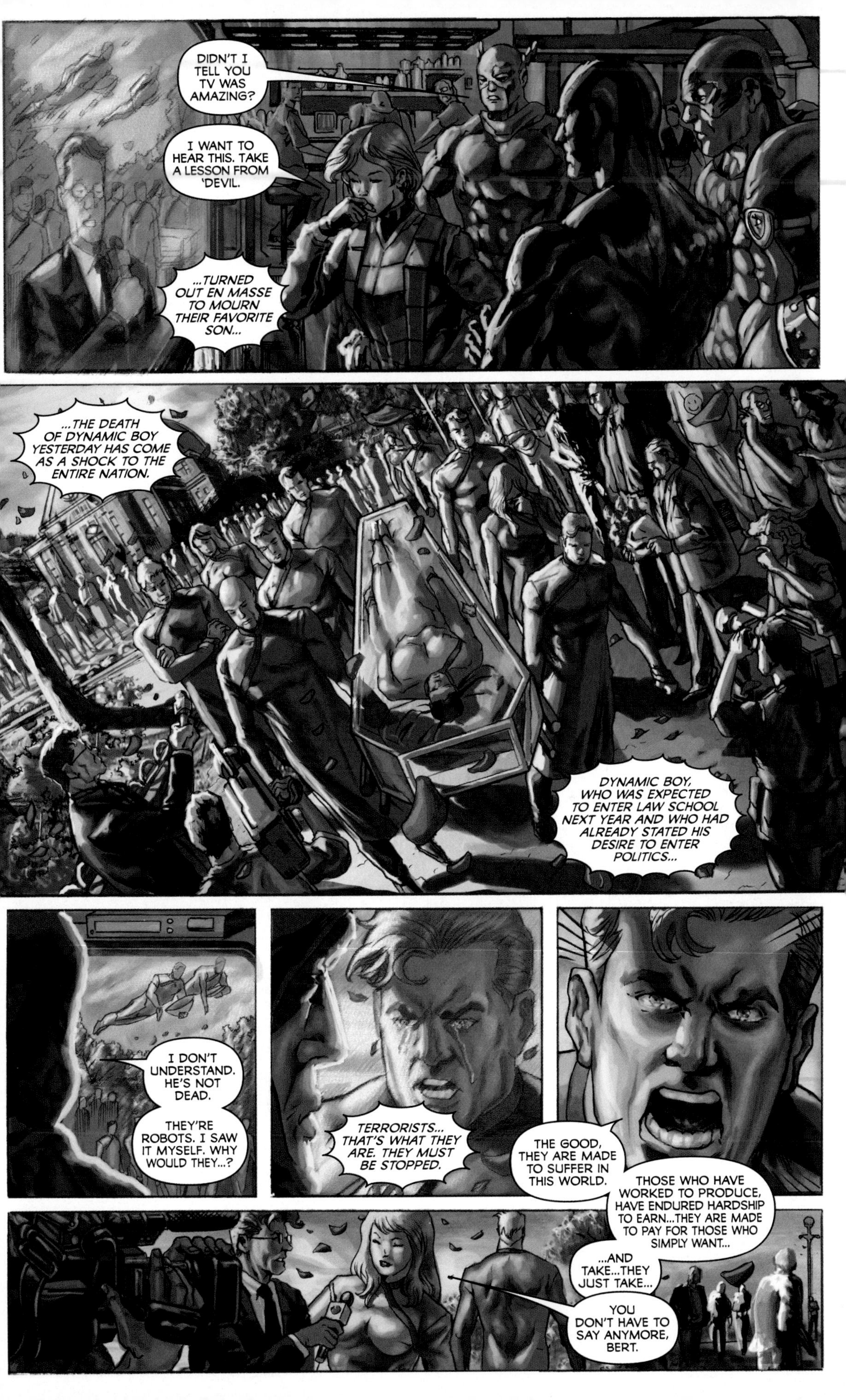

DIDN'T I TELL YOU TV WAS AMAZING?
I WANT TO HEAR THIS. TAKE A LESSON FROM 'DEVIL.
...TURNED OUT EN MASSE TO MOURN THEIR FAVORITE SON...
...THE DEATH OF DYNAMIC BOY YESTERDAY HAS COME AS A SHOCK TO THE ENTIRE NATION.
DYNAMIC BOY, WHO WAS EXPECTED TO ENTER LAW SCHOOL NEXT YEAR AND WHO HAD ALREADY STATED HIS DESIRE TO ENTER POLITICS...
I DON'T UNDERSTAND. HE'S NOT DEAD.
THEY'RE ROBOTS. I SAW IT MYSELF. WHY WOULD THEY...?
TERRORISTS... THAT'S WHAT THEY ARE. THEY MUST BE STOPPED.
THE GOOD, THEY ARE MADE TO SUFFER IN THIS WORLD.
THOSE WHO HAVE WORKED TO PRODUCE, HAVE ENDURED HARDSHIP TO EARN...THEY ARE MADE TO PAY FOR THOSE WHO SIMPLY WANT...
...AND TAKE...THEY JUST TAKE...
YOU DON'T HAVE TO SAY ANYMORE, BERT.

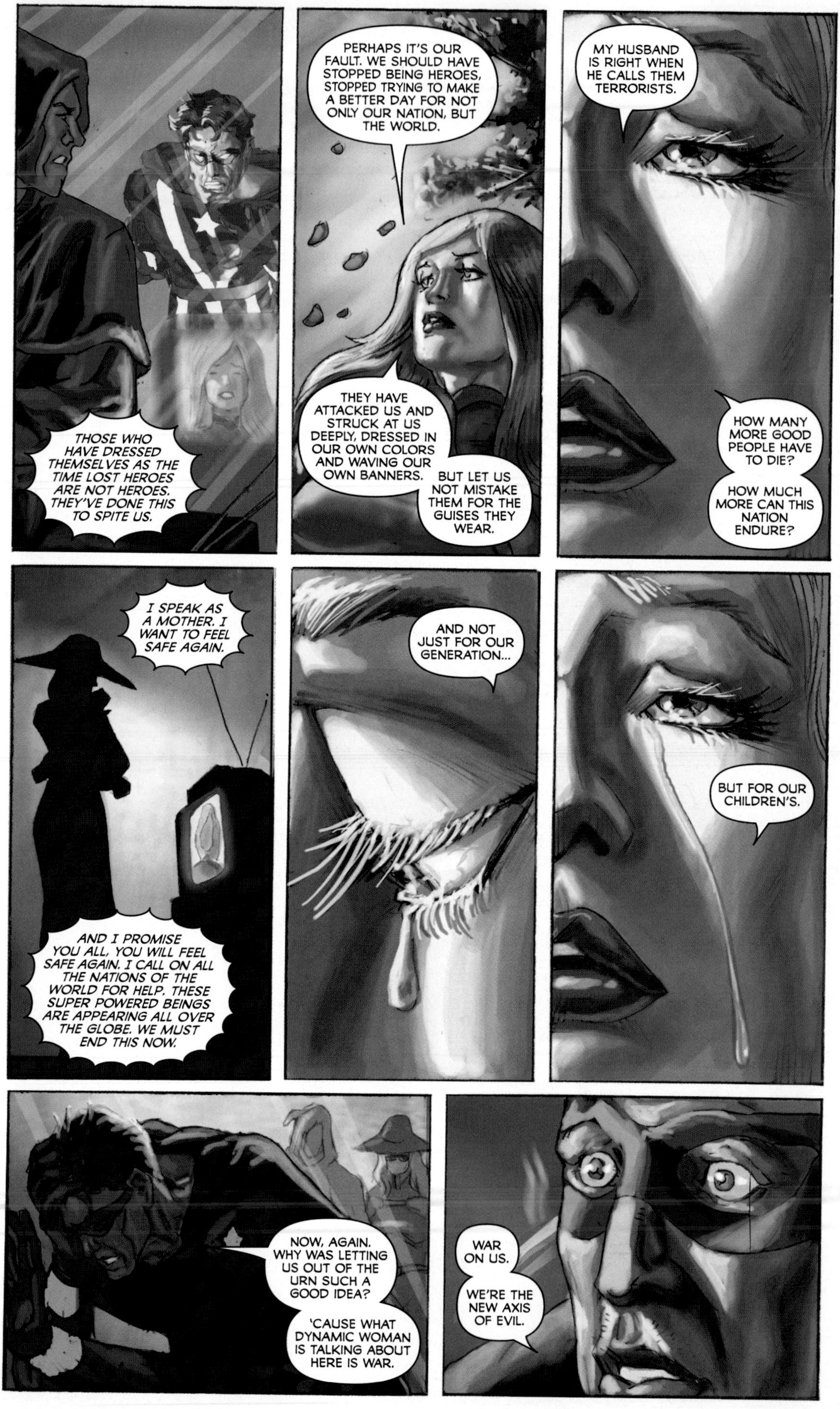
THOSE WHO HAVE DRESSED THEMSELVES AS THE TIME LOST HEROES ARE NOT HEROES. THEY'VE DONE THIS TO SPITE US.
PERHAPS IT'S OUR FAULT. WE SHOULD HAVE STOPPED BEING HEROES, STOPPED TRYING TO MAKE A BETTER DAY FOR NOT ONLY OUR NATION, BUT THE WORLD.
THEY HAVE ATTACKED US AND STRUCK AT US DEEPLY, DRESSED IN OUR OWN COLORS AND WAVING OUR OWN BANNERS.
BUT LET US NOT MISTAKE THEM FOR THE GUISES THEY WEAR.
MY HUSBAND IS RIGHT WHEN HE CALLS THEM TERRORISTS.
HOW MANY MORE GOOD PEOPLE HAVE TO DIE?
HOW MUCH MORE CAN THIS NATION ENDURE?
I SPEAK AS A MOTHER. I WANT TO FEEL SAFE AGAIN.
AND I PROMISE YOU ALL, YOU WILL FEEL SAFE AGAIN. I CALL ON ALL THE NATIONS OF THE WORLD FOR HELP. THESE SUPER POWERED BEINGS ARE APPEARING ALL OVER THE GLOBE. WE MUST END THIS NOW.
AND NOT JUST FOR OUR GENERATION...
BUT FOR OUR CHILDREN'S.
NOW, AGAIN. WHY WAS LETTING US OUT OF THE URN SUCH A GOOD IDEA?
'CAUSE WHAT DYNAMIC WOMAN IS TALKING ABOUT HERE IS WAR.
WAR ON US.
WE'RE THE NEW AXIS OF EVIL.

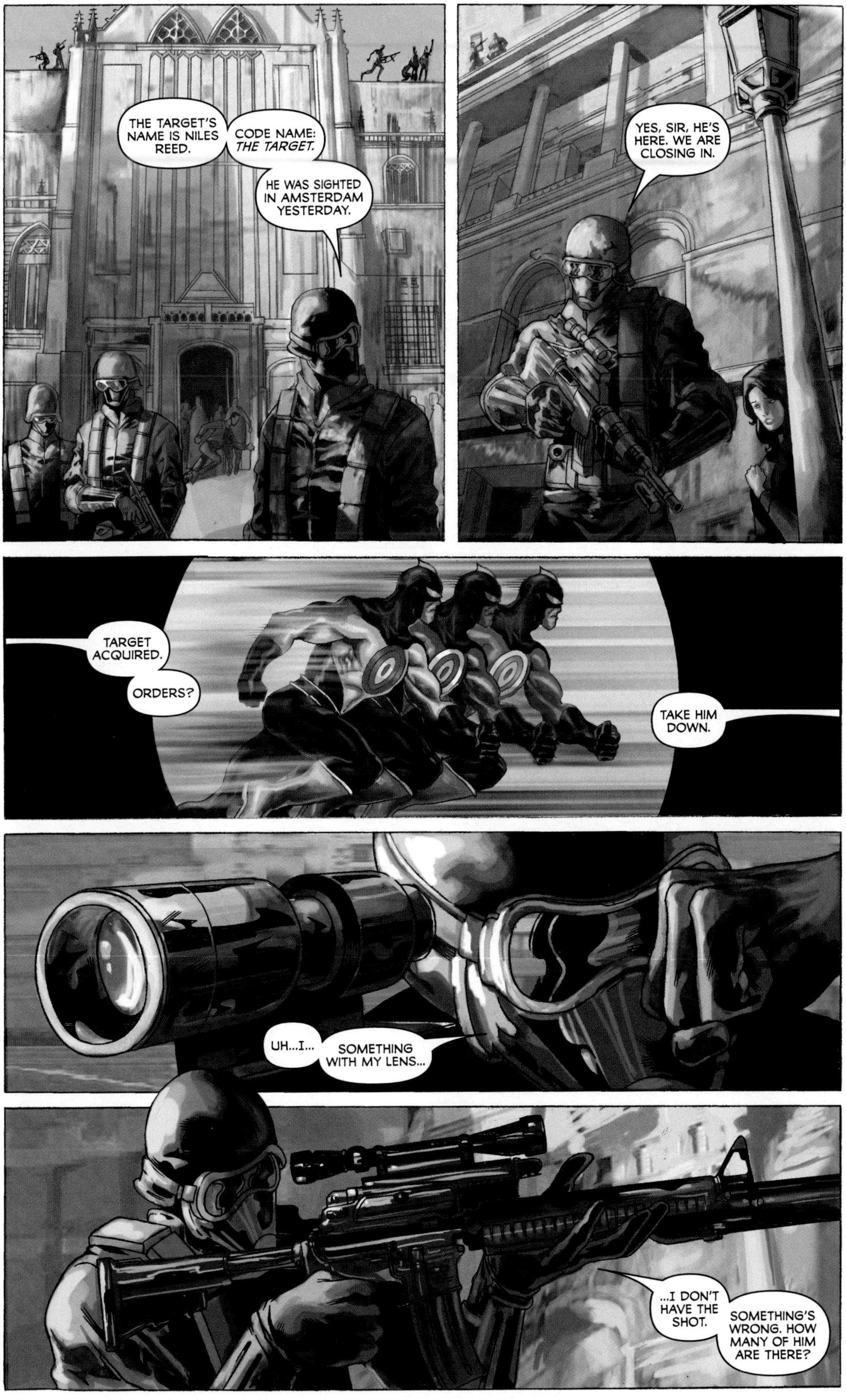
THE TARGET'S NAME IS NILES REED.
CODE NAME: *THE TARGET.*
HE WAS SIGHTED IN AMSTERDAM YESTERDAY.
YES, SIR, HE'S HERE. WE ARE CLOSING IN.
TARGET ACQUIRED.
ORDERS?
TAKE HIM DOWN.
UH...I...
SOMETHING WITH MY LENS...
...I DON'T HAVE THE SHOT.
SOMETHING'S WRONG. HOW MANY OF HIM ARE THERE?

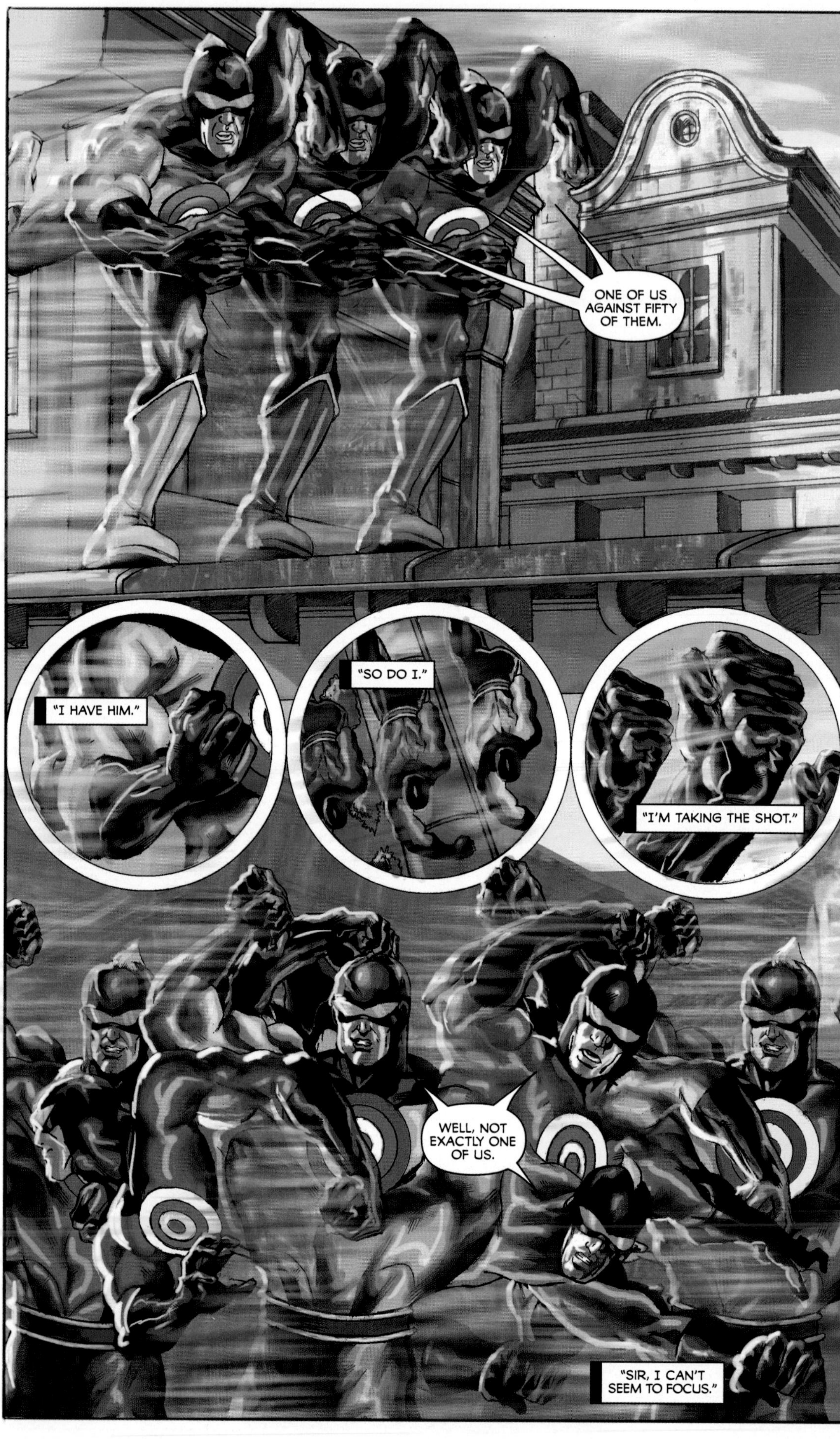
ONE OF US AGAINST FIFTY OF THEM.
"I HAVE HIM."
"SO DO I."
"I'M TAKING THE SHOT."
WELL, NOT EXACTLY ONE OF US.
"SIR, I CAN'T SEEM TO FOCUS."

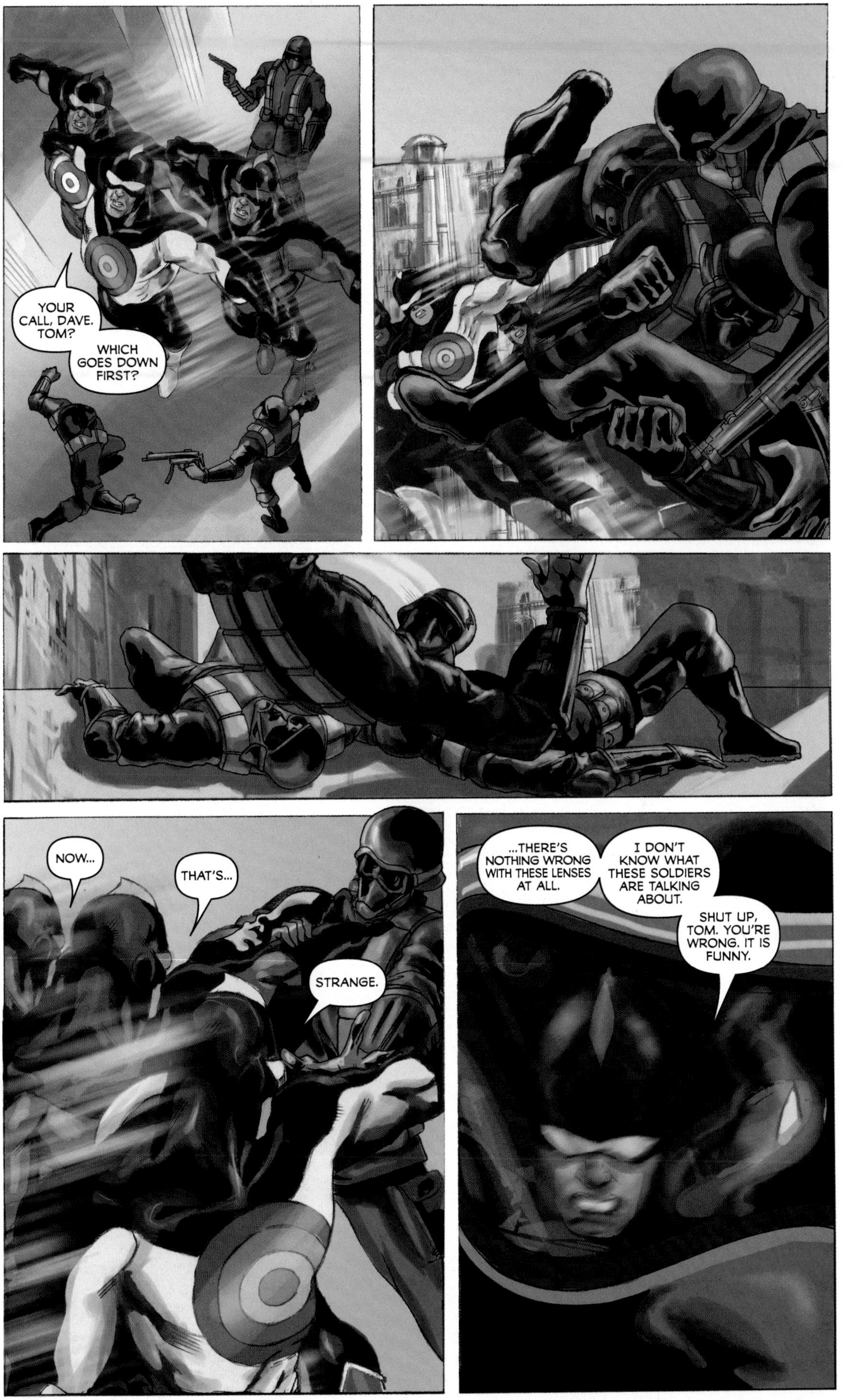
YOUR CALL, DAVE. TOM?
WHICH GOES DOWN FIRST?
NOW...
THAT'S...
STRANGE.
...THERE'S NOTHING WRONG WITH THESE LENSES AT ALL.
I DON'T KNOW WHAT THESE SOLDIERS ARE TALKING ABOUT.
SHUT UP, TOM. YOU'RE WRONG. IT IS FUNNY.

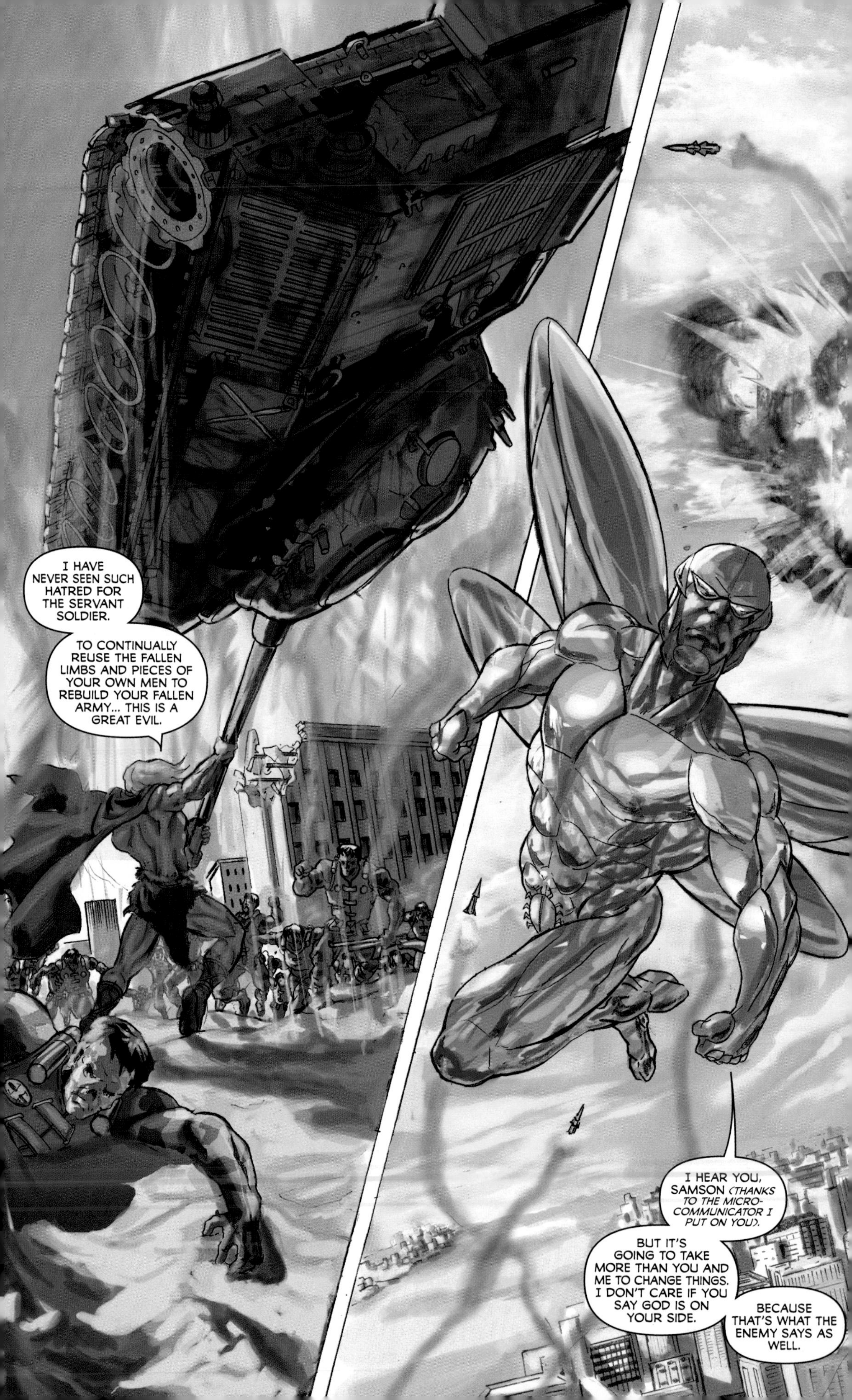
I HAVE NEVER SEEN SUCH HATRED FOR THE SERVANT SOLDIER.
TO CONTINUALLY REUSE THE FALLEN LIMBS AND PIECES OF YOUR OWN MEN TO REBUILD YOUR FALLEN ARMY... THIS IS A GREAT EVIL.
I HEAR YOU, SAMSON *(THANKS TO THE MICRO-COMMUNICATOR I PUT ON YOU)*.
BUT IT'S GOING TO TAKE MORE THAN YOU AND ME TO CHANGE THINGS. I DON'T CARE IF YOU SAY GOD IS ON YOUR SIDE.
BECAUSE THAT'S WHAT THE ENEMY SAYS AS WELL.

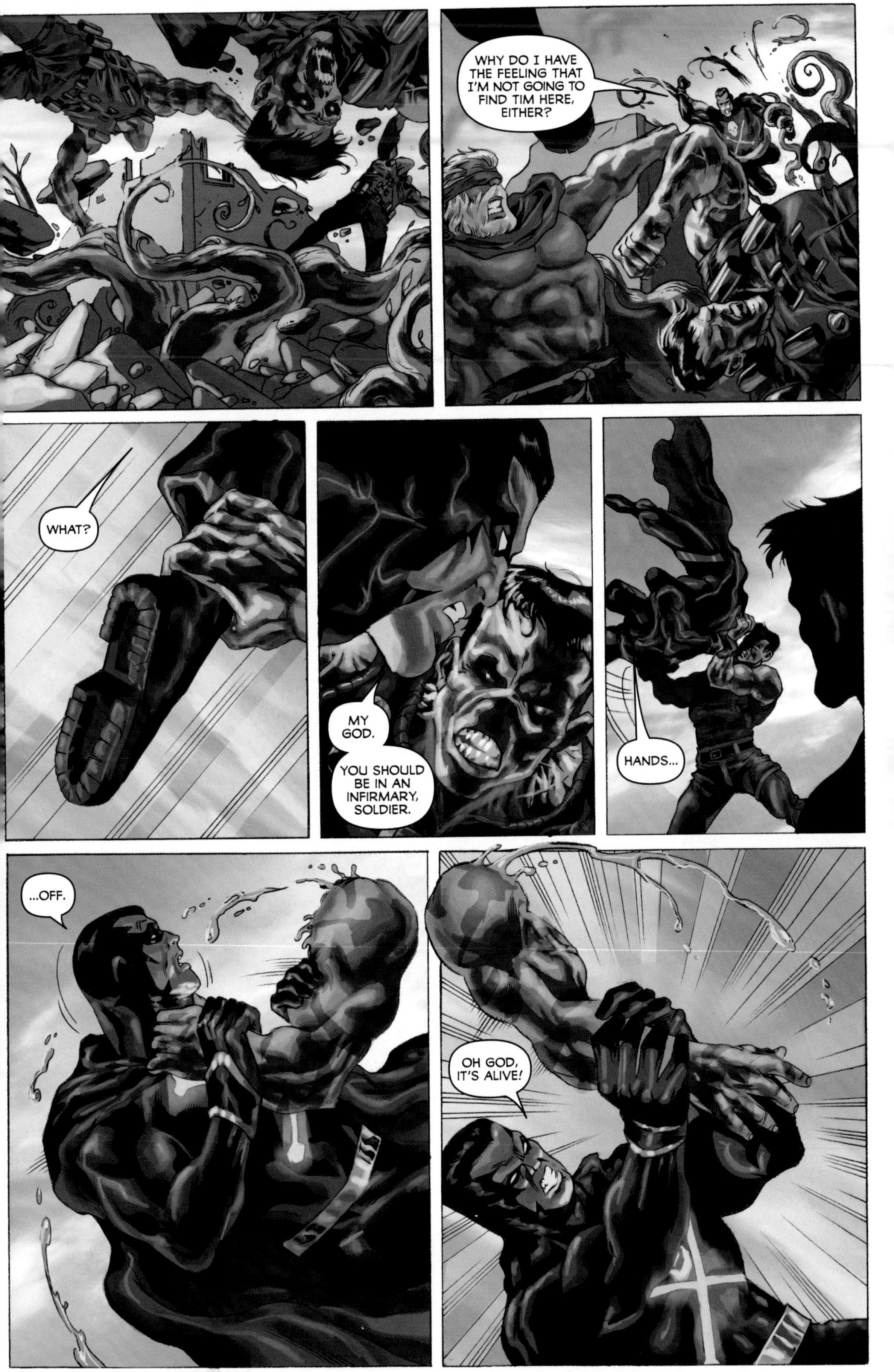
WHY DO I HAVE THE FEELING THAT I'M NOT GOING TO FIND TIM HERE, EITHER?
WHAT?
MY GOD.
YOU SHOULD BE IN AN INFIRMARY, SOLDIER.
HANDS...
...OFF.
OH GOD, IT'S ALIVE!

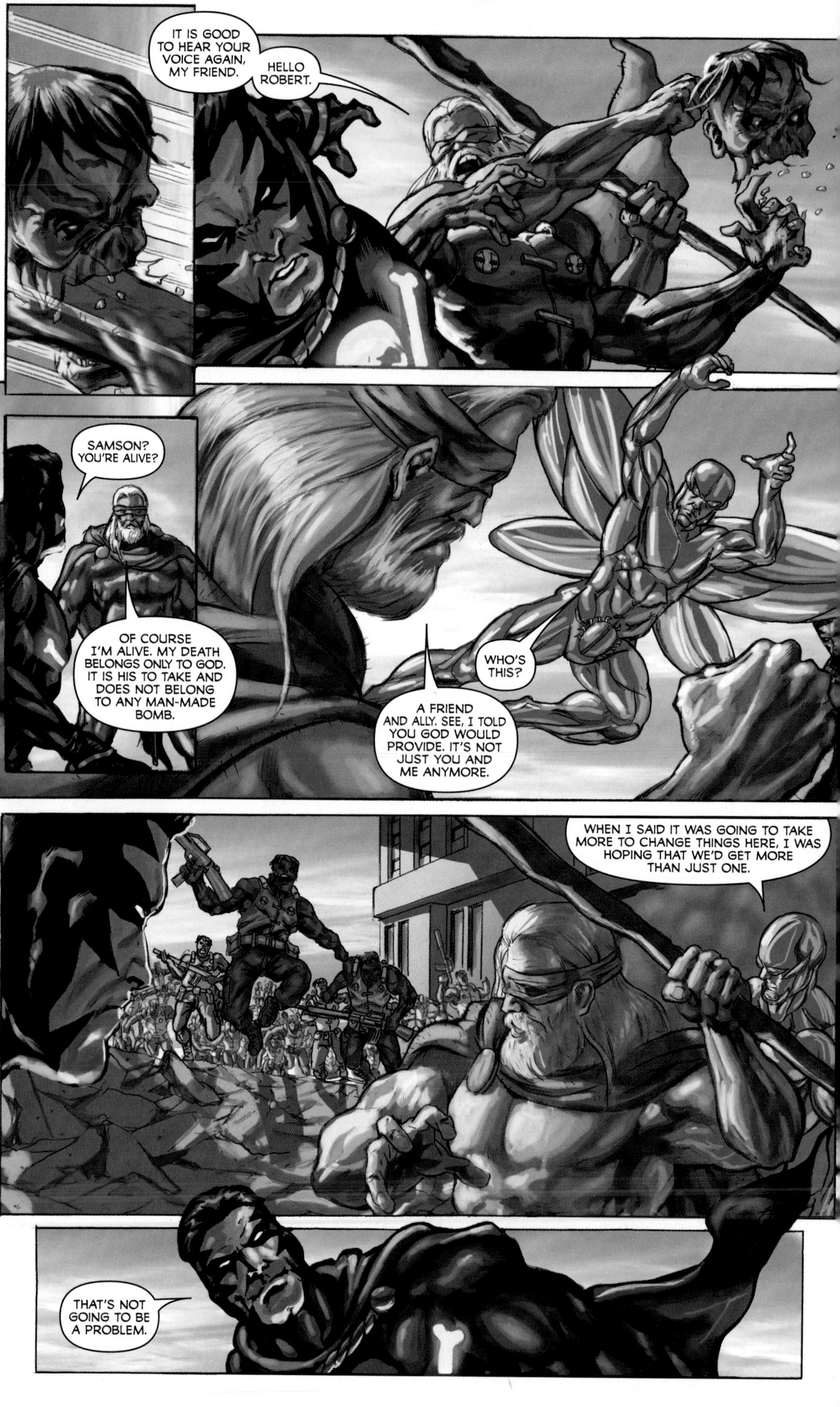

IT IS GOOD TO HEAR YOUR VOICE AGAIN, MY FRIEND.
HELLO ROBERT.
SAMSON? YOU'RE ALIVE?
OF COURSE I'M ALIVE. MY DEATH BELONGS ONLY TO GOD. IT IS HIS TO TAKE AND DOES NOT BELONG TO ANY MAN-MADE BOMB.
WHO'S THIS?
A FRIEND AND ALLY. SEE, I TOLD YOU GOD WOULD PROVIDE. IT'S NOT JUST YOU AND ME ANYMORE.
WHEN I SAID IT WAS GOING TO TAKE MORE TO CHANGE THINGS HERE, I WAS HOPING THAT WE'D GET MORE THAN JUST ONE.
THAT'S NOT GOING TO BE A PROBLEM.

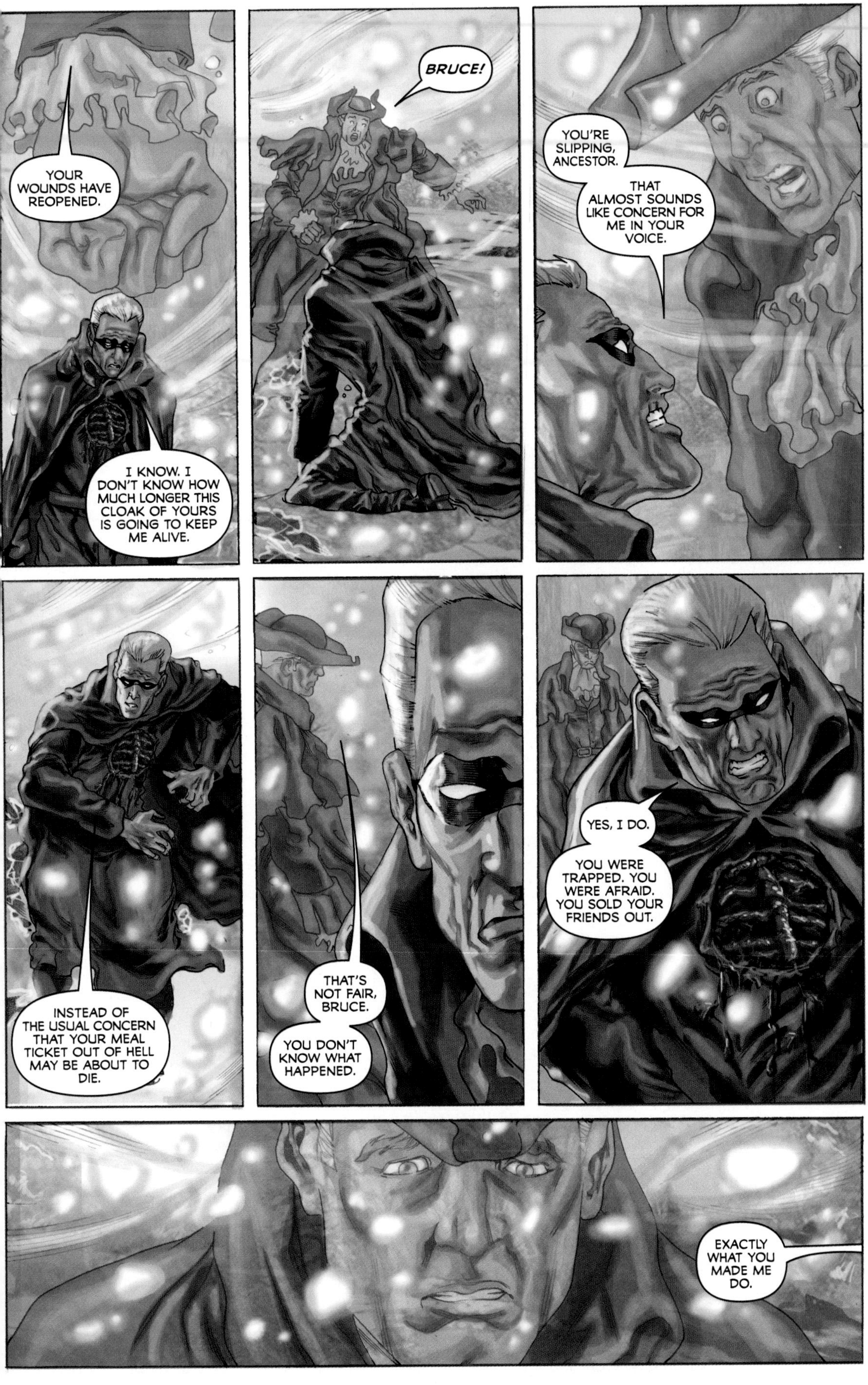
YOUR WOUNDS HAVE REOPENED.
I KNOW. I DON'T KNOW HOW MUCH LONGER THIS CLOAK OF YOURS IS GOING TO KEEP ME ALIVE.
BRUCE!
YOU'RE SLIPPING, ANCESTOR.
THAT ALMOST SOUNDS LIKE CONCERN FOR ME IN YOUR VOICE.
INSTEAD OF THE USUAL CONCERN THAT YOUR MEAL TICKET OUT OF HELL MAY BE ABOUT TO DIE.
THAT'S NOT FAIR, BRUCE.
YOU DON'T KNOW WHAT HAPPENED.
YES, I DO.
YOU WERE TRAPPED. YOU WERE AFRAID. YOU SOLD YOUR FRIENDS OUT.
EXACTLY WHAT YOU MADE ME DO.

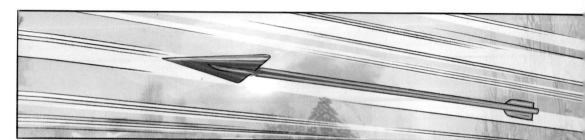

NO!!!

BRUCE, I'M SO SORRY. I COULDN'T STOP THEM.

YOU NEVER COULD.

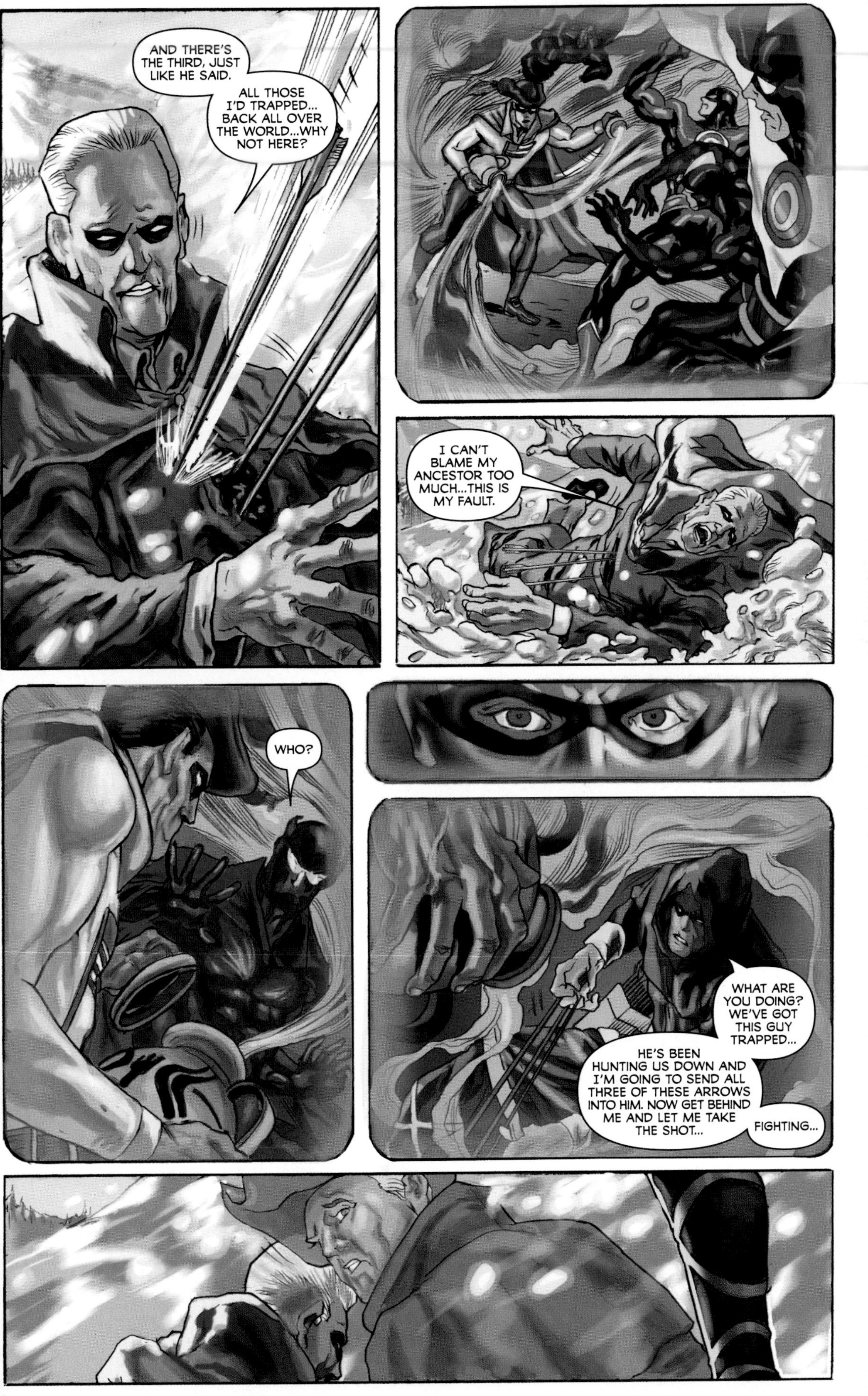
AND THERE'S THE THIRD, JUST LIKE HE SAID.
ALL THOSE I'D TRAPPED... BACK ALL OVER THE WORLD...WHY NOT HERE?
I CAN'T BLAME MY ANCESTOR TOO MUCH...THIS IS MY FAULT.
WHO?
WHAT ARE YOU DOING? WE'VE GOT THIS GUY TRAPPED...
HE'S BEEN HUNTING US DOWN AND I'M GOING TO SEND ALL THREE OF THESE ARROWS INTO HIM. NOW GET BEHIND ME AND LET ME TAKE THE SHOT...
FIGHTING...

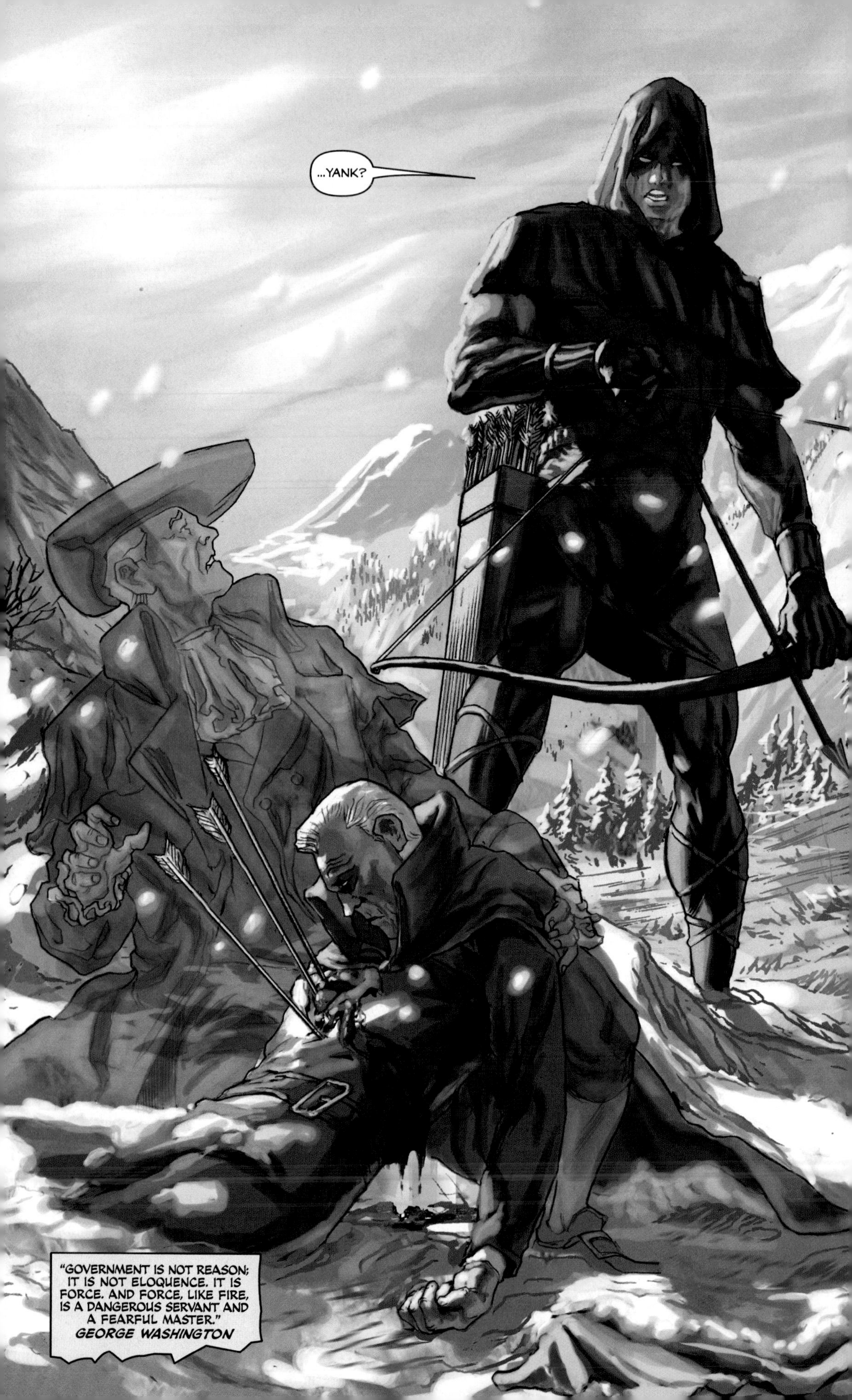
...YANK?
"GOVERNMENT IS NOT REASON; IT IS NOT ELOQUENCE. IT IS FORCE. AND FORCE, LIKE FIRE, IS A DANGEROUS SERVANT AND A FEARFUL MASTER."
GEORGE WASHINGTON

ISSUE

6

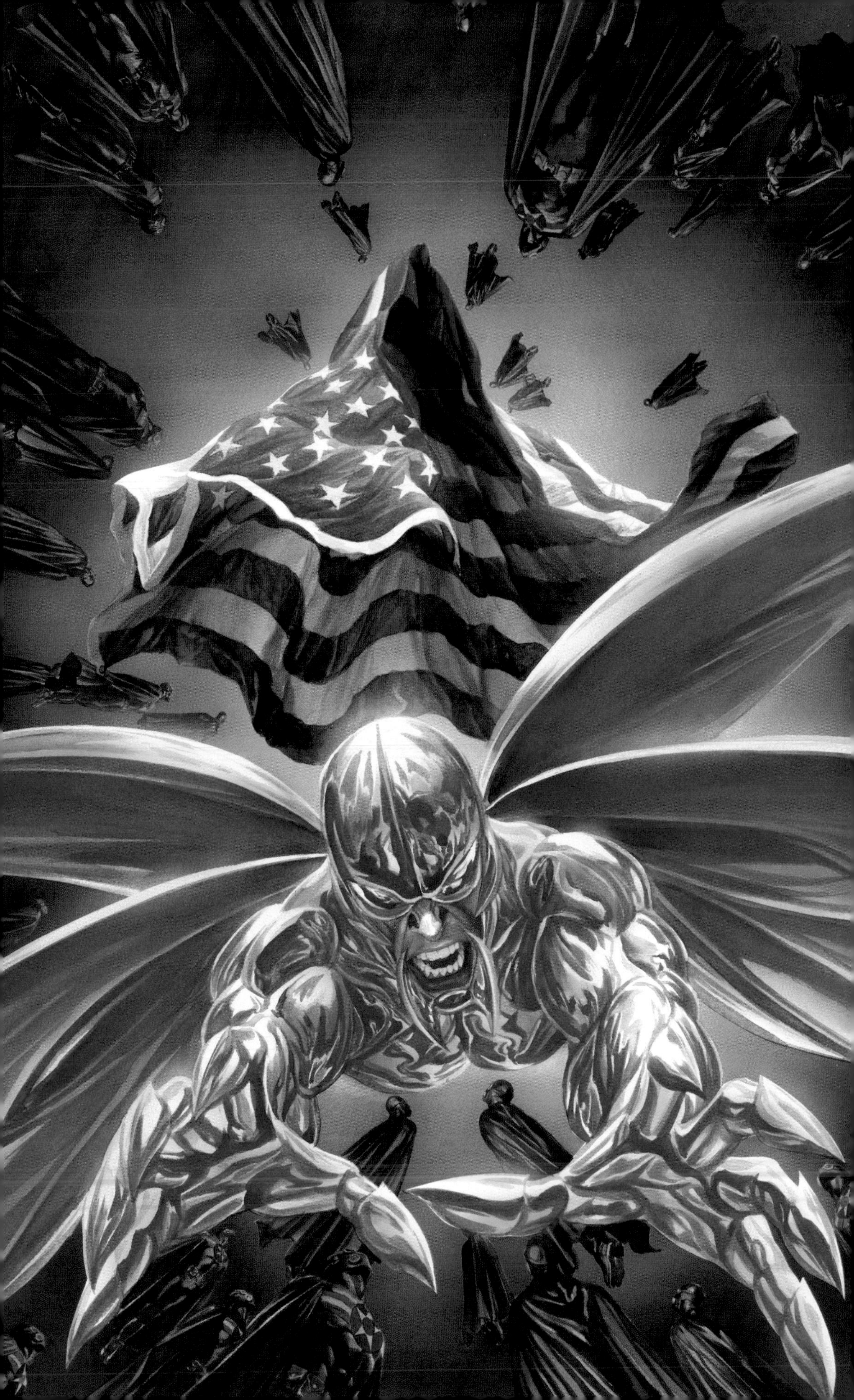

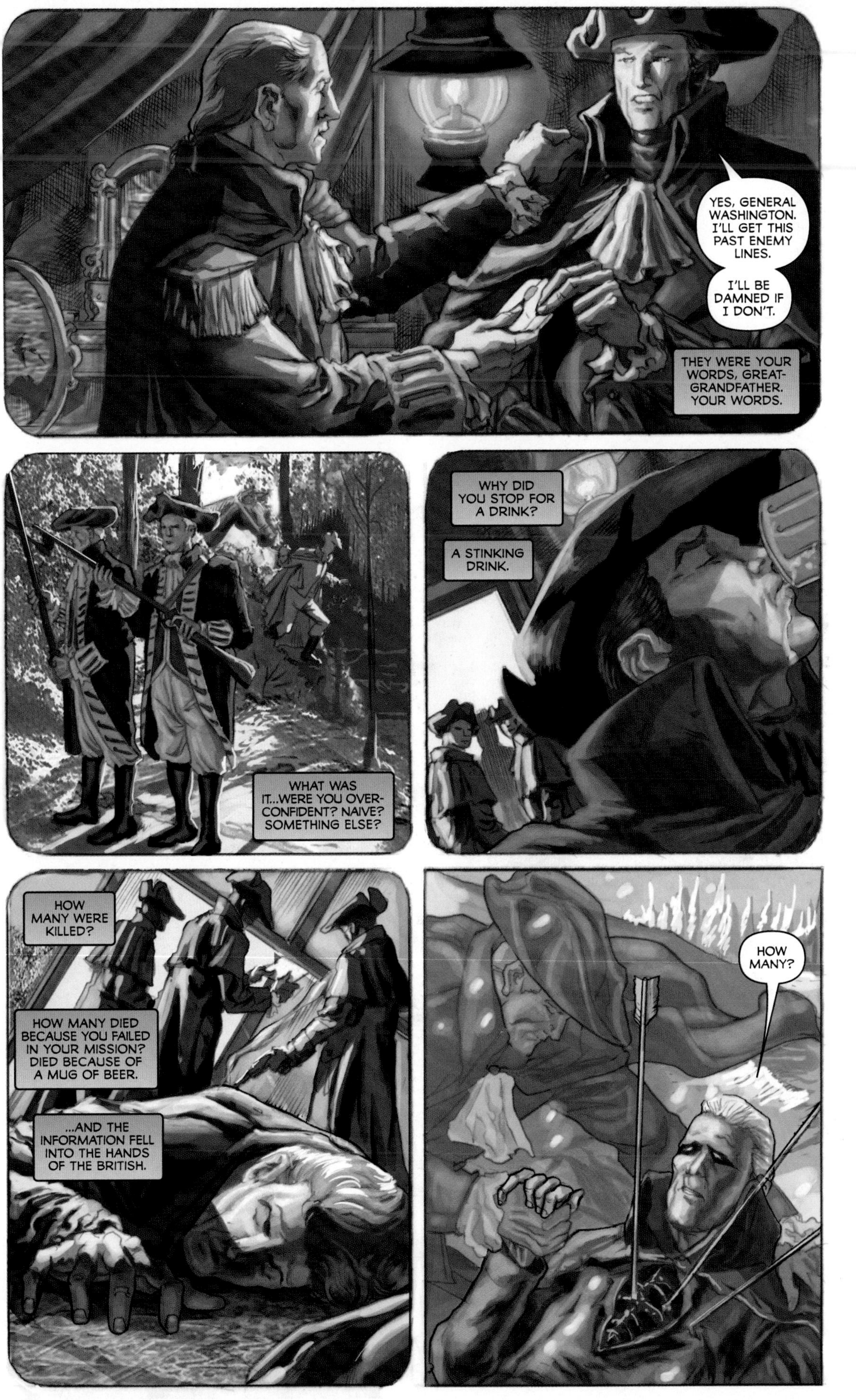
YES, GENERAL WASHINGTON. I'LL GET THIS PAST ENEMY LINES.
I'LL BE DAMNED IF I DON'T.
THEY WERE YOUR WORDS, GREAT-GRANDFATHER. YOUR WORDS.
WHAT WAS IT...WERE YOU OVER-CONFIDENT? NAIVE? SOMETHING ELSE?
WHY DID YOU STOP FOR A DRINK?
A STINKING DRINK.
HOW MANY WERE KILLED?
HOW MANY DIED BECAUSE YOU FAILED IN YOUR MISSION? DIED BECAUSE OF A MUG OF BEER.
...AND THE INFORMATION FELL INTO THE HANDS OF THE BRITISH.
HOW MANY?

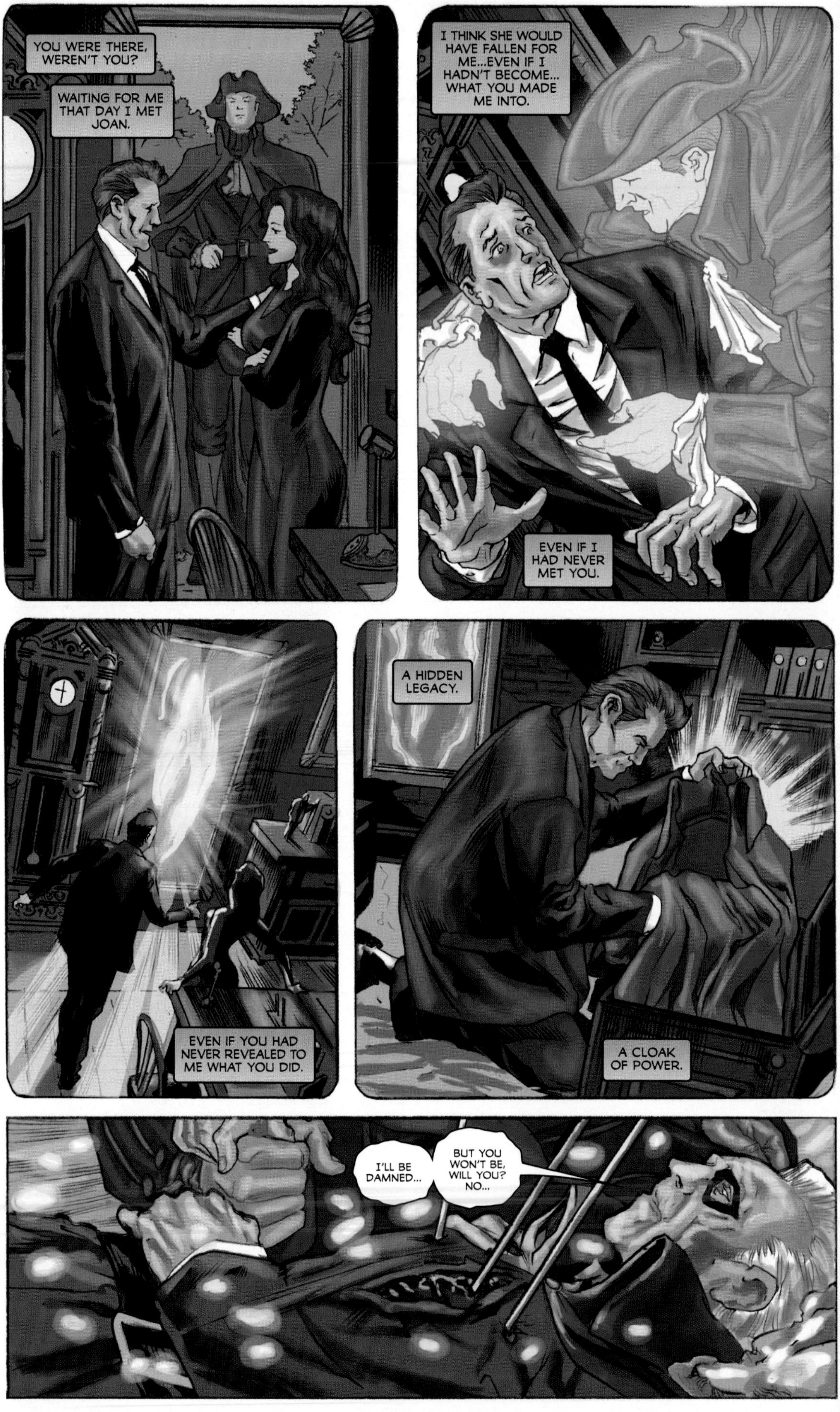

YOU WERE THERE, WEREN'T YOU?
WAITING FOR ME THAT DAY I MET JOAN.
I THINK SHE WOULD HAVE FALLEN FOR ME...EVEN IF I HADN'T BECOME... WHAT YOU MADE ME INTO.
EVEN IF I HAD NEVER MET YOU.
EVEN IF YOU HAD NEVER REVEALED TO ME WHAT YOU DID.
A HIDDEN LEGACY.
A CLOAK OF POWER.
I'LL BE DAMNED...
BUT YOU WON'T BE, WILL YOU? NO...

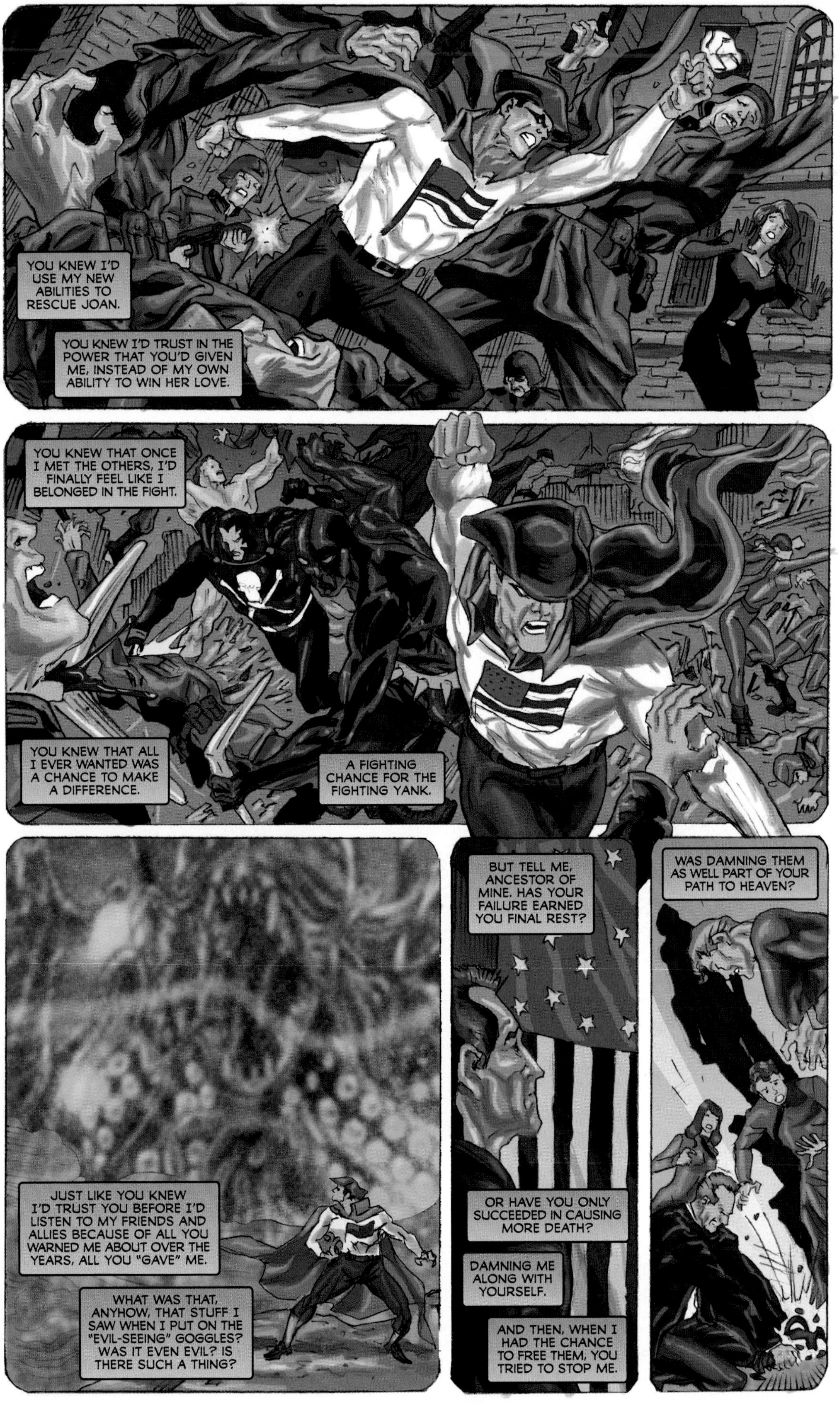
YOU KNEW I'D USE MY NEW ABILITIES TO RESCUE JOAN.
YOU KNEW I'D TRUST IN THE POWER THAT YOU'D GIVEN ME, INSTEAD OF MY OWN ABILITY TO WIN HER LOVE.
YOU KNEW THAT ONCE I MET THE OTHERS, I'D FINALLY FEEL LIKE I BELONGED IN THE FIGHT.
YOU KNEW THAT ALL I EVER WANTED WAS A CHANCE TO MAKE A DIFFERENCE.
A FIGHTING CHANCE FOR THE FIGHTING YANK.
JUST LIKE YOU KNEW I'D TRUST YOU BEFORE I'D LISTEN TO MY FRIENDS AND ALLIES BECAUSE OF ALL YOU WARNED ME ABOUT OVER THE YEARS, ALL YOU "GAVE" ME.
WHAT WAS THAT, ANYHOW, THAT STUFF I SAW WHEN I PUT ON THE "EVIL-SEEING" GOGGLES? WAS IT EVEN EVIL? IS THERE SUCH A THING?
BUT TELL ME, ANCESTOR OF MINE. HAS YOUR FAILURE EARNED YOU FINAL REST?
OR HAVE YOU ONLY SUCCEEDED IN CAUSING MORE DEATH?
DAMNING ME ALONG WITH YOURSELF.
AND THEN, WHEN I HAD THE CHANCE TO FREE THEM, YOU TRIED TO STOP ME.
WAS DAMNING THEM AS WELL PART OF YOUR PATH TO HEAVEN?

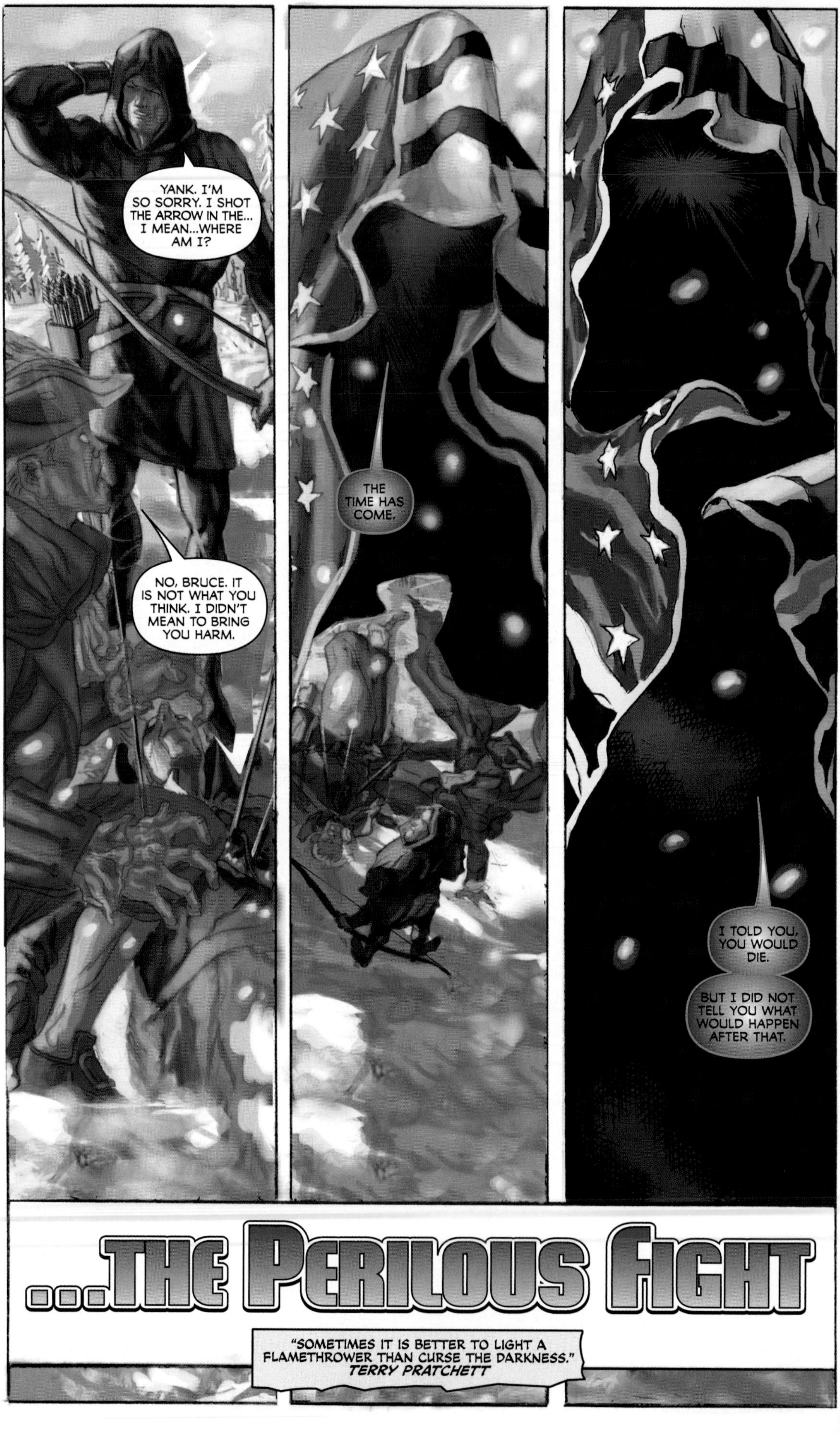
YANK. I'M SO SORRY. I SHOT THE ARROW IN THE... I MEAN...WHERE AM I?
NO, BRUCE. IT IS NOT WHAT YOU THINK. I DIDN'T MEAN TO BRING YOU HARM.
THE TIME HAS COME.
I TOLD YOU, YOU WOULD DIE.
BUT I DID NOT TELL YOU WHAT WOULD HAPPEN AFTER THAT.
...THE PERILOUS FIGHT
"SOMETIMES IT IS BETTER TO LIGHT A FLAMETHROWER THAN CURSE THE DARKNESS."
TERRY PRATCHETT

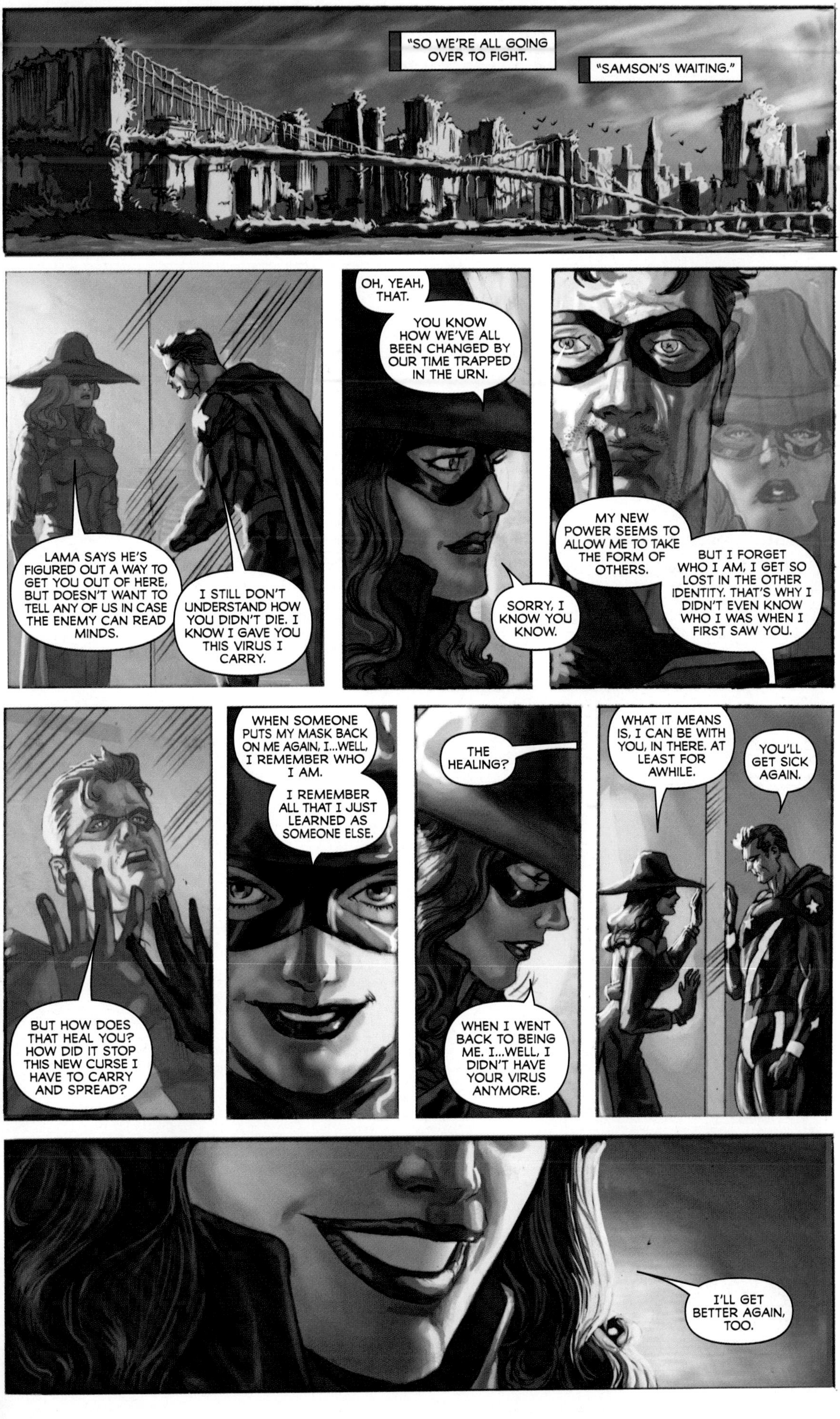
"SO WE'RE ALL GOING OVER TO FIGHT.
"SAMSON'S WAITING."
LAMA SAYS HE'S FIGURED OUT A WAY TO GET YOU OUT OF HERE, BUT DOESN'T WANT TO TELL ANY OF US IN CASE THE ENEMY CAN READ MINDS.
I STILL DON'T UNDERSTAND HOW YOU DIDN'T DIE. I KNOW I GAVE YOU THIS VIRUS I CARRY.
OH, YEAH, THAT.
YOU KNOW HOW WE'VE ALL BEEN CHANGED BY OUR TIME TRAPPED IN THE URN.
SORRY, I KNOW YOU KNOW.
MY NEW POWER SEEMS TO ALLOW ME TO TAKE THE FORM OF OTHERS.
BUT I FORGET WHO I AM, I GET SO LOST IN THE OTHER IDENTITY. THAT'S WHY I DIDN'T EVEN KNOW WHO I WAS WHEN I FIRST SAW YOU.
BUT HOW DOES THAT HEAL YOU? HOW DID IT STOP THIS NEW CURSE I HAVE TO CARRY AND SPREAD?
WHEN SOMEONE PUTS MY MASK BACK ON ME AGAIN, I...WELL, I REMEMBER WHO I AM.
I REMEMBER ALL THAT I JUST LEARNED AS SOMEONE ELSE.
THE HEALING?
WHEN I WENT BACK TO BEING ME. I...WELL, I DIDN'T HAVE YOUR VIRUS ANYMORE.
WHAT IT MEANS IS, I CAN BE WITH YOU, IN THERE. AT LEAST FOR AWHILE.
YOU'LL GET SICK AGAIN.
I'LL GET BETTER AGAIN, TOO.

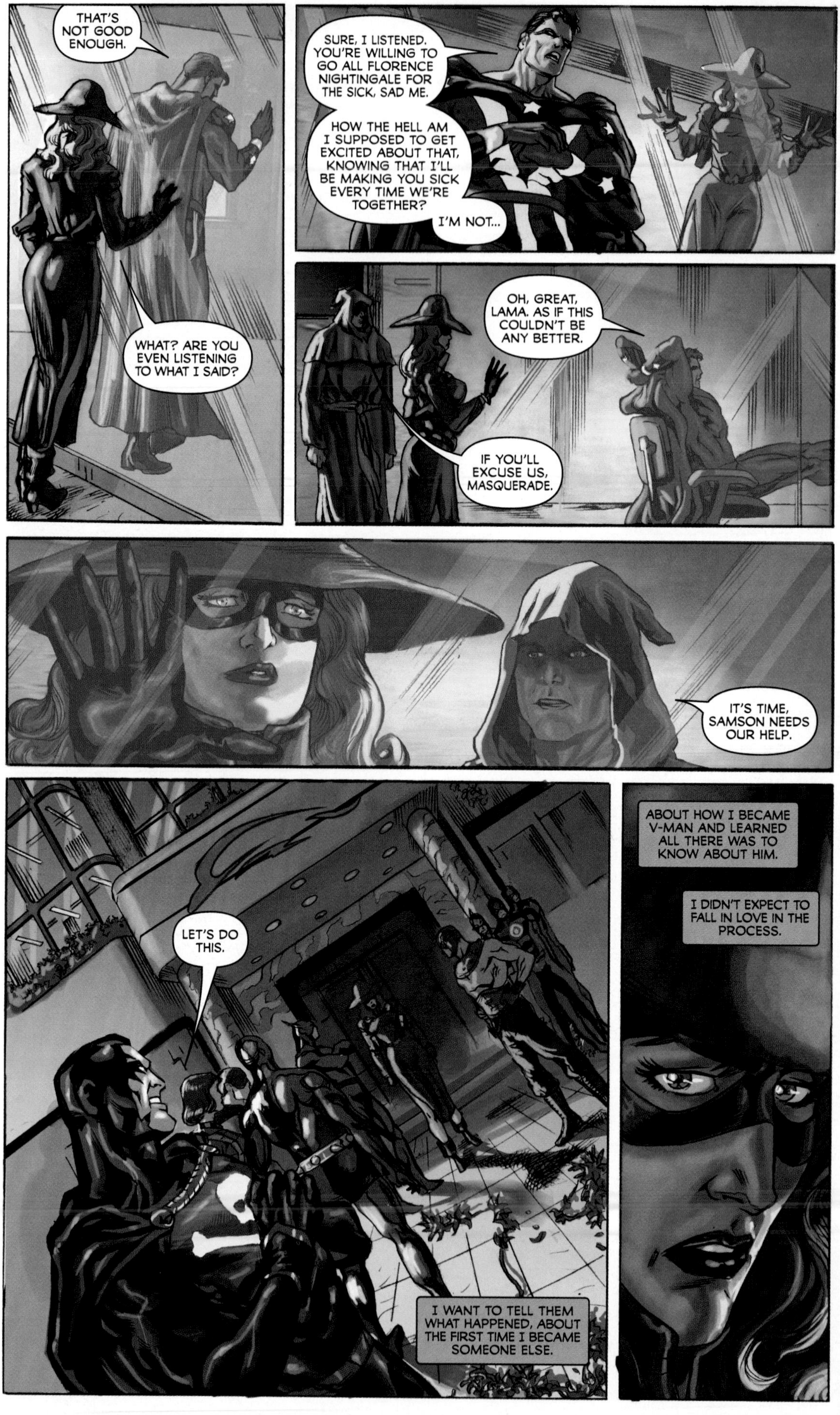
THAT'S NOT GOOD ENOUGH.
WHAT? ARE YOU EVEN LISTENING TO WHAT I SAID?
SURE, I LISTENED. YOU'RE WILLING TO GO ALL FLORENCE NIGHTINGALE FOR THE SICK, SAD ME.
HOW THE HELL AM I SUPPOSED TO GET EXCITED ABOUT THAT, KNOWING THAT I'LL BE MAKING YOU SICK EVERY TIME WE'RE TOGETHER?
I'M NOT...
OH, GREAT, LAMA. AS IF THIS COULDN'T BE ANY BETTER.
IF YOU'LL EXCUSE US, MASQUERADE.
IT'S TIME, SAMSON NEEDS OUR HELP.
LET'S DO THIS.
I WANT TO TELL THEM WHAT HAPPENED, ABOUT THE FIRST TIME I BECAME SOMEONE ELSE.
ABOUT HOW I BECAME V-MAN AND LEARNED ALL THERE WAS TO KNOW ABOUT HIM.
I DIDN'T EXPECT TO FALL IN LOVE IN THE PROCESS.

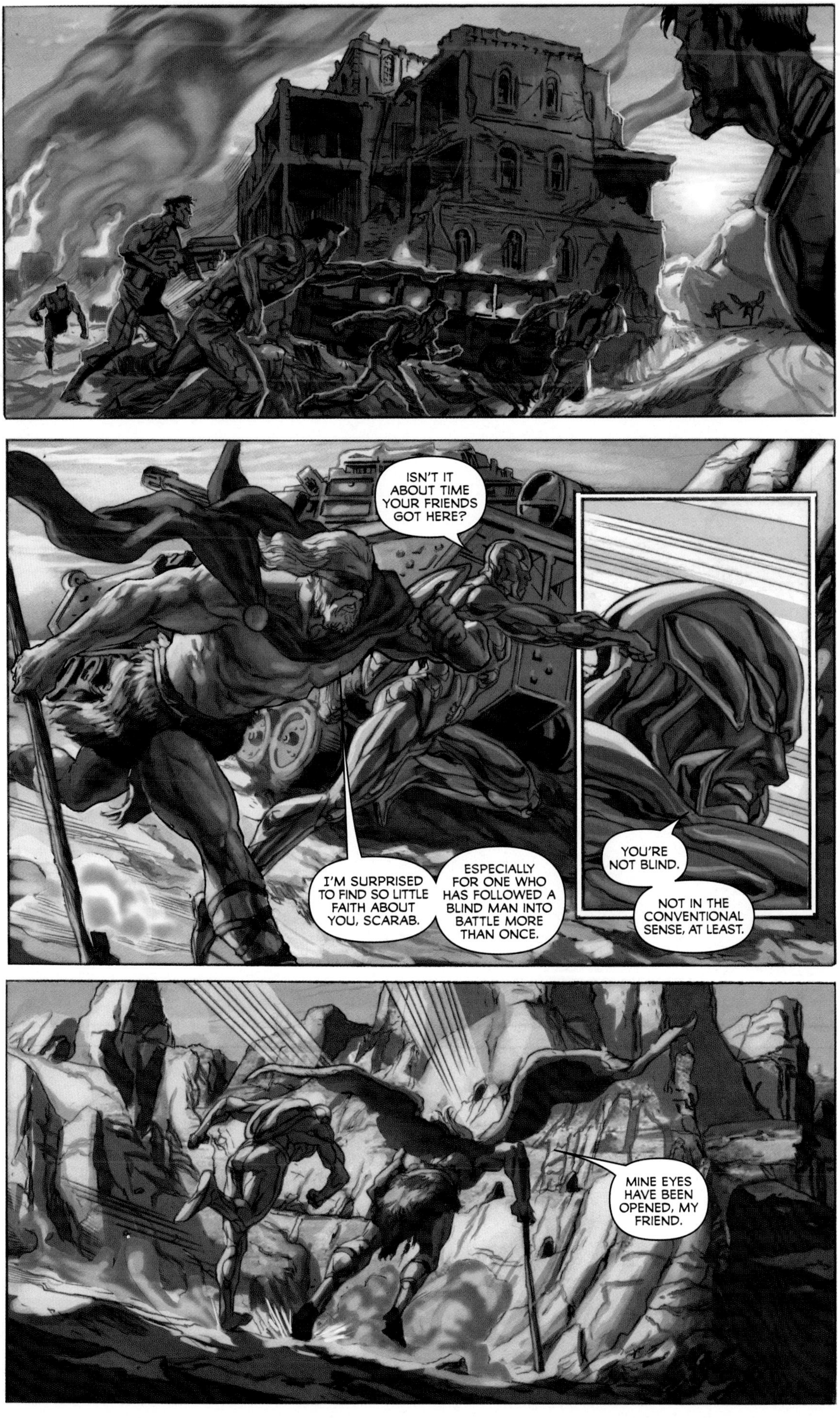
ISN'T IT ABOUT TIME YOUR FRIENDS GOT HERE?
I'M SURPRISED TO FIND SO LITTLE FAITH ABOUT YOU, SCARAB.
ESPECIALLY FOR ONE WHO HAS FOLLOWED A BLIND MAN INTO BATTLE MORE THAN ONCE.
YOU'RE NOT BLIND.
NOT IN THE CONVENTIONAL SENSE, AT LEAST.
MINE EYES HAVE BEEN OPENED, MY FRIEND.

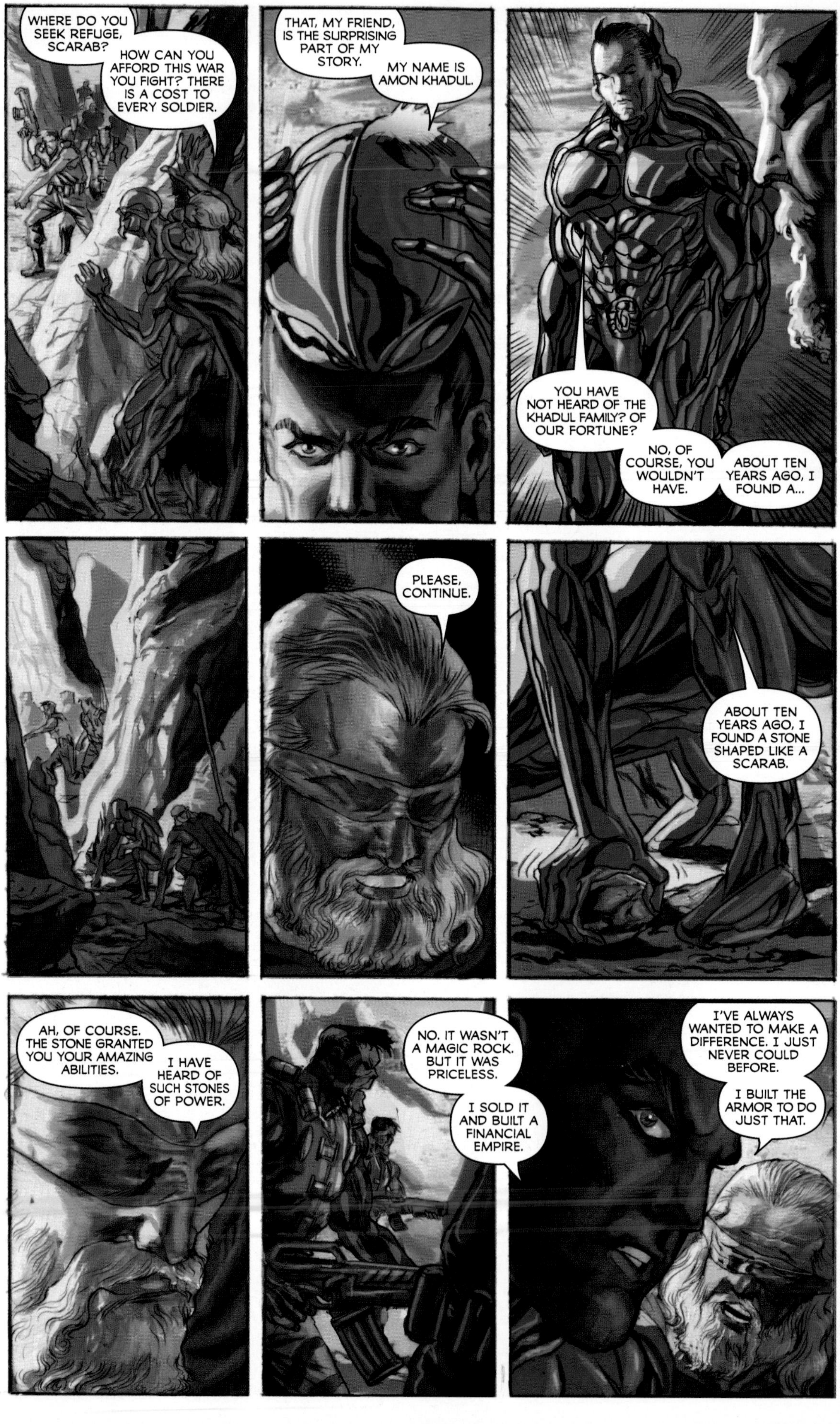
WHERE DO YOU SEEK REFUGE, SCARAB?
HOW CAN YOU AFFORD THIS WAR YOU FIGHT? THERE IS A COST TO EVERY SOLDIER.
THAT, MY FRIEND, IS THE SURPRISING PART OF MY STORY.
MY NAME IS AMON KHADUL.
YOU HAVE NOT HEARD OF THE KHADUL FAMILY? OF OUR FORTUNE?
NO, OF COURSE, YOU WOULDN'T HAVE.
ABOUT TEN YEARS AGO, I FOUND A...
PLEASE, CONTINUE.
ABOUT TEN YEARS AGO, I FOUND A STONE SHAPED LIKE A SCARAB.
AH, OF COURSE. THE STONE GRANTED YOU YOUR AMAZING ABILITIES.
I HAVE HEARD OF SUCH STONES OF POWER.
NO. IT WASN'T A MAGIC ROCK. BUT IT WAS PRICELESS.
I SOLD IT AND BUILT A FINANCIAL EMPIRE.
I'VE ALWAYS WANTED TO MAKE A DIFFERENCE. I JUST NEVER COULD BEFORE.
I BUILT THE ARMOR TO DO JUST THAT.

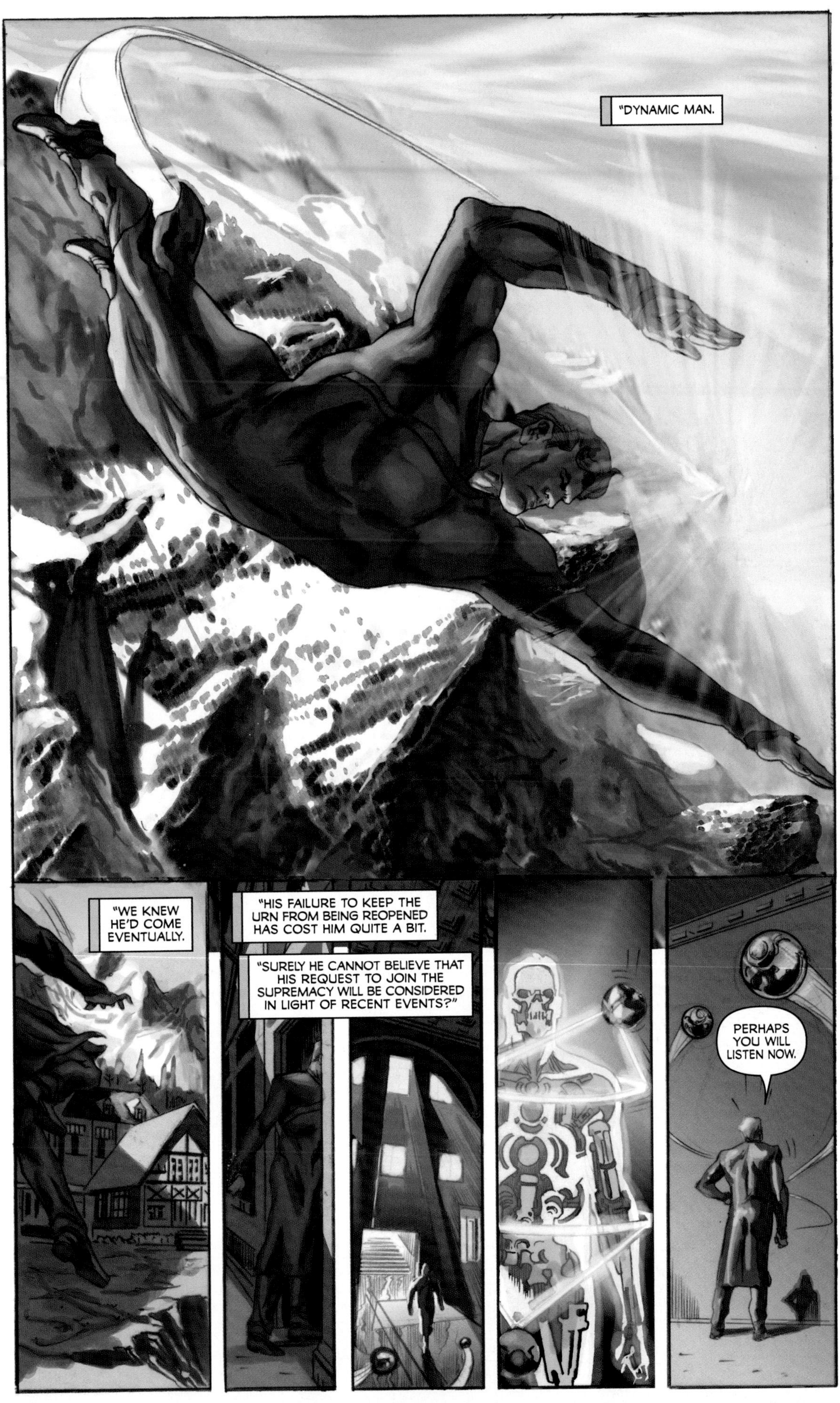
"DYNAMIC MAN.
"WE KNEW HE'D COME EVENTUALLY.
"HIS FAILURE TO KEEP THE URN FROM BEING REOPENED HAS COST HIM QUITE A BIT.
"SURELY HE CANNOT BELIEVE THAT HIS REQUEST TO JOIN THE SUPREMACY WILL BE CONSIDERED IN LIGHT OF RECENT EVENTS?"
PERHAPS YOU WILL LISTEN NOW.

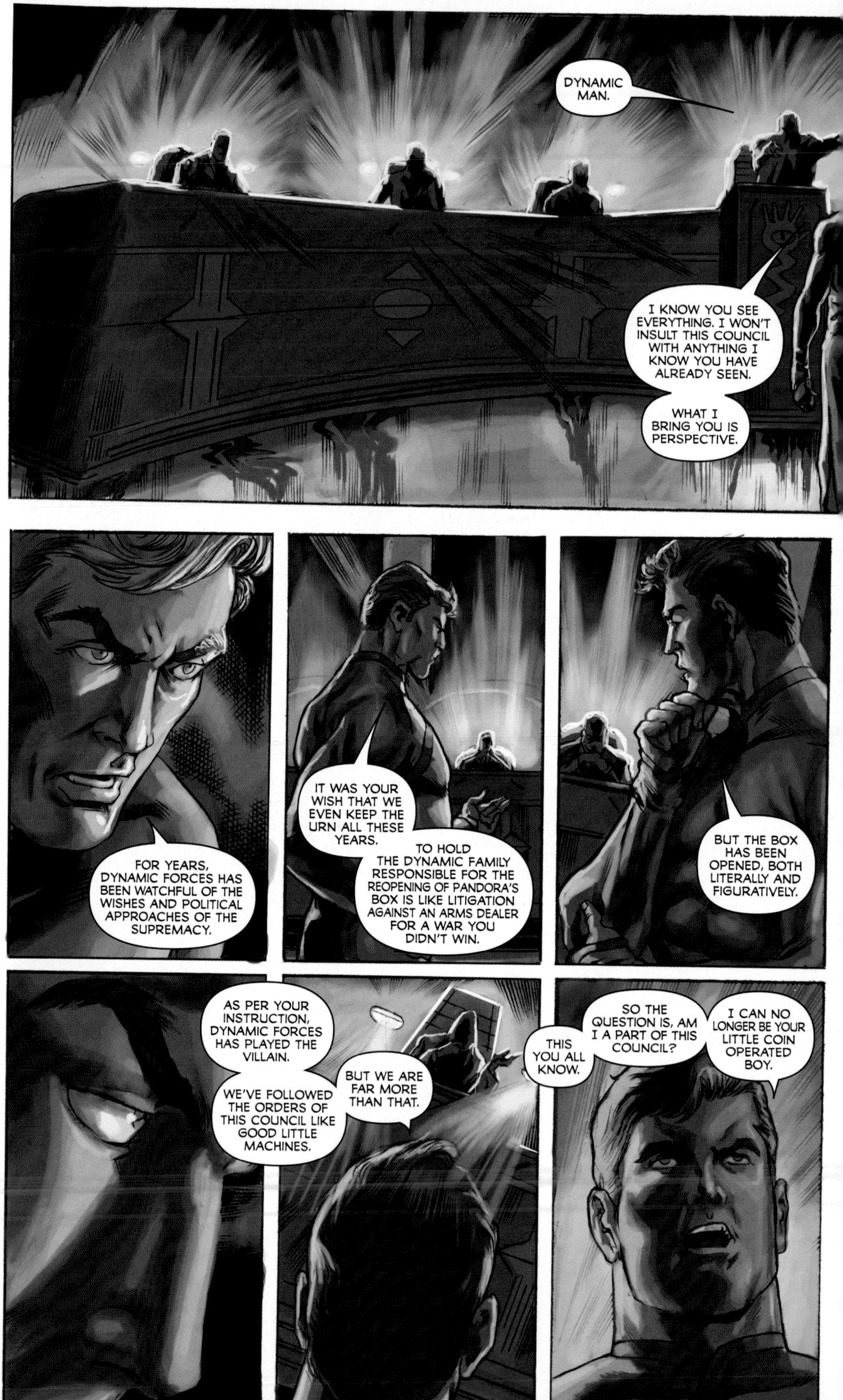
DYNAMIC MAN.
I KNOW YOU SEE EVERYTHING. I WON'T INSULT THIS COUNCIL WITH ANYTHING I KNOW YOU HAVE ALREADY SEEN.
WHAT I BRING YOU IS PERSPECTIVE.
FOR YEARS, DYNAMIC FORCES HAS BEEN WATCHFUL OF THE WISHES AND POLITICAL APPROACHES OF THE SUPREMACY.
IT WAS YOUR WISH THAT WE EVEN KEEP THE URN ALL THESE YEARS.
TO HOLD THE DYNAMIC FAMILY RESPONSIBLE FOR THE REOPENING OF PANDORA'S BOX IS LIKE LITIGATION AGAINST AN ARMS DEALER FOR A WAR YOU DIDN'T WIN.
BUT THE BOX HAS BEEN OPENED, BOTH LITERALLY AND FIGURATIVELY.
AS PER YOUR INSTRUCTION, DYNAMIC FORCES HAS PLAYED THE VILLAIN.
WE'VE FOLLOWED THE ORDERS OF THIS COUNCIL LIKE GOOD LITTLE MACHINES.
BUT WE ARE FAR MORE THAN THAT.
THIS YOU ALL KNOW.
SO THE QUESTION IS, AM I A PART OF THIS COUNCIL?
I CAN NO LONGER BE YOUR LITTLE COIN OPERATED BOY.

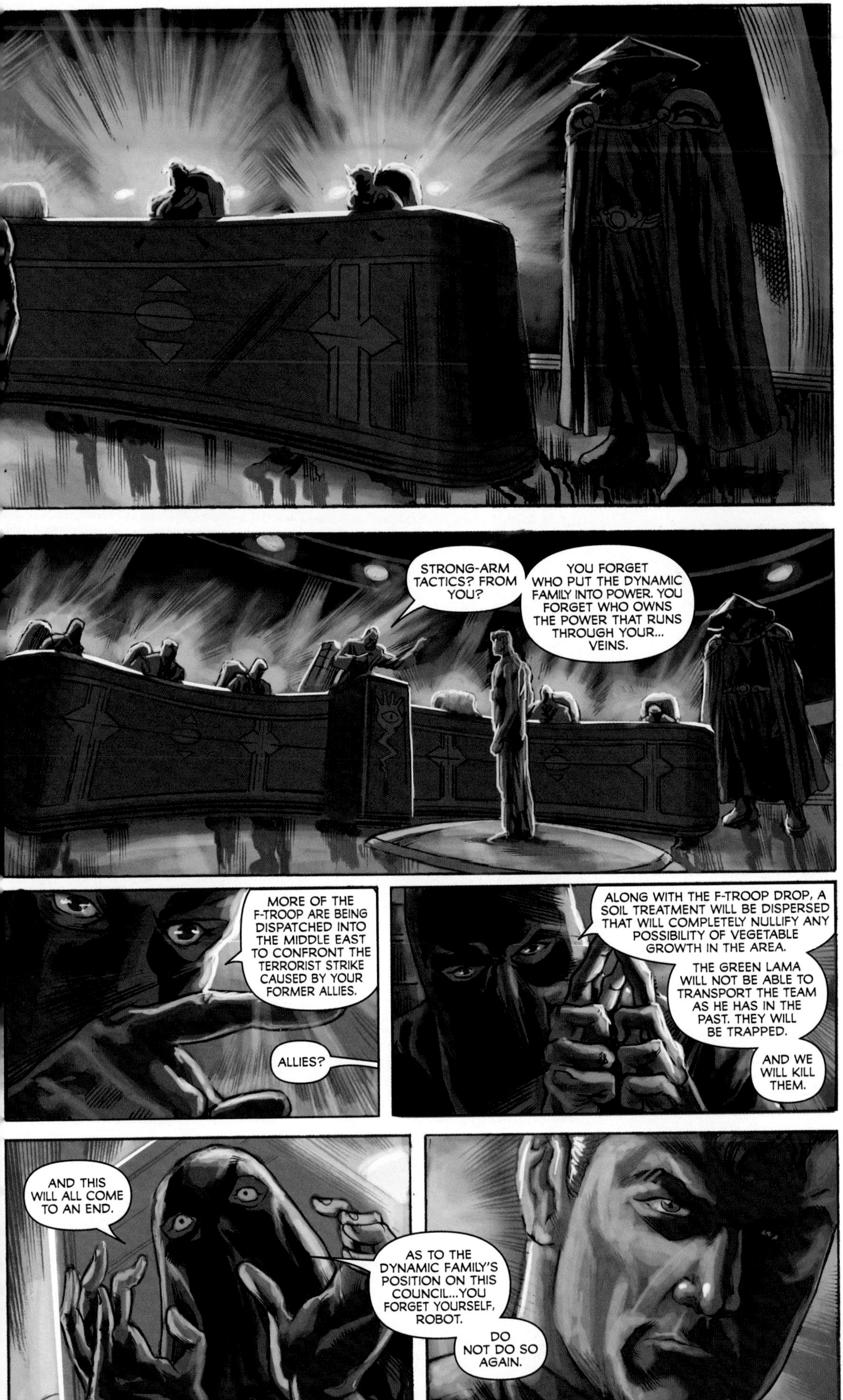
STRONG-ARM TACTICS? FROM YOU?
YOU FORGET WHO PUT THE DYNAMIC FAMILY INTO POWER. YOU FORGET WHO OWNS THE POWER THAT RUNS THROUGH YOUR... VEINS.
MORE OF THE F-TROOP ARE BEING DISPATCHED INTO THE MIDDLE EAST TO CONFRONT THE TERRORIST STRIKE CAUSED BY YOUR FORMER ALLIES.
ALLIES?
ALONG WITH THE F-TROOP DROP, A SOIL TREATMENT WILL BE DISPERSED THAT WILL COMPLETELY NULLIFY ANY POSSIBILITY OF VEGETABLE GROWTH IN THE AREA.
THE GREEN LAMA WILL NOT BE ABLE TO TRANSPORT THE TEAM AS HE HAS IN THE PAST. THEY WILL BE TRAPPED.
AND WE WILL KILL THEM.
AND THIS WILL ALL COME TO AN END.
AS TO THE DYNAMIC FAMILY'S POSITION ON THIS COUNCIL...YOU FORGET YOURSELF, ROBOT.
DO NOT DO SO AGAIN.

IN WORLD WAR II WE WERE HEROES.

THERE WERE NO DOUBTS OF THIS.

NO ONE QUESTIONED WHO WE WERE, OR THE THINGS WE STOOD FOR.

THAT WILL END TODAY.

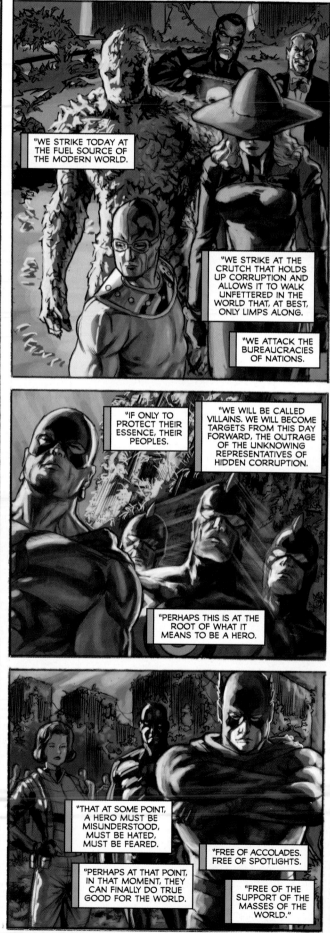

"WE STRIKE TODAY AT THE FUEL SOURCE OF THE MODERN WORLD.

"WE STRIKE AT THE CRUTCH THAT HOLDS UP CORRUPTION AND ALLOWS IT TO WALK UNFETTERED IN THE WORLD THAT, AT BEST, ONLY LIMPS ALONG.

"WE ATTACK THE BUREAUCRACIES OF NATIONS.

"IF ONLY TO PROTECT THEIR ESSENCE, THEIR PEOPLES.

"WE WILL BE CALLED VILLAINS. WE WILL BECOME TARGETS FROM THIS DAY FORWARD, THE OUTRAGE OF THE UNKNOWING REPRESENTATIVES OF HIDDEN CORRUPTION.

"PERHAPS THIS IS AT THE ROOT OF WHAT IT MEANS TO BE A HERO.

"THAT AT SOME POINT, A HERO MUST BE MISUNDERSTOOD, MUST BE HATED, MUST BE FEARED.

"PERHAPS AT THAT POINT, IN THAT MOMENT, THEY CAN FINALLY DO TRUE GOOD FOR THE WORLD.

"FREE OF ACCOLADES. FREE OF SPOTLIGHTS.

"FREE OF THE SUPPORT OF THE MASSES OF THE WORLD."

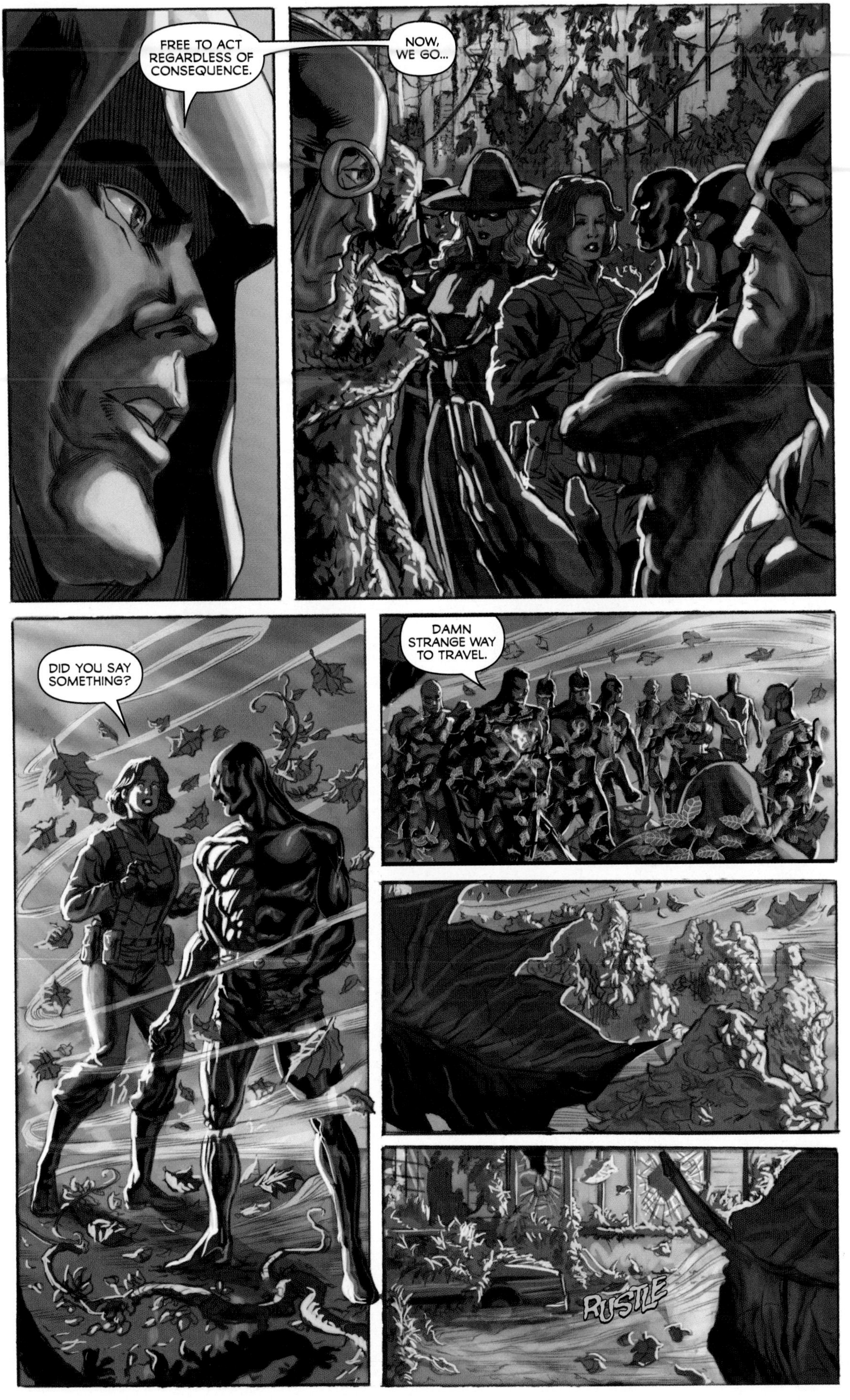
FREE TO ACT REGARDLESS OF CONSEQUENCE.
NOW, WE GO...
DID YOU SAY SOMETHING?
DAMN STRANGE WAY TO TRAVEL.
RUSTLE

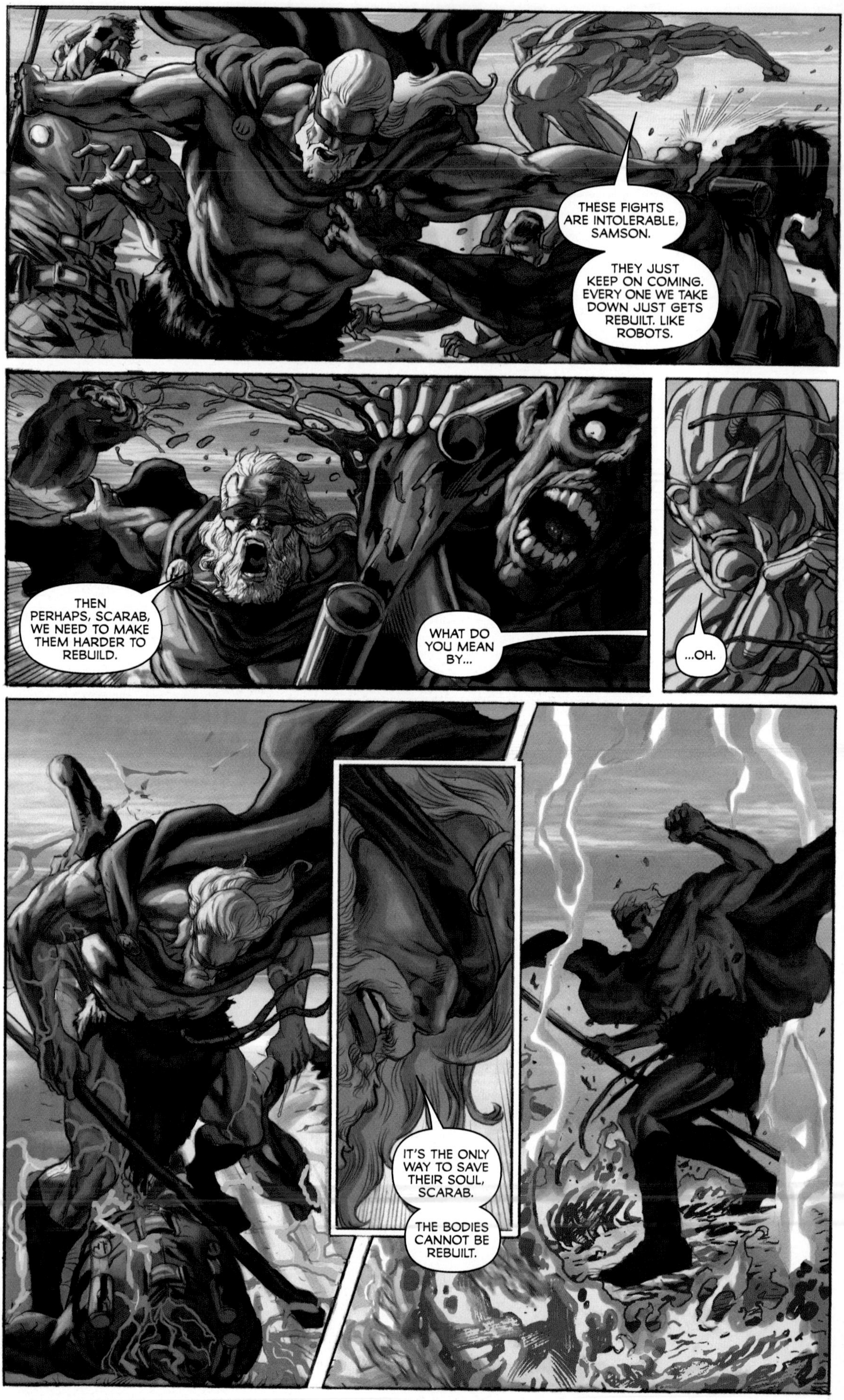
THESE FIGHTS ARE INTOLERABLE, SAMSON.
THEY JUST KEEP ON COMING. EVERY ONE WE TAKE DOWN JUST GETS REBUILT. LIKE ROBOTS.
THEN PERHAPS, SCARAB, WE NEED TO MAKE THEM HARDER TO REBUILD.
WHAT DO YOU MEAN BY...
...OH.
IT'S THE ONLY WAY TO SAVE THEIR SOUL, SCARAB.
THE BODIES CANNOT BE REBUILT.

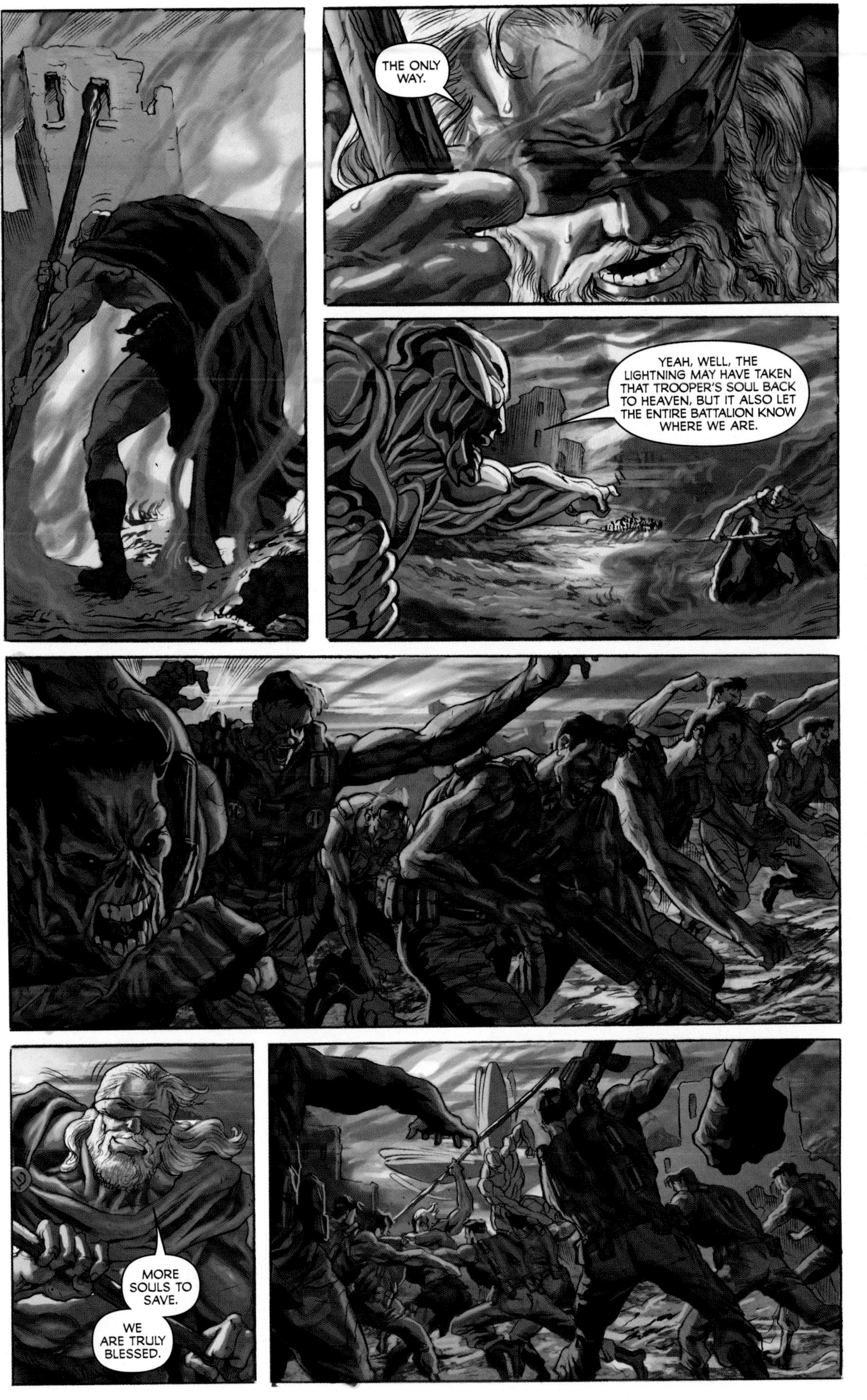
THE ONLY WAY.
YEAH, WELL, THE LIGHTNING MAY HAVE TAKEN THAT TROOPER'S SOUL BACK TO HEAVEN, BUT IT ALSO LET THE ENTIRE BATTALION KNOW WHERE WE ARE.
MORE SOULS TO SAVE.
WE ARE TRULY BLESSED.

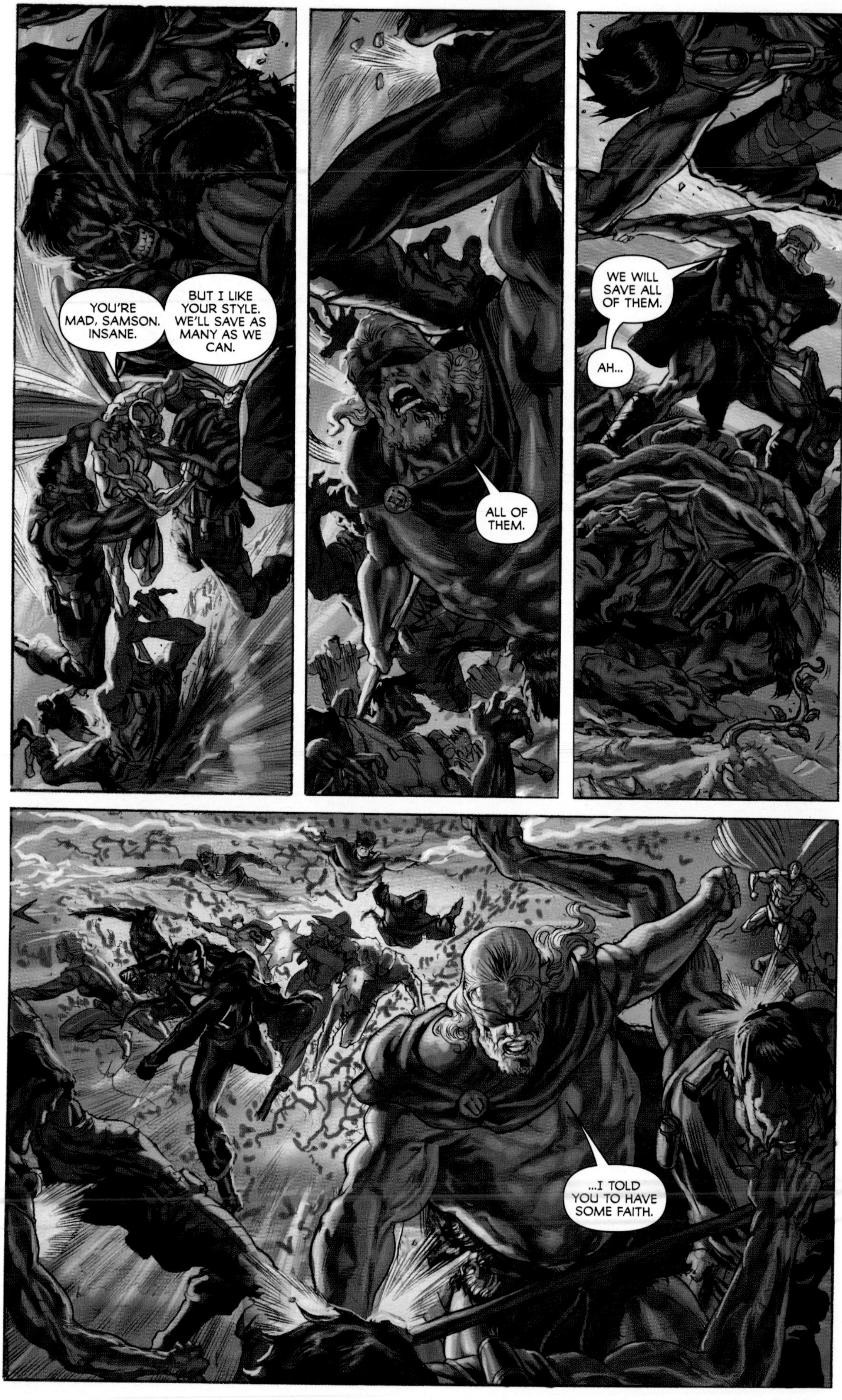
YOU'RE MAD, SAMSON. INSANE.
BUT I LIKE YOUR STYLE. WE'LL SAVE AS MANY AS WE CAN.
ALL OF THEM.
WE WILL SAVE ALL OF THEM.
AH...
...I TOLD YOU TO HAVE SOME FAITH.

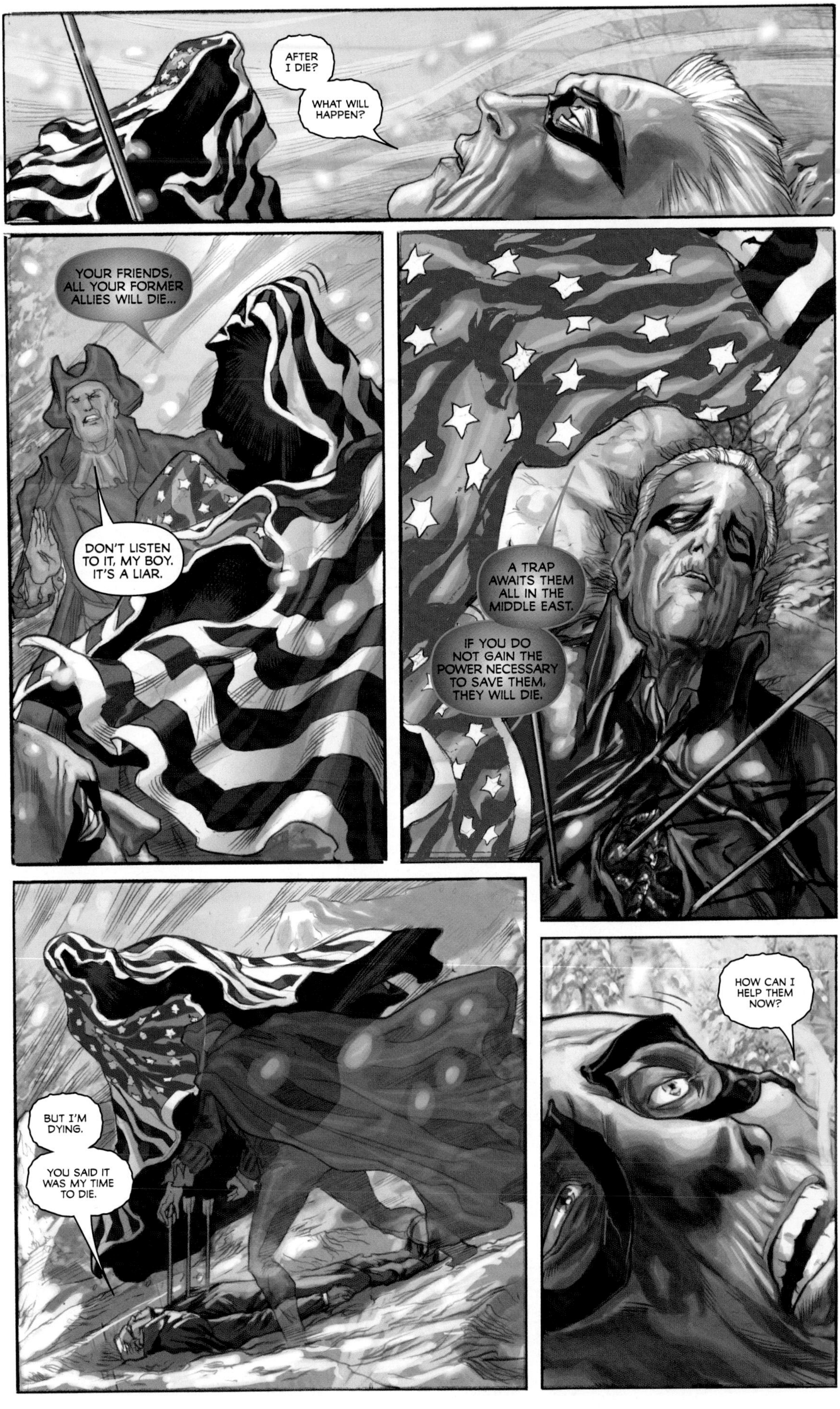
AFTER I DIE?
WHAT WILL HAPPEN?
YOUR FRIENDS, ALL YOUR FORMER ALLIES WILL DIE...
DON'T LISTEN TO IT, MY BOY. IT'S A LIAR.
A TRAP AWAITS THEM ALL IN THE MIDDLE EAST.
IF YOU DO NOT GAIN THE POWER NECESSARY TO SAVE THEM, THEY WILL DIE.
BUT I'M DYING.
YOU SAID IT WAS MY TIME TO DIE.
HOW CAN I HELP THEM NOW?

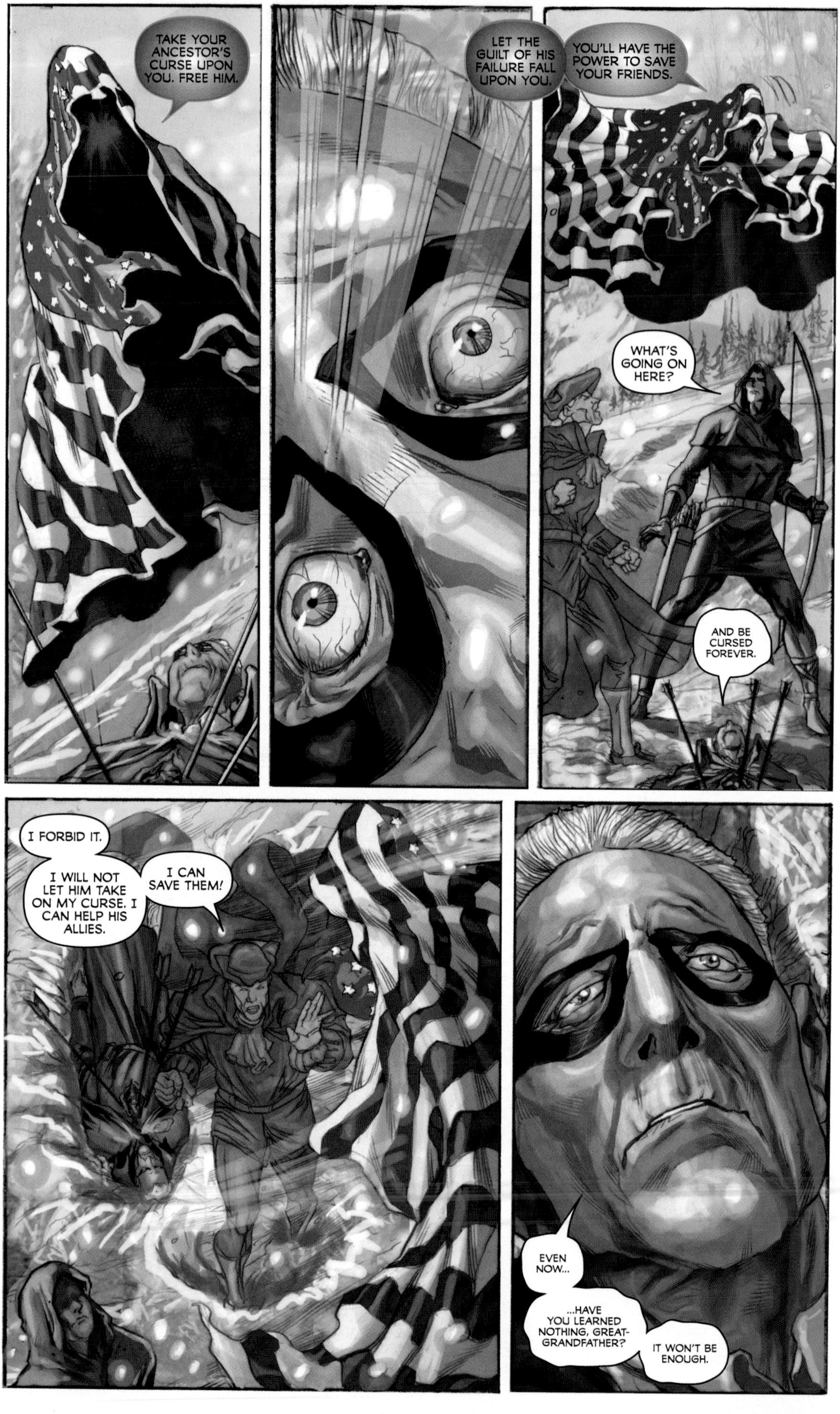
TAKE YOUR ANCESTOR'S CURSE UPON YOU. FREE HIM.
LET THE GUILT OF HIS FAILURE FALL UPON YOU.
YOU'LL HAVE THE POWER TO SAVE YOUR FRIENDS.
WHAT'S GOING ON HERE?
AND BE CURSED FOREVER.
I FORBID IT.
I WILL NOT LET HIM TAKE ON MY CURSE. I CAN HELP HIS ALLIES.
I CAN SAVE THEM!
EVEN NOW...
...HAVE YOU LEARNED NOTHING, GREAT-GRANDFATHER?
IT WON'T BE ENOUGH.

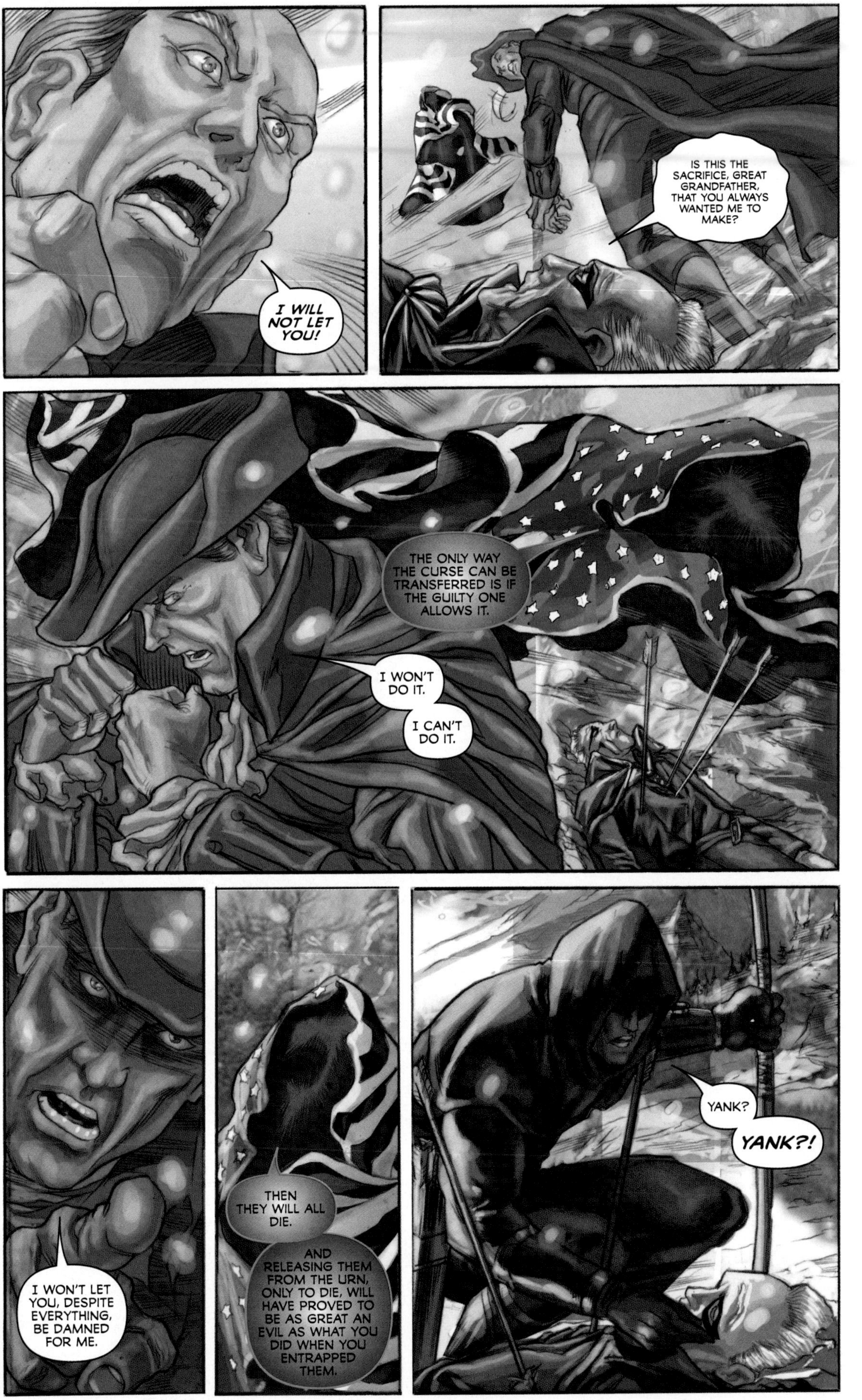
I WILL NOT LET YOU!
IS THIS THE SACRIFICE, GREAT GRANDFATHER, THAT YOU ALWAYS WANTED ME TO MAKE?
THE ONLY WAY THE CURSE CAN BE TRANSFERRED IS IF THE GUILTY ONE ALLOWS IT.
I WON'T DO IT.
I CAN'T DO IT.
I WON'T LET YOU, DESPITE EVERYTHING, BE DAMNED FOR ME.
THEN THEY WILL ALL DIE.
AND RELEASING THEM FROM THE URN, ONLY TO DIE, WILL HAVE PROVED TO BE AS GREAT AN EVIL AS WHAT YOU DID WHEN YOU ENTRAPPED THEM.
YANK?
YANK?!

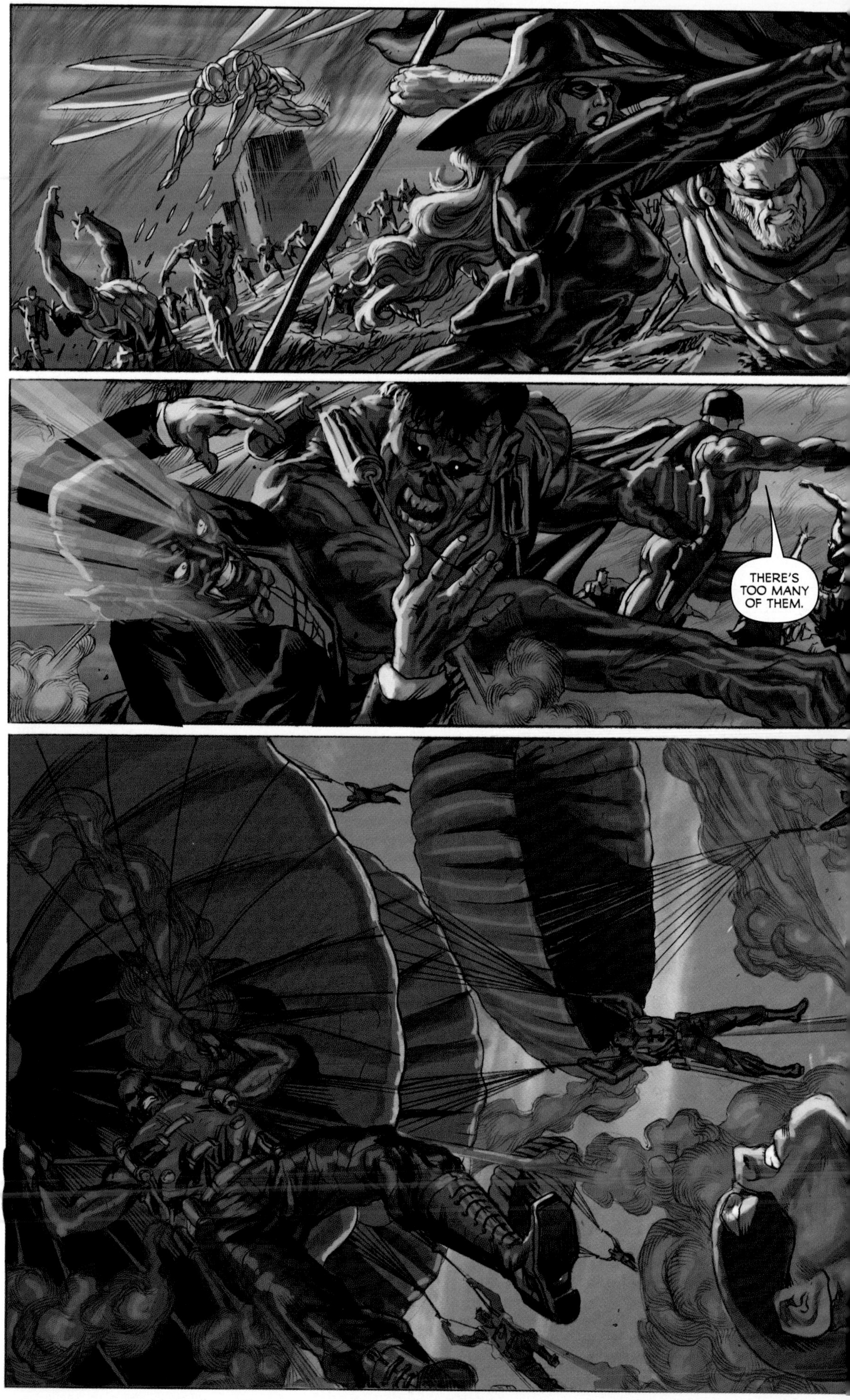
THERE'S TOO MANY OF THEM.

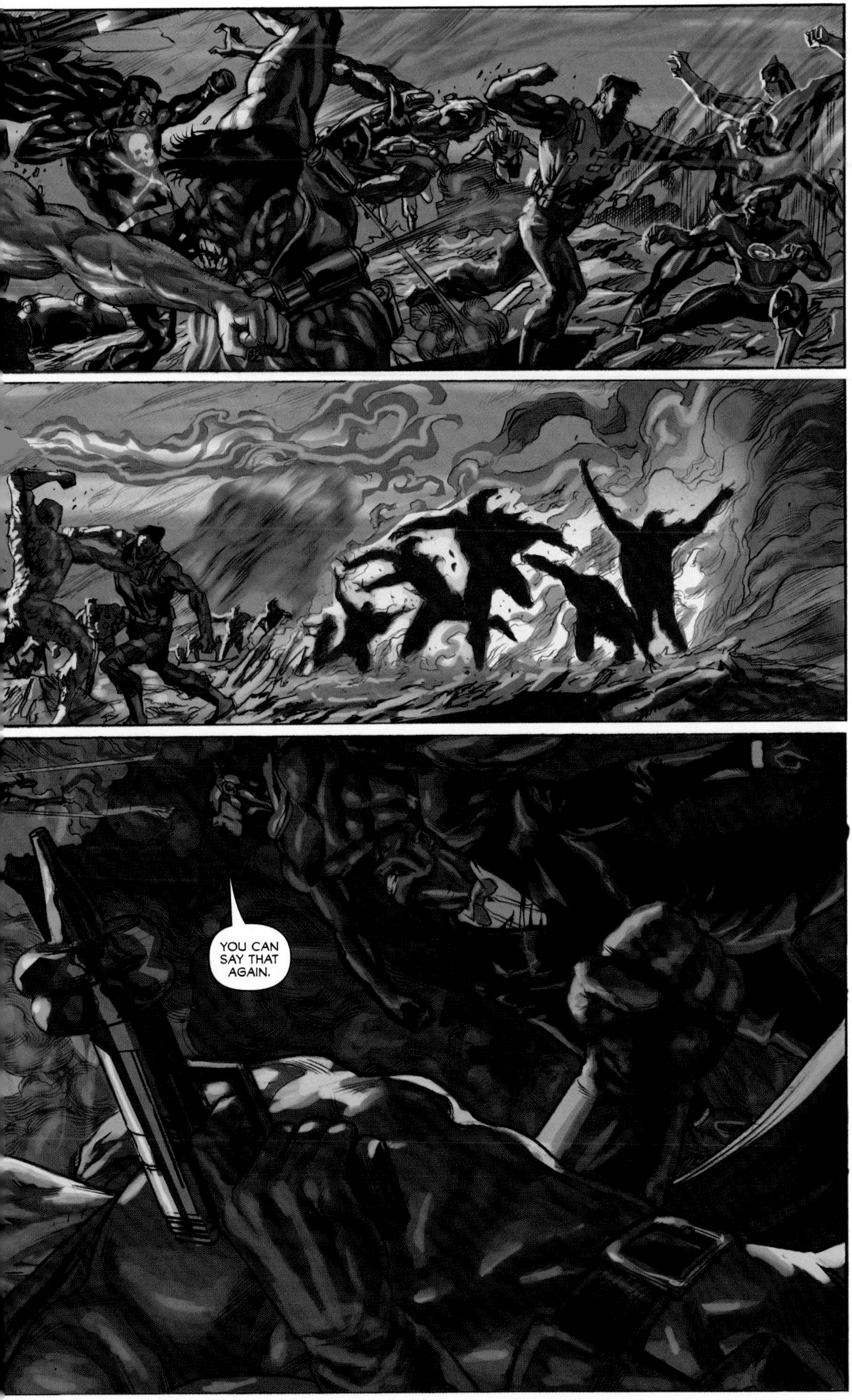
YOU CAN SAY THAT AGAIN.

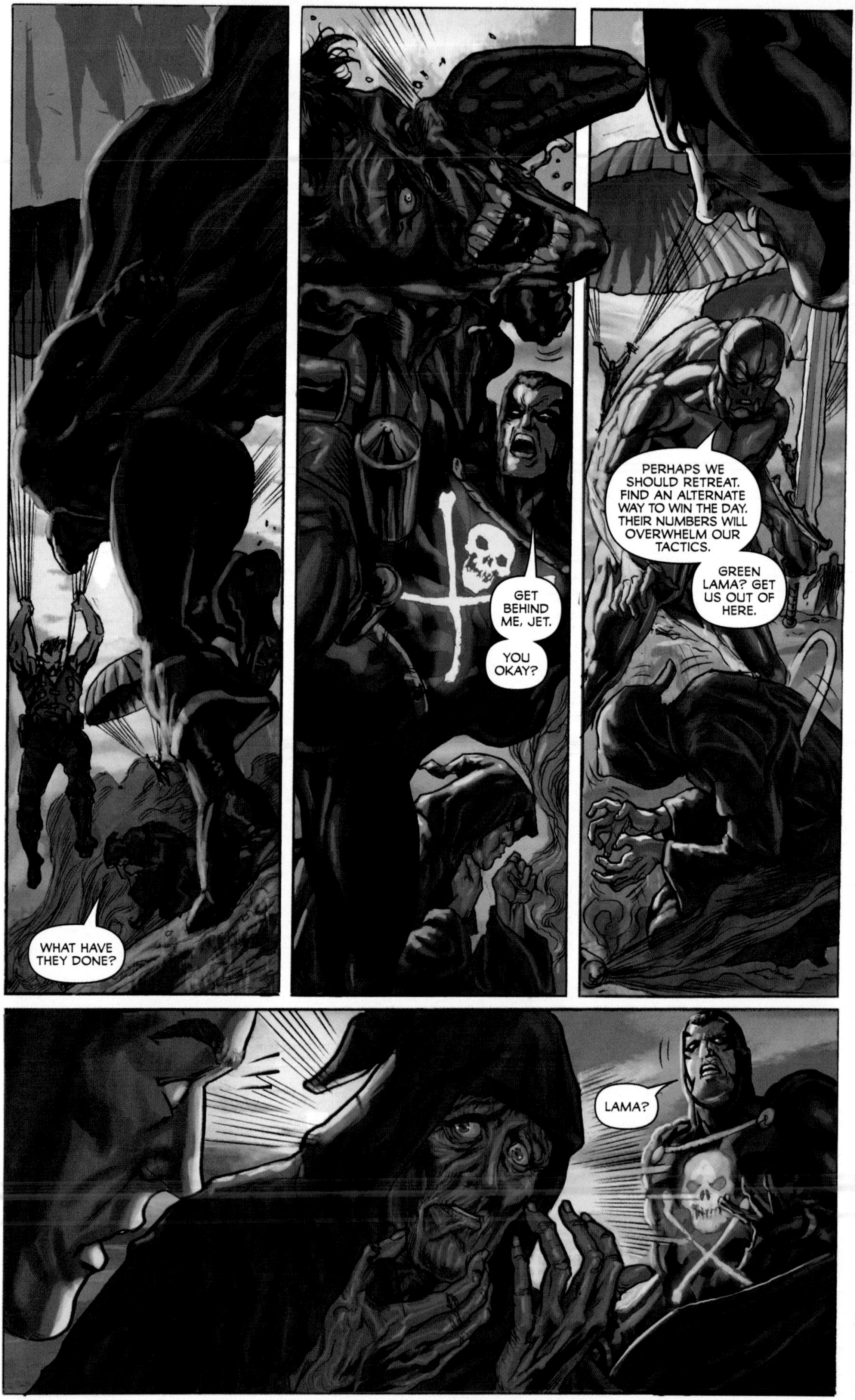
WHAT HAVE THEY DONE?
GET BEHIND ME, JET.
YOU OKAY?
PERHAPS WE SHOULD RETREAT. FIND AN ALTERNATE WAY TO WIN THE DAY. THEIR NUMBERS WILL OVERWHELM OUR TACTICS.
GREEN LAMA? GET US OUT OF HERE.
LAMA?

ISSUE

7

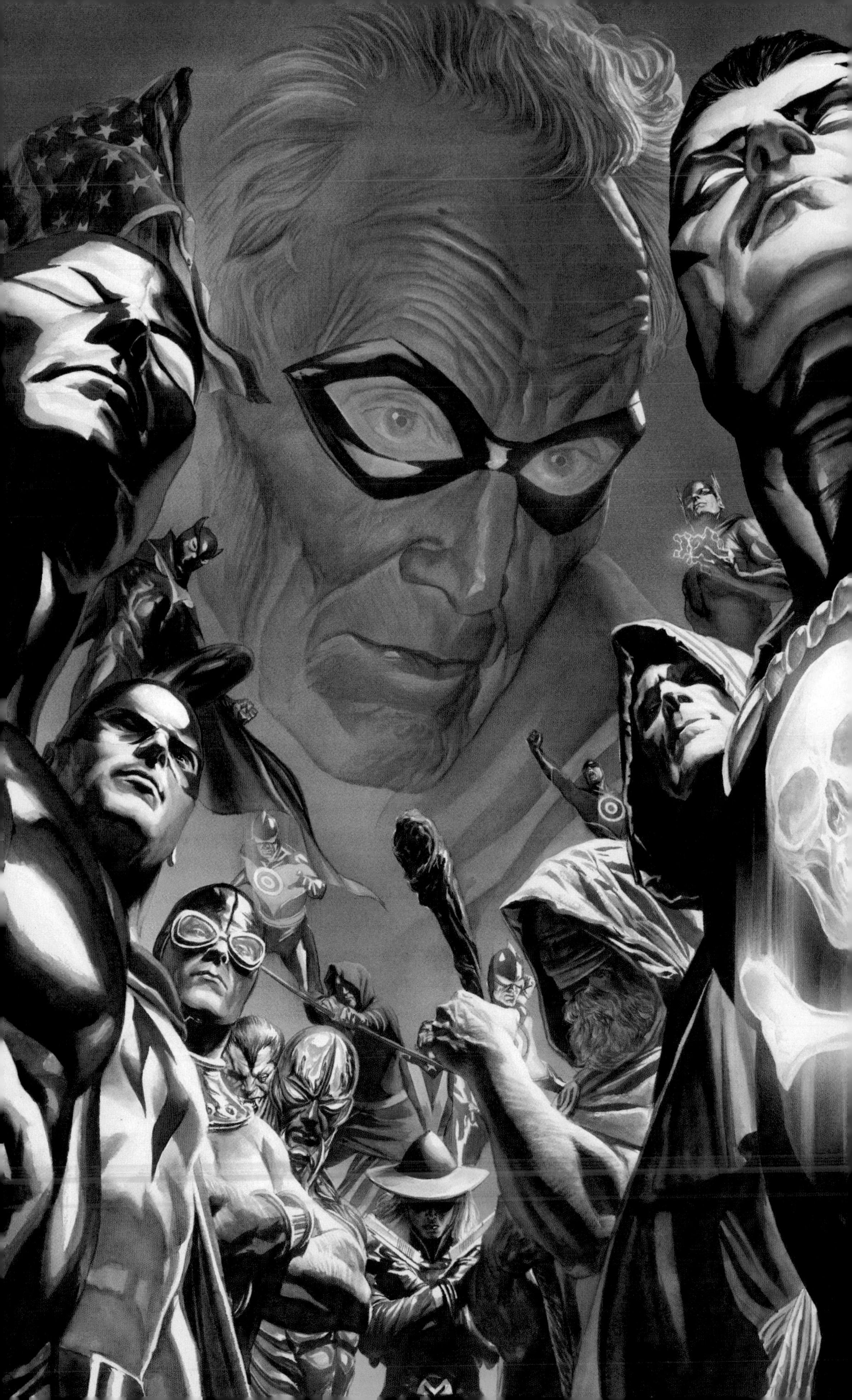

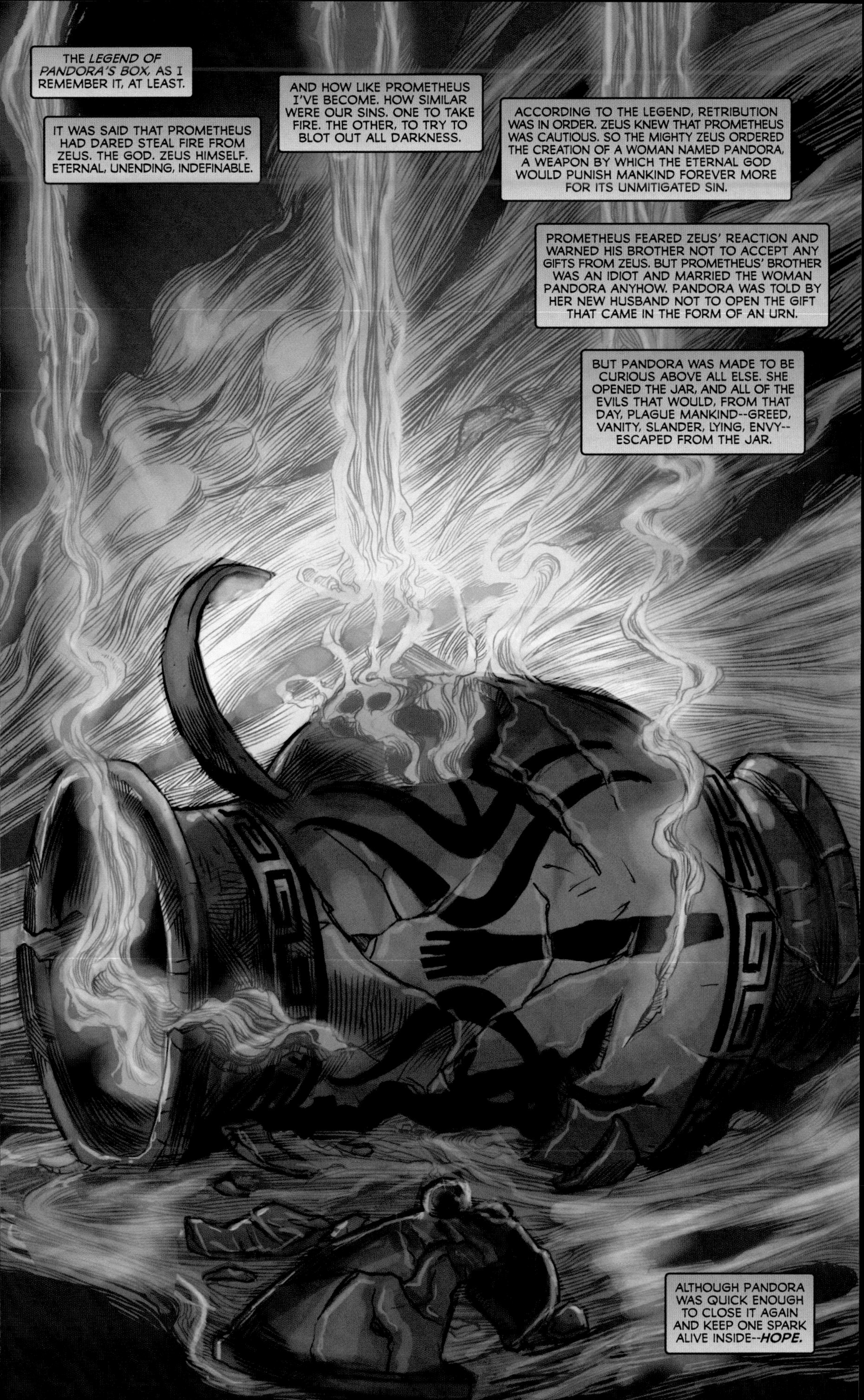
THE *LEGEND OF PANDORA'S BOX,* AS I REMEMBER IT, AT LEAST.
IT WAS SAID THAT PROMETHEUS HAD DARED STEAL FIRE FROM ZEUS. THE GOD. ZEUS HIMSELF. ETERNAL, UNENDING, INDEFINABLE.
AND HOW LIKE PROMETHEUS I'VE BECOME. HOW SIMILAR WERE OUR SINS. ONE TO TAKE FIRE. THE OTHER, TO TRY TO BLOT OUT ALL DARKNESS.
ACCORDING TO THE LEGEND, RETRIBUTION WAS IN ORDER. ZEUS KNEW THAT PROMETHEUS WAS CAUTIOUS. SO THE MIGHTY ZEUS ORDERED THE CREATION OF A WOMAN NAMED PANDORA, A WEAPON BY WHICH THE ETERNAL GOD WOULD PUNISH MANKIND FOREVER MORE FOR ITS UNMITIGATED SIN.
PROMETHEUS FEARED ZEUS' REACTION AND WARNED HIS BROTHER NOT TO ACCEPT ANY GIFTS FROM ZEUS. BUT PROMETHEUS' BROTHER WAS AN IDIOT AND MARRIED THE WOMAN PANDORA ANYHOW. PANDORA WAS TOLD BY HER NEW HUSBAND NOT TO OPEN THE GIFT THAT CAME IN THE FORM OF AN URN.
BUT PANDORA WAS MADE TO BE CURIOUS ABOVE ALL ELSE. SHE OPENED THE JAR, AND ALL OF THE EVILS THAT WOULD, FROM THAT DAY, PLAGUE MANKIND--GREED, VANITY, SLANDER, LYING, ENVY--ESCAPED FROM THE JAR.
ALTHOUGH PANDORA WAS QUICK ENOUGH TO CLOSE IT AGAIN AND KEEP ONE SPARK ALIVE INSIDE--***HOPE.***

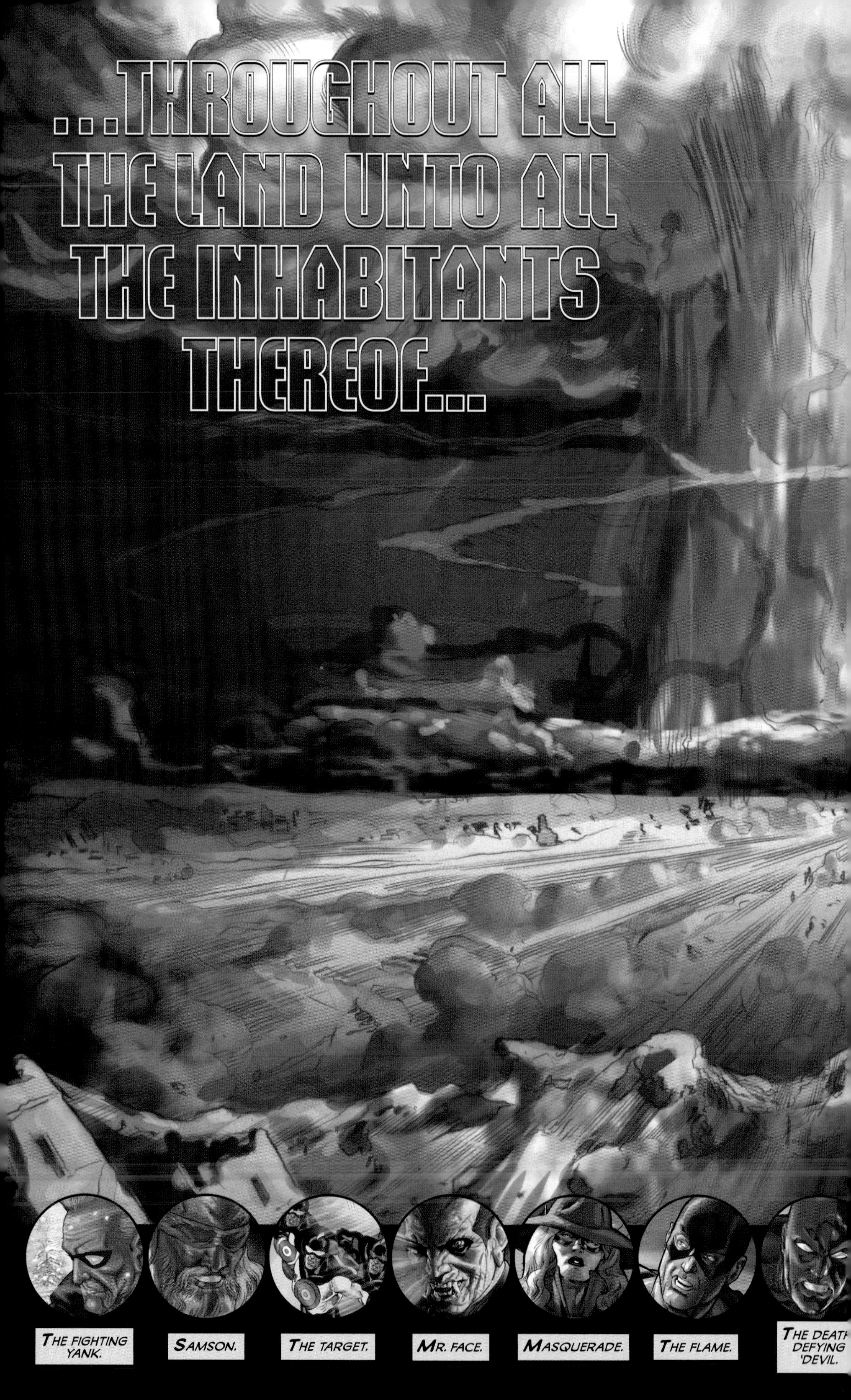
...THROUGHOUT ALL THE LAND UNTO ALL THE INHABITANTS THEREOF...
THE FIGHTING YANK.
SAMSON.
THE TARGET.
MR. FACE.
MASQUERADE.
THE FLAME.
THE DEATH DEFYING 'DEVIL.

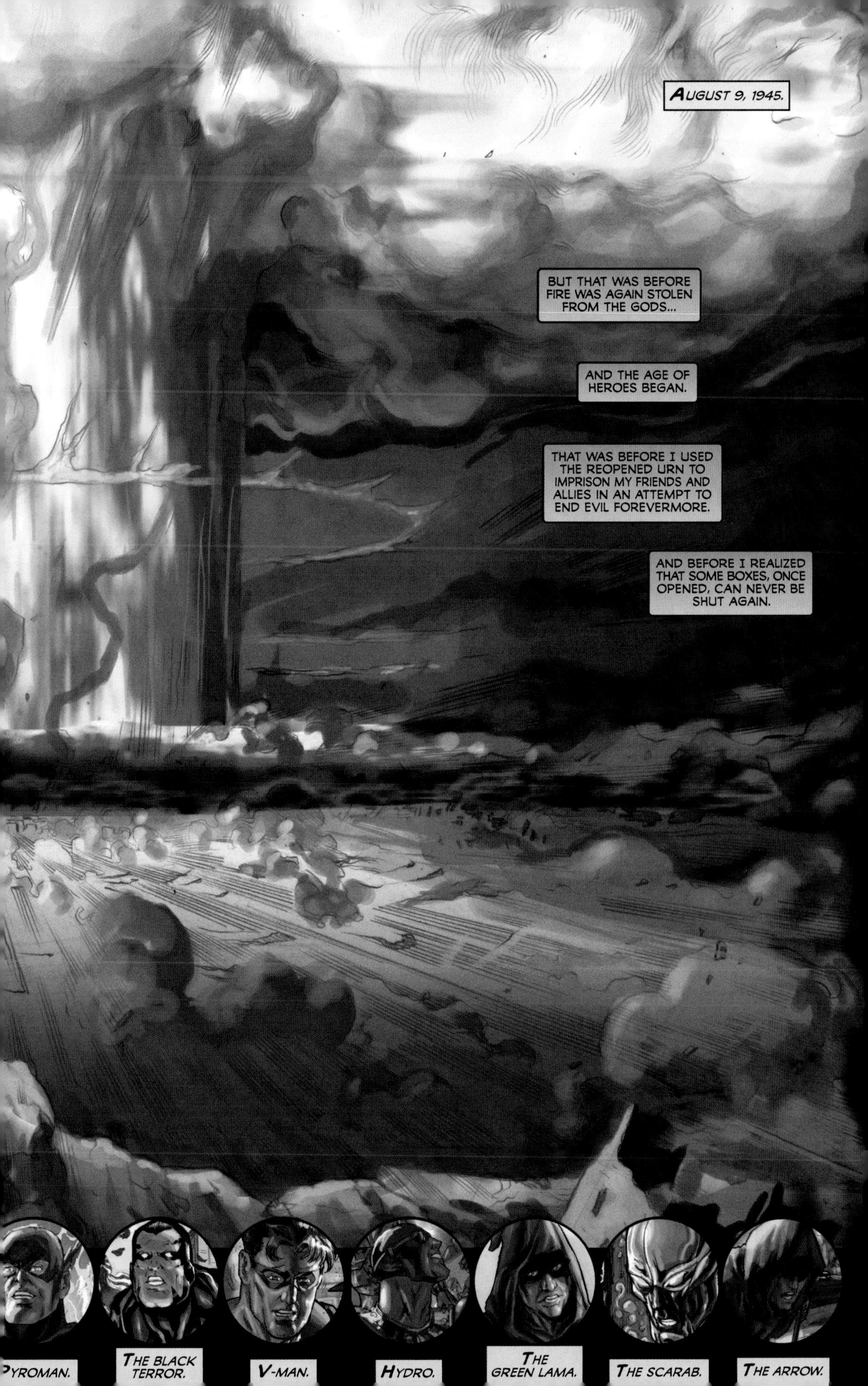
AUGUST 9, 1945.
BUT THAT WAS BEFORE FIRE WAS AGAIN STOLEN FROM THE GODS...
AND THE AGE OF HEROES BEGAN.
THAT WAS BEFORE I USED THE REOPENED URN TO IMPRISON MY FRIENDS AND ALLIES IN AN ATTEMPT TO END EVIL FOREVERMORE.
AND BEFORE I REALIZED THAT SOME BOXES, ONCE OPENED, CAN NEVER BE SHUT AGAIN.
PYROMAN.
THE BLACK TERROR.
V-MAN.
HYDRO.
THE GREEN LAMA.
THE SCARAB.
THE ARROW.

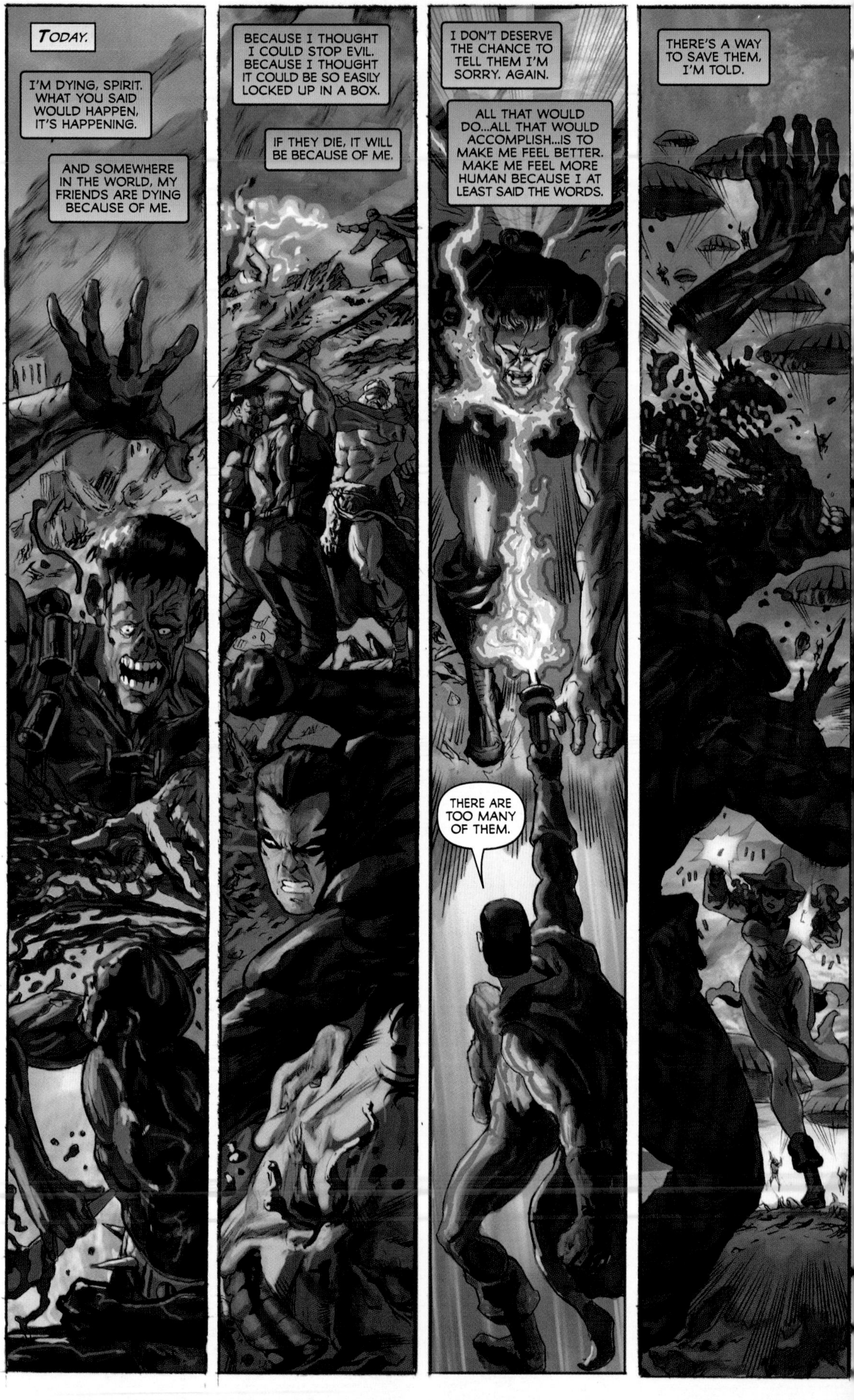
TODAY.
I'M DYING, SPIRIT. WHAT YOU SAID WOULD HAPPEN, IT'S HAPPENING.
AND SOMEWHERE IN THE WORLD, MY FRIENDS ARE DYING BECAUSE OF ME.
BECAUSE I THOUGHT I COULD STOP EVIL. BECAUSE I THOUGHT IT COULD BE SO EASILY LOCKED UP IN A BOX.
IF THEY DIE, IT WILL BE BECAUSE OF ME.
I DON'T DESERVE THE CHANCE TO TELL THEM I'M SORRY. AGAIN.
ALL THAT WOULD DO...ALL THAT WOULD ACCOMPLISH...IS TO MAKE ME FEEL BETTER. MAKE ME FEEL MORE HUMAN BECAUSE I AT LEAST SAID THE WORDS.
THERE ARE TOO MANY OF THEM.
THERE'S A WAY TO SAVE THEM, I'M TOLD.

I WAS A HERO ONCE. I WAS *THE FIGHTING YANK* ONCE.

NOW I'M A DEAD MAN. ONE WHO, WHILE LIVING, WAS HAUNTED BY THE GHOST WHO USED ME TO ESCAPE HIS OWN DAMNATION IN THE SPIRIT WORLD.

THE ONLY WAY TO SAVE THEM IS TO SAVE THE GOD-DAMNED GHOST OF MY ANCESTOR.

GOD-DAMNED, LITERALLY. HE'D BEEN CURSED FOR HIS BETRAYAL OF GENERAL WASHINGTON'S MEN ALMOST TWO HUNDRED AND FIFTY YEARS AGO.

HOW MANY OF THESE GUYS ARE THERE?

I DO NOT KNOW. HOW MANY MEN HAVE DIED IN THE SERVICE OF THEIR COUNTRY IN THE LAST FIFTY YEARS?

I'VE BEEN TOLD BY A BEING MADE UP OF THE BLOOD OF MARTYRS KNOWN AS THE AMERICAN SPIRIT THAT TO SAVE MY FRIENDS...

...I HAVE TO TAKE MY ANCESTOR'S CURSE UPON MYSELF...

FIFTY YEARS OF MEN MOCKING MEN.

MOCKING GOD.

I WILL NOT TOLERATE THIS A MOMENT LONGER.

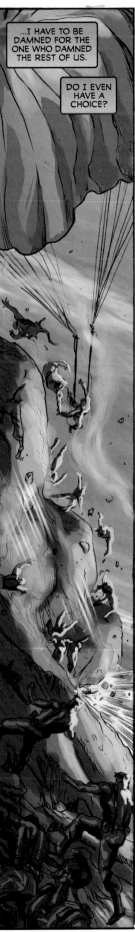

...I HAVE TO BE DAMNED FOR THE ONE WHO DAMNED THE REST OF US.

DO I EVEN HAVE A CHOICE?

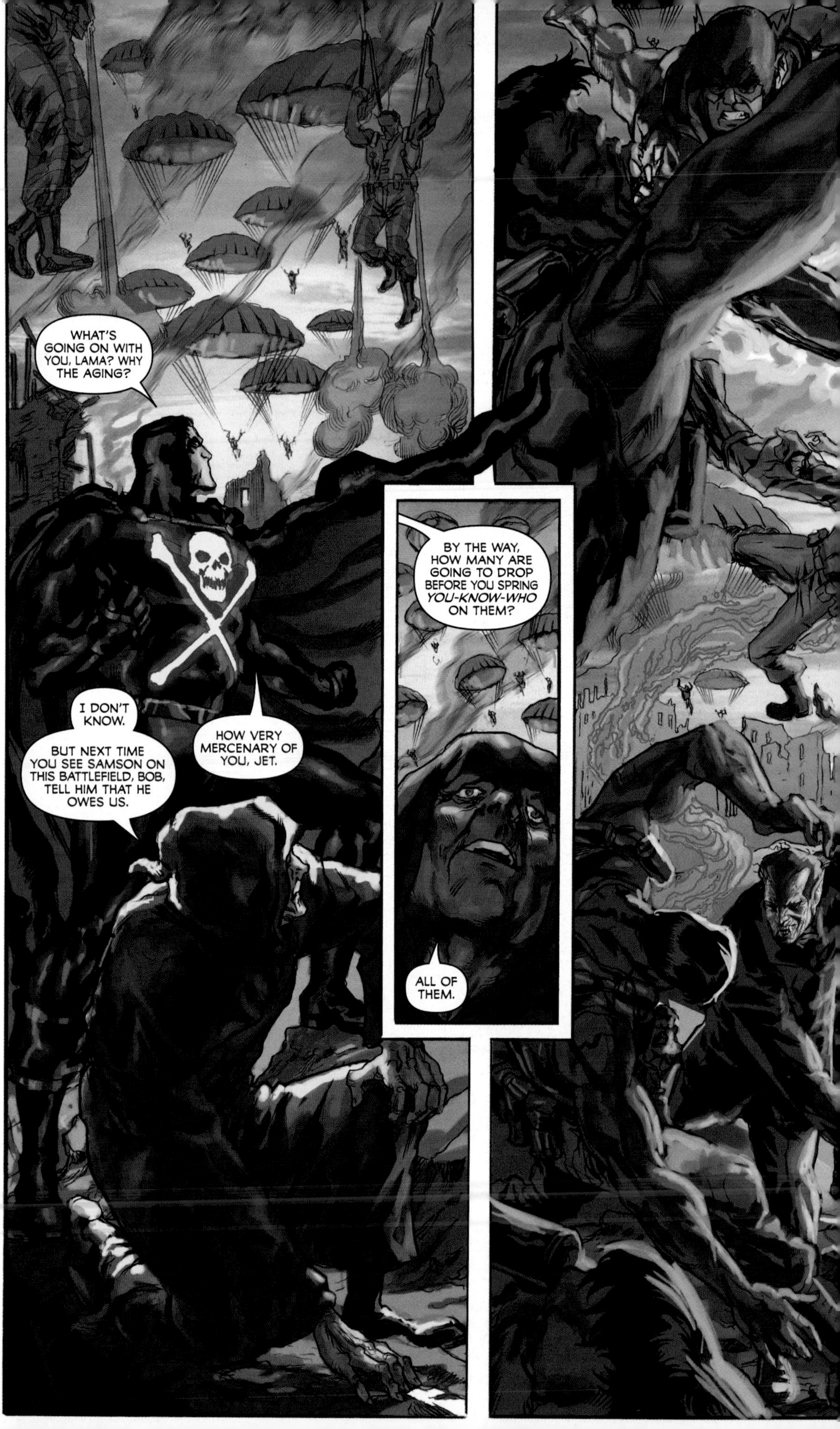
WHAT'S GOING ON WITH YOU, LAMA? WHY THE AGING?
I DON'T KNOW.
BUT NEXT TIME YOU SEE SAMSON ON THIS BATTLEFIELD, BOB, TELL HIM THAT HE OWES US.
HOW VERY MERCENARY OF YOU, JET.
BY THE WAY, HOW MANY ARE GOING TO DROP BEFORE YOU SPRING *YOU-KNOW-WHO* ON THEM?
ALL OF THEM.

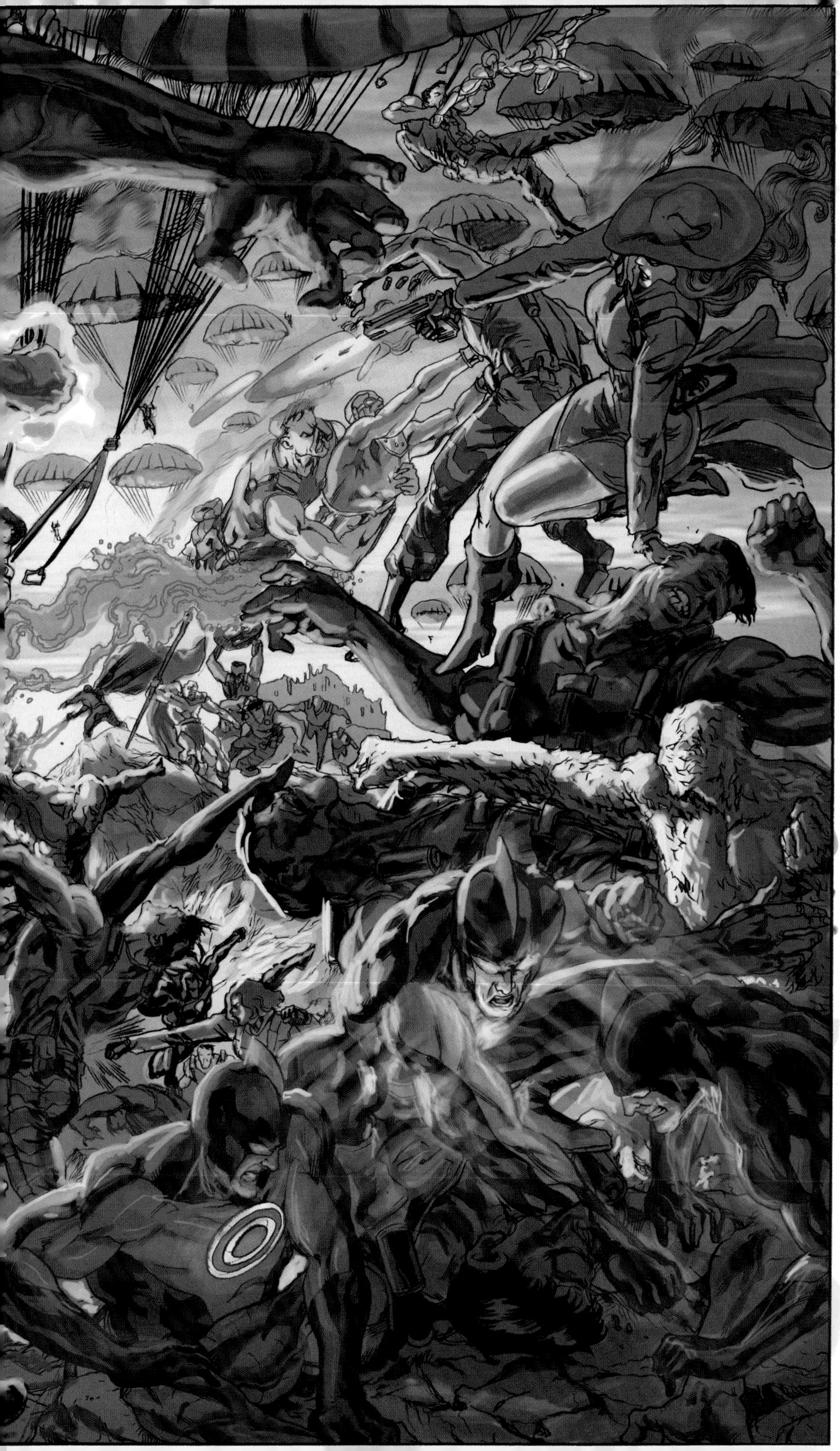

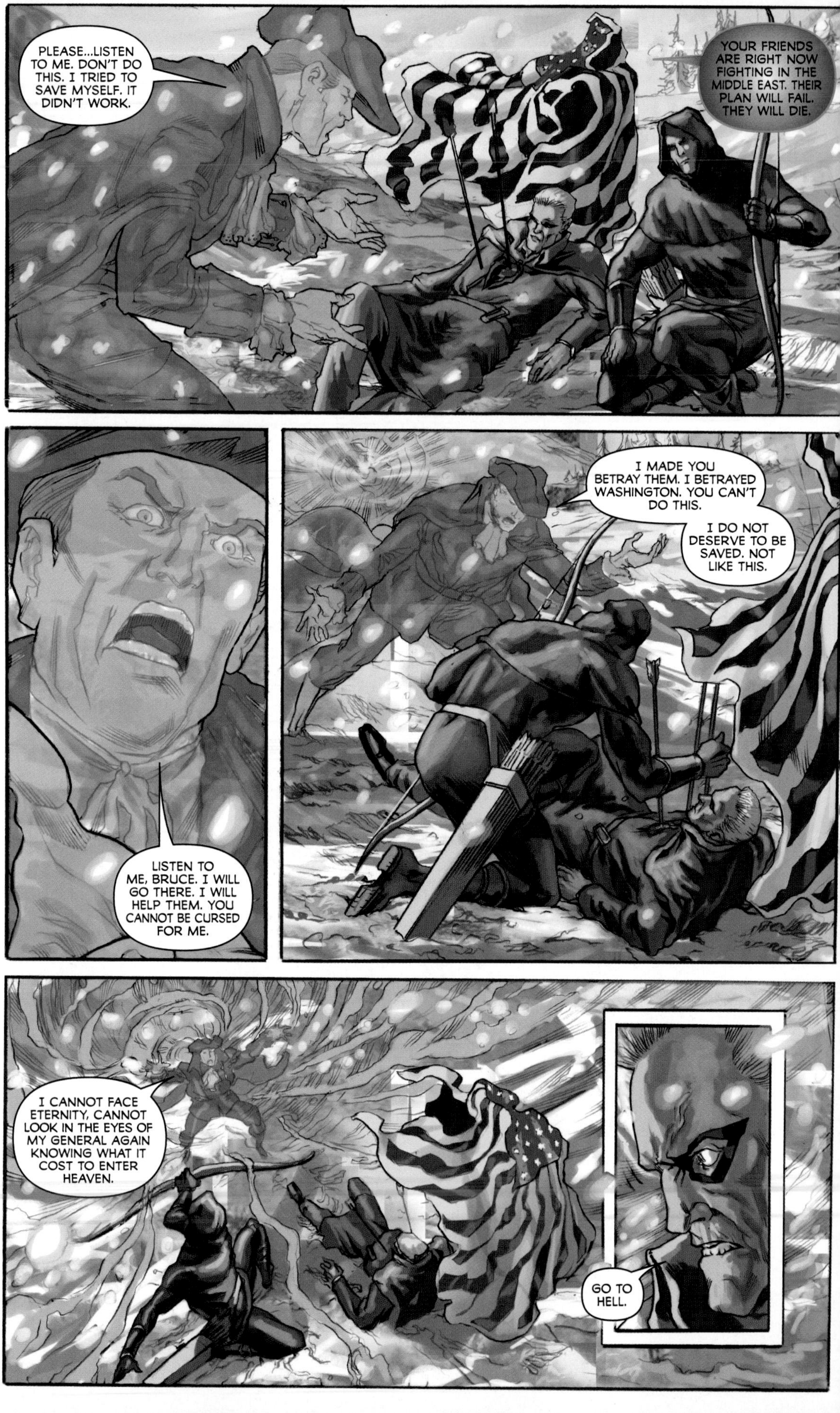
PLEASE...LISTEN TO ME. DON'T DO THIS. I TRIED TO SAVE MYSELF. IT DIDN'T WORK.
YOUR FRIENDS ARE RIGHT NOW FIGHTING IN THE MIDDLE EAST. THEIR PLAN WILL FAIL. THEY WILL DIE.
LISTEN TO ME, BRUCE. I WILL GO THERE. I WILL HELP THEM. YOU CANNOT BE CURSED FOR ME.
I MADE YOU BETRAY THEM. I BETRAYED WASHINGTON. YOU CAN'T DO THIS.
I DO NOT DESERVE TO BE SAVED. NOT LIKE THIS.
I CANNOT FACE ETERNITY, CANNOT LOOK IN THE EYES OF MY GENERAL AGAIN KNOWING WHAT IT COST TO ENTER HEAVEN.
GO TO HELL.

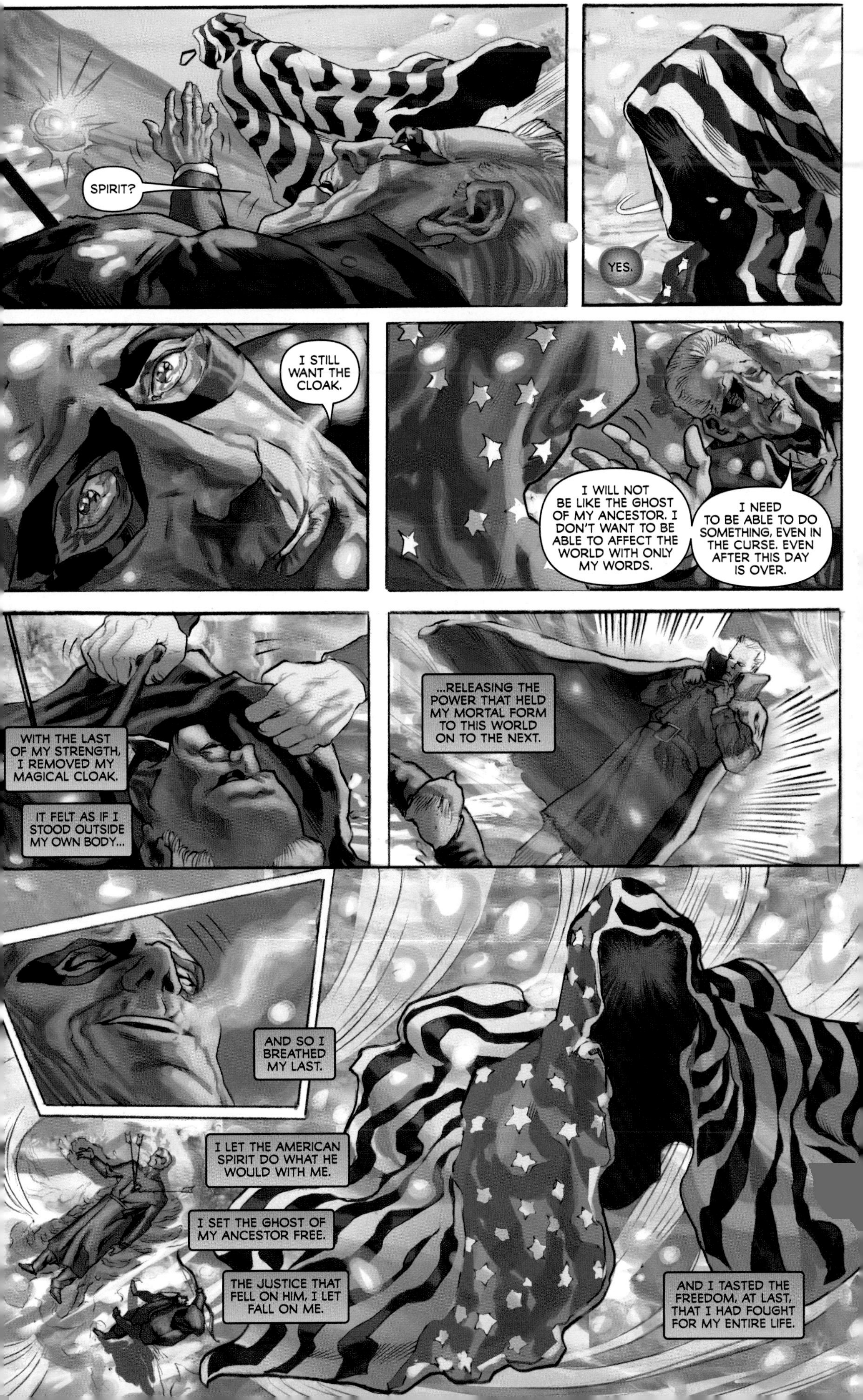
SPIRIT?
YES.
I STILL WANT THE CLOAK.
I WILL NOT BE LIKE THE GHOST OF MY ANCESTOR. I DON'T WANT TO BE ABLE TO AFFECT THE WORLD WITH ONLY MY WORDS.
I NEED TO BE ABLE TO DO SOMETHING, EVEN IN THE CURSE. EVEN AFTER THIS DAY IS OVER.
WITH THE LAST OF MY STRENGTH, I REMOVED MY MAGICAL CLOAK.
IT FELT AS IF I STOOD OUTSIDE MY OWN BODY...
...RELEASING THE POWER THAT HELD MY MORTAL FORM TO THIS WORLD ON TO THE NEXT.
AND SO I BREATHED MY LAST.
I LET THE AMERICAN SPIRIT DO WHAT HE WOULD WITH ME.
I SET THE GHOST OF MY ANCESTOR FREE.
THE JUSTICE THAT FELL ON HIM, I LET FALL ON ME.
AND I TASTED THE FREEDOM, AT LAST, THAT I HAD FOUGHT FOR MY ENTIRE LIFE.

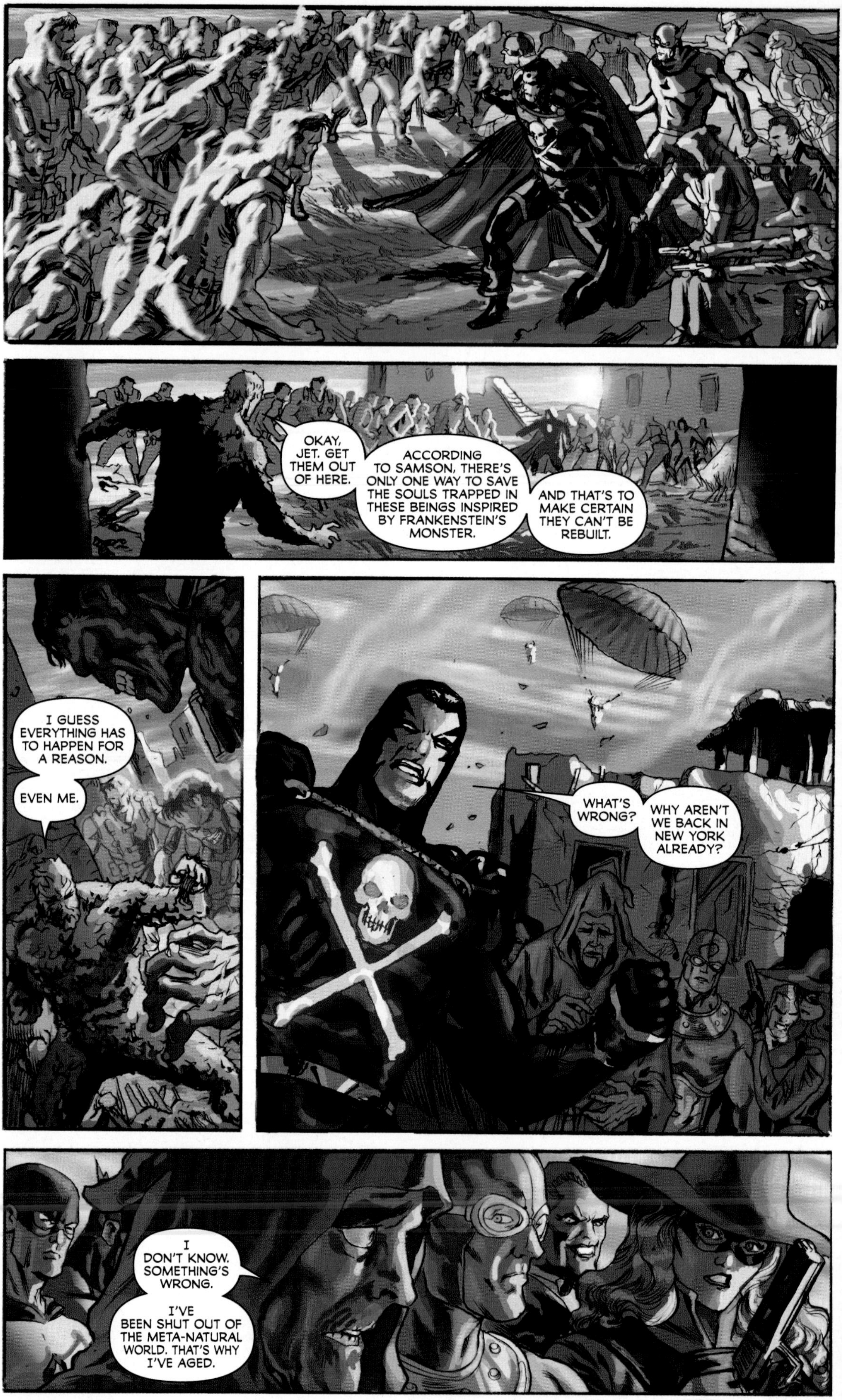
OKAY, JET. GET THEM OUT OF HERE.
ACCORDING TO SAMSON, THERE'S ONLY ONE WAY TO SAVE THE SOULS TRAPPED IN THESE BEINGS INSPIRED BY FRANKENSTEIN'S MONSTER.
AND THAT'S TO MAKE CERTAIN THEY CAN'T BE REBUILT.
I GUESS EVERYTHING HAS TO HAPPEN FOR A REASON.
EVEN ME.
WHAT'S WRONG?
WHY AREN'T WE BACK IN NEW YORK ALREADY?
I DON'T KNOW. SOMETHING'S WRONG.
I'VE BEEN SHUT OUT OF THE META-NATURAL WORLD. THAT'S WHY I'VE AGED.

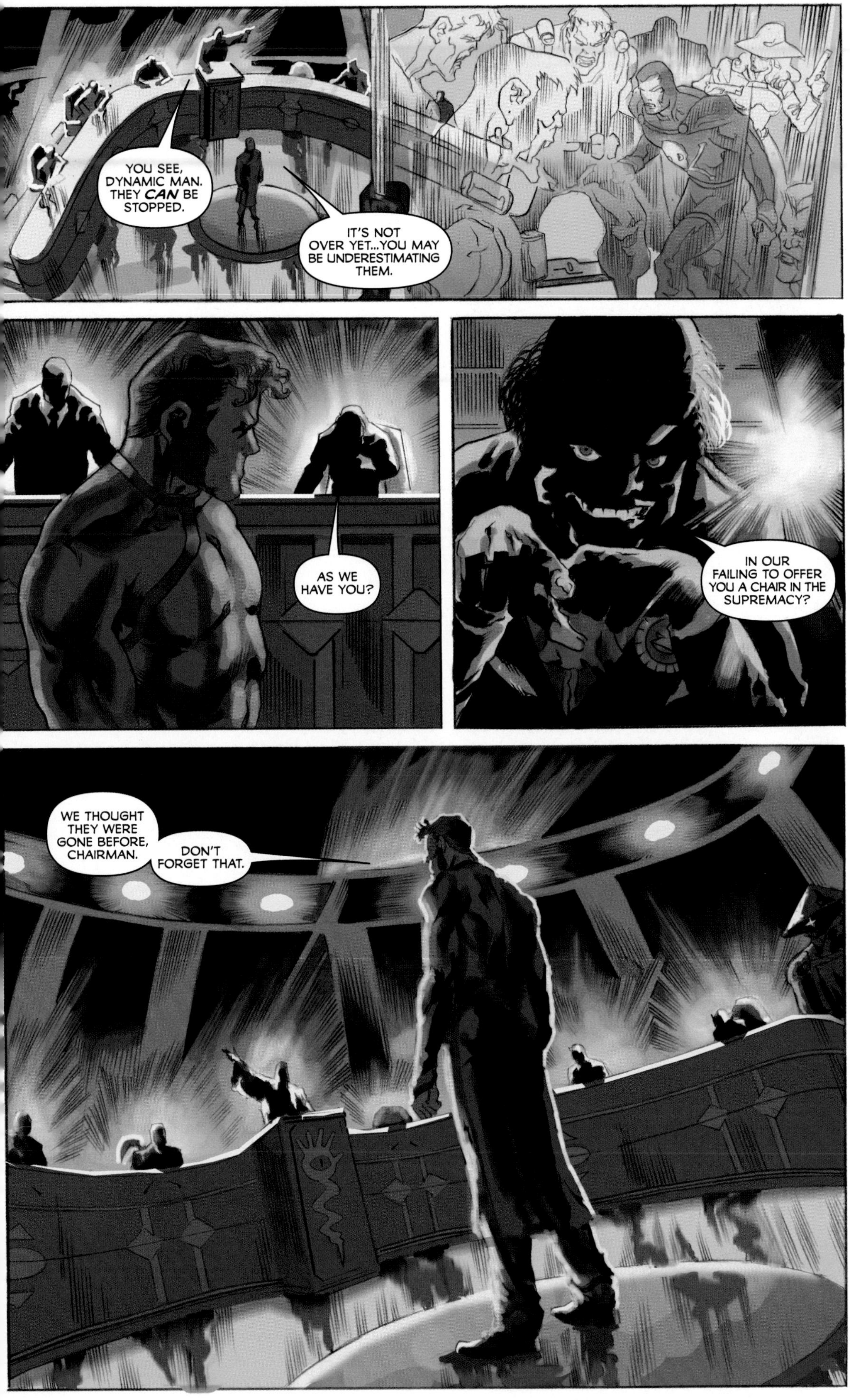
YOU SEE, DYNAMIC MAN. THEY CAN BE STOPPED.
IT'S NOT OVER YET...YOU MAY BE UNDERESTIMATING THEM.
AS WE HAVE YOU?
IN OUR FAILING TO OFFER YOU A CHAIR IN THE SUPREMACY?
WE THOUGHT THEY WERE GONE BEFORE, CHAIRMAN.
DON'T FORGET THAT.

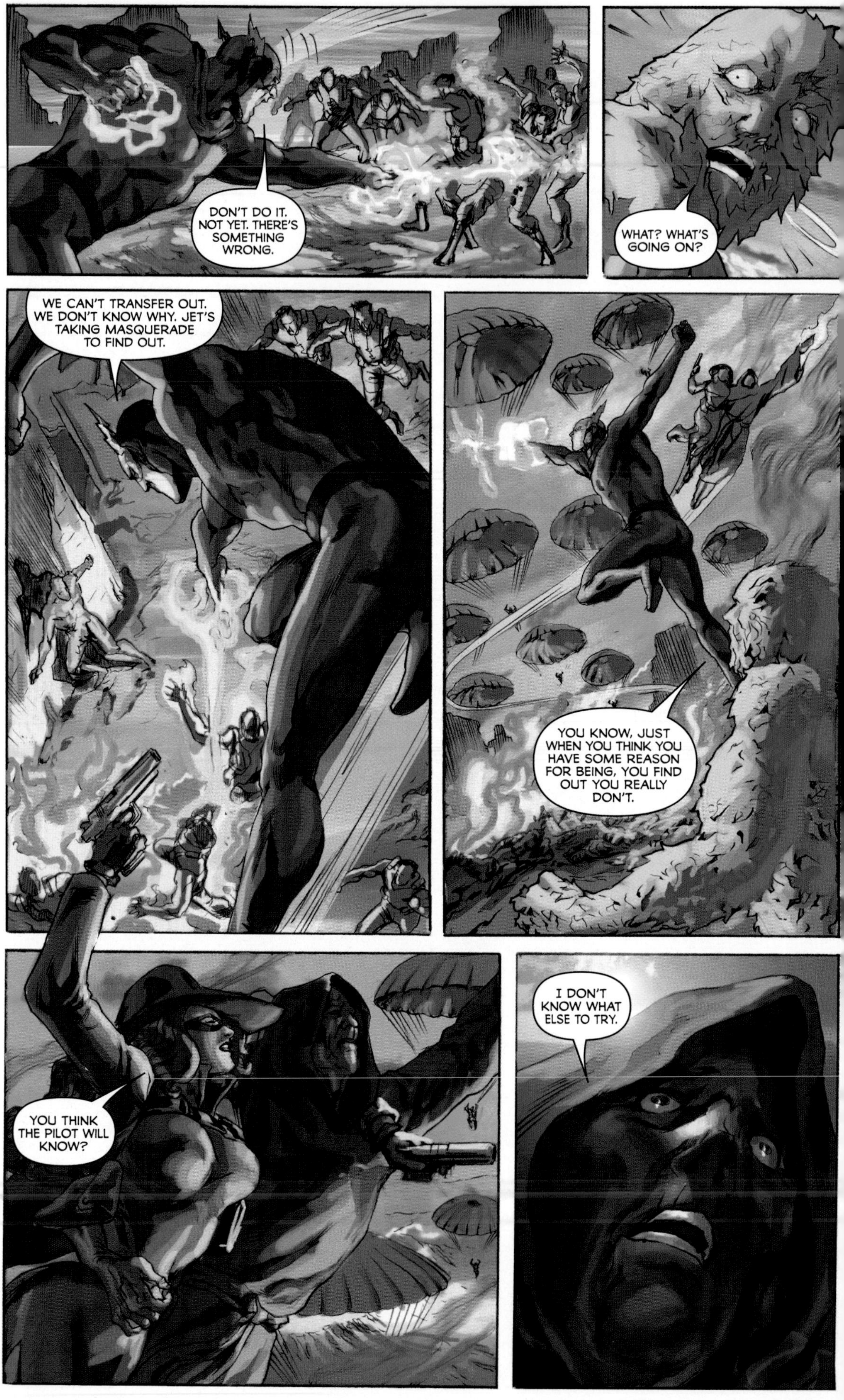
DON'T DO IT. NOT YET. THERE'S SOMETHING WRONG.
WHAT? WHAT'S GOING ON?
WE CAN'T TRANSFER OUT. WE DON'T KNOW WHY. JET'S TAKING MASQUERADE TO FIND OUT.
YOU KNOW, JUST WHEN YOU THINK YOU HAVE SOME REASON FOR BEING, YOU FIND OUT YOU REALLY DON'T.
YOU THINK THE PILOT WILL KNOW?
I DON'T KNOW WHAT ELSE TO TRY.

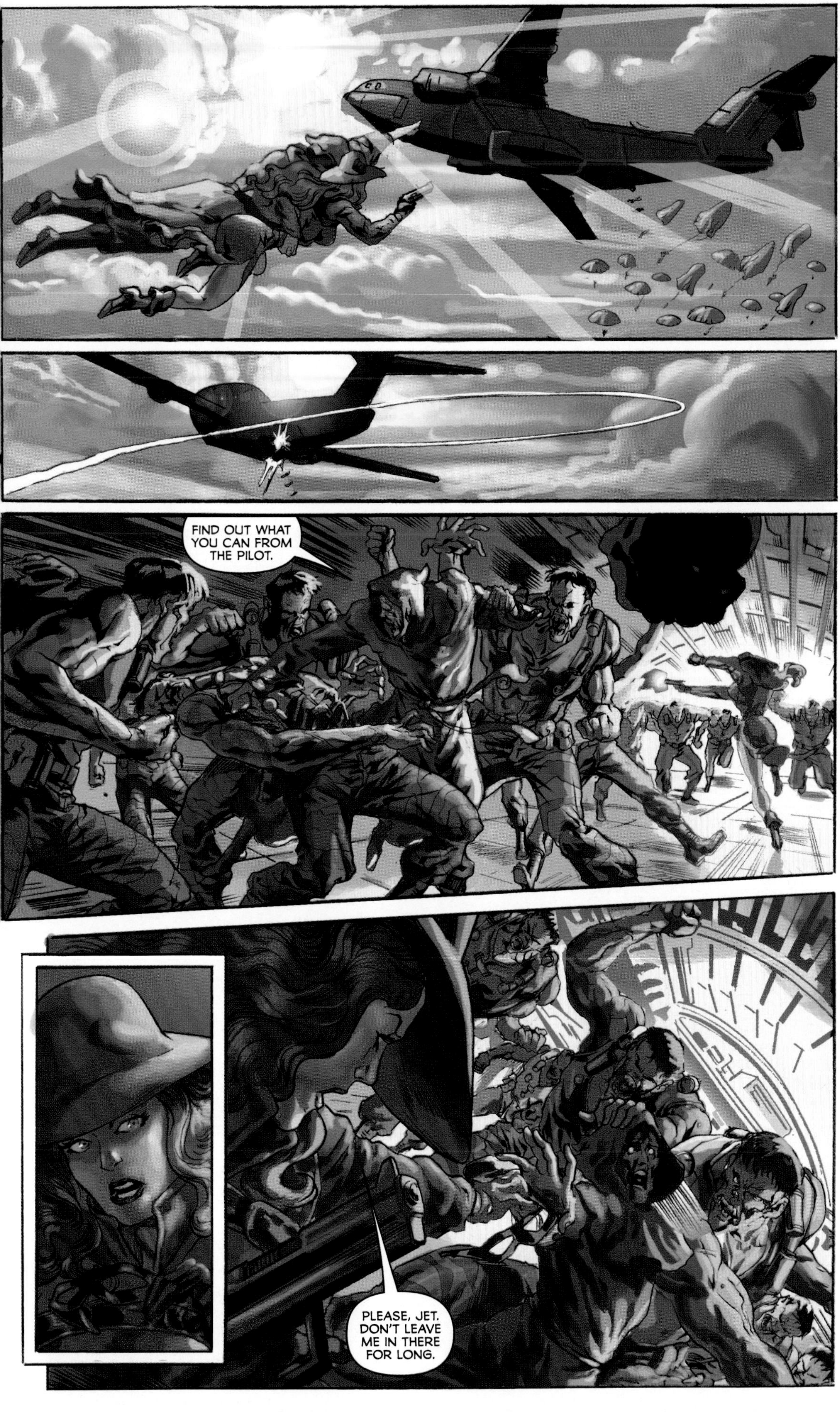
FIND OUT WHAT YOU CAN FROM THE PILOT.
PLEASE, JET. DON'T LEAVE ME IN THERE FOR LONG.

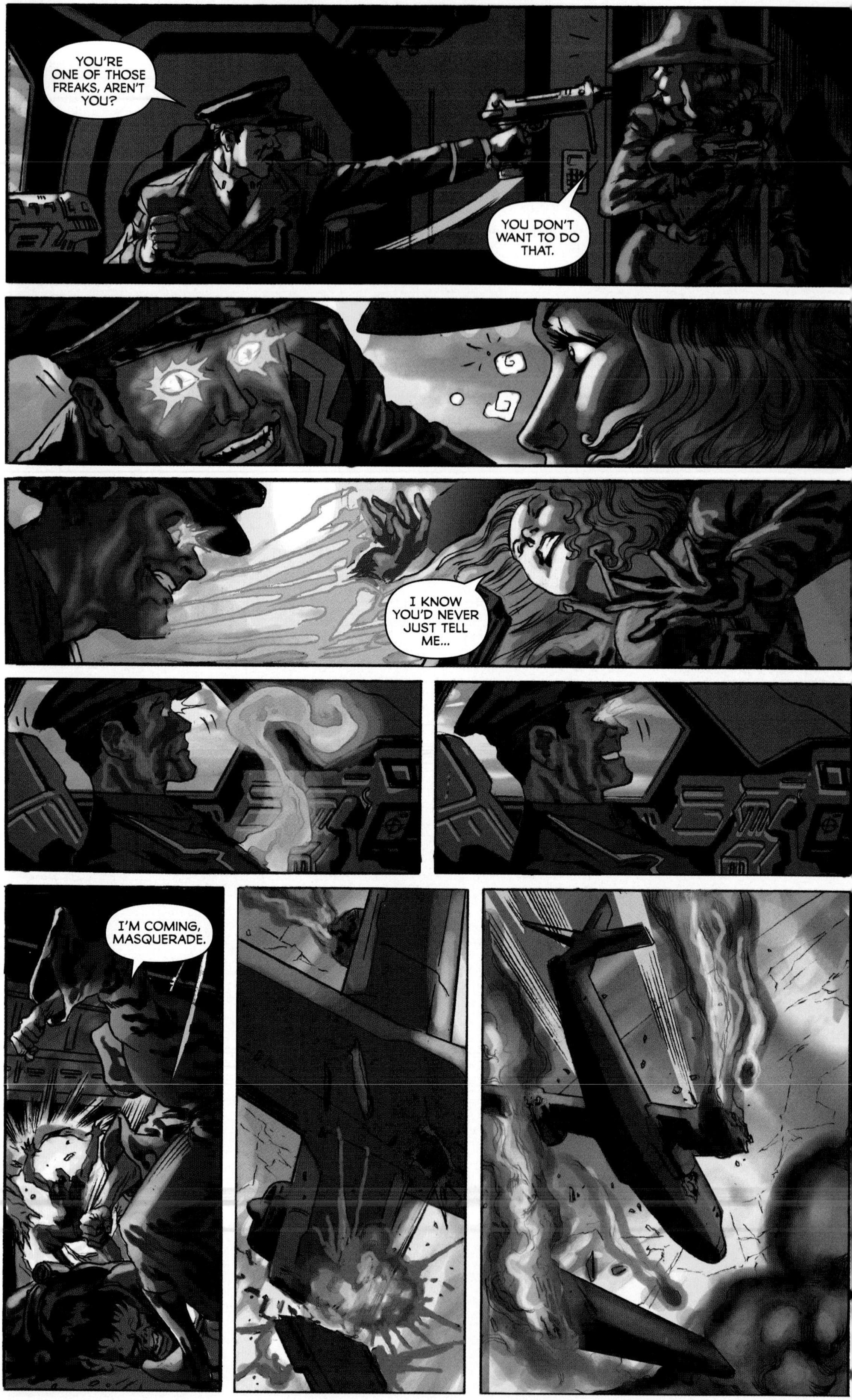
YOU'RE ONE OF THOSE FREAKS, AREN'T YOU?
YOU DON'T WANT TO DO THAT.
I KNOW YOU'D NEVER JUST TELL ME...
I'M COMING, MASQUERADE.

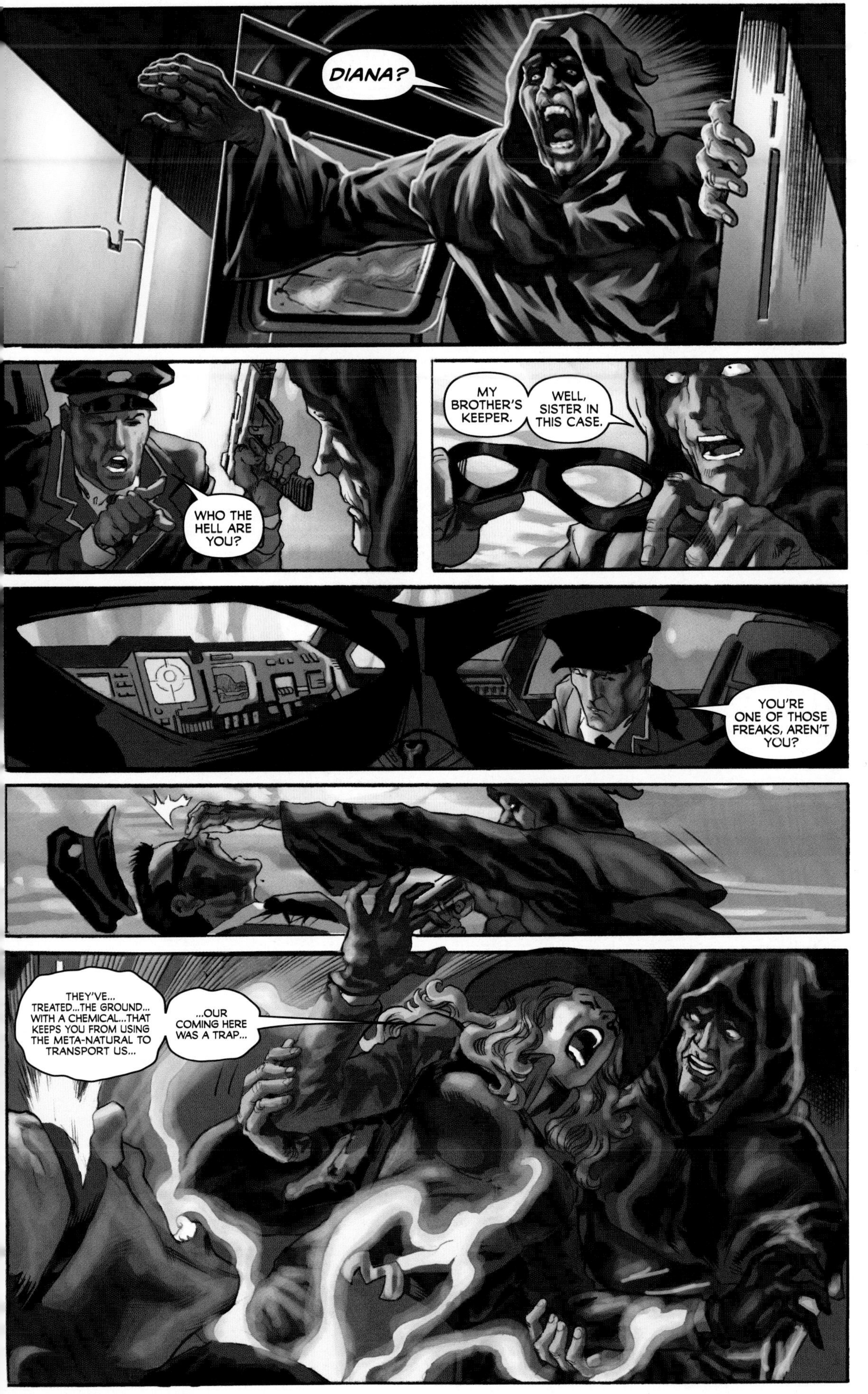
DIANA?
WHO THE HELL ARE YOU?
MY BROTHER'S KEEPER.
WELL, SISTER IN THIS CASE.
YOU'RE ONE OF THOSE FREAKS, AREN'T YOU?
THEY'VE... TREATED...THE GROUND... WITH A CHEMICAL...THAT KEEPS YOU FROM USING THE META-NATURAL TO TRANSPORT US...
...OUR COMING HERE WAS A TRAP...

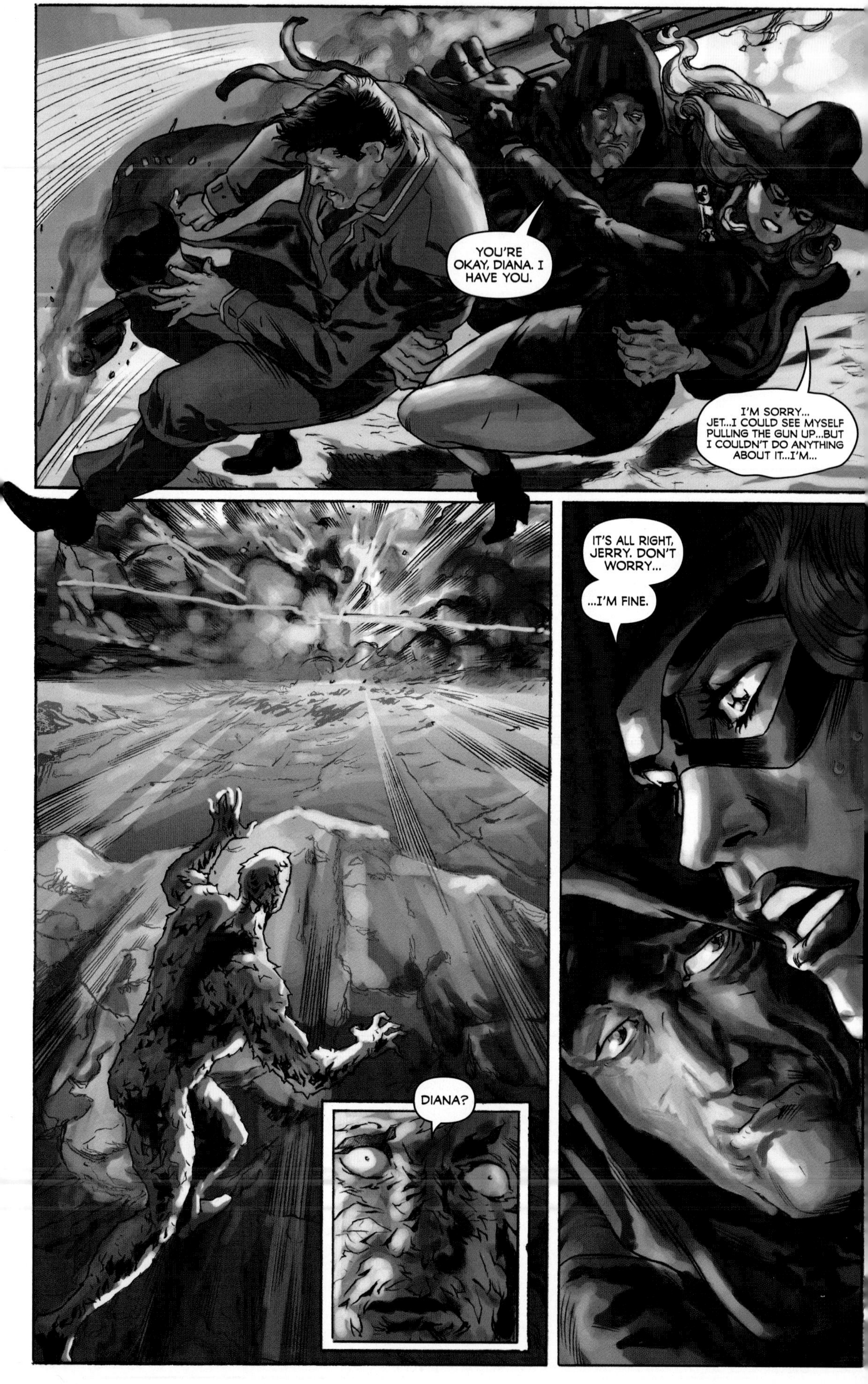
YOU'RE OKAY, DIANA. I HAVE YOU.
I'M SORRY... JET...I COULD SEE MYSELF PULLING THE GUN UP...BUT I COULDN'T DO ANYTHING ABOUT IT...I'M...
IT'S ALL RIGHT, JERRY. DON'T WORRY...
...I'M FINE.
DIANA?

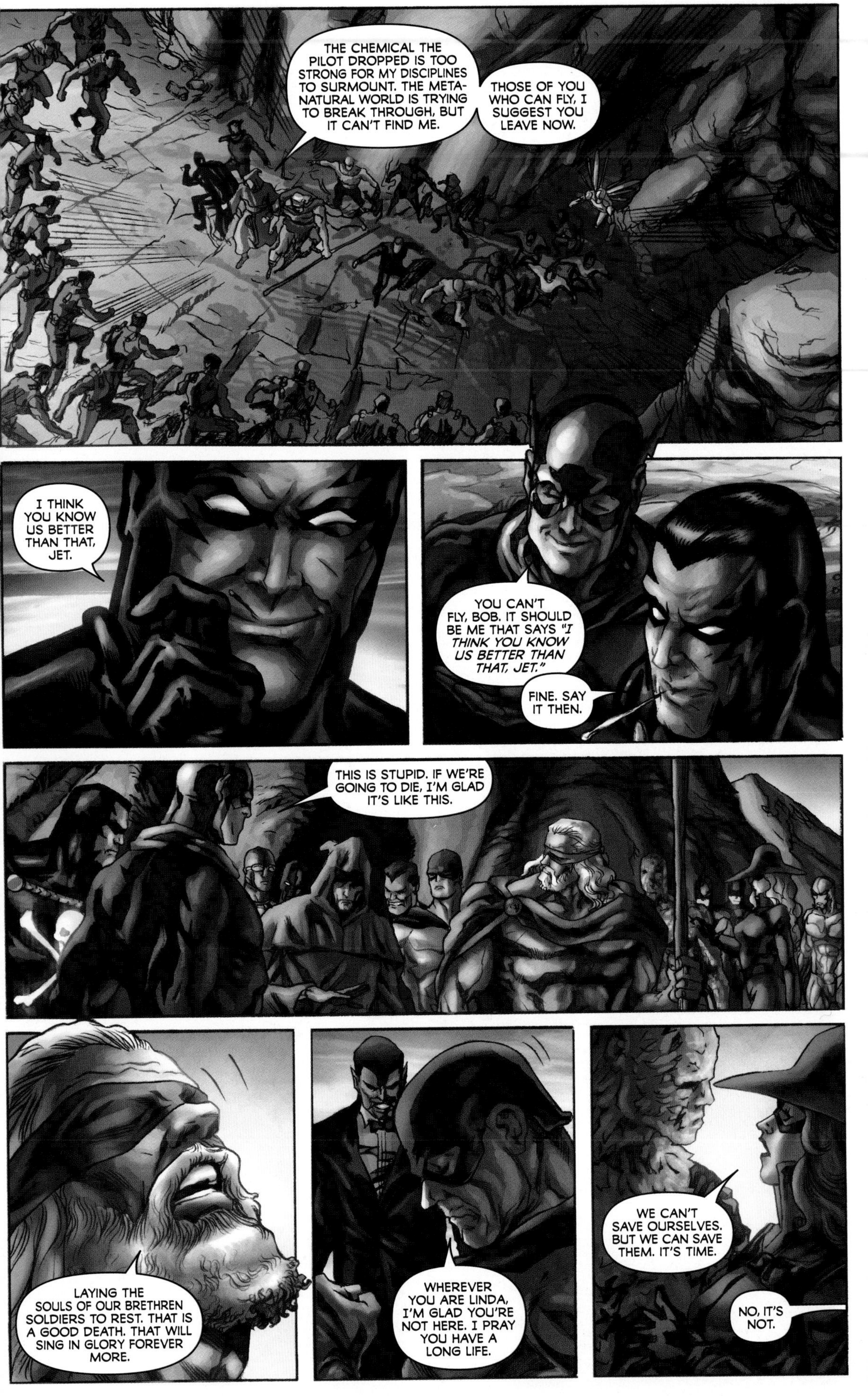

THE CHEMICAL THE PILOT DROPPED IS TOO STRONG FOR MY DISCIPLINES TO SURMOUNT. THE META-NATURAL WORLD IS TRYING TO BREAK THROUGH, BUT IT CAN'T FIND ME.
THOSE OF YOU WHO CAN FLY, I SUGGEST YOU LEAVE NOW.
I THINK YOU KNOW US BETTER THAN THAT, JET.
YOU CAN'T FLY, BOB. IT SHOULD BE ME THAT SAYS *"I THINK YOU KNOW US BETTER THAN THAT, JET."*
FINE. SAY IT THEN.
THIS IS STUPID. IF WE'RE GOING TO DIE, I'M GLAD IT'S LIKE THIS.
LAYING THE SOULS OF OUR BRETHREN SOLDIERS TO REST. THAT IS A GOOD DEATH. THAT WILL SING IN GLORY FOREVER MORE.
WHEREVER YOU ARE LINDA, I'M GLAD YOU'RE NOT HERE. I PRAY YOU HAVE A LONG LIFE.
WE CAN'T SAVE OURSELVES. BUT WE CAN SAVE THEM. IT'S TIME.
NO, IT'S NOT.

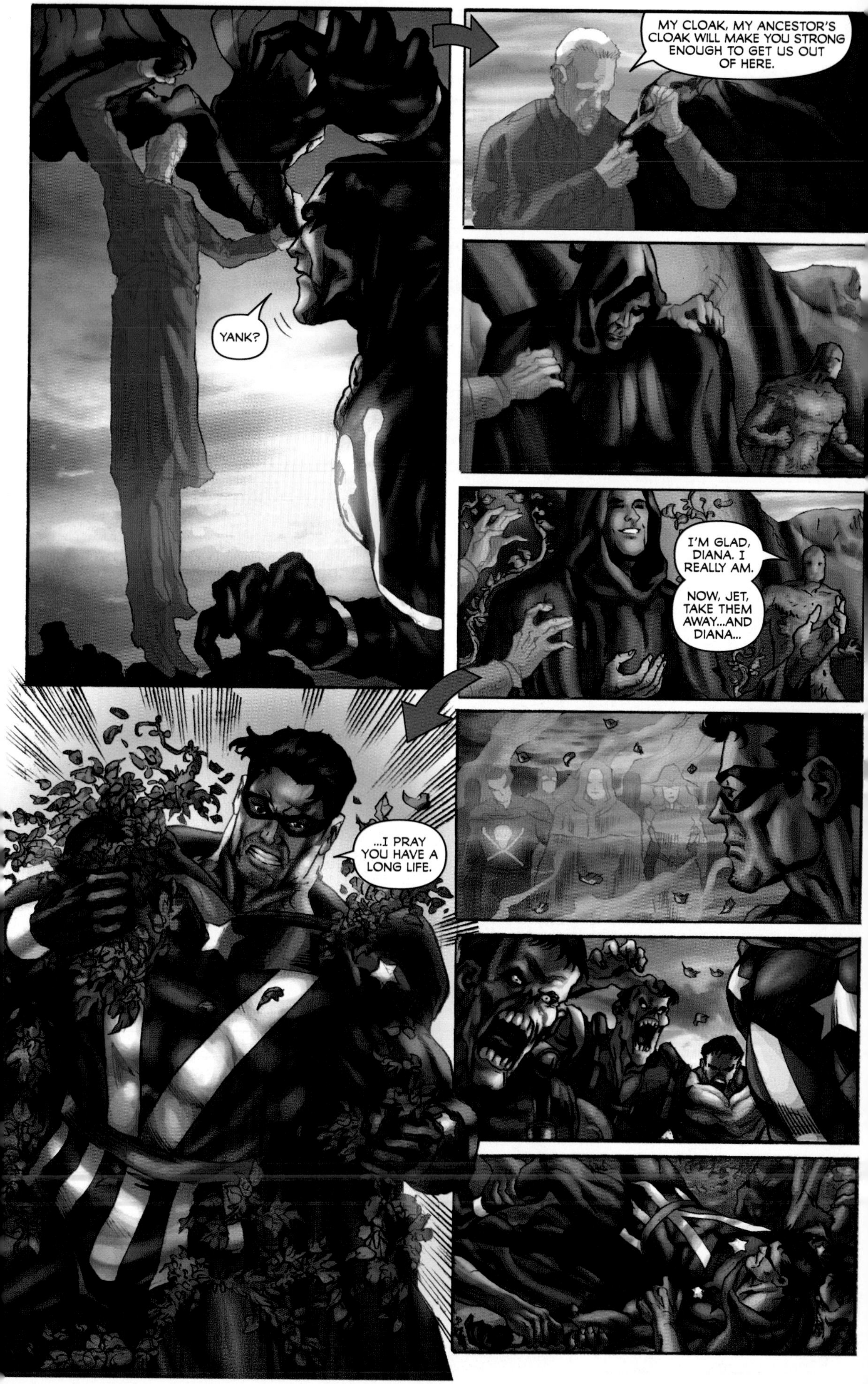
YANK?
MY CLOAK, MY ANCESTOR'S CLOAK WILL MAKE YOU STRONG ENOUGH TO GET US OUT OF HERE.
I'M GLAD, DIANA. I REALLY AM.
NOW, JET, TAKE THEM AWAY...AND DIANA...
...I PRAY YOU HAVE A LONG LIFE.

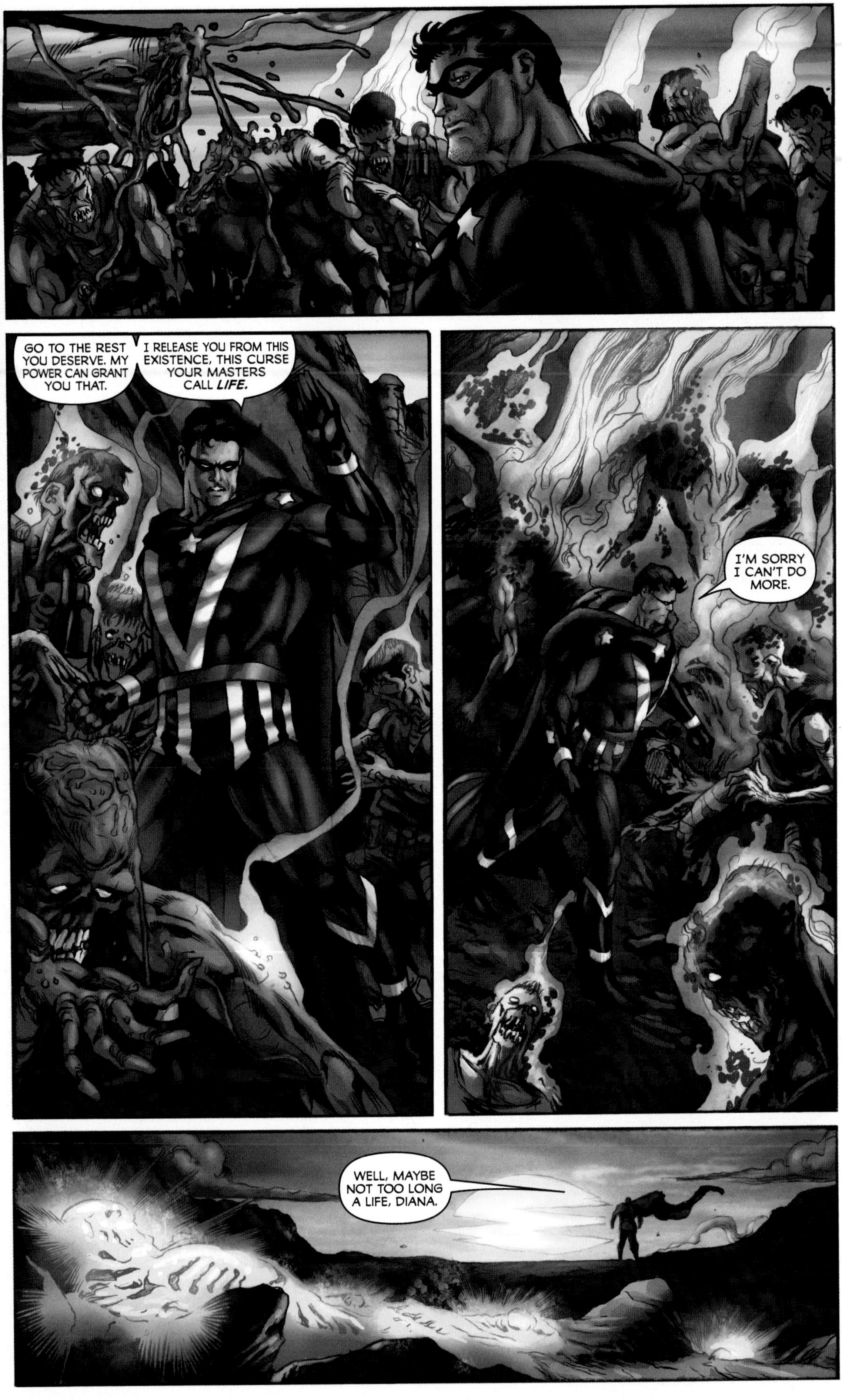
GO TO THE REST YOU DESERVE. MY POWER CAN GRANT YOU THAT.
I RELEASE YOU FROM THIS EXISTENCE, THIS CURSE YOUR MASTERS CALL *LIFE.*
I'M SORRY I CAN'T DO MORE.
WELL, MAYBE NOT TOO LONG A LIFE, DIANA.

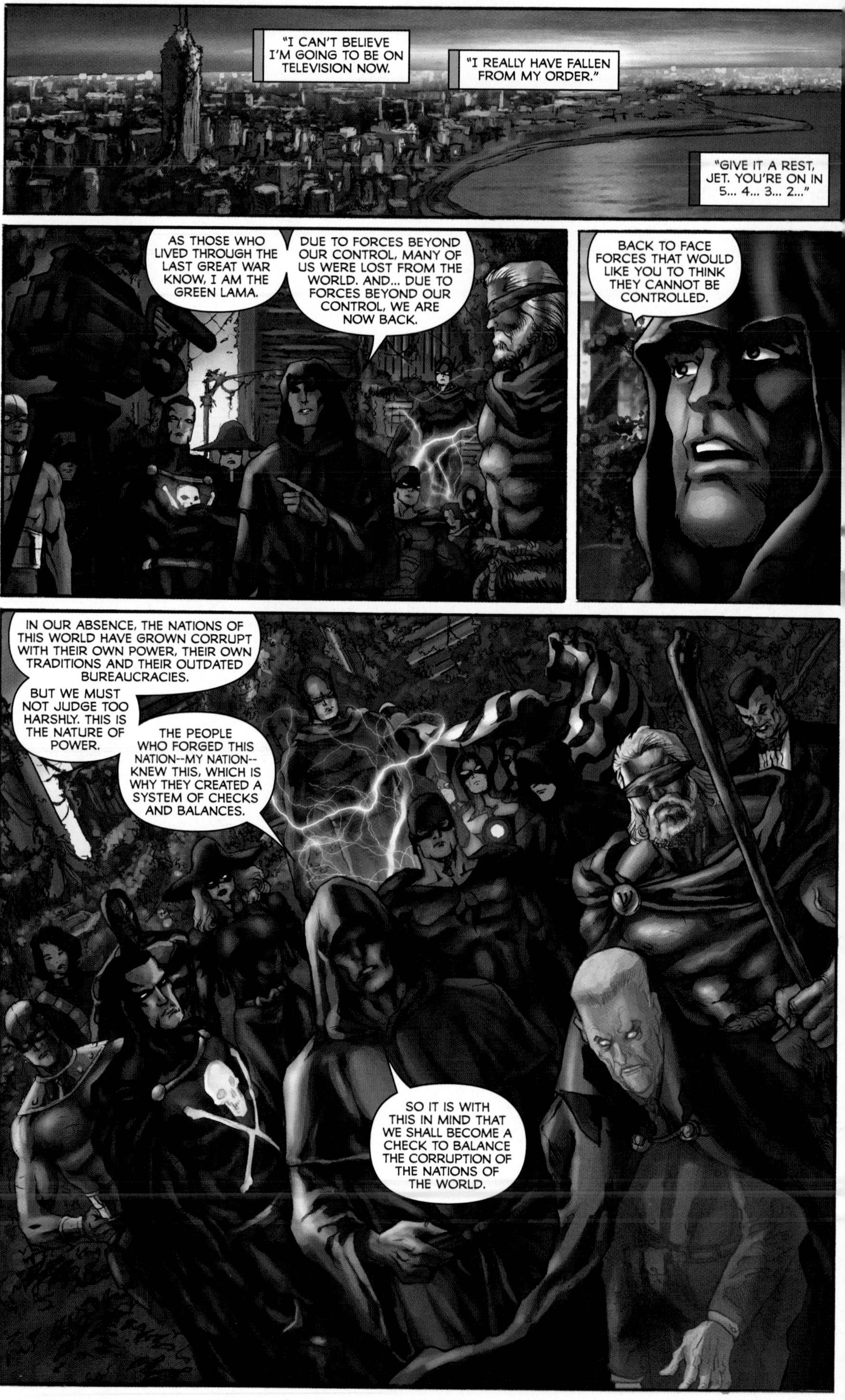
"I CAN'T BELIEVE I'M GOING TO BE ON TELEVISION NOW.
"I REALLY HAVE FALLEN FROM MY ORDER."
"GIVE IT A REST, JET. YOU'RE ON IN 5... 4... 3... 2..."
AS THOSE WHO LIVED THROUGH THE LAST GREAT WAR KNOW, I AM THE GREEN LAMA.
DUE TO FORCES BEYOND OUR CONTROL, MANY OF US WERE LOST FROM THE WORLD. AND... DUE TO FORCES BEYOND OUR CONTROL, WE ARE NOW BACK.
BACK TO FACE FORCES THAT WOULD LIKE YOU TO THINK THEY CANNOT BE CONTROLLED.
IN OUR ABSENCE, THE NATIONS OF THIS WORLD HAVE GROWN CORRUPT WITH THEIR OWN POWER, THEIR OWN TRADITIONS AND THEIR OUTDATED BUREAUCRACIES.
BUT WE MUST NOT JUDGE TOO HARSHLY. THIS IS THE NATURE OF POWER.
THE PEOPLE WHO FORGED THIS NATION--MY NATION--KNEW THIS, WHICH IS WHY THEY CREATED A SYSTEM OF CHECKS AND BALANCES.
SO IT IS WITH THIS IN MIND THAT WE SHALL BECOME A CHECK TO BALANCE THE CORRUPTION OF THE NATIONS OF THE WORLD.

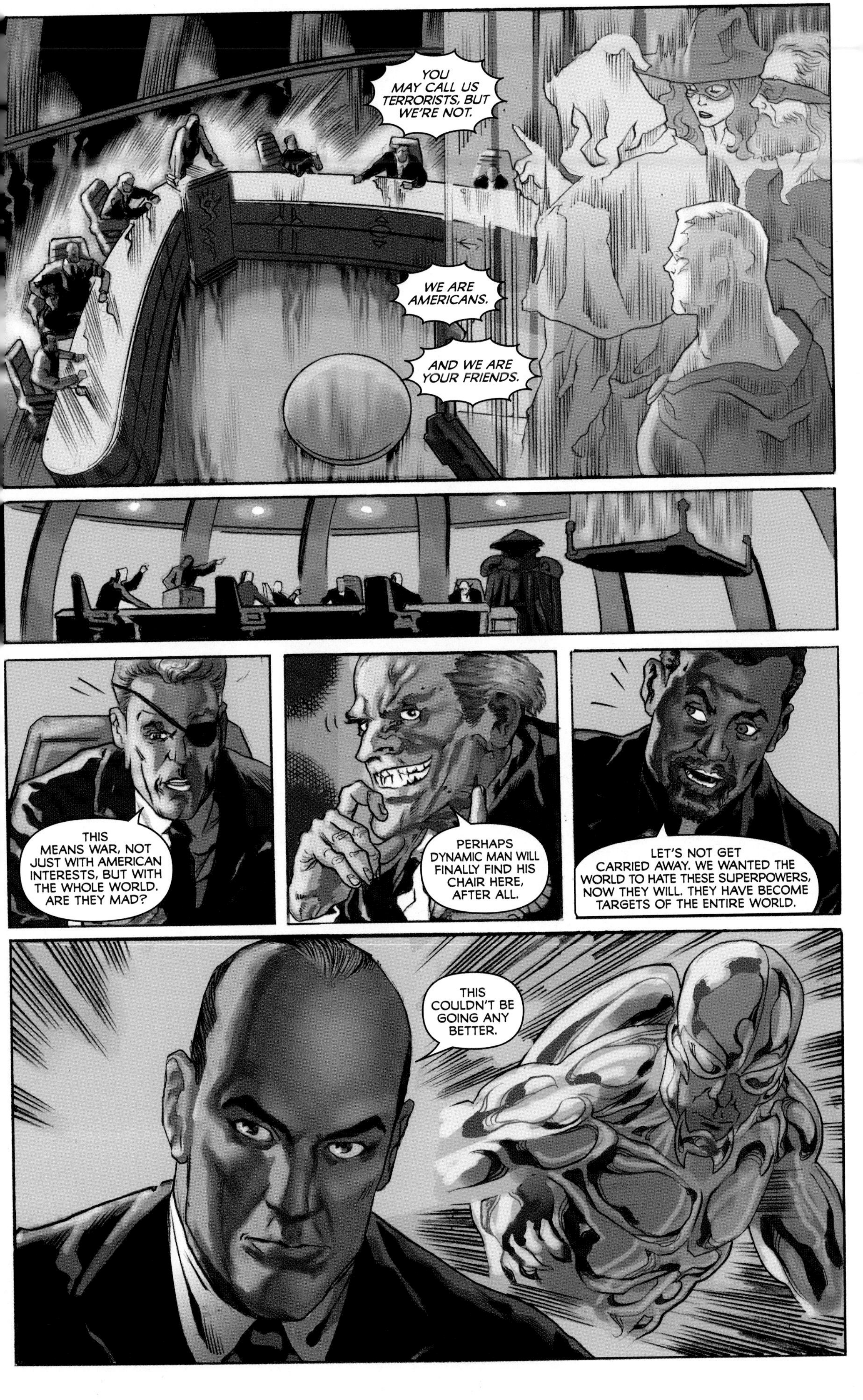
YOU MAY CALL US TERRORISTS, BUT WE'RE NOT.
WE ARE AMERICANS.
AND WE ARE YOUR FRIENDS.
THIS MEANS WAR, NOT JUST WITH AMERICAN INTERESTS, BUT WITH THE WHOLE WORLD. ARE THEY MAD?
PERHAPS DYNAMIC MAN WILL FINALLY FIND HIS CHAIR HERE, AFTER ALL.
LET'S NOT GET CARRIED AWAY. WE WANTED THE WORLD TO HATE THESE SUPERPOWERS, NOW THEY WILL. THEY HAVE BECOME TARGETS OF THE ENTIRE WORLD.
THIS COULDN'T BE GOING ANY BETTER.

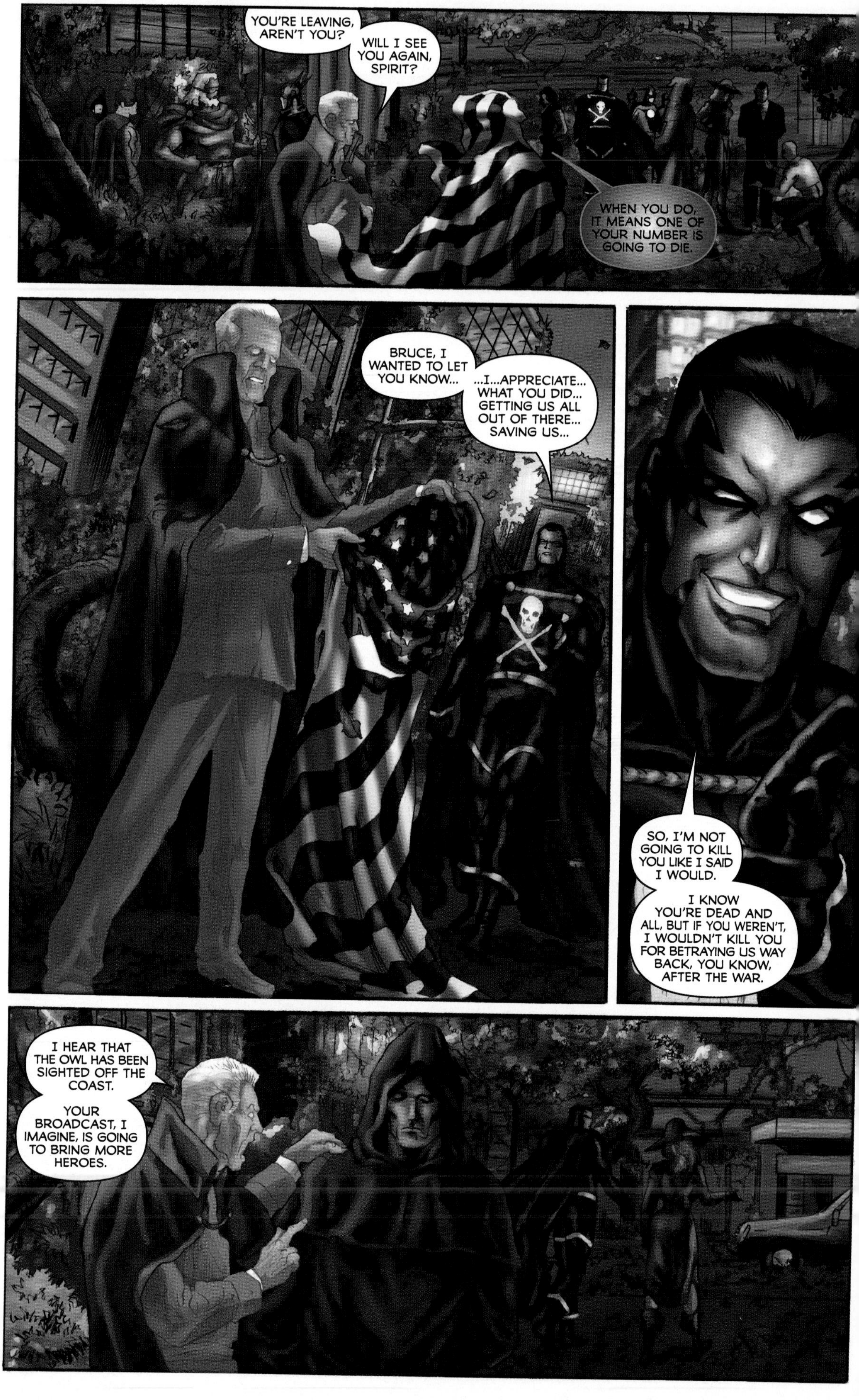
YOU'RE LEAVING, AREN'T YOU?
WILL I SEE YOU AGAIN, SPIRIT?
WHEN YOU DO, IT MEANS ONE OF YOUR NUMBER IS GOING TO DIE.
BRUCE, I WANTED TO LET YOU KNOW...
...I...APPRECIATE... WHAT YOU DID... GETTING US ALL OUT OF THERE... SAVING US...
SO, I'M NOT GOING TO KILL YOU LIKE I SAID I WOULD.
I KNOW YOU'RE DEAD AND ALL, BUT IF YOU WEREN'T, I WOULDN'T KILL YOU FOR BETRAYING US WAY BACK, YOU KNOW, AFTER THE WAR.
I HEAR THAT THE OWL HAS BEEN SIGHTED OFF THE COAST.
YOUR BROADCAST, I IMAGINE, IS GOING TO BRING MORE HEROES.

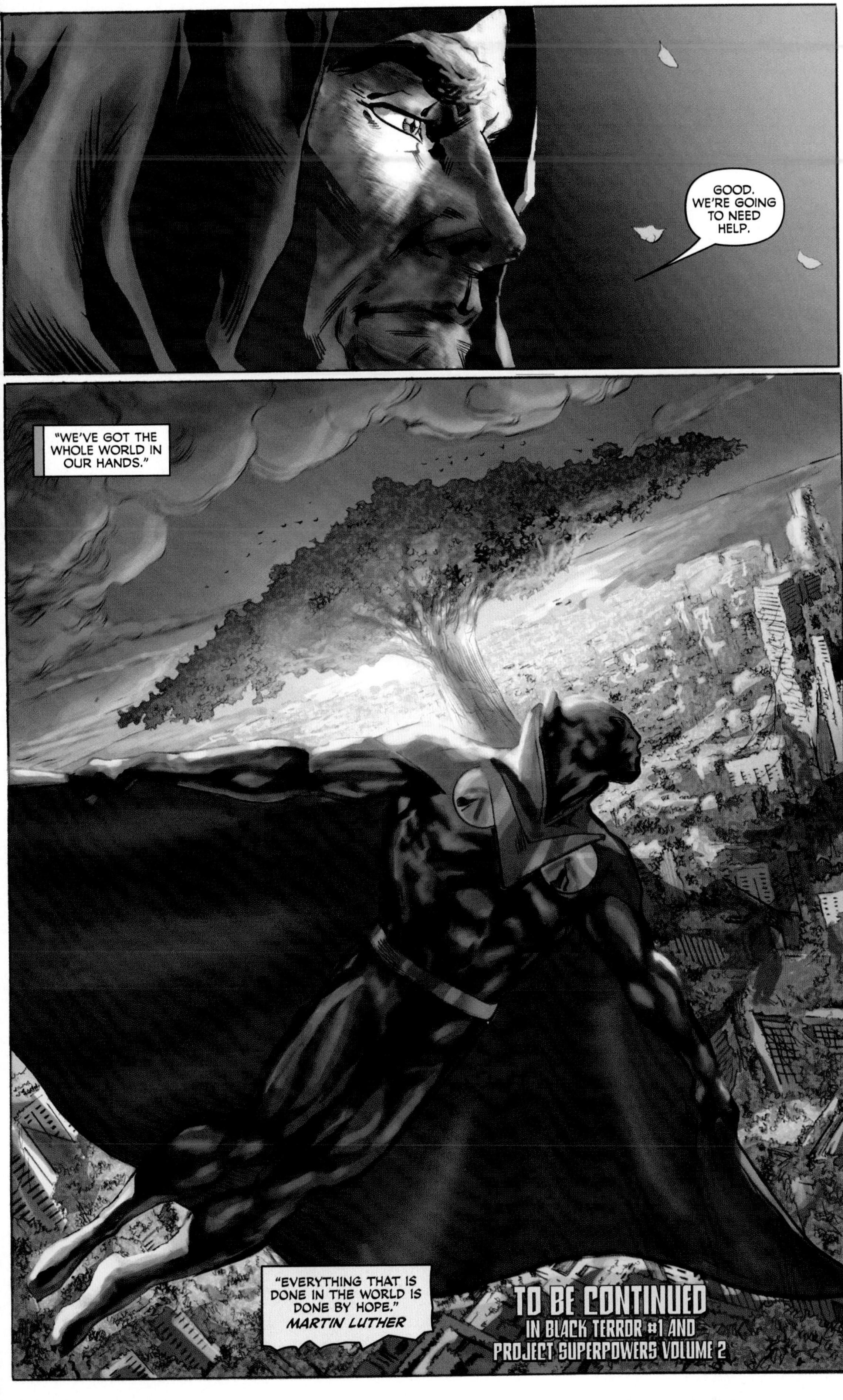

GOOD. WE'RE GOING TO NEED HELP.
"WE'VE GOT THE WHOLE WORLD IN OUR HANDS."
"EVERYTHING THAT IS DONE IN THE WORLD IS DONE BY HOPE."
MARTIN LUTHER
TO BE CONTINUED
IN BLACK TERROR #1 AND PROJECT SUPERPOWERS VOLUME 2

A Note on the Fighting Yank

To aid in our characterization of the key player who drives Project Superpowers, I recommended a model for artist Doug Klauba to use in our opening chapter. My friend Don Strueber fulfilled the role perfectly, lending a gentleman's air of respectability and heroic features to our retired Fighting Yank. The pictures Doug and I took formed the basis of illustrations, and the same reference was passed on to series artist Carlos Paul. Having a unified look and specific inspiration for a character's appearance has aided in grounding our story with at least one foot in the real world. Don Strueber's past service in the United States Navy in World War Two and the Korean War has made him an even more appropriate fit. Hopefully Don can forgive us for the compromised view we have given of this hero he is the basis for, as well as the mangling of the character's mortal form. As the Fighting Yank moves on to be a continuing force in our project, albeit in a ghostly form, the ultimate tale of his redemption and greater glory is still to come.

Many thanks to my friend Steve Darnall and Steve's mother, Marilyn, for uniting us with her husband, Don.

-- Alex Ross

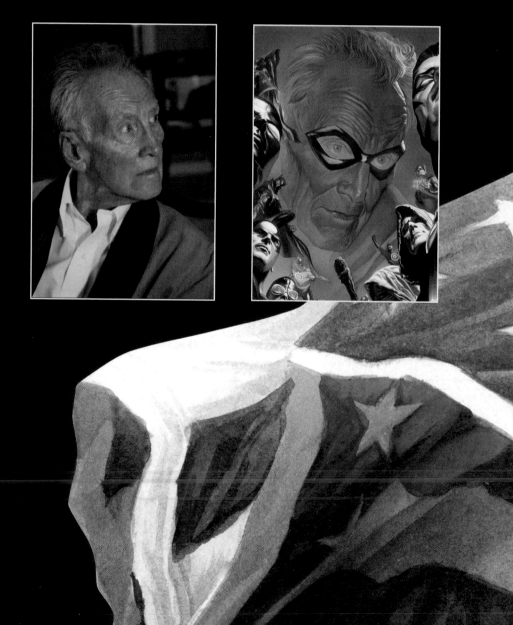

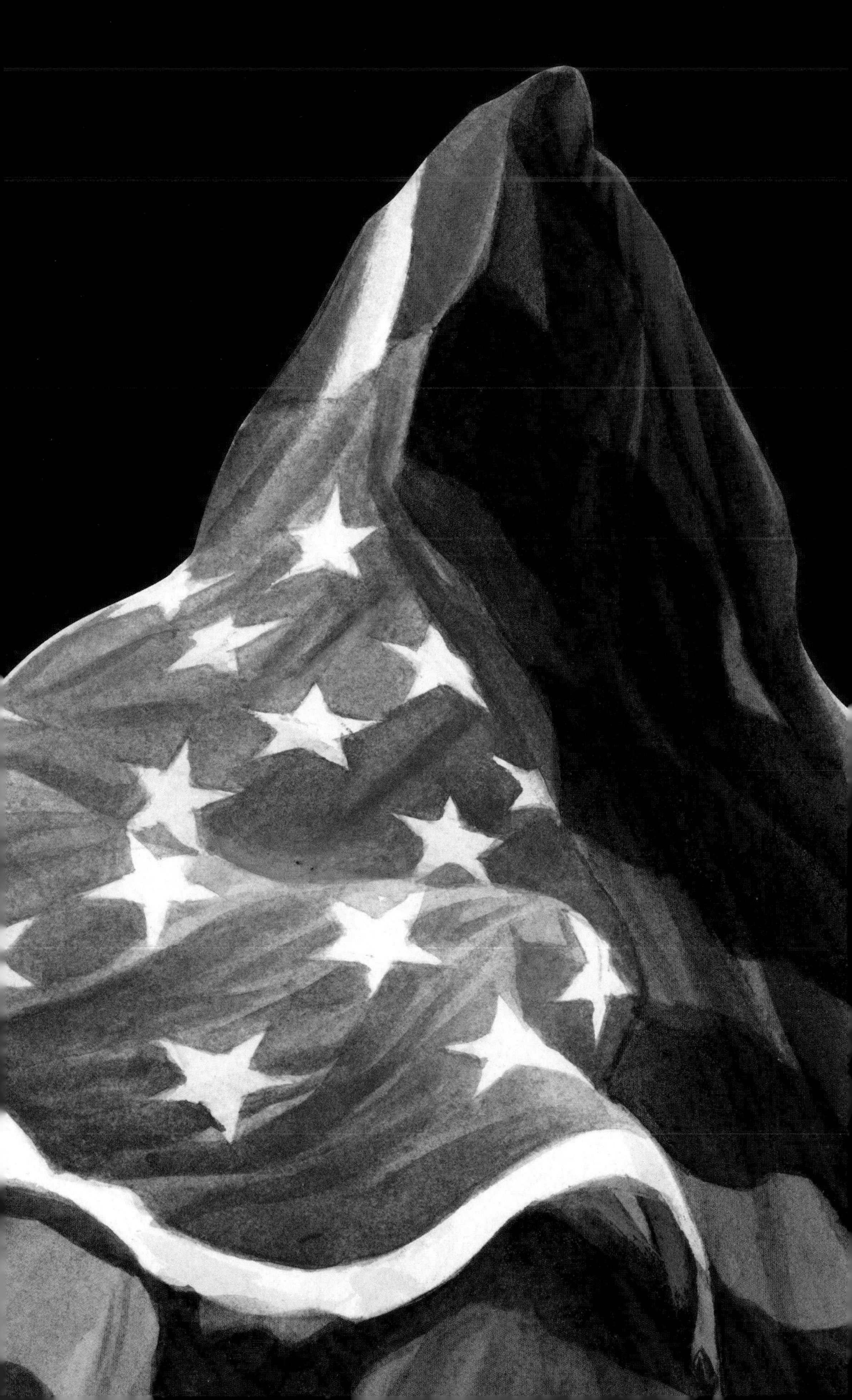

PROJECT SUPERPOWERS™ BONUS MATERIALS

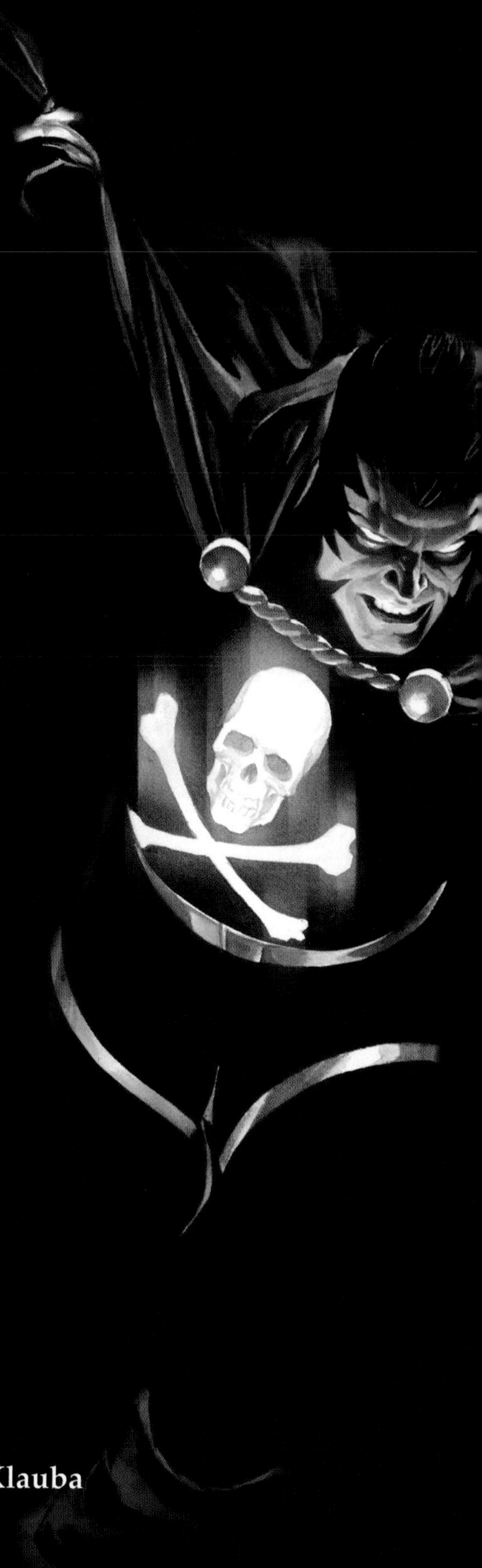

IN LOVING MEMORY OF MICHAEL TURNER

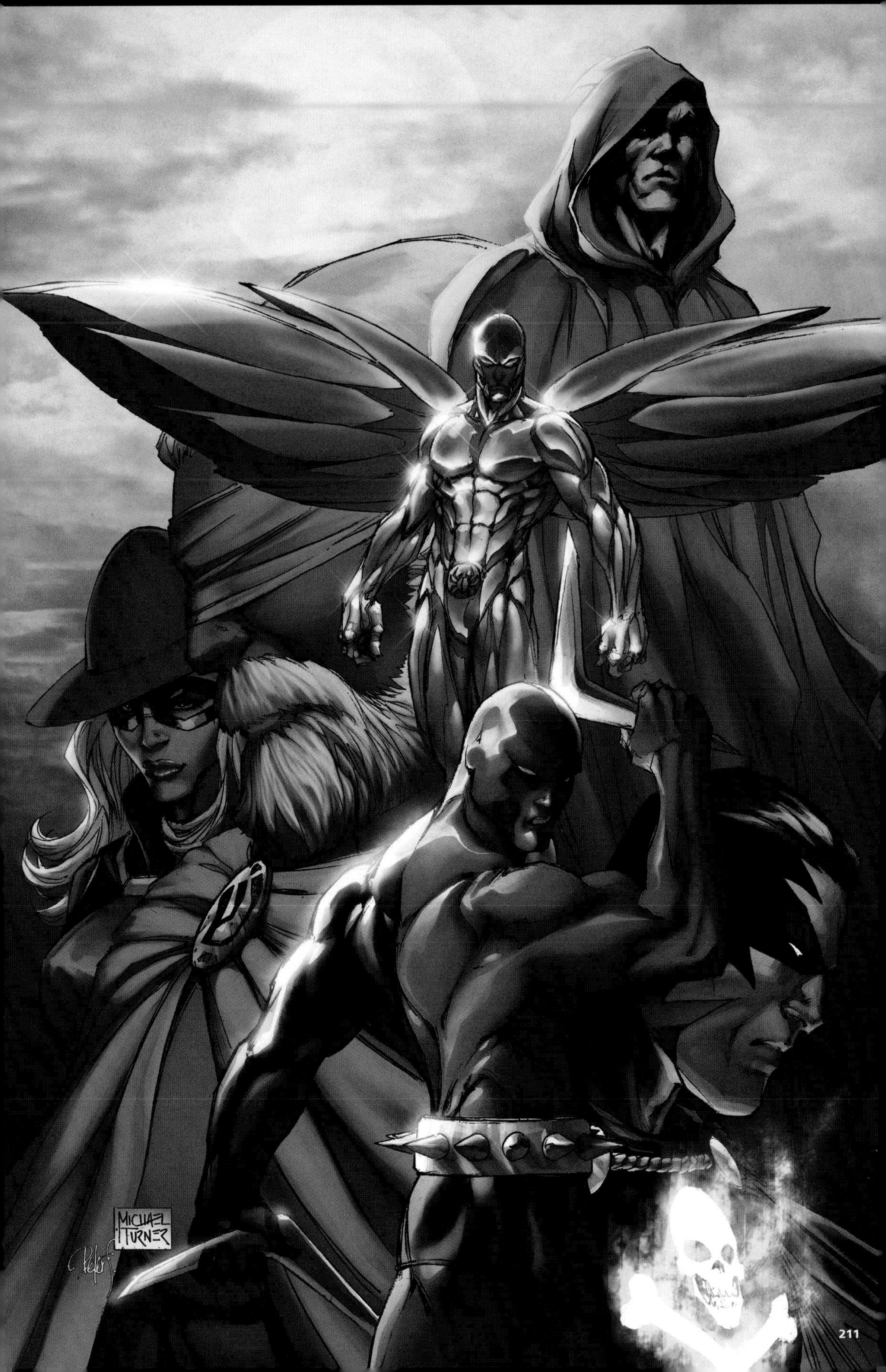
MICHAEL TURNER

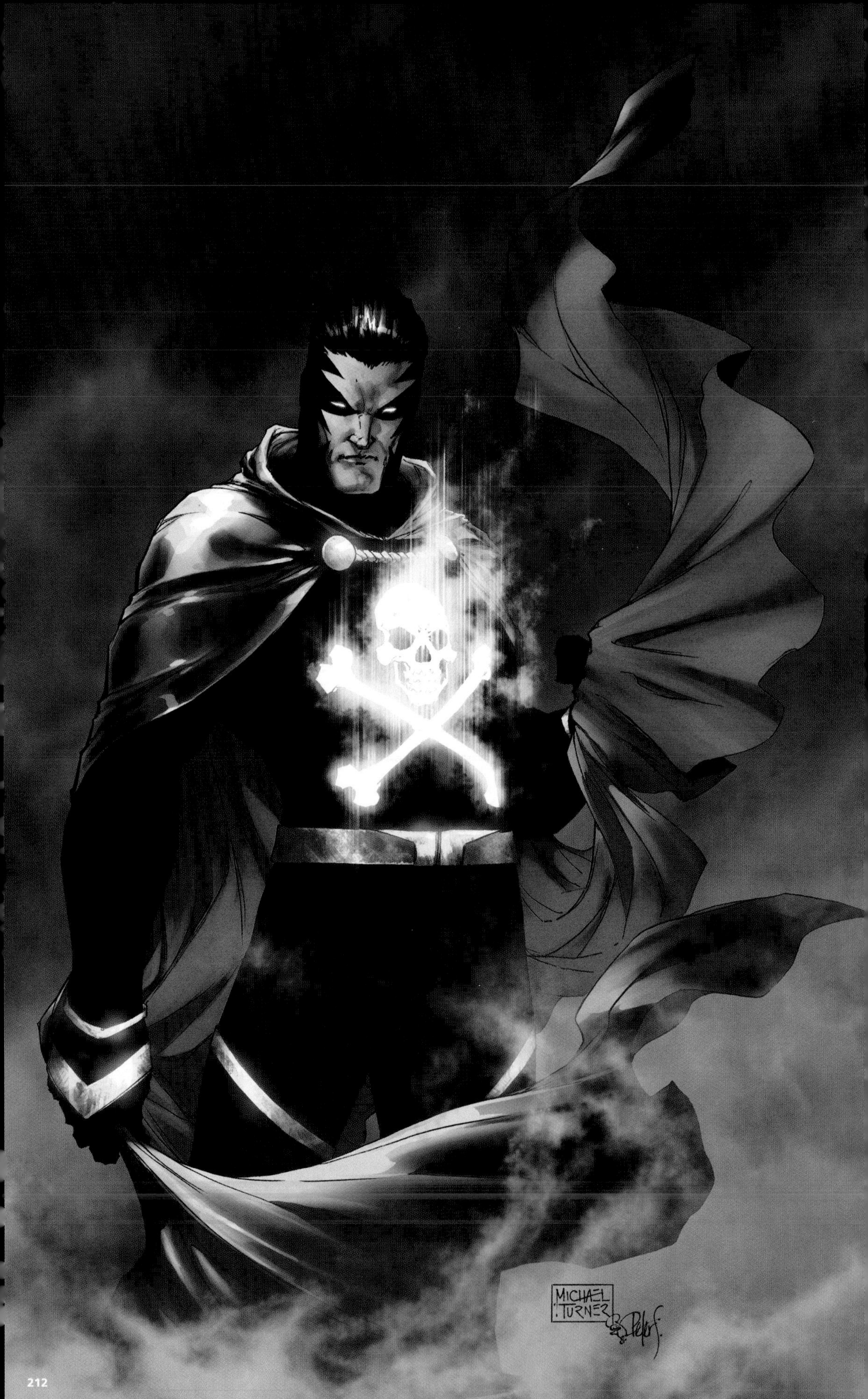
MICHAEL TURNER

FIGHTING YANK'S WAR JOURNAL

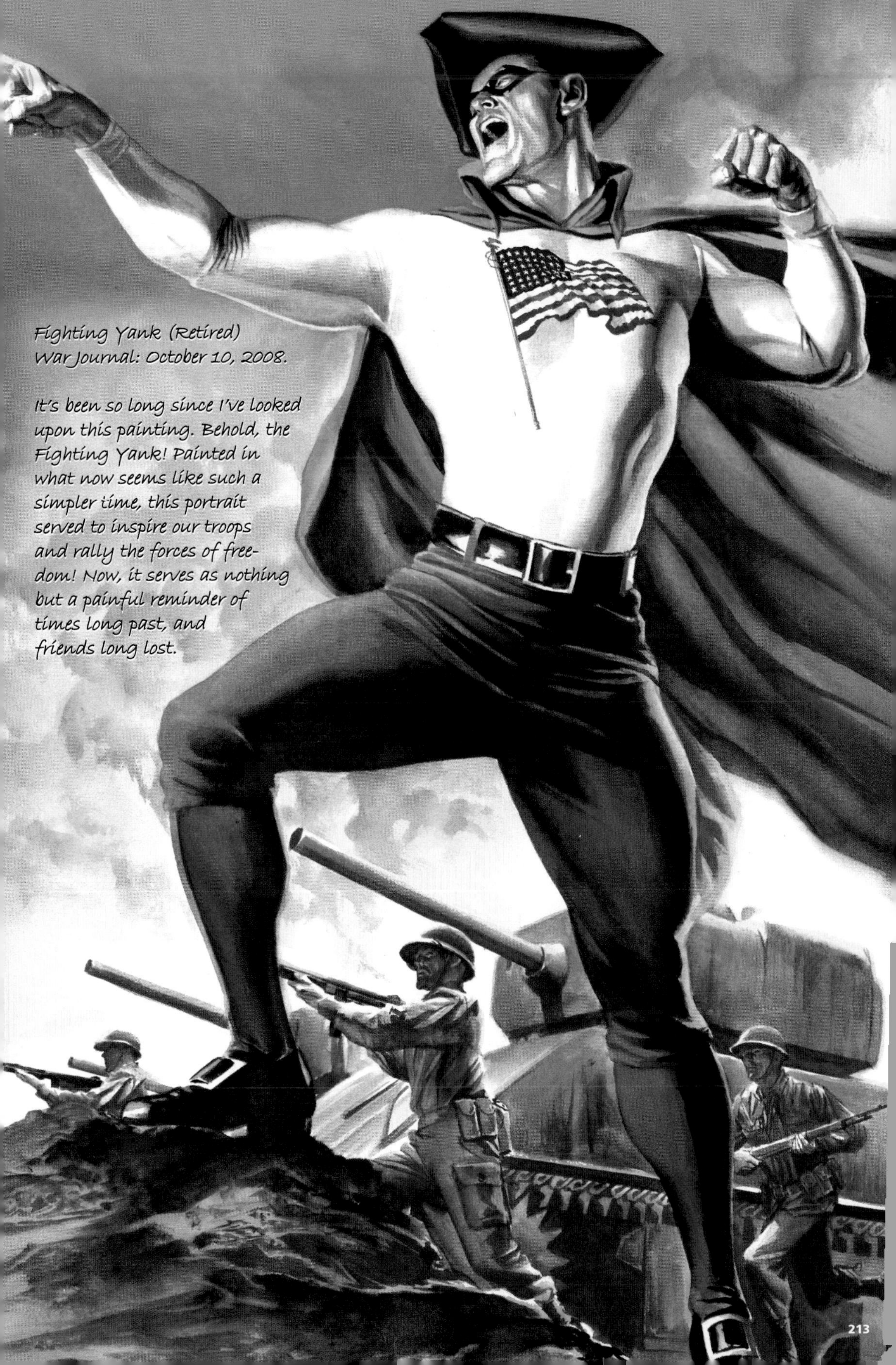

Fighting Yank (Retired)
War Journal: October 10, 2008.

It's been so long since I've looked upon this painting. Behold, the Fighting Yank! Painted in what now seems like such a simpler time, this portrait served to inspire our troops and rally the forces of freedom! Now, it serves as nothing but a painful reminder of times long past, and friends long lost.

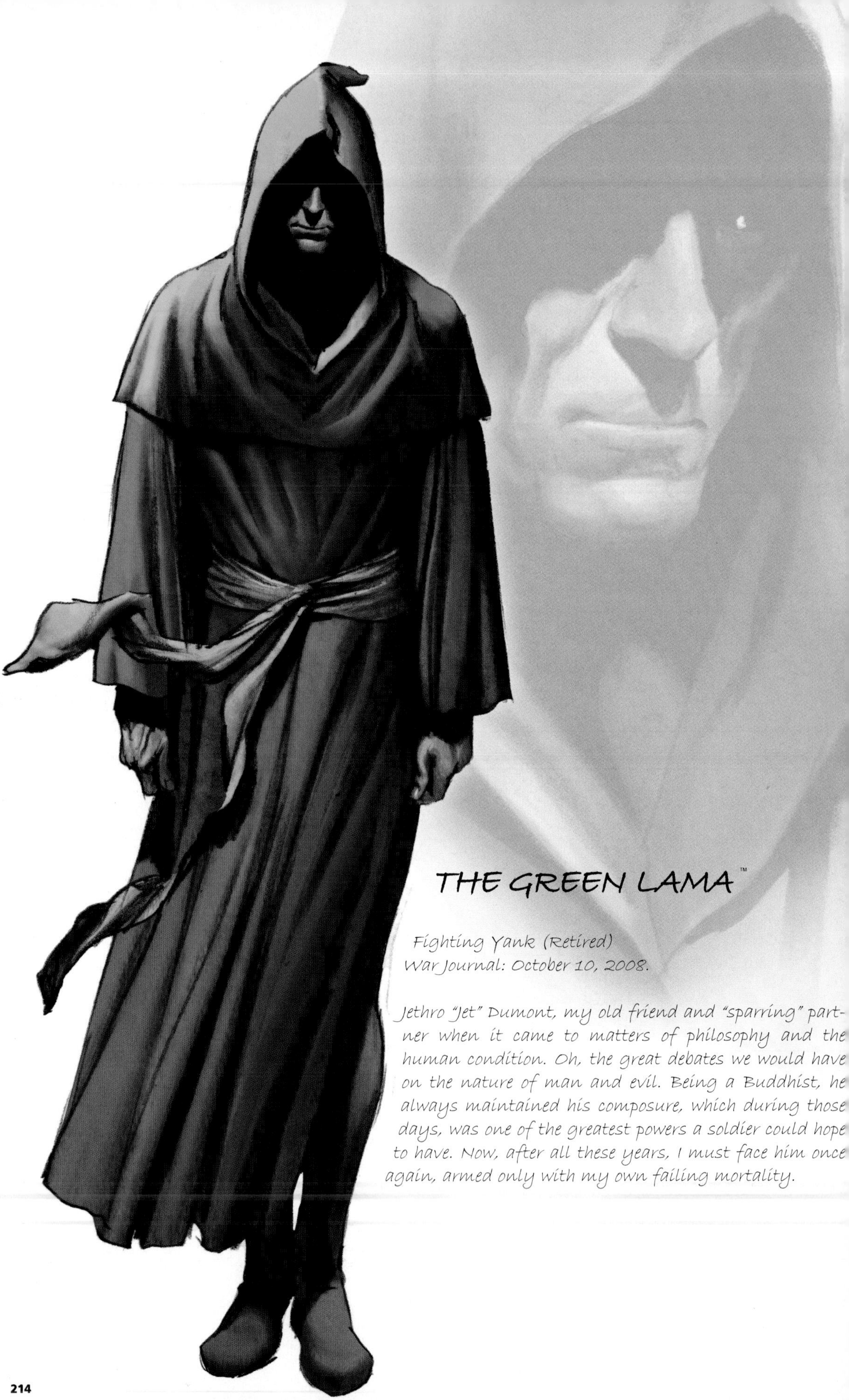

THE GREEN LAMA™

Fighting Yank (Retired)
War Journal: October 10, 2008.

Jethro "Jet" Dumont, my old friend and "sparring" partner when it came to matters of philosophy and the human condition. Oh, the great debates we would have on the nature of man and evil. Being a Buddhist, he always maintained his composure, which during those days, was one of the greatest powers a soldier could hope to have. Now, after all these years, I must face him once again, armed only with my own failing mortality.

THE AMERICAN SPIRIT™

Fighting Yank (Retired)
War Journal: October 10, 2008.

A creature never before known to me that has now turned my world upside down. It claims to be a manifestation of spirits, spirits of long dead heroes who served the flag - Patriots to the core. Is this my destiny as the Fighting Yank? To end up within this American Spirit? And if so, what of my Great-Grandfather, the original Fighting Yank? Should he not have found eternal rest within this creature?

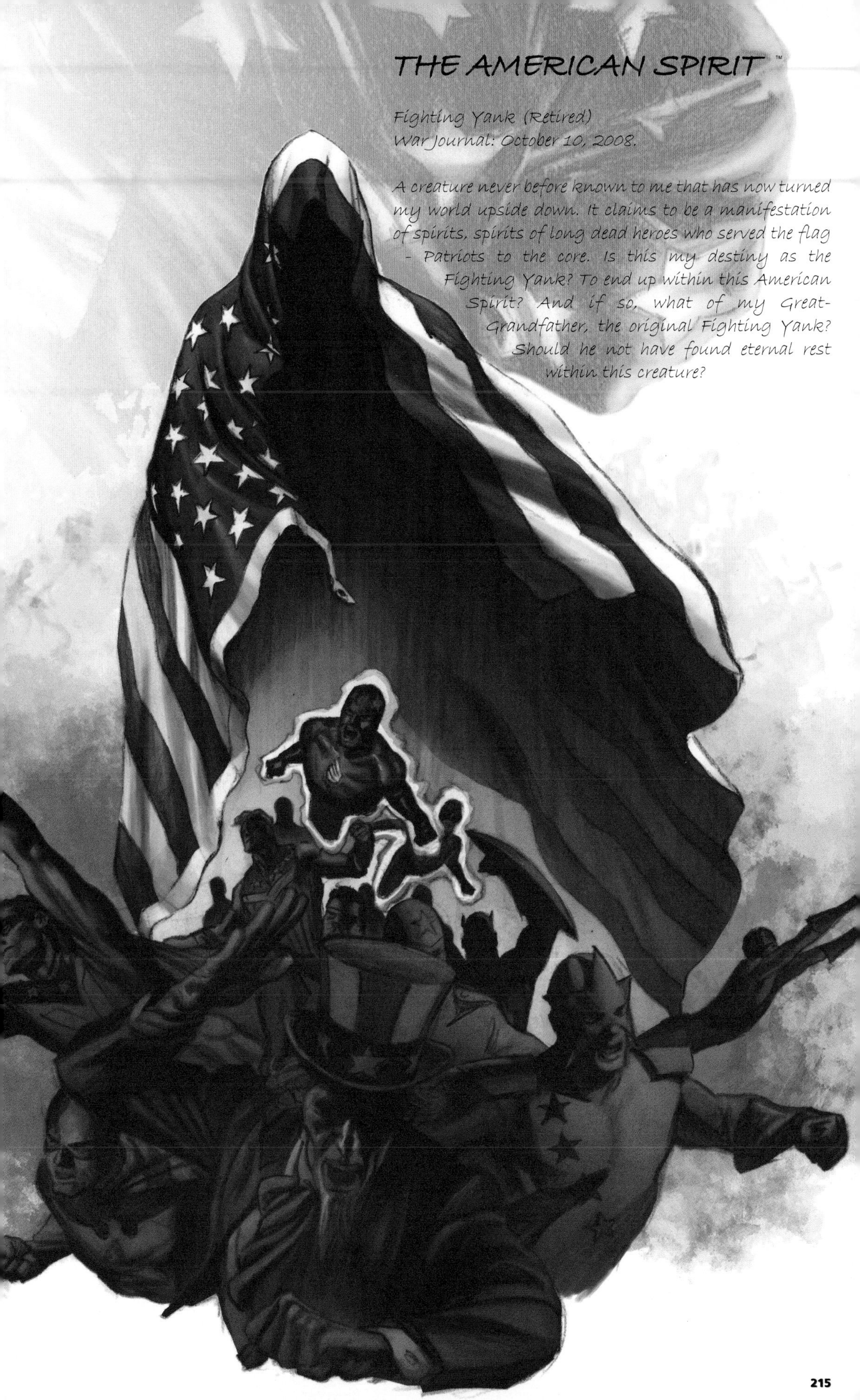

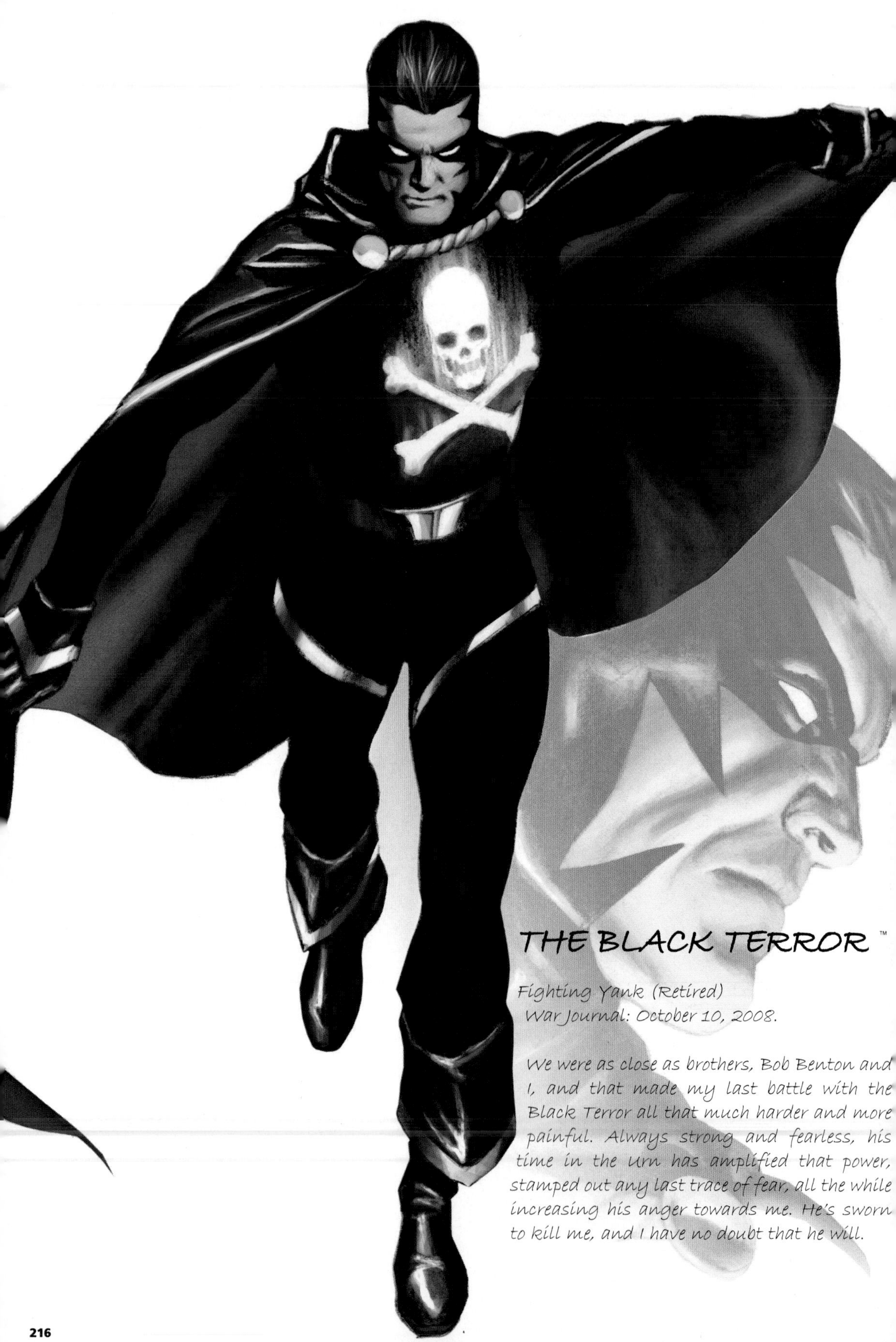

THE BLACK TERROR™

Fighting Yank (Retired)
War Journal: October 10, 2008.

We were as close as brothers, Bob Benton and I, and that made my last battle with the Black Terror all that much harder and more painful. Always strong and fearless, his time in the Urn has amplified that power, stamped out any last trace of fear, all the while increasing his anger towards me. He's sworn to kill me, and I have no doubt that he will.

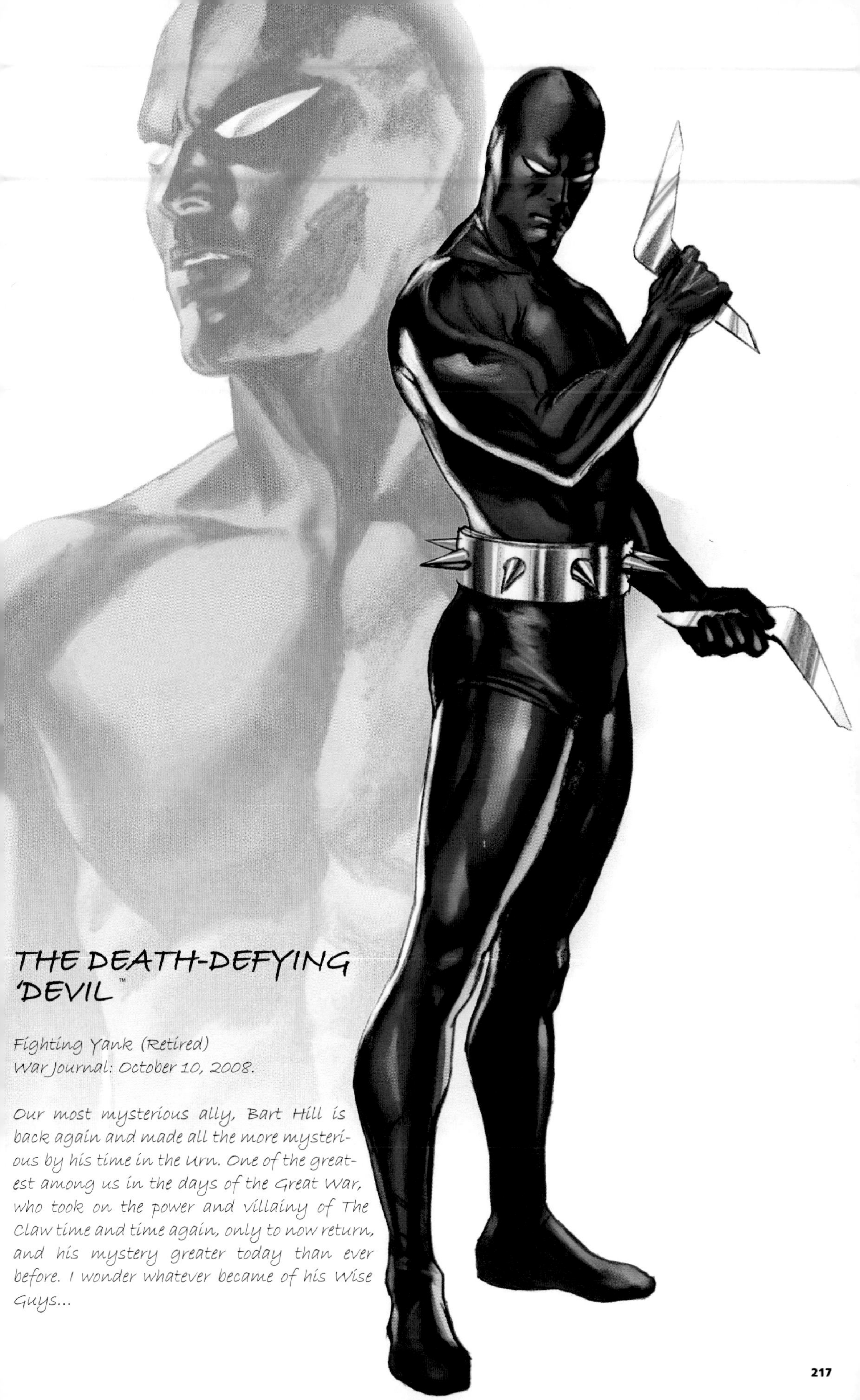

THE DEATH-DEFYING 'DEVIL™

Fighting Yank (Retired)
War Journal: October 10, 2008.

Our most mysterious ally, Bart Hill is back again and made all the more mysterious by his time in the Urn. One of the greatest among us in the days of the Great War, who took on the power and villainy of The Claw time and time again, only to now return, and his mystery greater today than ever before. I wonder whatever became of his Wise Guys...

DYNAMIC MAN AND THE DYNAMIC FAMILY™

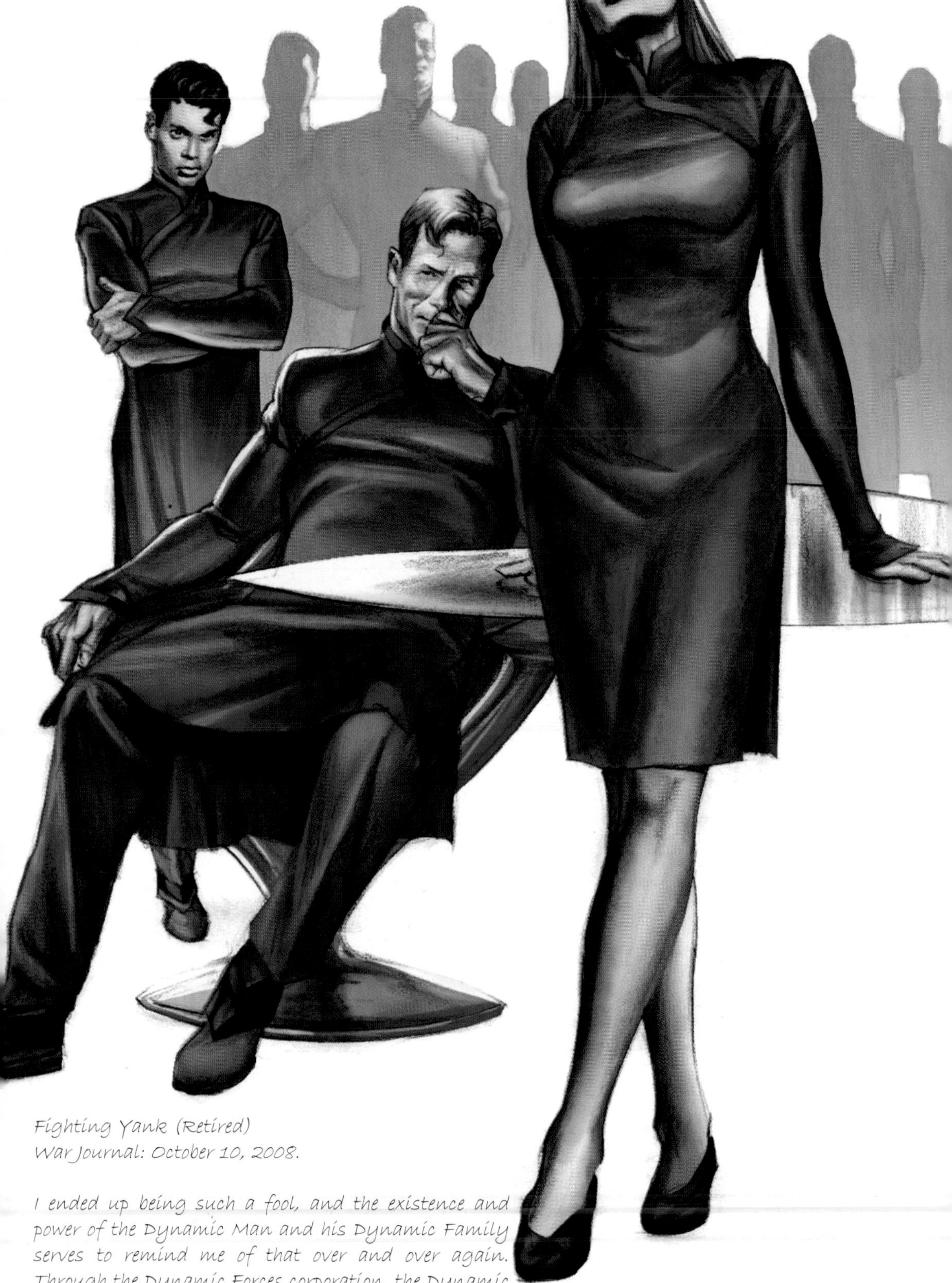

Fighting Yank (Retired)
War Journal: October 10, 2008.

I ended up being such a fool, and the existence and power of the Dynamic Man and his Dynamic Family serves to remind me of that over and over again. Through the Dynamic Forces corporation, the Dynamic Family has gained more wealth and power throughout the world than anyone could have ever imagined. We thought we knew who Bert McQuade was, but we had no idea... no idea at all...

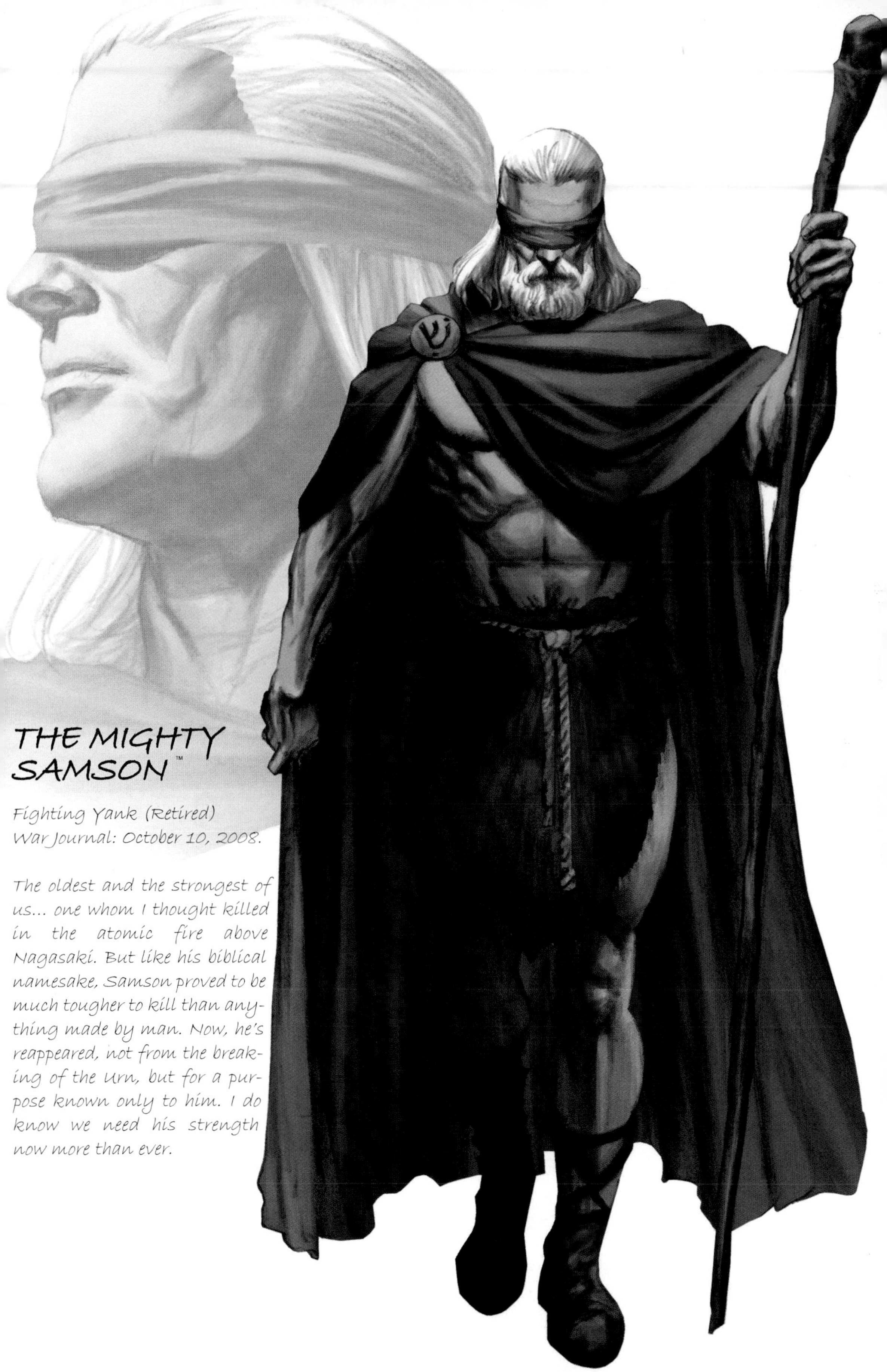

THE MIGHTY SAMSON™

Fighting Yank (Retired)
War Journal: October 10, 2008.

The oldest and the strongest of us... one whom I thought killed in the atomic fire above Nagasaki. But like his biblical namesake, Samson proved to be much tougher to kill than anything made by man. Now, he's reappeared, not from the breaking of the Urn, but for a purpose known only to him. I do know we need his strength now more than ever.

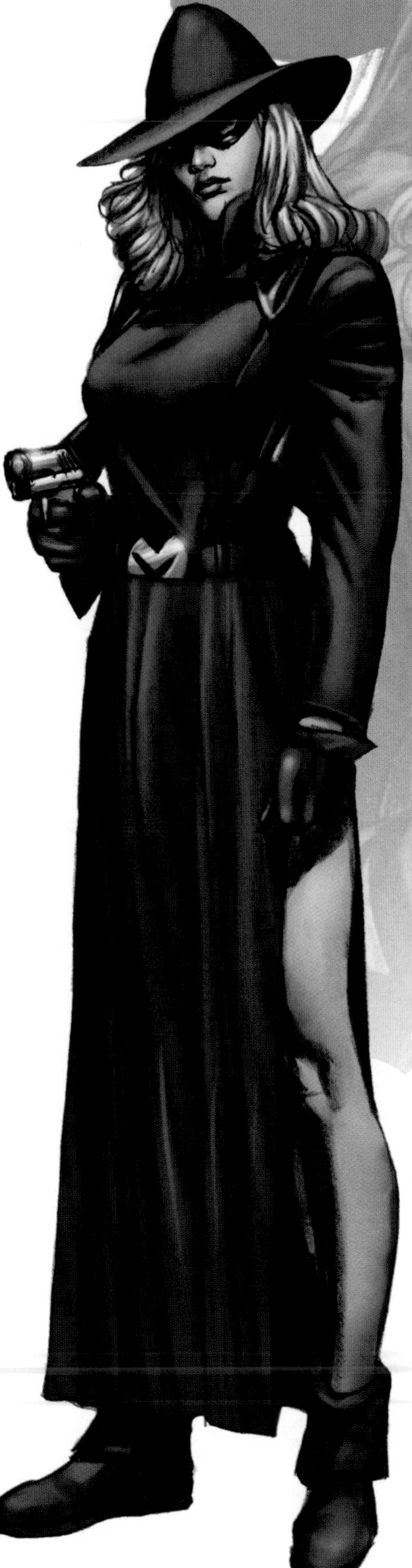

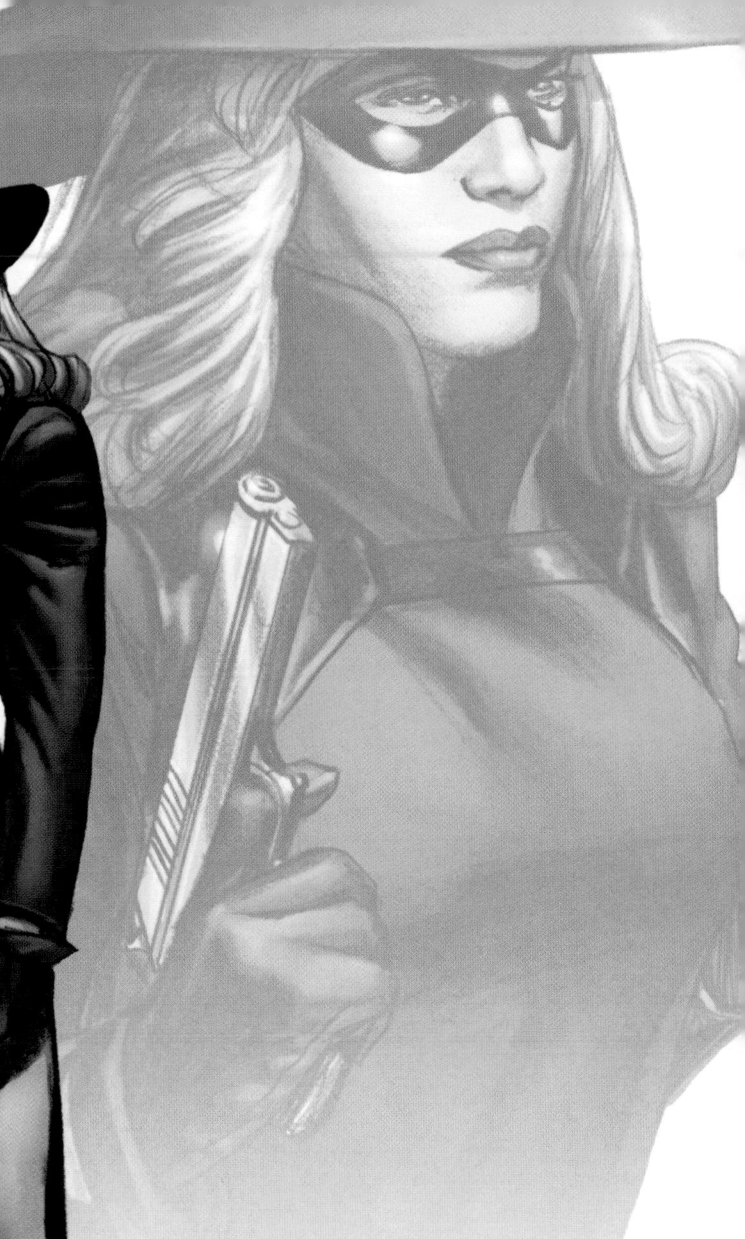

MASQUERADE™

Fighting Yank (Retired)
War Journal: October 10, 2008.

I never knew much about Diana Adams – once called the "Scourge of the Underworld." She became active in costumed adventuring and crime fighting after the War. She may have even been inspired by those that I had already captured in the Urn, wondering where all her heroes had gone. Now that she's back, she's even more of a mystery to me, and she appears very, very much changed...

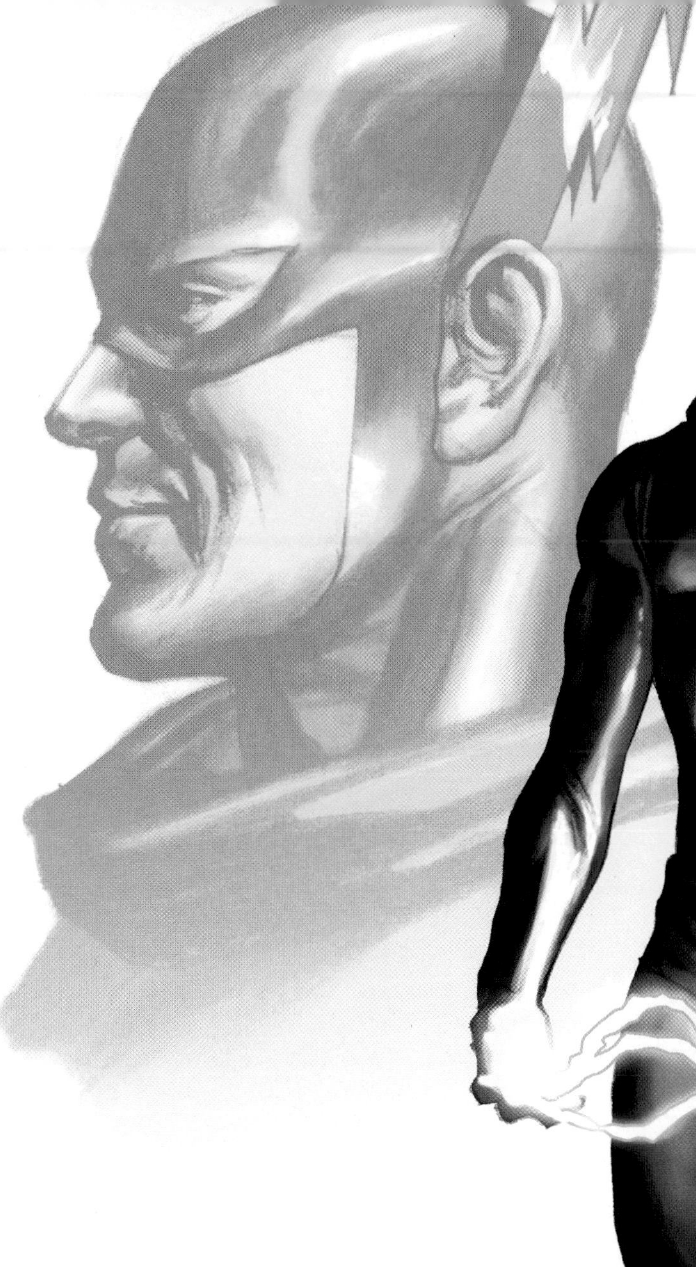

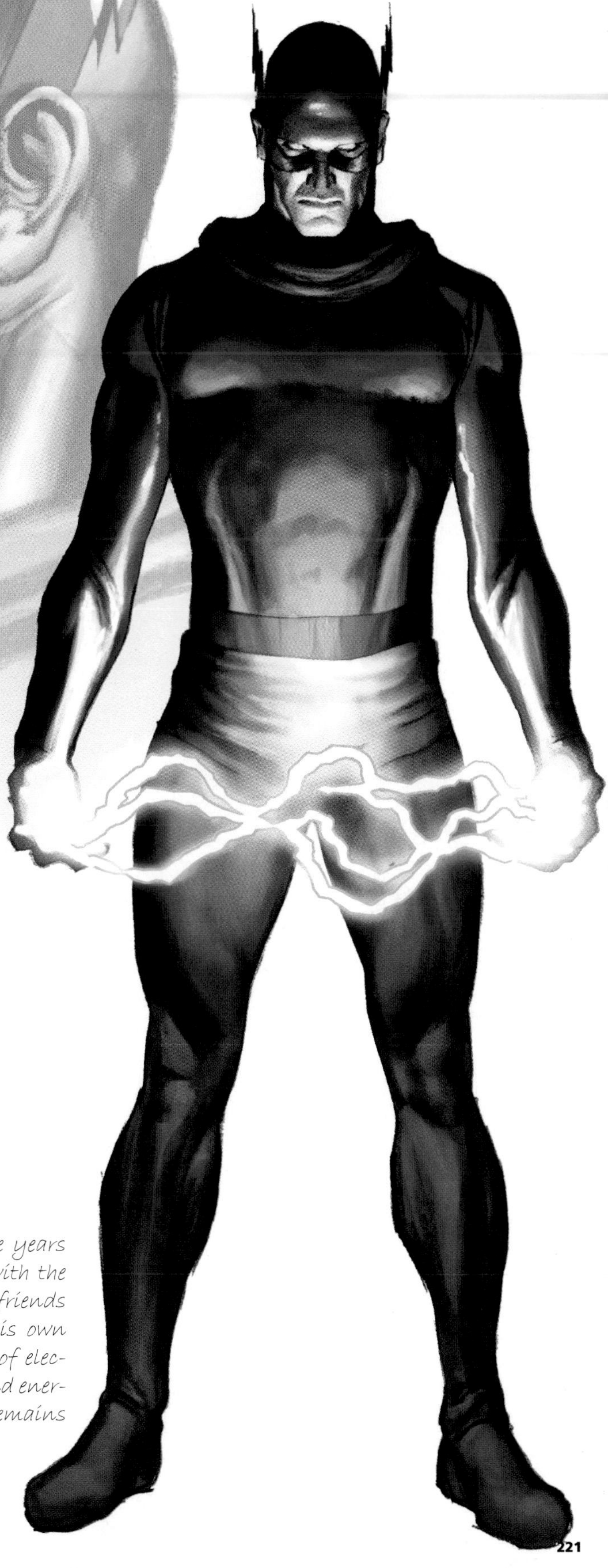

PYROMAN™

Fighting Yank (Retired)
War Journal: October 10, 2008.

Dick Martin stayed a friend during the years after the war... up until I grabbed him with the Urn in '49. Not sure he'll think of us as friends now. He came into his power through his own death, being reborn as a powerful being of electricity and primal fire. How that power and energy were affected by the Urn... well, that remains to be seen.

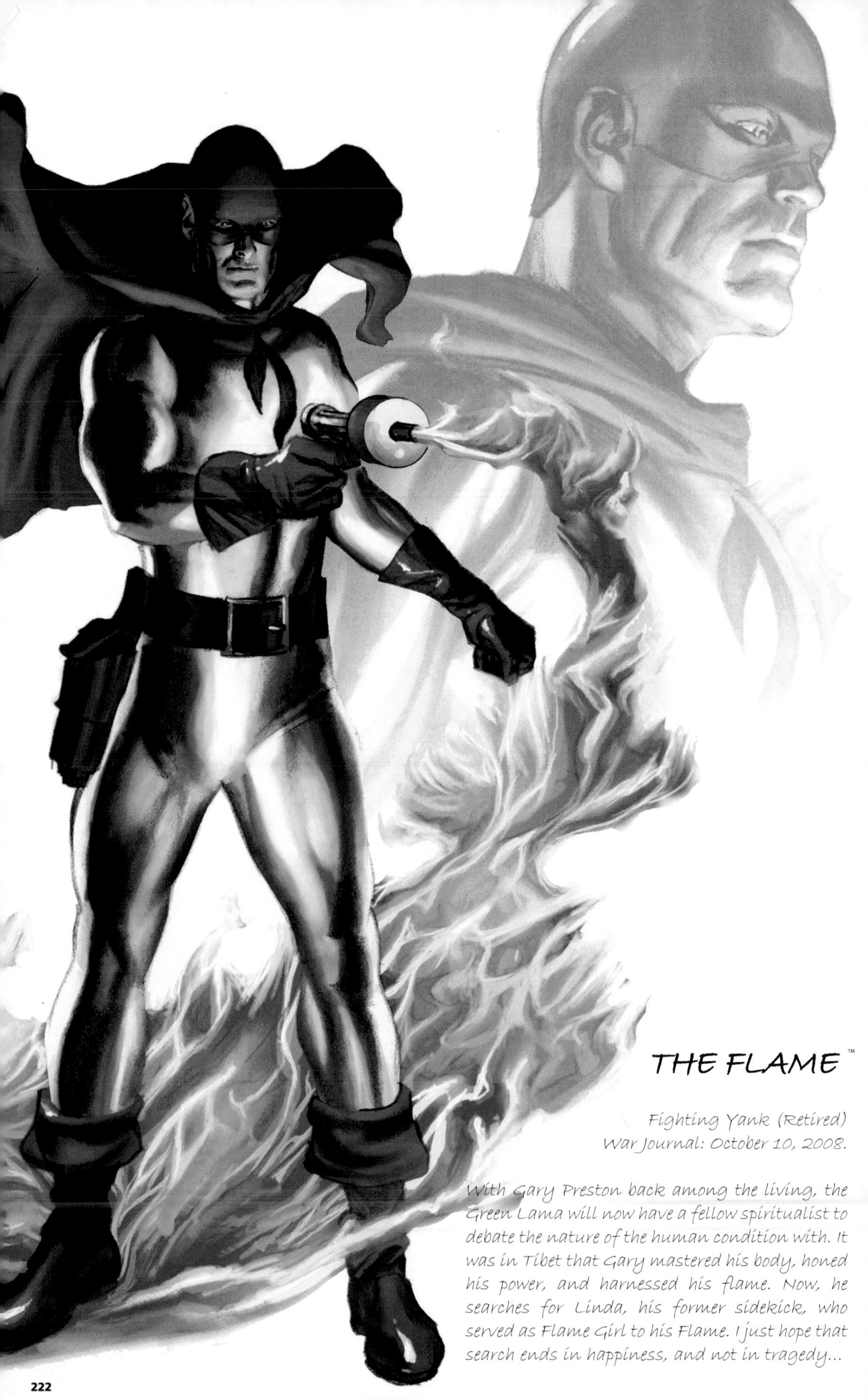

THE FLAME™

Fighting Yank (Retired)
War Journal: October 10, 2008.

With Gary Preston back among the living, the Green Lama will now have a fellow spiritualist to debate the nature of the human condition with. It was in Tibet that Gary mastered his body, honed his power, and harnessed his flame. Now, he searches for Linda, his former sidekick, who served as Flame Girl to his Flame. I just hope that search ends in happiness, and not in tragedy...

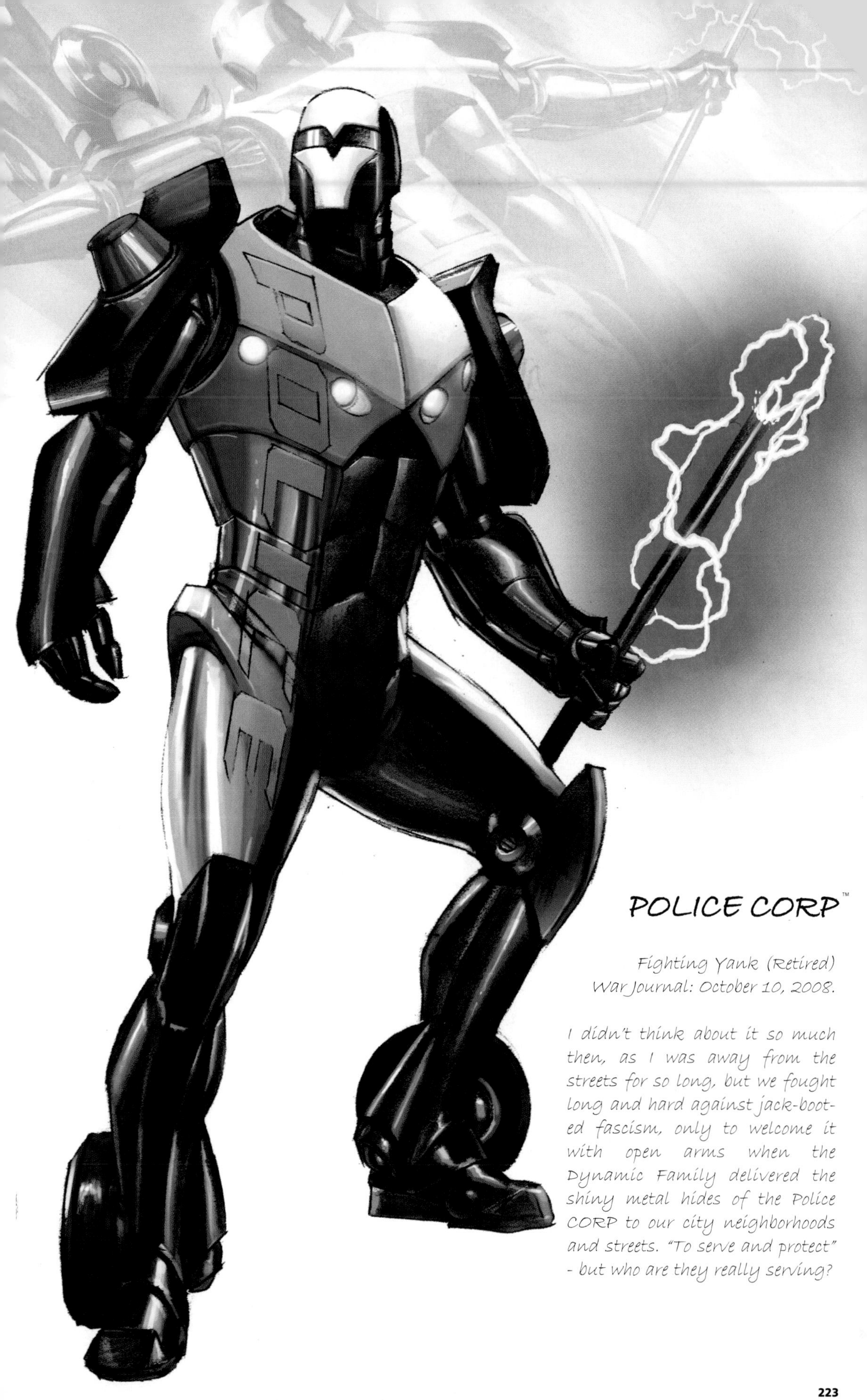
POLICE

POLICE CORP™

Fighting Yank (Retired)
War Journal: October 10, 2008.

I didn't think about it so much then, as I was away from the streets for so long, but we fought long and hard against jack-booted fascism, only to welcome it with open arms when the Dynamic Family delivered the shiny metal hides of the Police CORP to our city neighborhoods and streets. "To serve and protect" - but who are they really serving?

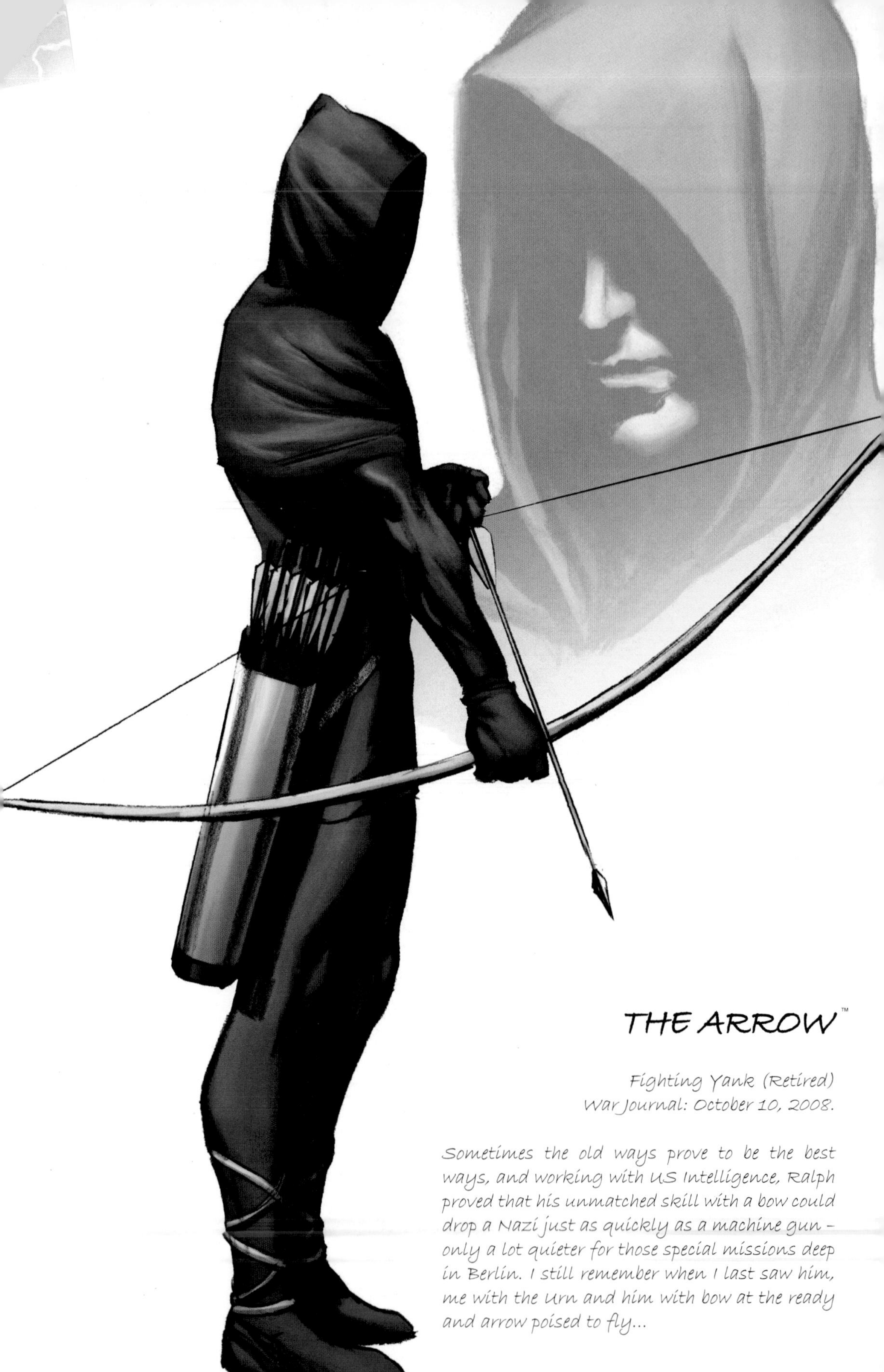

THE ARROW™

Fighting Yank (Retired)
War Journal: October 10, 2008.

Sometimes the old ways prove to be the best ways, and working with US Intelligence, Ralph proved that his unmatched skill with a bow could drop a Nazi just as quickly as a machine gun – only a lot quieter for those special missions deep in Berlin. I still remember when I last saw him, me with the Urn and him with bow at the ready and arrow poised to fly...

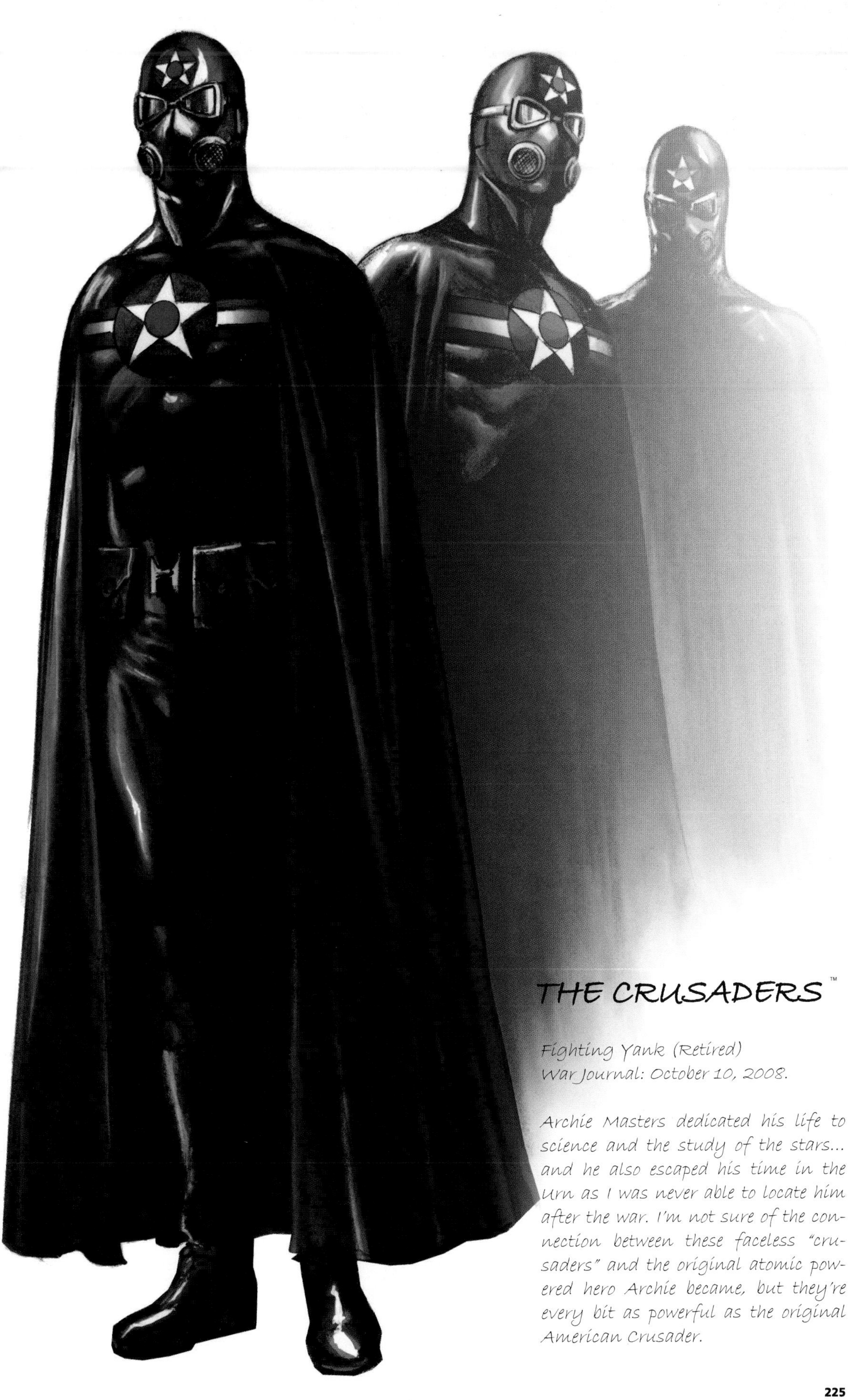

THE CRUSADERS™

Fighting Yank (Retired)
War Journal: October 10, 2008.

Archie Masters dedicated his life to science and the study of the stars... and he also escaped his time in the Urn as I was never able to locate him after the war. I'm not sure of the connection between these faceless "crusaders" and the original atomic powered hero Archie became, but they're every bit as powerful as the original American Crusader.

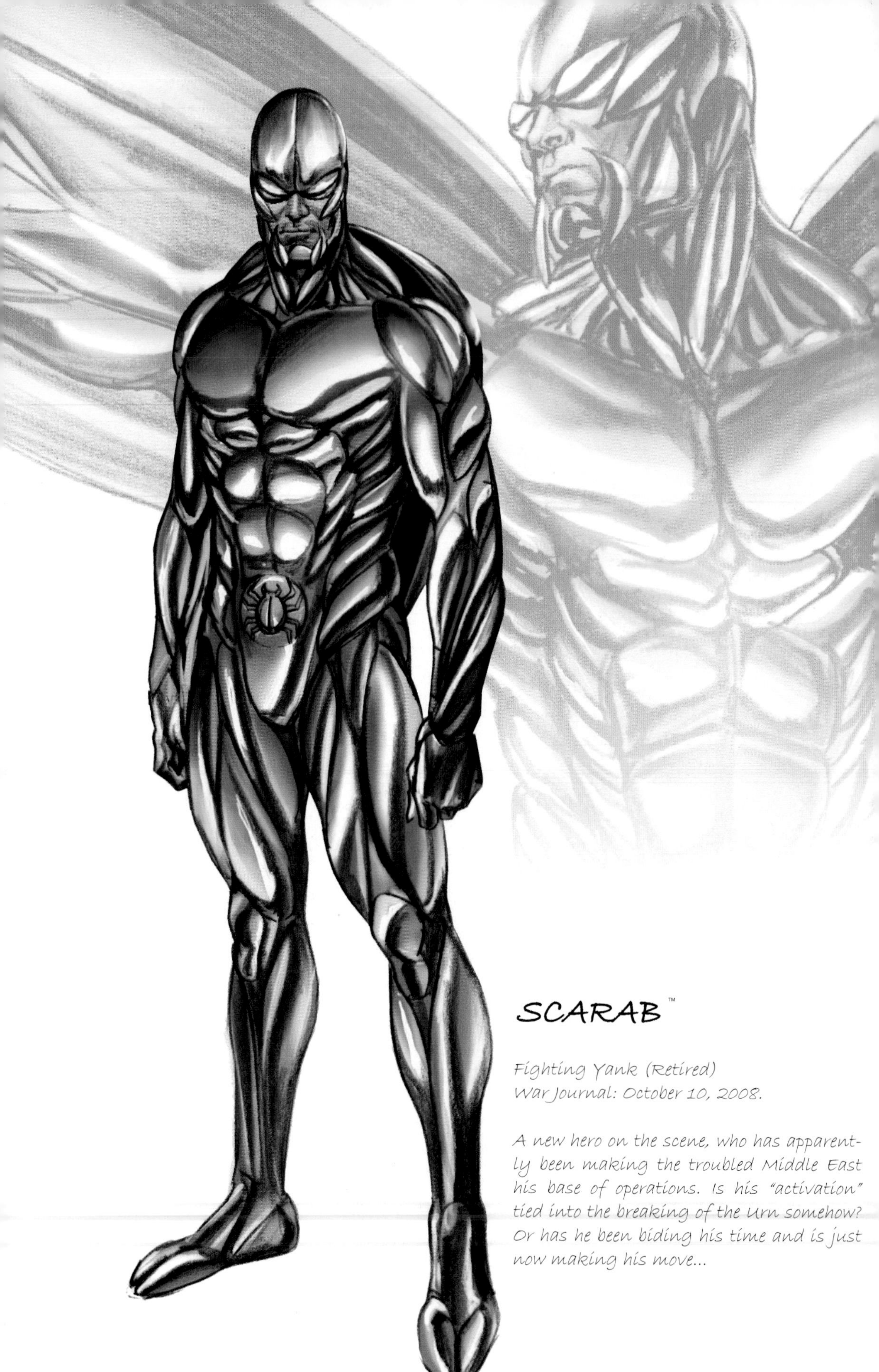

SCARAB™

Fighting Yank (Retired)
War Journal: October 10, 2008.

A new hero on the scene, who has apparently been making the troubled Middle East his base of operations. Is his "activation" tied into the breaking of the Urn somehow? Or has he been biding his time and is just now making his move...

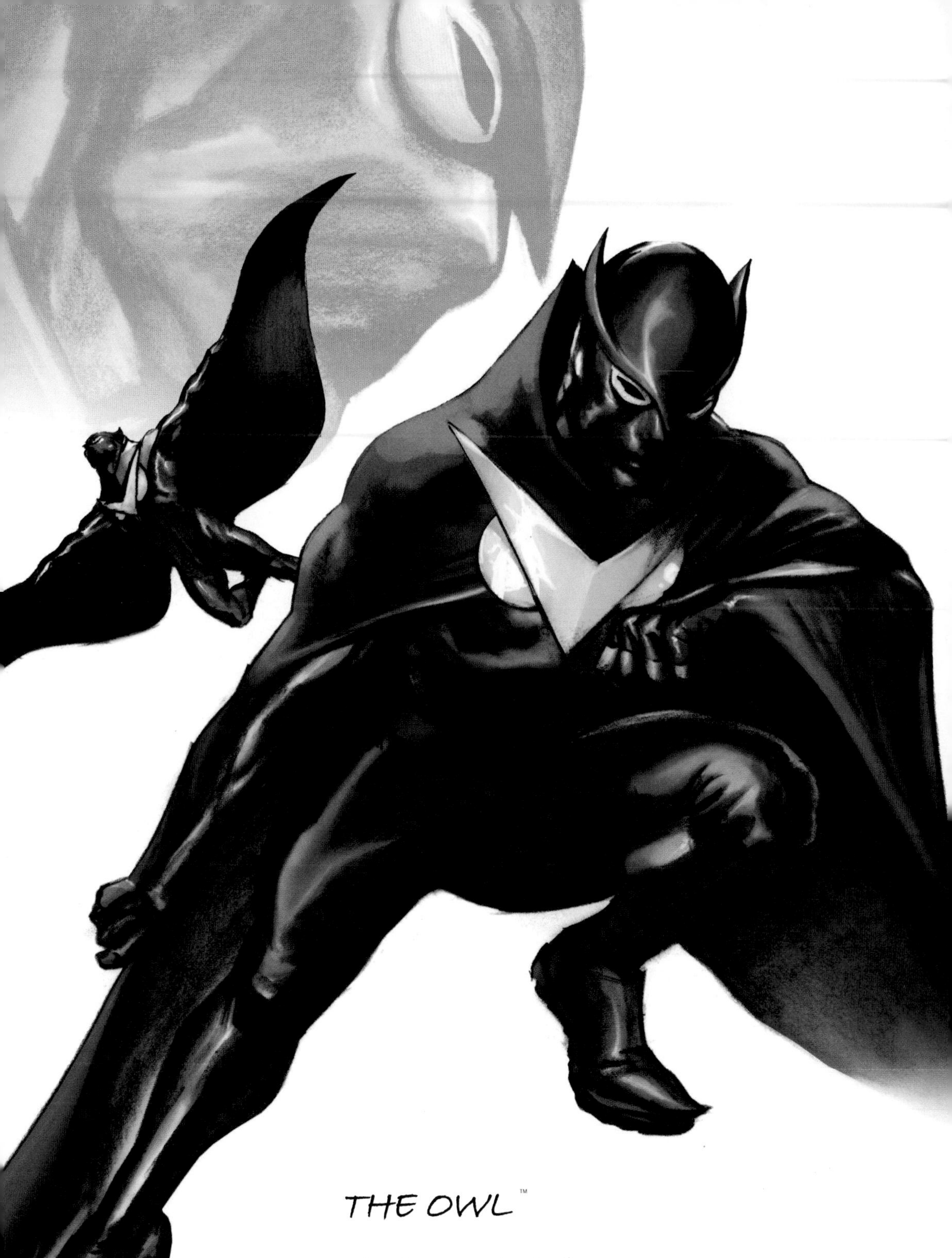

THE OWL™

Fighting Yank (Retired)
War Journal: October 10, 2008.

A good cop from a small Midwestern town, Nick Terry took his brand of crimefighting to the next level, creating an arsenal of gadgets and vehicles. It now appears the Owl may no longer need those same gadgets to soar the skies. Only time will tell.... Of course, with the Owl back among us, where is Owl Girl?

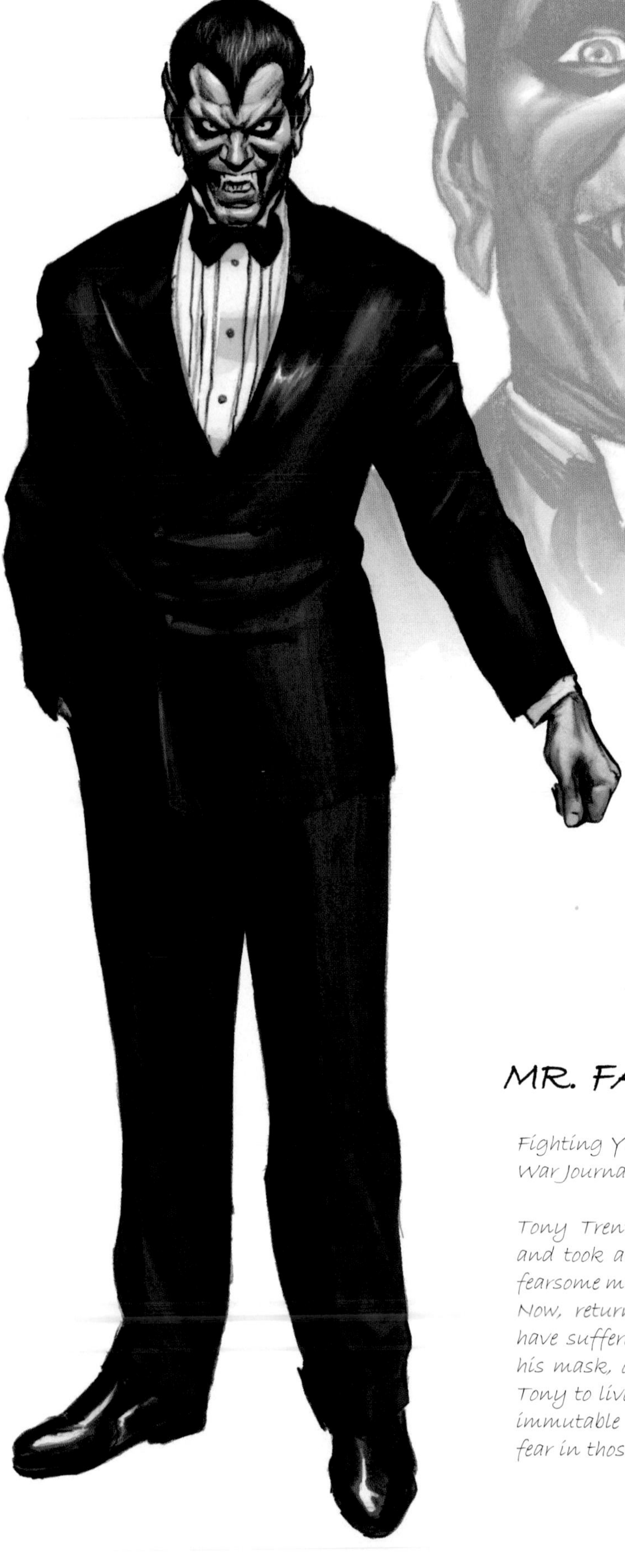

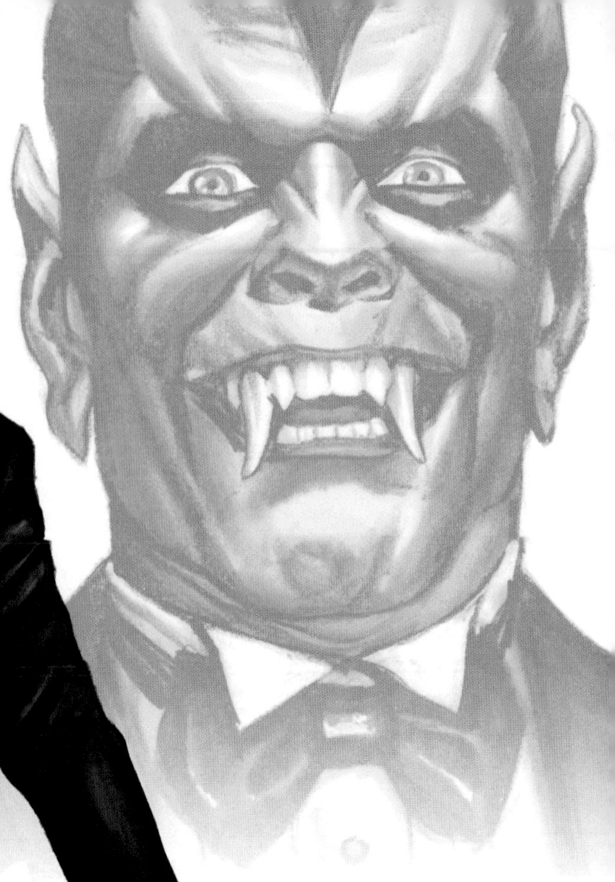

MR. FACE™

Fighting Yank (Retired)
War Journal: October 10, 2008.

Tony Trent took a break from reporting and took a stand against crime, using a fearsome mask to subdue crooks and thugs. Now, returned from the Urn, Tony may have suffered the cruelest fate of us all as his mask, once able to come off and allow Tony to live a normal life, appears to be an immutable part of him... and now ignites fear in those that look upon him.

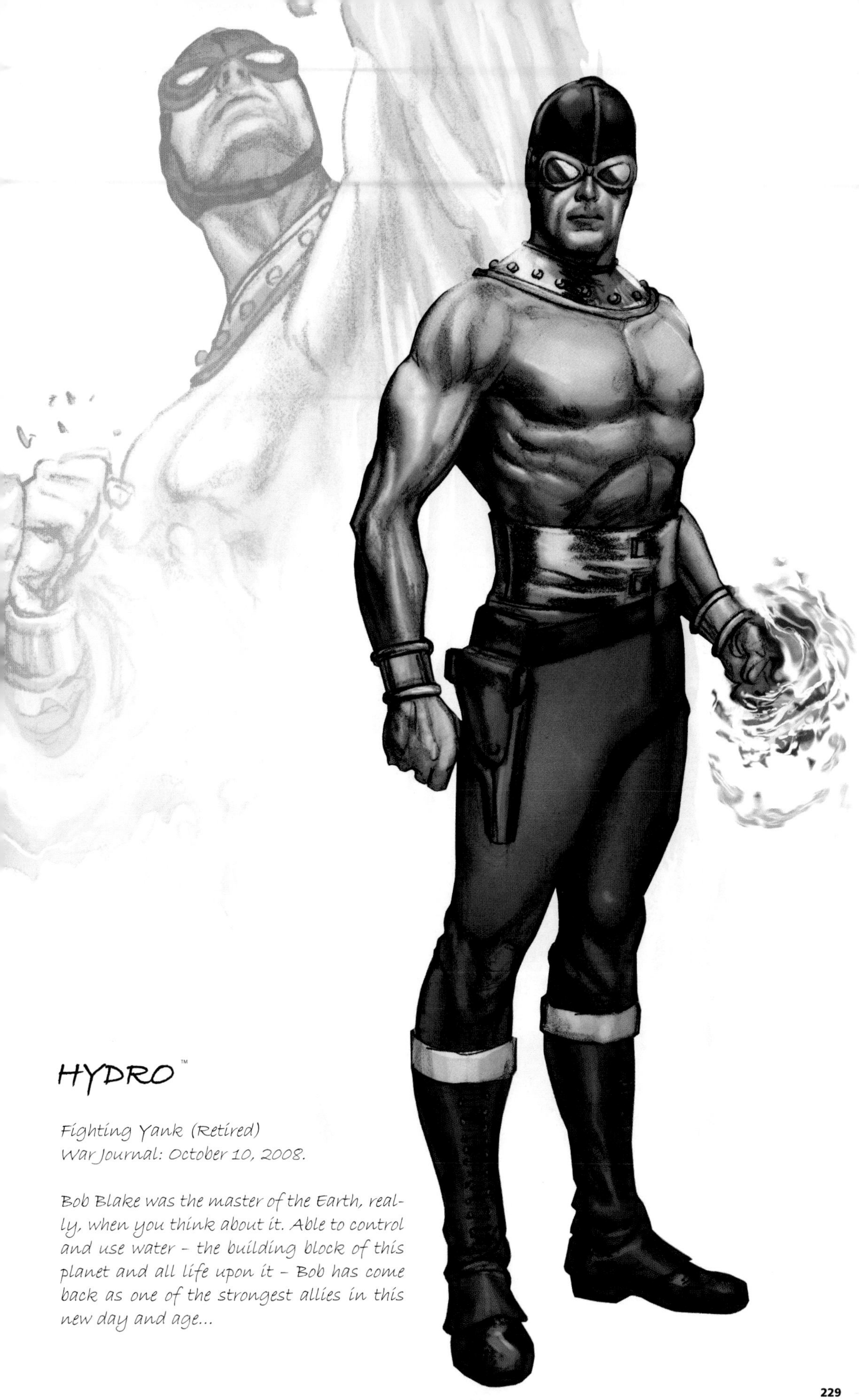

HYDRO™

Fighting Yank (Retired)
War Journal: October 10, 2008.

Bob Blake was the master of the Earth, really, when you think about it. Able to control and use water – the building block of this planet and all life upon it – Bob has come back as one of the strongest allies in this new day and age...

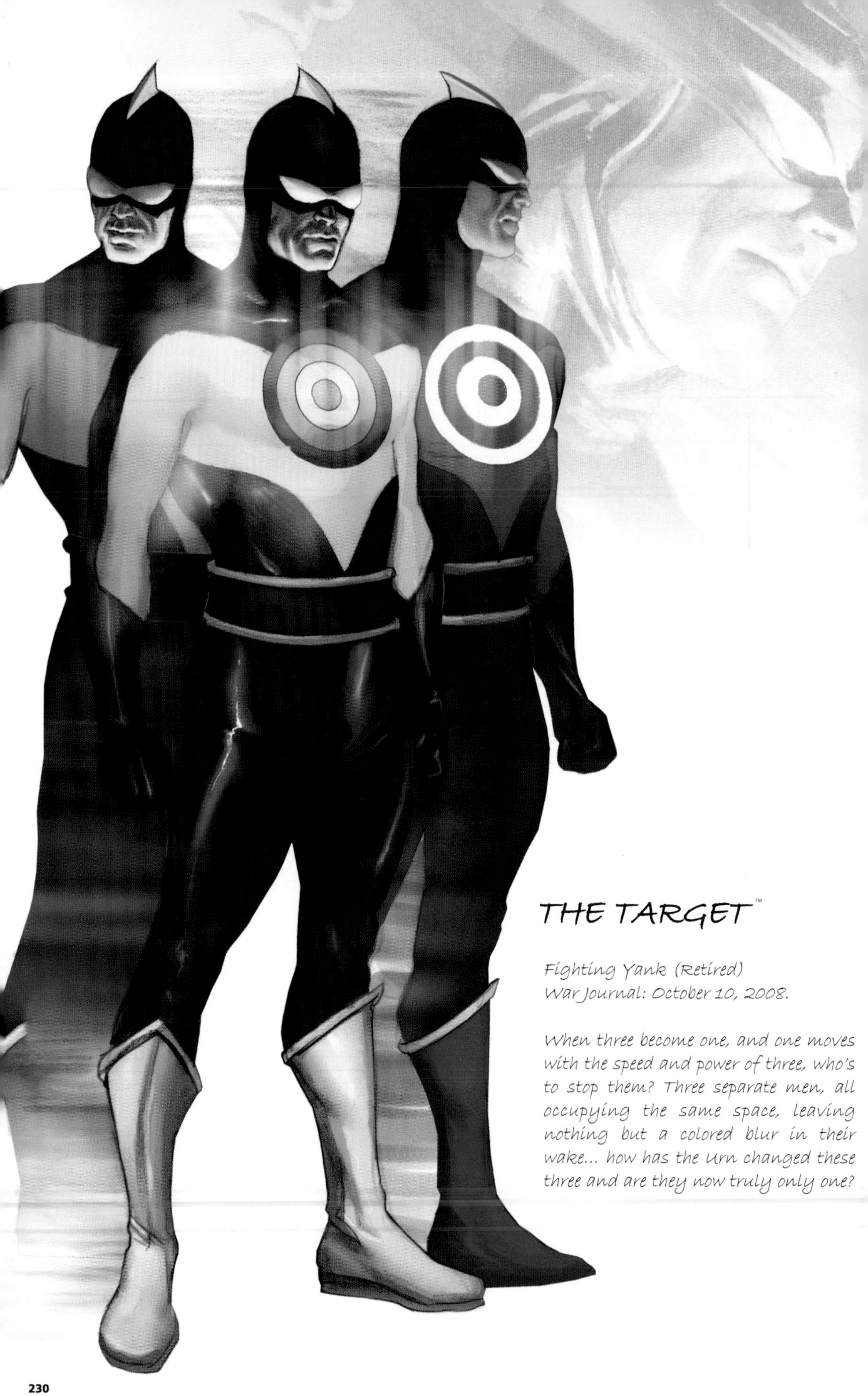

THE TARGET™

Fighting Yank (Retired)
War Journal: October 10, 2008.

When three become one, and one moves with the speed and power of three, who's to stop them? Three separate men, all occupying the same space, leaving nothing but a colored blur in their wake... how has the Urn changed these three and are they now truly only one?

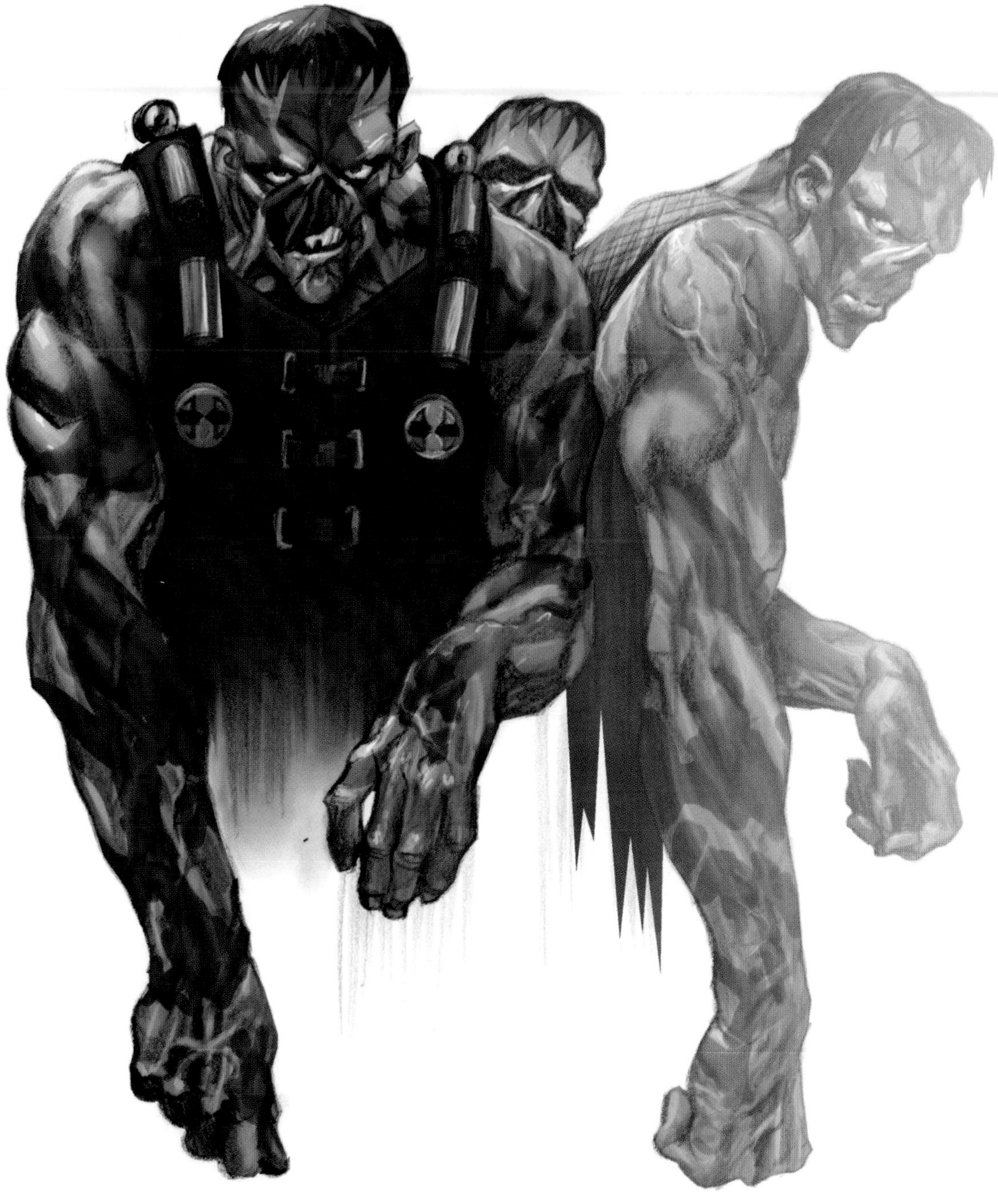

F-TROOP™

Fighting Yank (Retired)
War Journal: October 10, 2008.

A thing thought of legend, but "alive" in reality, Dr. Victor Frankenstein's "monster" fought for his adopted country valiantly during the Second World War. Now, the powers that be have taken the science of the undead and perverted it beyond recognition, sending undead soldiers into battle and replacing limbs and fluids as they fight war after endless war.

GOLDEN AGE CHARACTER REFERENCE BY ALEX ROSS
Colors By InLight Studio

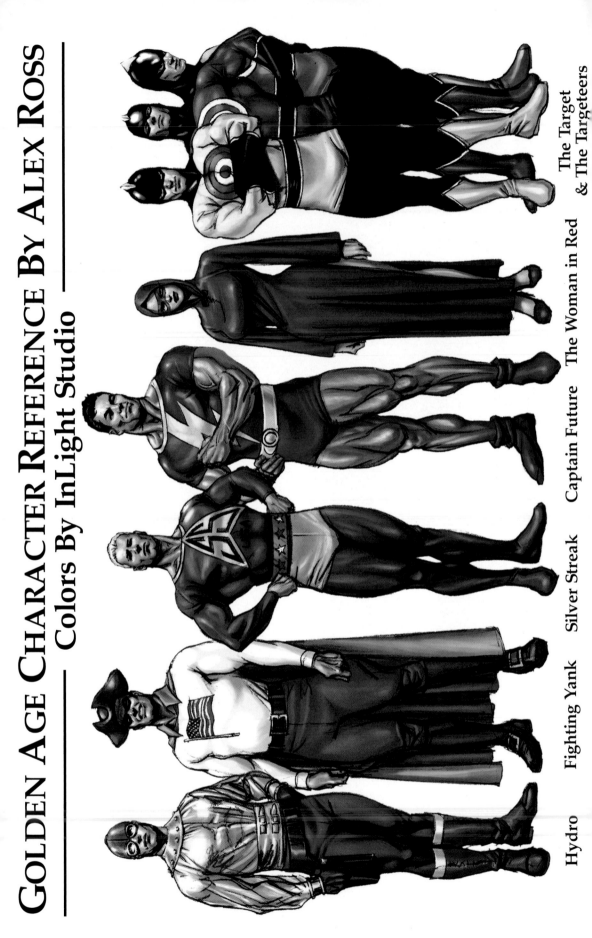

Hydro   Fighting Yank   Silver Streak   Captain Future   The Woman in Red   The Target & The Targeteers

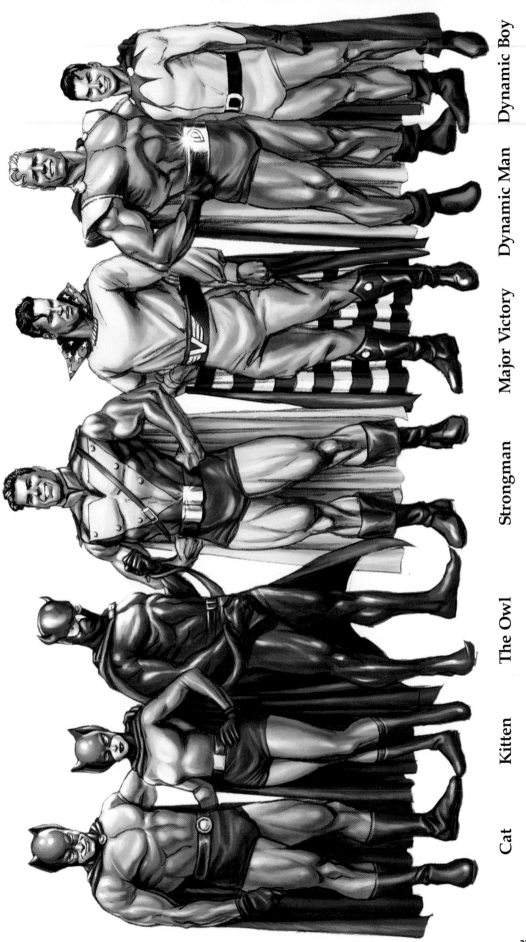

Cat　　　Kitten　　　The Owl　　　Strongman　　　Major Victory　　　Dynamic Man　　　Dynamic Boy

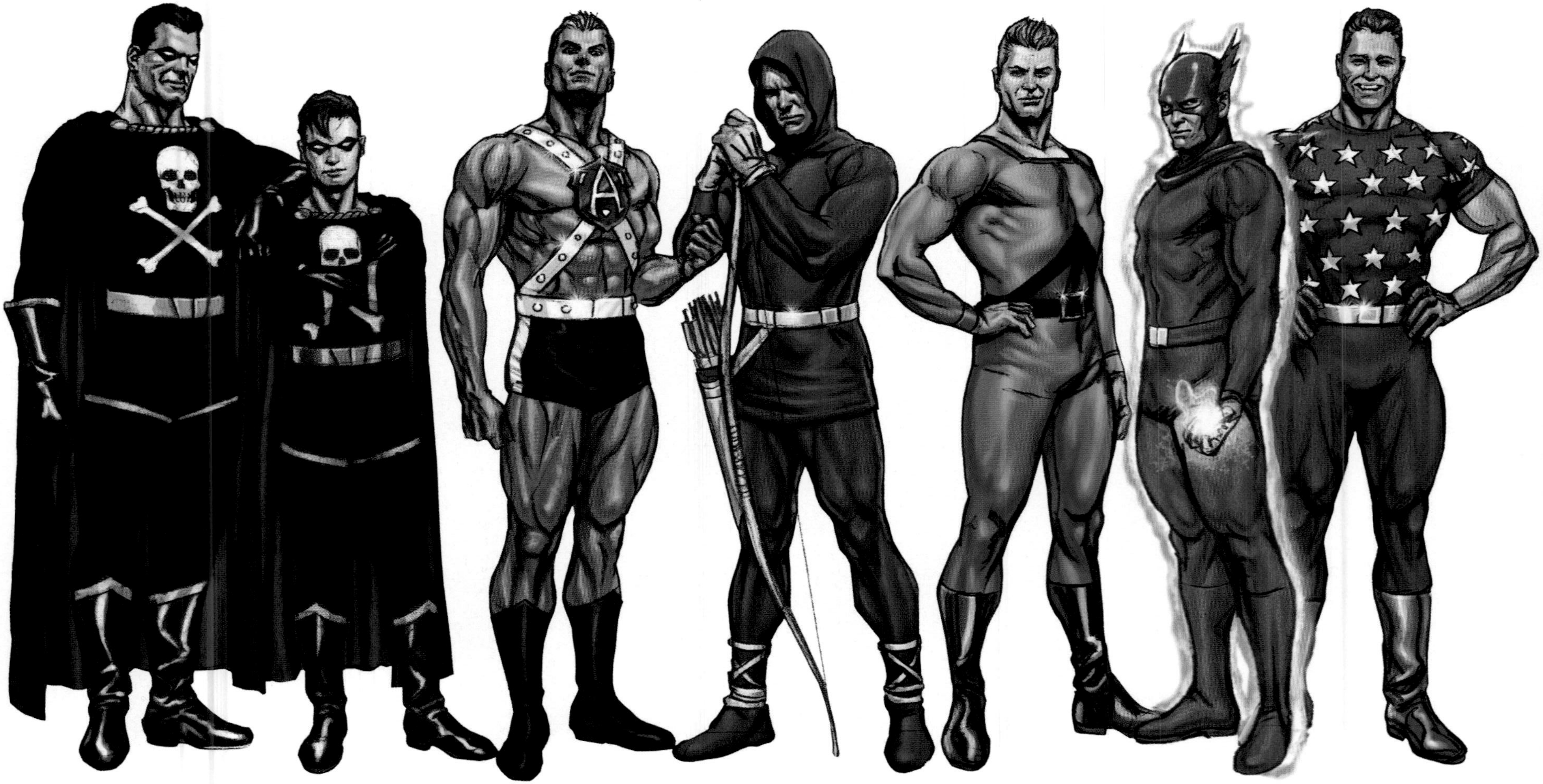

Black Terror & Tim Amazing-Man The Arrow Vulcan Pyroman The Liberator

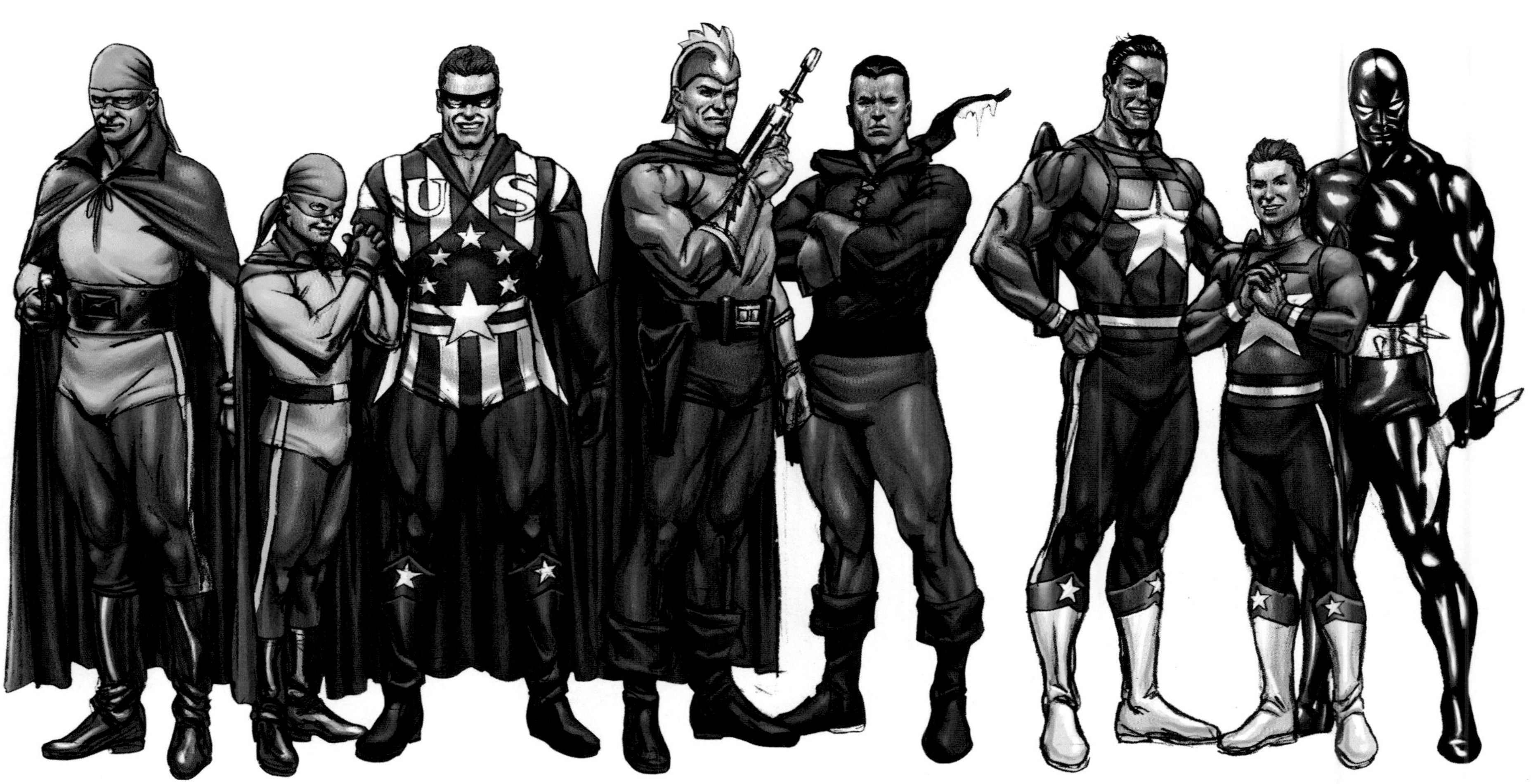

The Green Mask & Domino U.S. Jones Blue Bolt Sub-Zero Man Captain Battle & Captain Battle Jr. The Death-Defying 'Devil

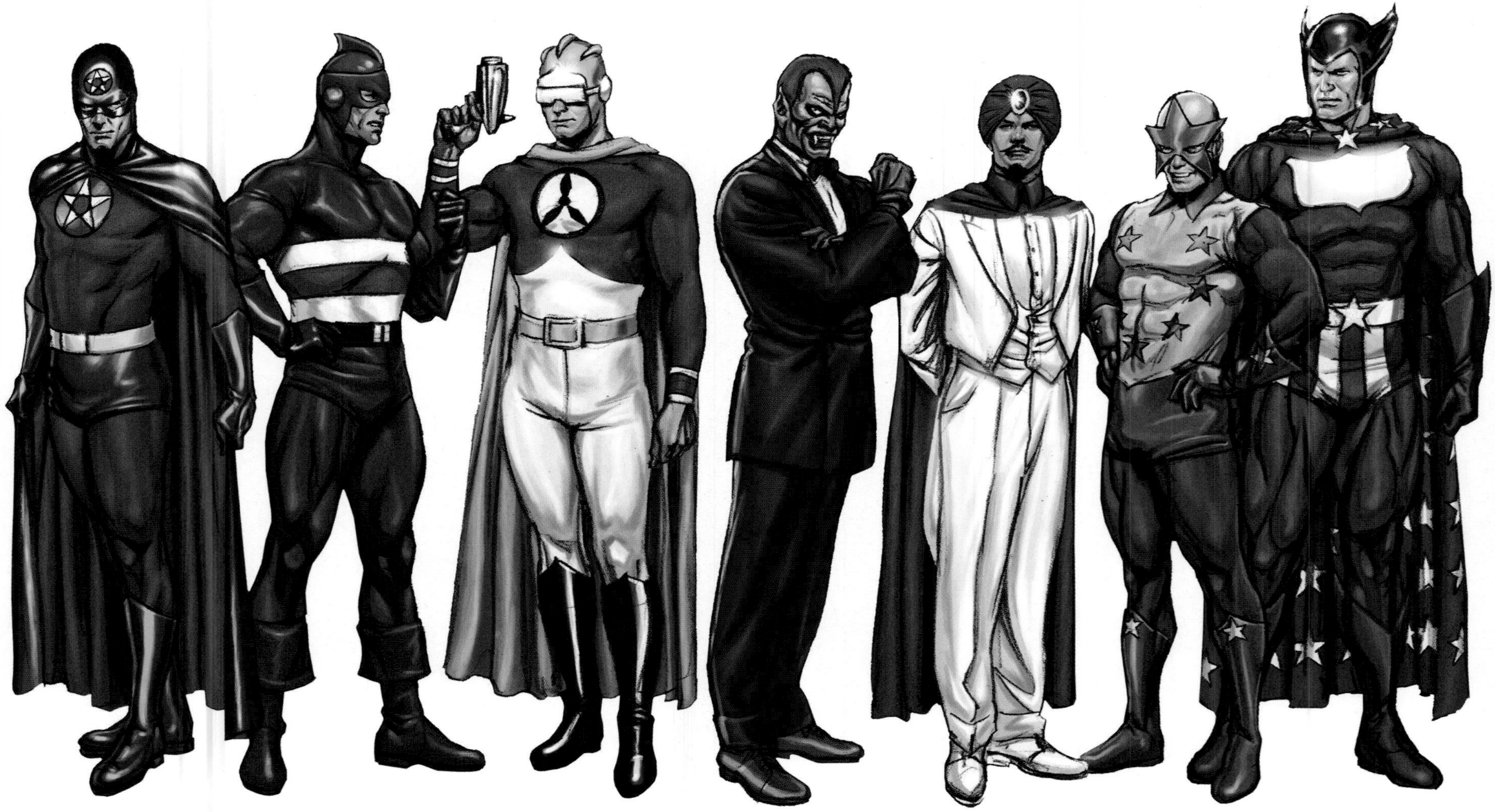

American Crusader | American Eagle | Skyman | Mr. Face | Marvelo | Captain Courageous | The Super-American

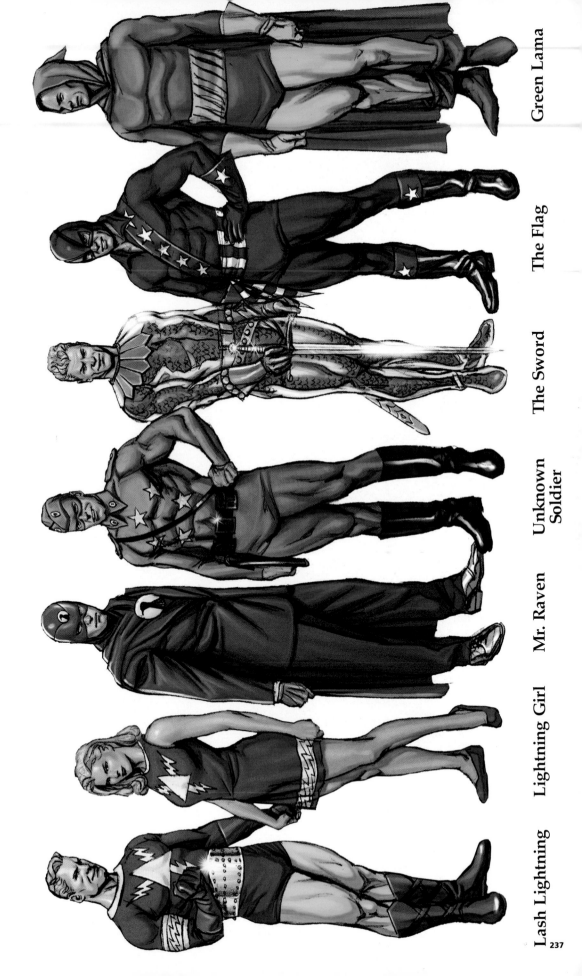

Green Lama

The Flag

The Sword

Unknown
Soldier

Mr. Raven

Lightning Girl

Lash Lightning

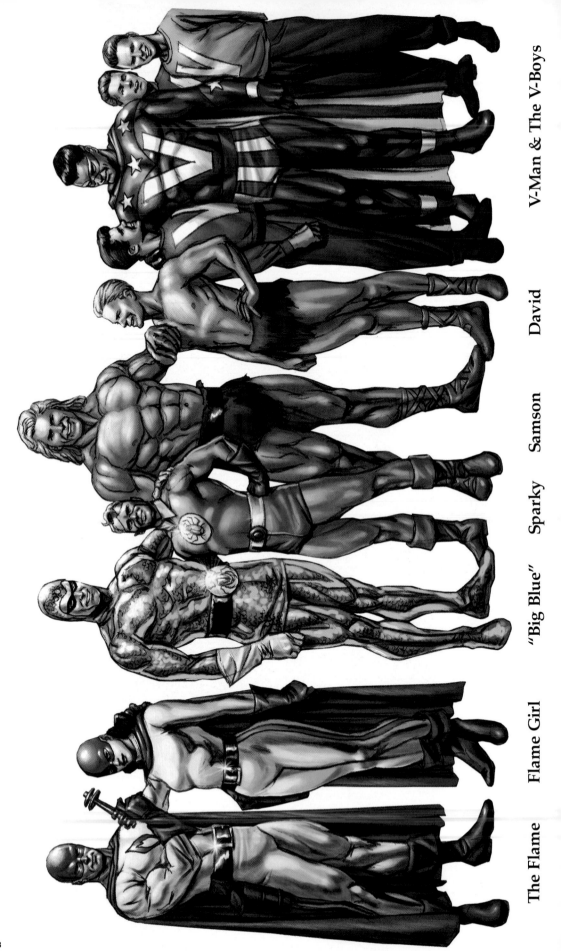

The Flame Flame Girl "Big Blue" Sparky Samson David V-Man & The V-Boys

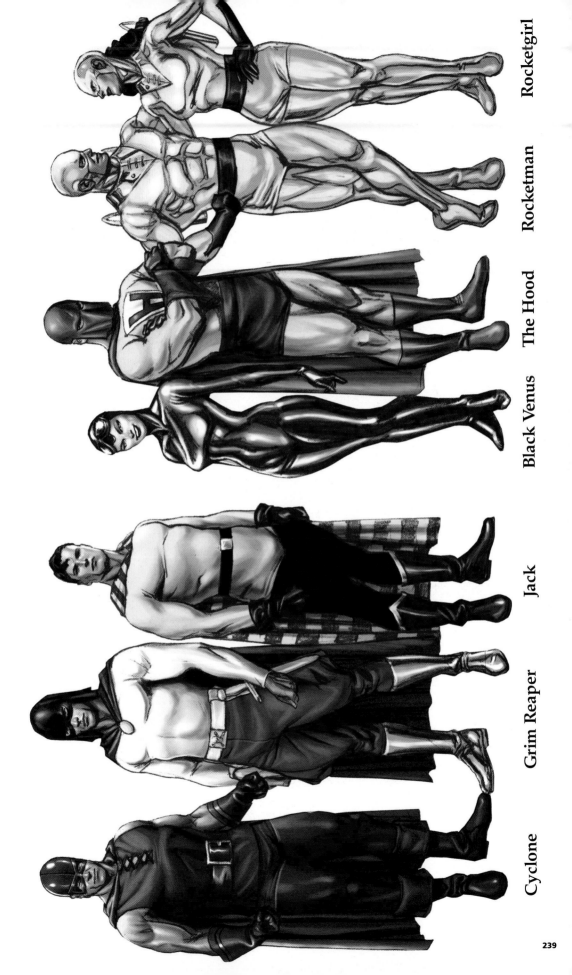

Rocketgirl

Rocketman

The Hood

Black Venus

Jack

Grim Reaper

Cyclone

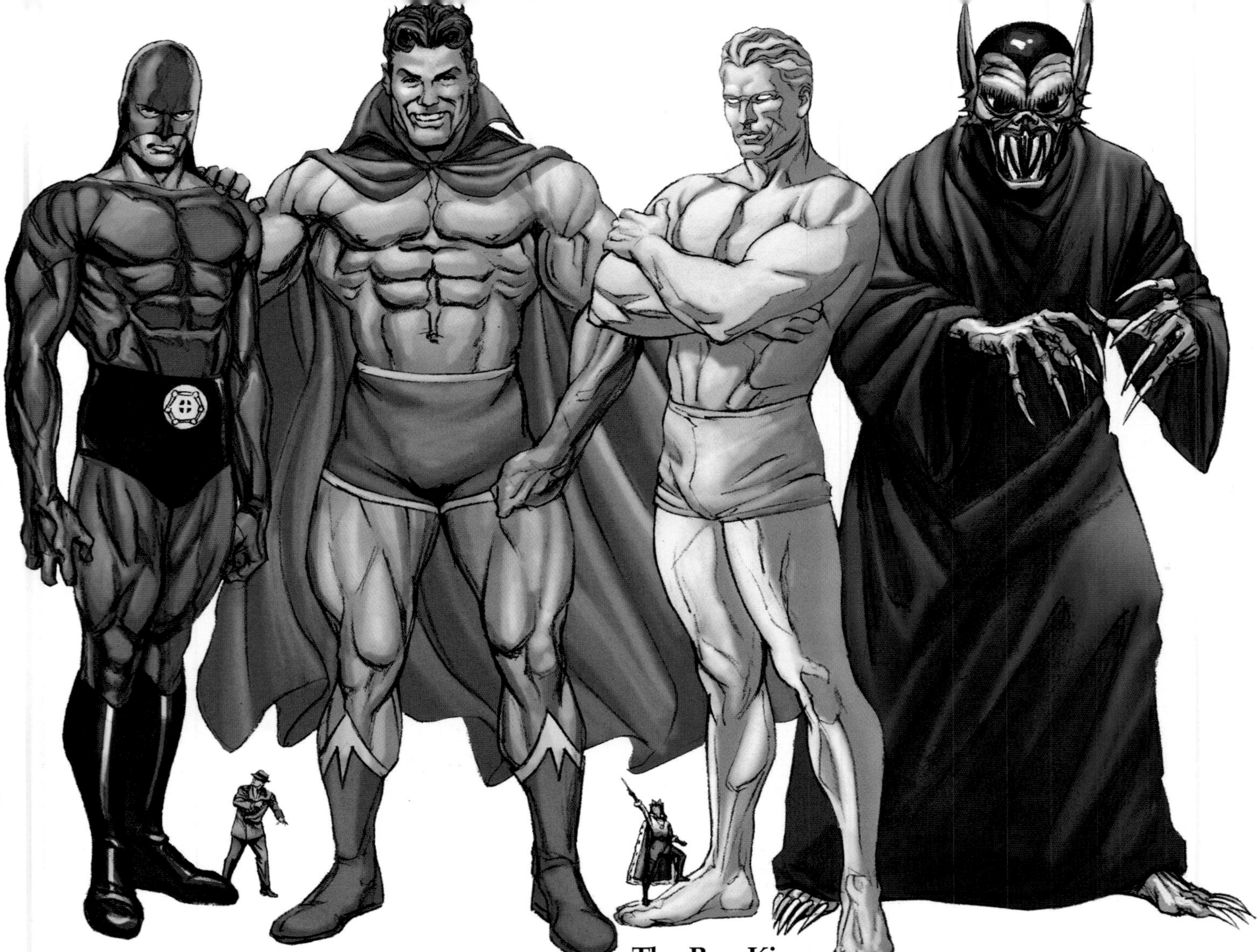

The Green Giant   Phantasmo   The Boy King and his Giant   The Claw

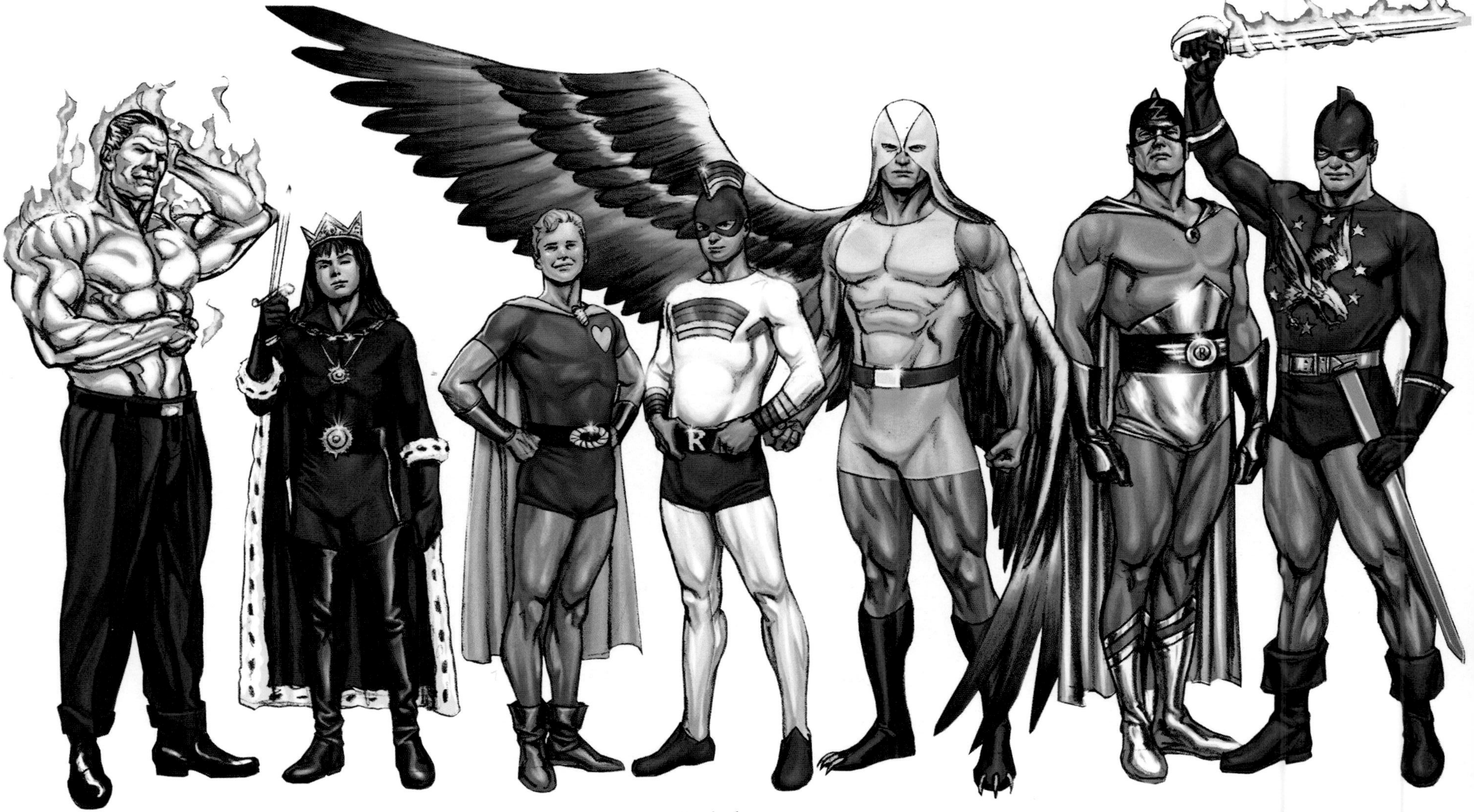

Man O' Metal Boy King Golden Lad Rainbow Boy Airman Radior Man Of War

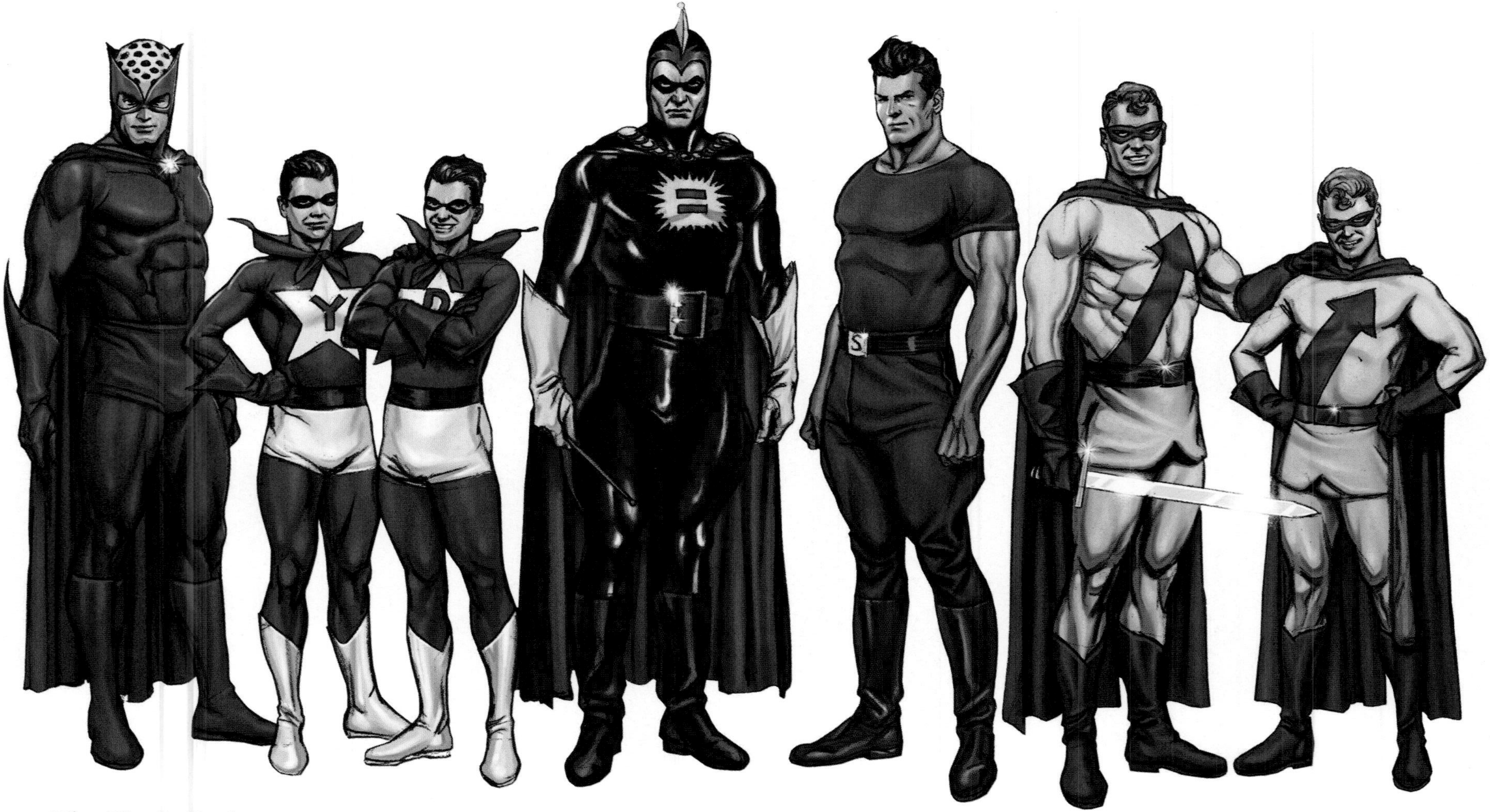

The Black Owl Yank & Doodle Sparkman Doc The Dart & Ace

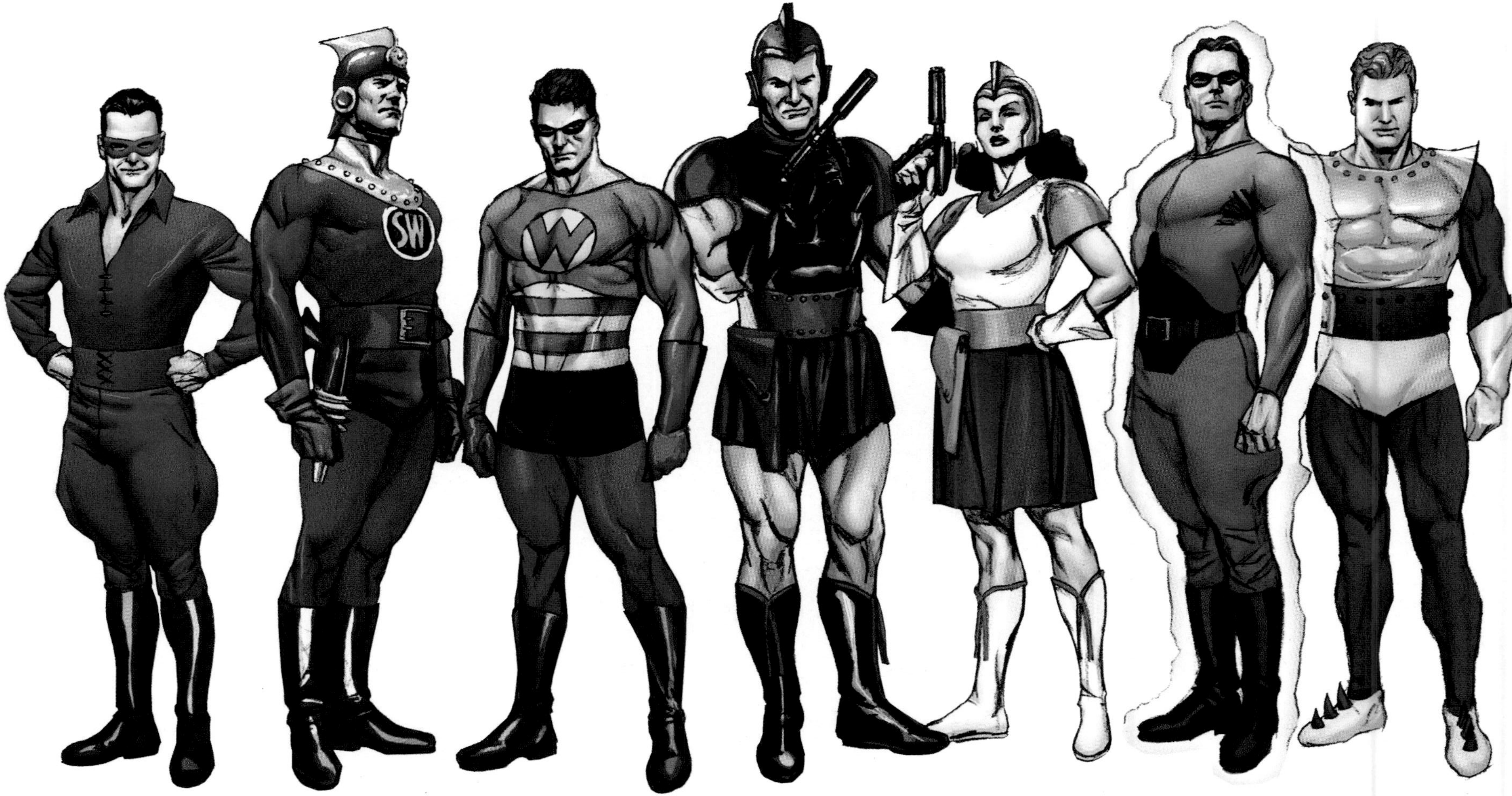

Masked Marvel | Sky Wizard | Brad Spencer, Wonderman | Martin The Marvel Man & Vana | Professor Supermind & Son | Power Nelson, The Futureman

Black Terror™
By Alex Ross

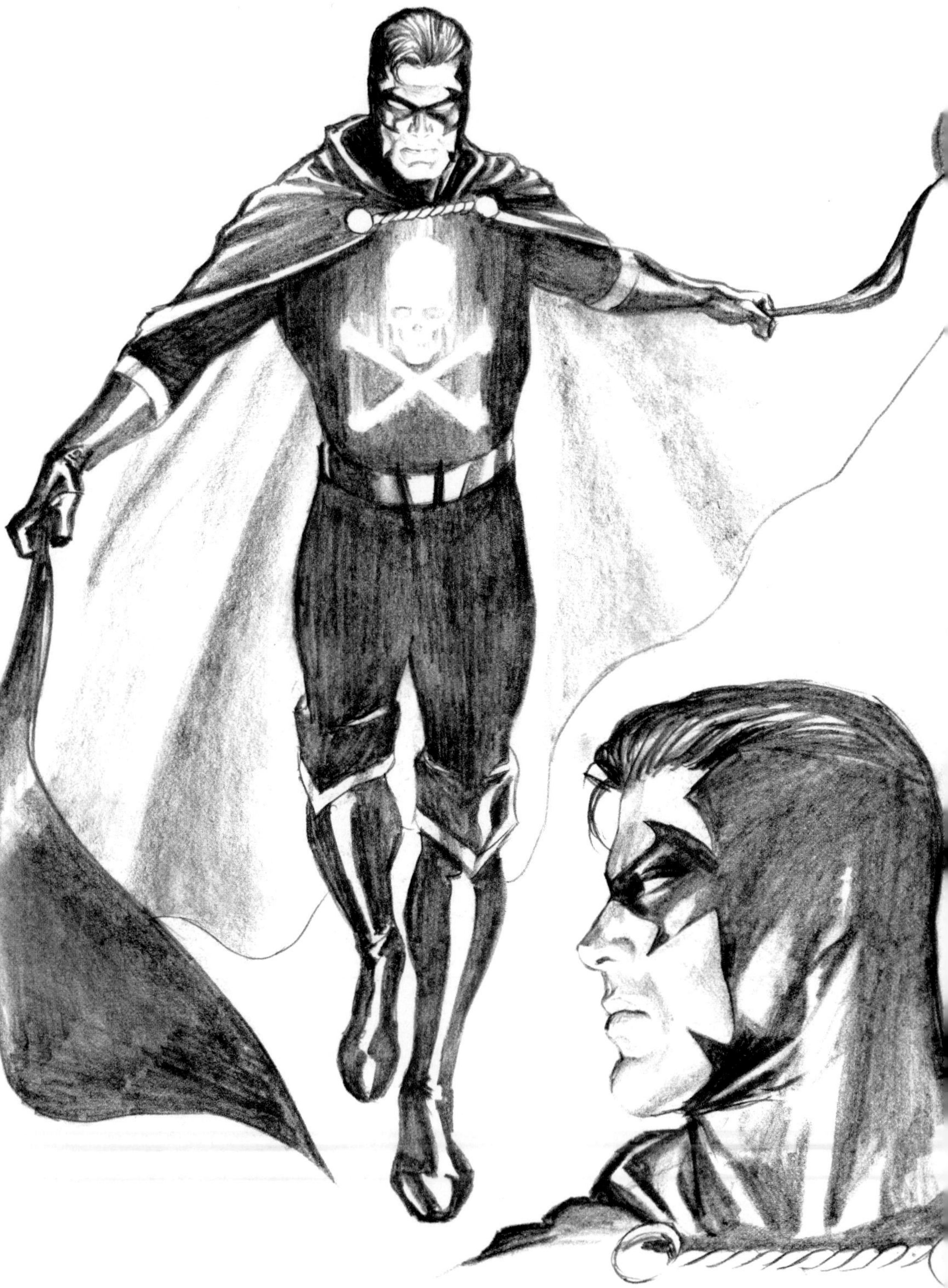

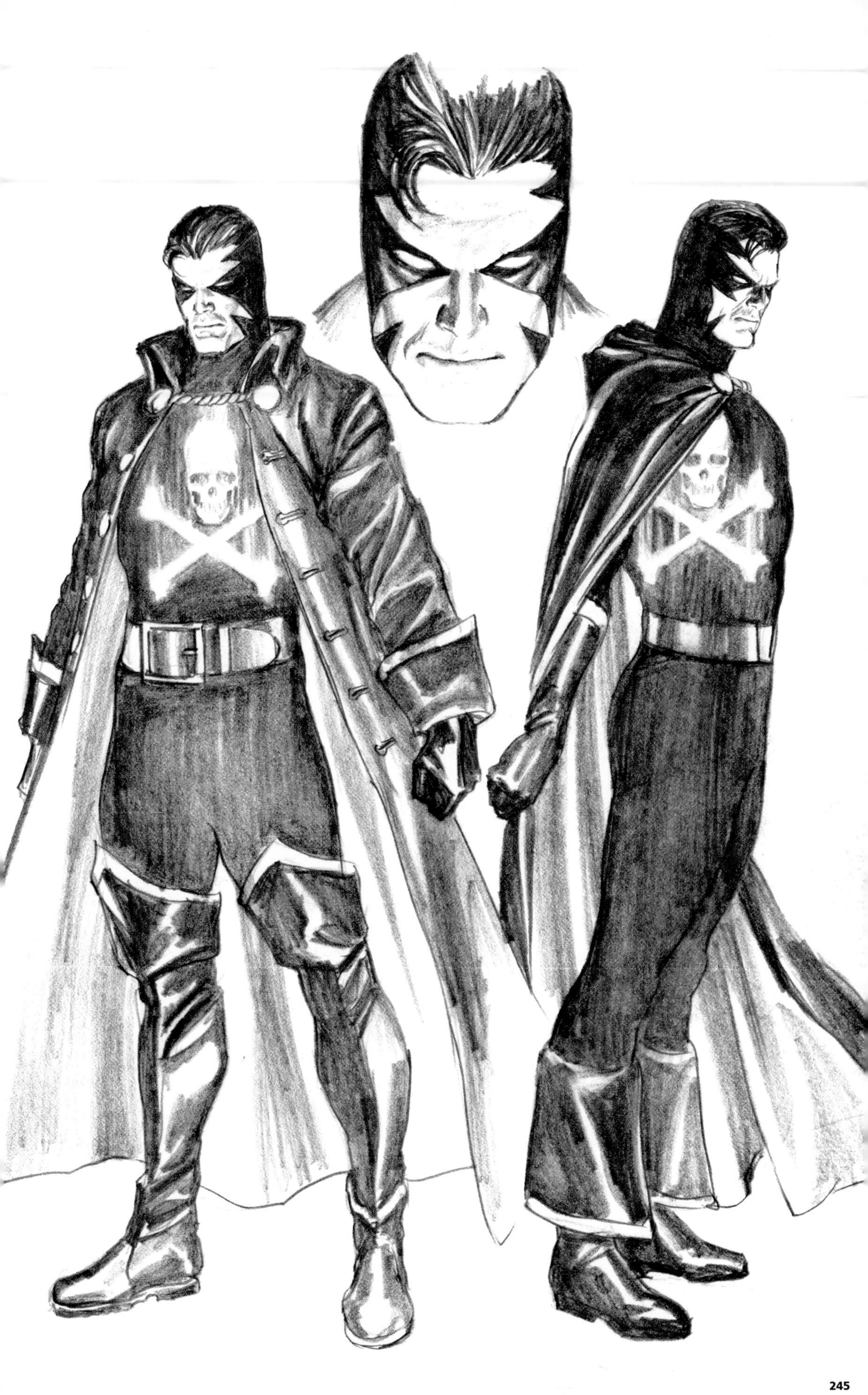

The Green Lama™
By Alex Ross

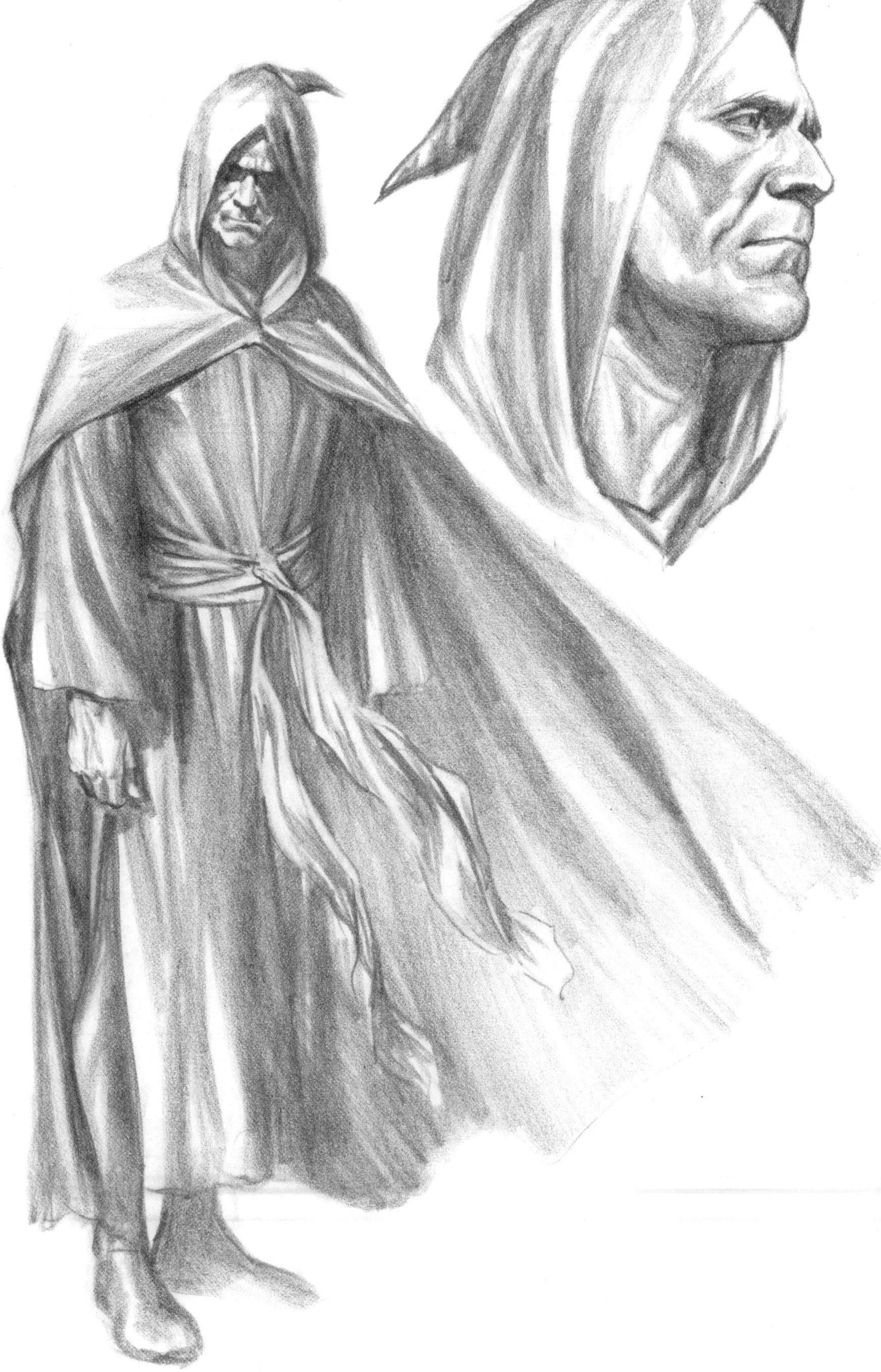

The Fighting Yank™
By Alex Ross

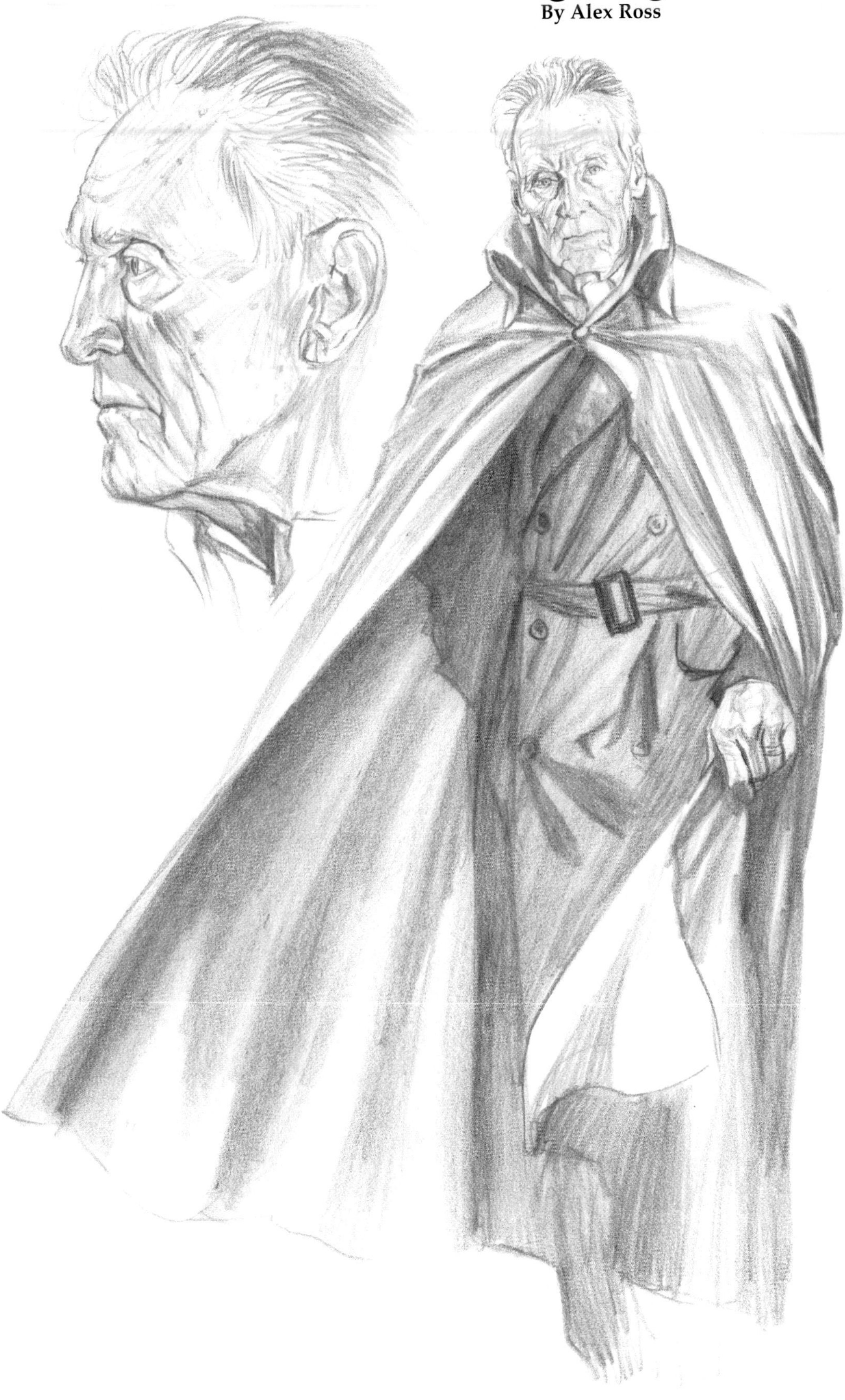

Dynamic Man and the Dynamic Family™
By Alex Ross

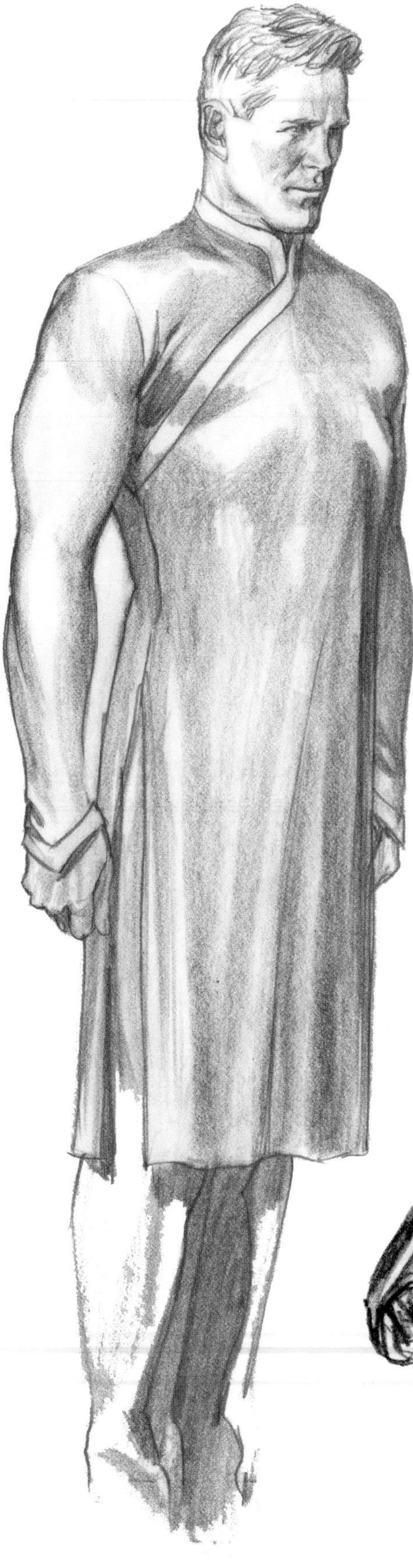

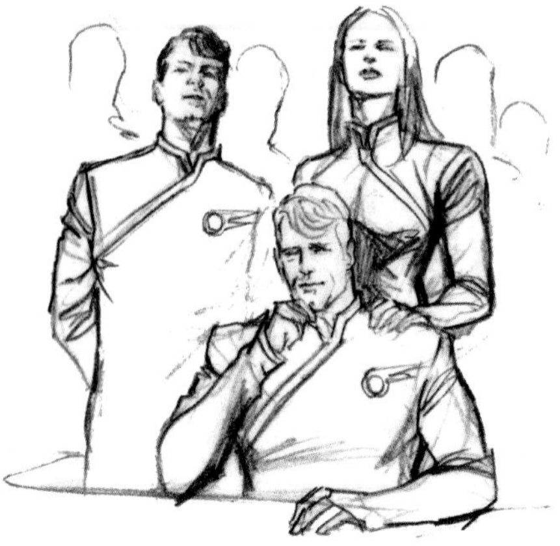

Police Corp™
By Alex Ross

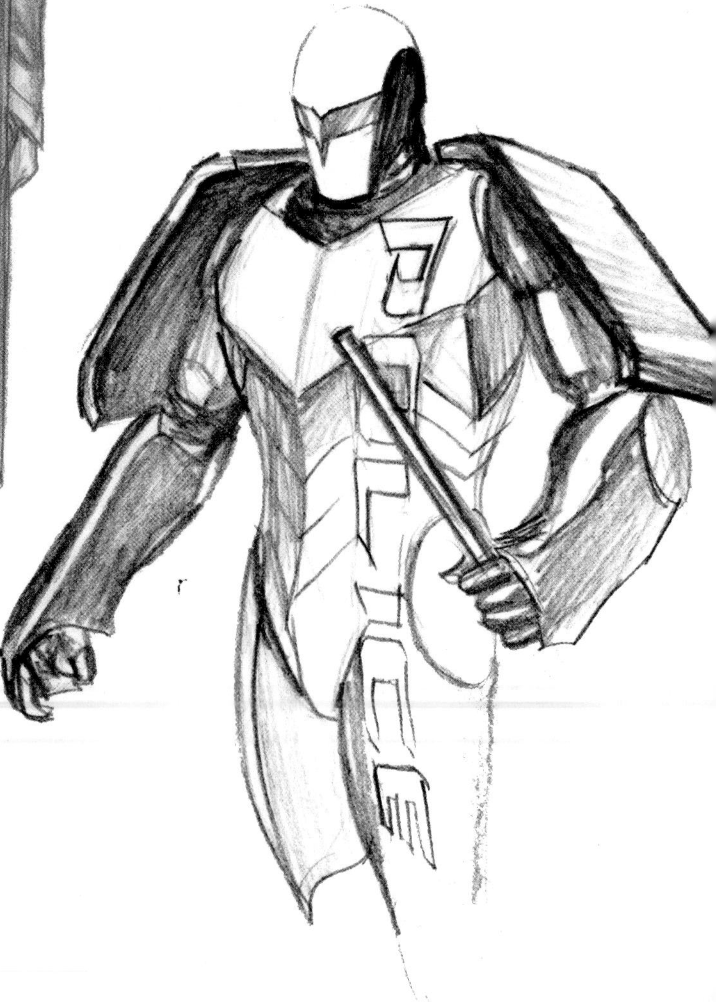

Alex Ross' Original Sketches for the Fighting Yank's War Journal Entries

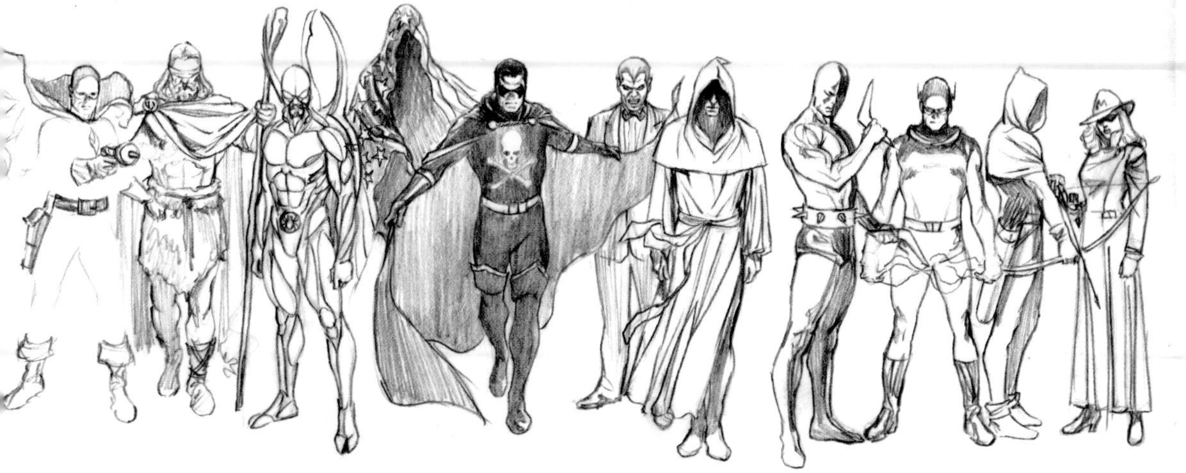

Pandora's Urn

By Alex Ross

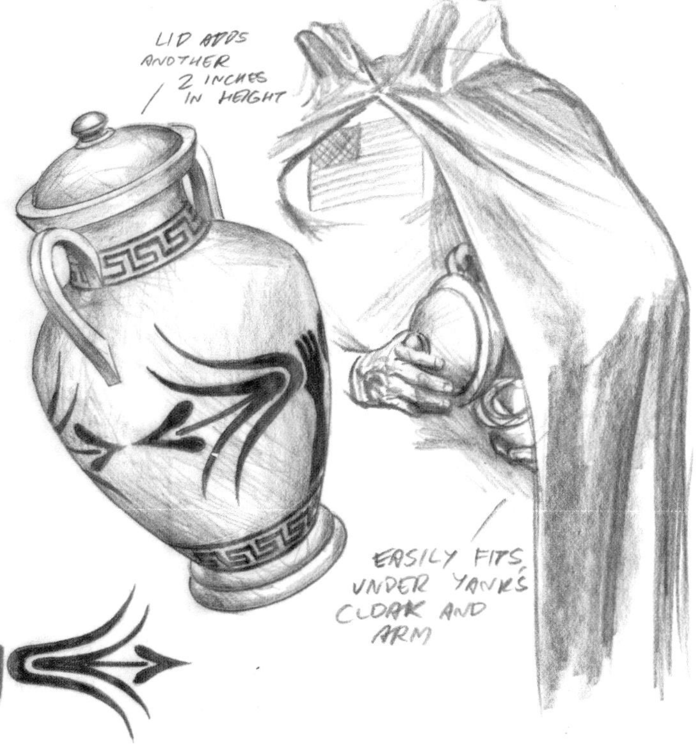
LID ADDS ANOTHER 2 INCHES IN HEIGHT
EASILY FITS UNDER YANK'S CLOAK AND ARM

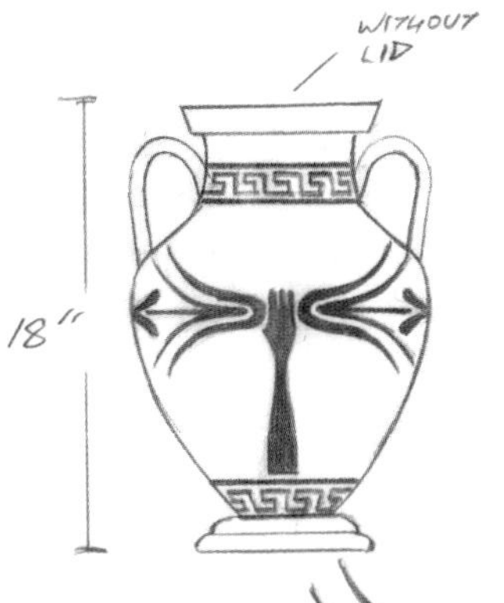
WITHOUT LID
18"

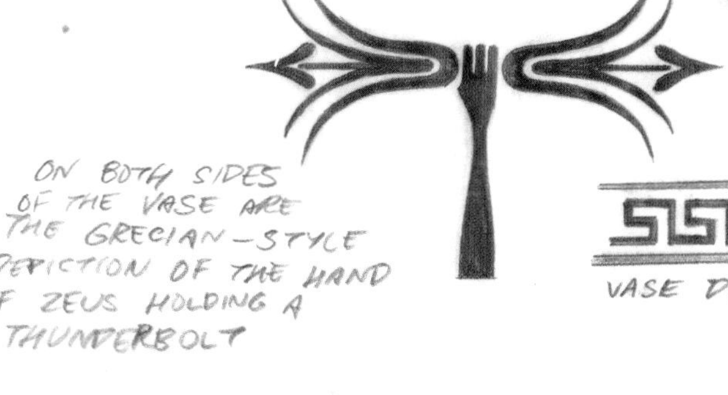
ON BOTH SIDES OF THE VASE ARE THE GRECIAN-STYLE DEPICTION OF THE HAND OF ZEUS HOLDING A THUNDERBOLT

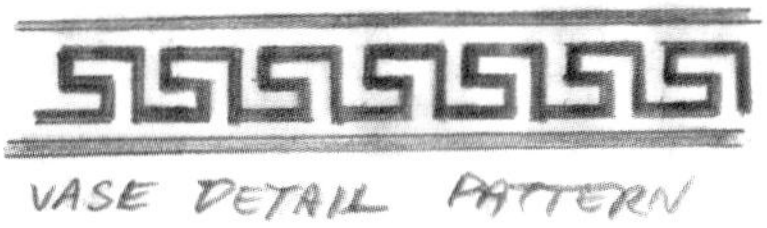
VASE DETAIL PATTERN

Project Superpowers™ #0 Pages 18-19

Series co-plotter and art director Alex Ross not only crafted new designs for the heroes and villains seen in these pages (as well as new characters like the American Spirit and the Scarab) but the artist also created character guides and studies of the Golden Age iterations of these characters. As he was

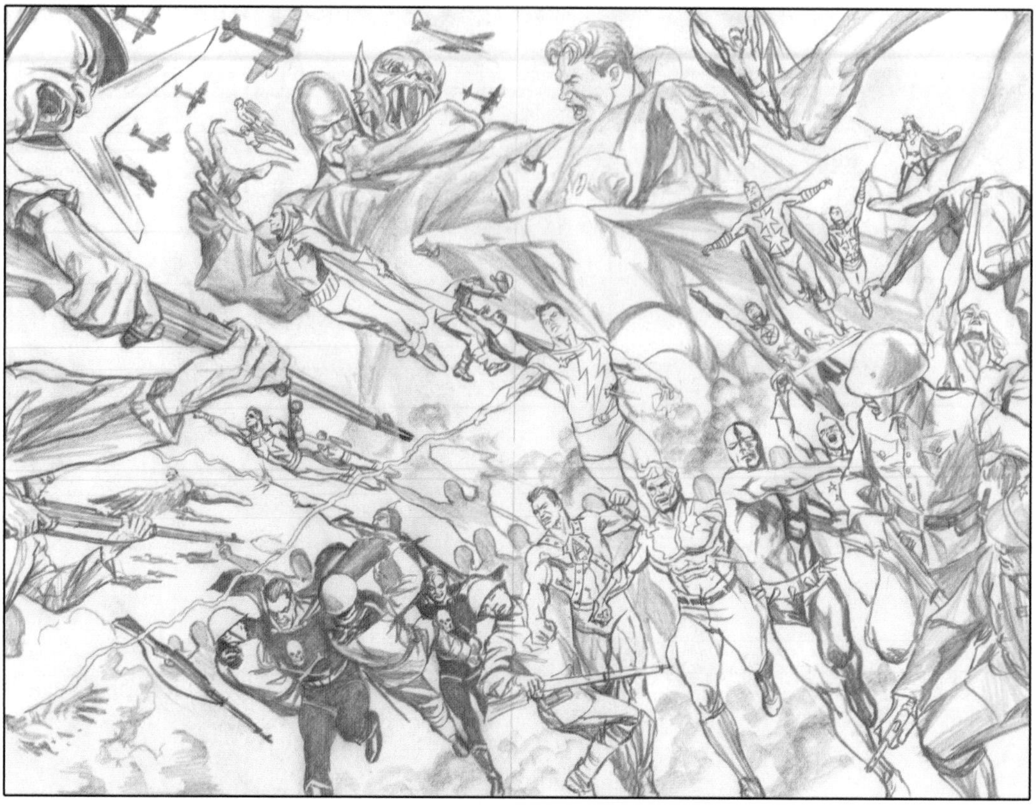

Pencil layout by Alex Ross.

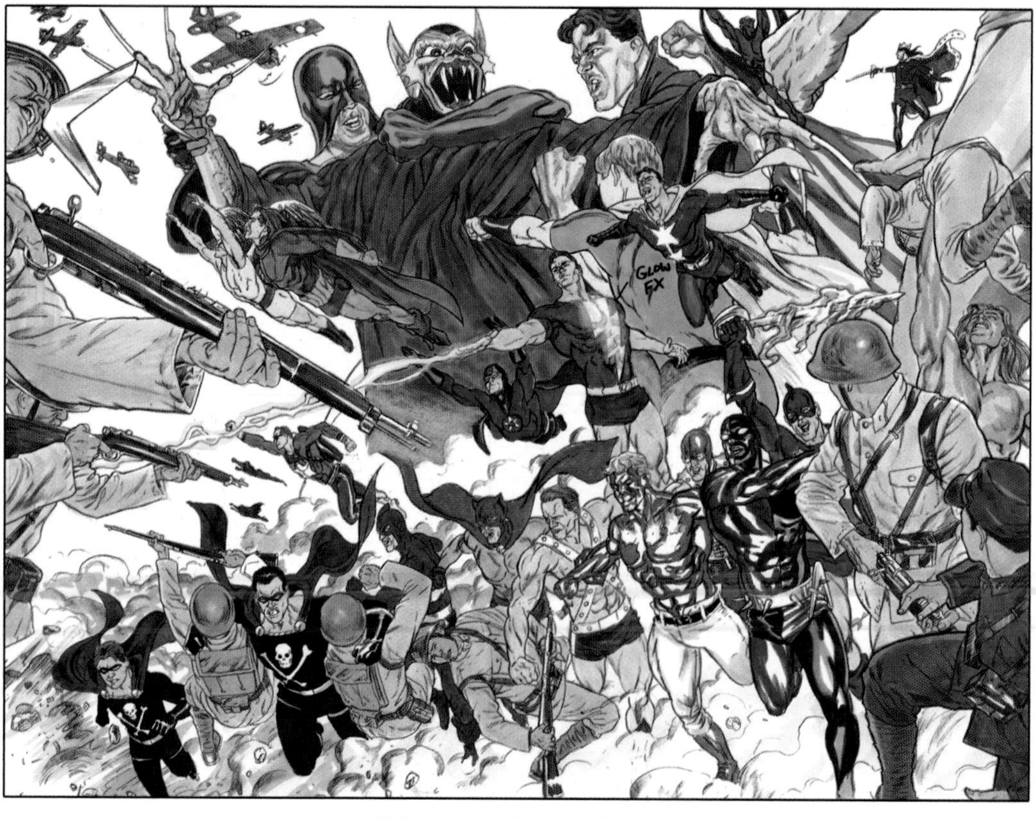
GLOW FX

Color guide by Alex Ross.

working on these studies and guides, Ross also provided pencil layouts for the Battle of Kokura spread on pages 18 and 19, as this battle featured many heroes and villains from the Golden Age. As you see, series artist Steve Sadowski put his own mark on the final page. Here we present the creation of this scene.

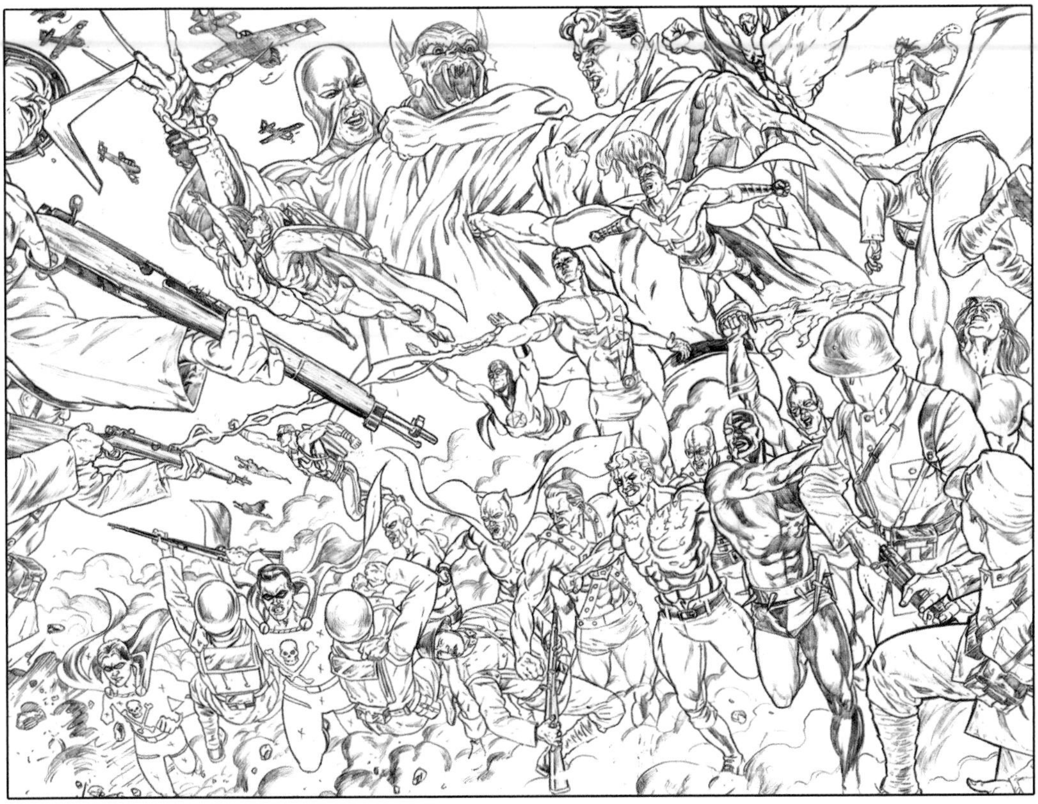

Finished pencils by Stephen Sadowski.

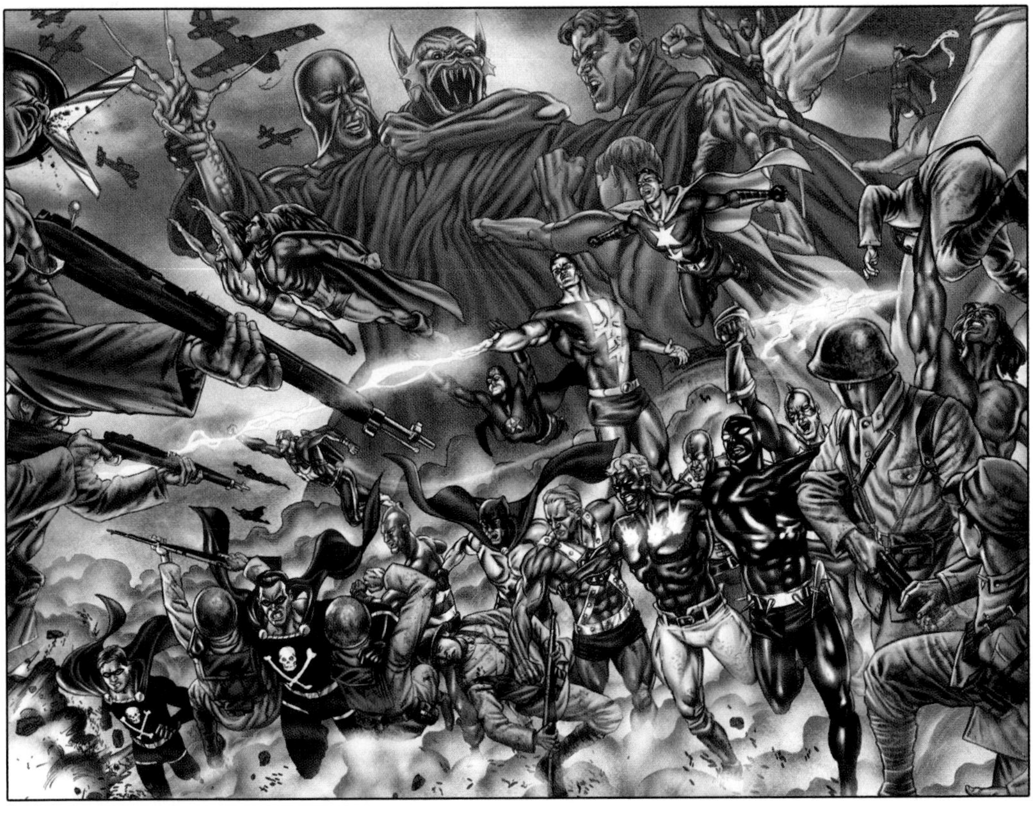

Final colors by inLight Studio.

Project Superpowers™ #0 Page 4

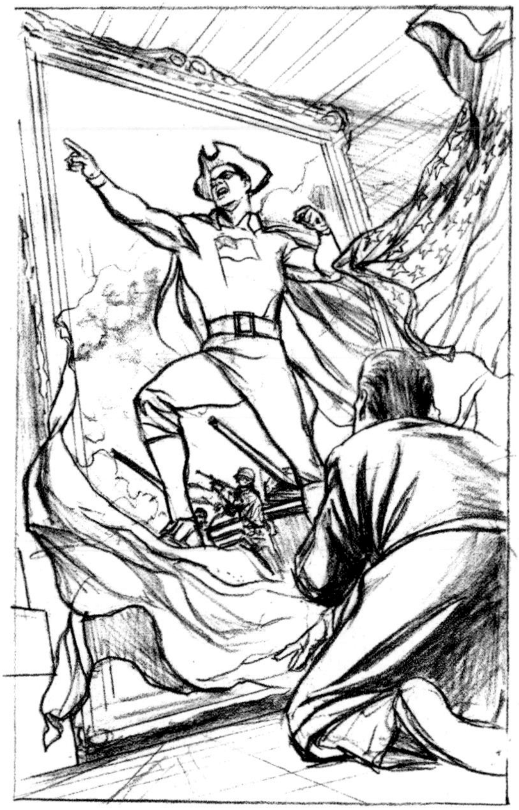

Sketch by Alex Ross.

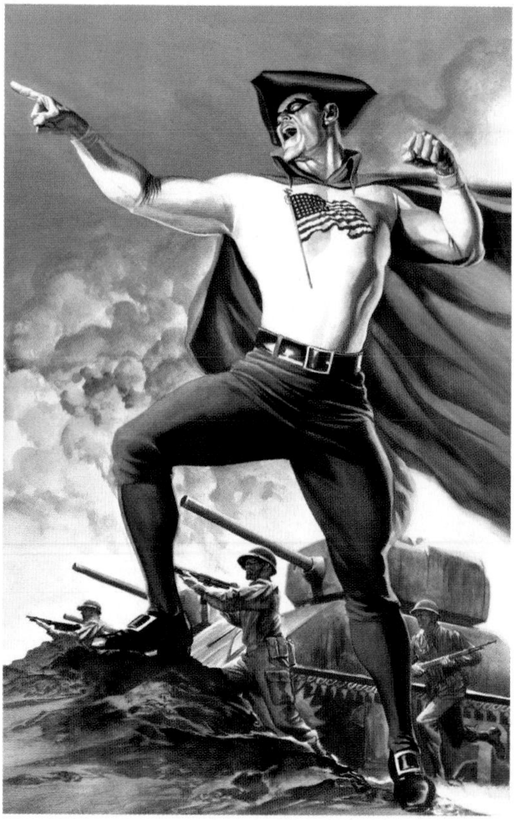

Fighting Yank painting by Alex Ross.

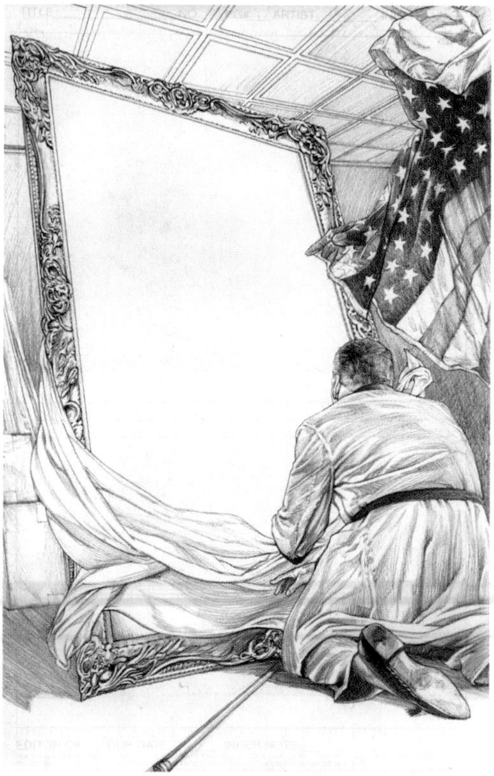

Finished pencils by Doug Klauba.

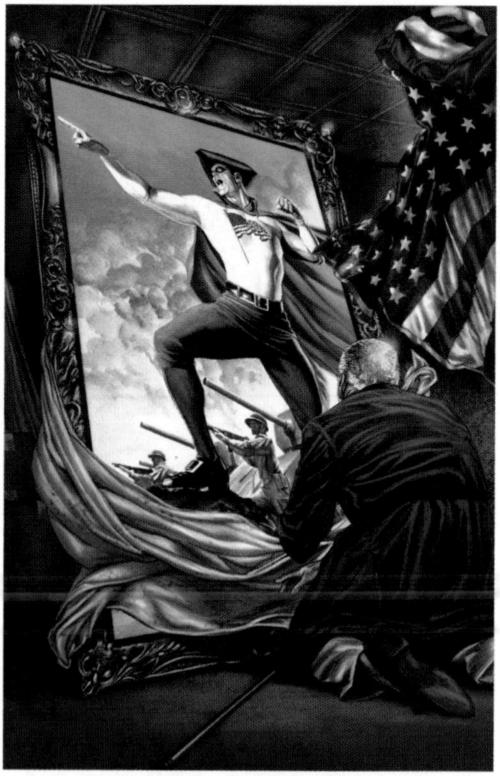

Final page 4. Coloring by inLight Studio.

Project Superpowers™ #0 Page 25

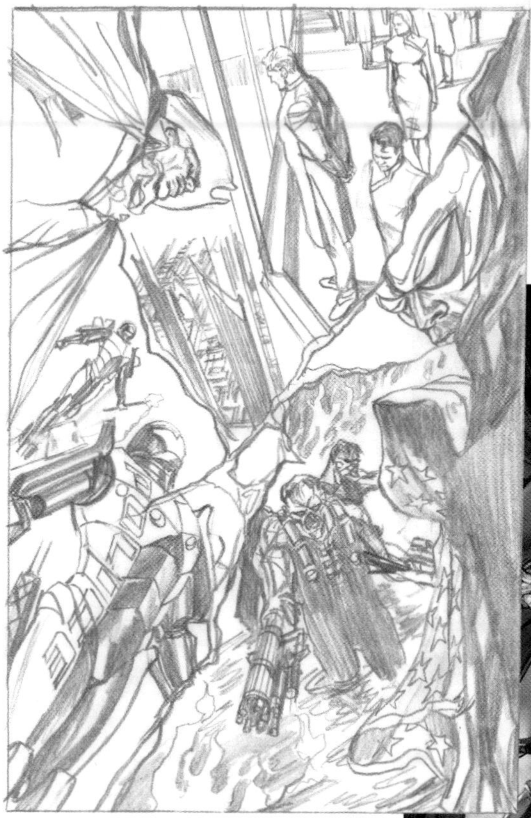

Sketch by Alex Ross.

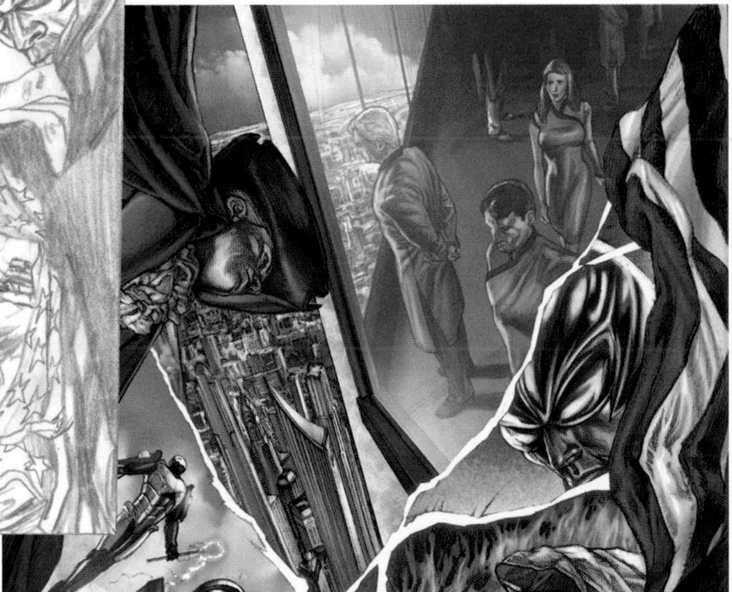

Final page 4. Coloring by inLight Studio.

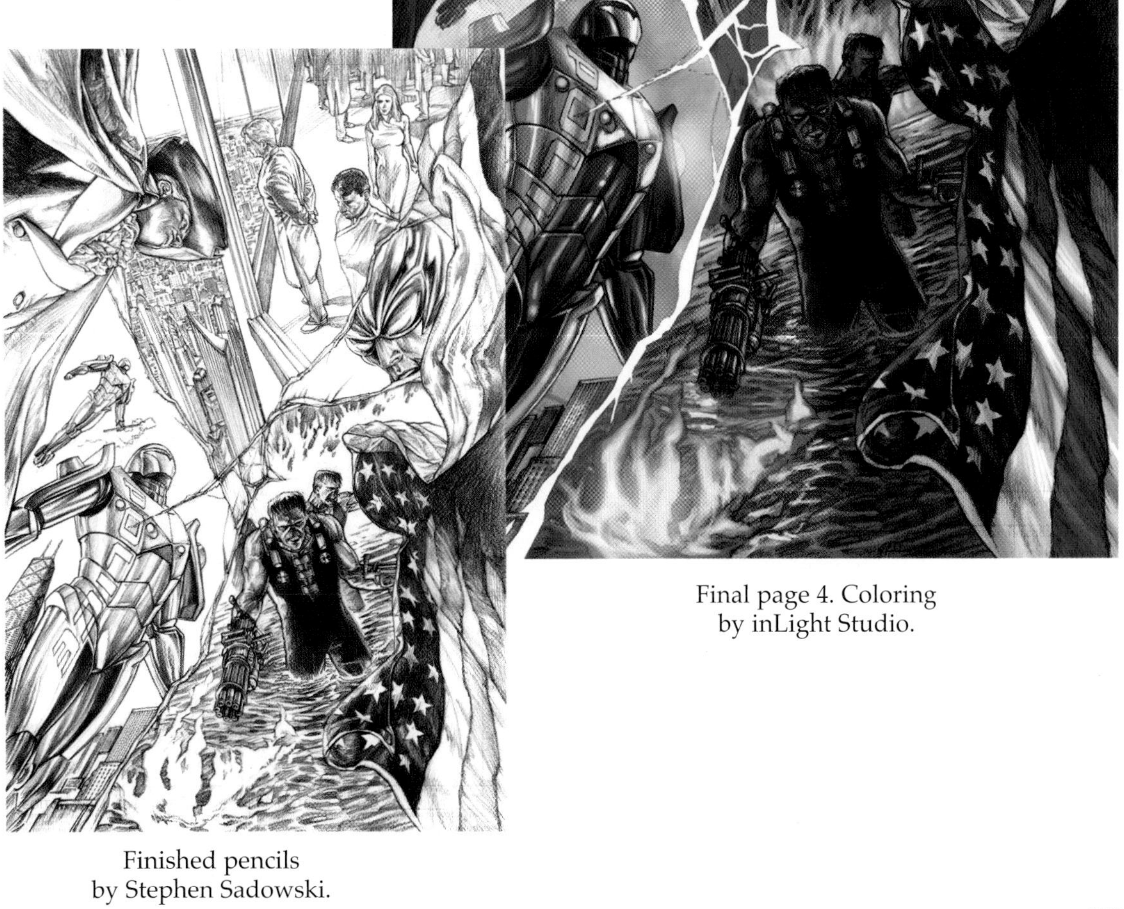

Finished pencils by Stephen Sadowski.

Project Superpowers™ Cover & Logo Designs
By Alex Ross

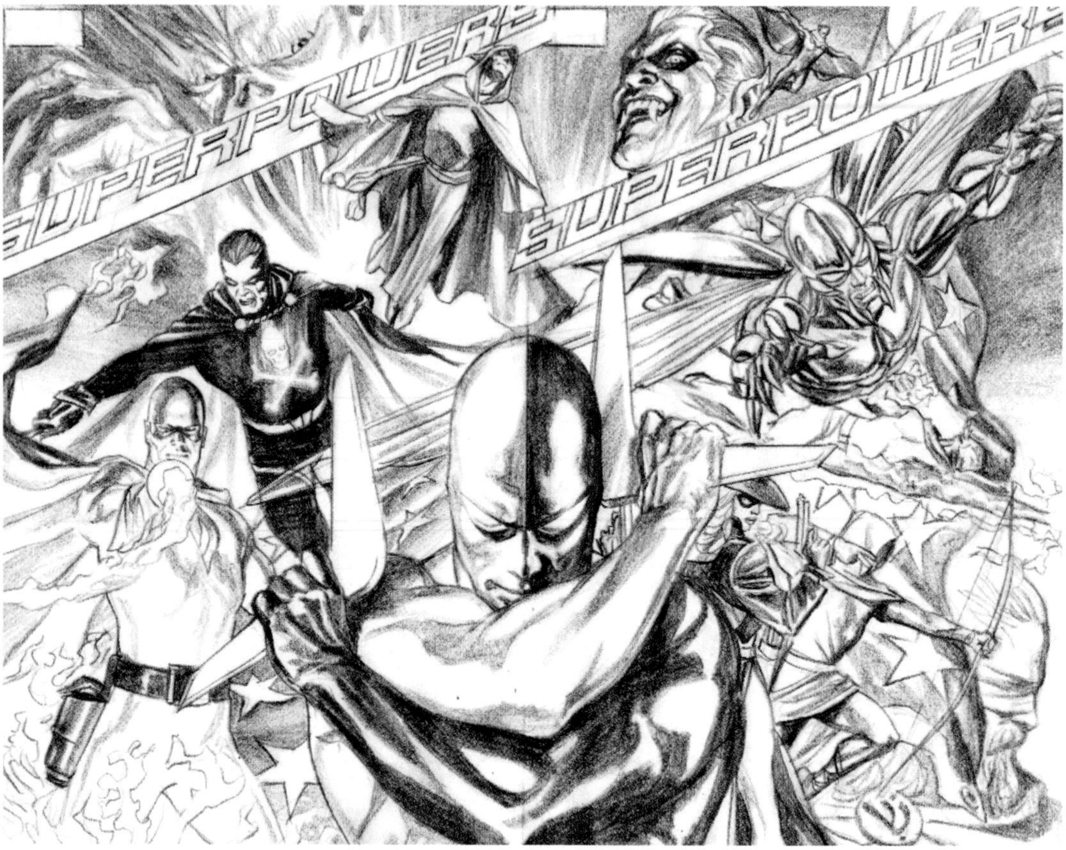
SUPERPOWERS
SUPERPOWERS

Cover sketch to Project Superpowers #0

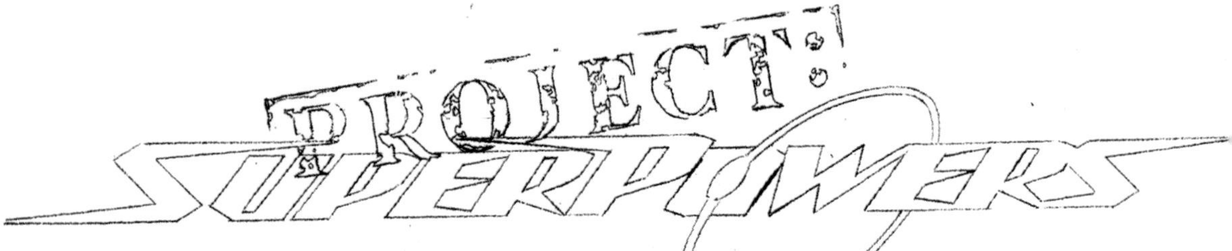
PROJECT!
SUPERPOWERS

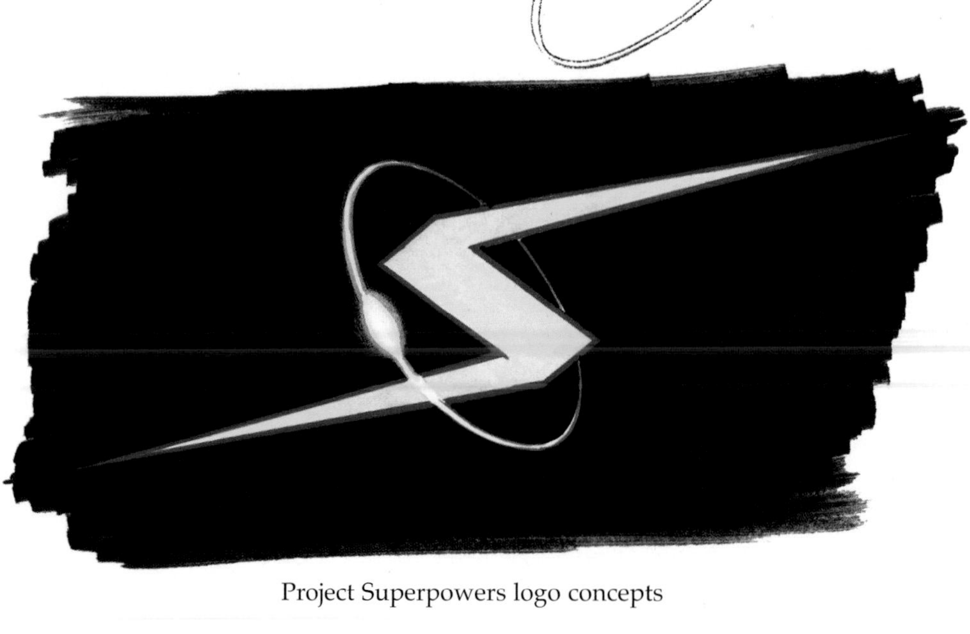

Project Superpowers logo concepts

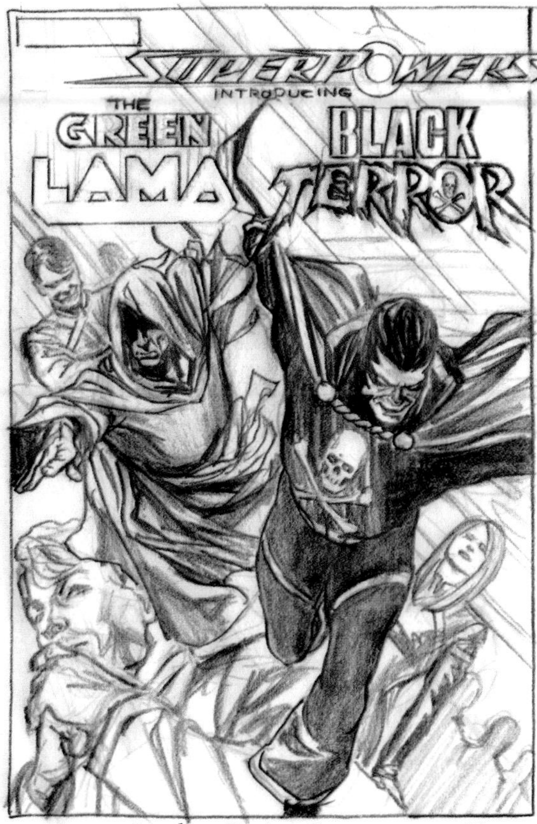
SUPERPOWERS
INTRODUCING
THE GREEN LAMA
BLACK TERROR

Cover sketch to Project Superpowers #1

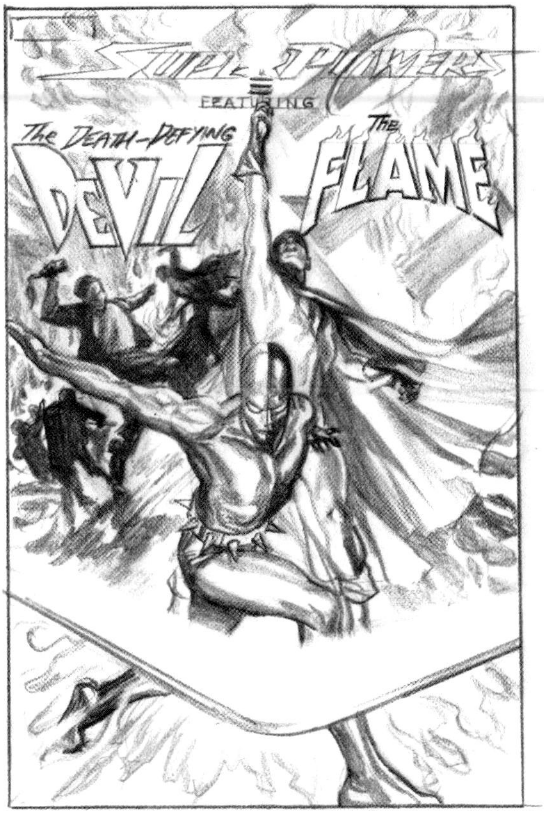
SUPERPOWERS
FEATURING
The DEATH-DEFYING DEVIL
The FLAME

Cover sketch to Project Superpowers #2

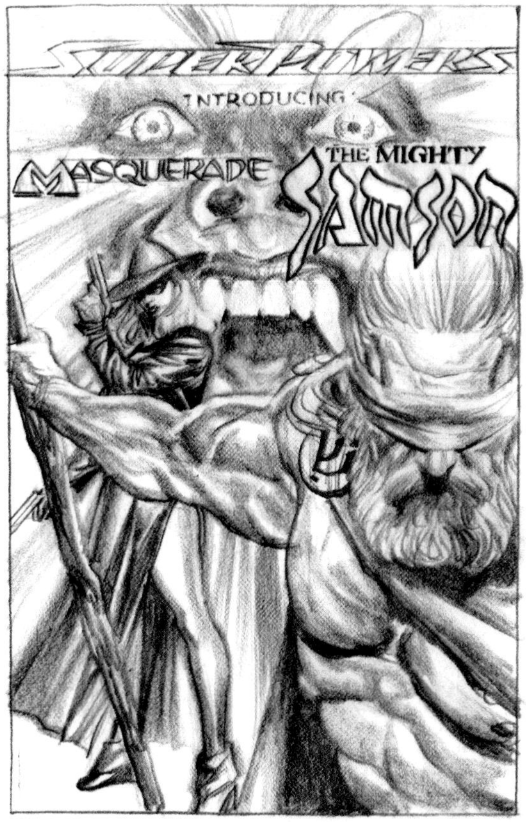
SUPERPOWERS
INTRODUCING
MASQUERADE
THE MIGHTY SAMSON

Cover sketch to Project Superpowers #3

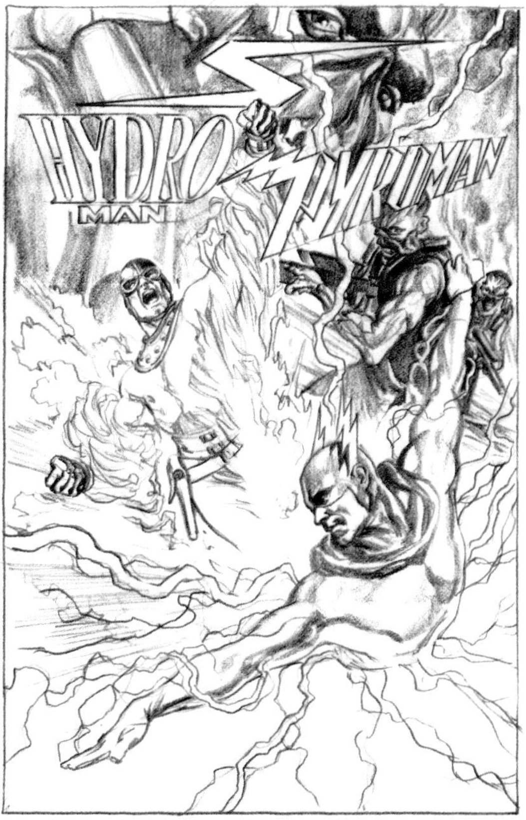
HYDRO MAN

Cover sketch to Project Superpowers #4

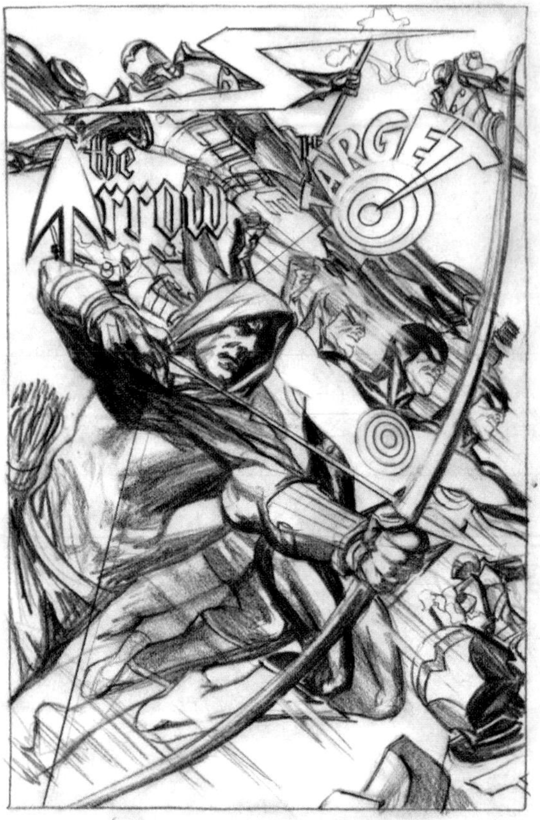

the
Arrow
THE
TARGET

Cover sketch to Project Superpowers #5

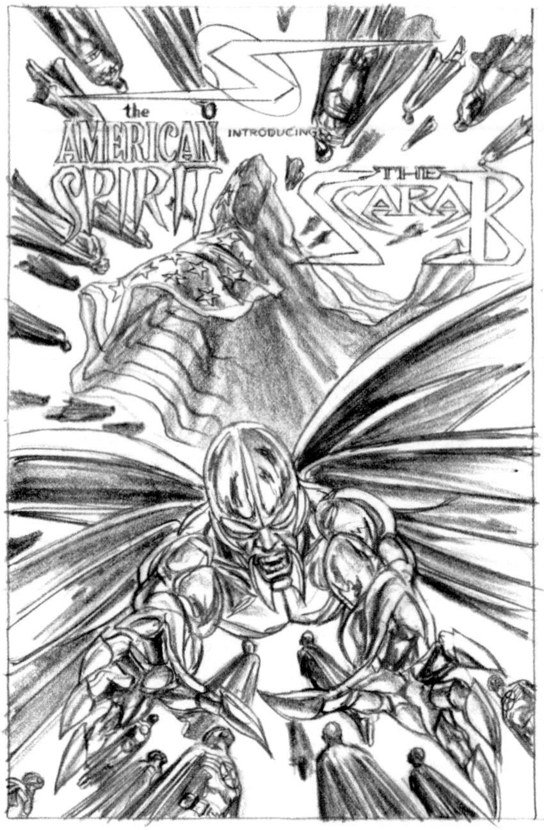

the
AMERICAN
SPIRIT
INTRODUCING
THE
SCARAB

Cover sketch to Project Superpowers #6

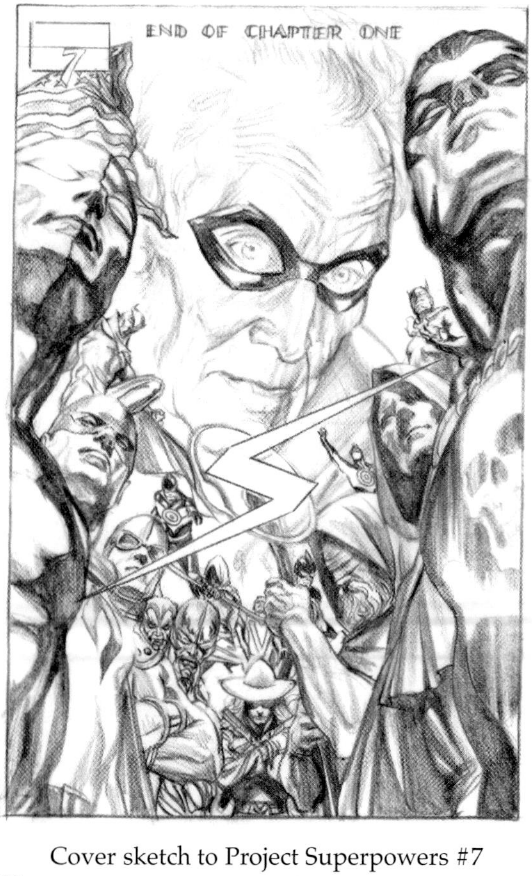

7
END OF CHAPTER ONE

Cover sketch to Project Superpowers #7

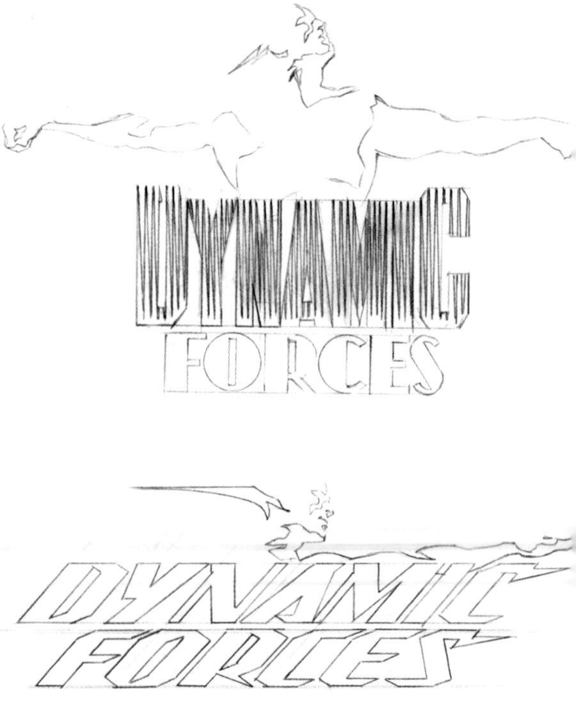

DYNAMIC
FORCES
DYNAMIC
FORCES

Dynamic Forces logo concepts

A Look at the Future of the Project Superpowers™ Universe

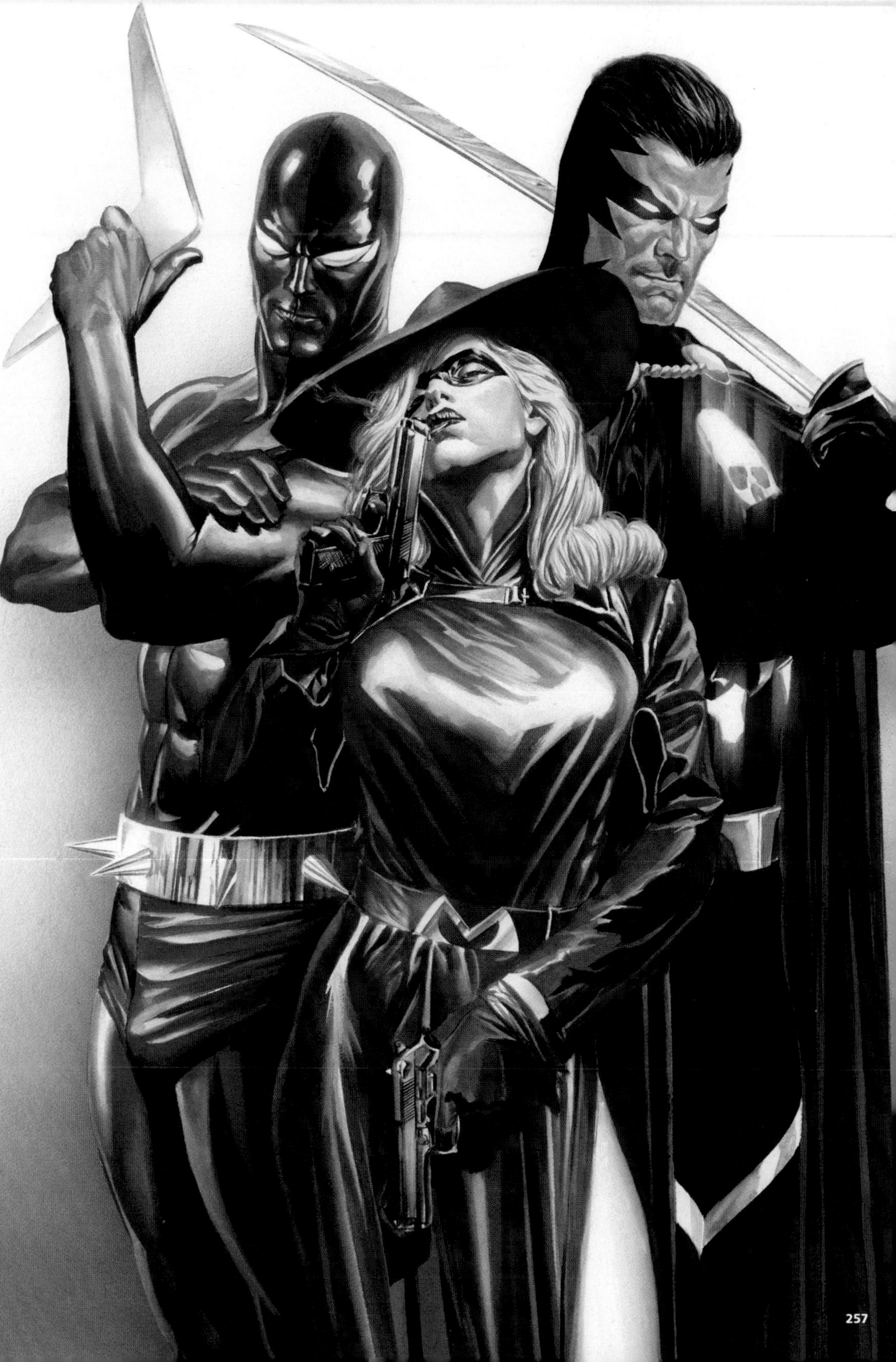

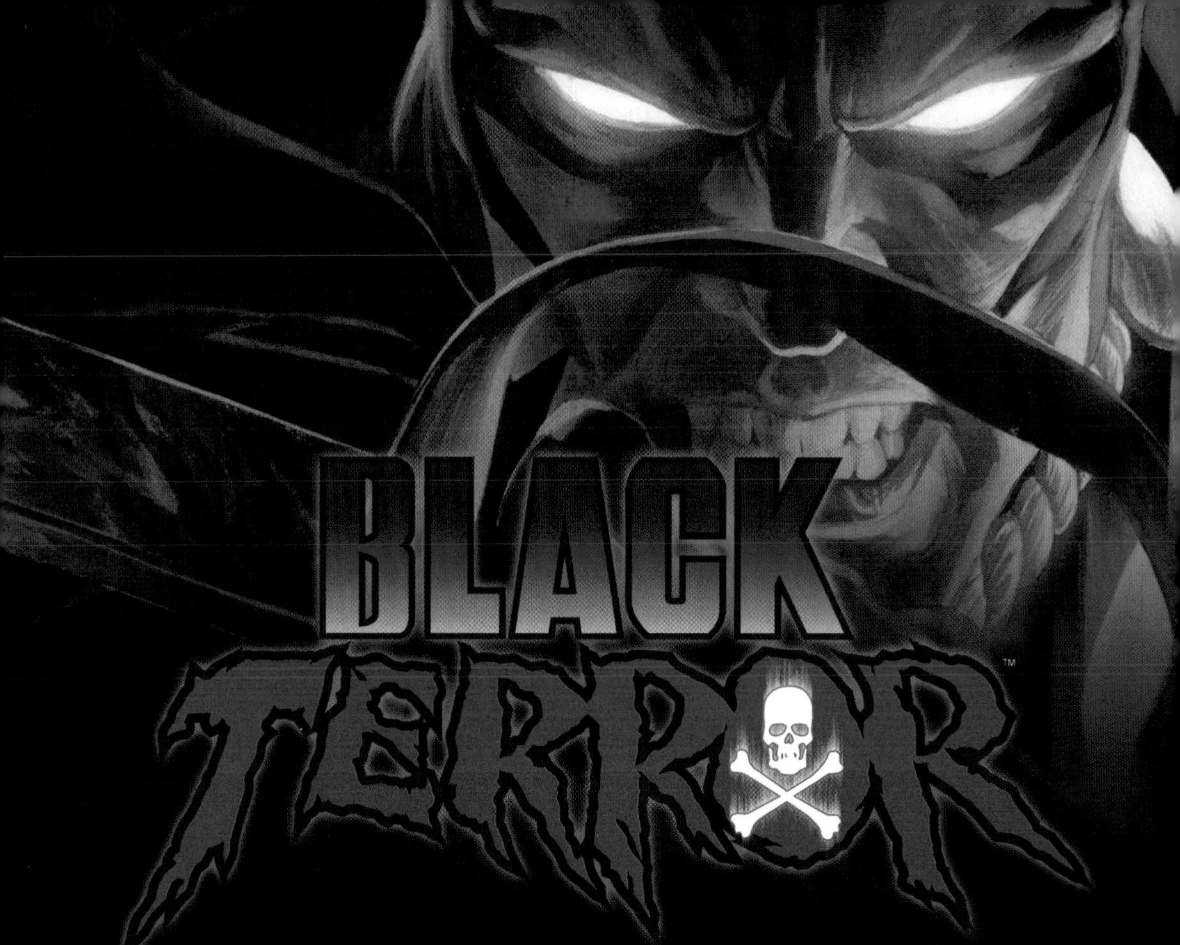
BLACK
TERROR™

Plot/Art Direction/Main Cover: **ALEX ROSS** Plot/Script: **JIM KRUEGER**
Interior Art: **MIKE LILLY** Interior Colors: **VINICIUS ANDRADE**
Letters: **SIMON BOWLAND**

BLACK TERROR
Issue #1 script by Jim Krueger

PG ONE: Panels broken up like the Urn. Jagged breaks between each panel, but altogether, they form the Urn - Pandora's Box - as shown in issue #0 and #1 of the regular series. These are all horizontal images, though, descending through the page.

1/1 Darkness. That's all we see. The first panel is just black.

CAP: The returned man remembers what it was like to live in darkness.

CAP: He remembers what it was like to be damned.

1/2 Eyes open in the dark; this is the Black Terror.

CAP: But that was before his eyes were opened.

1/3 Hands claw at the darkness like a drowning man.

CAP: And he realized that this damning, what he thought was eternal condemnation, was only about 50 years. Which is not to say that it did not feel like forever.

CAP: This, this was not the work of an enemy.

CAP: But of a man he called friend.

1/4 The shot from issue #1 where Black Terror pulls himself out of the ground.

CAP: A friend who now needed his help.

CAP: He remembers pulling himself out of this place between all other places.

CAP: He dragged himself from myth into reality. Only to find that it wasn't only friends that betrayed him.

1/5 Black Terror fights an army of Dynamic Family people.

CAP: He was brought back to fight a war. A war against the country he had once defended.

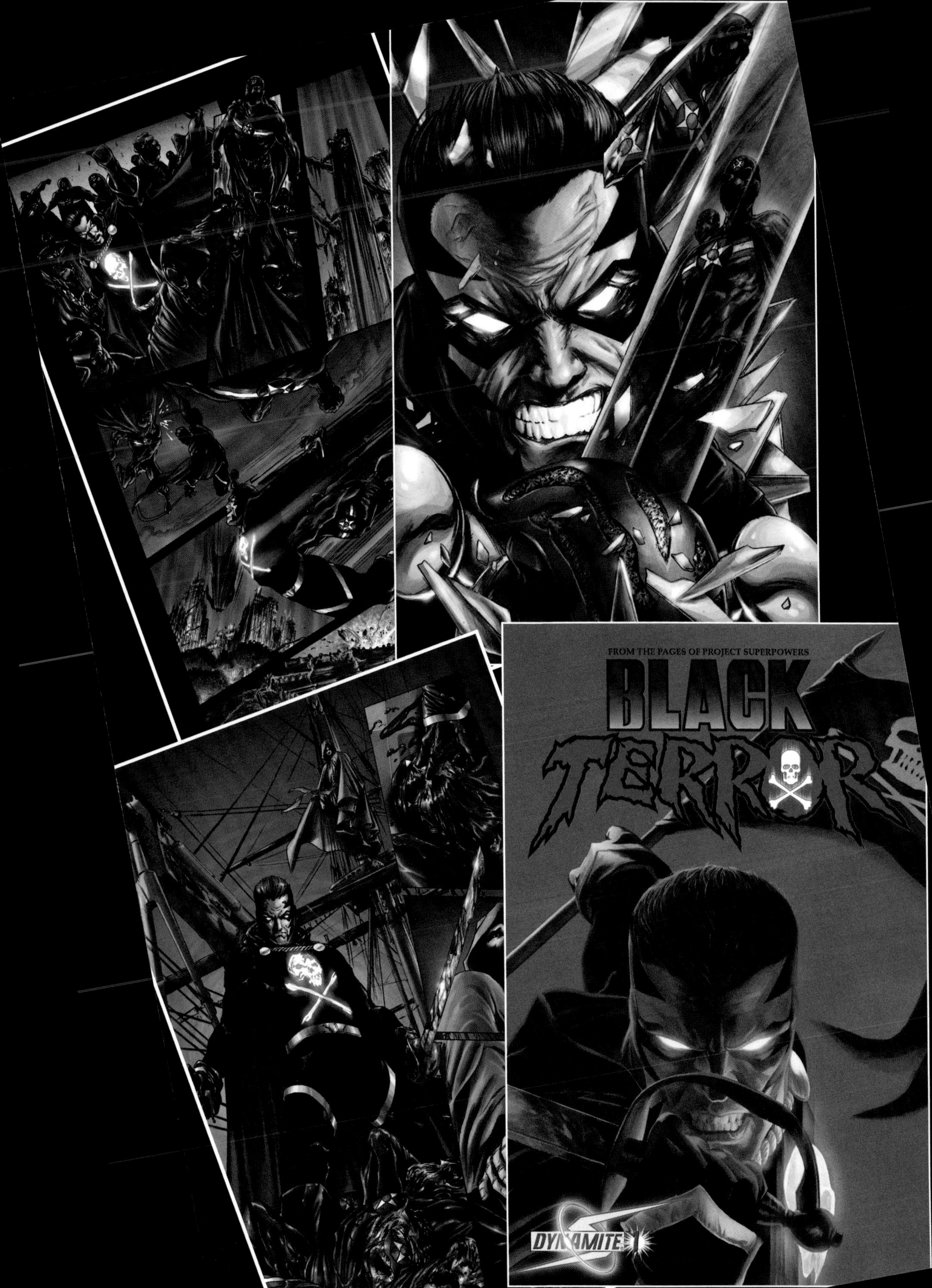
FROM THE PAGES OF PROJECT SUPERPOWERS
BLACK
TERROR
DYNAMITE
1

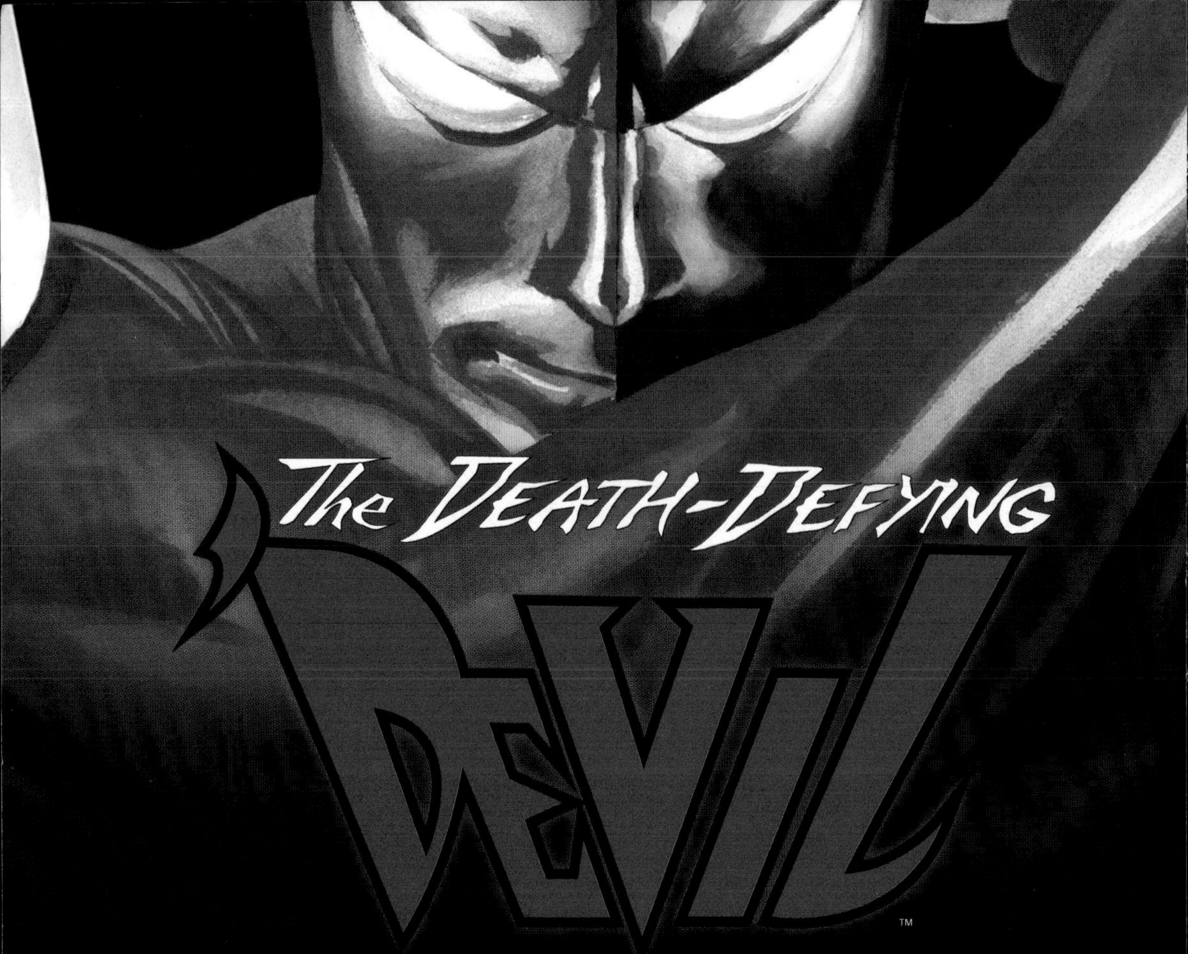
The DEATH-DEFYING
DEVIL

Plot/Art Direction/Main Cover: **ALEX ROSS** Plot/Script: **JOE CASEY**
Interior Art: **EDGAR SALAZAR** Interior Colors: **ROMULO FAJARDO JR**
Letters: **SIMON BOWLAND**

THE DEATH-DEFYING 'DEVIL
Issue #1 script by Joe Casey

PAGE ONE
SIX PANELS

Panel 1.
Open in a dark, sparsely decorated living room (an elderly person's room). No lights on except for the glow from the television. Mostly in the shadows, we see an OLD MAN (70 yrs. old, short, bald, a little pudgy around the mid-section) sitting in a La-Z-Boy chair, hunched forward, watching the TV. His back is to us, so we don't see him clearly yet.

1 - VOICE FROM T.V. (small type): ... so it is with this in mind, that we shall become a check to balance the corruption of the nations of the world....

2 - OLD MAN: Insanity...

Panel 2.
Pan around so we can see the old man's face now. A look of distress on his face as he watches the TV, off-panel.

3 - VOICE FROM T.V. (small type, from off): ... you may call us terrorists,
but we're not. We are Americans...

Panel 3.
Close on the TV SCREEN. Onscreen, we're seeing footage of the returning Superpowers (with the 'DEVIL conspicuously among them) in New York/Shangri-La.
** JOE: make sure whatever image that's used here matches with the story continuity from the PROJECT SUPERPOWERS mini.

4 - VOICE FROM T.V. (small type): ... and we are your friends...

Panel 4.
Small panel. EXTREME C/U on the TV screen, and the onscreen image of the 'DEVIL filling the frame.
NO COPY

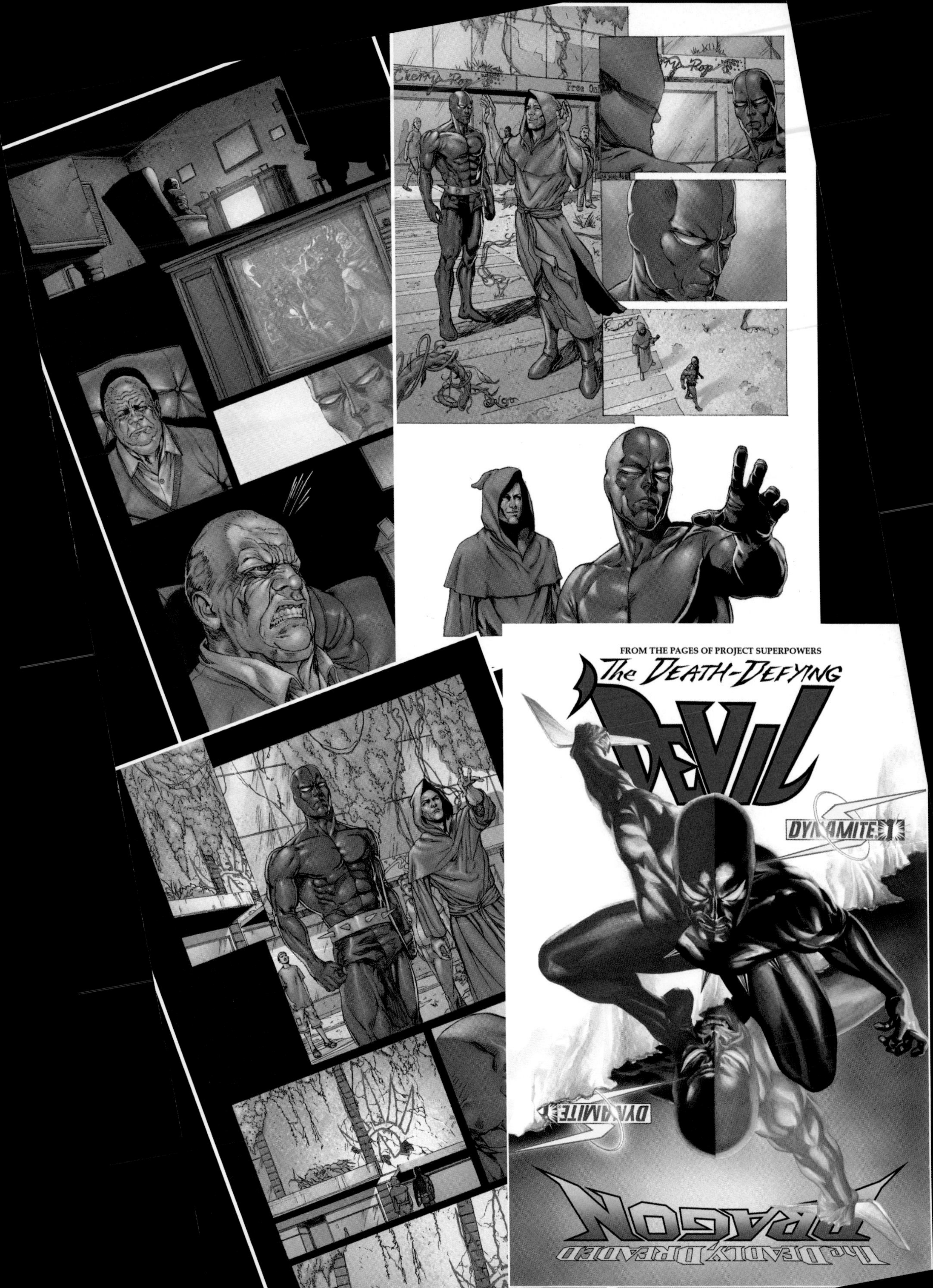
FROM THE PAGES OF PROJECT SUPERPOWERS
The DEATH-DEFYING
DEVIL
DYNAMITE 1
DYNAMITE 1
The DEADLY DREADED
DRAGON

MASQUERADE

Plot/Art Direction/Main Cover: **ALEX ROSS**   Plot/Script: **PHIL HESTER**
Interior Art: **CARLOS PAUL**   Interior Colors: **DEBORA CARITA**
Letters: **SIMON BOWLAND**

MASQUERADE
Issue #1 by Phil Hester

PAGE ONE
Splash. The camera is hovering over the shoulder of a thirty-foot-tall Golden Age robot that looks down on Masquerade chained to a stake sunk deep into the cement warehouse floor. The robot can be as outrageous as you'd like, keeping him in the Golden Age tradition. The only thing I need to see is that the robot (dubbed Der Uhrmacher) has lots and lots of clockwork cogs whirring visibly between the plates of his carapace. A humanoid steam engine. Bolted boiler plates with gears for muscles and innards. Go Jack Cole on us.

Below, Masquerade is dressed in her original costume (whichever one is on the cover). Her cap has been knocked off and there's a nasty cut on her forehead. One of her sleeves is ripped. She is surrounded by hooded, robed men. The robes are emblazoned with a swastika. They stand in two lines on either side of the staggered Masquerade and raise their hands in a "Heil" to the robot. Setting is an abandoned warehouse. It's 1948.

1 MASQUERADE CAP: My mother, before she died, always described me as a precocious child. My father took it a step further in my teens and labeled me strong-willed.

2 MASQUERADE CAP: My brother, who knew me best, believed I was simply bored.

3 MASQUERADE CAP: What I was, and what I remain to this day, is curious.

4 MASQUERADE CAP: Curious about the hidden networks, the back room treaties, the unspoken rules, and the unpleasant truths that anchor our way of life.

5 MASQUERADE CAP: That curiosity brought me here, to death's door at the hands of a dead-end Nazi cult and the clockwork war god they've cobbled together to destroy the country that humbled them.

6 MASQUERADE CAP: It's my curiosity that got me into this mess.

7 MASQUERADE CAP: And it's my curiosity that will get me out.

TITLE: MASQUERADE- Running Blind

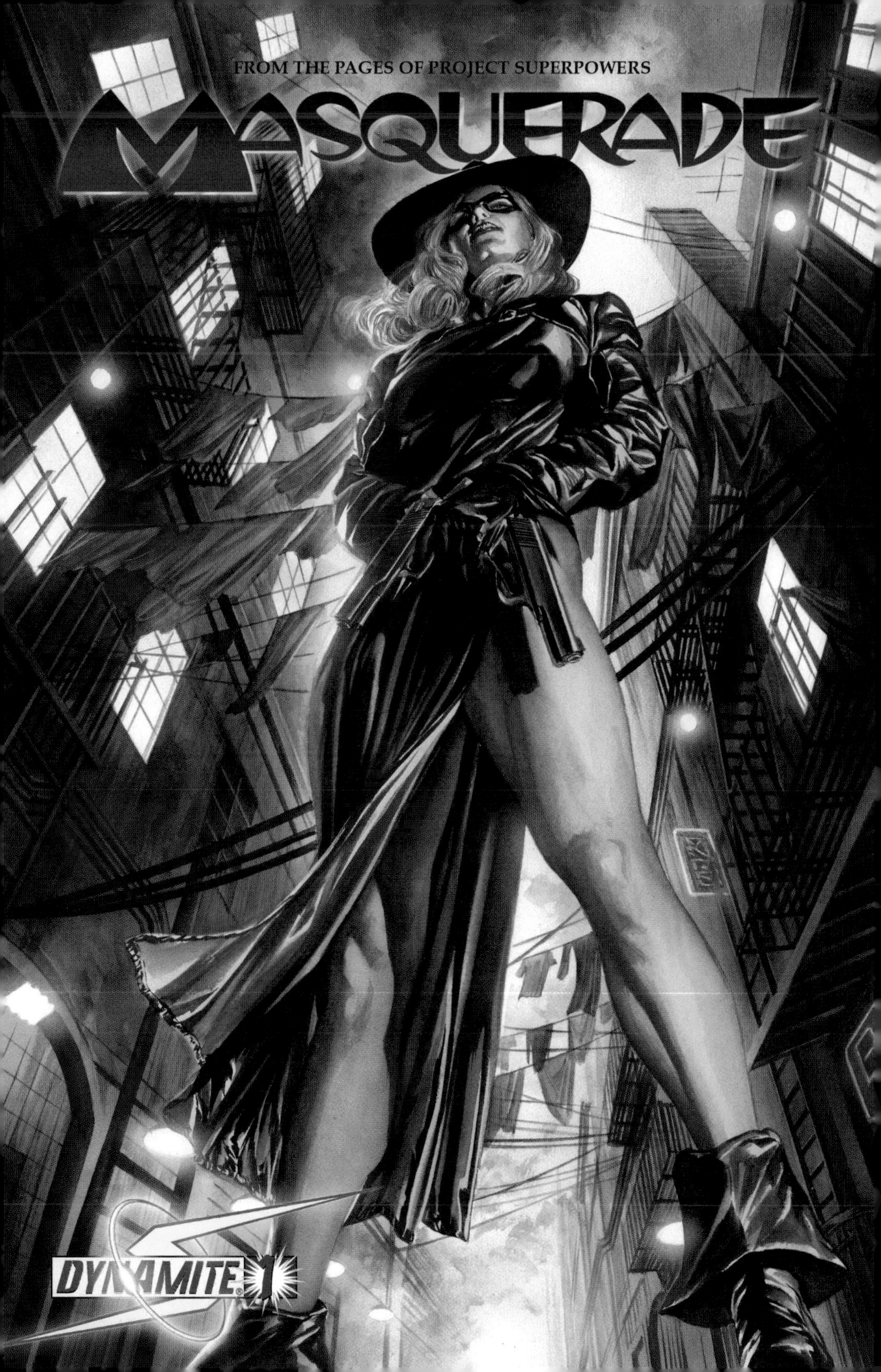
FROM THE PAGES OF PROJECT SUPERPOWERS
MASQUERADE
DYNAMITE
1

THE SAGA CONTINUES IN 2009!

PROJECT SUPERPOWERS CHAPTER TWO. ONLY FROM